Dorothy Rogers

State University of New York at Oswego

ADOLESCENTS AND YOUTH

Fifth Edition

PRENTICE-HALL, INC., ENGLEWOOD CLIFFS, NEW JERSEY 07632

Library of Congress Cataloging in Publication Data
Rogers, Dorothy
  Adolescents and youth.

   Bibliography: p. 470
   Includes index.
   1. Adolescence. 2. Youth. I. Title.
HQ796.R63 1985   305.2'35   84-18056
ISBN 0-13-008806-4

Editorial/production supervision and
  interior design: Kate Kelly
Cover design: Joseph Curcio
Manufacturing buyer: Barbara Kelly Kittle
Cover photos: (top) Ken Karp; (bottom) Marc P. Anderson

Printed in the United States of America

10 9 8 7 6 5 4 3 2 1

ISBN 0-13-008806-4 01

Prentice-Hall International, Inc., *London*
Prentice-Hall of Australia Pty. Limited, *Sydney*
Editora Prentice-Hall do Brasil, Ltda., *Rio de Janeiro*
Prentice-Hall Canada Inc., *Toronto*
Prentice-Hall of India Private Limited, *New Delhi*
Prentice-Hall of Japan, Inc., *Tokyo*
Prentice-Hall of Southeast Asia Pte. Ltd., *Singapore*
Whitehall Books Limited, *Wellington, New Zealand*

ontents

PART TWO   DEVELOPMENT OF THE ADOLESCENT 57

Chapter Three

Physical Development   57

PART THREE   SOCIAL ROLES OF THE ADOLESCENT   221

Chapter Eight
The Adolescent In The Family   221

Chapter Nine
The Adolescent In The Peer Group   252

Chapter Ten

Alienated Youth

Chapter Eleven

Sex Roles Of The Adolescent

PART FOUR   THE THRESHOLD OF ADULTHOOD   417

Chapter Fourteen

The Future Wage Earner   417

Preface

This text has been designed for use in adolescent psychology courses at the college level. It concerns not only adolescents—in the traditional sense of individuals growing from puberty into physical maturity—but also youth—those young people who are too mature to be classed as teenagers, yet who, for various reasons, have not fully achieved the status of adults. As adulthood (in the sociocultural sense) has been postponed with growing frequency in recent years because of college attendance, military service, or other reasons, the size of the youth category has increased correspondingly.

Both adolescents and youth share the same general problems and advantages of being in a transitional stage between childhood and adulthood; however, the two groups differ considerably in their activities, values, and overall maturity. For this reason, the reader is urged to note in the following pages whether a particular piece of research or discussion relates specifically to adolescents, to youth, or to both.

An integrated view of both adolescents and youth is built into the book's organization. Part One—*Who Is The Adolescent?*—concerns the overall definition and significance of adolescence, its relationship to the total life span, plus the goals and research methods of adolescent psychology. It provides a frame of reference for the ensuing chapters, outlines the special problems of the young, and critiques relevant research.

Part Two—*Development of the Adolescent*—evaluates the factors shaping the adolescent personality and explores the various aspects of growth: physical, emotional, mental, moral, and psychobiological. Each aspect of development is related to the others and to the total development of the individual.

Part Three—*Social Roles of the Adolescent*—analyzes the major social roles that adolescents are called upon to play in the family, peer group, school, and the sociocultural environment. Special attention is given to the psychosexual roles of men and women and to those alienated youth who reject the conventional social order.

Part Four—*The Threshold of Adulthood*—focuses on two special areas, choice of a career and transition to adulthood. The world that present-day youth will face as adults and the significance of their current experience for dealing effectively with what lies ahead are explored.

Special features add to the book's usefulness as a classroom text. Summaries of the salient points of each chapter underscore basic principles and provide convenient review. A glossary at the end of the book serves as a useful reference tool. Supplementary study material is suggested in annotated reading lists at the end of each chapter, compiled from a wide range of recent scholarly journals and books. At the end of each chapter are lists of questions, topics for class discussion, and suggestions for individual or class projects, which are designed to stimulate students' examination of controversial issues and to encourage the application of theory to practical life problems.

The text is written in a simple, lucid style, yet without sacrifice of intellectual depth. Concepts are carefully explained and often clarified by anecdotal illustrations, many of them from the author's own files. Most subtopics in this edition have been revised in some way, some being deleted because they have become less relevant, and others expanded because of their changing or growing significance for youth. Topics covered in greater depth in this edtion include, among others, historical factors, appraisal of research, identity theory, creativity, sexuality, and dropouts. Other topics not covered in previous editions have been added, such as wellness, loneliness, the rock and video youth cultures, leaving home, and sex differences presumed to exist in the brain.

Some topics are included that are rarely found in other adolescence texts or receive only a nod—among them the unwed teen parent, smoking, and dating. Such topics as social-sex role, sociocultural factors, and cultural pluralism are stressed more than in most textbooks because the author believes them to be of special importance.

The concept of pluralism, which is currently gaining increased attention throughout the world, is recognized with regard to both adolescents and the larger society. Adolescents ae recognized as having infinitely varied personalities and as forming highly varied subgroupings. They are also discussed according to their membership in various categories of the larger, pluralistic society, with its different social classes, ethnic, and racial groupings.

Supporting research throughout this edition is up to date, with most sources dating from the late seventies to the present; some earlier references have been retained because of their historic significance or importance, or because more recent material of the same caliber was lacking. An effort has been made to sense issues in the making and anticipate what may lie ahead. The key idea is to show that the status of adolescents is not static but fluid—rooted in the past and reaching into the future.

The approaches employed in this book can be more generally useful to students than merely for learning about adolescents. For example, because more attention is paid to concepts than to transient data, students should become oriented to the appreciation of basic principles and their underlying meaning. Similarly, the emphasis in this text on issues is useful because such issues represent the most significant and unresolved questions in the field. Citizens of today's fast-changing world, where ambiguity and complexity are the rule, need to be comfortable with and challenged by the issues that confront them. Some of the issues treated here are of long-standing and continuing significance: Do peers or parents exert greater influence? Of what value is stage theory for understanding adolescence? Do early or late maturers fare better? Other issues are especially relevant to the present: What causes violence in the schools? What rights should adolescents have? Are sex mores changing in fundamental ways?

The portrayal of adolescents has often been distorted because books and the research on which they were based were produced by adults. This edition, like the previous four, reflects a concern for youth's own perceptions. This concern is exemplified by anecdotal statements and issues of special interest to youth themselves, such as cohabitation, smoking, and student rights. Overall, the approach has been significantly influenced by the views of the students in the author's classes in adolescent psychology.

Chapter One

The Nature
And Meaning
Of Adolescence

THE ADOLESCENT IMAGE

Youth's Detractors

Society's image of the adolescent is a somewhat confused montage, varying from the extremely critical to the highly sentimental. The less-favored stereotype of the teenager has a venerable history. Adults have always looked upon the contemporary crop of adolescents as a lost generation. Socrates wrote 2350 years ago,

> The children now love luxury; they show disrespect for elders and love chatter in place of exercise. Children are tyrants, not the servants of their households. They no longer rise when their elders enter the room. They contradict their parents, chatter before company, gobble up dainties at the table, cross their legs, and tyrannize over their teachers.

In 1864, Ives described teenagers in these terms:

> For the last ten years I have been a close observer of what has passed among the rising generation in this great metropolis [New York], and I cannot suppress the humiliating conviction that even pagan Rome, in the corrupt age of Augustus, never witnessed among certain classes of the young a more utter disregard of honor, of truth and piety, and even the commonest decencies of life.

In the early 1900s, G. Stanley Hall branded the girl teenager as a flapper, or one "yet in the nest and vainly attempting to fly while the wings have only pin feathers." Several decades later, Hal Boyle (1951) portrayed the adolescent boy as "dressing like a bum, having the manners of an ape," and "if you look into one of his ears you can see daylight coming through the other ear."

Thus, after the social creation of adolescents as a category and high school attendance became the norm, adolescents became stereotyped in various unfavorable ways. They were associated with being wild, moody, silly, flighty, foolish, and lacking judgment. They were considered emotionally unstable, almost pathologically so. And since society regards persons who are pathological as incapable of properly handling full citizens' rights, the effect was to curtail the freedom of persons under legal age. Without intending to do so, well-meaning individuals, charged with supervising adolescents, conspired with those people who would deprive them of their rights (Starr, 1981).

Although adults' downgrading of adolescents is a centuries-old practice, it is something new that youth under age 21 are coming to look down their noses at those a bit younger than themselves (Willis, 1981). College students these days speak of high school juniors and seniors as though there was at least a generation gap in their ages. One 20-year-old said: "I can't believe what the seniors at my high school are doing now. Why, we wouldn't have considered doing such a thing when I was a teenager!" (p. 954). Student teachers often report that they are concerned about controlling high school students because they have gotten out of hand these days. Thus, the generation gap, in some cases, seems to have shrunk to just two years.

In any case, youth often have a somewhat unflattering view of themselves and, like most minority groups, accept the adverse views of the power groups whose authority they resent. For some years the author has had students write, anonymously, words they associate with the terms "infant," "adolescent," "adult," and "old person." The words they have associated with "adolescent" have been both positive and negative, but predominantly negative. Here is a sampling:

INFANT: helpless; cuddly; precious; tiny; innocent.
ADOLESCENT: open; eager; searching; mixed-up; bewildered; moody; pimply; obnoxious; cynical; healthy; frustrated; energetic; fun-loving.
ADULT: mature; stable; sensible; serious; hard-working; dull.
OLD PERSON: dependent; wise; sad; reserved; lonely; old-fashioned.

It may be conjectured that youth's acceptance of the negative stereotype becomes a self-fulfilling prophecy. Don't we all react to others' expectations of us? Questions of how youth feel about themselves, how they perceive others' view of themselves, and how these feelings affect their behaviors have not been adequately answered.

Youth's Defenders

Some writers praise youth for their idealism and their concern for the world. The youth of the 1960s and 1970s were the first whose life spans embraced a period when complete annihilation of the human race by biochemical and atomic means was possible. Also, they were the first for whom it was possible to introduce dramatic and massive behavioral and genetic engineering. In other words, it was the first time that human beings had the power to "nullify millions of years of evolutionary history or to take conscious scientific control of it. . . . This fact seems to be taken as mind-boggling, if not frightening, to a much greater extent by contemporary youth than by their parents" (Lambert, 1972, p. 39).

Lipsitz (1979) concludes that "we are entangled in stereotypes about young teenagers, stereotypes so negative that we would find them offensive were they racial, religious, or ethnic. Such stereotyping of the young . . . co-opts our sensibilities and blinds us to the realities of adolescence" (p. 4).

Reasons for Distorted Images

Willis attributes the downgrading of adolescents to several factors, one being that we attribute to young people the insecurities and foolish behaviors that we indulged in ourselves at that age. Also, it helps to excuse our own foolish behaviors at that age by rationalizing that they are natural at that time. The media, too, especially television programs, do their part in distorting views of adolescents. Ordinarily they are shown as "easily contented or unconventionally bizarre" (p. 956). Part of the reason is that few people would watch programs showing the rather dull lives of typical teenagers. There is a saying that "adolescents are like airplanes—the only ones you hear about in the news are the ones who crash" (p. 956). Hence, you can hardly obtain a valid picture of adolescents from the newspapers.

For several reasons images of youth become distorted, one being the under- or over-representation of certain categories. For example, because of the disproportionate amount of research among college students who are conveniently located for college researchers, the image of youth appearing in popular and professional literature is mainly upper-middle class (E. J. Smith, 1981).

Teenagers as an age category are underrepresented on television, being seen just a third as often as their numbers in the population (Gerbner, Gross, Morgan & Signorilli, 1980). Television is planned to appeal to the largest potential audience—and, as adolescents become increasingly drawn into peer activities, they depart further from the "mainstream focus" of television (Larson & Kubey, 1983, p. 15). Thus society may not provide adequate portrayal of roles for youth, and this may cause them to perceive themselves as less important relative to other age groups. Television's image of youth is also somewhat negative, often representing them as runaways, rebellious, confused, preoccupied with sex, alcohol, and drugs (Peterson & Peters, 1983).

In fairness, it should be added that television also affords images of positive role behaviors among youth. These images may display qualities of helping behaviors, friendliness, cooperation, adherence to rules, and delay of gratification (Rushton, 1982). Besides, the teenager also sees on television portrayals of developmental tasks, which include developing a positive body image, appropriate gender role orientations and healthy heterosexual relationships, emotional and economic independence from parents, and preparation for future occupational roles (Faber, Brown & McLeod, 1979).

Perspective on the Adolescent Image

None of the common portrayals of adolescents is entirely erroneous or entirely correct. Some teenagers may be little better than bums and some models of decorum, but in between these extremes can be found every possible type

A positive adolescent image.

and combination of types. Who are teenagers? They are all kinds of people—every shape, every color, and every temperament. They have been perceived as "idealistic and materialistic, sensitive and callous, conservative and liberal, bright and dull, optimistic and dispirited, as victims and as victimizers, as innocents and as decadents, and as almost anything else it is possible to imagine" (Adelson, 1979, p. 34). The way the young are perceived depends greatly on the view of the beholder.

Youth's image cannot be pinned down, observes Veysey (1976), because it varies continuously with time and circumstance. Many people "viewed with alarm" the youth of the 1950s, who appeared to have lost their hunger for adventure and experience and instead sought the comfort of security. But no sooner had this picture of youth been drawn than its facets changed. The younger generation, so recently portrayed as self-satisfied and pleasure-oriented, was perceived as alien and discontent in the 1960s. Youth of the 70s and early 80s were again sober and concerned about jobs; the youthful anarchists of the 1960s seemed almost a different breed.

DEFINITIONS OF ADOLESCENCE AND YOUTH

The term **adolescence** comes from the Latin verb *adolescere,* meaning "to grow into maturity." In this sense, *adolescence is a process rather than a time period, a process of achieving the attitudes and beliefs needed for effective participation in society.* It may also be defined as "a movement." It is a physical migration, the rapid and frequent passage through space: from home to college campus, or even through abundant intracity travel. Rock music and the dances to accompany it are only the latest form of physical arousal in this type of movement. It has always been the case—from the Aleut Eskimos to the Congolese, from Alexander the Great's trek across Asia to David's sling that slew Goliath, from Caesar to Christ—that "the movers, the adventurers, the conquerors, and the martyrs, have been the young people" (Wolfgang, 1973, p. 4). Adolescence may be defined in other ways: as a period of physical development, a chronological age span, a sociocultural phenomenon, and even as an abstract concept, suggesting an idea or an attitude toward life.

Some writers differentiate between early and late adolescence, and between adolescence and **youth.** The status of early adolescents is marginal, for they are treated neither like adults or children. They are required to stay in school and not allowed to drive or take full-time jobs until age 16. Hence, that age becomes something of a marker between early and late adolescence (Berndt, 1982). Although they can engage in sexual behaviors such relations are discouraged until late adolescence. The experiences of older adolescents differ in many respects from those of younger ones; at the same time, they differ profoundly from those of **adults.** An even more recent arrival on the age-stage scene is the youth who is adult chronologically and physically, yet still fails to function as a full-fledged citizen in society. This category includes the graduate student and the unemployed youth who lingers in the parental household after graduation.

Adolescence as a Period
of Physical Development

Physically, adolescence comprises several distinct periods. **Pubescence,** sometimes called preadolescence, refers to the two-year period preceding puberty and to the physical changes taking place during that period. The climax of pubescence is called **puberty** and is marked by certain indicators of sexual maturity: in girls by the **menarche,** or the first menses, and in boys by a number of signs, the most valid probably being the presence of live **spermatozoa,** or male reproductive cells, in the urine.

Early adolescence, in the biological sense, dates from the beginning of the pubescent growth spurt until a year after puberty, when the new biological functions are fairly well stabilized. Late adolescence is more difficult to define, lasting until physical growth is relatively complete, during the late teens or early twenties.

In general, the biological onset of adolescence occurred earlier as the twentieth century advanced, until recent years, when it stabilized. Until a decade or so ago, physiological maturity was achieved from one-third to one-half year earlier each decade in the United States, Britain, and the Scandinavian countries.

Adolescence as an Age Span

Adolescence is sometimes defined by chronological age. In America, the age of maturity is usually set at 18, although no rigid age limits are applied. The period from 12 to 15 years may be thought of as early adolescence, 15 to 18 as middle adolescence, and 18 to 22 as late adolescence (Konopka, 1973). There is no clear-cut time when adulthood begins, a fact underlined by the widely varied times that different states treat their citizens as individuals for particular purposes. Minimum age requirements for various functions, including driving a car and getting married, vary from state to state.

The age norms within a society produce "a social clock that is superimposed upon the biological clock in producing orderly and sequential changes in behavior and in self-perceptions . . . " (Neugarten, 1977, p. 633). Age itself is a somewhat meaningless variable because there is little significance in the mere passage of years. Rather, biological and social events occurring in that time give a particular period its significance. This social time system constitutes a form of social control that creates in people's minds obligations to do certain things at certain periods—that is, to be "on time."

Arbitrary age designations may be defended on certain grounds; they provide a definite frame of reference, and they are in keeping with the practices of a society that writes laws in terms of chronological years. For example, society decrees that an individual may not marry or drive a car or vote until specific ages have been reached. Although such limitations are arbitrary, the alternative would be chaos. How would it be possible to devise and conduct valid testing programs to determine when each individual in the country is ready to do these things?

Adolescence as a Stage in Development

Closely related to the chronological concept of adolescence is **stage theory,** which suggests that the life span can be defined less arbitrarily than by age, yet can still be subdivided into relatively distinct periods. In this sense, a society categorizes its members according to age groups, each with its distinctive characteristics, duties, and privileges. Transitions from one stage to another require several years, each constituting "both an ending and a beginning, a departure and arrival, a death and rebirth, a meeting of past and future" (Levinson, 1977, p. 102).

Prior to this century, adolescence was rarely recognized as a distinctive stage in the life cycle. Not until 1904, after G. Stanley Hall published his classic *Adolescence: Its Psychology and Its Relations to Physiology, Anthropology, Sociology, Sex, Crime, Religion, and Education,* did adolescence become recognized. After this time, "adolescence became a household word" (Keniston, 1975, p. 4). Hall did not "discover" adolescence, but he did recognize what was occurring: the arrival of industrial society in America and Europe.

Other factors parallelled those that originally produced recognition of a specific time of adolescence. These onrushing social changes created a need to attend college, just as the industrial revolution created a need to attend high school. In consequence a new stage emerged, sometimes called "late adolescence and young adulthood, a phrase whose very mouthfilling awkwardness attests to its inadequacy" (Keniston, 1975, p. 7). Certainly the term "adolescence," long associated with the teens, was inadequate to describe individuals from about 18 to 24 or 25 years of age. While the term "young adult" provides them a certain dignity, it suggests what is not true, that they have already assumed the full responsibilities of citizenship, including establishing a family and assuming a

Adolescence is a stage of development of transition from infancy to adulthood. (Courtesy of Public Relations Office, State University of New York at Oswego)

job. Psychologically, these individuals may indeed be young adults, in that they have attained a stable self-concept and have put adolescent rebellion behind them. Nevertheless, they differ greatly from those young adults who are not in college, who have married, and who have become fully committed to their occupational and citizenship roles. In time the term "youth" won over its competitors as the favored designation for this stage.

In summary, various factors have conspired collectively to designate adolescence as a discrete age stage. First, children inevitably became more separated from adults as society moved from a rural to an urban environment. Second, as cultures became more complex, the stages became increasingly refined, with a definite step-like transition from infancy to adulthood. While some societies ritualize the shift from youth to maturity, those lacking such rites have instead a **youth culture,** or institutionalized adolescence. Against this background various stage theories have evolved, all commonly portraying childhood, adolescence, and adulthood as three relatively distinct stages that can be identified sociologically, physiologically, and psychologically.

Adolescence as a Transition

Adolescence is often portrayed as a bridge linking childhood and adulthood, with no true essence of its own. Panelas (1983) points out that the adolescent period becomes a regulated span of time in which young people are brought through a "series of status passages that mark the transition from childhood to adulthood" (p. 62). These transitions are supervised by various social institutions, including family, school, workplace, and the military.

However, Lipsitz (1979) calls the idea that adolescence is transitional a myth. Actually, it is no more transitional than any other stage in life. People should recognize this period for its own significance, a period of great importance in its own right. The view of adolescence as transitional may cause one to believe that troubled youth will simply grow out of it, or that this period of life deserves no special attention because of its transience.

Adolescence as a Sociocultural Phenomenon

Physical adolescence is as old as the human race, but social adolescence is a product of modern Western culture. Thus viewed, adolescence is the period in an individual's life when society ceases to regard him or her as a child but does not yet accord full adult status. The period serves as an apprenticeship, filling the interim between biological maturity and sociocultural adulthood. Adulthood, in this sense, is a cultural creation which indicates that a person is ready to enter upon the full obligations and privileges of society. For example, individuals classified as adolescents have increased in number because of the earlier onset and delayed closure of adolescence (Matthews & Serrano, 1981). Also, individuals stay in school longer, which postpones social adulthood.

Proefrock (1981) stresses that the developmental period of adolescence is not a biological fact but is produced by social factors; and we may attribute to adolescents characteristics which have been socially derived and are not actually part of human development. For example, adolescents are sometimes labeled "delinquent" for engaging in behaviors that are illegal merely because the persons engaging in them are socially defined as adolescents. Thus, **status offenders** might be viewed as adolescents who have simply resisted society's decision that adulthood be delayed. Indeed, status offenders are different psychologically from delinquent youths engaging in illegal activities. That is, we look on such youths negatively merely because society has defined them as nonadult.

Adolescence in the social sense is not a universal phenomenon. Every society has its young people, but they are not necessarily adolescents, at least not in the sense of individuals who possess their own subculture with its characteristic way of life; therefore, the two terms are not completely interchangeable.

Within any particular society adolescents develop multiple-role identities through their experiences with their peers and other socializing agents; and they try out role identities in the peer group and other settings. Television plays a part in adolescents' developing multiple role identities by dramatizing role models of all sorts of people. Then the peer group becomes the setting in which adolescents view themselves in terms of these identities. Certain of these roles, which receive peer approval, may be incorporated into their own identity; others may simply be tried and abandoned. In this way youth "are involved continually in the process of negotiating identities out of which selves and realities are created and re-created" (Peterson & Peters, 1983, p. 76).

Society can more readily afford the institution of adolescence at present because adolescence now consumes a far shorter proportion of the total life span. Vastly increased longevity has lengthened the average total period of adulthood, while the years required for the physical transition from childhood to full maturity have remained the same. When individuals had few years remaining of adult life after total maturity was reached, they seemed ill-advised to devote a long time to preparing for adulthood.

Other Approaches to Adolescence

THE HISTORICAL VIEWPOINT Adolescence may be viewed historically by comparing the youth of one age in history with those of another. Such study is possible because societies have been concerned with their youth since the earliest ages of recorded history. In Homer's *Odyssey* we find the story of Telemachus, the only son of Ulysses. Aristotle described in some detail the secondary sex characteristics of adolescents in his *Historia Animalium* and treated the psychological aspects of puberty in his *Rhetoric*. Plato, too, discussed youth's outlook in the *Dialogues*, one example being Lysis's complaint to Socrates that he was not permitted to drive the family horses.

In earlier times there was no long gap between puberty and achieving adult responsibilities; however, today puberty may be separated from adulthood by several years. It is this historical discrepancy which "defines the character of adolescence" (Starr, 1982, p. 192). Historically, an individual might leave childhood by becoming independent; and whatever might delay its attainment would limit access to adulthood. Indeed, until the period of industrialization, about the middle of the nineteenth century, adolescence could hardly be said to exist, because young people—even children—had entered the work force. However, after American workers became unionized, there was opposition to adolescent labor. As a result, school attendance laws were passed in 1852 in Massachusetts and required by all states by 1918, thus delaying adolescents' entry into the work world (Proefrock, 1981).

In the earlier decades of the nineteenth century most youths were employed and had a good deal of independence. Working-class youths worked in mills, and middle-class youths in white collar jobs; hence, they were accorded what amounted to adult status. Some children even left home to work by the age of 7 and many, or most, had work contracts, paying for their lodging and expenses by age 14. And since they were economically independent, they often married by the midteens. As a result, until the War of Independence, young people had more rights than do present-day American youths. Boys, at least, were able to execute wills at the age of 14 and by 16 they fully became men, serving in the militia and paying taxes.

Their independence extended to their social lives. By the early nineteenth century in rural communities young people might congregate together unchaperoned at their dances, sleigh rides, and other social events. Parents simply assumed that the older youth would supervise the younger ones (Starr, 1982).

Early in the Industrial Revolution young children worked 12-hour days in mines and shops, receiving less pay than adults. Women were expected to be married by midadolescence; in contrast, most states now require that they be at least 16 years old before they marry (Matthews & Serrano, 1981).

Then, from around the late 1870s until 1900 youth's status speedily declined, mainly because of technological advances in industry. As a result the demand for low-skilled youth labor diminished rapidly, at the same time that their numbers were increasing, partly because of the higher infant and child survival rate. The result was a reduction in youth's social standing and political independence. As they ceased making money their status diminished, and because of their economic dependence, the minimum age for marriage was raised, especially in the middle class. Although older youths kept much of their formal autonomy, younger ones lost their access to adult society and became ever more subject to control by parents and institutions. In effect, their earlier "moral autonomy" became displaced by the conformity associated with their dependent status. Meantime, youth's earlier participation in social movements, in the first half of the nineteenth century, dwindled. Overall, young people "were no longer taken seriously on social and political issues . . ." (Starr, 1982, p. 196).

THE PSYCHOLOGICAL VIEW   Psychologically, adolescents are perceived in terms of their attitudes, behaviors, mental health, and developmental status. Hayes (1982) points out that "not all Americans become adolescents and not all adolescents become adults".

THE PHENOMENOLOGICAL APPROACH TO ADOLESCENCE   This approach, which involves consideration of adolescents from their own point of view, has been somewhat neglected. Adults have often portrayed adolescents as marginal personalities, lacking a clear-cut self-concept and caught in the no-man's land between childhood and adulthood. However, Bamber (1973) observes that most adolescents identify with the world of adulthood and that the majority of them do not have marginal personalities. Marginality is restricted to adoles-

Most adolescents identify with the adult world but have their own world-within-a-world view. (Photo by William J. Butcher)

cents in particular psychological environments. Without studies that gauge youth's views, adults will hardly be able to peer inside youth's world-within-a-world.

THE ECLECTIC APPROACH Finally, the interpretation of adolescence may be eclectic, from several points collectively. For example, adolescents are shown both to influence and to be influenced by all sorts of variables within their immediate settings—by the context of the family, the broader ecological environment, education, and political institutions as well as the historical evolutionary context (Hill, 1980a). For another example, note the decreasing mean age of menarche, presumably caused by changes over time in nutrition, health, and medical practice (Lerner & Spanier, 1980). Yet early adolescents who are capable of reproducing at earlier ages these days do not necessarily achieve an identity or arrive at formal thought earlier. Thus, the adolescent experience is affected by historical change within a sociocultural context and such changes then "feed back into the context to alter it" (p. 257).

Frames of Reference

Whatever the relative merits of the various concepts of adolescence, all must be taken into account, since all exist in modern society. We must alert ourselves to the specific frame of reference whenever adolescence is being discussed. The term "juvenile delinquent" is used in the chronological sense because legal responsibility is defined in terms of age. But allusions to early and late maturers often have reference to development in the physical sense. To say that a person's behavior is adolescent is to use the term in its social sense, implying failure to behave in a fashion appropriate to adults in this society.

So far as this volume is concerned—except where otherwise specified—

adolescence is socioculturally, yet flexibly, defined. No matter what a youth's chronological or physical status, he or she must operate in a social order. Adolescents must take into account the way society reacts to their behavior and progressively reorient themselves in terms of social expectations.

PERSPECTIVE ON A PSYCHOLOGY OF ADOLESCENCE

Psychology of Adolescence Defined

The psychology of adolescence is the study of the attitudes and behaviors of individuals during this period. As mentioned earlier, the first comprehensive psychology of adolescence was presented in G. Stanley Hall's classic two volumes published in 1904 and 1905. The next major text on the subject was by Leta Hollingworth in 1928. Thus, adolescent psychology, generally regarded as a science peculiar to the twentieth century, developed slowly and did not come into prominence until the 1930s.

Reasons for a Psychology of Adolescence

The psychology of adolescence has flourished since the 1930s, at first employing then popular though inadequate models. Psychoanalytic models of personality function, when applied to adolescents, resulted in viewing their behaviors as "severely pathological, bordering on psychosis or psychopathy" (Ellis, 1979). Equally inappropriate to explain adolescence were models of childhood. While they help to explain aspects of adolescent development, they do not account for the special features of adolescence itself. Such models are prone to "underplay the increased competence, strength, and adaptability that the adolescent may bring to bear on the strains of the adolescent period" (Ellis, 1979, p. 104).

The interest in adolescence has increased for several reasons. The record number of babies of the post-World War II baby boom became adolescents at the same time as the great social unrest of the 1960s; this resulted in waves of student activism, greater than ever known before in this country. Meantime, the woman's movement threw the spotlight on the professional aspirations of young women, which produced concern about the years just preceding their entry into the job market. It became evident "that many of the strands underlying the identities of adult women might well be disentangled by investigating their adolescent roots" (Hill, 1982, p. 1410). Longitudinal studies which demonstrated the importance of all segments of the lifespan, and how each related to the others, naturally included adolescence. Such studies also began to show that ages other than early childhood might have critical effects on the total life experience—hence the relative interest in early childhood declined. Although "it is difficult to say whether the new interest in adolescence only reflects, or has contributed to, the decline of the doctrine of early experience . . . that decline certainly has removed one of the earlier ideological barriers to research on adolescence" (Hill, 1982, p. 1410).

The psychology of adolescence gained credibility as a specialized discipline, perhaps because of the following special problems relating to this period of life:

There is confusion between the adolescent's role and status. **Role** is the pattern of behaviors expected of youth in a specific situation; **status** is the definition of the obligations and privileges attached to the role. For example, in the roles they play as adolescents, youth are expected to drive and sometimes to own a car, to smoke, to dress like their peers, and to spend much of their time with their peer group. Meantime, they may hold very low status in their part-time job, medium status among their peers, and high status in their families.

Neither adolescents' roles nor their statuses are clear-cut in today's society. No dominant set of expectations establishes their status as that of "the adolescent." Their roles may involve conflicting privileges and expectations. A boy may be treated like a man when working on his part-time job, but like a child in his own home. He may be a diligent worker at school, but an irresponsible pleasure-seeker in his peer group. He continues to be bossed like a child, but no longer enjoys the protected status of childhood. He must hold a part-time job to earn the money that his social life requires, yet he is expected to study hard and keep up his grades.

The adolescent's status is inferior to that of adults. Adolescents are in marginal situations, for they have neither the protected position of childhood, from which they are partially emancipated, nor the responsible position of adulthood, for which they are unprepared. They are uncertain as to when they cease to be adolescents. By the time they are sure that they are no longer children, they are beginning to wonder but are not yet sure whether they are now adults. Such vagueness hardly permits clear definition of responsibility.

The adolescent's status is also lacking in dignity. The term "adolescent" itself has overtones at once pedantic and erotic, suggestive of primitive fertility rites and of the orgies of classical antiquity. The term "teenager" is also unsatisfactory; it is patronizing and embarrassing. We have no neutral term, free from unfortunate connotations, to represent persons of this age period.

Many writers now question this concept of adolescence. Much apparently confused behavior is simply exploratory and exemplifies the frustrations normally accompanying problem-solving behavior. A certain amount of conflict during this period may be desirable, if it reflects the adolescent's efforts to find a place within society without sacrificing individuality. On the other hand, the identity crisis is often traumatic because it may bring to the surface previously repressed conflicts. Neurosis may leave its roots very early in life; however, it may assume pronounced forms during adolescence (Shenker & Schildkrout, 1975).

Youth constitutes a critical period in the life span. A concept called the *sensitive period hypothesis* suggests that there are critical moments when experiences produce their maximum effect. The same experiences, occurring at either an earlier or a later age, would have less effect than at the particularly affected age. Adolescence itself is viewed as such a critical period in various ways.

Certainly, adolescence is critical in that the likelihood of modifying undesirable behavior is greater then than it is later on. The instability of early adolescence makes it easier to sort out childish ways of thinking, feeling, and acting and to reorganize them on a more mature basis. Even by late adolescence, certain behavior patterns are deeply rooted and difficult to change. In the San Francisco Longitudinal Study of Transitions young adults showed increasingly greater stability over a period of eight years, moving as they had from high school years characterized by "emotional turmoil, role ambiguity and identity problems" (Thurnher, 1983, p. 58) to adult years.

For many individuals, adolescence will also be the last stage in their lives—at least until retirement—when they will have relatively large chunks of free time. Many youths use this time to construct "a social and cultural space, free from the direct surveillance of the major institutions that dominate their lives" (Panelas, 1983, p. 62).

Adolescence is also significant in the way that characteristics, attitudes, and behaviors established during this period relate to those in the years that follow. When high school students were followed for a 1- to 5-year period, life-style orientations initiated by the tenth grade established a pattern for certain "global aspects of adjustment" in the next stage of young adulthood (Newman, 1979). The young adult's life style is heavily dependent on choices, competencies, and aspirations acquired in adolescence. Moreover, the degree to which maturation proceeds through adulthood reflects the abilities to encounter and resolve conflict that were acquired in adolescence.

The very early years of life have been presumed to be those in which the basic directions of development were established (Lerner, 1981). It was, in effect, a "psychology of the permanent" (Livson & Peskin, 1980), instead of "one of change and plasticity" for all the years after childhood (p. 254). Features of adolescents were often treated as though they were merely regressions to earlier "oedipal phenomena" (p. 254).

Recent trends in the biological and social sciences have tended to produce a different way of viewing developmental processes in adolescence. The popular view that early experience permanently set the tone for the future simply failed to account for behavioral phenomena in later years (Baltes, Reese & Lipsitt, 1980). Accumulating data, especially longitudinal data, has shown many kinds of influences to be involved in changes over time, including maturational, social, and cultural factors. In consequence, scientists these days reject purely developmental theories in favor of multidisciplinary ones.

Brim & Kagan (1980) point out that the new view of human development suggests that humans can change throughout their lives and that early experiences do not constitute an inevitable barrier to changes across the life span. Indeed, many persons retain a very considerable potential capacity for change; and the effects of early childhood experience itself are modified by ensuing experience, thus causing life development to be far "more open" than commonly recognized (p. 1). That is, adolescent development has many dimensions and is interactional and dynamic.

The impact of adolescent experience on adult personality is apparently significant, so much so that some authorities believe adolescence to be the most critical period of life as far as society as a whole is concerned. Later crises, such as menopause and retirement, may seem more important to the individual, but a new generation is not at stake when they occur. Individuals who fail to make the normal transition to adulthood become misfits, delinquents, and criminals, and their problems spill over onto their children. The importance of a period is not measured by its length but by its influence, which in the case of adolescence seems to be persistent and pervasive.

College youth perceive their adolescence to have been important for varied reasons:

FEMALE: The realization that just because you get older and look older doesn't mean you feel older or more mature inside.

FEMALE: Learning about different people and different ways of life; deciding what to do in life.

MALE: I left home, bumped against reality, and learned alot about me.

A psychology of adolescence may help define adolescents' developmental tasks and roles—those their culture expects them to achieve before they reach the next age level. Three theoretical perspectives have emerged as focal points in discussing adolescence: acquiring sex-appropriate roles, achieving an identity, and establishing commitment to values, ideology, occupation, and life styles (Adams and Looft, 1977). Of these three, Keniston (1975) places special emphasis on roles. At the youth stage, individuals may assume deep commitment to specific roles, which may sometimes constitute the foundation of later roles. In other cases, as they move into adulthood, adolescents may view their earlier roles as experiments that failed.

There are many types of developmental tasks and roles, but they may be summed up somewhat as follows: (1) younger adolescents are concerned with what they are; older ones, with what to do about it. An integral part of the problem is defining one's ideal self, which limits the kind of self a person tries to be. Adolescents must also achieve satisfying social relationships. They live on the periphery of both child and adult groups, and belonging to their own group becomes a means of achieving stability. (2) They must achieve adjustment to a heterosexual world, which involves adaptation to sex role, solution of sex problems, and, for the vast majority, courtship and selection of a mate. (3) They must become independent. Lack of weaning, in the figurative sense, may result in adult dependency on parents, employer, or marriage partner. (4) Basic to, and foremost of, all tasks of adolescence is the need for teenagers to find themselves. This task requires "experiencing continuity between the inner and outer selves, a sense of continuity of one's self from one moment to the next, integration of past experiences, and experiencing for the first time a sense of the future—of knowing that one has a personal and social destiny" (Lipsitz, 1979, p. 5). Now for the first time the youth says, "I have a future, I have a destiny, I am part of a generation" (p. 5).

Adults, as society's agents, must understand adolescents if they are to transmit culture in a manner conducive to the welfare of that society. Havighurst and Dreyer (1975) observe that "every society must ingest a generation of children and digest or socialize them into adults who can carry on the business of the society" (p. 125). In other words, society must find new ways of absorbing youth into adulthood. With regard to this task, some adults know they are confused; others are confused without knowing it. Some of the latter are well meaning, but bumbling; others are hostile, though unconsciously so. Even the most well-meaning adults may utilize fear and anxiety as instruments of acculturation; they play on adolescents' emotions to implant the adaptations on which society depends.

Not much of real worth is written about teenagers for adult consumption (Willis, 1981). Many books on infant care for parents provide concrete, research-based information, but there is little regarding adolescence. Those who read adolescent psychology, without understanding it, may be worse off than before. For example, they may lack a sense of humor in evaluating what youth do because they have become obsessed with serious terms such as ego identity, self esteem, and intrapsychic conflict.

Adults also need help in understanding their own attitudes toward teenagers—attitudes arising from their own limited experience and special emotional needs. On one hand are the sentimentalists, who prefer to think positively of all teenagers; on the other are those who choose to believe mostly ill of young people. Every adult was once an adolescent. Some adults' disgust and annoyance toward teenagers are unconscious defenses against troublesome but repressed memories of their own teen years. Still other adults are intolerant of adolescents' foibles because they view their children as extensions of themselves. The daughter who displays bad manners is presumed to reveal her parents' inability to bring her up properly.

Another problem is that parents may unconsciously resent their children because they themselves are losing their youth at a time that their children are at the height of their physical attractiveness. That is, adults may unconsciously feel some resentment toward these reminders of their own lost youth (Fox, 1980). However justified parents' negative attitudes may be, adolescents are adversely affected by them. If others are anxious about them, adolescents will be anxious about themselves. If adults expect them to be obnoxious, they will probably live up to this expectation.

General principles of psychology cannot meet the needs of adolescents; special knowledge and skills are needed. Some individuals, among them Rousseau, believed that children should be permitted to grow up largely unguided by adult influence and control. They even deluded themselves into believing that boys with long records of delinquency would reform if people would only trust them to do so. But problems like these have a way of persisting, which proves the inadequacy of either the haphazard or the hands-off approach.

Others assume that the general principles of psychology are sufficient. These people see no more need for a psychology of adolescence than for one devoted to any other period of corresponding length, such as the twenties or thirties. Yet every stage is an important and unique link in the chain of life, and like every other period, adolescence has its own themes. Each generation of youth has a trademark different from persons older and younger and different from youth that preceded or will follow them. For example, in recent decades young people, especially in high-status groups, hold freer attitudes toward sex and feel less guilty about it. Laws of behavior that are sufficiently general to apply to all ages prove too abstract to provide help for specific problems. We all know teachers and parents who are relatively successful in dealing with one age but not with another.

Youth's relationship to a complex, rapidly changing age requires contemporary answers. The current world that youth will inherit as adults "suggests a caldron where the status quo is boiling; mutually supportive cultures are growing in plurality; traditional sex mores are relaxing; and ideological ferment is leading to novel role patterns and life styles" (Grinder, 1975, p. 442). Hence, youth cannot simply be bequeathed hand-me-down advice from their elders. Nor can they achieve a definitive adjustment. Instead, they must endlessly prove their adaptability. With "few signposts to direct them, they take the road to nowhere, somewhere, or anywhere" (p. 442). Meantime, the population explosion creates perils of anonymity, and rampant value confusion produces a crisis in moral development. Caught in the middle, youth vainly seek a basic value system to serve as glue to put their own pieces together. Note the testimony of these adolescents:*

> I am anxious about the societal forces which threaten; and I often find myself attempting to manipulate my environment. I cannot deny the existence of recurring anxiety concerning my ability to plan ahead. As a defense I have not so much resigned myself to living in the present as striving to accept the fact that all you can know about the future is that you cannot know.

> The bigness of our age is what has affected me the most. The lack of stature and influence that might have been present in another time has made me feel cynical. It is impossible for me to forget, or not see, such problems as the war, race, or whatever; and yet what I alone or even grouped with some friends can do seems small indeed. Our power structure is so distant and so out of tune that it seems to not hear or see us.

American youth and their culture serve as prototypes for youth around the world. American teenagers have an influence on their counterparts in other societies through the mass media, which transcends international boundaries. Margaret Mead suggested that "the campus rebel in Iowa can identify with his counterpart in Tokyo or Paris because events on one side of the earth become available, simultaneously, everywhere else" (Harris, 1970, p. 61). Certainly, if American youth are the pacemakers for younger sets around the globe, they should be helped to set a good example.

A final, and just recently acknowledged, task is to relate adolescence to the entire life cycle, an emphasis precipitated by two main developments. First, growth as a person is no longer perceived as ceasing with adulthood. Adults have come to perceive themselves as individuals capable of continuing growth throughout life. They are no longer judged as programmed for decline. They are perceived developmentally in terms of opportunities for continued actualization and development of their potential.

Until recently, adolescence was perceived as a time of wrapping things up and being ready for adulthood. Graduation exercises were presumed to represent youths' launching into the adult world—the die was cast for better or

---

* Unreferenced material is from author's classes.

American youth have influenced their counterparts in other societies. (Courtesy of Public Relations Office, State University of New York at Oswego)

for worse. Adulthood was viewed as homogeneous in nature and was represented as a plateau in the life span, culminating in death. Now, people also must be prepared for greater longevity than is common even now—hence the greater importance of developing sound physical and psychological underpinnings. Ultimately, some way may even be found of regenerating cells indefinitely so people would live well over a century. Donald Coffey of Johns Hopkins comments: "Can we? Yes. Will we? Probably. Will that be a good thing? I don't know" (Medicine dares, 1983).

A related point is that personality traits are not forever cast in early years but may change in significant ways in subsequent years. Early experience is still viewed as highly significant but not as deterministic in effect as formerly thought. At the same time, the life cycle approach helps to appreciate what effect each stage in life has on those to follow, even into late-late years (Renshon, 1977). All strands of development constitute the life cycle. The life cycle itself is a mode of "conceptualizing the aging process: a sequence of statuses and roles, expectations and relationships, constituting in the broadest meaning of the word, an individual's 'career'" (Van Dusen & Sheldon, 1976, p. 106).

Stages in the life span are interdependent, and particular stages in the life continuum represent the accumulated outcomes to date of all that has gone before, along with a certain "directional thrust" that influences the future (Rosenfeld, 1977, p. 32). Each stage has many facets involving all phases of development, although each has its own special characteristics and tasks. These characteristics depend to some degree on maturational factors; for example, adolescence is partly initiated by puberty and is partially determined by sociocultural circumstances. Even if an individual has not arrived at puberty, that individual is expected by society to behave like others his or her own age.

Each generation of youth goes through life experiencing the same historic periods at the same time; thus successive age groups or birth cohorts develop unique characteristics because of their common social environment at the same periods of the life cycle (Van Dusen & Sheldon, 1976). For example, the cohort that arrived at adulthood during the late 1960s still bears the imprint of the do-your-own-thing and peace philosophies of that period.

STUDYING ADOLESCENTS

Modes of Research

EARLY METHODS   Observations about adolescents have a long history. Aristotle (384–322 B.C.) turned his attention to adolescence and left the following description of physical changes in puberty:

> When twice 7 years old in most cases, the male begins to engender seed; and at the same time hair appears on the pubes, in like manner so Alcmaeon of Croton remarks, as plants first blossom and then seed. About the same time the voice begins to alter, getting harsher and more uneven, neither shrill as formerly nor deep as afterward, nor yet as an even tone, but like an instrument whose strings are frayed and out of tune; and it is called . . . the bleat of the billy-goat. . . . At the same age in the female, the breasts swell and the so-called catamenia commences to flow; and this fluid resembles fresh blood. . . . In the majority of cases the catamenia are noticed by the time the breasts have grown to the height of two fingers' breadth. In girls, too, about this time the voice changes to a deeper note. (quoted in Ross, 1910)

Of psychological changes Aristotle had nothing to say except that girls at this age needed constant surveillance because of developing sexual impulses. However, he believed that youth, in general, tended to be ardent, passionate, irritable, or sanguine because of their biological make-up.

Aristotle's method was simply to record what he believed he saw around him. No other method was used until near the beginning of the nineteenth century. Nor was there until this time any better description of adolescence than Aristotle's. True, in 1795, one finds an age-distribution table for the beginning of menstruation and, in 1748, an excellent general account of puberty. However, the lack of reliable facts concerning puberty was pointed out by Roberton (1832) only a little over a century ago.

INFLUENCE OF G. STANLEY HALL   The psychology of adolescence emerged as a topic in modern psychology in the late nineteenth century with the work of G. Stanley Hall (1846–1924). Hall assembled a monumental mass of data on adolescence. He sought, not too successfully, to apply to education the scientific exactness of the developing physical sciences. He directed interviews, had adults fill out questionnaires concerning their early reminiscences, and analyzed youth's self-expression in essays they had written. Hall's views, illustrated in excerpts below, continue to be reflected in contemporary methods of educating youth as well as in popular books.

> Adolescence is a new birth, for the higher and more completely human traits are now born. . . . Development is less gradual and more saltatory, suggestive of some ancient period of storm and stress when old moorings were broken and a higher level attained. . . . Important functions previously nonexistent arise. . . .Every step of the upward way is strewn with wreckage of body, mind, and morals. . . . Sex asserts its mastery in field after field, and works its havoc in the form of secret vice, debauch, disease, and enfeebled heredity, cadences the soul to both its normal and abnormal rhythms, and sends many thousands of youths a year to quacks, because neither parents, teacher, preachers, nor physicians know how to deal with its problems. . . . (quoted in Fleming, 1951, pp. 36–37)

With regard to the study of youth, Hall seems to stand halfway between the fictional generalizations of past centuries and the controlled observation and experimentation of the present. His chief contributions were that he focused attention on adolescents and attempted to apply scientific methods to their instruction. He brought to bear on the problems of adolescent education contributions from experimental psychology, physiology, anthropology, sociology, and literature.

Nevertheless, certain weaknesses are apparent in Hall's work, and his generally crude methodology renders all his findings suspect. He ignored the effects of cultural setting, disregarded individual differences, and failed to indicate deviations from norms. He reflected contemporary views as to the relative status of the sexes; and he opposed coeducation on grounds that girls mature earlier than boys.

FREUD'S VIEWS ON ADOLESCENCE   Second only to the influence of Hall in the early part of the present century was that of Sigmund Freud (1856–1939), the Austrian neurologist and psychiatrist who devised the technique that became the standard procedure for psychoanalysis. His theories emphasized the critical significance of early childhood experiences, but he disagreed with Hall's view that sexual instinct has its birth at puberty. That children should suddenly acquire sex feelings at about age 14, he observed, would be as nonsensical as to suppose that they are born without genital organs, which begin to sprout only at puberty.

The Freudian image of adolescence, popularized by Erik Erikson, emphasizes the importance of youths' identity crises. The neoFreudians overlook the sociocultural context and interpret youth as a stage of almost mystical withdrawal from the real world, a moratorium during which the person unconsciously gathers strength and gains a sense of direction for future engagement. Veysey (1976) challenges such an interpretation of adolescence for neglecting the influence of society. Institutional structures powerfully affect what we do, playing a vital role in the shaping of individual destiny and the assignment of roles.

Current Methods of Studying
Adolescents

HISTORICAL METHOD   Currently proliferating research about adolescents involves a variety of methods, one of the most useful being the historical method. According to this method, youth's characteristics may be compared at various stages in history, over longer or shorter spaces of time.

ANTHROPOLOGICAL STUDIES   Also helpful for studying adolescents are **anthropological** studies, which compare ways of living in different societies. Especially important were those of Margaret Mead (1928), whose interest was personality development among young people in the South Pacific. Significantly, she concluded that the stresses that frustrate our own adolescents are primarily due to civilization. Preadolescent and postadolescent girls in Samoa differed little except in certain bodily respects. Adolescence was tranquil, reflecting an easy, patterned way of living.

The anthropological method depends on field researchers' own observations and on explanations supplied by local persons. Inquiry may focus on such questions as: Is onset of puberty given social recognition, and if so, how? And is adult status assumed abruptly or gradually? Comparisons of cultures show the range of possibilities and help to put an individual culture in focus. However, there are certain dangers in cross-cultural comparisons. We cannot assume that what is good for one culture is desirable for another. Nor can we rely on the complete accuracy of such studies; without statistical evidence, their validity is uncertain.

THE LONGITUDINAL APPROACH   **Longitudinal** research involves studying one population of subjects over a period of time, with follow-ups at certain intervals. It helps us appreciate the significance of adolescence in the total life cycle, how this stage is built on the experiences of childhood, and how it becomes a transition to the future (Adelson, 1979). We can examine adolescence within the context of the total life span because of important longitudinal studies that have been going on for varying periods of time and will span the lives of the individuals concerned. Among the most important longitudinal studies are the Berkeley Study of Life Style and Personality, the Bonn Longitudinal Study of Aging, the Chicago Study of Life Events and Adaptation in Adulthood and the San Francisco Longitudinal Study of Transitions (Thurnher, 1983). In another important longitudinal project, the Guidance Study of the Institute of Human Development, subjects were intensively studied from birth to 18 years and in follow-ups at ages 30 and 40 (Peskin and Livson, 1972). For both sexes, psychological health could be predicted poorly, if at all, from measures taken at the age periods 5 to 7, 8 to 10, and 14 to 16. However, adult health was predictable from multiple behaviors assessed at ages 11 to 13—the preadolescent period. Subjects were likely to become psychologically healthy adults if, during this period, they had been relatively expressive, extroverted, and free of irritability and temper tantrums. Both outgoingness and impulse control over aggression were predictive of good personality development among males in adulthood. In women, psychological health in adulthood was predictable from certain pre-adolescent behaviors, including self-confidence, independence, intellectual curiosity, and, surprisingly, a hearty appetite.

Longitudinal studies yield information no other method can supply. They focus on growth patterns, permitting analysis of the complex interplay of factors affecting growth. When the research team is composed of scientists from different fields, their cooperation produces a well-rounded picture. McCall (1977) calls the longitudinal method "the life blood of developmental psychology" (p. 341). However, there are problems of maintaining rapport with subjects over the years, or even maintaining contact at all. These factors, besides the expense of getting in touch with the same subjects over considerable intervals of time, tend to trim the size of the group that can be studied, thus limiting the general applicability of findings. One also wonders what effect playing guinea pig over the years has on the subjects.

In many cases, such as the following, it is well to integrate contemporaneous with life-span research (Berzonsky, 1983). For the time being, early-maturing males and later maturing females have an advantage. The early-maturing male grows more rapidly than his peers at a time when physical prowess is an advantage and the later-maturing female is not projected too soon into a mature sexual maturity that might pose problems. Nevertheless, their opposites, early-maturing females and late-maturing males, in later years tend to become "relatively more open, independent, and adaptable", perhaps because of the experience gained in handling their adolescent stresses. As longitudinal data become increasingly available, developmental principles must be revised in terms of accumulated data.

CROSS-CULTURAL STUDIES   As the name suggests, these studies compare aspects of life and development in two or more countries, or in two or more subcultures, and provide perspective both on other countries and on ourselves. One cross-cultural study involved a comparison of views held in 1962 and 1970 by young American and Danish females regarding premarital relationships. The percentage of females in 1970 whose first coital experiences were followed by feelings of remorse and regret ranged from zero for Danish females to 11.1 percent for females in the midwestern United States (Christenson & Gregg, 1970).

MISCELLANEOUS METHODS   Other methods of studying adolescents, too numerous to analyze thoroughly, will only be mentioned here. Daydreams, when reported anonymously, are helpful clues to major frustrations and strivings. Panel discussions, when conducted by a person capable of establishing proper rapport, will yield considerable understanding of how adolescents think and feel. Diaries and letters are quite revealing because they express subjects' feelings when free from threat. Unfortunately, such documents are generally hard to obtain, especially from those afraid to reveal themselves to others. Questionnaires and interviews are widely used for studying all areas of development. However, they are subject to many sorts of error. It is difficult to make the questions definite, unambiguous, and natural. Subjects tend to answer questions the way they think they should be answered.

The case study approach, in which professionals pool for discussion all the evidence they have regarding an individual, has the weakness of depending greatly on the researchers' "intuitive skills" (Csikszentmihalyi, Larson, & Prescott, 1977, p. 282). Because this approach does not deal with youths in their natural environments, it has little relevance to the salient issues of adolescence as encountered in everyday life. Observational approaches are also weak because they are damaged by the impact of the observer's presence and by limitations on contexts that can be studied. Observers cannot easily do such studies in situations where young people normally gather, as in their private parties.

An aim of the ecological approach is to study adolescents' systems of interaction, their degree of involvement in various activities, and how they affect youths' developing cognitive and affective patterns. The technique attempts to answer questions regarding what adolescents do all day every day, their motivations for engaging in various activities, and how they are affected by engaging in them.

Especially in more comprehensive and complex research, various research approaches and instruments are used. In a longitudinal study of the adaptation of high school boys to two midwestern high school environments, over 30 researchers employed such varied tools as survey questionnaires, demographic data, collection, interviews, naturalistic observation, field experimentation, and various kinds of tests (Kelly, 1979).

Current Research

Modern research on adolescence leaves much to be desired. Conclusions often fail to take into consideration the nature of the sampling, which is often highly restricted as to population, social status, and the times. Most adolescent psychology to date is based on data drawn from the middle class; the upper-upper and lower-lower classes generally have been ignored. Although much research has been done with college youth, little has involved out-of-school youth and other special categories. Sufficient studies of youths' perceptions of themselves and their environments are also lacking.

It is also important to consider individual distinctiveness of development and not view adolescence in too global or universal fashion (Lerner, 1981). There is a tendency to overgeneralize, to speak of "the teenager," "the boy," or "the girl." Almost anyone who reads a statement about "the adolescent" will be able to think of teenagers to whom it does not apply. We should think of the range of differences, instead of lumping all cases at the mean. We cannot catch all individuals in the same widespread net, nor brand them all with the same label. We may even be giving up "the illusion that there is a single adolescent psychology, timeless and universal" (Adelson, 1979, p. 37). Adolescents are no one thing; they are very different in early, middle, and late adolescence. And adolescent girls appear to be somewhat different from adolescent boys.

Conclusions are often based on studies that overlook basic research essentials, such as the need for adequate controls. For example, it is commonly presumed that college attendance has a liberalizing effect; however, a comparison of Indiana undergraduates and a same-aged control group not attending college indicated that all had undergone a similar liberalizing effect. What has been interpreted as a liberalizing effect of the school environment may have been an environmental effect of the larger society acting upon all youth. Nevertheless, it is true that liberal arts and social science fields attract more liberal students than do preprofessional, physical science, and education areas (Rich, 1977).

Grinder (1982) concludes, after reviewing adolescence research, that the range of topics being investigated is proliferating; unification across disciplines is being encouraged; and empirically derived conclusions are "superseding conventional wisdom and intuition in forming youth development policies" (p. 224). A main problem, however, is that researchers focus on specific interests and fail to take into account data and hypotheses developed in alien frames of reference.

SUMMARY

The adolescent image, or society's view of what an average adolescent is like, is no single thing. Instead, it varies widely from one age or group to another. Some critics assume a highly negative view of youth; others take the youth-can-do-no-wrong attitude. Still others not only defend the younger generation, but perceive it as the hope of the future. Youth's image cannot be pinned down because it varies with time, place, and circumstance. The image is also distorted by the public's exposure to portrayals of selected segments of youth, as in the mass media. Meantime, youth themselves are significantly affected by these images because they tend to behave as they are expected to do.

Not only is youth's image somewhat unclear and confused, but the terms relating to this age stage are variously, often ambiguously, defined. Some writers differentiate between the teenager (or early adolescent) and the youth (or late teenager). Adolescence itself is defined in several ways: as a stage in physical development, as an age span, as a discrete stage in development, or as a sociocultural phenomenon. It is often interpreted as a period of transition between childhood and maturity. No longer are persons at any stage of development seen as they were some decades ago, as growing up in simplistic environments, but rather as within a complex sociocultural context. Adolescence can also be viewed historically by comparing youth from one age in history with another or cross-culturally from one country to another. It may even be viewed as the state of mind or mode of existence typical of individuals who are no longer children but not yet adults. Consideration of youth's self-perception, or self-image, is termed the phenomenological approach. Of diminishing significance are the psychoanalytic model, which views adolescents as tension-ridden, and the approach that seeks to explain adolescence in terms of childhood theoretical models.

The scientific study of this period of life—the psychology of adolescence—serves various important functions. It helps to define the adolescent's roles and status and to pinpoint the problems characteristic of the period. It defines in what ways and to what degree adolescence is critical and identifies both wholesome and unwholesome features of the period. Such a science further provides the data and ideas that society in general and adults in particular require for guiding youth. Adults need bases for understanding their own reactions to adolescents.

The study of youth is especially important today, when the demands of a complex, rapidly changing age make hand-me-down answers from older generations obsolete. Only through intensive study of each major life stage can life be viewed in clear and balanced perspective. Nor will youth be able to realize their whole life's best potential without laying adequate foundations in terms of decision-making and life-style engineering. For another thing, American youth, as portrayed in the mass media, serve as prototypes for many young people in other countries; hence, the image that American teenagers project can have a significant effect on adolescent behavior in other nations.

A historical perspective helps to place today's youth in proper focus. Fortunately, records concerning adolescents' status and education across the centuries have been pieced together. They have been studied formally for a brief span—indeed, only since the beginning of the twentieth century. Current methods of investigation, which include anthropological research and longitudinal and cross-sectional studies among others, are becoming increasingly varied and sophisticated. In addition, the literature concerning youth, both popular and scientific, has proliferated. It ranges from profound to highly superficial, from purely local to national and cross-cultural in coverage. Vast amounts of this research are still overly simplistic and parochial, yet a growing number of researchers are testing new approaches, developing more imaginative research designs, and tackling the crucial questions of youth in a postindustrial age. Great gaps in our knowledge still remain, and even those topics which are fully researched must continually be reexamined. In such a swiftly changing world, it is futile to seek definitive answers; instead, youth's status in society must always be adapted to the times.

DISCUSSION QUESTIONS AND ACTIVITIES

1. Consult textbooks on the psychology of adolescence dating from G. Stanley Hall's time, around the turn of the century, to the present. Note ideas that sound strange, along with dates and references. How do these ideas reflect the changing times?
2. Search old newspapers and magazines for references to adolescents. What conclusions can you draw concerning attitudes toward adolescents in those years?
3. Collect cartoons and comic strips from current newspapers and periodicals, and tell how teenagers seem to be viewed in modern society.
4. How are adolescents typically portrayed on television? Is this portrayal accurate and positive?
5. Report to the class on a research study of adolescents. Discuss the methods used, limitations of the study, and the general applicability and usefulness of the findings.
6. Write extemporaneously, during the first class meeting, a thumbnail sketch of today's adolescent. Turn it in to the instructor so that a comparison can be made with the way you come to view the adolescent by the end of the course. At that time, you will be able to determine the nature and direction of changes in your views.
7. Be prepared to discuss these topics in panel before the class: (a) Is a psychology of adolescence actually needed? (b) Which of the conflicting stereotypes of teenagers is most accurate? (c) Is adolescence as critical a period as childhood? (d) What do you believe to be the contemporary attitude toward teenagers in your own environment?

SUGGESTED READINGS

Adelson, J. (Ed.) (1980). *Handbook of adolescent psychology.* New York: Wiley. This comprehensive volume contains papers by experts in the field on many aspects of adolescents and is organized in three sections: "New Perspectives in Adolescence," "The Process of Adolescence," and "Variations in Adolescence."

Berzonsky, M. D. (1983). Adolescent research: A life span developmental perspective. *Human Development, 26,* 213–221. Life-span (including adolescence) research is considered in terms of current status and alternative research strategies, and a revised concept of socialization is presented which suggests new questions for investigation.

Eklund, S. J. (1982). The psychological rights of the child and a life-span developmental perspective. *Viewpoints in Teaching and Learning, 58*(1), 36–43. Rights of minors are considered in relation to developmental changes from conception through adolescence and within the context of the total life span.

Green, L. B. & Hubbard, J. P. (1982). The "minority psychology" of adolescence: A concept for adult equanimity and rationality. *Adolescence, 17*(67), 585–603. Both adolescents and adults are portrayed as faring better when the older generation treats the younger one with fairness and rationality rather than emotionalism and authoritarianism.

Grinder, R. E. (1982). Isolationism in adolescent research. *Human Development, 25,* 223–232. Recommendations are made that adolescence research be integrated with, and capitalize upon, other research and that such research be broadened to include socioeconomic circumstances that shape interpretations of the significance of adolescence.

Hart, S. N. (1982). The history of children's psychological rights. *Viewpoints in Teaching and Learning, 58*(1), 1–15. Minors' psychological rights are considered from the historical perspective with regard to the nature of childhood, children's rights movements, and decision-making guidelines regarding rights.

Kulka, R. (1982). Monitoring social change via survey replication: Prospects and pitfalls from a republican survey of social roles and mental health. *Journal of Social Issues, 38*(1), 17–38. Alternative means of conducting longitudinal studies are examined in terms of their relative strengths and weaknesses, with particular reference to studying women and social change.

Kulka, R. & Colten, M. E. (1982). Secondary analysis of a longitudinal survey of educated women: A social psychological perspective. *Journal of Social Issues, 38*(1), 73–88. A particular set of data is analyzed to illustrate how such information may be used for studying particular social-psychological issues.

Lamke, L. K. (1982). The impact of sex-role orientation on self-esteem in early adolescence. *Child Development, 53*(6), 1530–1535. An examination of the relationship between sex-role orientation and self-esteem among 12- to 15-year-olds revealed that the effect of sex-role orientation on self-esteem was greater for females than males.

Reese, H. W. (1982). Behavior analysis and life-span developmental psychology. *Developmental Review, 2*(2), 150–161. Examination is made of five criticisms of developmental behavior analysis as related to the life-span perspective in developmental psychology.

Shapiro, D. & Crowley, J. E. (1982). Aspirations and expectations of youth in the United States, Part 2. Employment activity. *Youth and Society, 14*(1), 33–58. This study of youth's vocational aspirations shows them to be unrealistically high, to be revised downward somewhat with age, and to differ according to sex, psychological factors, and family background.

Simons, C. J. R. & Thomas, J. L. (1983). The life cycle in historical context: The impact of normative history-graded events on the course of life-span human development. *Human Development, 26,* 117–120. A review is made of conclusions which emerged from the eighth West Virginia University Biennial Conference on Life-Span Development which focused on the influence of history-graded events on human development.

Starr, J. M. (1983). Toward a social phenomenology of aging: Studying the self process in biographical work. *International Journal of Aging and Human Development, 16*(3), 255–270. The life history approach to aging, including cohort differences in aging patterns and historical changes in life course differentiations challenges the older "stability" and "ordered change" theories of aging.

Stewart, A. J. & Platt, M. B. (1982). Studying women in a changing world: An introduction. *Journal of Social Issues, 38*(1), 1–16. Issues involved in untangling cohort developmental, historical, and other factors in change are discussed, with particular reference to studying women in a changing world, along with a consideration of design and method employed in such studies.

Weisfeld, G. & Berger, J. M. (1983). Some features of human adolescence viewed in evolutionary perspective. *Human Development, 26,* 121–133. Features of adolescent development and their possible functions are viewed in evolutionary perspective on the basis of cross-cultural, comparative, hormonal, and developmental research.

Chapter Two

Self-Concept
And Personality

THE RELATIONSHIP OF SELF-
CONCEPT TO PERSONALITY

The popular concept of personality reflects its origin in the Latin word *persona,* a mask worn by Roman actors. In this sense, personality represents the individual as others see him or her, one's social-stimulus value. For example, a person may be classified as an infamous swindler, a gruff person with a heart of gold, or a diamond in the rough. Almost 18,000 words in the English language can be used to describe someone's personality. Some people think of personality as a highly desirable but mysterious gift bestowed on a favored few, including politicians and movie actors, but psychologists define personality as the whole feeling, thinking, acting being. They do not think of the individual as *having* personality but as *being* one.

Individuals view their own personalities through the distorting lenses of their own experience. Depending on past failures, successes, hopes, and fears, they may say, "I'm not such a bad guy" or "I'm a dumbbell." These remarks reflect the speaker's self-concept or personality as viewed from within.

Ellis and Davis (1982) use the term "self" to describe "the psychological and physical totality of a person" (p. 695). The self system represents "the organization and integration of all experiences into the self, whether or not the individual [is] aware of that organization" (p. 696).

The adolescent self-concept has various significant dimensions as well as the total organization by means of which these particular dimensions function together. The self-concept may be asynchronized in that some dimensions of self-concept may change while others remain stable; but when any dimension of self-concept changes its modifications influence the whole self-concept. Thus the developing self-concept may be interpreted both as a changing entity as well as "evolving multi-dimensional parts" (p. 696).

How Self-Concept Originates

An adequate self-concept is so vital to an adolescent's well-being that we shall analyze this subject in detail. First, let us trace how a self-concept comes to be.

One assumption basic to understanding human behavior is that every significant act is done to satisfy some need. These needs may be thought of as ranging from lower- to higher-order needs (Maslow, 1954):

PHYSIOLOGICAL NEEDS: for satisfaction of hunger, thirst

SAFETY NEEDS: for security, order, stability

BELONGINGNESS AND LOVE NEEDS: for affection, identification

ESTEEM NEEDS: for prestige, success, self-respect

SELF-ACTUALIZATION NEEDS

The terms *lower* and *higher* as applied to needs merely indicate that some needs assert themselves earlier than others in the developmental process and are more directly concerned with biological satisfaction. The lower need must be reasonably well satisfied before the next higher need is sharply felt. A starving person will risk his or her life to get food; physiological needs take precedence over safety needs.

Other principles applying to need satisfaction may be summarized as follows: (1) Individual development is not a matter of definite steps, but of gradual shifting from one level to the next. It may involve setbacks, as in the case of the tired, discouraged art student who squanders on one big meal all the money she has saved for art materials. (2) Progression from one level to another will not occur if a need at any level is insufficiently fulfilled. For example, the chronically insecure boy is more concerned about feeling safe than about winning social success. (3) As a person moves up the need scale, lower needs do not disappear but assume a place of lesser importance in the motivational structure. Even an artist engrossed in painting a picture pauses to satisfy pangs of hunger. Lower-order needs no longer dominate, however. Many an ambitious youth has existed on a substandard diet in order to afford the education he or she desperately wanted.

DEVELOPMENT OF BEHAVIOR TRAITS   In the process of seeking to satisfy needs, each individual finds certain behaviors more effective than others. These behaviors, practiced until they become enduring characteristics, are called *traits*. Some persons' traits are central to their makeup; others are peripheral, or less fundamental in accounting for the kinds of persons they are. It is the unique way that traits are ordered that gives individuals their distinctive personalities. Note this teenager's description of herself:

> FEMALE: I don't have much initiative or creativity; nor am I one for responsibility. Another of my lovely attributes is my bad temper. I fly up at any little thing. I constantly make mountains out of molehills. Until I was 16 I was shy and bashful, but I have changed. My dislikes consist of cats and people. If I don't like someone I make it plain by telling him or ignoring him. I embarrass easily; I am very sensitive. I'm also sarcastic and say a lot of things I don't mean.

Each individual's personality traits become organized into a unique pattern, or personality syndrome, composed of those characteristics which have proven most useful and have become habituated. In other words,

> those traits closely related to the enhancement of a child's self-concept are especially crucial and become the bases for less fundamental traits. Thus a girl may identify closely with her mother and vaguely feel like a little mother herself. With great solicitude she tends her little brother; with complete conscientiousness she helps clean the house. These traits—motherliness, nurturance, and conscientiousness—become a cornerstone of her personality. In time, she develops other traits, too. For instance, she may be so home-bound that she becomes relatively reserved and overly serious. One readily sees, therefore, that traits do not arise in random fashion. All are part of a pattern that is integrated by central goals and values. (Rogers, 1969, pp. 107–108)

Traits themselves vary in the degree to which they are biologically or culturally determined. Temperamental traits are dependent on native endowment. They are highly resistant to change and constitute a core around which other traits are formed. Other characteristics are largely a matter of experience and environmental influence and are comparatively easier to change.

THE INDIVIDUAL'S ROLES   In the individual, traits interact with and modify each other because they are organized into patterns appropriate to roles. Roles are sets of socially expected behavior patterns associated with an individual's functions in various social groups. Sex and family roles are most important in early childhood, but others are enacted throughout life, simultaneously or in succession. In adolescence the student role dominates all the other roles. By this age, family role has diminished and the vocational role has rarely been assumed.

In a sense, adolescents' roles are more rigid than those of adults. Adolescents had no choice over their family of origin; they must attend school and they are restricted with certain peers. Adults have more control over their lives. Adults can change their careers, obtain a divorce, and select friends on bases of congenial interests from a broader area (Mortimer & Simmons, 1978). In this sense, adult roles are more flexible and encourage a wider range of behavior than do those of children and youth.

Youth draw on portrayals of television role models as they try out media life styles in their peer groups. Thus, they determine which roles harmonize with their own emerging identities by enacting them and receiving feedback from their peers (Peterson & Peters, 1983).

In time, individuals come to feel that they play their roles well, poorly, or in a mediocre manner. In other words, an individual develops a self-concept, which comprises the impressions and beliefs concerning the kind of person he

In adolescence the student role dominates all other roles. (Courtesy of Public Relations Office, State University of New York at Oswego)

or she is. Such remarks as "I lost my temper" or "I always seem to goof" afford glimpses of an individual's self-concept.

Although some persons perceive themselves far more favorably than they are perceived by others, no one is exactly what he or she would like to be. Coexistent with self is an ideal self, or *ego-ideal*, which would satisfy more of the individual's needs and would come closer to the individual's standards of what is admirable than the real self does. Stated otherwise, the ideal self is the sort of person an individual would like to become.

LIFE STYLE   The individual's own adaptation of roles and opportunities through life becomes that individual's **life style** on which individuals place their personal stamp. The adolescent's life style will continuously change and evolve and "represents [his or her] endless compromise between personal goals and environmental demands. Certain approaches prove rewarding and become habituated—distinguishing marks of the life style. Others may be rejected after being given a trial" (Rogers, 1982). A youth's life structure may be loosely or tightly organized, externally or internally directed, dominated by short- or long-term goals (Van Dusen & Sheldon, 1976).

On the individual level, life style reflects the continuing integration of personal goals and external requirements. One tries out various life styles, discarding aspects of them after finding them unrewarding. A young person may enter a commune or join a group drifting around the country but ultimately find that the values of a middle-class upbringing cannot easily be discarded. That is, each individual carries a certain emotional and cultural "baggage" that limits the choice of life style (Van Dusen & Sheldon, 1976).

A look at history shows that youth's life style is much more comfortable than in former generations. In times past rugged individualism, with its focus on dedicated work, enterprise, risk-taking, and achievement produced a well-to-do middle class (Archer, 1982). Even when such persons had "made it," they continued to expect more rewards in the future. Their philosophy was one of delayed gratification denying themselves now for prospects of a brighter future. In contrast, their children inherited a certain affluence—hence, looked forward to a rewarding life style, without delayed gratification (Logan & O'Hearn, 1982). Meantime, the frontier mentality, which "pulled people like a magnet toward the future" had declined; and the fact that many challenges had been overcome collectively conspired to focus youths' minds on the present.

The latest orientation of the "post-affluent" or "post-industrial society" (Brandwein, 1981), came into being after World War II, and has characterized the upper middle class of the past decade or so. The new focus is on experiencing life as fully as possible with the least effort possible. Another element of this scenario, produced by such events as the bomb, Vietnam, and Watergate, has been a fear of the future, causing a greater focus on the present.

This living in the present has caused young people to focus on their own age "and to experience the various ages or stages of the life cycle less as rungs on the continuous ladder of life, but as separate and distinct ways of life lived by different kinds of people" (p. 525). Nowadays, "being young is lived with such intensity that it ceases merely to be an age; it becomes, in effect, a culture or a land" (p. 525). Youth are separated these days psychologically from adults because the world has changed so rapidly that a great gulf separates them.

Self-Concept Formation
as a Developmental Process

The search for self begins in childhood. However, the intellectual and emotional awareness of self, which emerges from interaction with others, is especially characteristic of adolescents. Around age 13 an individual's family affiliations become increasingly clarified and the self-assertion dimension becomes more prominent (Ellis & Davis, 1982). Meantime, growth in self-acceptance is accompanied by more independent functioning; and by age 16, adolescents may begin their final thrust away from the family (Ellis & Davis, 1982).

In general, self-concepts become less concrete and more abstract with advancing years. When subjects in grades 4, 6, 8, 10, and 12 responded to the question "Who am I?" younger ones mainly described themselves in concrete terms, including references to their possessions, play activities, and physical appearance, while adolescents employed more subjective, abstract descriptions, including motivational, interpersonal, and attitudinal characteristics (Montemayor & Eisen, 1977). Many of the adolescents referred to themselves in terms of name and sex, suggesting that such characteristics have important significance to them. Fewer of the younger children portrayed themselves in abstract terms, except for the 12-year-olds who called themselves "a person" or "a human." Here are typical responses, the first from a 9-year-old boy in the fourth grade, which reflects the concrete flavor of the younger children's answers:

> My name is Bruce C. I have brown eyes. I have brown hair. I have brown eyebrows. I'm nine years old. I LOVE! sports. I have seven people in my family. I have great! eye site. I have lots! of friends. I live on 1923 Pinecrest Dr. I'm going on 10 in September. I'm a boy. I have a uncle that is almost 7 feet tall. My school is Pinecrest. My teacher is Mrs. V. I play Hockey! I'm almost the smartest boy in the class. I LOVE! food. I love fresh air. I LOVE school. (Montemayor & Eisen, 1977, p. 317)

The next example, from a twelfth-grade 17-year-old girl, indicates a movement toward the abstract, with emphasis on mood states and ideology.

> I am a human being. I am a girl. I am an individual. I don't know who I am. I am a Pisces. I am a moody person. I am an indecisive person. I am an ambitious person. I am a very curious person. I am not an individual. I am a loner. I am an American (God help me). I am a Democrat. I am a liberal person. I am a radical. I am a conservative. I am a pseudoliberal. I am an atheist. I am not a classifiable person (i.e., I don't want to be). (Montemayor & Eisen, 1977, p. 318)

Children tell about what they look like, where they live, and what they do, selecting a somewhat shallow and undifferentiated concept. Adolescents perceive themselves in terms of intrinsic personality characteristics and qualities, producing a unique self. They do not simply add abstract ideas to earlier concrete descriptions but perceive themselves quite differently, in an integrated, more complex fashion (Montemayor & Eisen, 1977).

It is sometimes assumed that an individual self-concept is significant in guiding and directing behavior; it is also assumed that people have a single global self-concept that they bring into all situations in which they are involved. Rather, it appears that an individual's self-concept depends very much on the context concerned. Even within a single role, such as that of son or daughter, when placed in a different context, self-ratings are multiple and distinct according to specific interactional settings. The idea of an undifferentiated global self-concept is "overly simplistic" (Griffin, Chassin & Young, 1981, p. 55).

M. Snyder (1980) agrees, saying that "as much as we might like to believe that the self is an integral feature of personal identity, . . . the self is a product of the individual's relationships with other people . . . there may be striking depths and contradictions . . . between the public appearances and private realities of the self" (M. Snyder, 1980, p. 32).

It has become "almost a canon of modern psychology that a person's ability to reveal the private self to intimates is essential to emotional health" (M. Snyder, 1980, p. 40). In this regard some individuals are high self-monitors, who have unusual ability to monitor the image that they project to others, and then to adjust their behaviors to the reactions that they elicit from others. In contrast, low self-monitors tend simply to act as they feel, rather than modifying their behaviors to fit their audience. These high monitors do not employ their special skills to deceive or manipulate others, but rather to promote healthier social interaction. The fact that high self-monitors are good at initiating conversations and are not shy, helps to maintain social relationships of a high quality. In addition, the overt behaviors of high self-monitors tell little about their inner feelings.

Self-images, whether revealed or not, are continually modified, undergoing elaboration as the individual moves through successive phases of development. By adolescence, the person's self-concept has become somewhat refined and sometimes operates unconsciously. At other times, as in the case below, it projects itself sharply into the forefront of consciousness.

> FEMALE: When I first discovered the mystery of my own being, . . . I still see myself standing in front of my mother's mirror marveling at myself. But the more I asked, the more those greenish eyes out of the mirror asked back; the more I tried to get into myself, the more I closed my inner self. Finally, the eyes began to flicker and glitter, and I said to myself in the mirror: "I hate you," and I really meant it. After that I was so frightened I ran out like I had done something very bad. (Moustakas, 1956, p. 204)

FACTORS MODIFYING ADOLESCENTS' SELF-CONCEPTS

Effect of Others' Attitudes on Self-Concept

The discovery of self and the capacity to develop to maturity involves examining the self in relation to the society in which one lives, and its development depends on differentiating "the self from the nonself" and on social interaction (Hayes, 1982). The process is furthered by systematic programs of education, designed to encourage an individual's development to higher stages, which should be the "central purpose of the high school curriculum" (p. 159). Thus, personal development depends on social interaction not just to take the perspective of others toward oneself and learn to assume the perspective of others, but to take the perspective of the entire community within which one works and lives. In other words, people who discover themselves as individuals must be able to place their selves into relations with other selves. Nor does one lose individuality in such relations but gains a sense of self through them (Youniss, 1980, p. 20). A youth's belief that he or she is attractive, smart, or silly is to a considerable extent formulated through labels applied by others. Especially important are the opinions of those who are significant others—persons having a central place in a person's scheme of things, notably parents and peers.

One might wonder whether adopted children have a poorer than normal self-concept since they are not their foster parents' "flesh and blood." Adoption per se appears to have no effect on self-concept scores when the child is adopted at a young age. That is, the adoptive status in itself does not produce a negative identity. When negative elements do become part of an adolescent's identity, they typically stem from problems within the home (Norvell & Guy, 1977). However, the initial motives that adults have for adopting children are very important for a child's later adjustment. The older the child was when adopted, the lower the individual's self-concept is likely to be, probably because the older child has undergone shifting family relationships. A healthy self-concept appears to develop independently of the assigned status of adoptee.

Adolescents' sense of self-worth is importantly influenced by their peers who are, in a sense, a closed corporation. They communicate with other young people, and their goods and services are increasingly provided by them. Most popular music is provided by rock bands and pop singers who themselves are part of the youth culture. By contrast, the entertainers of two decades ago were seldom young themselves. Thus, the youth culture sets standards against which its members continually measure themselves.

In the following examples, note the relationship between teenagers' self-concepts and the opinions they believe others hold of them:

> FEMALE: I'm self-confident at times; at other times I'm at a loss. I'm glad I'm me. . . . Most people think I'm a snob from the Big City. Close friends don't feel that way.

> MALE: I detest myself, knowing that I haven't utilized my powers for self-growth. . . . My presence evokes attitudes ranging from bellicosity to contempt.

> MALE: I have many idiosyncrasies that displease others, but they please me. . . . I am not well liked.

Youth who believe themselves poorly regarded by others, in an effort to bolster their self-concept, may resort to prejudice and bigotry (Logan, 1978). Condemning some group viewed as inferior raises one's own self esteem; and by interpreting some out-group as "threatening, one temporarily builds the boundaries of the self (and of one's group as well) into a kind of fortress identity . . ." (p. 506).

Effects of Age, Sex, and Culture

Age is a significant factor in self-concept. Society attaches importance to maturity, hence teenagers view themselves as less important than adults. Remarks like "Wait till you grow up" or "Mother and Dad know best" are constant blows to adolescent self-esteem. Parenthetically, this high estimation of adulthood constitutes an advantage in the socialization process, encouraging progress toward maturity.

Research supports the idea that the sense of self does indeed change over the years; for example, in a study of students in grades 4 through 8, the sixth graders expressed the poorest self-attitudes, perhaps because of anxiety about impending transfer from the neighborhood school to a larger junior high school. The eighth graders were least rejecting of themselves, and such negative perceptions as they had related largely to home and parents, at times reflecting increasing efforts to attain autonomy (Kokenes, 1974). Despite earlier changes, it would seem that once stabilized, self-esteem remains fairly constant. In one study, students' self-esteem was fairly high at the tenth-grade level and rose over the next eight years. Students' feelings of self-worth were relatively stable (Bachman, O'Malley, & Johnston, 1978).

Self-concept also relates to sex-role orientation. In a study of high school students, in grades 10 to 12, masculinity in females was consistently predictive of self-esteem, thus disproving the traditional assumption that a positive adjustment for female adolescents depends upon adopting a feminine sex-role orientation (Lamke, 1982). Among males both masculinity and femininity appeared important for high self-esteem.

A great deal of research relates to the relationship between positive self-image, self-confidence, and intelligence. The gifted tend to be more accepting of themselves, have a greater sense of direction, and are more adaptive. They are high with regard to "goal integration" and more confident of vocational choice (Hogan, 1980). Compared to less talented individuals they tend to be high on self-esteem and post-conventional moral reasoning ability, and low in anxiety (Monks & Ferguson, 1983).

In other research, a comparison of Indian, American, Australian, and Irish adolescents disclosed that the Americans had higher self-esteem (Agrawal, 1978). The Indian teenagers were rarely exposed to emotional situations outside the home and were subject to a long period of dependency. As a result, they were relatively immature as well as introverted, withdrawn, lonely, and isolated. Since they lacked adequate relationships with people outside the home, they had little empathy. In contrast, American adolescents seemed more capable of coping with social pressures. They also experienced greater release of aggressive and sensual impulses, partly because they understood sexual phenomena better. The Indian boys had poorer self-concepts because they were responsible for becoming their family's breadwinners, yet had little economic opportunity. Nevertheless, they had higher self-esteem and a better psychological integration than the Irish adolescents. On the other hand, the Irish boys adapted better in the areas of sex, family relations, and vocation.

We might question whether cultures that provide growing individuals relatively greater privacy afford a better environment for producing self-esteem.

Wolfe (1978) refers to the ego dimension of privacy—namely, that in private situations people feel free to choose their own movements. Privacy is also perceived as affording protection for the self, yielding feelings of personal dignity and self-esteem (Laufer & Wolfe, 1977).

IMPORTANCE OF SELF-CONCEPT

General Significance

For many reasons, self-perception has an important influence on an individual's behavior. Perception of self tends to determine what people experience and how they experience it. Individuals may try hard to ignore experiences that do not reinforce their concepts of themselves; or they may distort them so they do not conflict. A boy may perceive himself as an intellectual and spend hours in the library to convince himself and others of his scholarly tastes. When he fails to convince an instructor of his genius, he rationalizes that the instructor is a low-brow.

A strong self-concept provides a sense of continuity which is central to the process of personality maturation. It embraces sex and vocational roles and an integrated sense of values. In societies and situations where sex roles are blurred or highly varied and adequate identification models are scarce, role diffusion may develop.

Special Significance
at Adolescence

For several reasons, self-concept is especially important at adolescence. Because of their growing autonomy and physical strength, adolescents have a degree of freedom that makes a distorted self-concept dangerous. Moreover, adolescents' self-concepts, built upon their limited childhood experiences, hinder them in relating to new and varied situations.

Adolesence itself is important in the development of the self-concept. During this period, self-image is being crystallized at the same time that it is being revised. Expanding experiences characteristic of adolescence constantly force reevaluation of self and color feelings of adequacy or failure. For most adolescents, the self-image evolves subtly, without difficulty; but those with a sharply deviant make-up may have problems. Their very difference from others highlights the sense of self and compels insistent self-examination. The fact that most adolescents reject deviant traits may undermine the self-confidence of unusual individuals and set them brooding over their social isolation.

ENHANCING THE SELF-CONCEPT

Enhancement Through
Self-Actualization

NATURE OF SELF-ACTUALIZATION   Among the important ways of maintaining and enhancing the self-concept, perhaps the most basic method of all is self-actualization, or the process of becoming one's best and truest self. The term **self-actualization** implies a progression through sequential and increasingly higher levels of motives and organization. It emphasizes constructive development of potential, rather than obstacles to adjustment, such as fear, anxiety, and frustration. Self-actualization also implies a way of life compatible with one's unique pattern of traits, instead of slavish imitation of others.

The criteria for self-actualization and success are usually defined in terms of goals considered important in the western society (Monks & Ferguson, 1983). Rather, Maslow (1954) defined the self-actualized individual as "a creative, autonomous self, virtually independent of culture"; this definition encourages a duty-to-self ethic. Some critics insist that the search for self-fulfillment is nothing more than self-indulgence and self-centeredness—"the excesses of a me generation made decadent by too much affluence" (Yankelovich, 1983, p. 40). Yankelovich also speaks of the danger deriving from erstwhile theories of "self psychology" and "need language" and people's preoccupation with their inner and personal needs, and viewing themselves as simply an "assemblage" of those needs (p. 50). This credo benefits the individual but tends to ignore society's well-being. Rather, an individual should develop principles for integrating societal goals with personal values and behaviors.

Formerly, and until very recently, the contract between an individual and his or her culture was one of built-in self-denial and sacrifice and lay at the core of what is called "the American dream" (Yankelovich, 1983, p. 55). One would deny oneself and then, having worked hard, achieve material success for oneself and one's family. More recently most people have become more preoccupied with immediate satisfaction.

However, self-fulfillment, in the sense of finding a congenial life style, is not to be confused with selfishness. Youth, like their elders, consist of two main categories, says Yankelovich (1980). First there are those who hunger for the human experience of self-fulfillment. Other individuals represent a backlash against such sentiment, seeking to restore the older values. They seek to link political measures and religious fundamentalism to defeat the evils of what they term "secular humanism." This concept really means "social pluralism"—the freedom to choose one's own life style within certain generous limits, in one sense the very essence of self fulfillment" (Yankelovich, 1983, p. 40).

Of the two college students in the following quotations, we would judge the second more likely to achieve true self-actualization than the first:

> But I do want something out of life which I can consider as evidence that I am better than average—an ego booster, if you please. When I say "better," I don't mean in the social sense, or on account of my family, or anything like that. Better to me means more competent, more capable than the mediocre masses, whom I despise because of their apathy and mediocrity. This is why I work as I do—to insure that I will never fall into these masses.

> In life the thing I value most is happiness, which to me is roughly material comfort. I not only want this for myself, but also for the rest of the world. This is one of the reasons I am a scientist—so I can chip in my two-bits' worth toward the well-being of the rest of the world. If during my lifetime I make the rest of humanity, or humanity to come, just one iota more comfortable, then I will be content. (The "unsilent generation" breaks silence, 1958, pp. 113–114)

HELPING YOUTH TO ACHIEVE SELF ACTUALIZATION   Significant adults may fail to facilitate a youth's self-actualization. For example, teachers rate girls as better learners and harder workers than boys; however, they interact more with boys. Among either sex, teachers react most favorably toward high-achieving boys and most disapproving toward low-achieving boys, whereas they tend to treat all girls somewhat the same. Thus, teachers fail to encourage achievement among high ability girls as much as they do equally able boys (Parsons, Kaczala & Meece, 1982).

Where both sexes are concerned parents appear less preoccupied with aspirations for their children than in former years. In the 1960s, among American adults, "aspirations for children as a focus of personal hopes ranked second only to a desire for a decent, if possible, improved standard of living" (p. 39). By the early 1980s the percentage who named aspirations for their children had dramatically declined. This change might be interpreted as indicating greater concern by parents for their own continued self-realization or, as Watts (1981) believes, represents a growing tendency to allow children to design their own lives. The best solution is to encourage such initiative while, at the same time, providing encouragement and reasonable assistance.

Also essential is helping children and youth to develop the self-confidence and coping skills required to feel in charge of one's destiny. Smith (1983) points out that, over time, individuals develop expectations about the extent of personal control that they can have over events. Those who feel they have a measure of control proceed to develop modes of coping and to cope actively, whereas those who have no great hope proceed simply with withdrawal.

Under skilled guidance, a group may discuss various ideas of what constitutes a self-actualizing person. For one thing, self-actualizers are ready to endure privation to achieve what they truly value. They have achieved levels beyond mere concern for such lower-order needs as food and clothing. Of course, self-actualizers have biological needs, but they attach less importance to them.

In order that youth may understand how such characteristics contribute to an effective life style or fit into a pattern of living, it may prove helpful for them to discuss well-known persons like Lincoln, Beethoven, and Schweitzer in terms of the foregoing characteristics. Students may measure themselves in the same ways to determine their present status with regard to self-actualization.

Adolescents also need constructive outlets for interests and energies. Note this youth's despair at having no worlds to conquer: "I often regretted that there were no great causes left to fight for; that I could not be crucified, nor go on a crusade, nor choose to defend the cause of Saint Joan against the (then) wicked English, nor free slaves, nor kill tyrants. I thirsted for great injustices" (Spender, 1951, p. 2).

Enhancement Through Identification

Identity should be differentiated from identification. **Identification** is the merging of one's own purposes and values with those of another. The identification process, if carried too far, impedes establishment of identity. Accustomed to patterning after others, individuals who overidentify have difficulty integrating conflicting values of the various groups of which they are a part.

They identify with unreal people on television and films, and allow them to think and feel for them. However, youth are growing tired of this "second-hand living" and are becoming aware of their inner selves.

The matter of selecting identification figures or role models is complex, as shown in certain Texas high schools (Oberle, Stowers & Falk, 1978). Of these students, interviewed first as sophomores and again as seniors, blacks and whites preferred different kinds of role models. As sophomores, the black youths liked glamour figures such as famous athletes, while whites named parents, relatives not in the immediate family, close friends, and glamour figures about equally. Black senior boys, like the sophomores, preferred glamour figures, while white senior boys chose parents and relatives not in the immediate family. The black sophomore girls named about equally glamour figures, relatives not in the immediate family, parents, teachers, and school counselors, while white sophomore girls chose close friends. Among the seniors, black girls preferred teachers and school counselors about equally, while the white girls still preferred close friends. In general, more rural than urban youth preferred glamour figures, while the urban youth more often preferred close friends. The rural adolescents had fewer opportunities to make close friends who might serve as role models.

Overall, glamour figures were popular among the boys, being preferred by 40 percent of the urban boys and 49 percent of rural boys. As anticipated, almost no girls, rural or urban, picked famous athletes as role models; nor did either sex name siblings as role models. Relatives outside the immediate family were equally popular among urban and rural girls, and more so than among the boys (Oberle, Stowers, & Falk, 1978).

When college students were asked to name figures they had identified with from childhood to the present, family members were often included. Others were highy varied.

FEMALE: My high school gym teacher; an aunt who took me on a trip to Mexico; in college a professor who took an interest in me.

MALE: When I was between 10 and 13 I strongly identified with my best friend's older brother. I envied everything he did (good and bad) and wanted to be and act like him. Now I'm bigger than he is and haven't seen him in six years, but I still have his image in the back of my mind.

MALE: In my early years, I identified wth my parents; but as I grew and became more conscious of the world around me, I gained a great respect for a coach in my high school and idealized him for a time. Later I took great admiration in men who were trained in auto mechanics and racing. But now my greatest identity goes back to my father.

Enhancement Through Mastery and Achievement

MASTERY AS MOTIVE Also contributing to the adolescent's self-enhancement is mastery, a drive encouraged by competition within juvenile society. This need suggests both drive and goal and is especially important for adolescents. The mastery motive may be further subdivided into mastery of personal and social environment, each with its typical means of realization. For many reasons, mastery of others is essential to adolescents' ego-enhancement. Throughout

The mastery need suggests both drive and goal and is especially important to adolescents. (Photo by Margaret Hester)

their brief lives others have commanded their destinies. They have taken orders from their parents and, in order to ensure social acceptance, have acceded to their peers. Social realities have made them the puppets of others; for example, they may be required to attend a school that fails to meet their needs or settle for jobs that pay poorly.

THE ACHIEVEMENT MOTIVE   Researchers have tried, with varied results, to identify traits that characterize individuals who strive to master or achieve. Kline and Golombek (1974) administered questionnaires to high school seniors and their parents, and students whose achievement and educational plans were distinctly superior were identified. Such students felt that status and achievement were important, hard work was required, and mental work was desirable. In addition, they had well-defined goals that they valued and that had been directly influenced by their parents, either positively or negatively. Significantly, all the students could identify someone outside the immediate family who had played a special part in their feelings about higher education. Four of them indicated that their interest in a future vocation began with a certain teacher. Teachers singled out as being special ranged all the way from "warm, empathic, understanding" to "cold, aloof, brilliant." Kline and Golombek noted in conclusion that schools would do well to employ teachers with divergent and strongly individualistic personalities. The type of teacher preferred related to the type of student who was influenced.

In another study, involving business school students at the University of Texas, those who expected to start a company some day had no stronger motive to achieve than did the rest of the students (Shapero, 1975). Instead, "what set them apart was that they had a strong belief in internal control and a low belief in the ability of teachers to control their destinies" (p. 84). Such individuals were independent, inner-directed, somewhat alienated, and unsocial. Most of them would not consider working for someone else. Similarly, studies of adult entrepreneurs—those who establish a business, initiate a civic project, organize a new department at work—indicate that they worry less about what others think than other people do and that they are willing to take risks. They are not the valedictorians; instead they may be drop-outs. Nevertheless, concludes Cornuelle (1975), such individuals provide the spark for society and initiate its business.

It seems especially important that girls have access to adequate role models in higher education to develop interest in working and achieving (Ridgeway, 1978). However, men's opinions seem more critical in determining their feelings about the social acceptability of successful women. Women without high aspirations who become compelled by circumstances to work outside the home are unlikely either to aspire to or achieve a high-status vocation, yet young women's development of career aspirations and commitment to career-oriented life styles and thinking "are keys to future changes in women's standing within our society" (p. 290).

The peer group itself may have a negative effect on individual adolescents' achievement aspirations. Earlier studies have suggested that adolescents cared little for self-change, displayed a mixture of adult and childlike characteristics, and remained somewhat shallow and undeveloped. The most important determinant of peer status was athletic prowess, and cars were quite important. A study of boys in two high schools near Detroit partially supported these conclusions. In agreement with earlier studies, they attached great importance to their peer groups but they also showed at least some desire for personal change (Edwards, 1979). It seems that most of these adolescents may well develop into "shallow, dependent, childish, and undeveloped adults" (p. 103).

The question might be raised: How much achievement orientation is good? Eleanor Roosevelt, as an adolescent, proclaimed the importance of personal ambition.

> Those who are ambitious and make a place and a name in the great world for themselves are nearly always despised and laughed at by lesser souls who could not do as well, and all they do for the good of men is construed into wrong; and yet they do the good and they leave their mark upon the ages, and if they had no ambition, would they have ever made a mark? Is it best never to be known and leave the world a blank as if one had never come? It must have been meant, it seems to me, that we should leave some mark upon the world, and not just live and pass away. (Lash, 1971 p. 110)

VALUE OF ACHIEVING A SENSE OF IDENTITY **Identity** is not to be confused with *self-concept.* Self-concept includes a person's total picture of himself or herself, whereas identity refers to a feeling of distinctiveness from others. It implies consciousness of oneself as an entity with a definite place in the general scheme of things. The person with a sense of identity feels "all of a piece." The self-picture is integrated, not diffuse. Without consciously knowing it, a girl feels, "I am Joan Smith, a person. I am not simply a statistic, a one-among-many. I matter; I've a reason for being."

Marcia (1980) describes identity as "a self structure—an internal, self-constructed, dynamic organization of drives, abilities, beliefs and individual history" (p. 159). If this structure is well developed individuals are conscious of their own uniqueness as well as their likeness to others. If their identity is poorly developed they are confused about their own distinctiveness and commonly depend on others to evaluate them.

Donovan (1975) notes that "identity formation is one of the engaging, yet elusive, topics in contemporary psychology." It is also one of the most important. Erikson (1968) portrayed development in terms of successive psychosocial crises, the one specific to adolescence being the establishment of a stable sense of identity. If adolescents are able to make career decisions and to form sets of beliefs about religion and politics, they are said to have achieved **ego identity.** The absence of stable conclusions is called **identity diffusion.** The term **identity crisis** is defined as "a period of struggle or active questioning in arriving at a set of beliefs and a vocational choice. **Commitment** is defined as a firm, unwavering decision regarding occupational plans and belief systems" (p. 167).

Meacham and Santilli (1982) say that certain questions remain to be answered if Erikson's concepts of identity and intimacy in adolescence are to make sense within the context of total life development, and not simply as descriptions of "isolated crises" (p. 1461). These questions include, whether there must be a crisis, whether one can progress developmentally after unsuccessfully resolving some prior crisis; what are the developmental consequences of foreclosure; and what actually constitutes the successful resolution of a crisis.

Marcia (1966) expanded Erikson's basic theme into four identity statuses: *achievement, moratorium, foreclosure,* and *diffusion.* The **achievement** status connotes successful resolution of crisis and an ability to commit oneself "ideologically, occupationally and interpersonally" (Morgan & Farber, 1982, p. 204). Individuals who have arrived at identity achievement have consolidated their identities through clearly thought out decisions after examining alternatives. **Foreclosure** individuals never experience an identity crisis, but have prematurely established one mainly on the basis of parents' choices for them. Such an identity is too flexible to constitute an adequate foundation for resolving future crises. Those in the **moratorium status** are in the process of testing ideological and vocational alternatives but have made no firm commitments in these areas. They are involved currently in individual crisis. In other words, identity moratorium is crisis itself and is a time to struggle, to reevaluate and redefine one's goals before identity is actually achieved, and to try out different roles. **Identity diffusion** means avoidance of crisis and failure to acquire any sense of self-direction (Morgan & Farber, 1982).

A study by Coté and Levine (1983) failed to support Marcia's hierarchy of ego identity status along a developmental continuum. Among Marcia's four identity statuses only one, the moratorium status, could be differentiated from the others. Others perceive a rough continuum at least and suggest that an identity should be firmly established in adolescence. Still others view adolescents as not having yet established an identity and as undergoing identity crises before they decide who they are. Therefore, it would seem appropriate to deprive adolescents of full rights and to continue to control them until they know who they are. Thus, the invention of the social category of adolescents, along with theories invented relative to it, such as that they lack a feeling of identity, have contributed to forcibly delaying their assumption of adult roles (Starr, 1981).

This writer wishes to add that even an infant has a feeling of identity of sorts which gradually, over time, assumes greater clarity. Moreover, the process of defining and redefining the identity is one that persists throughout life; and the search for, and resolution of identity crisis, as commonly portrayed, represents it as too isolated and abrupt a phenomenon.

In general, older adolescents have made more progress in identity achievement than younger ones; however, such progress does not proceed in an all-or-not fashion. Archer (1982) found that older, more often than early, adolescents would, as identity achievers, make sophisticated decisions. Among early adolescents diffusion and premature foreclosure were the main identity statuses; however, some achievers and moratoriums were found even among sixth graders. In other words, individual identity statuses did not relate consistently to grade level. Hence, Marcia concluded that "the identity process neither begins nor ends with adolescence" (1980, p. 160). Also, consistent with research with older age groups—for example, that by Waterman (1982)—no sex differences were found in the pattern of identity development.

Identity achievement varies in different areas—for example, Archer (1982) reported identity achievement most often in occupational and religious areas. Identity achievement in the vocational area may be due to the school environment, where students are encouraged to think of college majors, employment, and curriculum tracks. On the other hand the study of evolution in science classes may result in some conflict with home religious teaching—hence, many tenth graders may be somewhat diffuse with regard to religion, suggesting that they are still exploring alternatives. In Archer's study, diffusion was especially apparent in the political philosophies area, partly because adolescents lacked actual experience in the political arena. This writer suggests also that adolescents are often taught such matters in a way that is hardly conducive to developing philosophical concepts. At any rate, the students expressed little feeling of "personal investment" in such matters.

There were a surprising number of foreclosures in the sex-role content area, perhaps due to adolescents' limited opportunities to explore alternatives, coupled with exposure to many alternatives provided in the media which appear unrealistic to them, or to parent and peer pressures to assume more limited "appropriate" roles. Apparently, traditional sex roles are still encouraged in high schools, and defections from narrower roles typically do not occur until the college years, when broader interpretations of sex roles become better accepted by their peer groups. Overall, looking at these contents individually affords a clearer overall view of adolescents' identity development than a report of overall identity status.

Mere sense of identity is not enough: It must be a healthy identity. A distorted sense of identity can have negative effects. Maladjusted individuals wrapped up in themselves believe that everyone is looking at them. They may play to this audience by showing off, driving recklessly, committing crimes, or wearing bizarre dress.

Identity in the positive sense has constructive values for adolescents. It suggests doing one's own thing—that is, being true to what one really is, instead of merely playing at being oneself. It connotes autonomy as a person, based on understanding of, and confidence in, self. Although it is the rare individual who is capable of clearly verbalizing this need, many adolescents feel it:

Now that I am rapidly approaching the end of my senior year I must inevitably think of the future. I am still unsettled in my plans, but I know some things I do not want. I will not accept regimentation or compulsion, whether in the army or anywhere else. The only control I respect is that which is self-imposed. I do not want an ordered life, regularity, or their concomitant responsibilities. My continuing problem, as I see it, is to find my identity, to find my place in a society which demands a total commitment that I cannot give. I believe in the sovereign individual and feel myself at bay. This I do want, to live in freedom, unrestricted by exterior compulsion. I want my contribution to life to be a living testimonial that individual freedom is compatible with the welfare and progress of society. (The "unsilent generation" breaks silence, 1958, p. 126)

PERSONALITY Progress toward establishing a healthy identity varies according to personality characteristics. A study of high school students in southwestern Virginia (Wilkerson, Protinsky, Maxwell & Lentner, 1982) showed that those individuals who had developed a stronger ego identity had fewer feelings of alienation, suggesting that each individual, in growing up, needs some success and feelings of achievement if he or she is to feel adequate to accomplish goals in subsequent years. Otherwise, individuals have feelings of little control over their own destiny.

The establishment of a clear identity also relates to being nontraditional. In a study of young women in a private Eastern college (Stein & Weston, 1982) individuals with nontraditional views had a clearer sense of identity than those with traditional views. Of course, nontraditional views which conflict with societal norms may contribute to a strong sense of identity because nontraditional persons are constantly confronted with the way they differ from most people in the society. These findings challenge the views of those clinical psychologists who continue to believe that well-adjusted women should accept traditional female roles, and of critics of the woman's movement who believe that few feminists are well-adjusted.

Particular personality characteristics and behaviors are associated with each identity status. Among a sampling of women college students Josselson (1982) found that those in moratorium status were trying to go it alone and when fearful they did not run to others for comfort. They could support their own anxieties and were more interested in what they could, rather than couldn't do—thus possessing considerable adaptive abilities. The achievement girls had already successfully established their identity through being able somehow to integrate divergent aspects of themselves. Their inner selves appeared to represent a healthy balance between their need to relate to others and to assert themselves. They emphasized their own potential. In contrast with the achievers, the foreclosures were somewhat preoccupied with their relations to others so that they could not free up their energies for more constructive use. The moratoriums, who were striving to develop independence, were still somewhat too anxious to have achieved it completely. They were still too absorbed in trying to define their own capacities to have yet established an integrated identity. Finally, the diffusions were a highly diverse group, often including individuals with various forms of character pathology.

For both sexes important identity issues relate to occupational choice, values and sex roles. (Courtesy of Community Relations Office, State University of New York at Oswego)

SEX AS A FACTOR IN IDENTITY STATUS   In contrast to the study just cited, most researchers have focused on researching identity formation in traditional male domains including politics and occupation (Thorbecke & Grotevant, 1982). Fannin (1979) believes Marcia's formulation applies these days to women as well. For both sexes important identity issues relate to occupational choice, values, and sex roles. College men are more advanced developmentally in matters of occupational choice and women more in sex-role concepts and sex ideology. However, with regard to identity development, the sexes show few significant differences. Indeed, "males and females are more similar than different in their use of developmental processes" (Waterman, 1982, p. 351). In most research female and male adolescents are represented equally among these four identity statuses, suggesting that they proceed at much the same pace and in a similar manner.

Various studies do suggest that the identity statuses may not have the same psychological significance for the sexes (Marcia, 1980; Waterman, 1982). Although neither sex deals well with identity diffusion and both sexes are about equally adjusted in terms of identity achievement, females more often than males adjust relatively well to foreclosure. It might be that society tolerates the foreclosure status for women more than for men—hence, they would adjust more readily to it (Marcia, 1980). However, this difference involves only a small fraction of persons who persist in the foreclosure status after adolescence.

Various writers, including Boynton (1978), believe that it was possible in the past for women to achieve identity without conflict. There was only one path open to women and that was marriage and motherhood. However, the presently available "alternative anchors for identity and for additional role definitions," especially for the middle-class, make this sort of "unidirectional model a vestige of the past" (p. 204).

In support of this view Fannin (1979) found that women who had achieved their identities had in general adopted more contemporary sex-role attitudes and had chosen less typical majors in college. It is clear that the Eriksonian model, based mostly on physiological factors, is incomplete and that psychosocial variables of today provide women with alternative options (Waterman, 1982).

These options, as in the case of men, result in some crisis. At the heart of Erikson's model of identity development is the discontinuous concept, which interprets crisis as occurring when the tentative identity, formulated at one stage, becomes inappropriate for later stages, and may, unless resolved, produce **identity confusion.** The issue of identity discontinuity is especially applicable to women reared under one set of norms and exposed to different ones after they move away from the family in adolescence or later on. Almost all middle-class women, at least, have experienced two contrasting value structures: the traditional one with marriage and motherhood as the core of the female identity and the nontraditional one which stresses vocation and individual choice.

This new perspective calls for a change in identification figures. In the past daughters' identification with their mothers might serve as a pretty reliable identity defining influence throughout their lives. However, these days such an identity is limiting to young women who enter the work world. Rubin (1979) feels that severe personal disappointments arise from accepting without question traditional roles as the woman's main source of identity in a society which has alternative options. Nevertheless, nontraditional women indeed need reinforcement and validation in the process of identity development, especially since their mothers' role modeling was probably traditional. In such cases their friendships with other females is highly significant in their identity formation (Yoon, 1978).

Because of contemporary social norms Morgan and Farber (1982) believe that Erikson's model, developed in a time of constricted social expectations, is an inappropriate model of female development. Changes over time tend to sanction the validity of current nontraditional roles as opposed to the traditional norms described by Erikson. Between 1970 and 1980 the number of adult women favoring efforts to strengthen women's status rose from 40 percent to 64 percent (Virginia Slims American Women's Opinion Polls, 1970, 1972, 1974, 1980). Over half of all American women (52 percent) also preferred a less traditional marriage with dual careers and shared household responsibilities. Almost half (46 percent) preferred having a job to staying at home.

These changes in attitude are reflected in changing behavior patterns. Over 50 percent of married women with school-age children are not working; and the fertility rate is also steadily declining (Hoffman, 1979); whereas the divorce rate has been increasing; and it is estimated that 40 percent of all present marriages will end in divorce (Hetherington, 1979).

Women have not completely rejected stereotypical sex-role concepts; however, they are not merging less traditional values with the more traditional model. They still assume most of the home responsibilities, yet, the majority go to work. That is, these two contrasting sets of role expectations make female identity conflict inevitable. Bardwick (1979) believes that the current generation of women has lost the "existential anchor" of sex-role definition which makes them feel secure (Everhart, 1982, p. 201).

Erikson (1968) perceived both sexes as experiencing the same sequence of developmental tasks until adolescence, but after that time as being confronted with divergent models. Erikson explained this difference on the basis of somatic differences between the sexes and claimed that the woman's inner space determines the way she relates to herself and to others. She achieves her identity through finding a husband to fill the void of her inner space, both literally and figuratively; whereas, young males achieve identity by interacting with society and testing alternative identifications.

Morgan and Farber (1980) question the acceptability in these times of Erikson's identity-through-intimacy formulation for females. Because of sweeping changes in society, not just among feminists but among all women, as Bardwick (1979) points out, "we are all affected by the changes, or the appearance of change, because our visibility in the media makes awareness unavoidable" (p. 2).

The Erikson model of female identity development was perhaps valid in times when women could attain a successful identity through the achievements of their husband. Until quite recent years a woman's status and self-definition were mainly determined by the man she married, because "most women's identities were achieved in the steroryped ideals of their family roles" (Bardwick, 1979, p. 22).

OTHER FACTORS IN ESTABLISHING AN IDENTITY   Marital status is an important factor in shaping identity. Lutes (1981) compared married and single college students and found the married ones more likely to be foreclosed. That is, they had made commitments without having examined many alternatives or having carefully examined and questioned their goals and values. The married men were highly conforming, perhaps because their foreclosure reflected a need to simplify choices and erase anxieties and doubts. In addition, the married students were lower on impulsivity; hence it took a longer time to make decisions. They showed greater cautiousness and inhibition in their emotions and were less sensation-seeking with regard to entertainment.

This writer suggests that the married students perceived themselves more as adults with adult responsibilities, hence allowed themselves less latitude for their behaviors. They are perceived as more settled by other individuals by the fact of being married; hence, they are more likely to perceive themselves that way.

Still another important factor in shaping identity is social class. In the upper-middle class, the model is that of the eventual leader, or "great man"—Luther, Gandhi, and Harvard student (Veysey, 1976). Ordinarily the identity crisis turns out to be a "luxury affordable only by the upper-middle class." For the great majority of youth, both in the United States and elsewhere, "adolescence is more likely to be shaped by relatively mundane pressures than by dreams and fantasies that are earthier, less transcendental" (p. 32).

In a sense each individual has many identities, in addition to sex and age. Youth may also possess an ethnic identity, a concept of special importance in a pluralistic society. That is, their personalities may result from having grown up in a particular ethnic group (Helson & Mitchell, 1978). Such an identity suggests a subjective sense of belonging and loyalty to a particular group.

Adolescent identity formation is also modified by changing times (Schippers, 1978). The traditional sex roles that provided a certain stability in human relationships are undergoing change, and what it means to be a man or woman is no longer clear. Nor is it clear what the distinctions are between normal and abnormal behavior. Many adolescents consider that being straighter or pursuing the accepted behaviors of society is boring and negative. Certainly there is a growing approval of varied personality patterns and life styles.

Modern times, in certain ways, are favorable to establishment of identity. The growing affluence and absence of great challenge now allows the leisure required to develop one's own personality and individuality. Hence, the self has become a focus of concern because youth are not compelled now to face outward, to cope with the demands of their environment or the frontier (Logan & O'-Hearn, 1982). Thus, "rugged individualism" has come to be displaced by a new type of individualism; and the focus is not on following some general guide but on developing one's own potential and self (p. 525).

The college experience, shared by increasingly large numbers of youth, favorably impacts on achieving identity. It is during the college years that the greatest gains in identity formation transpire, because "college environments provide a diversity of experiences that can serve both to trigger considerations of identity issues and to suggest alternative resolutions for identity concerns" (Waterman 1982, p. 346). Besides, college experience encourages exploration of alternative vocational goals, exposes students to ideological alternatives, and confronts them with a range of religious views (Waterman, 1982).

PATHWAYS TO IDENTITY Trying to establish their identity as adults, some youth employ symbols of age transition. Consider the young man who, upon assuming his new job, grows a beard, or the individual who bums around the country at some turning point in life. Doing something novel at a life turning point constitutes a certain rite of passage (Climo, 1975).

Newman and Newman (1978) see the path to identity as a complex interaction of sex and mode of child rearing. After reviewing the literature they conclude that the sexes achieve identity by somewhat different routes. For boys to achieve an identity, the parents should ideally combine "possibilities for a strong identification through the communication of warmth and responsiveness, with a clear, consistent use of limit setting and discipline" (p. 164). During this process the boy clearly distinguishes between himself and his parents while still reacting positively to them as role models. For girls, a warm parent-child relationship is also significant, but a combination of warmth with discipline simply overemphasizes her dependency and encourages acquiescence to her parents' desires. If girls are to become autonomous, they must be rewarded for efforts to be independent. A measure of conflict in the home helps girls to develop moral judgment and to encourage progress toward independent thinking, while a harmonious family setting helps boys develop a mature moral view (Newman & Newman, 1978). The combination of warmth plus restrictiveness produces too secure an environment to encourage girls to differentiate their personalities. Because of societal attitudes, the process of self-differentiation is harder for girls than for boys.

Both sexes should have access to alternative pathways to establishing identities and be encouraged to explore them. Educators and parents have wrongly assumed that early and midadolescents actively pursue alternatives before making their life-goal commitments; thus, parents and educators have inappro-priately timed their demands on adolescents (Archer, 1982). Adolescents may look toward a particular college major, or choose a particular curriculum track, or express interest in a particular first job, or a religious or political affiliation without feeling a genuine personal involvement in their choice. This lack of personal investment may be reflected in their future weak commitment to such matters, or lack of knowledge about them. Since prematurely foreclosed com-mitments often result from urging adolescents to arrive at conclusions, they should instead be allowed more time and opportunities for exploring alterna-tives.

FACTORS THAT RELATE TO ADOLESCENT PERSONALITY

Adolescents' efforts to build satisfactory self-concepts, whether through mastery or other means, will be abortive unless they are consistent with their total per-sonalities. For example, a girl likes small children so well that she plans to become an elementary school teacher, but she ignores the lack of psychological and physical stamina that would prove her undoing in so strenuous a job. Personality embraces the entire psychological structure and represents the unique patterning of all an individual's traits or characteristic ways of reacting to environment; traits blend and become patterned until the whole personality is more than merely the sum of its parts.

Biological Factors

Factors that account for personality are based either genetically or en-vironmentally (culturally). Where adolescents are concerned, genetic factors are likely to be ignored. Adults want to believe that they can transform teenagers, and they fall easy prey to the false concept of limitless flexibility of personality. Adults may also overlook the importance of heredity because its influence is hard to measure. Nevertheless, considerable evidence indicates that heredity lays the foundation for personality (Tanner, 1978b).

Environmental Influences

Factors external to the individual influence personality development. Some of these factors, like family experience, are widely recognized. Recent research, however, suggests that the power of parents and the passivity of chil-dren have been exaggerated. Certainly parents exercise considerable influence, but they do not have complete control. These models reckon without the child's own personality and the social circumstances under which the child is reared. Furthermore, earlier researchers have presumed that the parent-child influence was unidirectional, from parent to child. Studies indicate that the influence of parents on children could be interpreted as indicating children's effects on their parents. For example, the correlation between harsh punishment and children's aggressiveness is typically presumed to prove that severe discipline results in aggressive children. It might as easily indicate that aggressive children provoke parents to use harsh childrearing methods (Skolnick 1978).

Equally important is the effect of society. The relative lack of structure and rigid role-prescription in modern Western countries, as compared with earlier and simpler cultures, constitutes at once a hazard and an opportunity. The fluidity of Western society affords more alternatives and allows for individual differences. Modern adolescents face a heavy burden of self-determination because cultural patterns are changing, making former personality patterns nonadaptive. Hence, adolescents must decide how to relate to their culture (Keniston, 1975).

Especially in today's pluralistic society adolescents see models of many life styles of many cultures around the world and many subgroupings within the culture. The adolescent may experience the sort of confusion that an individual does who goes into a large department store with a tremendous supply of clothing to try on garments (Rogers, 1982).

Names and Clothes

Other factors, such as names and clothes, are subtle in their effects, but in the aggregate have powerful influences upon personality. The names that affect personality development most importantly are likely to be eccentric names or nicknames. Nicknames serve as a constant reminder of others' attitudes toward oneself. Less fortunate students are called by nicknames that reflect unfavorable attitudes. The 6-foot-tall girl nicknamed "Stackpole" was often reminded that others viewed her as oversized. A boy nicknamed "Sea Papa" after a stint in the navy had additional proof of his peers' failure to take him seriously. Yet, the more he protested his nickname, the more others reveled in its use.

Eccentric names are damaging, too. Among such names reported are Ima Hogg, Ura Hogg, Heza Hogg, Latina, Placenta, Bonadia, Panza Eta Burd, Trailing Arbutus Still, Icen Snow, Alpha, and Omega. Bearers of eccentric names at Harvard showed an excess of flunk-outs and neuroses (Savage & Wells, 1948). (One wonders about the home environment provided by parents who give children such names!) Unfortunate, too, are boys with names more often given the other sex. A Mexican boy named Dolores insisted on being called Jimmy instead.

Hoover (1979) speaks of name liberation as the quietest and most basic revolution. Hoover is referring to individuals who dislike their names and change them. For example, Marian Budorowski became Carla Colorado since it reminded her of her beloved outdoors. Hoover reminds us of such common stereotypes as: "Jane is cute and dull; Mary is virtuous; Kathy is traditional; Jennifer is interesting; Katie is spirited; Missy is prissy; Murial is plodding; John is stolid; Cecil is sissy; Harvey is bumbling; Bart and Mack are he-men" (p. 16).

Clothes are no less intimately linked with personality than names. Dienstfrey (1982) calls clothes "a billboard of the self . . . without them we are vulnerable and largely anonymous; with them we are clad in an armor of cloth" (p. 68). Of course, it is easy to misjudge what they mean. In personality tests given to college undergraduates, approval of skimpy bathing suits related in no way to sexual abandon. Rather, students who approved them believed that they had high moral beliefs and were somewhat detached in personal relationships.

Horowitz (1982) reported that the British tend to be fashion-oriented, and that fashions themselves are more age-oriented than class-oriented and that older and younger groups manifest different fashion behaviors. Moreover, younger consumers are more influenced by the excitement motive than older ones who are affected more by the economic motive. Younger individuals also pay more attention to style than to quality, and they are more influenced by the mass media and less by status symbols associated with social class.

Research shows, too, that younger people buy more these days, have more money, and are more likely to replace their clothing somewhat frequently. Since their parents are more prosperous they have larger allowances and beside, make more money themselves. Since people tend to associate youth and fashion together the young may have considerable impact on fashions.

We might also say that youth's purchases of clothing are more expressive than instrumental in orientation. Class-oriented fashions stress individuality; whereas age-oriented fashions are more uniform, with frequent changes making up for their lesser individuality (Horowitz, 1982).

We have interesting parallels to this description on high school and college campuses where students are continually in the presence of their peers and constantly pressured to behave in conformist ways and, at the same time, are searching for an identity (M. Snyder, 1980). Thus, we see that their clothes conform in the main to those of others, but they seek little ways to make their own clothes distinctive.

Over the years young people fluctuate in their degree of conservatism and dress. In the 1970s, as young college graduates prepared to "embrace regimented thinking," they attired their "public image in gray flannel suits, vests, and regimental striped ties. . . . In their private lives, today's youth are reinventing college proms, replete with long gowns and off-the-shoulder corsages; and they are returning in record numbers to Fort Lauderdale beaches, where, reminiscent of the 1950s, the police report beer is more in evidence than marijuana" (Shields, 1979, p. 50). However, not all the youth of the 1970s wore gray flannel. The alternative technology and anti-nuclear movements found expression in backyard gardening, interest in wind and solar energy, fights against corporate power, and block associations.

SIGNIFICANCE OF LIFE CYCLE

Since all life stages are interrelated it is important that young people come to think in terms of the whole life cycle. The life cycle may be perceived as universal, in that society dictates certain tasks at particular age stages; on the other hand it is infinitely varied, as individuals select from varieties of roles and opportunities throughout their lives.

Persistence of Personality Patterns

Personality development is a complex, often obscure process. Nevertheless, its basic design remains unchanged. Bower (1974) portrays "development [as] a cyclic process with competencies developing and then disappearing to reappear anew at a later age; development is not a continuous linear process but rather a series of waves, with whole segments of development reoccurring repetitively" (p. 302). Because of this basic consistency, in most individuals there is "a thread of . . . predictability of traits. Some personality characteristics are enduring; the mother who insists that her child was stubborn from his first day on earth may be speaking the truth" (Krech, Crutchfield, & Livson, 1974).

In contrast to the preceding observation, Kagan, Kearsley, and Zelazo (1978) stressed the potential for personality change, observing that longitudinal studies of American children do not prove that early behaviors are highly predictive of adolescent and adult behaviors. On the basis of cross-cultural research, especially in Guatamala, they assert that sharp changes in environment can effect considerable change in personality. This potential for change, observes Lerner (1981), "exists across the life course . . . as a consequence of continual, dynamic interactions between a changing person and his or her changing context" (p. 258).

In longitudinal research (the Grant Study), extending over four decades, of certain bright promising male undergraduates at a well-known eastern university, Vaillant (1977b) reported considerable personality change. He determined that it was not childhood traumas that shaped the men's future, but rather sustained relationships with significant people in their lives. Their lives did indeed change and possessed a certain discontinuity. Moreover, behaviors that might have been pathological at one period proved adaptive at another. Only the long-term perspective reveals the significance of behaviors at any given time.

The degree of perceived change in personality varies with age and individual. In the San Francisco Longitudinal Study of Transitions, which involved high school seniors facing transitions to college, first job, and marriage, newlyweds facing parenthood, middle-aged parents, and others facing retirement, a follow-up interview after eight years indicated that younger individuals, as might be expected because of their greater concern for self-knowledge and self-identity, more often reported changes in the self, 74 percent and 66 percent compared to 27 percent and 33 percent, among the older men and women respectively. For all the respondents 56 percent reported mainly positive, 25 percent neutral, and 19 percent negative changes (Thurnher, 1983).

Most individuals of all ages perceived turning points in their lives as producing mainly positive changes in themselves, their interpersonal relations, and their emotional state. Characteristics of individuals involved predicted the nature of events, rather than events producing changes in the persons concerned. Moreover, these personality characteristics remained stable over the eight-year period, only a degree of assertion showing any significant change (Thurnher, 1983).

Data concerning persistence of personality patterns raise certain questions yet to be answered: Would it be possible, given significant enough stimuli, to modify greatly even deeply ingrained traits? Or is it more practical simply to build on what the individual already is and to assume that presumably basic traits cannot be altered? Basic to these questions is another: Is consistency of particular characteristics attributable to genetic factors or to constant factors within the environment? On this last question there is considerable controversy, with the geneticists generally coming off second best, partly because genetic factors are never seen in pure form. With regard to this matter, Neugarten concludes that we have no firm evidence to date regarding the processes involved.

FUTURE PERSPECTIVES

Adolescence is a time of testing alternatives for the future in fantasy. This type of fantasy is different from the fantasies of childhood, when one played at being queen or king; it is reality-oriented, based on examination of alternative possibilities. Adolescence is a time of exploration, of trying out various roles and life styles. By this process youth determine those most congenial to themselves. Since their lives are less structured now than later on, youth can engage in freer exploration. Without such exploration, they may make premature decisions about the future, failing to consider alternatives that might prove more rewarding.

Of special help to youth, in this process of exploration, is the availability of role models and mentors, adults who take special interest in them. In reality, most youths lack a single role model but construct for themselves a composite of bits and pieces of ideals that they have seen exemplified in various admired persons.

However, in one sense, growing individuals will become more responsible for their own self-actualization and destinies and less dependent on being prodded by others (When family will have a new definition, 1983). As family forms become more flexible and less cohesive, youth will chart their own alternatives.

What makes such exploratory activity especially important is the growing recognition that early experience does not dictate future destiny. In the Terman study, in which bright people were followed for over six decades, people proved over time not to be completely "prisoners of the past" (Goleman, 1980b). Such findings add both obligation and opportunity to every age stage, including adolescence. To the extent that youth have the capacity for continuing growth, the more important it is that they deal with the future in constructive ways. Although we have always recognized the long-term continuity of such attributes as achievement and health, the greatest predictive value was for variables that measured no longer than ten years previously. Thus, personality characteristics of youth were assumed to relate most closely to those manifest in young adulthood.

Youth must come to recognize that their aspirations must be geared to future changes in external conditions, health status, and personal competencies. If they develop an achievement orientation that is unrealistic, they may face a lifetime of perceived failures. They must also be flexible if they are to adapt successfully; and they must continuously readapt to a new world constantly in the process of revision. In addition, they must become capable of a broad perspective, prepared for the greatest possible number of future worlds. The pace of change, coupled with increased longevity, means that long-lived individuals will experience a succession of somewhat different worlds (Rogers, 1982).

SUMMARY

The way individuals adapt both to themselves and to others depends upon self-concept and personality. Self-concept indicates the way people experience themselves. Personality represents all that a person is, the total configuration of personal characteristics. Some traits are central and highly resistant to change; others are peripheral or secondary and more modifiable. Temperamental character-istics are especially basic because they relate to an individual's native endowment. Traits, in turn, become organized into patterns appropriate to one's roles, or socially dictated patterns associated with particular functions in groups. The features common to all roles constitute the life style, or the self-in-action. In the process of playing roles, an individual gains impressions of the sort of person he or she is—whether competent or bumbling, social or antisocial, intellectually or socially inclined, and so on. That is, one develops both a self-concept, which comprises all one's impressions of oneself, and an ideal self, or the self he or she would like to become.

Various factors serve to modify the sort of self-concept a person devel-ops—among them, the attitudes of others. In effect, an adolescent's group pro-vides a looking glass, reflecting back how he or she looks to others. As a result, adolescents constantly engage in introspection and react to an imaginary audi-ence, testing in fantasy others' probable reactions. Such behaviors and their related effects on self-concept vary according to age and sex. Normally, as in-dividuals grow older and test themselves in a variety of roles and situations, their self-concepts grow more clearly defined.

The self-concept is maintained and enhanced through a number of processes. One of these, self-actualization, suggests a progression through se-quential and increasingly higher levels of motivation and achievement. Another process, achieving a sense of identity, involves attaining a feeling of distinctive-ness from others. It suggests an awareness of self and of one's place in the scheme of things. There are many pathways to establishing an identity—indeed, it must be continually redefined. A somewhat different process, identification, sometimes results in modeling after another, and if pursued too vigorously, obstructs the establishment of an identity. However, if identification is kept in proper perspective, it may enrich an individual's personality and improve upon identity. In this sense, the process simply involves recognizing congeniality be-tween one's own tastes, goals, and values and those of another.

Mastery, or the achievement of important goals, also serves to enhance the self-concept. An important aspect of mastery is achievement motivation, or tendency to seek and make progress toward goals. Of the sexes, males are relatively more achievement-oriented, and females are more affiliative. An ap-propriate degree of achievement motivation is essential to establishing and mak-ing progress toward goals; however, adults may impose on youth goals that are unrealistically high or difficult to attain.

Individuals' self-concepts and all their ways of seeking to define and defend them reflect their personalities or total trait structures. These frame-works, in turn, are shaped by both biological and sociocultural factors. Indeed, each individual's biochemistry is unique; it predisposes him or her to react selectively to a continuous barrage of environmental stimuli. Among those so-ciocultural factors which most importantly modify an individual's personality are family, peer group, school experience—and even one's name. The potential impact of each factor is modified by the individual's own trait organization to date; that is, he or she is no mere sponge soaking up the impressions that impinge on experience; instead, from the earliest weeks of life, the individual maintains certain traits that become increasingly refined and resistant to change.

These more typical traits become reflected in a correspondingly typical life style, or characteristic manner of organizing one's life activities. Often their influence is subtle, though very real, as in the choice of clothing. By adolescence, the broad outlines of individuals' life styles may be roughly defined. Within this framework, a person has plenty of latitude, either to develop effective ways of expressing basic characteristics or to choose patterns leading to perennial diffusion of self and dissipation of energy. Whatever the outcome, it may have a significant bearing on the years that lie ahead, though just how persistent or modifiable its bearing is disputable. In any case, the growing emphasis on continued personal development throughout the life span highlights the need to establish the outlines of rewarding life styles in adolescence.

DISCUSSION QUESTIONS AND ACTIVITIES

1. Make a case study, to be turned in at the end of the course, of some teenager you know well or of yourself as a teenager. The individual chosen should be discussed in terms of each aspect of development treated in this and succeeding chapters. If the instructor distributes an outline of points to be included, the outline should be suggestive rather than prescriptive.

2. Write an anonymous paragraph telling first how you view yourself and then how you believe others see you. All paragraphs may be collected, read to the class, and discussed.

3. Read a story or book whose chief characters are teenagers and write personality sketches of each of these characters.

4. Write down how you believe your ideal for yourself differs from society's ideal for you. Papers written by the class are to be collected and discussed.

5. Discuss the effect of popular stereotypes such as those found on television and in popular magazines on personality formation.

6. Write a paragraph analyzing the relationship between the type of clothes you prefer and your own personality.

7. Discuss effective ways of helping adolescents achieve self-enhancement in the various forms discussed in this chapter.

8. Write on a slip of paper anonymously how easy or difficult it has been to live with your name over the years. Papers will be collected and discussed.

9. Find a picture of youth in a teen magazine and write a paragraph concerning what the youth's attire tells about him or her and the youth culture.

SUGGESTED READINGS

Adams, G. R. & Jones, R. M. (1983). Female adolescents' identity development: Age comparisons and perceived child-rearing experience. *Developmental Psychology, 4*(3), 20. This study of female adolescents in grades 10 to 12 disclosed relationships between their identity status and the socialization styles that their parents employed.

Archer, S. L. (1982). The lower age boundaries of identity development. *Child Development, 53,* 1551–1556. A study of sixth, eighth, tenth, and twelfth graders which explored the lower boundaries of ego development with regard to vocational choice, religious beliefs, political philosophies, and sex-role preferences indicated the diffusion and foreclosure statuses to be common at all age levels.

Colombo, J. (1982). The critical period concept: Research, methodology and theoretical issues. *Psychological Bulletin, 91*(2), 260–275. A review of the literature suggests that the critical period concept is a viable one if certain limitations are taken into account.

Damon, W. & Hart, D. (1982). The development of self-understanding from infancy through adolescence. *Child Development, 53*(4), 841–864. A review of the literature is employed to develop a description and model of growth in self-understanding from infancy to adolescence, including genetic and conceptual relations among different aspects of self-understanding.

Elliott, G. C. (1982). Self-esteem and self-presentation among the young as a function of age and gender. *Journal of Youth and Adolescence, 11*(2), 135–153. Among individuals, ages 8 to 19, self-esteem and its components—including vulnerability to criticism, self-consciousness, and tendency to fantasize—affected the tendency to assume a false front in ways differing by age and sex.

Ellis, D. W. & Davis, L. T. (1982). The development of self-concept boundaries across the adolescent years. *Adolescence 17*(67), 695–710. Self-concept in the adolescent years is discussed in terms of its definition, significance, and theory, and a model is proposed for its development during this life stage.

Grotevant, H. D., Thorbecke, W., & Meyer, M. L. (1982). An extension of Marcia's identity status interview into the interpersonal domain. *Journal of Youth and Adolescence, 11*(1), 33–47. An extension of Marcia's Identity Status Interview to domains of friendship, dating, and sex roles proved to be a psychometrically sound method for evaluating interpersonal issues of contemporary adolescents.

Kness, D. (1983). Clothing deprivation feelings of three adolescent ethnic groups. *Adolescence, 18*(71), 659–674. In this analysis of factors that contribute to feelings of clothing satisfaction or deprivation, it proved that Afro-American adolescents held different values and views from those of Anglo- or Mexican-American heritage.

Lerner, R. M. (1982). Children and adolescents as producers of their own development. *Developmental Review, 2*(4), 342–370. Findings from this investigation of how children and adolescents may enhance their own development in consequence of their physical and behavioral characteristics are

conceptualized in terms of a person context or goodness-of-fit model.

Meacham, J. A. & Santilli, N. R. (1982). Interstage relationships in Erikson's theory: Identity and intimacy. *Child Development, 53*, 1461–1467. A system is suggested for evaluating Erikson's theories with regard to developmental progression, need (if any) for crisis, resolution of crisis, and consequences of premature foreclosure.

Morgan, E. (1982). Toward a reformulation of the Eriksonian model of female identity development. *Adolescence, 17*(65), 199–211. Examination is made of the implication of changing social norms for Erikson's model of female development and of broadening alternatives for women's identity achievement.

Muuss, R. E. (1982). Social cognition: David Elkind's theory of adolescent egocentrism. *Adolescence, 17*(66), 249–265. The author reviews Elkind's theory of egocentrism in terms of stages, research support, and educational implications.

O'Malley, P. M. & Bachman, J. G. (1983). Self-esteem: Change and stability between ages 13 and 23. *Developmental Psychology, 19*(2), 257–268. A review of longitudinal studies involving individuals, ages 13 to 23, indicates considerable stability in self-esteem over these years.

Openshaw, D. K., Thomas, D. L., & Rollins, B. C. (1983). Socialization and adolescent self-esteem: Symbolic interaction and social learning explanations. *Adolescence, 18*(70), 317–330. This study indicates that adolescent self-esteem can best be understood by viewing it from various perspectives.

Parsons, J. E., Adler, T. E., & Kaczala, C. M. (1982). Socialization of achievement attitudes and beliefs: Parental influences. *Child Development, 53*(2), 310–321. This study of fifth to eleventh graders and their parents regarding attitudes toward mathematics achievement disclosed that the parents, as role models of sex-differentiated math behaviors, did not directly affect their children's self-concepts, expectations, or life course plan.

Chapter Three

Physical Development

BODY IMAGE AND SELF-CONCEPT

Growth and Aging

To a certain extent adolescents, like people of all ages, age at different rates. Moreover, different functions within their bodies have their own special rates of aging (DeVries, 1977). Inherent in aging is the growth process, which proceeds at a decelerating rate from birth to maturity, with an extra spurt at puberty. In childhood and adolescence, boys' physical characteristics vary more than do those of girls, presenting more extreme dimensions in weight, height, and bone growth. By the time adolescence is over, there are more very tall and very short men, very light and very heavy men, than their counterparts among females.

In physical development, continuity—not discrete stages—is the rule. Distinctive stages may occur in certain creatures, such as insects at metamorphosis; however, only in adolescence does anything approaching a distinct developmental stage occur in human beings. Otherwise, different aspects of growth proceed on an even course, but somewhat independently and not collectively as in a stage. Even in adolescence the amount of synchrony is relative. For example, dental and skeletal age are mainly independent of each other, and the spurt in bodily development is not accompanied by any similar dramatic rise in intellectual capacity (Tanner, 1978a).

Importance of Physical Traits

Evidence of the external manifestations of growth and the importance of physical appearance are all around us. Daily advertisements in newspapers, magazines, television, and radio proclaim the benefits of "the body beautiful" and suggest ways to improve our image. Personal application blanks sometimes contain questions about appearance, partly because different physical characteristics become associated with different kinds of people. Bridgewater (1983) tells of a study in which students were to imagine themselves in the position of a company's employment interviewer. Half the students were given pictures of good-looking men and half unattractive men, employing identical resumes and interview transcripts for the two groups. Those who received the photos of the attractive applicants were more likely to hire them than the students with pictures of the less attractive ones. The attractive candidates also received higher ability ratings, except in two types of jobs which involved little personal contact.

THE SELF IMAGE   Damon and Hart (1982) point out that the self-picture in childhood is largely physical, but gradually it becomes more psychological in adolescence. That is, there is a movement in self-perception from surface features to deeper inner psychological characteristics such as thoughts and emotions. Also, various aspects of self-knowledge become linked together, and there develops an overall or dominant perception of self. Thus, the self-concept is in constant process of reorganization from childhood to adolescence.

The sexes react to their bodies somewhat differently. When college student volunteers (Collins, 1981) were photographed nude—front, side, and rear—

Self-concept is in constant process of reorganization from childhood to adolescence. (Photo by William J. Butcher)

and asked a month later to identify their own bodies and body parts from an array of photographs, the females required longer to identify themselves than males, and they identified the front of their body more quickly than the rear and the rear faster than the side. Among body parts the genitals were most important to the males and the breasts to the females. Pubic hair and legs seemed relatively unimportant to females, while body hair was a quite important secondary sex characteristic to the males.

At all ages, especially youth, the self-image is modified by how one believes himself or herself as seen by others. A study of 16-year-old adolescent boys indicated that self-evaluation of physical attractiveness and role competence depends to some extent, but not wholly, on their peers' opinions. Rather, feelings about self serve as "a filter through which the adolescent perceives and interprets social comparison data" (Eisert & Kahle, 1983, p. 103). Moreover, the degree varies, to which the self-view is influenced by one's own characteristics and by one's reaction to others' view of oneself. Perhaps the influence of group norms is greatest during periods of poor self-image and instability, when confidence in one's own views is low.

Image as Related to Self-Concept

Most people have several images of themselves: own-body image, or the way they believe they look; ideal physical self-image, or the projection of the physical traits they believe are best suited to the self they would like to be; and the daydream self-portrait, or physical self they assume when in a world of fantasy. For example, Alice perceives herself as flat chested and plain looking (own-body image), but looks forward to having enough money to buy attractive clothes appropriate to her hoped-for future role as wife and mother (ideal physical self-image). Since she lacks, for the present, both money and boy friends, she often daydreams of being the glamorous target of certain boys' glances (daydream self-portrait). Alice's ideal physical self-image determines the direction of plans for improving her appearance. For the time being, she may ignore possibilities that do exist and escape into fantasy.

Alice's own-body image may be somewhat different from the way she appears to others. Adolescents' views of themselves are distorted by past experiences and future goals. A girl like Alice, with feelings of inferiority, often sees her features in their worst light. The attractive girl, on the other hand, revels in the favorable picture she believes she presents to the world. Katherine Mansfield (1937) describes in "Prelude" Beryl's delight in herself:

> She ran into the dark drawing-room and began walking up and down. . . . Oh, she was restless, restless. There was a mirror over the mantel. She leaned her arms on the mantel and looked at her pale shadow in the mirror. How beautiful she looked, but there was nobody to see, nobody. Beryl smiled, and really her smile was so adorable that she smiled again. . . . (p. 10).

Similarly, each person's unique characteristics operate to distort his or her view of another person. Six people looking at the same person form six different images of that person's physical appearance. When someone asks several friends to help decide which of several picture proofs to have developed, there often is no consensus. Thus, the important thing about appearance is how people perceive themselves and are preceived by others. Of course, perception is not altogether haphazard. The individual's preferences are likely to be derived from the prevailing cultural ideal for one's sex and status.

Body Image in Adolescence

SIGNIFICANCE   The physical self is of more central concern in adolescence than in any other period of life except, perhaps, old age. Basic physical changes force the body into the adolescent's consciousness. He or she has lost the security of a familiar body; new sensations, features, and body proportions have emerged. Because of these dramatic body changes, the body becomes an important symbol itself, in which the adolescent invests emotions of security, self-worth, and competence (Maddock, 1973b). Adolescents must adapt to these changes and to others' perceptions of them. They cannot be sexually neutral; now they are perceived as sex objects. Physical change is rapid and often accompanied by temporary conditions of acne and obesity (Coleman, 1974).

Adolescents' feelings about their physical traits are not always negative. Here college freshmen tell what they like most about their appearance.

> MALE: Blue eyes and blonde hair—a combination most girls like. Also, I like the size of my ears, my general weight (150 pounds) and build, the size of my hands, and my height (5 feet 10 inches).
> FEMALE: I like the length of my lashes, the color and size of my eyes, and their expressive ability. They are outstanding. I like my legs, feeling

I am lucky to have small ankles, and neither heavy nor overly thin legs. This is supposedly feminine and attractive.

Physical changes at adolescence also symbolize the end of childhood; maturity is just over the horizon. Adult proportions begin to take shape, although it is impossible as yet to be certain of the nature, extent, or duration of changes still to come. Soon the outlines of mature features will be complete. So the adolescent is anxious—will one's mature physical self come reasonably close to his or her ideal? Adolescents do not realize that adult standards will be different. The high school athlete cannot comprehend that bulging muscles have little prestige for grown men. The plain girl does not realize that her lack of glamour will matter less later on.

The perceptual field of adolescents is narrowed by the tyrannical standards of their peers. Deviations from peer standards are looked down upon, or at best tolerated. The price of nonconformity is rejection. Regardless of how much a boy likes a girl, he will not date her if her appearance draws ridicule from his friends. Both sexes, therefore, typically desire to correspond to the approved stereotype for their sex. They want to be like their age mates in such characteristics as hairline, skin texture, and symmetry of features; marked variations in any physical characteristics may seriously disturb them.

REACTION TO PHYSICAL CHARACTERISTICS   The sexes differ somewhat in the way they experience their physical selves. For example, a male's genital organs assume special meaning during adolescence. His testicles and penis almost double in size between the ninth and fifteenth year (Maddock, 1973b). The erectile power of the phallus, added to its dramatic growth, makes it the prime focus of mature male sexuality. Thus the phenomena of ejaculation and erection become the symbols and proofs of masculinity, importantly influencing the patterning of male sexual behavior.

For the female, the situation is somewhat different, despite a similar acceleration of growth in primary and secondary sex characteristics. Freud believed that girls, from childhood on, suffer from penis envy. Others interpet penis envy as a metaphor—not as envy of the male organ but of males' power and status (Cory, 1981). Cory cites research by Sharon Nathan who collected dream reports of women from such diverse groups as Peruvian college students and Australian aborigines. Dream reports of penis envy were most common in cultures where women's status was lowest as among the aborigines in Australia and least where women's social status was higher, as in Argentina. In cultures where people often dress scantily and sex differences are more easily seen women had no more dreams of penis envy than where they were less visible. However, men were conscious of differences in their own organs and those of others.

At least in America, girls rarely experience penis envy; however, they are concerned about their developing breasts which, unlike the penis, are not functional in sexual response. Few girls can achieve orgasm through breast stimulation alone. Nevertheless, the accessibility of breasts makes them a common object of petting and invests in them a certain significance. Hence, they hold more significance for femininity than the enlargement of the clitoris or vagina, of which girls are largely unaware.

A study of college students, in a cosmopolitan population with high geographic mobility, disclosed that they fully recognized that personal appearance was an important factor in getting and keeping jobs and being promoted, and that the women recognized appearance as a factor more than the men. The women, it may be noted, were aspiring to professional level employment after graduation. In addition, those with previous employment had a greater awareness of the significance of how they appeared. A further factor was occupational choice, with those aspiring to jobs which would involve much direct contact with their clientele expressing greatest concern over appearance. In contrast, those who would experience less contact, such as engineering students, expressed less concern (Sweat, Kelley, Blouin & Glee, 1981).

Views about what constitutes sex appeal differ according to an individual's sex and personality. While a mustache or beard contributes to a man's attractiveness, even the least facial hair on a female is unappealing (Wilson & Nias, 1976). Girls care less than boys about the physical appearance of their future mates; but they do have their preferences. They prefer slender males with "thin legs, a medium thin waist and a medium wide chest, producing a kind of V-look." They don't care about "large biceps or a bulging crotch." Nevertheless, girls' perceptions vary somewhat according to their personalities; the more "extroverted, sporting women like muscular men, while neurotic, drug-using women prefer thin figures. Older, more traditional women prefer brawny males, while younger more liberated ones like the lean types" (p. 98).

The majority of youth feel reasonably satisfied with their physical appearance, although almost half dislike their body builds. Girls more often complain about their height and weight than boys do. Girls who see themselves as thin want to stay that way, or become thinner, while boys who perceive themselves as thin prefer to be heavier (Katchadourian, 1977).

Here college students describe the physical characteristics of their ideal male and female in a recent study by the author:

Ideal Male
FEMALE: Neat, layered hair, mustache, wider shoulders than waist.
FEMALE: Approximately 6 feet tall, collar-length hair, medium build, broad shoulders, slim waist, nice face.
FEMALE: Very athletic, but not overly muscular or burly, short hair, well-developed physique.
Ideal Female
MALE: Pretty face, nice eyes, slim, tall, small breasts, smooth skin, loving, warm personality, good sense of humor.
MALE: Thin, not too hippy, long curly hair, big eyes, well dressed and groomed.

Students were asked to name the one physical characteristic in themselves that they would most like to change and the largest amount of money they would be willing to pay to change it.

MALE: To be relieved of my asthma I would pay $5000+.
MALE: I'd like to be taller—$10,000.

MALE: I'm balding. I'd give whatever I had.

FEMALE: I'm pretty satisfied with being smaller than most; however, if I had to change something, I probably would want about 2 more inches on my breasts.

MALE: The amount of fat around my midsection (want to be in shape)—$1,000.

MALE: I would pay anything to free my body totally of acne and fat.

There may be a certain amount of defensiveness about perceptions of one's own looks. In one study college students were asked to evaluate an essay, presumably written by a college freshman. Through being shown a photograph, the subjects knew the writer's physical attractiveness (high, medium, or low) and sex. Attractive essay writers were accorded highest evaluations from students of the opposite sex, while writers of medium physical attractiveness received highest evaluations from same-sexed students (Anderson & Nida, 1978). The researchers hypothesized that since most people perceive themselves as moderately attractive, they give highest evaluations to people they view most like themselves—that is, same-sexed individuals of medium physical attractiveness.

Effect of Hormones on Adolescent Behavior

Thus far our discussion has concerned the relationship of physical traits to general adjustment. Now we shall consider physical characteristics that assume special significance.

During adolescence most of the **endocrine glands,** or glands of internal secretion, undergo an adolescent growth spurt. These glands affect growth, physical energy, emotionality, and health. The **pineal gland,** a tiny body located near the brain, functions chiefly during childhood and probably retards sexual development. The **thymus,** in the upper part of the thorax and the lower part of the throat, atrophies in late childhood and presumably inhibits precocious sexual development. The **thyroid,** located in the neck region near the larynx, controls the transformation of energy in the body. Overactivity of the thyroid may produce nervousness, irritability, and restlessness; undersecretion is associated with general physical and mental sluggishness.

The **pituitary,** located at the base of the brain, is called "the master gland" because it powerfully affects operations of the other glands and influences growth and metabolism. Although data concerning this gland are complex, it is generally agreed that the anterior lobe of the pituitary secretes hormones that stimulate the thyroid, the **adrenals,** and **gonads.**

Children without adequate growth hormones become small, short (about 130 centimeters) adults, but with normal proportions. They are sometimes called miniatures. Growth hormone extracted from human pituitary glands and injected into such children produces a normal growth rate, or even faster than normal, if they are already small when injections begin. Oddly enough, this growth hormone is species specific; and while insulin and certain other substances from animals work well in humans, animal growth hormone does not (Tanner, 1978b).

The main hormone regulating prepubertal growth is produced by the anterior pituitary, an endocrine gland; however, this hormone is simply one of several that regulate growth. This growth-producing factor in the pituitary affects overall body size and has a stronger impact on the growing child than on the adult. Only about four milligrams of growth hormone can be extracted from one pituitary gland; and to treat a single child lacking the hormone for five years necessitates processing 650 glands which must be removed soon after death occurs (Tanner & Taylor, 1969). Hormones from the thyroid gland located in the neck in front and on the sides of the trachia are essential for developing proper skeletal proportions, for forming and erupting teeth, for developing the brain, and for converting cartilage into bone (Katchadourian, 1977).

Adequate production of the pituitary hormones in the preadolescent prevents abnormal growth of the ovaries and testes, and indirectly, of the other reproductive organs. When the usual age of puberty is reached, if the pituitary gland has not been, or is not, functioning properly, the reproductive organs remain in an immature state and secondary sex characteristics fail to develop normally. An excess of the pituitary hormone in early life produces precocious sexual development.

The gonads, the primary sex glands located in the testes in males and in the ovaries in females, are stimulated by the pituitary hormones to produce mature sperm or ova, as well as **estrogens** (female hormones) or **androgens** (male hormones). In both sexes, the secretion of androgens by the adrenal cortex increases sharply at puberty; these hormones are especially important in girls, because they are responsible for the development of pubic and axillary (underarm) hair. Also among girls, about a year and a half before menarche, estrogen secretion becomes cyclical and increases in amount. Low levels of estrogen are found in both sexes until pubescence, after which the rate of production increases sharply in girls and ultimately evolves into a cyclical secretion culminating in menarche. No such cyclical secretions are found in boys.

Until puberty, the gonads of both sexes also secrete small amounts of ketosteroids (adrenal or male hormones). At puberty, the amount increases markedly for both sexes, but ultimately becomes twice as much for boys (Group for the Advancement of Psychiatry, 1968). The slight amount of estrogen se-

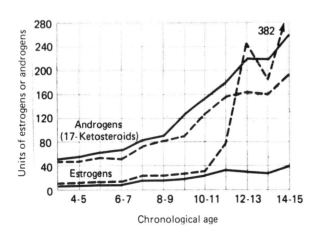

Figure 3–1   Excretion of sex hormones. Results are derived from urinary analysis. Note that the curve for estrogen secretion in males flattens during adolescence, while that for females rises precipitously. The androgen curve, however, tends to flatten for females and continues to rise for males.

cretion in boys during this period is quite minor in comparison to the ketosteroid secretion. Thus the hormones of the opposite sex may be found in the blood of each sex in limited amounts, but the balance is heavily weighted in favor of the hormones of one's own sex (Figure 3–1). In rare instances, an excess secretion of the hormone of the other sex may lead to development of some of the secondary sex characteristics of the other sex.

The adrenals, located above the kidneys, consist of an outer layer, the cortex, and an inner portion, the medulla. The medulla secretes adrenalin which affects body responses in emotion. Since the adrenal cortex, like the gonads, produces androgens, this gland also plays a role in sex development. Overactivity of the cortex in early childhood is associated with precocious sexual development; overactivity after puberty is associated with accentuation of masculinity. Women thus affected often develop masculine proportions, a deep voice, and hairiness.

Hormones and Adolescent Behavior

The relationship between hormones and behavior is complex but largely indirect. The direction of behavior is not determined, but the range, depth, and feeling tone of the accompanying emotions are affected. Variation in hormonal output may lead to greater or lesser reactivity to stimuli and thus may afford a physiological base for unpredictable adolescent behavior. Although experience undoubtedly modified this young girl's feelings, we infer that hormones played a part.

> My breasts, which until then had been hardly perceptible, began to swell softly and astonish me with charming but embarrassing sensations. My hips, which had been like a boy's, took on another undulation, and through my whole being I felt one great surging, longing, unmistakable urge, so that I could no longer sleep at night but tossed and turned in feverish, painful unrest. (de Beauvoir, 1953, p. 376)

Some endocrinologists infer, simply because new behavioral patterns manifest themselves at the time of hormonal changes, that a causal relationship exists between them. It seems more likely that such behavioral changes result from the mature social roles into which adolescents are pushed at about the time of puberty. Although physiological development may set limits on what these behaviors may be, social customs largely determine appropriate patterns.

Lerner (1981) speaks of the goodness of fit with regard to psychosocial adaptation, in that individuals participate in their own physical development, thus modifying the impact of pubertal events. Such adaptations vary greatly according to the individual and physical changes involved.

PUBERTY

The Nature of Puberty

CRITERIA FOR ASSESSING STATUS OF PUBERTY   The onset of puberty involves a succession of rapid changes in the reproductive system induced by hormones, coming shortly after childhood (Petersen & Taylor, 1980).

Puberty does not constitute one single event; instead it is "a slowly unfolding process beginning at conception" (Petersen, 1979, p. 47). The various changes of puberty do not all occur together or at the same rate. For example, reproductive capabilities and the growth spurt have slightly different hormonal bases and may occur at different rates.

No single standard exists for assessing pubertal status in either sex. The onset of maturity is indicated most noticeably by breast development and menarche in girls, by growth of facial hair and voice change in boys. Criteria of male development also include first ejaculation, and the appearance of axillary (underarm) hair, pubic hair, and other secondary sex characteristics. For both sexes, one of the more accurate methods is determining the stage of bone ossification,

Figure 3-2 When boys and girls mature.

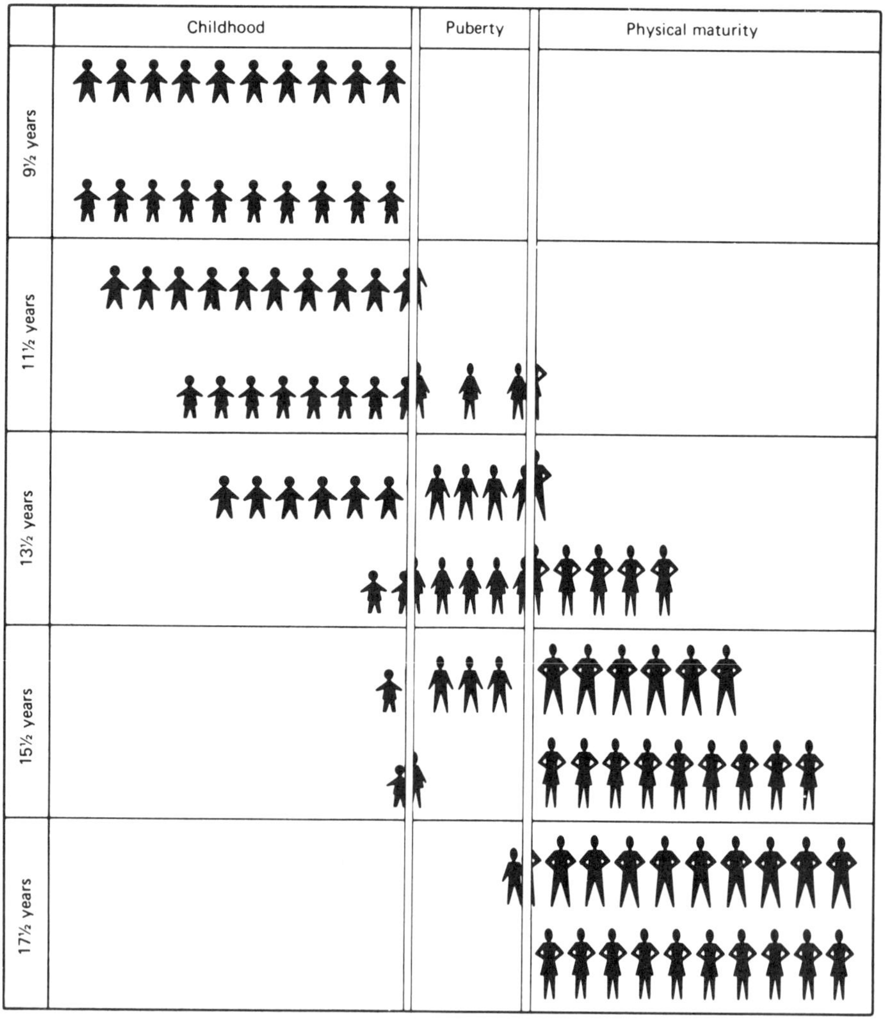

as recorded by means of x rays. A problem arises, however, in setting up standards with which to compare given x-ray pictures. Nevertheless, on the main point everyone agrees: boys mature about two years later than girls (Figure 3–2). Where adolescents are concerned, girls are prone to judge boys' maturity by changes in facial hair and in voice, whereas boys judge girls in terms of figure and breast development. In both sexes it must not be forgotten that "different tissues, organ systems, and physiological functions approximate adult levels at quite different ages" (Coleman et al., 1974, p. 97).

Pubescence is not a simple datable event but a period within which a constellation of changes occurs. Such changes affect blood pressure, blood composition, pulse rate, and the development of primary and secondary sex characteristics. Both sexes develop moderately coarse, pigmented hair in the armpit and groin regions. Muscle mass also increases in both sexes, much more in boys than in girls. For individuals of either sex, any particular change may vary in time of occurrence by more than five years. Normally, healthy individuals experience a period of rapid growth, or a growth spurt, which begins at any time within a six-year span, from age 8 to 14 in girls and from 9 to 15 in boys. Apparently the adolescent growth spurt is triggered by arriving at a certain critical metabolic rate, and, if it is to continue, about 17 percent of body weight must be fat. Female athletes in certain sports and teenage anorexics, who refuse to eat and therefore lose much weight, may cease to menstruate (Petersen, 1979).

Almost all muscular and skeletal dimensions participate in the growth spurt, but not equally (Tanner, 1978a). The diameter of the head, which is almost dormant from a few years after birth, manifests a small growth acceleration in most individuals. The face shows considerable change, with the forehead attaining more prominence because of the growth of the ridges of the brow and air sinuses beneath them. Such changes are more marked in boys than in girls; some girls undergo no detectable change in facial dimensions.

The greatest sexual distinction in the skeleton at puberty occurs in shoulders and hips. Boys experience a greater spurt in shoulder width, and girls in hip width. Some sexual *dimorphisms* date from birth; others are most prominent in puberty. Even at birth, girls have a wider pelvic outlet or opening at the bottom of the bony pelvis—the narrow passage through which babies must pass at birth. Pubertal changes serve to widen the pelvic outlet, broaden the hips, and thus provide room for uterus and baby to grow. At all ages, including puberty, boys' physical characteristics are more variable than those of girls.

PUBERTAL CHANGES IN GIRLS   In the typical girl, the adolescent growth spurt begins shortly after the age of 10 and peaks about age 12, after which there is a sharp decline. Ordinarily, her breasts begin to grow at about the age of $10^{1}/_{2}$, but in some cases enlargement begins earlier or as much as $2^{1}/_{2}$ years later. About three years are ordinarily required for full breast development; and a similar period is needed for pubic and underarm hair to attain full density. However, race is a factor. Among Chinese girls, pigmented and underarm hair begins growing later and is less dense. In white girls, the first few pigmented hairs begin to appear in the pubic region at about age 11, and a few are in the underarm region shortly after the age of 12. In rare cases, such hair appears even in early childhood.

Even among normally healthy girls, age of puberty varies. Ordinarily the first pubertal event is the occurrence of breast buds, or elevation of the nipple as a small mound with a slight enlargement of the areola (surrounding area), at an average age of 11 years or a range of 9 to 13 for 95 percent of normal girls. Pubic hair appears shortly later, although it appears before the breast bud in a third of all girls. These events occur quite independently so that, among girls having fairly advanced breast stage development, 25 percent have no pubic hair development, while 10 percent have reached the full adult condition (Tanner, 1978b).

There have been many investigations relative to the age of menarche. Among white girls in America today, about half reach menarche between the ages of 12 and 14, 80 percent between $11^1/_2$ and $14^1/_2$, and more than 95 percent between the ages of 10 and 16 years. Fewer than 2 percent experience menarche between the ages of 8 and 10, and fewer than 2 percent after the age of 16. For American black girls, variations in age of menarche are similar to those of white girls, but among South African Bantu girls, menarche averages about two years later. Instances of menarche even before school age and later than age 20 have been recorded.

There has been much speculation as to why age of menarche varies so widely according to historic period, culture, and place. In the nineteenth century menarche was reported earlier for girls growing up in the tropics. However, climate has little effect on age of menarche; most individuals in tropical countries have a late menarche only because of poor nutrition (Tanner, 1978b).

After menarche girls typically increase in height by about $2^1/_2$ inches, with only one girl in seven growing 4 inches or more. Very rarely does a girl have the ability of procreation at menarche. Usually there is a sterility interval of three or more years between first menses and fertile ovulation.

PUBERTAL CHANGES IN BOYS   In boys the first observable sign of pubertal change is increase in the size of the testes and penis. This enlargement usually begins before the age of 12 for the testes and near the age of $12^1/_2$ for the penis. Individual age differences may range from $9^1/_2$ to $14^1/_2$ years for the growth of the testes, and from 10 years to 15 years for the penis. The average length of the penis almost doubles from age $12^1/_2$ to age 17, and the average volume of the testes increases more than tenfold from age 12 to age 19. For the average boy, the growth spurt begins at about $12^1/_2$ years of age and reaches its peak shortly after age 14. Individual boys vary from $10^1/_2$ to 16 years for onset of the height spurt. Among white boys, pigmented hairs near the base of the penis appear between the ages of 10 and 16, with 80 percent of the boys showing this stage of development between ages 11 and 15. However, among Chinese boys, pigmented pubic hair is typically not seen before the age of 14, and some do not have any pigmented hair until after age 16.

Rate in growth of pubic hair also varies among individuals. For some boys, pubic hair growth is rapid; for others it is slow. One boy may have just a few pigmented hairs for a period of years; another may take less than six months to attain a moderately dense growth. The average time for acquiring a dense growth after the first pigmented hairs appear is about three years. Some boys have pigmented underarm hair by the age of 11, others not until the age of 17, but for most boys it appears between the ages of 12 and 16. Occasionally, children

Pubescence is not a datable event but a period within which a constellation of changes occurs. (Photo by William J. Butcher)

exhibit pubic hair growth and accelerated growth in the external genitalia even in early childhood.

After puberty the male's orgasm is usually accompanied by ejaculation or the discharge of semen (sperm from the testes and secretions of related sex glands). During sexual excitement women produce vaginal fluids quite profusely but do not ejaculate them. The mature woman conceives with or without orgasm, but the man's ejaculation is essential for fertilization (Katchadourian, 1977).

During puberty, boys experience a small to moderate amount of breast development. A node of firm tissue, sometimes exceeding a half inch in diameter, develops under each nipple. These nodes appear in a few boys by age 11 and in most boys by age 15. By late adolescence they frequently become too small to palpate. For many boys this enlargement vanishes in a year, for one third in two years, for 8 percent in three years. Boys who are unaware that this change is normal and usually transient may become anxious about its feminizing effect on their appearance. Because of their extra fat, obese boys appear to have enlarged breasts (Katchadourian, 1977).

PERSPECTIVE ON PUBERTY   Individuals experience puberty at varied ages, so that among any group of 14-year-old boys or 12-year-old girls some will not have begun their pubertal changes, while others will have all but completed them. Such variation, almost wholly genetic in origin, has significant educational and social consequences. Difference in tempo of growth, whether the pattern of growth proceeds quickly or slowly, is perceived most easily at puberty but exists at all ages (Tanner, 1978b).

Aging not only proceeds at different rates within different individuals but also within different organs of the same individual. Hence, not all same-aged adolescents are at identical stages of physical development; nor do all the bodily processes move in tandem. Note the asynchrony in adolescent features when certain features develop before others; it takes a while for some parts to catch up and give the face a more balanced appearance.

Across the years, the overall growth process has increased in momentum so that adolescents today are taller than their counterparts of a few decades ago. Such changes are not limited to the United States but apply to a wide range of ethnic and national groups: Italian, Polish, Chinese, Japanese, New Zealanders, and others.

Both sexes achieve their final height earlier than in former years. In 1880, boys did not attain their final height until age 23, 24, or even 25, whereas now the average youth reaches full height at the age of 18. At the turn of the century, girls achieved their final height at age 18 or 19, and today at age 16 (Tanner, 1968). As we stated earlier, at all ages boys' physical characteristics vary more than do girls'. Boys are more extreme in their dimensions of weight, height, and bone growth (Rogers, 1982).

Psychological Reactions
to Physical Maturation

BODY BUILD   Pubertal changes in body build may be related to emotional health in two principal ways: as an indicator of personality type and as a measure of an individual's variance from norms for one's sex. One well-known theory, developed by W. H. Sheldon and E. Kretschmer among others, states that body build is directly correlated with temperament and personality (Sheldon, Stevens, & Tucker, 1940; Kretschmer, 1951). Sheldon's classification, the most popular, identifies three body types: the **mesomorphic** (muscular, athletic), the **ectomorphic** (thin, lanky), and the **endomorphic** (round, pudgy). Sheldon described boys with an ectomorphic build as cautious, quiet, and hesitant to give offense; they were sensitive, lacked energy, and looked to adults rather than to peers for approval. For girls, the composite picture was similar, although ectomorphic girls showed more soberness of outlook (they were unfriendly, tense, and irritable). Consistent with other studies, mesomorphs proved well adjusted. Mesomorphic girls tended to channel their energies into social affairs; mesomorphic boys, into gross motor activities. Endomorphic children of both sexes showed a fondness for comfort and a need for affection and approval.

Later research has shown these correlations to be nonexistent or extremely low. Although body type has proved a poor indicator of personality in individual cases, one can easily conclude why some relationships have been found. For one thing, the same genetic factors that modify body build also contribute to basic temperament or typical emotional pattern. Particular body builds may also contribute to the development of related traits. The thinner ectomorph may be defeated easily in fights and become tense and shy; the mesomorph with a strong, athletic body may find it easy to win and may, therefore, develop aggressiveness as a means for gaining status.

For young boys, physical prowess means success and prestige and "the body is very much an instrument of the person" (Tanner, 1978b, p. 84). Strong, muscular boys mature earlier than others and experience an earlier growth spurt. They generally dominate their peers before puberty and have an earlier start to a favorable status for maintaining that domination. The "unathletic, lanky boy, unable to hold his own in the preadolescent rough and tumble, gets still further pushed to the wall at adolescence as he sees others shoot up while he remains nearly stationary in growth" (p. 85). Even younger boys may surge past him in athletic skills and size. Individuals of both sexes react to expectations that they conform to characteristics associated with cultural stereotypes.

In other research Brenner and Hinsdale (1978) studied perceptions of body-build stereotypes and self-identification among girls in three age categories: 6, 15, and 19 years. While side-view figures of a female endomorph, ectomorph, and mesomorph were shown, they were asked to circle adjectives from 27 antonym pairs indicating which was most like themselves and which they most wanted to look like. At all ages the girls preferred the mesomorph figure, viewed the endomorph unfavorably, and the ectomorph somewhat less negatively—and the unfavorable impressions of the ectomorph and endomorph grew stronger with age. The heavier girls rejected stereotypes associated with their own physique and denied any association between their own behaviors and those attributed both by themselves and others to persons of their physique. They identified their own behaviors with those of more favorable body builds and indicated preference for physiques other than their own. Because of such stereotypes, society responds to overweight individuals in ways that interfere with their social and emotional development.

HEIGHT A second structural feature of special concern in adolescence is height. Growth in height is rapid during infancy and early childhood. The rate of growth then slows down and becomes steady until early puberty, when it speeds up again. However, in northwest Europe and North America, the average boy practically stops growing in stature at age $17^1/_2$, and the girl, at $15^1/_2$, with a normal variation of about two years around these averages. After this growth, only about 2 percent of additional height is acquired. Meantime, there is great variation among both sexes in height and rate of growth until maturity (Tanner, 1978b). Girls are typically shorter than boys until about age 11, and their adolescent growth spurt occurs about two years earlier. At age 14 boys again become taller because their growth spurt has now begun and girls' is about complete.

In a heterogeneous population where height is a highly visible variable and varies with racial and ethnic background, it becomes a handy feature for assigning status. Since persons from the taller ethnic and racial groups founded and achieved leadership in this country, height has come to symbolize success, at least for males. Height deviations are a special problem for the shy person who dislikes feeling conspicuous. Well-adjusted individuals can absorb considerable physical variation into their self-concepts without being disturbed.

Concern over height increases with the degree of variation from the average, modified somewhat by the way individuals perceive variance. Tallness in the male is considered desirable, unless it is extreme or combined with excessive thinness. Even the very tall man may win distinction in sports if he is also well coordinated and muscular. If he is not, his ego may suffer from failure to live up to others' expectations. At the other extreme, shortness is incompatible with the male ideal of dominance. Society takes the short man less seriously. He, in turn, may exaggerate masculine behaviors—walking with great strides, or affecting pipe-smoking and drinking.

Very tall girls have greater problems than do very tall boys. Few males will date girls much taller than themselves. However, tall women today are less conspicuous than they were formerly. Women's entrance into the professions has made height something of an asset. The demand for tall fashion models has also helped make greater height in women respectable. Shortness is a problem for girls only when it is extreme or conflicts with personal aspirations for a career where height is expected. Actually, the short girl has something of a monopoly on the short boy. In any case, "acceptable height" continues to vary with the woman.

WEIGHT   Another source of concern to many adolescents is weight. Both overweight and underweight appear more frequently among girls than boys and among older than younger girls. The tendency to put on weight may be normal and temporary. The body may simply accumulate fat until the limbs lengthen enough to redistribute it. There is a weight spurt for girls between the ages of 10 and 14, and for boys about two years later. After puberty, the amount of fatty tissue normally decreases somewhat in boys and increases in girls. Fat deposits occur normally in females during adolescence, regardless of their eating habits; but since the girl does not understand this phenomenon, she may become alarmed by the excess weight and resort to crash dieting.

Excess weight may have both physical and emotional ill effects. Fat people meet constant frustration. They hear humorous allusions to "fatties" and "pot-bellies." Fat girls are spurned by boys. Besides, overweight individuals mature more rapidly and attain final stature earlier than their leaner peers. In consequence, overweight adolescents may be ready for sexual experience earlier than others, yet they may find themselves unable to obtain the attention they desire because of their physical unattractiveness.

Research confirms the common view that adolescents, girls especially, are extremely conscious of overweight. In a study of a thousand 15- to 16-year-old pupils categorized as overweight, underweight, or average, Hendry and Gillies (1978) found that average-weight adolescents were judged most favorably by their physical education teachers and had more positive images of their own bodies and of themselves, especially with regard to sports. Overweight adolescents, especially the girls, were very conscious of being overweight and, in consequence, had lower feelings of body esteem; nevertheless, they attempted to be sociable with their peers. Underweight adolescents perceived their bodies as less deviant from the average than did the overweight individuals; however, they felt inadequate and shunned heterosexual social affairs. Teachers' expectations of the different body types tended to reinforce the poorer self-images of underweight and overweight adolescents.

Self-perceptions regarding one's weight may diverge sharply from what may, in fact, be ideal. Most adolescent girls who are at least 30 percent overweight believe it ideal to be 10 percent underweight. Adolescents who are not overweight use as many uncomplimentary adjectives to describe their present appearance as do those who are overweight (Storz, 1982).

Considerable data suggest that a tendency to obesity depends on both genetic and environmental factors. A comparison of identical twins reared together and apart indicates that difference in body weight is greater for those reared apart. That is, environmental factors serve either to limit or to encourage obesity, regardless of any genetic tendencies involved. The tendency to obesity is established between birth and age 2, a critical period that determines the number of fat cells an individual will harbor until death. By this age, fat children have both larger and more fat cells than children of normal weight. After age 2, weight loss does not reduce the number of fat cells, although the cells themselves may become smaller. Fat children, it has been said, eat a broad pathway into adulthood because of their "permanent excess of fat-making machinery" (Rodin, 1978, p. 43). Dieting may reduce the amount of fat in the individual cells, but only surgery can reduce their number. The only real key to avoiding adolescent and adult obesity is to prevent the production of excess numbers of fat cells early in life (Shenker & Schildkrout, 1975).

Less well recognized are the problems of the underweight adolescent. The too-thin girl may yearn for the softness and curves generally associated with her sex, or the thin boy may envy the athlete's rugged physique. Either sex may be concerned over general appearance and the difficulty of finding suitable clothes. In some adolescents, underweight is related to other physical conditions. In others, excess fatigue, irregular meals, or poor food may foster habits of eating too little. Still others may find even the thought of food unpleasant, an attitude sometimes originating in early childhood when eating habits are established. Refusal to eat becomes an easy way to frustrate an impatient or unloving mother, or it may be a way to get attention. In such instances, eating has somehow come to arouse feelings of anxiety and guilt.

MOTOR SKILLS   Since motor skills reach their peak during the teens, some persons question the custom of designating adolescence as the awkward age. It is a biological principle that functional capacity must follow structural growth. Changes cannot be adapted to until after they have occurred. Therefore, some readjustments to growth, with accompanying awkwardness, are natural. For example, consider the boy who wrote, "When I'm nervous my legs and arms want to move real quicklike." The facts do not support the concept of adolescence as an overgrown, clumsy stage. In general, motor skills increase in proportion to body strength, with such elements as balance showing a continuous increase with age, with little, if any, adolescent spurt.

A review of the research indicates that acquiring sports skills helps adolescents to learn various tasks essential for their developmental level (Dozier, Lewis, Kersey & Charping, 1978). They help youth to adapt to changes in their body structure; to channel their impulses, especially their aggressive ones, so that they can become a constructive force in personal mastery; to develop effective and close relationships with others; and to become emancipated from the parents. In addition, sports participation helps adolescents to express their personal emotions and convictions, including "feelings of power, anger, or frustration; tenderness over a fallen teammate or opponent; affection and exuberance; stoicism, loss, and loneliness" (p. 484).

Traditionally, girls have received far less encouragement than boys in their motor development. They have been hampered by the concept of girls as being passive and having little real interest in sports. Fortunately the social climate is changing so that women are coming to be accepted increasingly in the sports world. Yvonne Slatton, a sports sociologist, points out girls' participation in Little League, bids to women to join professional teams, and televised programs of women's competition. While such events undoubtedly attract the more athletic, better-coordinated girls, they also help to establish athletics as appropriate for girls and to encourage girls' participation generally (Female jocks, 1978).

PRIMARY SEX ORGANS   The prepubescent growth of the reproductive organs, both external and internal, is slow, but their growth during adolescence is very rapid. The uterus is about 45 percent of final adult size at birth. Immediately after birth it shrinks and does not even recover birth size until age 5. After that age, it grows slowly until puberty, then increases rapidly in size through adolescence and reaches adult size at about age 20. On average, the boys' genitals reach the adult stage three years after they first begin to develop. Some boys complete their genital development in as little as 1.8 years, whereas others require as much as 4.7 years (Marshall & Tanner, 1970). The penis grows quite rapidly during the first four years of life and then more slowly until puberty. Rapid growth resumes with the onset of puberty and continues until the penis reaches full adult size at about age 21.

The male's external genitals include the penis and the scrotum. The testes are called internal sex organs, despite their location outside the abdomen in the scrotal sac. The penis begins to grow rapidly about a year after the onset of pubic hair and testicular development, ordinarily between ages 10 and $13\frac{1}{2}$, and continues until ages $13\frac{1}{2}$ to $16\frac{1}{2}$. In most boys, the penis and testicles almost double in size between the ninth and fifteenth years; added to the erectile power the penis has had since birth, this growth invests in them special value as "the primary locus of grown-up male sexuality" (Maddock, 1973b, p. 328). At the same time, the processes of erection and ejaculation attain significance as proof of masculinity; and the adolescent male becomes concerned to see whether he "measures up to his contemporaries, both in terms of size and performance" (p. 328). The shape and size of the penis are unrelated to the male's race, physique, virility, or effectiveness in the sex act. Although penises vary in size, these variations diminish during erection. Nor does the penis enlarge or diminish in size because of frequency or infrequency in sexual function. The male's preoccupation with his genitals results partly from the fact that they are quite apparent, functional, and intrinsically rewarding. His need to give these structures a proper part in his life may constitute an important motivating force in determining his sexual behaviors (Maddock, 1973b).

Boys whose genitals are relatively small may worry because of the traditional association of genital size with virility. Except where deviation is extreme, this notion is a myth and copulation will not be affected. Several factors may contribute to producing abnormally small genitals. The simplest is late puberty, a condition that will correct itself in time. If puberty has begun in other respects and genitals fail to develop normally, genetic or hormonal factors are probably to blame. The condition normally responds to treatment with gonadotropic or androgenic hormones.

The female genitals, or vulva, include the mons pubis, or soft protuberance above the pubic bone; the labia majora, or major lip below the mons which surrounds the minor lip; the clitoris; and the vaginal opening (Katchadourian, 1977). All structures within the vulva change significantly during puberty. They become enlarged and more erotic in sensitivity, particularly the clitoris. Although girls' external genitalia are not as visible as boys', girls may nevertheless be quite sensitive about them. Since information about the size of normal female organs is not readily available to her, an adolescent girl may suspect abnormality and may suffer anxiety, especially if the clitoris is unusually long.

Normally girls do not feel penis envy; they are principally concerned with the penis as the organ of copulation. Whether they view it as sexually exciting, repugnant, or frightening is important for later marital adjustment. A Viennese girl relates the following childhood experience:

> I had heard that it [the male organ] was 12 to 15 cm. long. During the fancywork period (at school) we took the tape measure and indicated the stated length on our stomachs, naturally reaching to the navel. This horrified us; if we should ever marry we would be literally impaled. (Stekel, 1926, p. 121)

BREASTS   A girl's breasts are important to her because they are obvious; in a manner similar to the male's penis, breast development may be a value-imparting occurrence that "interacts with supporting sociocultural factors (the breasts being traditional symbols of beauty and motherhood) to shape the patterning of female sexual expression" (Maddock, 1973b, p. 329). That is, the enlargement of her breasts produces more consciousness of being female than does the enlargement of the clitoris.

Welch (1980) cites research by Chris Klienke and Richard Staneski who had college students rate head-to-waist photographs of three college women. Each of three had used cotton to make her breasts appear progressively larger from one photograph to the next and each wore dresses that fitted closely enough to make her breast size clearly visible. In all three photos they had been trained to hold their facial expression neutral. The factor of breast size did not apparently affect the ratings of the women for overall personal appeal or likability. However, the smaller bust was associated with ratings of ambition, intelligence, competence, morality, and modesty. Such a study underlines the fact that we unconsciously modify our perceptions, certainly initially, in terms of physical characteristics; and such evaluations vary according to overall cultural evaluations attached to them.

Because of the breasts' symbolism, girls become correspondingly disturbed if their breasts appear abnormal in any way. Since it is not uncommon for one breast to develop faster than the other, a girl may become anxious, especially if she does not realize that balance is usually restored at a later time. Sometimes they grow so large as to become a matter of embarrassment. In such case there are effective and safe plastic surgical techniques—and some that are not so safe—that may correct these conditions after a woman has become adult. The shape and size of the breast do not relate to their efficiency in nursing or in responding to erotic stimulation (Katchadourian, 1977).

MENSTRUATION   Greif and Ulman (1982) point out that menarche, or first menstruation, is "a unique and concrete event which marks puberty" (p. 1413). Other pubertal changes, such as breast development, occur quite gradually; however, "menarche is unique in that it occurs suddenly and without warning, and involves bleeding. As the most discrete event of female puberty, menarche is a signpost of physical maturity and fertility" (p. 1415).

Many girls have unpleasant experiences relating to menarche and keep the event secret (Greif & Ulman, 1982). However, their experiences differ according to various factors including the girl's age when it occurs, her expectations, her information, her family support system, and her own personality characteristics. Its negative impact may be reduced by adequate psychological and physical preparation, showing that these changes are normal. Timing is also important, and knowing that other girls their age are having the same experience. Girls for whom menarche is exceptionally early or late typically have more difficulty accepting it.

Early menarche may be especially stressful, partly because early maturers often have received no preparation at all—hence find the experience frightening and shocking (Koff, Rierdan & Rheingold, 1982). Among girls who were incompletely prepared for menstruation, themes in their memories of the experience included those of "dying or of dire illness; of shame, guilt and concealment; and of being somehow abnormal. . . . " (p. 7).

Reactions to menarche are varied, from highly positive to highly negative. Some girls are proud of attaining adulthood. Note this comment in Anne Frank's diary: "I have the feeling that in spite of all the pain, unpleasantness, and nastiness, I have a sweet secret." By contrast, other girls—and society as a whole—attach negative values to the process. In William Faulkner's *The Sound and the Fury,* Quentin Compson's father portrays women as maintaining a "delicate equilibrium of periodical filth between two moons balanced." James McGregor Allan opposed women's suffrage on the grounds that every woman is more or less an invalid. Lois Gould's *Such Good Friends* contains a comic horror episode in which the protagonist learns to insert a tampon, aided by two friends in the school lavatory. The instruction is horrifying: "The diagram—terrifying cross sections of the female interior, full of squiggly Suez canals—showed a cute little cotton wad nestled in there like an eensy white mouse with its tail hanging down and out."

Even today society treats menarche as a hygienic crisis, with the emphasis on cleanliness. The event's significance is ignored as it relates to such factors as the teenage girl's "newly acquired ability to reproduce, the changing relationship with her mother, and her emerging identity as an adult," all critically tied to the onset of her first period (Menstrual myths, 1979, p. 60).

A study of women college students' memories of menarche, or first menstruation, indicated that the more adequately one was prepared in advance the more positive was the experience. Important aspects of such preparation are knowledge of the physiology of menstruation and the mechanics of menstrual hygiene (Kott, Rierdan & Rheingold, 1982).

Although mothers were named most often as sources of menstrual preparation in one study (Block, 1978) over 20 percent of mothers with young adolescent daughters had told them anything about menstruation; another 16 percent had given only the most minimal information, mainly regarding the mechanics of menstrual hygiene; and just 26 percent had given any information about the physiology of menstruation or its relation to pregnancy. None of these mothers had any awareness of how to deal with the psychological correlates of menstruation. It is hardly surprising, therefore, that the preparation commonly received fails to reduce the negative impact of menarche.

The question might then be asked: Does the experience with menarche somehow increase interest in children, in infants, and childbearing? A study of 12- and 13-year-old girls, half of whom were premenarcheal—had not gone through menarche—and half who had more often preferred pictures of infants to those of adults. In a second study premenarcheal girls, postmenarcheal girls, and boys, all rated pictures of infants, peers, college students, and 30- to 50-year-olds. The postmenarcheal girls rated the infants most positively, the boys second, and the premenarcheal girls least (Goldberg, Blumberg & Kriger, 1982). The question might be raised: Was it a matter of the individual's maturity or the factor of menarche itself? The postmenarcheal girls might simply have been more mature than the premenarcheal ones, because of general biological factors related to early maturity as well as to girls' generally earlier maturity than boys'.

Girls' reactions to menarche are highly varied. When researcher Jon Meccarello asked graduate women students about their first menstrual period, some recalled feeling excited and joyous about it; others felt uncomfortable and mentioned it to no one except their mothers; and others had forgotten about it. Those who as graduate students reported high tension levels a week before their menses more often had experienced trauma at first menstruation (Menstrual myths, 1979).

Girls obtain little help from their mothers in preparing for menarche. In a study of 124 California mothers of 12-year-olds, Doris Block found that few had discussed with their daughters the relationship between menstruation and pregnancy, and "an overwhelming majority" had never discussed birth control with them. Even more had not given their daughters any significant information about the father's role in reproduction. Even today young mothers still feel uncomfortable about giving such information and rationalize that their daughters are not interested in such things, or that they have already somehow obtained the information (Blinking at the birds and bees, 1979).

It has often been assumed that women are more emotionally unstable than men because of their menstrual cycle; however, the research does not bear out this notion. In a study of college students (Curtis, 1981) no significant effects among them related to the menstrual cycle. Nor did the premenstrual women appear to be either generally depressed or aroused. It appears that so-called menstrual blues may simply "fulfill, to a large extent, culturally induced expectations" (p. 710).

Also, when men and women were led to succeed or fail at a particular task there were no differences in actual performance between the sexes or between women in different menstrual phases. The men were more accurate than women in estimating their own performance but did not overestimate it. The women appeared to underestimate their performance and to reward themselves less than they deserved. The women, overall, were less confident than the men and their low expectations not easily overcome (Curtis, 1981).

In other research, Diane Ruble found that presumed associations between menstrual cycle and bodily symptoms have led women to exaggerate what are normal fluctuating bodily states. Young women aged 18 to 24, after presumably being monitored by an electroencephalogram (EEG), were told either that their period would arrive in a day or two or not for a week to ten days. They were then asked to rate themselves on 48 symptoms generally associated with menstruation. Those young women who thought their periods were close at hand reported greater water retention, pain, and changes in eating habits than those believing otherwise but who were actually at the same stage in their cycle. The latter group did not mention any greater depression, irritability, or other unpleasant feelings (Gaylin, 1978).

Wellness

The current emphasis on wellness in America, which has also caught on among youth, should be supported by appropriate instruction on relevant programs. As a case in point, consider a comparison of high school males in Reno, Nevada who did nor did not use supplements—that is vitamins and minerals. Those who used them did so primarily because they believed them quite important to health. Statements they often agreed with were: "They make me healthy" and "They keep me from being sick." Among reasons for use, maternal influence ranked very high as did "They give me energy," which is nutritionally incorrent. Calories, not vitamins, give energy. Little significance was given to teachers' and coaches' influences, although 32.4 percent of the users of multivitamins said they did so because "they help me in sports". The most common reasons for nonuse of food supplements were, "I eat right so I get my vitamins/minerals/proteins from food"; "I never really thought about them"; and "I don't need them."

Many young people have their own health programs, often jogging. Moderate and regular exercise can be quite healthful if it is not too strenuous (Scanlon, 1979). A danger inherent in individually developed health plans is that some adolescents fall for health and diet fads.

PHYSICAL PROBLEMS OF ADOLESCENTS

Nutrition

Nutrition is of special importance in adolescence, when certain food elements are essential for accelerated growth, particularly calcium for the skeletal system and protein for tissue growth. During adolescence, nutritional needs are greatest during puberty, peak requirements for girls being reached between ages 12 and 15 and for boys between ages 14 and 17. Adolescents at these ages require more calories than nursing mothers or adults performing physical labor (Katchadourian, 1977). A major problem is adolescents' preference for snack food over proper diet. Snacking is especially common in families where both parents work. In addition, adolescents may become addicted to whatever diet fads their parents assume or become the victims of their parents' ignorance regarding nutrition (Diets and children's health, 1977). Their diet is often deficient in essential elements, even when calorie intake is sufficient. They are establishing eating habits and attitudes for the rest of their lives. Whatever adolescents eat

Nutrition is important but adolescents' preference for snack food is a major problem. (Photo by Frank M. Guines, III)

will influence their mature physiques, their overall stamina, their resistance to infectious diseases, and their health for all the years ahead.

A computerized study of University of Tennessee students' eating habits indicated that they did not overeat, but that they ate the wrong things (Rating the student diet, 1979/80). Those who went without eating breakfast tended to make up for it later. Those who ate at a campus school food service ate a wider variety than did others, while those who lived mostly on fast foods tended to lack sufficient vitamins C and A. Many of the dieters ate chef's salad as an entree, not realizing they were eating over 500 calories of cheese, meat, and salad dressing. In general, they ate too much meat and too few fruits and vegetables.

Smoking

Smoking cigarettes, the most hazardous form of tobacco smoking, is a habit usually established in adolescence. A vast amount of research has identified its health hazards. High school students who have smoked from one to five years already have sustained pulmonary damage. Even healthy young persons who smoke experience increased blood pressure and heart rate. They must also exert greater effort than nonsmokers to complete various physical tasks. More serious effects of smoking gradually develop over the years. Young smokers can greatly reduce or avoid future damage "by quitting, or at least reducing the number of cigarettes, the number of draws, and the extent of inhaling, or by switching to brands that contain less tar and nicotine and by smoking only the first part of a cigarette. (The last third contains 50 percent of the harmful substance.)" (Katchadourian, 1977, p. 215).

Because cigarette smoking has been reported as the largest single preventable cause of death in the country, programs designed to reduce or prevent the smoking habit are important (Surgeon General's Report in Pomerleau, 1979). Most of these programs focus on long-term health hazards; however, this approach may be ill-adapted to adolescents. Adolescents have trouble relating themselves to health hazards many years away. Besides, to many adolescents smoking benefits may outweigh health risks (Leventhal & Cleary, 1980). Often, high school youths' image of adolescent smokers is "sophisticated, attractive, and socially successful" (the kinds of images portrayed in cigarette advertising); and they wish to create such images in the eyes of their peers (Barton, Chassin, Presson & Sherman, 1982, p. 1499). In contrast, among most college students the incidence of cigarette smoking has declined dramatically over the past two decades.

Attempts to help youth avoid or stop cigarette smoking should, of course, take into account the personalities and attitudes of the individuals involved. For example, in other research in San Diego County, California, Lotecka and Lasselben (1981) compared high school smokers, ex-smokers and nonsmokers and found considerable differences among them. The smokers did not like to talk about smoking. Almost all had some nonsmoking friends, at least among those smokers who wished to stop smoking. The ex-smokers had wanted to stop because of pressure from parents, sports, health, repulsive image, and unpleasant sensations. They said such things as "its unhealthy—it hurts the lungs and causes cancer—it's dumb, disgusting—I want to breathe" (p. 518). The ex-smokers used various devices for avoiding smoking. They might walk, meditate, or simply be alone.

The nonsmokers wanted nothing to do with cigarette smoking and appeared to avoid hanging out with smokers. They had simply avoided smoking by saying "I don't smoke" and felt somewhat superior about it. Smokers had more problems than nonsmokers and did less homework. The nonsmokers viewed smoking as a dirty habit, bad for their health, dumb, and poor for sports performance.

Most of the students felt that nonsmokers conveyed a better image. With regard to popularity, 44 percent of all the students indicated smokers were just as popular as nonsmokers or ex-smokers; 44 percent felt smokers were a little less or much less popular; and 9 percent said they were a little more or much more popular. When asked if smoking is a dirty habit 82 percent said yes, and 17 percent no.

The smoker groups seemed to be somewhat different in personality. They showed a strong desire to be themselves and to have their own life style. They tended to reject anything that was imposed on them such as schedules, goals, or assignments, and they distrusted adult guidance on the subject of smoking, preferring peer leadership and books designed to break the habit.

Mental health professionals themselves often fail to recognize the seriousness of youth's smoking. A survey of youth agencies in Ontario, Canada indicated that over half (54 percent) placed great emphasis on physical fitness, but gave less formal teaching about smoking than any other health topic. In those agencies where the adult leaders themselves were nonsmokers, policies more often forbade smoking during agency activities and far more of the youth smoked (Goodstadt, Larson & Langford, 1982).

Alcohol

INCIDENCE   Although youth's rate of alcohol consumption may now have stabilized, a study by Ruth Engs of students' drinking patterns on 15 university campuses, compared with earlier studies, indicated no significant increase in the percent of students who drink or have drink-related problems (Student spirits, 1979). Over half said they drank at least once a month; a fifth, not at all. The number of heavy drinkers and abstainers also continued about the same. A few more of the men (82 percent) than women (75 percent) drank and about five times as many men as women drank heavily. There were no significant differences in drinking patterns of freshmen and seniors, suggesting that drinking habits remain constant during college years.

EFFECTS   Heavy use of alcohol may result in such conditions as pancreatitis, acute gastritis, and acute depression. Various mental and physical complications associated with chronic alcoholism, including cirrhosis of the liver, do not appear among youth. Alcoholism among youth ordinarily constitutes more of a social than a medical problem.

On the other hand, heavy drinking by adolescents also leads to heavy drinking as adults, who use alcohol more than ever before, at least in the United States (Ziomkowski, Mulder & Williams, 1975). Many alcoholics who come for treatment in their thirties admit to dependence on alcohol since their early teens (Blume, 1975).

Alcohol abuse by youth is associated with vandalism, violence, and vice. It is a factor in half of all homicides and a third of all suicides. Another danger is reckless behavior, especially drunken driving.

A study of students at Oklahoma State University indicated that the single most important factor in determining how much and how often the student drank was how much the student drank before coming to college. Neither parental attitude nor religious commitment appeared directly or indirectly to affect quantity or frequency of drinking or problem drinking itself (Hughes & Dodder, 1983).

TREATMENT   Finn and Brown (1981) suggest that those who counsel youth should recognize that many heavy-drinking youth understand more about the negative effects of their behavior than their drinking would indicate. A survey of 1269 high school students in Massachusetts indicated that a large majority recognized both short- and long-term risks involved in getting drunk, although a considerable minority did not. Those who drank the most had the most realistic understanding of the dangers of intoxication and getting high. Yet many of the respondents believed that the dangers were worth taking. Therefore, it appears that adults should focus their efforts on helping youth to analyze their motivations for drinking as well as on whatever benefits they feel are involved and spend less time convincing them of the dangers of their behaviors, which they recognize anyhow.

The motivations and perceived benefits involved vary according to sex and individual; one should not generalize about any particular adolescent's attitudes toward drinking on the basis of a youth sample. It should also be noted that in many communities the girls get drunk as often as do the boys (Finn & Brown, 1981).

Other Drugs

EXTENT AND NATURE OF USE   Of great social concern is youth's growing use of drugs, especially marijuana. Among 682 junior and senior high school students in a middle-class suburb of New York City, two thirds of the students confessed to drinking alcohol and 29 percent to having smoked hashish or marijuana in the half year before the study, although only 1 to 7 percent got high every day. The use of hard drugs or LSD was rare (In one ear . . . ,1977). Marijuana use is still popular; however, youth are coming, increasingly, to wonder about its safety. Of over 17,000 high school seniors questioned in 1980, about half felt that regular marijuana smoking constituted a health risk, up from 35 percent in 1978 (Youth on the move, 1980).

Research has disclosed a relationship between drug use and medicine-taking, namely, that usage of any drug may lead to stronger drugs and dependency. Alcohol, tobacco, and medicines all relate to drug-seeking behavior; therefore, drug-abuse problems should be linked to the more general problem of using tobacco, medicines, and alcohol.

Some studies have indicated that youth unemployment has been associated with increased use of tobacco, drugs, and alcohol, increase in delinquency, and a growth in cynical attitudes about the work ethic (Chase, 1982).

MISCELLANEOUS CAUSES OF DRUG USE   Various causes have been advanced for youth's attraction to drugs. Most youths use drugs for several reasons (Wogan & Elliot, 1972). Girls sometimes use them to control weight; some youth use them when studying for examinations; still others want to get high. In other cases, drugs may be used to expand the boundaries of the ego and to overcome its limitations. Adolescents' drug use may relate to the need for thrills and novelty. Experimentation may include such variations as sniffing glue, lighter fluid, or gasoline. Another cause may be group pressure or the need to belong.

The effects of marijuana fall into several main categories. Somatic effects include feelings of warmth, lightness in the limbs, and effortlessness of movements. Cognitive effects are reflected in "a stream of disconnected ideas that flows rapidly and unhindered. Even ordinary statements acquire new meaning and apparent profundity. Perceptions are altered as the senses become sharper; colors seem brighter, sounds clearer" (Katchadourian, 1977, p. 222). In addition, the sense of time is altered so that a few minutes seem like an hour. Nevertheless, the marijuana user keeps in touch with reality and appears sober even when intoxicated.

A survey of eighth through twelfth graders in four high schools in a northeastern city indicated no significant relationship between marijuana use and selected social and aggressive tendencies. Rather, there was a positive relationship between such use and property offenses, probably for the purpose of getting money to finance the habit (Thornton, 1981).

TREATMENT The problem of dealing with drug users and abusers is a complex one involving many elements including peer pressures, family problems, cultural values, and individual psychology (Jalai, Crocetti & Turner, 1981). Therefore, therapy must be comprehensive, yet tailored to the individual and the situation involved.

The home environment is especially important. Reese and Williams (1983) found that parents of drug abusers had less skill and confidence in dealing with their children; and the parents had less confidence in their childrearing ability compared with parents of nonabusers. The more confident parents tend to employ more consistent discipline and rules, thus being more adequate models for their children in developing problem-solving skills and attitudes which would contribute to avoiding drug use (Reese & Wilborn, 1983).

In other research which involved a comparison of high school-age adolescents in a residential chemical dependency program and a control group of high school seniors, the treatment group more often came from one-parent, poor, disadvantaged families, and made poorer grades although they were average or above in ability (Svobodny, 1982). With regard to causation the treatment group often mentioned "poor family relationships, non-caring attitudes about school, peer pressure to use drugs, no one to talk with," as part of the total problem. Most of them had begun with experimenting and then used drugs more frequently to escape their problems. However, all of them said that drugs did not really help them deal with their problems, but would need support from others if they were to go straight. Most of them were "scared and anxious when they were at the threshold of leaving the program." This is the time that counselors call the grieving period, when youth feel uncertain of their support system and fearful of entering the "real world again" (p. 851).

Beyond the foregoing generalities, each individual has unique reasons for using drugs. Here some reactions to drugs are given by college students:

> It was a new experience, but seemed no better than a cheap drunk.
>
> People seem to be less barbaric on grass than on alcohol.
>
> When drinking I get loud, but pot calms me down. Sometimes it makes me oversexed.

POTENTIAL HARM OF DRUG USE Tests have shown little pronounced impairment among ordinary marijuana users, although frequent use has been associated with various unfortunate reactions, including nausea, vomiting, and respiratory ailments. While adverse reactions to moderate use are unproved, potentially harmful effects of continued and heavy use are controversial. Heavy marijuana use has been reported to contribute to aggressive criminal behaviors, social apathy, and personality deterioration, among other outcomes, but definitive answers must await results of on-going longitudinal research (Nahas, Paton & Idanpaan-Heikkila, 1976).

A main danger of LSD is potential harm to future offspring. The threat to the health of the offspring exists even if the mother quits taking the drug during pregnancy. To what degree or whether this danger actually exists is uncertain (Jaffe, 1975). While LSD has been proved to cross the placental barrier in mice, thus far it has not been shown to do so in humans.

Drugs are dangerous in that they may create a psychological dependence on pharmacological crutches and may produce entanglements with narcotic addicts and dope peddlers. In this company, the youth may be introduced to more potent drugs and become addicted. The bulk of evidence suggests that, just as excessive, long-term use of alcohol has unfortunate social, psychological, and physical effects, so may use of any drug, including marijuana.

Gullotta and Adams (1982) reviewed the research literature concerning controlling substance abuse among adolescents to determine which kinds of programs have been most effective. Some approaches stress both genetic and cultural factors. Others emphasize both social factors and the individuals concerned, and their complex interaction. Another approach is through legislation, intended to control the availability of a substance. Programs designed for drug control among adolescents are most effective when they take into account the multiple factors involved (Gullotta & Adams, 1982).

Wherever possible it is important to identify and treat drug problems early. Adolescents commonly employ a particular sequence in their use of both legal and illegal drugs (Svobodny, 1982). About two years after their first experience with alcohol and tobacco they may have their first experience with marijuana and then other illicit drugs. Multi-drug use patterns are a common problem of drug abuse. In general, the earlier an individual begins drinking or using drugs the more likely an addictive problem will follow.

Accidents, Suicide, Health Status, and Disease

ACCIDENTS Adolescents are especially vulnerable to certain types of accidents and disease. Among causes of death among teenagers, accidents rank first accounting for 60 percent of deaths, of which 40 percent are due to motor vehicle accidents. The accident rate per mile driven is highest in youth, declines steadily until late middle age, then rises slightly. Serious traffic violations and careless driving account for 77 percent of accidents producing injuries. Twenty percent may be attributed to excessive speed, 17 percent to refusing to yield, 7 percent to driving on the wrong side of the road, 10 percent to careless driving, and 7 percent to mistakes in overtaking (Katchadourian, 1977). Although motorcycles comprise only 3 percent of all motor vehicles, the risk in operating them is about four times as great as for cars per hour driven (Metropolitan Life, 1973). Over 90 percent of motorcycle accidents occur to males, two thirds in the 15- to 24-year-old group. Other causes of adolescent deaths are homicide, malignant growths, and suicides (Teenagers in the 60s, 1974).

Adolescent males are far more likely than females to become the victims in accident fatalities, including motor vehicle, swimming, and boating mishaps. Drowning ranks second in the 15- to 19-year age group (12.2 for males and 1.0 for females per 100,000). The next greatest cause of accident fatalities is fires for females (0.7 per 100,000) and firearms for males (4.9 per 100,000).

Suicide is the third leading cause of death among adolescents, after accidents and homicides, and is on the increase among both sexes (Tischler,

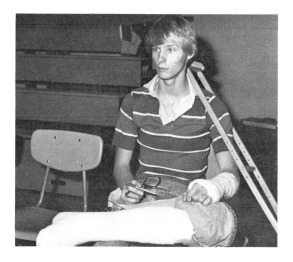

Adolescents are especially vulnerable to accidents. (Photo by Frank M. Guines, III)

McHenry & Morgan, 1981). In the United States about 25,000 individuals commit suicide each year, almost a fifth of these are between 15 and 24 years of age. It is estimated that a much larger number of adolescent suicides are unreported and that half of these are simply called accidents. In general, the data indicate a history of psychological maladjustment, some sort of family loss or disruption, and incapability of adapting to certain adult roles. Males are more likely than females to have engaged in acting out behaviors such as delinquency, whereas the females have more often made previous threats of suicide. Also, males are more often successful in their suicide attempts as they commonly use guns, whereas females use drugs or poison which often fail in their intended result (Cosand, Bourque & Kraus, 1982).

In a study of high school youth in twelve public high schools in the greater Boston area, school professionals identified thirty clues warning of an adolescent's potential for suicide. Seventy per cent had shown signs of depression including despair, sadness, and indifference as well as certain physical signs including problems of eating and sleeping. On some occasions they have been alerted to the problem by the individuals involved or by those in whom they had confided. At other times the communication was indirect as through morbid or suicidal themes in written work and art. Those most common were signs of withdrawal, social isolation, and lack of peer support. Most of the schools had some informal ways of dealing with suicide attempts but just 20 percent had any kind of formal system such as a crisis team (Grob, Klein & Eisen, 1983). In general, the single greatest predictor of suicide is "severe, long-term psychological disability" and a history of maladaptive behaviors and unfortunate incidents with the family. Young suicides rarely show evidence of any physical illness. Overall, it appears that "multiple problems, many of them psychological, and any external trauma, regardless of its source, may have been sufficient to motivate suicide" (Cosand, Bourque & Kraus, 1982, p. 928).

The incidence of suicide also relates to the following factors: previous suicide attempts; being male and nonwhite; living in socially disorganized urban areas; belonging to families where suicidal behaviors have occurred; having abnormal electroencephalograms and sometimes organic brain dysfunction; being unmarried and pregnant; and having chronic and acute physical illness including medical complications (Petzel & Cline, 1978, in Feinstein & Giovacchini, 1978). Contrary to common opinion, college students are not a high-risk group. Suicidal behaviors proceed "within a complex psychological-biological-historical context, suggesting a suicidal process rather than an impulsive, isolated, or circumstantial occurrence" (p. 259).

Prognosis and intervention must focus on a combination of social, biological, and psychological factors. One problem that arises in connection with treatment is that of confidentiality. To what extent do counselors have the right to breach adolescents' confidence and discuss their problems with their families. Some of the families, armed with such information, might simply make matters worse (Grob, Klein & Eisen, 1983).

HEALTH STATUS   Adolescence is one of the healthiest periods in life, but is less so than teenagers assume. About 60 percent of adolescents rate their health as excellent or very good, 36 percent as good, and fewer than 5 percent as fair or poor, a rating consistent with their parents' view about their children's health (U.S. National Center for Health Statistics, 1975). Nevertheless, physical examinations prove young people to be less healthy than they think they are (Katchadourian, 1977).

A major problem among youth is venereal disease, or sexually transmitted disease, especially gonorrhea. This disease is very common yet very difficult to control (Silber, 1981). Two million people develop it each year, a third of them adolescents. It is the most common infectious disease in the country and is three to eight times as common in adolescent girls as boys, and adolescent teenagers, ages 15 to 19, account for 25 percent of all cases.

Yet gonorrhea is difficult to control—because it has a short incubation period; patients whose gonorrhea is cured are not immune to future infection, and both school and community take little interest in the problem. Many individuals are also symptomatic infectious carriers—that is, they do not show symptoms, but are carriers of the disease. Females unaware of their infection may suffer from sterility as well as from pelvic inflammatory disease, which is quite serious. The incidence of syphilis increased during the 1950s, but it has leveled off. In many parts of the country, minors may now be treated for venereal disease without parental consent.

Adolescents themselves are poorly informed about such matters. In one study, 28 percent of 14- to 17-year-olds could not name a single sexually transmitted disease; and in another, a survey of adolescent girls, over 40 percent thought birth control would prevent venereal disease (Silber, 1981).

STUDENT REACTION   Of 95 students in the author's classes at State University College, Oswego, New York, who responded to the question: "I am careful to maintain health habits that will help to preserve good health in the future," 80 percent agreed, 4.2 percent disagreed, and 15.7 percent were uncertain. These comments are typical of youth's growing concern about health.

MALE: I am careful to maintain health habits. Anything that I feel is harmful to me I will not do. I used to smoke. But one morning I woke up with a problem breathing and threw them away and haven't had one since. I don't believe in taking hard drugs because they can harm your body. I try to stay in shape, although I admit I am not in the greatest shape right now. I can't see how anybody can smoke cigarettes. Since I've quit I've tried to get others to quit with very little success. It annoys me now to even breathe the smoke of other people's cigarettes.

FEMALE: I am very careful to maintain my health habits. I do not smoke, drink, take drugs, or overeat. I run two miles every day and try to be as active as possible. I want my later years to be enjoyable, so now's the time to start doing something about it.

PROBLEMS OF PHYSICAL VARIATION

The Early Maturer

Prominent problems of adolescence are those of the early and late maturer. In the guidance study of the Institute of Human Development (Peskin & Livson, 1972), early maturers of both sexes fared better than late maturers over the long run. From the onset of puberty through middle adolescence, early maturers were more inhibited socially, cognitively, and athletically. However, by age 30 early maturers had significantly passed the late maturers in psychological health.

Certain other observations should be added: first, that rapid maturing may unduly shorten the period needed for a satisfactory transition to adulthood. Early maturers may no longer feel at home among their age mates, who still linger physically in childhood's afterglow. However, individuals vary greatly in their responses and they may report personal feelings at odds with what might be expected.

The Late Maturer

For both sexes, the problems of late maturers are traumatic. Late-maturing boys suffer especially because of the premium males place on genital size and sexual adequacy. They may be self-conscious about their childish genitalia when they must undress before their peers. They cannot compete successfully at sports and often withdraw. Girls still think of them as little boys. In consequence, such boys often adopt undesirable compensatory behaviors, including attention-getting devices. A follow-up study of late maturers at about age 33 indicated that the same behaviors that differentiated them in their teens from more physically precocious age mates had persisted into adulthood. Although physical differences had largely disappeared, personality differences remained about the same (M.C. Jones, 1957). For most boys, late puberty is a real handicap and rarely provides any special advantages.

Sometimes hormonal treatment has been employed with late male maturers, with some success. Certain arguments have been offered against providing hormonal therapy for late-maturing boys: An adolescent might feel that his sexual maturity was artificial; or the comparatively rapid development of secondary sex characteristics might intensify incipient neurotic patterns. However, tentative findings indicate that such complications rarely arise if appropriate psychological therapy accompanies hormonal therapy (Stempfel, 1967).

The late-maturing girl has problems, too. The girl's "lack of breasts is obvious and she may doubt she will ever develop as well as certain of her peers." For both sexes late maturity may "act as a trigger to reverberate fears accumulated deep in the mind during the early years of life" (Tanner, 1978b, p. 86). Members of either sex whose variation is extreme may be ignored or ostracized by their peers and either go it alone or retreat to a younger group.

Sexually Inappropriate Characteristics

Physical attractiveness is measured in terms of sexually appropriate stereotypes. Women judged attractive in the feminine sense have more experience with petting and intercourse, even when they differ little from less attractive women in other ways. They are also targets of more sincere and persistent romantic interaction. Sexually inappropriate physiques are especially anxiety-producing for teenage boys. Their fears are realistic, for girls react sharply to physical aspects of masculinity. In the following quotations, girls tell how they think a male's body size relates to his masculinity:

> The bigger the better. A real skinny guy with no "body" just turns me right off. I like guys who I know are stronger and bigger than I am. It gives me a sense of security in case of danger, etc.
> I could not feel feminine or attracted to a male smaller than myself.
> A well-built man is sexy.

Here two boys react to the same question:

> I have seen big guys that are as queer as a three-dollar bill.
> How the hell can someone be turned on by a little puny runt?

Physical characteristics that may be regarded as appropriate for either sex vary with the times and reflect subtle changes in sex role. The recent trend toward a more androgynous sex role, which stresses total personality development rather than high masculinity or femininity, has resulted in subtle changes in the physical ideal for the sexes.

The Physically Handicapped or Invalid Adolescent

Less common than problems associated with physical deviation from the norm, but usually more serious, are those relating to physical handicaps. About half of all severely handicapped persons are under age 50, and one fifth are under age 25. Although such handicaps are always serious in effect, they assume special significance at adolescence. Handicapped boys or girls cannot expect many dates. Unpublished research by this writer indicates that, although a large minority of women would marry a physically deformed man, males would more often reject a physically deformed woman; however, the gap has been decreasing.

Victims of illnesses like rheumatic fever and epilepsy have a special problem. These individuals appear normal but must not engage in certain activities. Peers, and even adults, often assume they are faking in order to avoid competition or gain attention.

Various factors—for example, the extent to which a defect can be camouflaged—limit the effects of crippling. A facial disfigurement, being quite visible, may play an important role in the development of self-concept, but a scar on the body is not often observed by others. However, adolescents whose handicaps are not visible may be at a special disadvantage. A teenage boy with a heart condition may find himself ignored because he cannot participate in vigorous play. The age at which crippling occurred is particularly important, for the earlier individuals are crippled, the easier it is for them to adapt.

Also significant in evaluating a particular handicap is society's attitudes toward specific handicaps. At the University of Kentucky, 455 students and rehabilitation workers ranked certain disabilities in terms of the social distance they felt toward different kinds of handicapped people. Of 21 handicaps, those rated as most acceptable were, in this order: ulcer, arthritis, asthma, diabetes, heart disease, amputation, blindness, and deafness. More unacceptable ones, beginning with the least acceptable, were: mental illness, alcoholism, mental retardation, tuberculosis, hunchback, and cerebral palsy (J. Horn, 1975).

FUTURE PERSPECTIVES

The physical aspects of adolescence have a significant impact in later years, when physical characteristics assume adult size and appearance. During youth appearance becomes part of an individual's wares when seeking a mate. The especially attractive young person whose appearance becomes his (or more often her) passport to acceptance can pay a heavy price in later years after physical attractiveness declines.

Adult alcohol and drug use often has its roots in adolescence. By the end of their senior year in high school, over a third of all students have used at least one drug other than marijuana at some time, and the percentage using marijuana rose substantially in the 1970s (Bachman & Johnston, 1979). Sixty percent had tried marijuana themselves; a third had used it twenty or more times; and 10 percent of all seniors used it daily or almost daily. The percentage who reported drinking daily had remained steady over the previous five years, at around 6 percent. The college experience has the effect of increasing such consumption. In two universities, the number of students who reported drinking wine, beer, and hard liquor more than once or twice a week increased from 47 percent to 58 percent; the incidence of abstainers decreased from 23 percent to 14 percent (Igra & Moos, 1979).

Certain effects of excessive drug use—for example, abnormalities of the red blood cells—are apparent even in youth and young adulthood. Indeed, concludes Dr. Harry Ward of the University of Colorado School of Medicine, almost every drug produces toxic reactions, and such reactions are fairly common among young adults (Scanlon, 1979, p. 36). However, the long-term effects of marijuana use are still controversial. One problem is that generalizations do not always hold for individuals, because the amount of drug use or smoking that results in addiction for one individual may not for another, for whatever combination of genetic or experimental factors involved. Habits of smoking and poor diet, established during adolescence, are danger signals for the period ahead.

Dr. Edmund Pellegrino, a professor of biology and medicine, calls attention to the increasing incidence of coronary disease among young adults, especially young women. He speculates that such increase may relate to the growing use of contraceptive pills (Scanlon, 1979). The effectiveness of medical care in later years depends greatly on whether diseases are identified as early as possible. Thus, "the early identification and treatment of young adults who have a family history of heart disease, diabetes, arthritis, emphysema, and other diseases of genetic origin may well be a way of lowering the cost of their medical care in later years, when these diseases have their greatest impact" (Scanlon, 1979, p. 55).

An individual's overall health status in earlier years tends to persist; accordingly, some youth's characteristic indifference to future consequences is unfortunate. Among the Terman long-term study of bright individuals, there was a distinct continuity of health, as measured in adolescence, over the next five decades (Goleman, 1980b). Object lessons abound all around us of adults who established habits in early life that proved harmful to health in old age.

It seems possible, within not many years, that people will live much longer than now. Thus, it will be critical that young people develop a life-span way of looking at health, instead of the all too common present orientation (If you live to be a hundred, 1983).

Of particular significance for youth is the growing emphasis today on positive concepts of health. Many youth have embarked on their own health programs, especially jogging. Donald King, chairman of the College of Physicians and Surgeons of Columbia University, when asked what young adults might do to prolong their lives, suggested that sustained moderate exercise can be extremely helpful, so long as it is not too strenuous (Scanlon, 1979). The danger is that some young people will embrace various health and diet fads without fully understanding them.

With regard to the effect of physical fitness programs on mental health, much of the research has been flawed in its methodology and its conclusions dubious (Folkins & Sime, 1981). However, a review of the research does indicate that physical fitness programs contribute to "improved mood, self concept and work behavior . . ." (p. 373). Personality traits are unaffected, except for self-concept, which might be improved by a more favorable body image.

In the future it will become increasingly important that young people learn more about their own bodies and practice keeping on the edge of changing medical treatments. Else they will be unintelligent consumers of dramatic medical marvels that are becoming commonplace. Adolescents are on the threshold of adulthood and parenthood—hence, should be fully aware of choices they may have to make regarding unborn or newly born children (Medicine dares, 1983).

On the other hand, this gene therapy might also "turn the U.S. into a science fiction fantasy land in which parents can manipulate personality, intelligence and physical appearance in future generations" (p. A6). The question arises: Just how bright, tall, friendly, or attractive do parents want their children to be? There is tremendous concern about development of guidelines to prevent abuse in genetics research (Medicine dares, 1983).

A special need for young people is better genetic education and counseling, so they can be aware of genetic susceptibilities and defects that they might pass on to their offspring, as well as what their alternatives are. They should also know about precautions that might be exercised by individuals with family histories of breast or lung cancer and become aware of the special dangers of smoking and drinking during pregnancy (Scanlon, 1979).

Only lately has the medical profession taken any real interest in adolescent medicine; even now few youths have access to physicians who are well acquainted with this speciality. To date, a considerable body of scientific knowledge has been amassed regarding children's health; however, much less is available concerning the special health problems of adolescents (Scanlon, 1979).

Also, most research studies deal with individuals and what they are like at a particular period in time, failing to reflect that they are continuously growing and developing (Nydegger, 1981). That is, in focusing on a specific period in time, they fail to appreciate human beings as dynamic, growing individuals. Nor should the study of biological changes in adolescence be narrow and unidisciplinary, for biology impinges on behavior only as mediated by the social framework (Petersen & Taylor, 1980).

Also deserving attention are ethical issues relating to adolescents' health— for example, whether the state might have authority regarding medical treatment of minors without parental consent. In 1983 an adolescent whose parents had denied her treatment for cancer on religious ground received treatment by order of the court, after an appeal. Most conflicts relating to medical treatment of minors have been decided in favor of the state under the so-called *parens patriae* doctrine and the "best interest and welfare philosophy—for example, regarding treatment of minors for venereal disease, drug abuse, alcoholism, etc." (Crutchfield, 1981, p. 175).

In some states laws have been passed recently for discouraging minors from seeking abortions by requiring parental consent or notification (Family Planning/Population Reporter, 1980). In most cases current policies limit minors' rights to certain areas such as medical treatment, drug addiction, and venereal disease. The situation is much fuzzier regarding fertility-related behaviors.

SUMMARY

Adolescence is one stage in the life-long process of aging; it proceeds continuously, with some asynchronies and characteristic changes in puberty. Adolescents incorporate perceptions of these changes in their own bodies into certain images of their physical selves: *own-body image,* or the way they believe they look; *ideal physical self-image,* or those characteristics of the self they desire to be; and *daydream self-portrait,* or the physical image they assume when in the world of daydreaming. For several reasons, these self-perceptions are of special concern in adolescence. At this time, physical changes project the body into adolescents' thoughts; they must adapt to these changes and to others' perceptions of them. These physical changes signify the end of childhood and point to maturity just ahead. Finally, body image relates to broad social and psychological phenomena that define the adolescent's status in the group, especially with members of the other sex.

Also basic to adolescent adjustment are less visible physiological factors, among them the working of the endocrine glands. Two of these, the pineal and thymus glands, inhibit sexual development until such time as it is appropriate. However, the overall relationship between hormones and behavior is complex and largely indirect. The pituitary gland is called the master gland and influences the operation of other glands affecting growth and metabolism. If the pituitary gland is not functioning properly at puberty, neither the reproductive organs nor secondary sex characteristics develop properly. The gonads (sex glands) are stimulated to produce mature sperm and ova as well as estrogens (female hormones) and androgens (male hormones). Low levels of estrogen are found in both sexes until puberty, after which time estrogen production increases greatly among girls and androgen secretion increases significantly in boys.

Perhaps the main function of the hormones is to induce puberty, which involves a complex of changes resulting in the capability to reproduce. However, no single standard exists for determining the onset of pubertal status for either sex. Indeed, pubertal changes, like all aspects of aging, vary widely among individuals. Pubescence is not a single datable event but a period within which a constellation of changes occurs.

These changes may have a profound effect on body image. Increase in size of the primary sex organs because of the presumed relationship to virility, is especially important to boys. Breast development and onset of menstruation, because they herald the arrival of feminine maturity, have a strong symbolic significance for girls. There is little, if any, substance to the common view that girls are prone to instability during the menstrual period.

Certain generalizations concerning puberty help to explain its significance. For one thing, various pubertal characteristics have changed across the years with each generation. Boys are affected by these more than girls. Both sexes are taller than their counterparts of former generations, and both sexes attain their final height earlier than in previous years. It is uncertain, however, what optimum human size might be and whether a reversal in this trend may occur.

Whatever the nature of pubertal changes, the fact that they are noticeable makes them important symbols of maturity, influencing the attainment or withholding of adult privileges. Moreover, the pace of physical development ordinarily parallels a corresponding development in the individual's ability to reason. However, some writers insist that emotional and ethical maturity are not keeping pace with youth's physical and social development.

Various factors have been found to relate to changes in puberty, one being nutrition. In general, the better the climate and the more wholesome the nutrition, the earlier puberty occurs. In addition, according to the hybrid vigor hypothesis, when individuals mate outside their own group, their offspring experience puberty at an earlier age. Climatic and geographic factors also play a part, with puberty occurring earlier in hot, humid climates at low altitudes.

Each of the pubertal changes relates somehow to the adolescent's emotional health. The thin, lanky ectomorph adjusts somewhat better than the endomorph, but more poorly than the mesomorph. An individual's height is important, too, because it is both visible and highly variable among individuals and racial groups. Another important physical characteristic is weight. A tendency to be fat may be normal or temporary; it may have physical and emotional ill effects. The cause of overweight can be either physiological or psychological or a combination of the two. Underweight may also be a problem, especially in a culture that values softness and curves. Less well recognized are problems relating to primary sex organs, in terms of their relationship to body image; males feel anxious if their genitals are small or slow in developing; girls are less concerned about their genitals because they are less conspicuous.

Certain other physical problems relate to adolescents generally, among them nutrition and fatigue. Nutrition is particularly important to adolescents because accelerated growth at this period makes certain foods essential. Other common health problems of teenagers relate to drinking and smoking. Older teenagers, who have been bombarded with continuous reports of the negative effects of smoking, are sharply curtailing the practice, but their drinking continues unabated. Another, and especially severe, problem is the adolescent's use of drugs, which has aroused particular concern in recent years. Youth may use drugs for a variety of reasons: because friends use them, to gain a sense of self-transcendence, to escape the clutch of reality, or simply to satisfy the need for novelty. The choice of drugs may depend on the effect produced as well as the sort of individual involved. Dealing with youth's drug habits is difficult because neither adolescents nor adults fully understand or appreciate drugs' potential consequences.

Certain other problems are associated with manifestations of physical variation, among them early and late maturation. Late maturing is especially disadvantageous for boys because size is thought to relate to athletic prowess and sexual adequacy in the male. Late maturers of both sexes find social adjustment difficult. Another especially acute problem of variation is the sexual inappropriate physique. Women who are judged unattractive are ignored by males; teenage boys who appear unmasculine are rejected by both sexes. Physical handicaps are also anxiety-producing because they have pervasive effects on all aspects of personal and social adjustment. In general, physical handicaps are more devastating if they are acquired after birth, particularly during adolescence. Indeed, physical development and its related problems are probably more significant for an individual's adjustment at adolescence than at any other period except old age.

The most striking recent change regarding physical health in adolescence, as at all ages, has been the emphasis on optimum health. While the search for more effective treatment of pathologies continues, the main stress now is on preservation and enhancement of sound health.

DISCUSSION QUESTIONS
AND ACTIVITIES

1. If there is an elementary or junior high school near your campus, from its office records compile data concerning the seventh or eighth grade, including general status of health, range of height and weight within the grade, differences in physical development, and health problems of boys and girls. What general picture of this age emerges?

2. Interview a physician or nurse on your college medical staff concerning the health status of youth. Ask for clarification on problems of diet, fatigue, and other trouble areas common to this age group. Report your findings in class.

3. Bring to class newspaper columns advising young people on how to improve their health and appearance. The class may discuss the value and effect of the advice offered.

4. Collect advertisements designed to arouse adolescents' concern over their physical selves and analyze their probable psychological impact.

5. Prepare to participate in panel discussions of these topics: (a) Would it be wise to have special diet tables in high school and college cafeterias for those wishing to lose weight? (b) How should the physical education program in your institution be modified to meet better the needs of students?

6. Interview a coach or physical education teacher on either the high school or the college level concerning his or her health philosophy and obtain suggestions for maintaining and improving the health of teenagers.

7. Write answers to the following questions, identifying your replies only by your age and sex. The class may divide into groups, each of which will compile replies to one question and report to the class. (a) What was your reaction to changes that took place in puberty? (b) How do you think that your physical self has affected your own life and adjustment? (c) If you ever attempted to go on a diet, describe the experience. If not, describe the experience of someone you have known. (d) Describe as nearly as you can how you feel toward an individual with each of these physical traits or manifestations: body odor, unusually good looks, acne, sexually inappropriate physique, an obvious physical handicap, a facial blemish. (e) Describe your ideal for the physical appearance of a teenage boy and girl. (f) How do you feel about your own looks and physical self?

8. Examine stories in novels or popular magazines or watch television programs to determine the physical traits commonly possessed by youthful heroes and heroines. Write a report analyzing your findings.

9. As a class, discuss the status on campus of drug use, including alcohol, marijuana, cigarettes, and common medications and pills.

10. Discuss, as a class, the topics of accidents, suicide, and disease, in terms of causes, effects, and what to do about them in situations and localities familiar to you. (Statistics for the local campus may be obtained from the health service.)

11. Your instructor may show slides of teenagers who vary widely in appearance. Write a personality sketch of each and then compare results with the rest of the class.

SUGGESTED READINGS

Adler, I. & Kandel, D. B. (1982). A cross-cultural comparison of sociopsychological factors in alcohol use among adolescents in Israel, France, and the United States. *Journal of Youth and Adolescence,* *11*(2), 89–113. Comparisons are made of patterns of adolescent alcohol use in three cultures—France, Israel, and the United States—including the differential impact of parents and peers on such use.

Barton, J., Chassin, L., Presson, C. C., & Sherman, S. J. (1982). Social image factors as motivators of smoking initiation in early and middle adolescence. *Child Development, 53*(6), 1499–1511. A study among nonsmoking early and middle adolescents indicated that the smoking image held by both categories was ambivalent and suggested certain modifications in preventive strategies.

Brook, J. S., Whiteman, M., & Grodon, A. S. (1983). Stages of drug abuse in adolescence: Personality, peer, and family correlates. *Developmental Psychology, 19*(2), 269–277. This questionnaire study of high school students discloses that stages of drug abuse may be differentiated according to various personal, familial and social factors.

Brooks-Gunn, J. & Ruble, D. N. (1982). The development of menstrual-related beliefs and behaviors during early adolescence. *Child Development, 53,* 1567–1577. This study of girls tested both prior to and several months after menarche determined expectations regarding the experience, to what extent the experience matched anticipation, and how sources of information regarding menstruation influence attitudes toward it.

Brown, S. V. (1982). Early childbearing and poverty: Implications for social services. *Adolescence, 17*(66), 397–408. The implications of deficiencies found through a national survey in public social services for teenage mothers are considered in terms of these individuals' future welfare and needs for upgrading such services.

Cash, T. F., Cash, D. W., & Butters, J. W. (1983). "Mirror, mirror, on the wall . . . ?" Contrast effects and self-evaluations of physical attractiveness. *Personality and Social Psychology Bulletin, 9*(3), 351–358. In this experiment in which 51 female college students rated their own attractiveness and body-parts satisfaction following exposure to same-sexed stimulus persons who were or were not physically attractive, the predicted contrast effect was found.

Fleischer, B. & Read, M. (1982). Food supplement usage by adolescent males. *Adolescence, 17*(68), 831–845. A specific sampling of male adolescents was studied to determine the types, appropriateness, and amount of food supplements they used, as well as demographic factors relating to such use.

Gaines, C. & Butler, G. (1983). Iron sisters. *Psychology Today, 17*(11), 64–69. Female body building and exercise are discussed in terms of their current status and appropriateness for their sex.

Goodman, N. R. & Barenblatt, L. (1983). Adolescent mobility potential and socio-political attitudes. *Adolescence, 18*(70), 457–472. This study of high school seniors was designed to consider the effect of various factors—including sex, social class, and mobility potential on sociopolitical orientation.

Monagan, D. (1983). The failure of coed sports. *Psychology Today, 17*(3), 58–63. After analyzing research regarding coed sports the writer concludes that both sexes still experience certain anxieties and conflicts on this matter, with regard to its impact on their respective sex roles.

Stubbs, M. L. (1982). Period piece. *Adolescence, 17*(65), 45–55. Theories about and personal experiences with menarche are examined and more enlightened approaches to this marker event are foreseen.

Svobodny, L. A. (1982). Biographical self-concept and educational factors among chemically dependent adolescents. *Adolescence, 17*(68), 847–853. A comparison of adolescents in a chemical dependency program and a control group of high school seniors disclosed significant differences between the two categories and suggested improvements in programs for prevention and treatment.

Trotter, R. T. (1982). Ethnic and sexual patterns of alcohol use: Anglo and Mexican college students. *Adolescence, 17*(66), 305–325. A survey of alcohol use patterns among Mexican-American and Anglo-American college students disclosed significant differences in terms of ethnicity and sex.

Weithorn, L. A. & Campbell, S. B. (1982). The competency of children and adolescents to make informed treatment decisions. *Child Development, 53,* 1589–1598. The results of this study indicated, with regard to certain hypothetical treatment dilemmas, that children and adolescents, ages 14 and 18, did not differ from older subjects in terms of reasonable preferences regarding informed health treatment decisions; even 9 year olds could participate meaningfully in such decisions.

Winick, M. (Ed.) (1982). *Adolescent nutrition.* New York: John Wiley and Sons. This in-depth analysis treats the role of nutrition in adolescent development from the standpoint of both normal needs and stress-related problems.

Chapter Four

Emotional Development

THE NATURE OF EMOTION

Characteristics and
Dimensions

Emotional response to stimuli has three main aspects: mental, physical, and motivative. It has a mental component since it involves such feelings as happiness, anger, excitement, or fear. It has a physical component since it embraces a vast complex of internal changes, including muscular, chemical, glandular, and neural activities. It has a motivative component since it involves continuous readaptations to problems inherent in an ever-changing environment. The motive is often the center, or core, of the person's emotional state.

Emotional experience can be thought of as having certain dimensions. These include: (1) Intensity of feeling: The emotion can range from a barely noticed twinge to the most powerful passion. (2) Strength of motive or impulse toward action: The individual who is sad desires to isolate himself; the one who hates wants to destroy. (3) Hedonic tone: The experience of emotion has a quality of pleasantness or unpleasantness, or both. (4) Complexity: Such basic emotions as delight, love, and anger combine in varying and unknown degrees to produce complex patterns like romantic love, patriotism, awe, and contempt. Sometimes emotion is simple, as in pure grief; at other times it is so complex as to be indescribable. Most emotions are mixed, blending like adjacent colors in the spectrum. In fact, unnamable feelings occur more often than others. Even pleasant and unpleasant feelings are often mixed together, giving rise to ambivalent emotions. The fifth characteristic of emotional experience is its integrative or disintegrative effect: the extent to which emotion contributes to or detracts from goal-directed behavior. The experiencing of emotion can serve such integrative functions as energizing the individual's behavior, maximizing strength in an emergency, and lending positive tone to experience. Disintegrative effects can include unhappiness, mental confusion, and undue demands on one's energy resources. Whether its effect is positive or negative, emotion infiltrates every aspect of human life. The organism operates as a whole, and every cognitive state may have its feeling tone.

Emotionally Healthy Behavior

Persons concerned with guiding adolescents should be able to identify integrative emotions. Adolescents' emotional health must be judged on the basis of their stage of development. In the Grant Longitudinal Study at Harvard, those individuals who were judged by the staff as having "negotiated adolescence best" were not always those who made the best adjustments in adult life. The traits "friendly" and "having vital affect" rated high for adolescent adjustment but not for adult adjustment. Maladjustment in adolescence was associated with such traits as shyness, ideation, introspection, inhibition, and lack of purpose and values. Such characteristics did not relate to later development. Instead, they seemed part of that "self-limiting, psychiatric malady called adolescence" (Vaillant & McArthur, 1972, p. 421). The adolescent characteristics "well-integrated" and "practical organizing" did correlate positively with middle-age outcomes. According to another longitudinal study (Peskin & Livson, 1972), preadolescent to adolescent changes predictive of good emotional health can be summarized as development from a self-directed, controlled preadolescence to a more crisis-ridden, stressful adolescence. Individuals who evidence no inner unrest in adolescence have apparently built up excessive defenses. In adolescence a lack of consistency in surface behaviors signals better progress toward a healthy outcome.

Such research makes clear that adolescent adjustment must be judged in terms of satisfactory progress toward emotional maturity. Well-adjusted adolescents are on their way to accepting those unfortunate facts of life that they cannot change. They are coming to realize that life's developmental issues are never fully resolved and that conflict is never completely overcome. Anyone whom we classify as young may nevertheless "contain some persistent childishness, some not-outgrown adolescence, and some precocious adulthood in his make-up" (Keniston, 1975, p. 23). Adolescents also are beginning to recognize the inevitability of struggle between individual and social needs. They are gradually adjusting to the facts of emotional conflict and their effects on the body economy. They are trying not to hide from themselves.

Teen behaviors are often judged according to distorted criteria of normality. Thus, adults may judge as lazy the daydreamer whose mind is preoccupied with probing questions. They may label as "deviant" the youth who questions his elders' well-worn, perhaps old-fashioned value system, or may judge as recalcitrant a girl who dares defend her dignity against an unreasonable parent. Meantime society smiles benignly on "well-rounded" youths whose efforts are spread so diffusely that they will never achieve excellence in anything.

Factors that Modify Emotion

GENETIC INFLUENCES Constitutional factors may form either strong or weak links in the chain of life; however, the simple fact that the body is involved in emotion is no proof of the genetic origin of a particular emotional state. A teenager's outburst of anger may relate to fatigue and excessive exertion rather than to organic weakness. Nevertheless, research does support the contention that heredity affects emotion. After studying twins admitted to mental hospitals, Gottesman and Schields (1972) concluded that genetic background plays a role in certain psychological disorders, in the sense that schizophrenia is the outcome of a genetically determined developmental predisposition. That is, an individual's basic constitution may be relatively more or less susceptible to the stresses and strains that produce schizophrenia. Given this genetic potential, some individuals become schizophrenic and others do not, depending on the stresses in their environment (Krech, Crutchfield & Livson, 1975).

Other evidence of genetic factors in emotion is the early appearance of temperamental traits and their resistance to environmental influence. Even by two or three months of age a child's temperament and behavior profiles are evident. In longitudinal research (Thomas & Chess, 1977) involving 141 children from birth to their midteens, two thirds demonstrated three general temperaments or patterns of emotion: (1) About 40 percent displayed adaptability, positive mood, and regular body function. (2) Another "difficult" group (10 percent) usually withdrew from new situations, were ordinarily negative in mood, and adapted slowly to environmental changes; such individuals had irregular body functions and tense reactions. (3) A "slow-to-warm-up" group (15 percent) adapted slowly to new situations, were rather negative in mood, and were extremely low in activity level. The study indicated that each category of individual adapts best to certain modes of handling. Adaptable individuals react best to varied life styles; difficult ones need consistent, patient treatment; and slow-to-warm-up ones must be allowed to become accustomed to their environments at their own pace.

All human beings have similar physiological mechanisms, but each one develops a unique pattern of emotional arousal. Some individuals have **parasympathetic dominance;** consequently, they exhibit more emotional inhibition than normal and less emotional excitability and fatigue. Others with **sympathetic dominance** have greater problems of emotional control. Everyone has a hereditary tendency either to build up a residual load of tension or to discharge it. As a result, individuals vary in basic activity level, intensity of response, distractability, and adaptability.

THE FAMILY   Much research supports the common assumption that family experiences importantly influence emotional development. Indeed, all members of a family soak up its tensions. For example, severing relations with the nuclear family produces feelings of loneliness, fear, and anxiety, as well as challenge and elation in young people.

On the other hand, adolescents also absorb positive emotions in happier home settings. A study of eighth graders disclosed a positive relationship between adolescents' feelings of well-being and the time that they spent with their parents in recreational activities in their homes (McMillan & Hiltonsmith, 1982).

It has been commonly assumed that troubled adults are simply the product of such early trauma as lack of love, loss of a parent, or family strife. Many such individuals do come from unhappy homes, or have rejecting or domineering mothers and aggressive, weak fathers. However, most people who experience such situations in childhood become reasonably adequate adults. Moreover, samplings of normal and superior adults indicate that such pathological conditions in childhood occur in the same or even greater proportions. Hence, there appears to be only a weak link between such child experiences and adjustment as an adult. In a study at the University of California's Institute of Human Development directed by Jean Macfarlane, about 200 children were studied from infancy through adolescence and again at age 30. Although the researchers had predicted that children from troubled home environments would become disturbed adults, they were wrong in two thirds of their predictions. On the other hand, many children who grew up under presumably ideal circumstances became rather immature, unhappy adults, a pattern especially common for boys who had been athletic leaders and girls who had been pretty and popular in high school (Skolnick, 1978).

SEX   Adelson (1980) said that adolescent psychology is still mainly concentrated on boys and the common view of adolescence as a time of "impulsiveness, turbulence and struggle against authority" is more characteristic of males (p. 68). However, adolescent girls may be as emotionally unhealthy as boys.

In some ways, girls appear to be healthier emotionally; in other ways, boys do; in still others, the picture is mixed. In the Berkeley Longitudinal Study, girls' behavioral patterns over the years became somewhat disrupted by early adolescence, but they stabilized sooner than boys' behaviors did (Hunt & Eichorn, 1972). Girls also benefited from the relative openness associated with their role. Among college students, pairs of women conveyed emotional states to one another better than did pairs of men, perhaps because of the culture's greater permissiveness for women to express their emotional states (Buck, Savin, Miller, & Caul, 1972).

From infancy the sexes are taught to deal with emotions differently. Emotions such as gentleness, sentimentality, compassion, and tenderness have been called feminine, while aggressive feelings such as hostility and anger are portrayed as masculine. As a result, men may find themselves in "an emotional straight jacket" and have trouble in a modern society that demands that they be both "achieving and affiliating, seeking and merging, argumentative and empathic" (Skovholt, 1978, p. 8). These differences in the socialization of the sexes may pose problems in marital relationships and the family. In the current world of changing sex-role expectations, males will be called upon to play more expressive roles, especially within the family, while females will be called upon increasingly to fulfill themselves away from the home (Balswick & Avertt, 1977).

THE "TIMES" Problems of adolescents vary according to the times and the political and social climates in which they live. In the late 1960s young people were perceived as irresponsible, radical, and rebellious—characteristics often related to the youth counterculture (America's youth, 1977). By the late 1970s youth had settled down and dedicated themselves to adult values of education, hard work, and helping others. College students perceived little to alienate them, felt no great need to protest, and questioned whether they could change anything significantly anyhow (America's youth, 1977).

TELEVISION AND MUSIC Undoubtedly, television affects youth's emotional health although its specific effects are hard to determine. Lambert (1972) observed that youth of the 1960s were the first generation to be reared on television. They were the first for whom, from birth, the entire world had the visibility of a village. Television provided an escape on one hand, and the painful realities of the world on the other. Thus, their impressions were ambiguous—fantasy mixed with reality. The result may be some confusion between what is real and what is unreal.

The major portion of research concerning emotional response to television has concerned aggression. In one such study (in London) by William Belson, matched groups of boys, ages 12 to 17, were questioned by using visual aids regarding how many particular episodes from 68 television series they had witnessed. In addition, they were asked to place in "yes" or "no" boxes over 50 cards listing acts ranging from slightly to very violent, such as "I deliberately dropped a lighted match into a shopper's bag"; "I kicked a boy in the crotch as hard as I could"; "I took a hammer to a car and laid into it" (Muson, 1978, p. 53). The boys averaged six serious acts, although half had committed none of them. Twelve were the main perpetrators, each having committed ten or more major acts of violence in six months. Belson concluded that certain forms of TV violence have greater effect on real-life performance than others, such as physical

Music is especially for youth and mirrors their emotional experiences. (Photo by William J. Butcher)

and verbal violence in stories of close personal relationships, stories where violence is presented very realistically, and westerns. Comedies featuring violence, violent cartoons, sports other than wrestling and boxing, and science fiction shows including violence were too unrealistic to produce an effect. Constant exposure to violence did not appear to change boys' conscious attitudes toward aggression. It seems that whatever changes occurred took place below the conscious level.

Since music is designed especially for youth, it has greater impact on them. It gains their attention more easily, engages their emotions more strongly, and attracts them to new emotions, values, and symbols (Larson & Kubey, 1983). It also mirrors their intensely emotional experiences as they move through their daily lives.

One might raise the question: Why do youth spend more time watching television than listening to music when they associate it with less intense mood states? One reason, conjecture Csikszentmihalyi and Kubey (1981), is that it allows them a brief escape from the intense emotions of their lives, and helps regain "a measure of control over their inner lives" (p. 27).

CULTURE It is uncertain to what extent adolescents' emotions might be influenced by more subtle social and environmental forces. For example, does the constant concern about energy resources and nuclear power develop a basic insecurity in the fabric of youth's current personalities (Rogers, 1982)? Consider the common incidence of shyness among American youth. In a survey that included college students, naval cadets, and others, 42 percent labelled themselves as shy (The significance of shyness, 1975). The Chinese show no shyness, presumably because the ideology of service to the group has displaced the ego orientation from which shyness derives; by contrast, American culture stresses individuality, achievement, and success.

LIFE CIRCUMSTANCE   It is often overlooked that the impact of life events can have a significant effect on mental health and happiness. If life events are especially stressful, they may interfere with the developing individual's adaptive capacities; nevertheless, the relationship between life events and emotional health is complex. At times, unusually traumatic life events can have a constructive mobilizing influence, so that an individual sets about effecting some solution to a problem (J. S. Strauss, 1979).

The occurrence of such events may have no relevance to the period when they occur, but their effects do. The college youth who loses his parents in an automobile accident and simultaneously loses their financial support may have to go to work immediately. An 18-year-old girl who has always relied on her good looks and is badly burned on the face will, with startling abruptness, be placed in a difficult position in the adolescent peer culture. Events of lesser impact, collectively, influence emotional stability in important ways.

Although most research has focused on the impact of major life events, "generally conceptualized as discrete and radical situational changes," their total effect may be somewhat overrated. More common and less dramatic conditions, existing day after day, may also have a significant impact on mental health status and psychological functioning (Pearlin, 1980). Indeed, it would appear that "daily hassles . . . have a greater impact on moods and mental health than the major traumatic events of our lives" (Lazarus, 1981, p. 58). In general the effect of traumatic events is cumulative and the more life changes and events that occur the greater chance there is of problems.

These findings about the significance of daily hassles would lead us also to take note of the effect of those little things that cheer us up each day, such as hearing good news or getting a good night's rest or solving a hard problem. These "uplifts" become antidotes to the daily hassle, helping to restore an individual's resources.

Intelligence alone is insufficient insulation against the impact of such events. A comparison of ninth graders in gifted classes with other ninth graders not in such classes in the Philadelphia area (Ferguson, 1981) indicated that there was no significant difference between them in how upset they became by important life change events such as being arrested, fighting with parents or siblings, entering a new school, or having a friend die. The gifted experienced fewer such events but they were just as sensitive to them as less gifted classmates when they occurred.

THE NATION'S MOOD   Adolescents cannot help but absorb, to some degree, the emotional crises and status of the larger society. Consider the situation of the Germans after they were defeated in World War I and humiliated at Versailles. As a result, as a people they appeared to be searching for values to adhere to and to support (Logan, 1980). America, too, was seeking a nationwide identity in the late 1960s, a social crisis reflected in the increase in "existential neuroses" among youth and demonstrated by their modes of escapism as in drugs, and also in their questioning behaviors. Perhaps Watergate, Viet Nam, and the riots of the 60s created an identity crisis for America, especially among its young people. More remote but as real perhaps is youth's focus on the present and on the "me."

Youth's search for "a focus for their fidelity" concludes Logan, can be perceived in "what they are buying, both figuratively and literally" (Logan, 1980, p. 411). He notes that they are purchasing "the genuine (The Real Thing!) and other things that are 'basic,' 'honest,' and functional (the 'gear look') from Ivory Soap to Wella Balsam, to pottery. They are also buying the pure ('organic,' 'natural'), and the enduring (jeans, the natural world)" (p. 411). He notes a parallel preoccupation with those things that are "the nongenuine, the impure and the nonenduring," under the umbrella term "plastic."

EMOTIONS IN ADOLESCENCE

Adolescence—A Period of Storm and Stress?

ADVOCATES OF STRESS THEORY A long-standing issue in adolescent psychology is whether or not adolescence is a period of unusual storm and stress. Is adolescence turbulent or tepid? Are adolescents simply exuberant, or are they the hypertensive sum of their emotions? Authoritative views on this question are often polarized, although some may be found in the middle. Among the adolescence-is-stressful theorists, Keniston (1975) portrays the youth as trying to break away from the roles ascribed to him, "out of his culture, out of history, and even out of his own skin" (p. 11).

Adolescents appear to delight in extreme emotions even if they are, at times, disturbing. Around the country teenagers have their own "spooky stories regarding ghosts, witches, maniacs or unexplained curses that haunt nearby locations" (W. Ellis, 1983, p. 68). They jump in their cars to go to places to examine legends for themselves and try to get some experience with the supernatural. Most of the time these trips involve drugs and drinking, sex experimentation, and—many times—vandalism; they are ways of "giving the finger to grownup rationality."

All teenagers may agree that a certain road is haunted, but the nature of ghosts will vary. According to some of their legends "a statue glows, bleeds, weeps, screams or walks about. In others a ghostly corpse hangs from a bridge overhead or a phantom truck looms up ahead" (p. 69). Some of the legends, says W. Ellis, become excuses for "antisocial acts against symbols of adult morality," such as when adolescents might tear gravestones apart. Another reason, he says, is that these trips to investigate legends represent ways of "playing chicken with adolescent anxieties" (p. 69). Thus, they at once provide ways for teenagers "to rebel against adult authority [and] provide psychologically safe ways to confront anxiety about death" (p. 69). Fears which can haunt adolescents seek release in some manner and their parents ordinarily don't wish to talk about them. Therefore, visiting these haunts becomes a way of releasing the "psychic burden" that teenagers may carry, for teenagers do lose their lives in automobile accidents and "drinking sprees" (p. 69). The key to this reasoning is that when you "strip away their melodrama, the heart of nearly all legend trips is the same violent death found in the news headlines" (p. 69). Thus, "the legends give structure to the day's violence, transposing it into a night ritual" (p. 69). The main time for such participation becomes "the cruising age," which begins when one first receives a driving permit and ends the day one can legally buy alcohol. That is, "cruising feeds on the excitement for breaking the law—marijuana and beer both being forbidden fruits" (p. 69).

A CONTRARY VIEW   Many current authorities question the storm and stress theory, among them Hill (1980), who writes that there is no strong support for the storm-and-stress theory of adolescence. Adelson declared that adolescents are "*not* in turmoil, *not* deeply disturbed, *not* at the mercy of their impulses, *not* resistant to parental values, *not* politically active, and *not* rebellious" (1979, p. 37). In confirmation Offer, Ostrov and Howard (1981a) reported normal adolescents, as distinct from disturbed and deviant ones, to have a positive self-image, to be comparatively happy, and to have a healthy relationship with their parents. Most conclusions that adolescence is stormy have derived from studies of patients, including adolescents sufficiently stressed to seek professional help (Rutter, 1980).

In cross-cultural research, American teenagers seemed to be happier, better satisfied, and more optimistic than their peers in Israel, Ireland, and Australia. The American boys and girls more often realized their hopes and aspirations and appeared more in control of their destiny (Offer, et al., 1977).

Adolescents view themselves more positively than mental health professionals do (Offer, Ostrov & Howard, 1981b). The latter tend to see even normal adolescents as somewhat unhappy with low self-image and somewhat poor relationships with their parents. Parents do a better job of assessing their adolescent children's self-perceptions (Offer, Ostrov & Howard, 1982). Unlike mental health professionals, parents seem to agree with adolescents' mostly positive self-perceptions.

SIGNIFICANCE OF ADOLESCENT STRESS   Although debate has focused on the question, to what degree is adolescence stressful, more important is the long-term significance of teenage stress. George Vaillant (1977b) interviewed nearly 100 men, originally chosen from the most promising male undergraduates at an eastern university, and concluded that it is not the isolated traumas of childhood that determine one's future, but the quality of continued relationships with significant people. Also, individual lives change and the life cycle is characterized by discontinuities. What is mentally unhealthy at one point may be adaptive in another. Much behavior that looks pathological may reflect healing processes. Development persists throughout adult life, and its signficance for particular behaviors can only be seen within the context of the total life span.

AMOUNT OF SERIOUS DISTURBANCE   The storm-and-stress controversy applies to adolescents in general. Also controversial are estimates of the extent and significance of serious disturbance or pathology in youth. A survey of research on adolescents disclosed that, although certain periods of disruptive behavior did occur, turmoil and pathology did not characterize the adolescent period (Holzman & Grinker, 1974). The studies also disclosed many styles of adaptation in adolescence, few of which pointed to later psychopathology.

Even if the overall adjustment of adolescents had been exaggerated, certain disturbances and symptoms are more common at this stage than others. Certain personal and social pathologies commonly appear first in adolescence, including delinquency, out-of-wedlock pregnancies, depression, and schizophrenia (Adelson, 1979). Adolescents make more suicide attempts than do adults, and far more adolescent suicides go unreported, often being described as accidents. Often the act is impulsive, relating to some specific stressful situation, usually as a result of complex factors that have influenced the adolescent's behavior over a long period. The problem frequently relates to achieving a healthy sexual identity and good relationships with the parents. Other precipitating causes may be the struggle for autonomy, break-up with a close friend, or loss of someone significant, especially a parent.

SIGNIFICANCE OF ADOLESCENT STRESS FOR LATER ADJUSTMENT   Longitudinal research lends perspective to judging adolescent emotionality. Some empirical evidence suggests that emotional health at middle age relates to early adjustment (Scanlon, 1979). However, certain characteristics apparent in adolescence have little relationship to outcomes at mid-life. Livson (1976) determined that both adolescents who are traditional and those who are nontraditional (whom she calls independent) may arrive at a psychologically healthy middle age. Among women identified as psychologically healthy in middle age, she distinguished two main personality styles—the traditionals and the independents. The traditionals were gregarious, feminine, and traditional as adolescents and remained so into middle age. Throughout the period they gave much of their time to serving others. From early adolescence, the independents were more intellectual, introspective, unconventional, and achievement oriented. During the next two decades, independents became depressed and irritable, probably because their housewife-childbearing role interfered with their inclinations and ambitions. Nevertheless, they experienced a rebound in their 40s, after they were emancipated from child care, and continued to grow psychologically and emotionally. While they had not openly resented their wife-mother role, their earlier adolescent identities appeared to revive by age 50. The traditionals were able to maintain psychological health from adolescence to middle age because their styles fit their personalities. The independents did not fit the conventional definitions of femininity; however, in middle age, when sex roles become less distinct and even converge, their life styles became more compatible with the sort of people that they were. Apparently, young women of the independent type should deliberately plan life styles in young adulthood that are congenial with their temperament so that they might continue to grow during this period. This goal appears to be more achievable in androgynous households.

Emotions During Adolescence

LOVE   For a long time, researchers focused almost exclusively on such negative emotions as anxiety, fear and aggression. However, there has been a growing interest in prosocial or positive emotions, among them love.

The achievement of intimacy is a basic task of young adults. (Courtesy of Public Relations Office, State University of New York at Oswego)

Erik Erikson (1950) describes the achievement of heterosexual love, or intimacy, as the basic task of young adults. Presumably, having firmly defined their own identities in adolescence, they can now, without threat to their egos, become deeply involved with others. Those who cannot establish such relationships become inner-oriented and isolated. All of life is a search for and redefinition of identity, but it is not firmly enough established until adulthood to support intimate ties with another without some threat to the identity.

Research would tend to refute the view that youth lack desire for deep and lasting relationships. In its love and romance survey of *Psychology Today* readers (who are generally somewhat better educated and younger than the general population), a trend toward greater traditionalism was clear. The respondents ranged in age from 14 to 86, half married with children and one third never married. Although this group cannot be considered typical, it might be regarded as a trend-setting category. In comparison with a similar 1969 survey, when 17 percent of the men and 29 percent of the women said sex without love was either unenjoyable or unacceptable, 39 percent of the men and 32 percent of the women felt this way in 1983. This conservative view appeared most commonly among young people—half of those younger than age 22 believed sex without love unacceptable and unenjoyable. The majority of all ages believed that a single love can last a lifetime and the majority said that romance was important. The three most commonly named ingredients in love were friendship, devotion, and intellectual compatibility, which won out over such characteristics as "sexual electricity, irrational longing and mysterious chemistry" (Rubenstein, 1983, p. 45).

Changes in traditional notions about intimacy and love are reflected in popular adolescent song lyrics. In the 1950s the themes of marriage and love were at the core of much of adolescent music; people in love eventually intended to get married. During the 1960s the themes of rock music became more specific regarding sexual relationships that had no future orientation. It may be inferred that "instant intimacy without responsibility is more acceptable than the ideals of marital bliss for many" (Schippers, 1978 p. 146). The inference is that love should be treated on a temporary basis and that commitment be delayed in favor of open-ended relationships, at least for the time being.

Apparently females establish an earlier and sounder foundation for adult intimacy than do males. In a study of high school students (Mark & Alper, 1980) from early ages, the males had established somewhat widespread relationships with many others, whereas females had more intimate and intensive relationships with a smaller number of friends. In addition, female friendships were "emotionally richer and more oriented toward sharing personal concerns than were friendships between males" (p. 165). In confirmation, females more often than males wrote stories with themes of intimacy, although no sex differences were found in nonintimate affiliation themes. Those males who wrote intimacy imagery stories were less likely than other males to employ stereotypical male role themes.

Earlier-than-common or frequent love episodes in adolescence can impact negatively on social development. Rubin (1982) cites a study by Michael Johnson and Leigh Leslie of young lovers' relationships to their friends. At Pennsylvania State University couples in love listed fewer individuals as friends than did those not so involved, and those students who had become engaged or were married listed the fewest of all. The more involved a couple became the less significance they attached to their friends' opinions and the less they confided in them about their personal affairs. They also confided less in their relatives but their relatives lost less influence than did their friends. As they became deeply involved they tended to remove some relatives from the list of significant others but to become even more attached to others.

ALTRUISM AND EMPATHY The emotion of altruism is difficult to understand because it is a complex and fluid concept (Yarrow, Scott & Waxler, 1973). It suggests a wide variety of responses, including helping, sharing, sympathizing, and rescuing. If individuals are to become nurturant (manifesting warmth and support), they need opportunities for modeling themselves after altruistic people.

Yet another study of prosocial behaviors in a camp situation revealed no differences according to sex, although females are typically thought of as more nurturant. After only four days of camp these young adolescents accurately identified individual differences in prosocial behaviors. Although males offered more physical assistance and females more verbal support, there was no overall difference in amount of supportive behavior (Zeldin, Small & Savin-Williams, 1982).

Research regarding differences between the sexes in prosocial behaviors (spontaneous, unsolicited acts that help another) is conflicting. Perhaps the majority are tilted in favor of females. For example, a comparison of undergraduates with others having a history of greater self-interest, showed the former to be more empathetic. In addition, females scored higher than males both on empathy and on their history of helping behaviors. This result supports the cultural stereotype of females as more sensitive, caring, and supportive of others' needs than males are (Van Ornum, Foley, Burns, DeWolffe & Kennedy, 1981).

In another study of children in grades 1 through 12 who responded to four hypothetical situations in which a same-sex friend was experiencing some form of emotional stress, the subjects were asked to tell what they might say to make the distressed friend feel better (Burleson, 1982). The results indicated that the variety, number, and degree of sensitivity of these comfort-designed messages increased with age and that females' strategies were greater in number, variety, and sensitivity than those of males. The latter finding may reflect a greater focus on girls' developing nurturance skills as well as their faster rate of maturing. Also noted was a general consistency over the several situations with regard to comforting behaviors.

In other research, which involved 72 ninth, eleventh, and twelfth graders, Eisenberg-Berg and Mussen (1978) related level of affective role-taking or empathy ("matching one's own feelings with the corresponding feelings of someone else") with socialization practices (p. 185). Among both sexes, level of empathy related to level of moral reasoning, and maternal child-rearing practices to sons' empathy but not to daughters'. The mothers of the highly empathic boys were unrestrictive, equalitarian, nonpunitive, and affectionate toward them. Only rarely did parental practices relate to the girls' empathy scores, possibly because girls are more empathic than boys anyway. Since empathy is a basic component of the stereotyped female sex role, girls are automatically socialized to become empathic; therefore, "a ceiling effect may be operating so that specific parental socialization practices may not appear to influence girls' empathic capacities" (p. 186).

Other research reveals no significant sex differences in such behaviors. Adelson (1980), in a study of politics, found boys to be as compassionate and humane as girls. In another study, empathy or appreciation of the feelings of others, emotional responsiveness, sympathy, and willingness to help others with problems, G. R. Adams (1983) found no difference according to sex, except that females were higher on empathy than males. There was some relationship among social competence and sexual knowledge, empathy, and self-initiated social contacts.

HOSTILITY AND AGGRESSION   By contrast with the largely positive emotions just discussed, other feelings, such as hostility, are largely negative in effect. A common cause of hostility is frustration, and serious frustration raises hostility to its maximum pitch. Hostility may be directed toward specific persons or toward no one in particular. It may be turned inward on the self or outward on others.

Social class, sex, family, and culture all influence the expression of hostility. Lower-status boys may express anger freely; in the middle class, both sexes are taught to curb their hostility. Note this boy's concern over his failure to control hostile emotions when he was accidentally pushed during a basketball game:

> I looked at him [the opposing player] and saw nothing but a red spot where his face should have been. I swung my fist as hard as I could right where the red spot was and hit him square in the face. As soon as I hit him I once again saw his face. His eyes were crossed, and he was beginning to fall. As soon as I saw him I had such a feeling of regret and

disgust that I almost broke down in tears. Once inside the locker room and by myself I broke down completely.

Girls of all social classes are encouraged to restrain hostility. By adolescence, the girl faces expectations, especially from her mother, that she be "ladylike." Consequently, her feelings of hostility may find disguised expression in somatic symptoms and various defensive behaviors. By contrast, boys feel subtle pressures from peers, from the larger society, and even tacitly from their parents to be aggressive, despite adults' presumed efforts to restrain them.

The question arises: How much restraint of hostility is good? Does some mysterious sex-role mystique condemn both sexes to strains of unhealthy emotion? Sexton (1969) suggests that the problem is not one of "suppressing aggression but of turning it to good uses. Since aggression involves a drive to mastery over oneself, others, or the environment, we can use it to fight wars or build cities. We hope to choose the latter" (p. 29).

INFERIORITY AND POWER Inferiority feelings involve emotions of depression and shame arising from unfavorable self-evaluation and are based on deficiencies, either imagined or real. Individuals may have inferiority feelings in areas where they excel, simply because they fall below their own standards. People are most likely to feel inferior in areas where they fail to live up to their self-concepts. A boy who perceives himself as a social leader is crushed when he is not elected fraternity president.

Among individuals, inferiority feelings generally derive from a variety of factors, as in the following case:

MALE, AGE 16: I was scared to look at people, or to date girls, because I was slightly cross-eyed. Also I had to work to pay my way through the last two years of high school, which made me think that I was inferior to other students, and this fact made me keep to myself. I hated Jews—because I thought that they had all the money and were the cause of all the troubles. I was ashamed of my name because it identified me with the Polacks, who lived in the slum section and were looked down upon.

At graduation I was miserable for about six months because I couldn't decide what to do with my life—and could not imagine myself spending the rest of my life in a factory.

During their first weeks in school freshmen have traditionally experienced "homesickness," "college culture shock," or "early adjustment problems," including inferiority feelings (Margolis, 1981, p. 634). Such anxieties may derive from feeling different from those around them racially, religiously, or financially, which makes them feel isolated. They may also feel differences between themselves and their peers with regard to competencies—academic, athletic, and social, believing themselves less confident than others. Since students typically mask their fears individual freshmen may feel that they differ in experiencing anxiety. At the same time that they are having such negative feelings, they very much want to succeed.

The fact that this is usually their first extended time away from home, and that colleges no longer act *in loco parentis* further increases their anxiety. They must themselves organize all aspects of their lives including what they eat, wear, and do, what courses they take and their social lives. All this decision-making is occurring within a strange new environment. Nor do most freshmen receive immediate feedback concerning how well they are doing or how well they are adjusting. Meantime, the same timidity and depression that makes them anxious may prevent them from being confident enough to seek help (Margolis, 1981).

On the other hand, some youths may experience a certain omnipotence. They experience a "feeling of absolute freedom, of living in a world of pure possibilities, of being able to change or achieve anything. . . . One feels capable of totally transforming another's life; or creating a new society with no roots whatsoever in the mire of the past" (Keniston, 1975, p. 11).

Are such feelings genuine or simply defensive reactions to feelings of inadequacy and inferiority? Hendin (1975) observes that "feeling unable to cope with their emotions, many youth yearn for the invulnerability and efficiency of an IBM machine. They wish they could switch themselves on and off. The same students who complain of being programmed by parents and schools are often attracted to the behavioristic utopia Walden II. It is not the idea of being programmed that bothers them, but of being badly programmed" (p. 26).

GUILT   Another troublesome emotion is guilt or feeling of having done wrong. When people see their actions as having violated what is "right" or "moral" in a certain situation, they usually feel guilty. Their feelings may range in degree of unpleasantness from a twinge of conscience to agonizing self-condemnation. The source of guilt feelings is sometimes clearly recognizable to the person experiencing them: "I feel guilty because I let the boy go too far;" "I cheated on the examination." Or the source may be vague and complex, and the individual may feel only discomfort and anxiety. Like the prisoner in Kafka's novel *The Trial*, the guilty person may not know with what crime he or she is charged. Again, the source of guilt feelings may be only imagined transgression, caused by the mere contemplation of wrongdoing.

Here several teenagers describe behaviors that made them feel guilty:

MALE, AGE 13: Not doing all of my homework or bad homework.

FEMALE, AGE 14: Smoking, swearing, fighting with my mother.

FEMALE, AGE 13: Sometimes I have to sneak out of the house because my mother won't let me go.

MALE, AGE 13: Tipping a man's backhouse over. Stealing a man's car and putting it in the creek.

FEMALE, AGE 13: Lying or trying to make myself look better in front of other people.

ANXIETY   Anxiety is more ambiguous in its feeling components than fear or worry, largely because it is blended from many emotions. Both worry and fear have an object. The object of worry might be money; the object of fear might be snakes. Anxiety is more generalized, having reference to a vague feeling of impending doom. The anxious person feels fearful, on edge, uneasy, irritable, depressed, and generally uncomfortable.

Because youth, at their stage in life, are uncertain about their relationships to themselves and their own commitments, they may feel anxious and insecure (Bensman & Lilienfeld, 1979). As incompletely formed personalities, they are uncertain about how to relate to the establishment, how to climb the pyramid of achievement, and how to resolve various sexual problems. At such a time they are especially likely to seek sympathetic social support from others.

Many adolescent experiences are likely to tap reservoirs of anxiety. Anxiety arises chiefly from strong impulses that are blocked by social taboos—for example, masturbation and sex impulses. Another threat to contentment is the need to make vocational decisions. At school, examinations hang over students' heads while they make the social rounds. To compensate for their uncertainty, teenagers may "put on" a poised social self that belies the insecure private self beneath. Perhaps youth also experience vague anxieties about the threat of nuclear war or accidents, since this topic is given such wide publicity (M. B. Smith, 1983).

LONELINESS   This emotion is not the same as aloneness or solitude; rather it involves ineffectiveness in, and dissatisfaction with, personal relationships. It is discomforting, reflects ineffective social skills and relates to a broad variety of unfortunate cognitive and emotional states including low self-esteem, anxiety, depression, and interpersonal hostilities (Jones, Freemon & Goswick, 1981). Although adolescents have relatively frequent social contacts, the degree of satisfaction with those contacts is what is most important (Cutrona, 1982).

In any period of several weeks, over a quarter of all American adults feel "painfully lonely," and the rate for adolescents is somewhat higher (Rubin, 1979, p. 85). Loneliness relates to physical ills and even to suicide, as indicated in case reports. Even individuals who have firm emotional attachments may feel very lonely in certain settings.

Most available data about loneliness concern college students, and information about that in younger ones is rare. Yet early adolescents are more vulnerable to loneliness than older youth are. Besides, most college students' interpersonal problems are rooted in earlier social experience, and their coping strategies, interpersonal relationship styles, and intimate skills are based on earlier experience. Moreover, measures of adolescent relationships significantly predict adult levels of friendship, romantic relationships, and family relationships (Russell, Peplau & Cutrona, 1980). In short, the failure to develop intimate relationships and to become effective participants in social networks, as reflected in adolescent loneliness, reduces one's chances of developing satisfactory relationships at all later life stages.

In a study of the experience of loneliness among 100 adolescents (Moore & Schultz, 1983) the lonelier ones were more depressed, self-conscious, unhappy, and relatively dependent on others in decision-making. They were generally more dissatisfied with life and reluctant to take social risks. They had little confidence in their ability to attract others—thus, they were quite shy, self-conscious, and socially anxious. At the same time the experience of being much alone caused them to feel empty, bored, and isolated (Moore & Schultz, 1983).

Loneliness derives from a variety of factors. It may develop as a result of unsatisfactory relationships with significant others, especially peers. One of the main causes of loneliness is possession of somewhat inadequate social skills. Both high school and college students' peer relationships constitute the standard by which they measure the adequacy of their interpersonal involvements (Goswick & Jones, 1982).

One reason for people's loneliness is society's stress on being with other people. Individuals have been taught to abhor being alone. If a child does not play with others, something is assumed to be wrong. By adolescence individuals come to dread and fear loneliness. Society has taught them that if they are alone on Friday nights, something is amiss with their adjustment. A major reason for loneliness among the elderly is that they did not, as younger people, come to appreciate the value of solitude, such as having time to think things through and to be independent of pressures from others (Rubin, 1979).

Feelings of loneliness do not inevitably derive from circumstances of solitude. They depend mainly on how people feel about their circumstances and whether they perceive themselves as lonely (Rubinstein, Shaver & Peplau, 1979). Surprisingly, older people feel less lonely, on the average, than young adults do. Although more older than younger people live by themselves and see their friends less often than younger ones, they express more satisfaction with their friendships, have greater self-esteem, and feel more independent. They get drunk far less and join more civic and social groups than the young. They complain less than the young about psychological and physical symptoms such as headaches, depression, irritability, poor appetite, and poor concentration. Young people may experience loneliness more because of the gap between their need for intimacy and their success in attaining it. They are idealistic and romantic and believe it is essential to find a romantic sexual partner more than older people do.

This writer suggests that in the past we have overemphasized the need for many social relationships. Adolescents who try to maintain broad social relationships may suffer from a diffusion of interests when a greater concentration would result in more achievement. Besides, such individuals may become unduly manipulated by their peers. In short, how much in the way of social activities is healthy and to what extent does the desirability of such relationships vary with the individual?

It is important to distinguish between the kind of relationships—that is, social networks—adolescents have and the satisfaction that adolescents take in such experiences. In a study of eastern junior and senior high school students Avery (1982) found that males were lonelier than females and that androgynous males were less lonely than undifferentiated or feminine males. The masculine individuals were not as lonely as feminine ones. The masculine and androgynous males did not differ in their own feelings of loneliness, but for females the results were unclear. Androgynous females were less lonely than undifferentiated ones, but feminine, androgynous, and masculine females differed little in loneliness. Perhaps one reason that males were lonelier than females was that more females than males were androgynous. If androgyny produces better adjustment obviously more males would experience loneliness.

Although loneliness related to sex-role orientation the impact of that orientation on adjustment was less clear. There was only partial support for the traditional view that the traditional sex role should be acquired in adolescence or that masculinity is the main predictor of adjustment. Masculine and androgynous males differed little in their own subjective feelings of loneliness. Both these types were less lonely than feminine males. The results also agreed with Massad's (1981) report that higher masculinity related to greater peer acceptance for males. This writer points out, however, that as these individuals move into adulthood, high masculinity becomes less valued because adult activities are less stereotypically male or female, especially in recent times.

Note, however, that high masculinity was not the only predictor of male loneliness; high femininity also contributed to loneliness. Overall, androgyny was the best predictor of positive adjustment. Avery (1982) conjectures that the link between androgyny and adjustment may reflect androgynous persons' lower expectations from relationships—hence, they are more easily satisfied.

DEPRESSION Although depression lacks the excited, drive-like qualities that characterize anger, fear, and anxiety, it is thought of as an emotional state. It possesses the physiological qualities of stress, including slower heart beat, lowered blood presure, and retardation of activity.

Depression may stem from failure to achieve some important goal, inability to solve some persistent problem, or from involvement in a life plan that one does not enjoy. Essentially, it is a self-punishing, harmful manner of adjustment, representing passive acceptance instead of constructive solution. Often, as in the film *Feeling of Depression,* an individual seizes upon an explanation for his feelings that obscures the real cause. The film hero believes his depression stems from his business difficulties. The more basic, though unconscious, causes of his depression are feelings of guilt and unworthiness. Looking himself in the eye would have disturbed his picture of himself as a kind, worthy individual.

Adolescent depression also may result from failure to achieve the self-ideal, from persistent unpopularity, or, as in the following illustration, from feelings of spiritual isolation:

> I thought of the book I had been reading this morning—a book written for boys and all about boys—and I compared the characters in it with myself—compared the darkness that weighed upon me now with the troubles they had experienced. It seemed to me that I must be different from everybody in that book—from the bad just as much as from the good. I had feelings which apparently none of them felt. I wondered if I were really different, or if the book were untrue—but how could I even find out unless I confided in someone, and unless I were truthfully answered? At present I was hopelessly shut into the little circle of my own desires and feelings. . . . I knew no one but myself, and of myself I knew much that filled me with shame. I was alone spiritually, as alone as one might be in a dead or dying world. The whirling flakes of snow fell ever faster out of the winter sky; the barren frostbound land was wrapped in stillness; the only sound I heard came from the breaking waves. And it seemed to me that the darkness gradually approaching was like the final extinction of life, and I could imagine that there would be no further awakening—that the end had at last been reached. (Reid, 1939, p. 237)

The manner in which individuals handle feelings of loneliness and depression depends on the ego strength they developed as children (Shenker & Schildkrout, 1975). Depressive moods may vary from short "down moods," quite normal in adolescence, to states of despair and apathy that sometimes precipitate suicide. Such extreme reactions are becoming more common. Psychoanalyst Hendin (1975) declares that the "culture is at war and young people are in the front lines. . . . Some are the obvious victims: The suicide rate among young men and women has risen more than 250 percent over the past 20 years" (p. 24). Depression may also manifest itself in impotence and drug abuse.

Adolescents may also find it stressful to leave the comparative security of elementary school for the more demanding and heterogeneous environment of the middle or junior high school (Baumrind, 1978). Middle-class students' resistance to school is often subtle and frequently directed at the self. Some take drugs, often marijuana; others may run away or commit suicide. Suicides among teenagers and young adults have tripled over the past two decades (Starr, 1981, p. 214).

In a study of junior high school adolescents, Friedrich, Reams and Jacobs (1982) found that depression related most to recent life experiences and stresses, lower family cohesion, and lower paternal income suggesting a somewhat transient quality of depression at this age. In contrast, suicidal fantasy at the junior high school age appears to relate, not so much to recent life stresses, as to family social climate variables, including less cohesiveness, less independence, and greater achievement orientation.

In general, females are more prone to depression than males. Since females have traditionally been trained to be helpless, and since they continue to face inequities in their life situations that are beyond their personal control, it is hardly surprising that "psychotic depression is so much a female specialty" (M. B. Smith, 1983, p. 395).

Both sexes, ages 18 to 29, feel more optimistic about their own futures than that of the country and less positive about the country's future than do older age groups (Watts, 1981). Nevertheless, they have higher than average feelings of optimism about their own personal futures. Perhaps, theorizes Watts, these young people may lack confidence in their elders' guidance of the nation, but feel confident in their ability to take care of their own personal destinies.

M. B. Smith (1983) believes that hope, which is "the conviction that a good future is possible and worth striving for," is essential. Else, we will not make an effort, and our worst fears will be realized. On the other hand, optimism, which is "the conviction that a good future is relatively certain or at least probable, is a mistake. We should all be running scared, [if we are] to bring potentially lethal problems under control" (p. 398).

Interviews with thirty-three teenagers after the death of a sibling produced a typical portrait (Balk, 1983). Most of them felt "shock, afraid, lonely, confused, depressed, and/or angry" (p. 154). They had thought of the dead sibling frequently, had experienced upset in sleeping but not eating habits, experienced holidays as unpleasant, maintained poorer study habits, and sometimes thought of suicide. After a time these emotions diminished but did not disappear, at least over a two-year span.

There was some difference between individuals with very close families and those whose families were less emotionally close. In very close families teenagers had been accustomed to using the family as a resource and felt more depressed by the loss. All felt that their lives had been greatly influenced by the sibling's death, in only a few cases adversely. Some said that it caused them "to grow up fast"; all said it had been an avenue to growth. They saw themselves as more grown up and mature than most of their peers, and they valued their time more. They felt that their selves had changed and that they had learned certain lessons: that bad things will happen in life; people should be valued while they are living; and there are ways of coping with distressful experiences. For a large majority religion had been of help—nineteen said that it had helped them after the death and twenty-seven that it had helped them to accept it.

Pattison (1977) believes that a significant task for adolescents in coping with death relates to their self-awareness as unique human beings. At this age an individual "has a sense of being, a sense of person, a sense of me. Characteristically the adolescent does *not* have a sense of longevity. The length of life is not at issue, but the quality is. Thus we see many romantic notions of death in the thoughts of adolescents. Who cares how long one lives, so long as one lives and dies as the real me? Adolescents make brave soldiers because they do not fear annihilation so much as whether they are brave and glorious" (p. 23).

Emotional Problems of the Adolescent

PROBLEM AREAS   Early adolescents have their own special problems, says Baumrind (1978). As they forfeit their childhood status, they loosen their dependency on their parents. At the same time, they participate more with their peer groups. In order to cover up their still strong feelings of helplessness, they may appear to rebel, and on the surface act very independent. Parents may be fooled into thinking that they are ready to go it alone, when they actually need firm assurance and authority from the family.

When 240 white, middle-class adolescents were administered a questionnaire designed to determine the seriousness of certain adolescent problems, they identified the three most bothersome ones as physical appearance, careers, and grades, in that order (Eme, Maisiak & Goodale, 1979). Several somewhat unexpected and interesting results appeared. Although experts on adolescence have recognized the importance of physical appearance, it was surprising that this area proved the most worrisome of all. One reason is the accessibility of outward appearance to others in social interaction and its importance in interpersonal attraction with both sexes. Yet the so-called experts have attached little serious significance to this factor.

Other findings were hardly surprising. Concern about career has long been recognized as a cause of identity crisis. It is also expected that adolescents will feel concern about such matters as parents, independence, peer relations, and sexual impulses. The least worry was attached to alcohol, extra-curricular activities, smoking, and drugs. Since most adolescents use but do not abuse drugs, drugs would hardly cause major worry. Overall, the study indicated that storm and stress do not exist in all problem areas nor apply to all adolescents.

Emotional problems vary in degree and kind over the life span. In the San Francisco Longitudinal Study of Transitions older individuals reported somewhat more negative emotions but not significantly so. Younger ones more often encountered problems of love, marriage, and career formation, whereas older ones more often experienced stresses of illness and bereavement. Among younger men the impact of stresses and life relations related significantly to education; among older men it related more to income (Thurnher, 1983).

INDIVIDUAL DIFFERENCES   Emotional problems reflect the personality and experiences of the individual involved. What are "lions-to-be-fled-from" for some are what Camus called "the fleas of life" for others, as may be seen in the following comments by students.

> FEMALE: During adolescence I was self-conscious because of a complexion problem and wearing braces on my teeth. I also experienced friction within a close-knit family when I insisted on being independent.
>
> MALE: In my early teens I worried most about acceptance from my peers. My stress grew even worse as I fought with myself over the question whether I cared or not about being accepted. Now in college my chief source of stress is the question: What the hell am I going to gain from this?

DEALING WITH ADOLESCENTS' PROBLEMS

Prevention of Emotional Problems

How best may adults help tame the turmoil in youth's troubled breast? How can a youth whose defenses are as hard as a bullet-proof vest be approached? The most important aspect of helping adolescents is prevention—eliminating conditions that threaten mental health and structuring environments conducive to positive emotions. In contrast to this approach, there is an abundance of negative advice. There are long lists of evils to avoid, such as emotional deprivation, overprotection, and severe discipline; usually the "don'ts" greatly outnumber the "dos." The positive side of counseling has been somewhat neglected, and the calmer phases of emotional life are little investigated and less understood. Nevertheless, enough of the positive approach is known to prove effective if put to work.

1. Adolescents need assured and steady contact with persons of integrity and kindness, partly to offset the mass media's steady diet of emotionally distorted situations. Positive emotions are often neglected in favor of moods of hate, violence, jealousy, and passion.

2. Adolescents need varied opportunities for wholesome expression of emotions. If emotions are properly channeled, they are unlikely to spill over and cause destruction. The boy in the following example has found a safety valve for his emotions.

> Music plays an important part in my life. There are some songs that seem to shake all my emotions. The chords in one song in particular give me goose-flesh whenever I hear it. Another song makes it difficult

to hold back the tears. My greatest pleasure is my guitar because I can create music with my two hands. When I am playing it my roommate can't get through to me. I'm in another world.

3. Adolescents need plenty of success in legitimate behaviors, so that fantasies become fulfillment, not just deferred pain. When positive emotions exist, it is hard for unhealthy ones to move in—but a healthy emotional climate is not enough. If adolescents are to achieve emotional maturity, they must be helped to organize their lives according to sound principles of mental health. For instance, the aggressive behaviors of a juvenile delinquent may become the approved drive of a scientist attacking some problem.

4. Adolescents also need defense mechanisms, which, within moderation, serve as reasonably adequate coping behaviors. In a study of humor and laughter, it was observed that 12- to 14-year-old girls told jokes to displace their own uncomfortable feelings about physical development and maturation. By joking, they could reduce frightening matters to "cozy and familiar ones . . ." (Ransohoff, 1975, p. 161). They reduced somewhat frightening physical phenomena to the silly and less frightening—for example, by describing big-breasted girls as "fivezies" or "sixzies."

    It may be that pressures of college life are such that too little time is left for fantasy as an outlet for frustration. A study of adolescents in grades 9 through 11 indicated more daydreaming in high school than in college. This finding would appear to agree with the fact that college students watch television less than do high school students because of alternative attractions.

5. Robert Coles (Coles & Woodward, 1975) advises that youth be "brought up to recognize that life is inherently complicated and full of lies and inconsistencies . . ." (p. 77). They cannot expect to find final answers to current problems, such as the energy crisis, foreign policy, the right way to live, or anything else. They must learn to develop tentative solutions and a philosophy of simply doing the best they can.

Resources for Helping Youth

NONPROFESSIONAL HELPERS   Adolescents most commonly rely on nonprofessionals, especially their peers, for help. Among a group of tenth graders, only 16 percent would go to teachers and 21 percent to school counselors. Over 80 percent would turn to friends (Ziomkowski, Mulder & Williams, 1975).

    In a Gallup Youth Survey June 24, 1981, in which 1013 teenagers were interviewed by telephone, 84 percent of the males and 77 percent of the females named parents as their main source of advice. Just 20 percent of the girls and 12 percent of the boys often went to their friends. The truth is that teenagers turn more often to their parents for help on some matters and to their peers on others.

PEER GROUP THERAPIES   Many specific responses to youth's problems including suicide, drug abuse, delinquencies, and teenage pregnancies—including unrest, growth of youth culture, the creation of "alternative communities

Adolescents often rely on their own peers for help in dealing with problems. (Courtesy of Public Relations Office, State University of New York at Oswego)

such as communes, and the proliferation of alternative mental health services such as rap centers, free clinics and drop-in centers," have been developed by youth themselves (Shore, 1981, p. 195).

Crisis centers have been established in order to provide immediate help for adolescents in difficulty who do not have access to professional help or who prefer peer helpers. They are operated by and for youth in order to deal with special problems that the "straight world" would not comprehend. They also serve as community centers for youth, dealing with youth's problems in a non-judgmental way.

Other innovative programs for counselling youth include telephone hotlines; houses where adolescents who leave home can find shelter and counselling, medical, obstetrical, and gynecological services; group homes for runaways; and centers for teenagers who simply want to talk. Telephone hotlines have several advantages—including their availability for immediate help in times of crisis. The individual is not placed on a waiting list. In case of more serious problems, the hotline operator may refer the caller to a local agency for longer-term assistance.

Opinions of such approaches are varied, though generally favorable. Mondale (1974) notes that "hotlines, runaway houses, and other similar programs actually initiated and supported by youth [are often] more effective than existing social agencies" (p. 12). By contrast, Baumrind (1974) believes that youth who have gotten themselves into trouble should not be catered to but should be dealt with firmly by adults. She believes that we "reinforce the antisocial choices of disadvantaged or affluent youth by providing free clinics, runaway centers, and counterculture high schools" (p. 81). Instead, youth's obligations should be "clearly stated and rigorously enforced."

The development of alternative services for young people has had two main effects: more traditional agencies have begun providing youth services which they had neglected before and, since youth often distrust traditional agencies, alternative services have been devised to create a bridge between alienated youth and means of help (Shore, 1981, p. 195).

PROFESSIONAL HELP   Adolescents with more serious problems who seek professional help may sometimes be treated with currently popular behavior modification techniques. Traditional therapists "favored the past and the unconscious as determining a person's behavior, while behavior therapists emphasize current factors, such as rewards and punishments that follow behavior, as well as other sources of social influence on the behavior" (Wilson & Davison, 1975, p. 59). Growing evidence indicates that behavior therapy may be successful in treating a wide variety of psychiatric disorders, such as social withdrawal, delinquency, phobias, and aggression.

Opponents of such therapy, especially the humanists, attack it as mechanistic, totalitarian, and arbitrary in its control of subjects. However, its defenders say that behavior modification therapy is consistent with humanistic philosophy. Indeed, argue Wilson and Davison, it is probably "the most effective means of promoting personal freedom and individualism because it enhances the individual's freedom of choice" (p. 60). All forms of therapy involve social influence; the behavior modifier simply acknowledges this influence. By stressing specific, clearly defined goals, the therapist avoids the "covert manipulations and subtle persuasion inherent in less structured therapies" (p. 60).

Ellis (1979) points out that the study of adolescent development has, until just recently, been dependent on the fields of child and adult personality functioning. Practitioners accustomed to dealing with adults, who see adolescents in clinics for private practice, may relate only to that aspect of adolescence that appears disturbed. They overlook what may simply be normal, even healthy, behavior at this stage. Although the majority of adolescents manifest some transitory symptoms of disturbance, only 20 percent display any major symptomatology, a figure almost identical to that of the population at large.

Models of adult personality function are inappropriate for those dealing with pathological conditions in adolescence. Ellis cites the case of a 17-year-old girl who panicked when he left the country. She was interpreted as being completely disorganized and was sent to a hospital, diagnosed as suffering from acute schizophrenia. Then an adolescent psychiatrist whom Ellis arranged to interview her gave her appropriate support and sent her home. Her difficulty had simply been a matter of working out her problem of separation from a psychiatrist who had been supportive of her.

Recently, advances in understanding the phenomena of adolescence have made psychotherapists who specialize in this stage aware of the shortcomings of earlier models of this period. They have also come to appreciate the significance of the environment in which adolescent development occurs. Although a recognition of the importance of cultural factors in human development is not new, greater emphasis is now being placed on understanding the interaction of complex developmental forces and how they impinge on adolescent problem solving and life styles.

Therapists' qualifications as appropriate identification models are also significant. Therapists who are secure in their own adult identities inspire adolescents' confidence in their own ultimate ability to surmount present problems and to achieve mature solutions (Meyers & Zegans, 1975).

It should be added that, for severe disorders, prompt and efficient psychiatric help is required—for example, when a youth displays bizarre behaviors, as in schizophrenia. Bauer and Bauer (1982) say that schizophrenia accounts for more human suffering than any other medical condition and it is seen with growing frequency. It is often disguised by drugs and depression, may be perceived as representing retardation or learning disabilities, and may come on as an abrupt "catastrophic, delirium-like illness" (p. 685). Some youth suffering from this condition receive long sentences as delinquents; some may die from drug addiction or in bouts with police.

The clinical picture varies with the individual and according to the severity of the illness. Certain common symptoms include poor judgment, narcissistic self-centeredness and inability to be concerned about others; and constant indecision about choices of behavior. Those with early and mild schizophrenia may be tired, edgy, anxious, and dress impulsively, just the way they feel and often inappropriately for the situation.

It is important that adolescent schizophrenia be diagnosed early and proper treatment undertaken so that the individual does not establish a psychological identity. Otherwise, the individual's behavior may progress toward psychotic symptoms and chronic illness, making treatment difficult and the prognosis poor.

EVALUATING ADOLESCENT THERAPY   Nadler (1978) helps to place the psychotherapeutic process in perspective. For various reasons, the same youth may be ascribed different degrees of mental health. A relatively normal youth who bothers his parents may be sent to a psychiatrist who assigns him a sick role; the youth, in turn, is led to perceive himself as emotionally ill.

While psychotherapeutic treatment works reasonably well in helping most youthful patients to achieve better techniques of living, some are undoubtedly abused in the therapy situation. In any case, the therapeutic process is a difficult one. Processes that are temporarily harmful may be therapeutic in the long run or the reverse.

In attempting to avoid seeming to be authoritarian, the therapist may not provide firm enough external limits. Or in trying to help a youth establish adequate structure, the therapist may be too directive. Thus, guidance of adolescents, whether by teacher, parent, or therapist is a "fine art" (Nadler, 1978, p. 459).

FUTURE PERSPECTIVES

Certain considerations help to place temporary or situational emotional problems in appropriate perspective. Longitudinal research, for example, has helped to distinguish persons who maintain sound emotional health and effective life styles from those who do not. On the basis of such studies, Norman Garmezy concluded that children and youth can thrive despite genetic disadvantages and environmental problems (Pines, 1979). Among those considered high risks for developing schizophrenia or other major disorders later on, only 10 to 12 percent actually did so—and several important factors distinguish the two categories.

Whether people believe they can cope or not makes a big difference in life adjustment and modifies their perception of traumatic events. Not only parents, but other persons and factors in a youth's environment may provide alternative sources of support and love, for example, warmly loving grandparents, siblings, and teachers, or special interest or recreational opportunities. Peer relations, as in street life, may provide the support that a growing individual needs. Some individuals gain a feeling of helplessness from being incapable of controlling circumstances and henceforth prove incapable of dealing with unfortunate events. Others with greater feelings of control over their environment can sustain unusual trauma without undue self damage.

General mental status in early years, as well as coping skills, are further indicators of later adjustment. The impact of future life turning points will hinge upon overall emotional stability (Thurnher, 1983). Coping skills which facilitate adaptability are developed in earlier years and tend to persist. A successful and effective adulthood depends on underpinnings of coping abilities constructed in earlier years (Rogers, 1982).

Adolescence is often described as a period of stress; it is less well recognized that young adulthood is also fraught with strain. Dr. Harold Visotsky, chairman of the Department of Psychiatry at the Northwestern University Medical School, points out that the highest incidence of psychological disorders is among people ages 25 to 40. The most common disorder among them is schizophrenia, followed by alcoholism, anxiety and depressive neuroses, and various other psychoses (Scanlon, 1979). It is unclear, however, to what extent such conditions are rooted in the experience of adolescence. Adult emotional health has proved more predictable from the preadolescent than the adolescent period; however, assessments of adolescent health may have been inadequate (Livson, 1976). Behaviors that convey the impression of instability in adolescence may be normal, even healthy, for that period.

Certain emotional attitudes are critical in adolescence because adolescents do not remain there long. They need to have some hope for what adulthood may bring. Traditionally, adulthood has been viewd as a time "for continuation, consolidation, application and stabilization, and eventually decline of one's powers, but certainly not the time for imaginative dreaming of what could be" (Menge, 1982, p. 438). From the more optimistic point of view adolescents develop a real confidence that their tomorrows will not simply fade away after age 35.

Preparation for adult life may be indirect, as in establishing sound foundations of mental and physical health, or direct, through identifying and preparing for the stresses to be encountered. To date, little has been done to provide such preparation in terms of formal education, although programs like Outward Bound help some young people to deal with stresses, to learn self-reliance, and to know where to seek help with problems (Scanlon, 1979).

Another important aspect of preparing for future years is developing the habit of keeping abreast of developments in medicine, psychology, and psychiatry. For example, safe, effective drug therapies may be developed to deal with unfortunate emotional states. However, adolescents should learn to distinguish between advancements that are sound and those that are dangerous (Medicine dares to dream of the impossible, 1983).

It is even more difficult to relate adolescent characteristics to emotional health in middle age (Vaillant, 1977). Since individuals who are psychologically healthy at that age may arrive there by different routes, the establishment of causality is unclear (Livson, 1976). However, it is likely that the anxiety neuroses of middle age have their roots in adolescence, when they first become well developed (Silverman, 1974). Patterns of worry, anxiety, and depression established then can, in time, become a way of life.

A certain amount of empirical evidence supports the view that emotional health and satisfaction at middle age do relate to early adjustment. In the Terman study, women who were satisfied in midlife had strong self-concepts from early years, and rated themselves low in inferiority and high in self-confidence. Those who felt self-confident in earlier years more often developed or followed a life style that produced greater satisfaction (Goleman, 1980b). Early feelings, especially about self, proved to be especially significant (Goleman, 1980a). Also predictive of longer range and broader mental health problems are poor peer relationships (Achenbach & Edelbrock, 1981).

Feelings of well-being in middle age may also relate to youth in more direct ways. It might be conjectured that males in the generations to come will enjoy a fuller, richer life because they are now escaping the emotional straightjackets that previously limited emotional expression, especially with regard to sentimentality, tenderness, compassion, and gentleness (Skovholt, 1978).

Looking ahead, but probably within the lifetime of today's youth, effective therapies may be found for such conditions as depression, schizophrenia, and senility as the brain's mysteries are unraveled. Possibly there may be "200 to 300 chemical messages in the brain—neurotransmitters—that influence function and behavior. By targeting drugs to specific sites in the brain, doctors can achieve better results" (Medicine dares, 1983, p. A7).

SUMMARY

Emotion, which constitutes a stirred-up state of the organism, has mental, motivational, and physical components. Particular emotions are distinguished by differences in intensity of feeling, complexity, and degree of integrative or disintegrative effect. Emotionally mature individuals have certain distinguishing characteristics: They accept their right to be human, they accept facts of life that they cannot change, but they do what they can about those factors that should and can be changed. Emotional maturity may also be described in terms of normality which, in turn, is viewed from four perspectives: health, utopia, average, and process.

Certain factors contribute to confusion in the search for valid standards of emotional maturity. For one thing, adjustment may be achieved at too great a cost to the individual. Besides, apparently healthy behaviors may mask truly unhealthy feelings underneath. Finally, what consitutes normal behavior, in terms of what is most typical, may simply reflect unhealthy features of the society itself.

Factors that determine a particular individual's pattern of emotions are both biological and sociocultural in nature. Constitutional factors may either facilitate or obstruct the acquisition of healthy emotional patterns. Individuals with parasympathetic dominance are more resistant to the negative effects of unpleasant emotions, whereas others with sympathetic dominance have greater problems of emotional health. Each individual is unique in terms of these biological factors, including body chemistry, degree of sympathetic or parasympathetic dominance, and general health. Other evidence of genetic factors in emotion is the early appearance of temperamental traits and their resistance to environmental influences. Just what part puberty plays in emotion is uncertain, although it is generally assumed to relate to heightened emotionality.

The influence of sex is important because of both genetic and sociocultural factors. Though it has not been conclusively proven, each sex may become naturally more or less susceptible to particular stresses. However, most authorities attribute sex differences in emotionality chiefly to sociocultural factors. From infancy, girls are encouraged to be more emotionally expressive while boys are encouraged to repress such emotions as compassion, tenderness, and gentleness. While this situation is changing somewhat, it tends to persist.

Individuals of both sexes follow their own patterns of emotional development. Even from the earliest weeks of life, individuals manifest characteristic emotional behaviors. Such patterns persist over the years, although different individuals and different characteristics within the same person vary in their susceptibility to modification. By adolescence, basic habits of emotion have become pretty well established; hence, youth must strive to understand themselves and to adapt their life styles accordingly.

Other influences on the individual's emotional development are environmental in nature. Primary among these is family experience. Another factor is the times—for example, youth's cynicism of the early 1970s, which reflected their disillusion with the Vietnam War, gave way to a realistic mood in the late 1970s, as obtaining a toehold in the work world grew more difficult. Other environmental influences include religion, which produces emotional crises much less often than formerly; social class, which modifies the kinds of crises and problems an individual may face; and cross-cultural factors, which limit the sort of emotional problems youth will experience in particular countries. The impact of television on youth's emotional health is undoubtedly large, although its particular effects are difficult to assess.

A long-standing issue in adolescent psychology is whether or not the period of adolescence is charcterized by unusual storm and stress. Some writers portray the period as unusually turbulent and adolescents' own behaviors as almost pathological in nature. Others admit that adolescence is indeed stressful, but that stress at this period is normal and even desirable. Such stress, they claim, helps individuals to clarify their values and, if these are satisfactorily resolved, to cope with future problems more effectively. In any case, degree of stress varies according to age, sex, and individual.

Even if the overall stress of adolescence has been exaggerated, certain symptoms are more common than others at this time. Certain pathologies, including delinquency, depression, and schizophrenia, commonly appear first in adolescence. The suicide rate also rises rapidly from early to late adolescence. Longitudinal research allows better perspective on behaviors that seem, on the surface, to suggest pathology. Although emotions rarely are experienced separately, it is sometimes helpful to isolate them for purposes of analysis.

Among the potentially positive or prosocial emotions, love is especially important. There is little empirical research concerning adolescents' attitudes about love; however, such data we have indicate clearly that young people are romantically and idealistically inclined, especially where love toward the other sex is concerned. Other positive emotions in youth, about which there is little research, are joy, altruism, and empathy. Whether or not contemporary young people are realistic in their search for happiness is still unresolved. Some authorities believe youth seek happiness in a frivolous fashion; others claim they are overly serious and grim. Although altruism has been studied very little, available research suggests that most adolescents, at least in America, grow somewhat more altruistic during their teens.

Other emotions are largely negative in effect. With regard to aggression, the sexes are socialized quite differently. Males are encouraged to express hostility in some areas and to restrain it in others. By contrast, females are consistently encouraged to curb their hostility, although it spills over in disguised and indirect ways. A second negative emotion, inferiority feeling, is relatively common among both sexes during their teens. Inferiority feelings connote sentiments of deficiency, whether imagined or real. Individuals may feel inferior even in areas where they excel. The negative feelings of shyness or self-consciousness are particularly troublesome during adolescence, which is the most social age of all. The social stratification of the teen society makes individual adolescents acutely aware of their status within the group. A further source of trouble is guilt, or feelings of personal wrongdoing. This emotion is accentuated in cultures such as ours which examine all acts in terms of their "goodness" and "badness."

Certain other negative emotions—fear, worry, anxiety, and loneliness—relate to individuals' apprehensions about factors within their environments. Fears may be classifed as normal, exaggerated, or irrational. Normal fears represent average response to average threat. Extreme fears, or phobias, may be obscurely rooted in the past and often require skilled professional help to overcome. Specific fears vary considerably according to the individual's age and sex; however, age does not in itself dissolve fear. Worry, like fear, suggests concern over a potentially threatening environment, but worry is more diffuse and persistent than fear. Worry is to be differentiated from the sensible concern which causes a person to take suitable steps to correct an undesirable situation. Characteristic adolescent worries relate to vocation, schoolwork, social adjustment, and sex. Females have more fears and worries than males, probably because they are taught to view the world as a threatening place. Even more troublesome than fear and worry is anxiety, partly because it is blended from many emotions. In addition, its object is unclear and therefore difficult to define. It has many unhealthy by-products, including unhappiness, loss of self-confidence, and unhealthy physical effects.

Two less insistent but devastating emotions are depression and boredom. Depression often stems from failure to achieve some important goal or from involvement in an unhappy life situation. Among adolescents, depression often results from failure to achieve the ideal self, from persistent unpopularity, or from failure to make the grade among peers or members of the other sex. A second somewhat passive emotion, boredom, involves feelings of becoming jaded and disinterested in life. Perhaps in these times it derives partly from experiencing too many emotions in too short a time. Growing children are exposed to so many intense and diverse stimuli that by adolescence only the spectacular and bizarre can arouse them. As a result, adolescents may seek to get "kicks" wherever they can—from rock and roll, drug use, acts of delinquency, or whatever.

Certain problems—for example, those relating to sex role, body image, peer acceptance, and college achievement—are especially likely to arouse negative emotions during the teens. Other problems of adolescence concern such matters as personal appearance, career, and, in some instances, death. The emotions thus produced have a diffuse effect, influencing all the individual's behaviors—for example, driving, smoking and taste in music.

Therapies for adolescence, until just recently, have derived from those employed with children and adults. However, recent advances in understanding the phenomena of adolescence have made psychotherapists who specialize in dealing with troubled youth aware of the shortcomings of these earlier models. Therapists may still err in building treatment on theories with a weak empirical case. While psychotherapy produces reasonably good results with many youthful patients, others may be helped little or even harmed by such treatment.

Certain considerations help to keep adolescents' problems, both minor and major, in better perspective. Individuals' beliefs in how well they can cope, as well as their perceptions of their environment, modify their response to traumatic events. Longitudinal research helps to distinguish life styles which are, or are not, conducive to maintaining sound emotional health.

DISCUSSION QUESTIONS AND ACTIVITIES

1. What stresses and strains are experienced by modern adolescents that were not experienced by former generations?
2. What common high school situations tend to arouse stressful emotions among adolescents? To what extent are these situations avoidable?
3. Analyze several popular songs in terms of their emotional appeal to teenagers and youth.
4. Describe some adolescent you know well, or yourself as an adolescent, in terms of emotional reactions, quality of adjustment, and environmental situations conducive to emotionality.
5. Examine newspaper advice columns for teenagers. About what types of emotional problems are the teenagers seeking counsel? Criticize specifically the advice given.
6. Be prepared to serve on student panels to discuss any of the following questions: (a) Is adolescence a more difficult period than childhood? (b) Do adolescents need a certain amount of guilt, fear, anxiety, and tension? (Discuss each emotion separately.) (c) Are adolescents who manage to muddle through problems on their own stronger than those who seek advice? (d) Do adults go too far in encouraging adolescents to suppress their emotions? (e) Is it unhealthy for males to repress their needs for dependency and gentleness?
7. Invite a psychologist from the college counseling or mental health service to discuss with the class major emotional problems of students on campus, probable causes, and effective therapies.
8. Analyze the college environment on your campus, both inside and outside the classroom, in terms of factors that tend to reduce or improve students' emotional health.

SUGGESTED READINGS

Balk, D. (1983). Adolescents' grief reactions and self-concept perceptions following sibling death: A study of 33 teenagers. *Journal of Youth and Adolescence, 12*(2), 137–161. An analysis was made of the impact of sibling death on 33 teenagers in terms of emotions, study habits, grades, and religious beliefs.

Bauer, W. & Bauer, J. L. (1982). Adolescent schizophrenia. *Adolescence, 17*(67), 685–693. Schizophrenia is discussed as it applies to adolescence in terms of its significance, dynamics, clinical features, and treatment.

Compton, M. F. & Skelton, J. (1982). A study of selected adolescent problems as presented in contemporary realistic fiction for middle school students. *Adolescence, 17*(67), 637–645. An analysis of the fifteen most popular realistic fiction books indicated the situations encountered in them to be more "mature" than those found in earlier fiction for young adolescents.

Cosand, B. J., Bourque, L. B., & Kraus, J. F. (1982). Suicide among adolescents in Sacramento County, California 1950–1979. *Adolescence, 17*(68), 917–930. Data collected in a California County are analyzed to determine factors relating to suicide among youth including sex, age, and socio-demographic factors.

Donohue, K. C. & Gullotta, T. P. (1983). The coping behavior of adolescents following a move. *Adolescence, 18*(70), 391–402. This study indicated differences in ways that adolescents cope with the stresses of relocation, in terms of individual, age, and sex.

Friedrech, W., Reams, R., & Jacobs, J (1982). Depression and suicidal ideation in early adolescents. *Journal of Youth and Adolescence, 11*(5), 403–407. Among a sampling of young adolescents differences between depressed and nondepressed categories indicated a significant relationship between life stress and depression and an inverse relationship between family cohesion and depression.

Gilligan, C. (1982). Why should a woman be more like a man? *Psychology Today, 16*(6), 68–77. A revised and more appropriate psychology of sex roles would indicate the female's emotional development to be healthier than when evaluated according to standards devised by and for males.

Godenne, G. D. (1982). The adolescent girl and her female therapist. *Adolescence, 17*(65), 225–242. A woman therapist of adolescent girls who interviewed other such therapists of both sexes concluded that often a female therapist is to be preferred, at least partly to allow role modeling.

Goswick, R. A. & Jones, W. H. (1982). Components of loneliness during adolescence. *Journal of Youth and Adolescence, 11*(5), 373–383. Among samplings of high school and college students factors relating to loneliness were negative in tone and, for the most part, similar for the two age levels.

Hawton, K. (1982). Attempted suicide in children and adolescents. *Journal of Child Psychology & Psychiatry & Allied Disciplines, 23*(4), 497–503. The literature is reviewed regarding demographic and background characteristics of teens who commit suicide.

Seidl, F. W. (1982). Big sisters: An experimental evaluation. *Adolescence, 17*(65), 117–128. An evaluation of a Big Sisters program, conducted by volunteers and supervised by professionals, indicated it to be quite effective.

Stein, M. & Davis, J. K. (1982). *Therapies for adolescents.* San Francisco, California: Jossey-Bass Publishers. This book embraces digests of over a hundred articles regarding the application of therapies to particular problems; many approaches are outlined for treating adolescents' physical and emotional disorders.

Thurnher, M. (1983). Turning points and developmental change: Subjective and "objective" assessments. *American Journal of Orthopsychiatry, 53*(1), 52–60. On the basis of recent developmental theories and a study of the interrelationships of self-defined turning points in life and longitudinal change in psychological health and self-concepts among younger and older adults, self-concept dimensions were found to be stable over time and to predict the impact of turning points.

Weiner, I. B. (1982). *Child and adolescent psychopathology.* New York: John Wiley & Sons. This comprehensive description of the nature, causes, treatments, and outcomes of psychological disorders of children and adolescents distinguishes between normal and abnormal development and details the current status of major pathological patterns during these years.

Williams, J. G. & Solano, C. H. (1983). The social reality of feeling lonely: Friendship and, reciprocation. *Personality and Social Psychology Bulletin, 9*(2), 237–242. In a study in which college freshmen filled out a loneliness scale and a social network questionnaire, lonely persons named as many best friends as did nonlonely ones and were equally likely to have this choice reciprocated; however, there was less intimacy in the lonely persons' relationships.

Chapter Five

Mental Potential

The American adolescent's mental development is currently a source of much concern. Every nation is anxious lest its next generation of adults be intellectually unable to cope with the increasingly novel, complex, and sophisticated problems of the modern world. This chapter will deal specifically with the adolescent's mental development; related matters will be discussed in Chapter 12 on the adolescent in school.

CONCEPTS AND DEFINITIONS

Intelligence is an individual's capacity to comprehend a situation or pattern or "to get rapidly and efficiently to the essence of whatever is being considered . . ." (Trachtman, 1975, p. 37). It is often confused with certain other attributes, among them **ability, creativity,** and **genius.** While intelligence refers to the mental potential of an individual, ability encompasses all the factors which that individual is able, at a given time, to put to work in coping with the environment. Ability, therefore, is a compound concept comprising not merely intelligence but also such factors as persistence, physical endurance, attitudes, and cumulative learning experience. Creativity would involve those aspects of intelligence that enable a person to find novel solutions to problems and individual modes of expression. Genius, though sometimes ascribed to all those who score very high on intelligence tests, is more often reserved for those with unusual creative ability. In recent years, psychologists have come to feel less confident of their ability to pigeonhole people in various mental categories.

However, as a frame of reference, we can define mental categories as follows: The bright individual we shall classify as one who performs above average (over 120) on currently respected intelligence tests. On the Stanford-Binet scale, this category would include roughly the highest 12.6 percent of the population, or about one person in eight. Below-normal (but not defective) people we shall define as having **intelligence quotients** (IQs) of 70 to 90; these number about 21.1 percent of the population, or about one in five. Mental defectives, with IQs below 70, constitute 2.6 percent of all individuals, accounting for one in 46. Most people—roughly three out of five—fall either in the average (90 to 100 IQ), or high-average (110 to 120 IQ) group. Another group, who are usually, but not always, bright by current IQ standards, are the creatives, who possess unusual capacity for producing novel solutions. The percentage of creatives is unknown.

Kagan (1978) points out that all human beings have the capacity to symbolize, to reason, to abstract, to categorize, to recall. Rather than speaking of generalized intelligence, it is best to speak of competence in the individual mental processes that collectively constitute mentality. Some individuals possess excellent visual memory but have trouble learning a new language. Hence, mental profiles should be developed for each individual, instead of deriving a single IQ number that presumably indicates overall mental ability. The mere "concept of general intelligence," says Kagan, is "useless because it distorts the nature of cognitive functioning" (p. 192).

PATTERNS OF MENTAL DEVELOPMENT

The Typical" or Normative Pattern

For better perspective on the mental traits of adolescents, let us briefly summarize the typical pattern of mental development. Intelligence rises rapidly during early years and continues to increase at a decelerating rate into the teens. Apparently most mental functions peak somewhere between late adolescence and the 30s. Then they remain on a relatively flat plateau, declining slightly in duller persons, remaining about the same for average ones, and rising slightly for brighter ones, until old age when all groups experience decline. The age of onset and extent of this decline is highly variable from one person to another.

There is disagreement concerning the nature and amount of mental growth after adolescence. Why later gains have not been shown by the average individual are not clear. In the Fels Longitudinal Study, the subjects' mean IQ continued to rise during the years 1939 to 1944, men with initially high IQs gaining the most. Women with the highest preadult IQs gained little in the adult years, indicating that bright women do not fulfill their intellectual potential (McCall, Hogarty & Hurlbut, 1972).

In discussing "normal" mental growth, note that typical mental growth patterns are derived from testing presumably randomly selected persons on different age levels or at successive ages. IQ scores represent average performance on a variety of subscores. Actually, some cognitive functions move toward greater differentiation and others toward greater synthesis. Moreover, particular individuals vary widely from the general pattern in their mental development. Finally, the general mental growth pattern indicates nothing about how individuals at the same age vary among themselves. Even by adolescence, the range in mental abilities among individuals on the same age level is wide.

Theories of Mental Development

THE CONSTANCY QUESTION   Persistent controversy has surrounded the question: "How constant is an individual's intelligence, relative to others of the same age-stage, throughout the life span?" Certain researchers believe that it remains relatively constant, programmed in broad outline by heredity. Cleary, Humphreys, Kendrick, and Wesman (1975) observe that the organism has certain innate capacities for cognitive development, although the limits are somewhat nebulous. No amount of education can change a chimpanzee into a human being, nor the mongoloid into a genius. However, the majority of psychologists support the anticonstancy position. They point out very considerable gains in IQ, resulting from special school programs and improved home environments. According to this theory, intelligence is not a fixed characteristic. Instead, it evolves as the biological substrate of intelligence interacts, throughout life, with psychosocial factors. Baltes and Schaie (1976) believe that considerable changes in IQ may occur even in adult life. They conclude that changes themselves may be programmed by genetics, or may reflect changes in the environment, or may result from both.

STAGE THEORY   Further controversy relates to the concept that mental growth proceeds according to relatively discrete stages, each with its own distinctive mental characteristics. According to Piaget, the best known of the stage theorists, mental development proceeds through four main stages (Flavell, 1963). The first involves **sensorimotor activity,** ranging from largely reflexive behavior during the first month, to exploratory activities, and finally to response to objects not immediately observable, in the second year. During the second stage, **preoperational thought,** children ages 2 to 4 are egocentric and categorize objects on the basis of single characteristics. Gradually, between ages 2 and 7, children shift from associational to cognitive verbal function and expand their capacity to observe that physical properties of an object are invariant despite appearances to the contrary. Thus, a distant object may form but a minute image in the retina yet be perceived as the size it actually is. During the third stage (**concrete operations**), ages 7 to 11, reasoning begins to be based on logic, and classification consists not merely in labeling a set of stimuli but in imaginatively combining objects within a category. Thus, a child may group together all items having wheels or any other common feature.

Before adolescence few individuals are capable of much abstract thinking. For example, at age 15 children have hardly developed political concepts, and they have only just begun really abstract thinking. Very few 18-year-olds can go so far as to describe an ideal society (Adelson, 1980). In his interviews Adelson found that not a single 11-year-old child could give a completely abstract response regarding political concepts (Adelson, 1980). Even very bright children, who had listened to political conversations at the dinner table simply had no idea of what political concepts were about, despite the fact that they were taking civics. Some of their teachers, when approached, said that the children couldn't grasp such concepts, therefore they didn't try to teach them.

The most significant cognitive development of adolescence is the emergence of formal operational reasoning which connotes the ability to think in hypothetical terms, to conjecture a broad range of alternatives and future events, and to think systematically of one's own thinking (Keating, 1980). It differs in several ways from mental processes of younger children. Concrete reasoners have trouble dealing with hypothetical statements at variance with reality, while formal reasoners can appreciate hypotheses and consider not-yet-proven possibilities (Berzonsky, 1978). Formal reasoners propose various solutions to a problem and speculate about several mutually exclusive causes of the same event. For example, consider this question: "A man was found dead in the back seat of a car that had hit a telephone pole. What happened?" Most 7-year-olds would suggest a single reason: Perhaps the man hit a pole and was thrown into the back seat and was killed. But the adolescent may think of several reasons: The man might have been put in the car after it crashed, so that the incident would appear to be an accident; or he could have been placed in the back seat by his companion after the crash; and so on.

Also, as adolescents move from childhood into adolescence most individuals come to evaluate others increasingly in terms of deeper and not merely surface characteristics (Higgins, Ruble & Hartup, 1980). In addition, almost all young adolescents can tell what life means to them and can quite fluently discuss their own lives as well as can older groups (De Vogler & Ebersole, 1983).

In other words, the adolescent becomes able to think abstractly, without the requirement of concrete "props." By age 15 to 16, the shift to formal operations is considered to be complete in the average person. This shift observes Lipsitz (1979), "is an exhilarating phenomenon because it is uniquely human. [Individuals] begin to be able to think about thinking, to generalize, to consider metaphors, to appreciate theorems—everything that has to do with ability to deal with abstract thought" (p. 7). This change is critical for all aspects of development at this stage. Until it occurs, adolescents "have probably not been able to truly become individuals with a coherent, cohesive sense of identity . . . they are also unable to respond to prevention programs that are based on the ability to consider contingencies or to predict" (p.7).

The fact that adolescents may have arrived at the formal reasoning stage in no way guarantees that they will reason at that level. For example, though adolescents express skepticism about advertising, they seem to abandon critical thought in appraising it. Indeed, in one study (Linn, de Benedictis & Belucchi, 1982) intellectual competence related just very slightly to reasoning about advertisements. Although over 95 percent were skeptical of advertisers and could even identify misleading portions of so-called product tests in advertisements, over 40 percent believed advertisements that reported private tests, even after acknowledging that procedural flaws may exist. They also believed that other people were more susceptible to being fooled than they were. Thus, they may have acquired the ability for critical thought, but they viewed advertising somewhat uncritically. The challenge is to determine why adolescents fail to apply critical thinking to broader aspects of their daily lives.

Critics of Piaget's stage theory question whether cognitive growth proceeds in a neat, stage-like fashion with children at any particular age level displaying a homogeneous or uniform level of complexity and developmental maturity. Flavell (1982) considers the matter unsettled—just how much homogeneity one might see in an individual's information-processing capabilities at any particular level would depend on the kinds of tasks and experimentation employed in research. The question might also be raised: If children are "cross-situationally homogeneous and consistent in intellectual level," could it simply be due to the way they are treated . . . ? (p.8) This writer suggests that our own age-grading system in school tends to result in an apparent age-gradedness in intellectual performance. At any rate, the results of intelligence tests show that some children are far more intellectually homogeneous than others. That is, some children display a far greater diversity in performance level on the various intellectual functions measured in intelligence tests than do others.

Despite widespread general acceptance, Piaget's theory has evoked considerable criticism. Broughton (1977) observes that a stage of formal operational thought is neither inevitable nor universal. It is not attained by all adolescents, nor is it the chief mode of cognitive functioning in adulthood. Moreover, education for formal thinking is too limited a goal and is insufficient for optimal life-span cognitive development. In particular, "comprehensive critical thought seems to be an important component of scientific, social, moral, and political consciousness—a consciousness beyond or apart from formal logical thought" (p. 97). Through acknowledging "broader, qualitatively different, and more reflective domains of cognitive affective development," educators may encourage the development of "cognitive functions of critical thought and interpretive abilities . . ."(p. 97).

Also, mental development is not a unitary process. A review of the research (Berzonsky, 1978) suggests that formal thinking normally emerges in adolescence, ages 11 to 15, but that the ability to utilize such thinking is not all-pervasive. That is, a particular adolescent may be capable of applying formal reasoning in science but perhaps not with semantic content.

Some authorities point out that although individual variation in the age at which successive stages appear is very great, any composite pattern (statistical average) will round out whatever stages, if any, exist. Nor is progression wholly one way, for regressions may occur. Indeed, young adults may display a lower level of formal operations than do most people in late adolescence and college years. This level becomes restored in a few years and ordinarily persists through the 30s and early 40s, when a plateau persists at least until the 60s (Botwinick, 1977).

There is also some speculation that cognitive development does not stop with Piaget's formal concept of formal operational thought, but that a fifth stage deals with problem finding (Arlin, 1975). Arlin concluded that formal operations or problem solving is essential but not sufficient for problem finding, while Cropper, Meck and Asch (1977) report the opposite to be true. Problem finding is defined as a "divergent process" reflected in ability to formulate problems, while problem solving is a convergent, "essentially hypothetical deductive" process (p. 517). Of their 86 subjects, 51 were problem finders and nonsolvers, while only 35 were both problem finders and solvers. They speculate that problem finding, as indicated in question-asking behavior, relates more to high tolerance for ambiguity than to divergent thinking. Possibly problem solving does not indicate a level of cognitive development but instead a predisposition to making creative responses.

Jerome Bruner believes that some individuals reach a still higher stage—of thinking about thinking—which involves "a consciousness of consciousness,

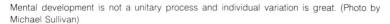

Mental development is not a unitary process and individual variation is great. (Photo by Michael Sullivan)

awareness of awareness, and a breaking-away of the phenomenological 'I' from the contents of consciousness" (Keniston, 1975, p.20). This higher state of consciousness may constitute the basis of a youth's special disturbances because of the "hyperawareness of inner processes, the focus upon states of consciousness as objects to be controlled and altered, and the frightening disappearance of the phenomenological ego, and an endless regress of awarenesses" (Keniston, 1975, p. 20).

Broader Concepts of Mental Development

In the past 15 years or so, observe Jeanne and Jack Block (1983), developmental psychologists have been preoccupied with issues of cognitive development; however, as ordinarily researched, cognitive psychologists have dealt with only a small segment of mental life. Yet an individual's psychological world rarely involves solely cognitive problems with which researchers have mainly concerned themselves. Everyday cognition does not revolve around tasks such as evaluating the dispensing of water into different containers or factors that might influence the swings of a pendulum. Moreover, psychological thought about development of cognitive structures has derived mainly from considering how individuals interact with their physical world. Such a world is far more orderly and subject to perceivable rules than cognitive problems embedded in a more personal world. Just as studies of cognitive development in the physical world may provide a relatively clear picture, those of cognition in the interpersonal world would involve far more complex elements.

For example, as growing individuals test interpersonal relationships and experiences, social feedback may be considerably delayed, often quite indirect, or ambiguous, calling for alternative explanations. The result may be the development and application of less-than-cognitive structures for dealing with the interpersonal environment, regardless of one's stage of mental development. Perhaps these modes of thought will be better understood after cognitive researchers come to explore growing individuals' cognition within the context of complex ambiguous situations. Such research may also lead to a better appreciation of intrinsic limitations in thinking and modifications in such limitations over a period of time. Also within the context of such emotions there are other emotions such as anxiety, fear, or positively, hope and joy. In other words, our perception of cognitive development has been too stripped down from the context in which such functions occur, thus leading to a seriously spurious and overly simplistic concept of how adolescents actually think.

Relevant Influences on Adolescent Mental Function

Family experience is especially important for development of appropriate attitudes toward intellectual matters. In one study of eighth graders, the more time they spent watching television the less they perceived their family's social climate as culturally and intellectually oriented (McMillan & Hiltonsmith, 1982). In other research, when boys and girls were matched in mathematics aptitude, more parents of daughters believed their child must work harder to do well than did the parents of sons (Parsons, Adler & Kaczala, 1982). Parents of sons believed that advanced math was more important for their sons than for their daughters, and they encouraged them more.

The Fels Study (Crandall, 1972) found it impossible to identify the genesis of intellectual achievement behaviors in the first three years of life. The early childhood precursors of academic effort and of intellectuality proved quite different. For both sexes, individuals who worked hard in college had been, as children, oriented toward adults, sensitive to their responses, and dependent upon them. In childhood they had often been rejected by, and were rejecting of, their peers, showed concern about others' approval, held somewhat conventional orientations toward vocational achievement, and had traditional sex-role characteristics and interpersonal relationships. On the other hand, [those] with well-developed intellectual interests exhibited a disregard for conventional socialization pressures from childhood on.

It has been widely believed that mode of child rearing importantly influences performance on intelligence tests. However, after studying children, ages 16 to 22, from adoptive and biologically related families, Scarr and Weinberg (1978) decided that family environmental differences have little influence on IQ variations among adolescents. Sibling and parent-child correlations suggest that genetic differences among families are largely responsible for the long-term effects of "family background." That is, the intellectual differences found among children in early adolescence bear little relationship to environmental differences among the families concerned.

Traditionally, the consistent finding that social-class differences relate to adult achievement has been perceived as indicating that differences in family environments during childhood operate to enhance or obstruct future educational, occupational and intellectual achievements. Kagan (1978) notes that one of the most firmly established findings in psychology is the relationship between children's social class and various indices of cognitive function, including achievement tests and IQ scores, richness of vocabulary, memory, and school grades. Middle-class children have greater expectation of succeeding in intellectual matters and are more reflective. In contrast, the Scarr and Weinberg research suggests that differences in family influences affecting IQ are mainly a matter of genetic differences among parents which at once affect their own status attainments and are passed along genetically to their children.

HEREDITY VERSUS ENVIRONMENT   Despite such evidence, authorities' opinions differ concerning the significance of heredity for mental performance. While all human populations have a vast number of genes in common, within those populations individuals also have genes influencing many differing characteristics. Each population of humans contains individuals whose abilites are above or below the average of all humans. Social policies should take human diversity into account to afford maximum chances for all persons to realize their potential, not as social classes or races but as individuals (Genetic differences in intelligence, 1977).

After reviewing the research, Carroll and Maxwell (1979) conclude that in representative populations heritability of at least some cognitive abilities can be at least as high as 0.4 or 0.5. Nevertheless, the matter of whether, and how much, cognitive abilities differ in heritability has not been determined. Even if degree of heritability ranges as high as 0.8 there is still room for the play of

Some environmentalists argue that experience can have an unlimited effect on an individual's capacity to deal with his world. (Courtesy of Public Relations Office, State University of New York at Oswego)

environmental variables, and various studies indicate that cognitive abilities can be improved somewhat.

Other writers stress the overall influence of environment, including all cultural effects, on mental development. Some environmentalists argue that "experience, if provided at properly sequenced stages, can have an almost unlimited effect on an individual's capacity to deal with his world" (Rogers, 1969, p. 127). Some basic level of intelligence, which itself involves a complex organization of statistics, is required for creative activity (Trachtman, 1975). Nevertheless, high intelligence alone is no guarantee of creativity.

For adolescents, a matter of concern has been how much drug use may impact negatively on their mental development. After reviewing the research Loftus (1980) concluded that "there is little evidence that moderate use of either [marijuana or alcohol] causes permanent physical damage to the brain, the center of memory" (p. 43). Neither does research confirm the common theory that drinking alcohol causes an actual loss of brain cells. However, there can be considerable difference in effect, according to individual variations in body chemistry.

The quality of school experience may impact on mental development, often in indirect but significant ways. Kelly (1979) identified high school students in two midwestern high schools as either high, moderate, or low explorers in terms of active desire to engage in the social environment. The high explorers at School One found many chances to express their initiative and interests within the school. The high explorers in School Two were less openly expressive, more reserved, and engaged in more deviant behaviors than low explorers or than the high explorers at School One. Possibly the challenge of School Two, which was quite stable, was to direct energies outside the school rather than to modify the school, and since the high explorers had comparatively greater needs for activity and interaction, they found the stable environment somewhat repressive.

SEX DIFFERENCES   In recent years a great deal of publicity has been given research which suggests that male and female brains are different (Weintraub, 1981). Such research tends to support the long-held belief that the male's greater aggressiveness and the female's greater domesticity are somehow legitimized by their differential physiology, especially in the brain.

Feminists say that sex stereotyping and rearing the sexes differently accounts for males' mathematical superiority. Psychologists Camilla Benbow and Julian Stanley reported that among seventh and eighth graders with high IQs, boys outnumbered girls two to one, scoring 500 or better on the math portion of the Scholastic Aptitude Test.

Most of the relevant research has been done with animals, among which male and female brains have been shown to be different. Thus, scientists have shown variations between the sexes in the hypothalamus, the focus of sexual drives, and the cerebral cortex, the seat of thought. It is conjectured that such differences are caused by sex hormones—male androgens and female estrogens and progesterones secreted by the sex glands and transported through the blood stream to all parts of the body.

However, scientists have not yet nailed down physiological differences between the brains of women and men. Many believe that brain development parallels that of genitals. If the fetus is male, they claim, the testosterone that produces a penis masculinizes the hypothalamus tissue and nearby structures within the brain, but, "if the fetus is a girl, estrogen secreted by the ovaries feminizes brain tissue and the surrounding cerebal cortex" (p. 15). Some scientists believe that brain structure controls behavior; however, Anne Petersen thinks that the reverse may be true, that behavior may modify the brain structure. For example, boys who are good in athletics excel in spatial reasoning, a skill directed by the right hemisphere of the cerebral cortex, spatial reasoning being "the ability to understand maps and mazes or objects rotating in space" (p. 17). As Petersen explains, athletes must constantly be aware of the position of their own bodies in space which, in turn, may, by some "mysterious mechanism," modify the brain structures (p. 17). This writer would like to add that almost from birth the kinds of toys given boys are far more conducive to the development of spatial reasoning than those given to girls.

Endocrinologist Anke Ehrhard believes that society importantly shapes gender behavior; nevertheless, certain sexual behaviors are influenced significantly by sex hormones. For example, she notes cases of girls whose adrenal glands, because of enzyme defects, have produced unusual amounts of androgen while in the womb; these girls are found to be very tomboyish and career-oriented. Boys exposed before birth to drugs containing large amounts of feminizing hormones do less "roughhousing than other boys" (p. 17).

Jerry Levy, neuropsychologist, believes the cortex of men and women is different, because of her research with split-brain patients, "epileptics whose hemispheres had been surgically separated as a means of controlling violent seizures" (p. 19). She concluded that the right hemisphere is concerned more with spatial relationships, as in solid geometry, and the left with language and rote memory. She also believes that females may reach puberty earlier, before their brains have fully lateralized. Hence, the hemispheres of the female brain might communicate more rapidly—an advantage "in integrating all the detail and nuance in an integrated situation but . . . a disadvantage when it comes to homing in on just a few relevant details" (p. 20).

Whatever may be the physical differences between male and female brains their implications are quite unclear. Certainly, abundant evidence shows that many men have talent in language and many women great talent in mathematics, although sociocultural factors are shown to possess highly significant effect on the direction and growth of mental potential.

Such research holds implications that could be both positive and negative. To the extent that brain differences exist the sexes' environments might be modified in such a manner as to maximize strengths and minimize weakness. On the other hand, premature and vastly exaggerated conclusions may be drawn to support arguments against equal rights, or unnecessarily confining each sex to a particular life style.

In summary, although no consistent sex differences exist longitudinally in overall intellectual abilities, differences in specific abilities persist through the life span. In general, males' test scores vary more over time and are less predictable than those of females.

Various methodological and interpretive deficiencies in research reviews raise questions about the strength of the foregoing conclusions. These deficiencies have to do with such matters as sampling, cognitive measures employed, measurement errors, and longitudinal design.

Significance of Adolescent Mental Traits

IMPORTANCE OF DEVELOPMENTAL PATTERNS   For both sexes, characteristics of mental growth in adolescence have special significance for their education and adjustment. First of all, adolescents develop mentally, even though the rate of their mental growth declines. Statistical analysis suggests that at least half an individual's final mental growth takes place after age 11. Furthermore, cumulative experience permits older youths to make much fuller use of their abilities than they had earlier. Adolescence is the last period, for most persons, when individuals can allocate a high proportion of their time specifically to mental growth.

It is also important to remember that each individual's mental growth pattern is unique. Growth curves of some individuals are labile, showing rapid increases and drop-offs in rate of growth. Others are relatively stable, manifesting fairly steady progress without spurts or lulls. Still others alternate between labile and stable patterns. Hence, curricula should be individualized. Some adolescents are ready for deeper subjects earlier than others.

Money (1977) points out that achievement cannot take place without an appropriately supportive environment; yet our environment tends to favor one sex over the other in the way chldren are reared. For example, boys are given more types of games that provide hand-eye coordination and that would lead to superiority in mathematical achievement. In college, boys have more same-sex role models of intellectual achievement. Yet the young intellectual woman needs an effective female role model "to give integrity to her own role, to invest her aspirations with greater reality, and perhaps offer her some clues about ordering her spheres of action" (Douvan, 1976, p. 5). The research supports Douvan's recommendation. Certain successful women, in writing their biographies, stressed the important role that older female role models played in their academic development (Angrist & Almquist, 1975).

In general, the lower the woman's status and opportunities are within a culture, the poorer her intellectual performance is. When Chinese and American adolescents were given three Piagetian tasks of formal operations, the 15-year-olds performed better than the 13-year-olds, the Americans better than the Chinese, and the Chinese females most poorly of all (Douglas & Wong, 1977). The aptitude for experimentation and hypothesis testing involved in formal thought demands searching, active modes of behavior, characteristics not especially encouraged in Hong Kong, especially in females.

COGNITIVE STYLE   Adolescents of both sexes differ among themselves in cognitive style—ways of perceiving, organizing, and labeling various dimensions of the environment. That is, most individuals have a preferred style for dealing with problems (Ewing, 1977). They superimpose on problems their own ways of dealing with it rather than swinging from one cognitive style to another. Few people are "cognitive switch hitters" and even those people hardly possess over two or three main styles (p. 73). Some people are systematic and methodological, revising plans and then determining ways of completing them. Others are more intuitive and unsystematic, nevertheless often with a coherent underlying rationale. Some people are perceptive, beginning with some idea about how to organize information and hypotheses. Others are receptive, concentrating on details without beginning with some preconceived organization. They suspend judgment until the facts are in and fall into place—the Sherlock Holmes approach. Some individuals make decisions cautiously, whereas others seem almost haphazard by comparison. Such a tendency stabilizes by age six; the degree of caution or brashness persists until after they have entered another growth spurt, following a period on a plateau.

At times a plateau is mistaken for cessation of mental growth. In such a case, a teacher may fail to encourage adolescents to continue their education, wrongly believing that they would fail the requirements of college. Indeed, such adolescents might fail if they went to college immediately. However, many veterans with mediocre high school records have resumed their education with great success after discharge from the military. Although some of the improvement may be attributable to greater maturity and stronger motivation, part may also be due to a late increment in mental potential.

SIGNIFICANCE OF INTELLECTUAL STATUS AT ADOLESCENCE   In many ways adolescents' needs relate to their mental abilities. In matters of role-taking they come to view the world from another's perspective, a process made possible by abstract, cognitive abilities developed during this period (Muus, 1983). At the same time, adolescents consciously employ their social experiences for enhancing the self, which they do with a degree of caution, an approach described as *strategic interaction* (Elkind, 1983). These individually designed interactions, says Elkind, are possible because of adolescents' growing mental capacities. By this time they can see the consequences of their behaviors and test them in advance before an imaginary or hypothetical audience.

The onset of puberty apparently has no great effect on the stability of relationships or developing mutually intimate friendships. Rather, changes with age in intimacy and mutuality of responsiveness are influenced more by cognitive development. As cognitive abilities increase, adolescents are able better to share their feelings with their friends and to establish a greater mutual understanding (Berndt, 1982).

It is also during adolescence that the structure of politics is usually first understood. Because of their growing capacity for hypothetical thought adolescents come to understand political hierarchies, competition for power among politicians, the role of political parties, the citizen's role in the social and political system, and their own role as future citizens (Damon, 1981). They can by now construct in their imagination alternative social worlds (Keating, 1980). They can also conceive of social conditions different from the realities around them—for example, a world of social equality and peace.

Becoming interested in politics by no means applies to all adolescents. Some remain "apolitical" and continue so throughout their lives. Even those who are politically active are often so only sporadically and superficially—that is, they do not understand the basic issues (Damon, 1983).

POTENTIAL FOR ACHIEVEMENT DURING ADOLESCENCE Unfortunately, we have failed to provide the sort of life experiences that will permit many adolescents to make outstanding intellectual contributions to society. We have erroneously concluded that real achievement must wait until adulthood. However, many persons have achieved significantly in their teens. William Cullen Bryant wrote "Thanatopsis" at age 18; and Jacob Perkins discovered the first synthetic dye at the same age. Galileo was 17 when he arrived at the principle of the pendulum.

Of course, there is tremendous variation in potential from one adolescent to another. In a random sample of 16-year-olds, test scores may vary from a mental age of 10 to one of 20. This spread underscores the need for much wider differentiation of learning experiences than most classrooms currently provide.

ADOLESCENTS WITH SPECIAL PROBLEMS OF MENTAL DEVELOPMENT

The Bright or Gifted Student

Among the schools' most disadvantaged students are the very bright and gifted. Few schools have the teachers, curriculum, or physical resources to provide the challenge such students need. Hill (1972) calls gifted youth the neglected students in today's schools, and talented students the grossest under-achievers. He concludes that equality in education is wrong, for "there is nothing more unequal than treating unequals equally" (p. 326). In addition, most current programs for helping bright children are inadequate; yet the needs of these students are just as great and specialized as those of the mentally retarded.

Baumrind (1972) agrees, declaring that some form of "tracking" (grouping by level of performance) by subjects is necessary if better students are not to be held back by less motivated, less able ones, at least in areas of their special talents.

Gifted adolescents are higher on autonomy, self-reliance, and self-assertiveness than are less gifted ones, and the achievement of gifted children also relates to the amount of independence training they receive (Hogan, 1980). However, some questions remain unanswered. It is uncertain whether time can be made up in dependent gifted children by encouraging autonomous behaviors, or whether they can be encouraged to be too autonomous. In any case, giftedness must be viewed as "always embedded within a constellation of personal and situational factors."

Note also that, despite much research, comparing gifted to less talented samples, it is unclear in what ways the samplings differ otherwise. Often gifted samples were chosen from some particularly highly motivated group of individuals, such as those involved in some talent search, and it is unclear whether the results can be generalized to the unknown numbers of gifted individuals in general. Also, many reports about the gifted rely on parent and teacher reports of "unspecified validity and reliability" (Monks & Ferguson, 1983, p. 14).

The gifted require utmost ingenuity if they are to profit by the school's offerings. Einstein once recalled that studying for final exams "had such a deterring effect on me that . . . I found the consideration of any scientific problem distasteful to me for an entire year. . . . It is little short of a miracle that modern methods of instruction have not already completely strangled the holy curiosity of inquiry, because what this delicate little plant needs most, apart from initial stimulation, is freedom" (Broad, 1979, p. 40). The lesson here is that teachers should provide such individuals encouragement and broad latitude for developing their interests and modes of inquiry.

Einstein summed up his lifelong search in this way: "Out yonder there is this huge world, which exists independently of us human beings and which stands before us like a great, eternal riddle, at least partially accessible to our inspection and thinking. . . . The road to this paradise . . . has proved itself as trustworthy, and I have never regretted having chosen it" (Broad, 1979, p. 42).

The Slow-learning or
Learning-disabled Adolescent

At the other extreme are the slow learners whose first requirement is that someone discover the cause of their individual impediments. Many are mentally normal but poorly motivated. Others are simply late maturers. IQ tests and interviews are needed to distinguish among these conditions and to devise treatments. Obviously, help for the individual who is alienated from school will be vastly different from that prescribed for the youth with physical or mental learning disabilities.

For the poorly motivated, assistance must relate to whatever complex of causes contributed to their feelings of apathy or alienation. Often a student's attitudes are so strongly held and deeply rooted that both individual counseling and remedial work are needed. Such a youth often makes dramatic gains when provided appropriate tasks and encouragement.

The plight of mentally retarded youths is somewhat different. Teachers often scold them, believing that they could learn if they only would. By adolescence, they stand dejectedly on the lowest rung of the intellectual hierarchy, already firmly entrenched. Early diagnosis of the type and extent of retardation, along with appropriate physical and psychological treatment, is essential.

Youth from a Lower Social Class

Another adolescent who often lags behind is the lower-class youth. Middle-class youth receive parental assistance with homework, obtain considerable training at home in the verbal skills they need at school, and are provided with more of the conditions they need for study, such as a quiet room, an encyclopedia, and a typewriter. Lower-class students usually have not received systematic instruction from their earliest years. At the bottom of the school status hierarchy, they have become unhappy and discouraged. They may decide in high school that they would like to go on to college; however, deficiencies in school subjects are cumulative and much time might be required to correct them.

THE UNDER-ACHIEVING ADOLESCENT   Some adolescents underachieve, not due to mental retardation, but because their basic learning skills are deficient. With regard to acquiring these skills, that is, the so-called 3 Rs—reading, 'riting, 'rithmetic—recent evidence is more encouraging than were earlier reports. Some "students will fail in traditional schools, but skillfully designed and executed compensatory education programs, from preschool to high school, can repair earlier deficiencies" (Hobbs & Robinson, 1982, p. 217). One effective approach to teaching adolescents, especially those not culturally oriented to academic learning, is to employ in regular classrooms those techniques developed for special education.

Often underachievement develops in secondary schools, because their curricula and methods are poorly adapted to adolescents' cognitive status.

RELATED ASPECTS OF MENTAL DEVELOPMENT

Skills

Skills—abilities to perform competently in various fields—are important to an adolescent. Skills are basic to achieving a sense of security; the wider the range of their skills, the more at home adolescents feel in a variety of situations. Some adolescents are equally at ease on the baseball diamond, on the dance floor, at the bridge table, and in the classroom. Skills also promote a sense of freedom and autonomy. Those who can do things for themselves are less susceptible to manipulation by others; their skills free them from being passively dominated by their peers.

Certain skills are especially important if adolescents are to succeed at their tasks. Skill in reading is highly desirable because of heavy library assignments in high school and college. Various study skills, including note-taking, typing, and using the library, also contribute to a student's adequacy.

In contrast with earlier times modern technology has dramatically increased the preparation and skills required for adulthood, thereby delaying entry. It also produces comparatively rapid obsolescence of skills, vocational and otherwise (Rogers, 1982). For example, it is becoming increasingly important that youth possess computer skills. Kiesler, Sproull and Eccles (1983) predict that, within a few years, computers will be the main tools in 25 percent of all jobs.

In this respect female youth are disadvantaged because the world of computers is primarily male. Men design the machines, and teach the course; most games are designed for boys; boys outnumber girls at computer camps by a rate of three to one. Moreover, video arcades "are dens of teenage male culture, a place where boys gather with their buddies" (p. 43). Sometimes the boys bring their girl friends, but the girls' role is simply to admire them, not to play the games themselves. In an informal survey taken at a Pittsburgh shopping mall, of 175 teenagers playing the games, just 30 were girls and not a single girl was playing alone. The games themselves are designed to appeal mostly to males. In one store such games were found as Olympic Decathlon, with four male athletes on the cover, and Cannon Ball Blitz, showing five men in battle. In all, on the packages, twenty-eight men were shown on the covers compared with four females. Also, the software developed for use in computers reflects the male culture, being concerned with such matters as sports, war, and violence.

The computer culture appeals to "the rebelliousness of teenage boys" and it has "bred a new kind of male punk, who prides himself on his talents at breaking codes, illegally copying computer games, and overloading time-sharing systems" (p. 46). They don't learn any useful computer etiquette; instead their exposure is to "mostly male role models who teach them to break rules" (p. 46).

It appears then that there is a male bias in teenager exposure to computers. True, many females are enrolling in computer classes in college. However, they would do much better if their earlier exposure had been greater and less male-oriented.

For optimum mental development in adolescents Hobbs and Robinson (1982) suggest the following: that research regarding intelligence relate to a life-span perspective; that experimental curricula be developed for high schools to assess cognitive skills and instruction in information processing and problem-solving strategies; and that basic academic skills be taught in secondary schools for all students with deficiencies. They recommend that alternative programs for adolescents, such as job training, include "general cognitive training" as well as instruction in basic academic skills. And they recommend that industry, business, and the military develop experimental programs for teaching cognitive competence and the basic academic skills as well as job related skills, and that the programs be evaluated for their short- and long-term effectiveness. Such an approach is especially vital in these times and years to come because, as older individuals increase in numbers relative to younger ones, the younger generation correspondingly must be more productive.

It should be added that youth should have a realistic understanding of the status of their skills or they will not know how, appropriately, to capitalize on their abilities or remedy their deficiencies. Yet, when the College Board asked a million high school seniors who took its aptitude test to indicate how they felt, compared with other people their own age, in particular areas of ability, their self-concepts appeared unrealistically high. In leadership ability 70 percent rated themselves above average, 2 percent below; in athletic ability, 60 percent better than average, 6 percent below; in ability to get along with others, 0 percent below and 60 percent above; and 25 percent saw themselves in the top 1 percent overall (Myers, 1980).

Attitudes

Attitudes represent states of mind, favorable or unfavorable, toward anything and everything—work, friends, religion, racial groups, life, and death—and they are especially important in mental development. They influence the individual's receptiveness to learning: the youth who hates mathematics is often unable or unwilling to concentrate on it. Attitudes also give substance to fact. A fact by itself is "like a sack which will not stand up when it is empty."

The influence of adolescence on shaping attitudes may have been exaggerated, judging by the results of a longitudinal study of two thousand young men at the University of Michigan. The Institute for Social Research followed these individuals from tenth grade until five years after high school and were impressed by the persistence of their attitudes. Nor did college education seem to have any special socializing effect on students. By the twelfth grade racial attitudes were already in place (Dogmatic teens, 1978).

Periodically, national polls assess the current status of youth's attitudes. A poll taken in 1979 refuted the common view that youth's views are predominantly liberal, if not far to the left. Of a national sampling of college freshmen, 57 percent were predominantly middle-of-the-road in their political views. A mere 1.8 percent identified with the far left, 0.8 percent with the far right, 23.6 percent with liberals, and 16 percent with conservatives (ACE Survey, 1979, p. 557).

Interests

An interest suggests a favorable attitude toward an activity and a desire to participate in it. Interests are becoming increasingly important as people have more leisure time. Many persons are engaged in occupations so confining or so monotonous that diversity of activity during their free time becomes imperative to their mental health. Those who play their life roles adequately tend to have leisure patterns that are vital and ego-integrative.

GENERAL CHARACTERISTICS OF ADOLESCENTS' INTERESTS   The interests of adolescents differ from those of younger chldren in several ways: (a) Adolescents' interests reflect their greater social maturity. They relinquish their bicycles, which have been associated in this culture with childhood, for cars, which belong to the world of adults. They also become more interested in personal appearance and clothes. (b) Adolescent interests often are introspective and egoistic, sometimes taking the form of poetry-writing and diary-keeping. (c) Activities often are more social. Those activities carried on alone, like horseback riding and fishing, decline rapidly. Construction-type activity diminishes, except in camps where work may be in groups. Reading lags after age 14, and the adolescent reads less for fun than the child does. (d) Interests become more serious. For example, interest in comic books diminishes. (e) Interests become more stable. Adolescents cease wandering from one interest to another. (f) Finally, interests become both less active and fewer. In one study (DeLong, 1975), preadolescents indicated both active and varied interests. Three fourths or more of them indicated interest in "pets, athletics, working with hands, outdoor games, travel, association with peers, spending money, living outdoors, and watching cartoons and comedies. . . . Items of least interest concerned living far from other people, doing factory work, and being lazy as much as possible"(p. 189).

The sexes differ significantly in their interests. Males score higher than females in investigative, realistic, and enterprising scales on the Strong-Campbell Interest Inventory while females score higher in social and artistic areas. Nevertheless, interests differ more between older adult men and women than between young adult men and women, which suggests that sexual differences in interests are becoming less marked than they used to be. The new generation of women is coming to feel freer to participate in scientific, outdoor, and mechanically oriented activities (Grotevant, Scarr & Weinberg, 1978).

Much research has focused on the effect of environments on people's interests but people also develop their own environments. In order to determine differences in interests among three groups of late adolescents—high school dropouts, high school graduates, and college students—graduate students surveyed the contents of their rooms (Manaster & Novak, 1977). The reading matter found in the youths' rooms related to defining love and sex roles; school and work orientation; family, peer, and social relationships; and personal roles. The literature included erotica, escape fiction, family living and childrearing guides, and vocational materials. Both girls' and boys' rooms contained such magazines as *Playboy* and *Playgirl.* Males in the high school graduate and high school dropout categories often had shop manuals and vocational magazines, such as *Popular Mechanics* and *Hot Rod,* while many rooms of all groups contained religious or self-awareness literature.

All the rooms contained television sets and music equipment, including stereo equipment, tape decks, and popular music collections. The high school dropouts favored western and country music while all categories liked rock-and-roll and "easy listening" music. The rooms varied widely in appearance, the majority containing brightly colored advertisements, slogans, newspaper cutouts, and photographs. The college students and high school graduates preferred more intricately designed decorations and were more selective in what they displayed than the dropouts. The dropouts' decorations included pictures of teenage idols, popular cars, and miscellaneous items, such as beer posters.

Youth's interests continuously change in nature and intensity with the times. In the future their interests will undoubtedly be modified somewhat by further technological developments, just as students now find it very important to own stereos (Age of miracles, 1983).

SPECIAL INTERESTS IN MUSIC, TELEVISION, AND READING   Almost all adolescents have some interest in television. By the time the average young person reaches 18, he or she will have watched approximately 22,000 hours of television, compared with 11,000 hours spent in the classroom. During this period, adolescents will have been exposed to about 35,000 commercials (LeMasters, 1974). However, the amount of televiewing is lower during adolescence than at any other stage of life and declines through those years (Larson & Kubey, 1983).

Psychologists have their own explanations for youth's television favorites. William Glasser says that adolescents aren't much different from the rest of society in their choices. They, like adults, want uncomplex characters and simple solutions. They want plots that "tie everything up in tidy, happy packages" (Torgerson, 1977, p. 6). Other shows have special appeal to teenagers. Teenagers have a certain sense of powerlessness and often become frustrated, hence like easy solutions. The "bionic marvel" always maintains control and always wins. Attractive young girls provide fantasy sex subjects for the boys and role models for the girls. Adolescents like cops who are free-swinging and are never called upon to account to their precinct captains. Adolescents also like TV characters of their age because it is easy to identify with them. They like comedy situations that appeal to their own relatively unsophisticated sense of humor. They like warm, permissive adults with sensitivity and patience for teenagers' pranks. Chaytor Mason, a professor of psychology, says they like heroes who are what the teenagers themselves would like to be (Torgerson, 1977, p. 6). They like a certain hero who is antiadult—a wise guy, yet polished. They also gain a certain education from television; and a detective show may represent problem solving for them.

In a nationwide four-year study that involved a random sampling of individuals age 13 and older, Frank and Greenberg (1979) found that television audiences could be divided into 14 main segments characterized by the leisure interests they had in common. The members of the youngest of the groups, whose average age was 19, were interested in getting away from the responsibilities and pressures of home life and indulging in athletic and social activities. For movies they liked "escapist fare—they are heavy frequenters of science fiction, horror and disaster films—as also are their television preferences" (p. 100). As compared to other age groups, they were above average in viewing children's programs (21 percent above the average), television movies (8 percent above), science fiction (22 percent above), and situation comedy (15 percent above). They were below average in viewing cultural and information programs. For them, television was chiefly for entertainment and situation comedies a mode of defusing family strains.

Annette Baran, a licensed clinical social worker, concluded that adolescents like any programs that ridicule adult authority or cater to their sense of fantasy (Torgerson, 1977). They also like reruns because they provide a certain sense of security to the "little kid" remnant that exists in all of us. Watching reruns represents "security, like sucking on a blanket, very much as small children like to be told the same bedtime story over and over" (Torgerson, 1977, p. 7). Adolescents like to return to familiar themes when they confront the world as a frightening place.

Some teenagers admit liking soap operas, with their somewhat preposterous themes. They, like the average worker, come home tired from school and simply want to relax. For the teenager, television is "an antidote to loneliness and the boredom of not having anything to do. [He] doesn't want to talk to anyone in his family anyhow. They'll only hassle him. TV doesn't talk back or make demands. And it can be a relief from doing homework or worrying about the terrible present or the impossible future" (p. 7). TV is much like aspirin: It is easy to obtain and relieves pain; and its side effects are not fully known, although we suspect it may be unfavorable (Torgerson, 1977).

Adolescents report music as a primary activity seven times as often as do adults (Csikszentmihalyi & Kubey, 1981). They even play it while they study;

Special interest in music, television and reading are common among adolescents. (Courtesy of Public Relations Office, State University of New York at Oswego)

and the amount of interference varies with the type of music played. According to a study of college students (La Voie & Collins, 1975), rock music interferes with the effective study of school subjects by adolescents; classical music does not. Nevertheless, more than four in five said that they listened to music while studying. All but twelve said that rock music did not interfere with their concentration, yet the data indicate that those who regularly study while listening to television, radio, or records do not retain factual material as well as those who do not study under such conditions. Why does rock music interfere with studying, but classical music exerts a minimal effect? According to one theory, youth find rock music especially appealing because it is written especially for them and somehow communicates with them. We also know that anything with a strong beat attracts our attention more than regular rhythms do. Rock has words to distract the listener, but classical music usually does not. In addition, the sheer dissonance of rock music helps to account for rock music's interference with studying.

Here teenagers answer the question,

Does the music of today have a message for you?

MALE: Yes. It gives me a feeling of the times, such as speed, revolution, and change.

MALE: Yes. It portrays a generation of people searching for something they can't quite find.

FEMALE: Yes. It expresses what is wrong with society; and some songs seem to express what I feel or some part of my life.

Youth may also seek messages in books, as suggested by cults that revolve around certain authors or topics. Changes in reading habits reflect youth's chang-

Table 5–1: Degree of Interest College Students Express in Selected Activities

TOPIC	FEMALES (N = 60)					MALES (N = 60)					TOTAL (N = 120)				
	G.D.	C.	L. OR N.	D.S.	D.M.	G.D.	C.	L. OR N.	D.S.	D.M.	G.D.	C.	L. OR N.	D.S.	D.M.
	%	%	%	%	%	%	%	%	%	%	%	%	%	%	%
Watching television	3	45	46	5	0	6	41	38	5	5	5	43	42	5	2
Reading	31	53	10	1	1	23	46	23	5	0	27	50	16	3	0
Observing or participating in sports	23	36	38	0	1	33	36	30	0	0	28	36	34	0	0
Socializing—spending time with friends	66	30	1	0	0	50	45	5	0	0	58	37	3	0	0
Working at special interests or hobbies	43	45	11	0	0	38	48	13	0	0	40	46	12	0	0
Devoting free time to various organizations (scouts, etc.)	6	43	48	1	0	5	15	68	6	1	5	29	58	4	0
Engaging in inside-the-house activities (sewing, cooking)	18	46	16	10	6	3	28	40	16	10	10	37	28	13	8
Engaging in outside-the-house activities (gardening, mowing)	18	38	31	8	3	8	36	35	16	1	13	37	33	12	2
Hiking, camping	33	41	23	0	1	31	38	23	3	1	32	40	23	1	1
Driving a car	28	50	18	0	1	30	45	20	3	1	29	47	19	1	1
Just sitting or drifting around doing nothing in particular	3	36	38	6	13	5	31	36	10	16	4	34	37	8	15

G.D.—Great deal
C.—Considerably
L. or N.—Little or none
D.S.—Dislike somewhat
D.M.—Dislike much

ing concerns. In the 1960s, youth's favorite books dealt with relevance, alienation, disillusion with government, escape from reality through drugs, the generation gap, social injustice for minority groups, and people caught up in a society and a war they did not believe in. Youth of the 1970s often looked for heroes worth modeling after, a sense of hope, and values worth upholding (Big change in adolescent reading, 1975).

In unpublished research by the author (Table 5–1), college undergraduates expressed unusual interest in spending time reading (50 percent), working at special interests and hobbies (40 percent), hiking and camping (32 percent), and driving a car (29 percent). Few expressed great interest in television (5 percent), working in various organizations (5 percent), or just sitting or drifting around, doing nothing in particular (4 percent).

Here are some illustrative comments concerning individual interests:

Television

FEMALE, AGE 19: TV is the end of a creative mind. Sure, lots of new ideas are introduced but children and even adults should experience life. Life is for living, not intellectualizing.

MALE, AGE 20: It's really good to watch TV. It lets me relax and still have something to do. TV is one way by which society can find answers to questions about themselves and other people.

Sports

MALE, AGE 21: I used to enjoy watching sports but I have lost interest in this during college. I think activities which keep your body in decent physical shape are important.

FADS   A special type of adolescent interest is the fad, which is a sporadic short-term fashion bordering on a cult. Fads are by definition temporary and unpredictable, and they are especially prevalent among teenagers. Among fads cited by upper New York State boys and girls, ages 16 and 17, were the following: gold caps, bleaching streaks of hair, beginning words with "y," speaking in supposedly "Chinese language," hot-rodding, and football and basketball pools. A strange fad, in 1974, was "streaking," or dashing naked, singly or in groups, through public places.

Various factors may explain the popularity of fads: the desire to attract attention; the urge to conform to what peer groups prize; the need for distinctiveness as individuals and as age groups; and the fascination with the unusual. Fads also depend on an environment favorable to their growth. Fads are typically seen as escapist, bizarre, or dysfunctional—for example, goldfish-eating contests, 50-mile walks, streaking. Such fads are not intended to change norms; rather, they represent attempts by individuals to establish meaningful roles for themselves and to attain a certain status. Where there is considerable autonomy, such as on college campuses, fad behavior flourishes. Such places have a higher-than-normal level of tolerance for unusual behavior (Manning & Campbell, 1973).

At the same time, fads permit adolescents to express their individuality by being the first to use a new slang phrase or by wearing more and crazier charms on their bracelets. Fads such as calypso and rock-and-roll may also produce enjoyable tension. They may compensate for boredom and low morale—

especially for adolescents who are marking time until they become adults. Or fads can represent a pioneer spirit and a yearning for freedom from regimentation. A senior high school boy advances further explanation: "High school is a good time to act kind of crazy and get it out of your system. Sometimes we do things because they cost less money—and sometimes we do things just because it's fun. And then there's always a crowd who's out to get attention. . . ."

Logan (1978) conjectures regarding youth's apparently meaningless fads—"for example, stuffing phone booths, swallowing goldfish, lining up dominoes, streaking, participating in trivia contests, taking the longest shower" (p. 506): Certain fads have "elements of social satire and rebelliousness (for shock value); they may also be indulged in as an effort to cope with one of the core problems of identity—diffuse adolescence—meaninglessness—by trying to make it meaningful through the sheer force of commitment to the fad, by trying, as it were, to make a career of meaninglessness and thereby transform it into something else" (p. 506). Or fads may be viewed as simply another form of "intense, immediate experience—an escape from the struggle to find meaningfulness in a changing world" (p. 506).

CREATIVITY

Definition and Values of Creativity

It is fitting to conclude our discussion of mental development with a consideraton of creativity. Creativity may be defined as the capacity to recombine, with unusual sensitivity and spontaneity, the products of experience into new forms. Creativity is more than mere acquisition of further data; it implies new integration of the data. It "sees beyond the tasks which it is called upon to perform; it forges new connections; it develops novel and unique relationships; it creates unexpected and unanticipated syntheses" (Trachtman, 1975, p. 37).

Creativity enhances many values, as great artists testify. "It is only in creative work that joy may be found," wrote Robert Henri. And Robert Schumann wrote, "If ever I was happy at the piano it was when I was composing." The same pleasure, in fact, may stem from the smallest details of creative achievement. "One day I leapt for joy," recalls Stravinsky. "I had indeed found my title—Petroushka."

Creativity serves utilitarian functions as well. It provides the answers to the knotty problems of a complex world. It permits individuals, after they have acquired basic techniques, to strike out on their own into new territory. In today's rapidly changing world, more and more young people must be prepared to cope with the new and unfamiliar in creative ways. The knowledge explosion has brought to an end the day when anyone can feel well educated merely in terms of available knowledge.

Creative youth should be encouraged to develop their potential because newer technologies will rely on the expertise of such individuals for developing and maximizing the use of these miracles (Soon, exciting new ways, 1983). For example, various professionals—including accountants, lawyers, and doctors—by means of "artificial intelligence advisors or electronic data banks—will have at their finger tips the latest wisdom for diagnosing and solving problems" (p.

A19). Much of this sophsticated technology may simply be unused because society will not know what to do with it.

Traits of Creative People

Gruber (1981), in his case studies of scientists, observed that many were highly productive and creative, even in adolescence. When Einstein was just 16 he "imagines himself riding a beam of light. This empathetic image of the observer travelling with the thing observed was carried over into his mature theory of relativity" (p. 67). And Freeman Dyson, the physicist, tells "how, as an adolescent, he discovered calculus and spent the whole summer working like a madman, solving every problem in a big calculus textbook. After that calculus seemed to be almost instinctive" (p. 70). And Bertrand Russell, at the age of 15, began to write about his religious doubts, but since he was afraid they would upset his family he invented a "secret notation consisting of Greek letters and a phonetic spelling of English" (p. 70).

Gruber concluded that certain characteristics distinguish such highly creative people. One is that each is different, although almost all show certain characteristics, one being very hard work—indeed such individuals find their work great fun. They are also generally "strong, robust, and energetic" with an "overall sense of purpose, a feeling of where they are and where they want to go" (p. 69). In contrast to just ordinary people, who have a tendency to shut their eyes to problems that appear to them to be complex or almost unanswerable, they "favor a course of daring, of challenging the world" (p. 70). Creative individuals are also selective in their associates. Courage is another factor, "not only to say new, and possibly dangerous things that need saying, but also the courage to refashion one's personal world" (p. 70).

Other research showed that creative individuals possess to a greater than usual degree, ideational flexibility (open-mindedness), personal independence, and relative freedom from conventional restraint and restrictions. Gifted adolescent boys who scored in or above the 98th percentile in verbal or mathematical talents possessed a rare combination of originality, intelligence, perseverance, and a desire to please. They were interested, responsive students in class, and they were warm and friendly (but not just for the sake of sociability). They lacked any special concern about possessions or physical surroundings. In contrast, boys with low verbal or mathematics scores were "practical, realistic, matter of fact, [with] a natural head for business" (Viernstein, McGinn, & Hogan, 1977, p. 176). They were interested in "the mechanics of things," and were good at organizing.

Another essential for more sophisticated thought is detachment, yet adolescents' focus on "my goals" and "my experience" (p. 527) may result in a frame of mind that interprets "analytical reasoning" as "antihumanistic" (Logan & O'Hearn, 1982, p. 527). The detached researcher or observer is the one most likely to employ "abstract conceptual tools," because abstraction is essentially "a form of removal from the concrete here and now." The mode of thinking which confines the self to immediate surroundings and the present is "almost by definition a concrete thinking style" (p. 527). This self-centered thinking, "comprising as it does a one-perspective rather than a multiple-perspective focus," is more like "preoperational and concrete thought than formal operational thought . . ." (p. 527).

Elements Essential to Creativity

An element conducive to creativity is the appreciation of everyone's gifts and achievements, whatever their nature or level. The creative approach exists in every area, whether art, music, craftsmanship, human relations, or technology. The boy who produces shop projects, however crude at first, should be accorded the same approval as the one who writes poetry. Every individual must be convinced that he or she has some potential. However, the school as traditionally organized does not capitalize upon the nonverbal types of intelligence often found among students who have not had access to, or constant contact with, books. Schools often do not recognize the emergence of high intelligence and creative behavior in forms other than the abstract, verbal type long fostered by the school.

A second essential, especially for complex tasks, is freedom from anxiety. An atmosphere free from threat encourages flexibility in devising new solutions. Adolescents must feel assured that their efforts will not produce rebuke, hostility, or shock. Work groups should be organized to permit free flow of intellectual communication. Shy children should be protected from dominance of the overly aggressive or the too self-assured. A few "strong men" in a group can stifle initiative with as much force as an authoritarian parent. Adolescents, more than most people realize, are self-conscious and uncertain. They often affect brashness simply because they are in need of self-confidence.

Adolescents must also come to appreciate the advantages in becoming self-motivated. Creativity is essentially a self-actualizing process. Rube Goldberg once said in a television interview, "to create, you must have a little motor inside you." Constantly encouraging adolescents to think and do for themselves on increasingly difficult levels tends to set in motion the initiative required.

Highly creative individuals usually are not very sociable. However, they are generally neither antisocial nor asocial (Cropley, 1972). They simply have less than the usual regard for peer approval and less fear of negative evaluation. They are inner- rather than outer-directed, and they do not mind being the only ones to hold a particular opinion. That is, they are more concerned about problems that absorb them than in social evaluation.

Many characteristics of creative people are also found in healthy-minded individuals (Ward, Kogan & Pankove, 1972). They may be anxious, but their anxiety is quite different from that of personally disturbed neurotic persons. Their anxiety may simply represent discontent with their progress in comparison with their own self-expectations.

Environmental Climates Conducive to Creativity

It is rarely recognized that among the most disadvantaged students are talented individuals for whom curricular offerings are barely adequate. Often such individuals grow bored and discouraged; sometimes they drop out of school. Many of them fail to enter college at all because they have never been challenged, and they resign themselves to jobs which they do not find satisfying (Phelps, 1978). Despite this situation, few states have special programs for the gifted and talented. The challenge is twofold: how to distinguish and provide the elements of a climate conducive to achievement, and how to instruct youth so that creative talent will flourish.

Although giftedness is a critical factor in creative achievement, motivation to achieve is also necessary and is embedded within especially supportive environments. Family clearly plays a role in establishing the motivation to succeed. Parents who criticize their children and fail to reward successes appear to have children who are not interested in success (Freeman, 1979).

High achievement motivation and actual achievement of gifted children may derive partly from the high socioeconomic status of their families, which also correlates with achievement. Some investigators (Freeman, 1979) indicate that where socioeconomic status is controlled the personality advantages of gifted over average-IQ children disappears. That is, high economic status, rather than giftedness, accounts for the personality advantage. The peer group environment is not ordinarily conducive to creative thought. The typical high school group's interests are symbolized by football, a soda bottle, rock and roll, and popular singers. School is tolerated as a necessary evil, redeemed somewhat by being the place where one meets one's friends. Also, the peer situation allows but limited opportunity to test different roles in "nonthreatening, nonevaluating settings" (Wolf & Larson, 1981, p. 347). Neither society nor their peers will allow adolescents this experimentation when they are beginning to think seriously about future professions and programming their future lives. Thus, the sort of fantasy that might produce creative thinking is obstructed by reality testing of their plans. The school environment, too, offers little encouragement of creative activity, especially of less conventional kinds.

Engaging in apparently pointless time-wasting, silly behaviors is not always anti-intellectual in effect. Pfeiffer (1981) believes that such behaviors may serve a utilitarian purpose in the long run. He observes how certain of the wilder youth in other times might have had their "flings with drag races and games of chicken and sailing vessels, daring one another to go further and further out into unknown waters . . . ; and all the time they were tinkering with new boat designs and uncovering secrets of the sea" (p. 36). Over time the collective benefits of such apparently pointless explorations enabled people to leave their overpopulated homelands and migrate to new lands. As younger people continue to fritter away their time in apparently crazy behaviors and older people mutter about the "crumbling values of the younger generation," youth are opening up "a fantastic abundance of possibilities" (p. 38). Future generations, concludes Pfeiffer, will confront problems of an even more formidable magnitude than ours today; and "the readiness to do or believe practically anything, to indulge in the most far out of lunatic fringe behaviors, [becomes] a form of survival insurance." It insures flexibility and a capacity for adapting (p. 38).

Another little recognized fact is that the very process of growing up and becoming continuously confronted with the realities of life may reduce one's ability to fantasize in ways not congruent with immediate realities. In the stage of concrete operation, around 7 or 8 years, children can engage in certain logical reasoning processes within the context of applying specific operations to concrete events or objects in their immediate presence. In contrast, in the formal operations period of adolescence an individual becomes capable of hypothetical thinking and alternative solutions. It might be assumed, therefore, that the adolescent should become more creative than the child; however, the reverse is true (Wolf

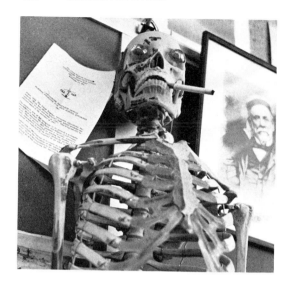

Engaging in pointless time-wasting, silly behavior is not always anti-intellectual. (Photo by Carl Purcell, National Education Association)

& Larson, 1981). There is an increasing relationship between formal thinking and creativity from early to middle adolescence but a drop after that, despite the greater egocentricity of children and their lesser ability to place themselves in another situation or take another point of view. Possibly the children's own cognitive limitations account for their apparently greater creativity since they make assumptions about reality which they do not change even when confronted with new and opposing evidence. In other words, "this ignorance of all the facts and the inability to change their opinions in light of new facts may help account for the unique and hence creative character of children's play fantasy and imagination" (p. 347).

FUTURE PERSPECTIVES

IQ and mental abilities in youth relate in various ways to outcomes in adulthood. Women in the Terman group cited previously, who had special mathematics ability as children and youth, proved to be more career-oriented than the average and to have more ambition and concern for excellence in work during their early and late adult years (Goleman, 1980b). On the other hand, Christopher Jencks (1979) found only slight correlations between IQ scores in school and successful performance in later years.

What happens to an individual's IQ after adolescence seems to depend on that individual's personality development and experience. In the Terman group, those individuals who became most successful appeared to become brighter as they grew older; the less successful group was still superior in intelligence to the general population, but their IQs did not increase as much (Goleman, 1980b). Ambition in successful men has been found to be a constant theme in their lives. They are more self-confident, have greater perseverance and are more goal oriented.

Critics of traditional intelligence tests have argued that their results do not necessarily predict what young people are capable of doing in the years ahead. They propose that these tests be replaced or supplemented by measurements of coping skills, social intelligence, cognitive style, learning potential, electrical responses of the brain, and audiovisual perception. Tests for entrance into professional schools would thus measure human dimensions, including sensitivity. For example, business-school students would be asked to respond as "supervisors to video-taped employers who present problems like requests for raises or promotions" (Rice, 1979, p. 37). Students would also be tested for their cognitive style and problem-solving strategies and be counseled to choose careers that capitalize on their personal approach.

Looking toward the future, youth should become increasingly concerned about the life of the mind and more sophisticated in developing its potential. In years to come, as machines assume the most burdensome tasks, their minds and energies for all their future lives will be freed up for satisfying and fulfilling kinds of experience (Rogers, 1982). Already, the by-products of technology have exposed adolescents to a much greater amount of information and intellectual stimulation than earlier youth experienced. The lengthened preparation required prolongs dependence on parents and the state but, at the same time, allows a longer period for gaining perspective on the future.

In the future it will become even more important to learn how to utilize the products of technology to enhance individual mental performance (Age of miracles, 1983). Even now laboratories of certain companies have devised "computers that talk, televisions that pull in hundreds of channels, and telephones small enough to be worn on the wrist but able to handle calls from anywhere in the world" (p. A19). People using computers may issue commands by voice and the computer will reply in "everyday language" (Soon, exciting new ways 1983). Researchers are also investigating means of linking computers to the brain

In the future it will become even more important to learn how to utilize the products of technology. (Courtesy of Public Relations Office, State University of New York at Oswego)

"with information carried on radio sequences tuned to a person's brain waves" (p. A19). Often the medium for transferring information will be light instead of wire or air, riding a laser beam traversing very thin transparent glass filaments or optical fibers (Soon, exciting new ways, 1983). Those individuals who, as youth have developed traits of curiosity, openness to the new, and flexibility will be best positioned to take advantage of such developments.

SUMMARY

Although considerable interest has been shown in children's thinking in past decades, the adolescent's mental development has only recently become a focus of interest. An appraisal of the research in this area requires a knowledge of certain terms: Intelligence refers to the capacity of an individual to act purposefully, to think rationally, and to deal effectively with his or her environment. A related term, ability, comprises not only intelligence but such factors as attitudes, persistence, endurance, and accumulated learning experience. Another concept, creativity, involves those aspects of intelligence that permit a person to discover novel solutions to problems. Many tests have been designed to measure intelligence, but such tests have certain limitations. For one thing, there are problems of standardization, notably in finding a random sampling of the population. For another, total scores, however valid, are less revealing than the subscores that contribute to them. Finally, intelligence testing fails to reflect the importance of such personality traits as self-confidence and independence in the learning process.

There is general agreement about the overall pattern of mental growth from birth until adolescence. Intelligence rises rapidly at first and continues to increase, although at a declining rate, into the teens. Precisely when the peak of intelligence occurs or when the plateau in adult intelligence turns into a decline is still widely debated. Probably there is no single peak age for the onset of such decline. In the meantime, certain cognitive functions move toward greater differentiation, while others attain greater synthesis.

Certain generalizations lend perspective to the normal growth pattern just described. This pattern represents norms from presumably randomly selected persons at successive age levels. It does not indicate how individuals of the same age vary among themselves or how a particular individual's growth pattern will proceed. Also, this composite pattern tends to obscure whatever relatively discrete stages, if any, exist in the course of mental development. Some authorities, notably Piaget, believe that such stages do exist. Others doubt both the validity and usefulness of stage theory. Many studies suggest that distinctive stages in cognitive development do indeed exist and that sequences of mental development are relatively well defined. However, the ages at which individuals pass through the stages are subject to sociocultural modifications. Certain critics also point out that many individuals never arrive at the formal operational stage, while some achieve a still higher problem-finding level. Finally, some individuals leapfrog over stages through which others crawl laboriously.

The adolescent's mental characteristics and development relate to many factors, one being heredity. However, authorities differ greatly concerning the significance heredity has on mental performance. Changes in IQ may occur even in adulthood, but to what extent they are genetically programmed or influenced by environment is uncertain. Mental growth also differs for the sexes, despite considerable overlap in distribution of scores. Certain sex differences—for example, the male's characteristic activity drive and aggressiveness—may be genetically based. Other sex differences in mental performance derive from sexually differentiated patterns of childrearing. Those individuals reared more like girls develop considerable passivity and dependence and do well in subjects like language and spelling, which depend on rules. However, boys and more masculine girls are more creative and independent in their thinking. Mental achievement cannot take place without a supportive environment, and societies generally, including ours, are more supportive of boys' intellectual efforts. Recently, increasing emphasis has been placed on the overall impact of environment on mental development, including all sociocultural effects. The quality of school environment, in particular, may influence such development, often in indirect but significant ways. All the foregoing factors interact and operate so complexly that it is difficult to assess the influence of specific factors.

Members of both sexes differ among themselves in cognitive style—special ways of perceiving, organizing, and labeling dimensions of their environments. Such styles may be labeled in various ways—for example, as field-dependent or field-independent, concrete or abstract. Recognition of such differences in style, both for the sexes and for individuals, is necessary if adolescents are to realize fully their mental potential. Also basic to such realization is the proper structuring of life experience. If the groundwork for ultimate development of mental potential was laid properly from earliest years, the period of early adolescence could prove far more productive than it normally does.

Certain adolescents have special problems with mental development—for instance, the bright individual who often feels no real challenge. Some critics contend that bright youth manage to achieve in spite of, not because of, the quality of their school experience. Other adolescents with special problems include mentally subnormal and poorly motivated individuals and those whose early learning experiences were so ineffective that they always lag far behind their classmates. Still other adolescents who lag behind are the lower-class youth, who often lack encouragement from their parents and proper facilities for preparing their homework.

The results of adolescent mental development include skills, attitudes, interests, and creativity. A wide range of skills is of special help to adolescents in their adjustment. For example, reading skills are necessary to efficient learning, and motor skills are essential to progress in athletics and social adjustment. Attitudes provide favorable or unfavorable orientation to objects and events and a readiness to respond in a particùalr manner to those objects and events. Individuals' attitudes influence their receptiveness to learning and the actions that they will take toward everything they do in life. Such attitudes are continuously in the process of revision, as indicated especially by national polls and longitudinal research.

Closely related to attitudes are interests, which suggest favorable inclinations toward an activity and a desire to participate in it. Adolescents' interests tend to be introspective, egoistic, social, serious, and less active than those of children; they focus especially on certain areas, such as music, television, special interests, and hobbies. A particular type of adolescent interest is a fad, which is a sporadic fashion. Fads are temporary and unpredictable, and they are particularly popular with teenagers. Fads and interests vary according to individual, sex, youth subgroups, and the times.

Perhaps intellectual activity in its highest form is represented by creativity, which is the capacity to recombine the products of experience into new forms with unusual spontaneity and sensitivity. It represents more than mere acquisition of further data; instead, it suggests a new integration of data. Creative individuals possess such traits as spontaneity, independence, sense of humor, and capacity for feeling. Certain environments are far more conducive to creativity than others. Neither traditional socialization processes, the peer environment, nor typical school curricula are especially supportive of creative behaviors. A truly congenial intellectual environment is characterized by freedom from anxiety and appreciation of every individual's gifts and achievements, whatever their nature or level.

DISCUSSION QUESTIONS
AND ACTIVITIES

1. Discuss measures that might be taken at home and in school to create a climate more favorable to adolescents' mental development.
2. The instructor may demonstrate how an individual intelligence test is given to an adolescent or administer a group test of intelligence to the class. At the conclusion of the test, discuss the results.
3. Write an anonymous paragraph exploring your own interests and some of the factors you think shaped them. A committee may analyze and summarize all the paragraphs and report to the class. What influences seem to have been most important? Is the general feeling among the students one of satisfaction or dissatisfaction with their interests?
4. Discuss the following topics as they relate to the education of bright children: (a) traits needed by their teacher; (b) merits of special classes or homogeneous grouping.
5. Discuss the effect on adolescents' mental development of the following: (a) television; (b) reading matter on newsstands; (c) digest magazines; (d) the public's attitude toward education; (e) typical modes of instruction.
6. If you have been given an IQ test on some occasion and were told your score, describe on an unsigned sheet of paper the conditions under which you were tested, how much guidance (or lack of it) accompanied your being told your IQ, and your reactions to your IQ standing. A committee may compile the results and report to the class.
7. Describe learning situations that you have found either unusually stimulating or the opposite.
8. Should adolescent social development be de-emphasized in favor of mental development? If so, to what degree, and how?
9. Examine and discuss several well-known tests of interests, attitudes, and intelligence designed for the adolescent level.
10. Evaluate the attitude of present-day adolescents toward, and their aptitude for, mental achievement. What, if any, modifications in their attitudes are needed to ensure effective development of their mental potential?
11. What are the advantages or disadvantages of students' being told their intelligence-test scores?
12. What do you consider to be your own creative abilities? What have you done, or what might you do, to develop them effectively?

SUGGESTED READINGS

Adamson, W. C. (1982). The gifted child: A psychodynamic profile. *Journal of Developmental & Behavioral Pediatrics, 3*(3), 170–178. A psychodynamic profile of the gifted child is developed, along with social, psychological, and cultural determinants that impact on their personality development.

Baker, C. D. (1982). The adolescent as theorist: An interpretive view. *Journal of Youth and Adolescence. 11*(3), 167–181. The conception of the adolescent as theorist stresses the practical and intermittent nature of youth's theoretical activity; theorizing becomes a part of identity and "world-building" work.

Davis, D. D. & Friedrich, D. D. (1983). Memory performance of young, middle, and old adults. *International Journal of Aging and Human Development, 16*(3), 311–324. A comparison of young, middle-aged, and older adults on memory tasks showed minor age-related differences as well as differences in structural capacity and organizational strategies in all three groups.

Flavell, J. H. (1982). On cognitive development. *Child Development, 53,* 1–10. The research concerning cognitive development is reviewed to determine to what degree such development is stagelike and to what extent it is homogeneous at specific stages.

Kerr, B. (1983). Raising the career aspirations of gifted girls. *Vocational Guidance Quarterly,* 1983, *32*(1), 37–43. This brief report concerns a study of the effects of a one-day comprehensive career guidance laboratory on the career aspirations of twenty-five gifted girls and twenty-five gifted boys.

King, P. M., Kitchener, K. S., Davison, M. L., Parker, C. A., & Wood, P. K. (1983). The justification of beliefs in young adults: A longitudinal study. *Human Development, 26,* 106–116. A two-year longitudinal study of adolescents and adults, tested on the Reflective Judgment Interview and the Concept Mastery Test, supported seven hypothesized shifts in epistemic assumptions over time.

Konopka, G. (1983). Adolescent suicide. *Exceptional Children, 49*(5), 390–394. The problem of adolescent suicide is discussed in relation to causes and modes of prevention.

Kramer, D. A. (1983). Post-formal operations? A need for further conceptualization. *Human Development,* 1983, *26*(2), 91–105. The question is considered whether the formal operational stage of cognitive development is the highest level or is another, more advanced stage needed to account for certain advanced forms of thought.

Linn, M. C., deBenedictis, T., & Delucchi, K. (1982). Adolescent reasoning about advertisements: Preliminary investigations. *Child Development, 53*(6), 1599–1613. In research among seventh and eighth graders competence factors related just slightly to reasoning about advertising, and performance factors suggested when adolescents use critical thinking and what rules of evidence they employ.

Logan, R. D. & O'Hearn, G. T. (1982). Thought-style and life-style: Some hypothesized relationships. *Science Education, 66*(4), 515–530. Changes in the culture are related to changes in life style as well as their consequent effect on reasoning skills and thought styles.

Menge, C. P. (1982). Dream and reality: Constructive change partners. *Adolescence, 17*(66), 419–440. Through employing analysis of ideals of past, present and the projected future, the argument is made that dreaming and imagination are not a waste of time but can be a meaningful part of life.

Monks, F. J. & Ferguson, T. J. (1983). Gifted adolescents: An analysis of their psychosocial development. *Journal of Youth and Adolescence, 12*(1), 1–18. A review of the literature discloses a positive view of gifted adolescents' social adjustment; however, the narrow scope of existing research on this topic prevents firm conclusions.

Paulsen, K. & Johnson, M. (1983). Sex-role attitudes and mathematical ability in 4th-, 8th-, and 11th-grade students from a high socioeconomic area. *Developmental Psychology, 4*(3), 19. This study of differences in sex-role attitudes and mathematical ability of children and adolescents of high socioeconomic status indicated differences according to sex-role attitudes and personal characteristics.

Silber, T. J. (1982). The differential diagnosis of functional symptoms in adolescence. *Adolescence, 17*(68), 769–778. Functional disorders of youth are discussed according to definition, classification, and techniques for the management of such conditions.

Wattanawaha, N. & Clements, M. A. (1982). Qualitative aspects of sex-related differences in performances on pencil-and-paper spatial questions, Grades 7–9. *Journal of Educational Psychology, 74*(6), 878–887. An analysis of the performance on spatial questions of Australian seventh to ninth graders indicated male superiority but that the manner of testing was also important.

Chapter Six

Moral And Religious Development

CONCEPTS AND DEFINITIONS

A human being's relationship to the universe is described in terms of morals, values, ideals, religion, and philosophy of life, all of which interrelate and overlap. Adequate orientation to this chapter requires a working definition of each of these concepts.

Morals are standards of right and wrong, determined for individuals by the values of the culture of which `they are a part. Moral behavior, in turn, embraces actions of social concern. Behaviors judged to be ultimately conducive to social advantage are called moral and right; those judged to be adverse to the social welfare are called immoral and wrong. These judgments are made by dominant groups that serve as arbiters; hence, the judgment that a behavior is moral indicates that it conforms to the standards of the arbiting groups. Since what is held to be good for a society depends upon situational factors and upon traditions, the nature of morality varies from time to time and from place to place.

People's morals are reflected in their values and ideals. *Values* refer to the relative worth attached to objects and behaviors. A value favorable to its object would result in positive reactions; the opposite attitude would lead to negative ones. Persons who value education expend money and time to support it. Those who do not value it vote down school bonds and deny their children funds for college. Values vary greatly in intensity. Individuals may react strongly or mildly to matters of honesty. Some administrators expel from school students who cheat; others simply lower their grades. Values also may range from the fully conscious to the completely unconscious. A teenage boy may know he values masculinity, but he refuses to acknowledge, even to himself, how much he values security.

Ideals, like values, predispose the individual toward positive or negative action, but they are more abstract than values. Ideals represent standards of perfection that extend youth's reach to more distant horizons. One may hold ideals of honesty in a particular setting. A youth may rob the public towel dispenser for the gang's picnic without violating a personal ideal of honesty. According to his code, public property is anybody's property.

Personal *religion* is harder to define. The religion of some individuals is little different from their philosophy of life; both account for their relation to the universe. Religion is a more conventional interpretation than a personal philosophy of life; it represents a system of attitudes, practices, rites, ceremonies, and beliefs, defining the individual's relation to God or a supernatural realm.

PATTERNS OF MORAL DEVELOPMENT

The early psychoanalytic concept of superego (conscience) development provides an underpinning for any current study of moral development. Nevertheless, this idea omits certain of the dynamic and structural complexities involved. It stresses the formation of the superego through identification with the same-sex parent but omits subsequent developments. By contrast, Piaget's (1948) account of moral development emphasizes changes in the logical structure of moral reasoning through childhood. From a similar frame of reference, Kohlberg (1975) portrays moral reasoning as developing through certain main stages. The first, or preconventional stage, involves relatively egocentric, or self-centered, concepts of right and wrong concerning what one can do without getting caught, or what leads to greatest personal gratification. In the second stage of conventional morality, in late childhood, good and evil are first identified with concepts of "good girl" and "good boy," which, in turn, are allied with social standards of law and order. In this stage, individuals may not behave according to their perceptions of right and wrong, but neither do they question the fact that morality is immutable and objective, deriving from parental edicts, community standards, or divine laws. The third level of moral development is post-conventional, which Kohlberg calls the ethical stage. It involves a reasoning more abstract than at earlier stages and may produce a clash between personal and conventional standards. In this postconventional stage, the individual becomes an adherent of personal principles, transcending not only conventional morality but even a social contract. In this sense, the social contract represents an agreement that members of the society enter into for their common good; it is, therefore, subject to alteration or revocation. Those who—and many never do—attain postconventional levels generally do so during late adolescence. In recent years Kohlberg (1977) has identified a still higher stage, somewhat like Erikson's (1959) stage of integrity. This concept connotes coming to terms with the self and developing interpersonal commitments within the more comprehensive historical and social frames of reference.

Apparently, most individuals never proceed beyond the conventional level. However, perhaps it is better that way. Society depends for its stability and "continuity on a certain cohesiveness and on the masses respecting its dictate. Modifications of morality and values, made necessary or desirable by changing times, can be affected by the minority who do achieve the post-conventional level and who, fortunately, possess greater intelligence and insight than the average person" (Rogers, 1982, p. 411).

A longitudinal study which followed the same individuals from early adolescence through middle adulthood supported Kohlberg's theory (Colby, Gibbs, Kohlberg & Lieberman, 1983). The subjects' moral development proceeded according to Kohlberg's stages and their respective moral levels persisted throughout this period, supporting Kohlberg's view that moral development possesses considerable internal consistency even while it continuously evolves into higher levels.

There have been various criticisms of Kohlberg's theory. The most significant challenge for Kohlberg's theory, concludes Damon (1983), is the relationship of his findings to "real life morality" (p. 283). That is, do individuals' expressions of moral views carry over into everyday events? To what degree "are they largely an intellectual exercise, unconnected to the subjects' social behavior?" (p. 283). Another objection is that stages 5 and 6 do not represent stages so much as they do individual differences. From this point of view stage 5 represents an orientation toward social welfare and stage 6 toward individualistic concerns. In effect, Kohlberg has simply dropped stage 6 and has revised stage 5 to encompass some of stage 6, thus including both individualistic and societal orientations. That is, he acknowledges that individual differences in moral judgment may derive from personality characteristics instead of a developmental stage.

Joseph Adelson feels that Kohlberg's work appealed because his ideal of arriving at a high level of morality would indicate a "greater maturity and purity of spirit" (p. 64). However, Kohlberg's stage 6, in which people put their own personal principles above all else, tends to sanction "unbridled individualism," and places it above the social contract (stage 5) in which individuals give precedence to society's conclusions about morality.

Muson perceives the manner in which Kohlberg derived his theory as flawed. His concept of stages of moral development is derived from having children react to certain moral dilemmas. These dilemmas are portrayed in stories that represent certain values important to the society. Authorities holding other values would interpret these moral dilemmas in such manner that different pictures of development would emerge. Besides, an individual's moral judgments of stories such as those used in Kohlberg's tests may not be a valid indicator of that person's own morality; that is, there is a gap between adolescents' moral judgments and behaviors. Also, some people cannot be placed in one stage or another, because some responses embrace several stages at once. The question also arises: Does the progression always proceed in only one way? At times people appear to regress to earlier levels (Muson, 1979).

The question also arises: Is each higher moral stage, as proposed by Kohlberg, a better stage? (Callahan & Callahan, 1981) Is fear of punishment, at the lowest end of Kohlberg's scale, of little worth as a form of ethical behavior? Kohlberg assumes that morality is somehow autonomous, universal, and impersonal.

Others object that Kohlberg's stage theory, which was derived from studying males, is inappropriate for assessing females' maturity. Females score lower than males in Kohlberg's moral interviews. Most often, says Gilligan (1982), women score at stage 3, which is based on the social-relational perspective. Thus women would be lower than men on Kohlberg's scale because men often score at stages 4 and 5. However, Gilligan argues that women's morality probably should not be measured on Kohlberg's scale since their moral problems and developmental experiences are different. From early childhood girls are taught to be nurturant and concerned about others' welfare. Boys, on the other hand, are encouraged to become independent of others, to acquire moral rules regarding their conduct, and to reconcile conflicts between their own and others' interests and values. Hence, women's interpersonal concern is neither superior nor inferior to men's more formal morality. Other research indicates little difference between men's and women's moral development, even on Kohlberg's scale. What little difference is shown tends almost to disappear when educational and occupational backgrounds are controlled (Walker, 1983).

This writer would explain any reported sex differences in this manner. According to the way women were reared traditionally and performed their adult roles, the social-relational perspective of stage 3 naturally emerged and was more functional, as women's role has been traditionally interpreted. However, in recent years as modes of rearing girls and women's adult roles have dramatically changed, the difference would tend to disappear, if, as Walker points out, educational and occupational backgrounds are controlled (Walker, 1983).

A new stage 7, proposed by Kohlberg, seeks to answer the question: why be moral? Is there some transcendent religious morality of love which would cause one to "seek some ongoing and ultimate order in the universe" (p. 86). Those who attained this last stage would recognize some universal natural law of morality, above and beyond cultural relativism. Moral education would no longer amount to indoctrination into currently prevailing mores but be a type of education "universal in its ethical content and rooted in respect for justice and individual human dignity" (p. 87).

This writer would make this observation. What anyone decides is universally and naturally good is modified by personal and sociocultural background. Perhaps the ideal can more nearly be approximated as the world's peoples learn to communicate with each other and to understand each others' views and needs.

Morality of Adolescence

SIGNIFICANCE   Questions about morals acquire heightened significance at adolescence. Teenagers are confronted by many new problems for which they are not prepared, such as those related to drinking, sex, and driving. They are expected to make decisions and to accept the consequences of their choices. While allowances are often made for them because of their age, they find it hard to live down a serious mistake. Meanwhile, books, teachers, and friends bring them into contact with sharply conflicting views, and their own increased intellectual powers stimulate them to test moral boundaries. At the same time, they are largely cut off from the guidance they need, for youthful groups are somewhat insulated from the larger society. Their cars enable them to leave the areas where they are recognized. No chaperones accompany them; they have freedom other generations of youth never had.

Factors Influencing the Adolescent's Morals

PARENTAL INFLUENCES   By adolescence, morals already have been shaped by a complex of factors, especially family experience. For the very reason that moral values are basic, parents tend to take a firm hand, denying their offsprings' self-determination in this area. As a result, adolescents and their parents are more alike in matters of morality than either generation realizes. Vern Bengtson and Alan Acock asked middle-aged parents and their 16- to 26-year-old children their views about various issues and also asked the children to predict how their parents would reply (Misunderstood parents, 1978). Parents were much less conservative in their views than their children had expected, and on some issues the parents were more liberal than their children. The only exception was an item about marijuana on which the parents were less liberal than their children believed they were. While there was no significant correlation between the actual views of parents and children, what the children thought their parents believed was strongly predictive of the opinions the children actually held. The researchers speculated that parents may deliberately represent their attitudes as more conservative than they are so that their children will adhere to more traditional behaviors. Even somewhat radical youth ordinarily are not in conflict with their parents; liberal parents have a high proportion of liberal children (Fengler & Wood, 1973).

Often values in the home are portrayed as unambiguous; in reality youth may find themselves exposed to parents whose value systems are in conflict. Here several youths describe their own situation:

> MALE: I was positively affected by the similarities in my parents' views because I was not constantly torn between two conflicting viewpoints, not knowing which to follow.
>
> MALE: The difference in my parents' views helped me to see things in different ways. Sometimes this may have caused anxiety; but overall it may have proved very beneficial.
>
> FEMALE: When it came to my parents' differences in views concerning me I was most affected in religion and dating. My mother was raised Baptist and my father Roman Catholic. My sisters and I were baptized Catholic; however there were problems. About ten years ago we all changed to Episcopalian; now all is well. When it came to dating, Mom was more eager than Dad for me to start. Maybe because I was the oldest he felt it hard to let go.

It is said that many parents have become uncertain about their own moral standards, hence, are poor role models in this regard. The combination of rapid change and diverse codes in a pluralistic society contributes to this uncertainty. Adults' conflict, in turn, becomes reflected in competing values in family, school, and society (A new generation, 1976).

Apparently parents and their adolescent children affect each other in terms of their respective stages of moral development. In a study of 30 urban family triads, each triad consisting of a mother, a father, and a son within the 10- to 13-year range, half the sons had already reached the moral judgment stage of one or both parents, which suggests that a high percentage of the sons would eventually surpass their parents in moral judgment. The sons' moral judgment level was higher than average, perhaps because of their high socioeconomic background. Some made principled statements though none had reached the fully principled level, which ordinarily must await the broader role-taking experiences of adulthood. Parental involvement with their sons' moral development often involved conflict and tension, but was more typical where sons at higher moral levels were involved.

Theorists believe that parental views in such matters are influenced somewhat by the child's, but the effect of parent on child is probably greater than the reverse because of the parent's greater power. Anyhow, the process varies among different categories of parent. In this study principled parents held longer family conversations with their sons than did the conventional parents and more often compromised in their childrearing methods. Principled parents also interacted more with their sons and revised their views to a certain extent after hearing their sons' views, in consequence, reaching some compromise. Conventional parents often reasoned with their sons but did not consider their son's views as frequently; nor did sons of more conventional parents receive as much time in family discussion.

The sons in higher moral stages had a warmer relationship with their parents than did the other sons. They gave more attention to their parents' views and engaged in more reasoning in the family discussion. They were less likely to lie to their parents, which indicated a greater mutual understanding between them and their parents (Buck, Walsh & Rotham, 1981).

COLLEGE EXPERIENCE   Another important influence on moral development is college experience. Often the values adolescents have learned from their parents are seriously challenged when they reach the university, with its stress on objectivity and its "questioning of taken-for-granted assumptions about life which the parents have spent all the previous years inculcating into them. As one student put it, 'When I came here the world was all one piece and ordered; now, as I leave it, it seems very fragmented and disjointed. All that couldn't have happened in just four years' " (Gunter & Moore, 1975, p. 203). Here, too, youth become exposed to varied life styles and values, including "rejection of materialism, exploration of drugs, dress—as symbols of revolt and rejection, sex—open rather than concealed—and activist politics, of a style the parents never experienced" (p. 203).

College experience also importantly affects the level of moral maturity ultimately achieved. The evidence suggests that adults in general advance little beyond what may be explained by level of education. Adults prove more heterogeneous than student groups in level of moral judgment because of broad educational backgrounds that are controlled in student groups. Few adults employ chiefly principled moral considerations in stages five and six when making moral decisions (Rest, Davison & Robbins, 1978).

An important influence on moral development is college experience. (Courtesy of Public Relations Office, State University of New York at Oswego)

MILITARY SERVICE   Many factors related to military service, in addition to cross-cultural contacts, significantly influence an individual's morals and values. Note these testimonies about the effect of military service:

> It broadened my horizons and made me realize that there are other things to consider in life besides my own welfare.

> It helped me to realize the plight of other people more intimately; it also broadened my knowledge of myself through being placed in a foreign and unplanned-for environment.

> The service taught me to take care of myself—washing, ironing, cooking, housekeeping, sewing, etc. It also taught me the value of an education, which motivated me to do well in college.

PART-TIME WORK EXPERIENCE   Part-time jobs, often portrayed as character builders, may have the reverse effect considering the types of jobs that teenagers hold—for example food service, retail sales, manual labor, and clerical jobs.

There are certain important potential sources of job dissatisfaction and undesirable behaviors among youthful workers. First, many work at technically unsophisticated and menial jobs. In one study (Greenberger, Steinberg & Vaux, 1981) regardless of job type, sweeping floors and carrying objects from one place to another were the two activities most frequently observed. An insignificant percentage of teenagers' time was spent at such developmental tasks as job training, informal discussion, and contact with supervisors or adults. A second complex of factors encouraging deviance involves stressful environmental conditions including time pressure, exposure to noise, and uncomfortable temperatures. Third, since they are relatively untrained, adolescents may be closely supervised and have no part in decisions about their work. Fourth, occupational deviance may be encouraged in settings characterized by little social support. In a survey of teenage workers the majority reported feeling less close to their coworkers and work supervisors than to almost any other persons in their lives (Greenberger, Steinberg, Vaux & McAuliffe, 1980). Fifth, occupational deviance thrives in situations where pay is perceived to be low. Teenagers typically work for low wages and may feel entitled to such extra compensation as theft may provide. Finally, the work setting may be set up so as to encourage crime. For example, material goods are often within easy reach and a considerable amount of money may change hands.

There are various ways of interpreting adolescent workers' deviance. Such deviance may "validate membership in a peer culture" (p. 441). It is more common when there is a positive social environment—that is, when adolescents work in the company of their peers and spend considerable time unsupervised (Greenberger & Steinberg, 1980). The company of same-age coworkers may provide both motivation and support for their activities. Such common deviant activities as working while intoxicated and giving away goods "serve to bond adolescents; drinking and drug use are social activities, and recipients of giveaways are often other teenagers" (p. 442).

An alternative explanation is that deviance is a reaction to job stress caused by job dissatisfaction and poor working conditions. However, these investigators found little evidence to support that hypothesis, especially in cases of nontheft deviance.

Worker characteristics are a significant factor in the incidence of deviance; however, the higher frequency of male than female theft at work is consistent with sex differences in delinquency in general. Interestingly, findings regarding the importance of attitudes are mixed. It would seem that an individual's feeling that certain forms of deviance are acceptable would relate to commission of that deviance, but this study indicated no such relationship. Possibly occupational deviance is "so familiar and so often winked at that an individual's general tolerance of unethical practices is not a sound predictor of what he or she personally does on the job" (p. 443). This writer suggests a parallel analogy: People with relatively high moral standards do not look on themselves as lawbreakers when they jaywalk because of generally casual attitudes toward it.

Additional predictors of worker deviance are an individual's materialism, as well as a young person's cynical attitude about the intrinsic value of work. Cynical workers are more inclined "to lie to their employer, vandalize property and thumb their collective nose at conventions by working while under the influence of alcohol or drugs" (p. 443).

The broad finding that the workplace provides chances for occupational deviance which adolescents exploit may not surprise the reader, but "what *is* surprising is that so many youth policy experts fail to anticipate this outcome" (p. 444). Various national panels have insisted that work eases the transition to adulthood by teaching youth socially approved attitudes and allowing them to perform socially valued tasks. They have tended to buy the notion that working is a deterrent to teenage delinquency. They have not acknowledged the possibility that working encourages at least certain forms of youth deviance.

The study also concluded that employment does not discourage deviance outside the workplace. Rather, it may encourage such deviance, in addition to that on the job. Thus, occupational deviance seems to "supplement rather than substitute for other forms of crime and delinquency" (p. 444).

This writer is quite impressed by the preceding study but adds the following: In many classes in adolescent psychology, she has asked students to write anonymous reports about their part-time work experience, and overwhelmingly they have reported the effects on them to have been positive. Perhaps both overall and long-term effects of holding part-time jobs in youth should be studied for better perspective on the problems cited above.

SEX ROLE   Another significant factor in moral development is sex role. Girls are more precocious in terms of introjecting adult-approved standards. Nevertheless, girls' acceptance of parental standards assumes different forms in early and late adolescence. Younger girls accept parental direction unself-consciously, seldom questioning its correctness; whereas older ones offer reasons for identifying with their parents' point of view. Older girls may assume in fantasy the role of mother and seek to justify views that they will soon be required to defend.

By contrast, boys proceed toward moral maturity in broken-field fashion, often by trial and error. They pose as ad hoc critics of whatever moral dilemmas they meet, often questioning and testing the limits. They may ultimately arrive at the same conclusions that many girls adopted somewhat earlier. But who is the more mature? It could be argued that each sex develops according to the moral pattern better suited to its future role of mother or father.

It should be added that the effect of the women's liberation movement on girls' values is still uncertain. College women, at least, reject the idea that they are any more unthinking and compliant in accepting values than are men. In any case, both sexes, after graduating and having children, will modify their views somewhat because of their status as adults and the so-called parenting effect. As they shift from the role of youth to the role of those charged with developing the morals of yet another generation of youth, they correspondingly become somewhat less innovative and more conservative.

PERSONAL ROLE   An individual's role—for example, whether instructor or student—may result in different moral judgments of behaviors. At a southwestern state university fifteen behaviors that faculty members judged to be dishonest were also judged dishonest by undergraduates, but there was no complete consensus on any one item (Eve & Bromley, 1981). Students showed considerable ignorance regarding various academic norms, notably "copying material without footnoting" and "adding sources not read to the bibliography." Certain common forms of cheating, such as copying answers, received greatest agreement; whereas "gray areas," such as submitting the same paper several times or feigning illness, produced greatest disagreement. Initiating and active behaviors were regarded as more dishonest than supporting behaviors—for instance, 90 percent believed it dishonest to copy papers during a test but just 79 percent thought that giving answers was dishonest. All but a few (89 percent) called submitting a paper written by another person dishonest, but just 77 percent called the student who loaned the paper dishonest.

The cheating practice was pervasive—just 37 percent had never cheated during their college careers and 22 percent said they had cheated on five or more occasions. Nor could their dishonesty be charged to ignorance of academic norms. For example, most of those who copied answers during a test also rated it as dishonest.

The writers suggested several ways of reducing cheating. One was to hold better college admission screening procedures to insure that students be capable of performing at an acceptable level. Colleges should not stress social involvement in contrast to intellectual involvement which becomes a "temptation in the face of declining enrollments [and] a buyer's market" (p. 19). It is also unclear "whether colleges and universities are capable or desirous of establishing a more monastic, aesthetic quality of existence . . ." (p. 19). Thus "cheating may be an acceptable price to pay to avoid a campus of students living in an egoistic, socially isolated pattern with over-zealous superegos and attendant psychosomatic disorders. Perhaps our pursuit of the cheating-free school should follow the ancient maxim, 'all things in proportion and nothing in excess' " (p. 20). The present writer suggests instead that faculty members continually strive to develop in students the personal integrity that would not allow them to cheat.

PEER INFLUENCE   Youth's views are also strongly modified by those of their peers. At this stage, adolescents' peers and parents constitute for them "contrasting social worlds" (Montemayor, 1982, p. 1517). The time spent with parents focuses on such social and home activities as shopping, eating, performing chores, playing games, or talking. About one and a half hours of free time are spent with parents each day, mostly watching television for which adolescents care little, because it is essentially a passive experience.

The effect of time spent with parents or with peers is complementary, in that both provide socializing experiences. The time spent with their parents focuses on completing instrumental activities, fulfilling duties, and attaining a sense of responsibility. In contrast, unstructured free hours spent with their peers afford opportunities for developing role-taking skills (Youniss, 1980). The differences in what they do with parents and peers explains why adolescents prefer to be with their peers. Time spent with peers involves egalitarian relationships and shared interests, which is more rewarding than task-oriented hierarchical relationships with their middle-aged parents.

These differences in life style of parents and their adolescent children cause them to interpret the morality of behaviors from different perspectives. Then, when bickering results, the young people take refuge in their peer group, relying on its standards and rejecting those of their parents (Hill, 1980).

COMMUNICATIONS MEDIA   Among more subtle influences on adolescent morals are media of communication; and their effectiveness is acknowledged by efforts at censorship. Do their views represent healthy alternatives or rival hypocrisies battling for immature minds? Comic books are berated for their emphasis on violence. Newspapers are scored for playing up the bad and the sensational and thus encouraging the idea that evil predominates in the world. Television has been charged with making the viewer callous to distress. Its commercials are blamed for elements of hedonism (the compulsive pursuit of personal pleasure) and programs that stress individual pleasure. Thus people begin to seek self-gratification, simple solutions to complex problems, and escape from firm self-discipline. Research on this question is still inconclusive. Communications media are changing so fast that large-scale research studies are out of date before they are completed. It is also difficult to determine the significance of research findings for individual adolescents. Every adolescent sees something different when he or she watches movies or television, depending on personal tastes and background. A boy with antisocial impulses concentrates on the way the hero handles a gun. His sister may be hardly aware of the gun but notes how he succumbs to the wiles of the heroine.

"THE TIMES"   Kohlberg's longitudinal research since the 1950s illustrates the effect of the times on values. During this period the country has experienced student protests, the civil rights movement, Watergate, the Vietnam War, and the woman's movement, all of which have involved issues of justice, and focused the country's attention on moral matters. Since these events have undoubtedly modified concepts of justice, changes in moral judgments over the past three decades reflect changes in cultural concepts of fairness as well as development of individuals' moral concepts. Individuals who lived through these decades of change under varying cultural conditions, acquired different concepts of justice. In such cases adults might appear to regress rather than progress in their moral development (Rest et al., 1978).

Smith (1983) believes that "modern urban life, with its segregated roles and bureaucratic impersonality, leaves notorious deficits in occasions for true human intimacy, tenderness and love" (p. 390). As a result, young people have taken refuge in encounter groups and communes and in sexual mores which approve sex with affection (Chilman, 1979).

In such times, a "profusion of cults and irrational belief systems stand ready to fill the vacuum" caused by the modern world's giving up its dedication to "external verities." This vacuum, believes Smith, is part of the fallout "of war and holocausts, secular faith in science, technology, and progress" (p. 390).

Others perceive the current situation more positively. Opinion poll expert Daniel Yankelovich (1981) sees Americans in the 1980s searching for new meanings—"an authentic grass roots phenomenon," which involves four Americans in five. Thus, young people live in a highly challenging time in defining their lives, lives that are now more open and allow them more options.

Yankelovich sees in America an eagerness for greater meaning in life and broader self-expression, but also "a touch of adventure and grace to their own lives and those of others." Besides the traditional quest for economic well-being, the search for self-fulfillment creates "new demands for intangibles—creativity, leisure, autonomy, pleasure, participation, community, adventure, vitality, stimulation, and tender loving care" (p. 39). Thus, they wish to add a true pleasure in living to the "efficiency of a technological society" (p. 39).

All the foregoing influences operate in ways so complex and subtle that accounting for any individual's moral code is almost impossible, even by the person himself:

> MALE, AGE 20: I'm not sure what influenced my moral code. I just know it departs considerably from conventional ones. I only know I always have a reason for what I do and seldom feel sorry for it.

MORAL GUIDANCE

Youth's Perennial Need for Guidance

Throughout the centuries, adults have written their prescriptions for the manners and morals of youth. In the fifteenth century at the University of Paris it was decreed that "among the students no other game than tennis can be played without the master's permission. However, sometimes the students secretly played cards and chess . . . and the naughtiest boys played dice" (Ariès, 1962, p. 88). Indeed, the students made no bones about visiting taverns and brothels, playing dice, and going dancing. Perhaps today's youth, with all their sophistication, need guidance as much as their fifteenth-century forebears did. But all too often, adolescents, like the one in the following quotation, fail to find mature guidance when they most need it.

> Still the imperative clamor of my mind remained unallayed. Was all my life to be a hunger and a questioning? I complained of my teachers who stuffed my head with facts and gave my soul no crumb to feed on. I

blamed the stars for their silence. I sat up nights brooding over the emptiness of knowledge and praying for revelations.

Sometimes I lived for days in a chimera of doubts, feeling that it was hardly worthwhile living at all if I was never to know why I was born and why I could not live forever. . . . (Antin, 1912, p. 333)

Present-day authorities, like their counterparts in former eras, continue to warn that the younger generation needs guidance. Schwartz (1977) observes that society does not teach values and that the American family with its [high] percent divorce rate is "in disarray and retreat" (p. 18). She believes that literary works assigned to young people today give them little help for coping with life. Jensen and Moore (1977) point out the negative consequences of living in a competitive self-oriented society and suggest that socialization processes should deliberately offset such effects. Otherwise, young people continuously ask themselves what they are getting out of situations in which they are involved. They receive little encouragement to care deeply for others.

Issues in Moral Guidance

Although adults concede that moral guidance for youth is desirable, they disagree on its particulars. There are two distinctively different modes of internalizing morality. In the first mode, anxiety and guilt are evoked in the youth when norms are violated. The second mode builds on the growing individual's potential for empathy. Recent decades have seen a shift, at least in the middle class, from the first to the second mode of socialization. As a result, middle-class youth are now expected to consider extenuating circumstances and to resolve moral conflicts in favor of human ends; they are encouraged to question institutional norms that do not serve such ends. Such a situation accounts, at least partly, for the protest, activism, and anomaly of many of today's middle-class educated youth.

A second issue is whether moral education should be consciously pre-planned or whether it should be handled incidentally as situations arise. In recent years, the indirect approach has prevailed, although some persons insist that schools need a more conscious approach to inculcating ideals and a more dedicated commitment to instilling values. Another issue arises from the common recommendation that successive levels of moral education be related to Kohlberg's interpretation of stages of moral development.

Keniston (1975) raises questions about encouraging all youth to arrive at Kohlberg's postconventional stage. According to this view, youth ideally come to trust their own moral perceptions, regardless of traditional views. Can society at any one stage absorb more than "a few postconventional individuals" like Socrates, Christ, Luther, or Gandhi? Does society not depend for its survival on a certain inertia or uncritical acceptance of most societal norms? Keniston concludes that it is not possible to regress to some past age when societal inaction underwrote societal stability; if attainment of higher developmental levels is coupled with interpersonal mutuality, the result need not be anarchy or social chaos, "but instead, viable new forms of social organization" (p. 26).

It should be added that the functional effectiveness of morals varies somewhat with the culture; therefore, different societies have correspondingly varied modes of moral education. For example, in the United States such training proceeds informally, in bits and pieces, through transactions of family, schools, youth organizations, church, and press. In contrast, in Russia such training is carefully programmed, beginning with the central committee of the Communist party and involving all institutions that deal with the young. Activities and programs for the Young Pioneers, the Russian organization resembling the American scouting movement, is designed to help children become "disciplined, responsible, courageous, and patriotic, and to work hard, take initiative, value education, respond to duty and love nature" (Cole, 1983, p. 76). The same values are encouraged in American individuals as well, the chief difference being the relative emphasis that each society places on formal training.

Most theorists accept certain broad principles of socializing children and youth in moral behaviors (Lickona, 1976). First, moral education should be suited to their present level of cognitive powers and personal development (Aronfreed, 1976). They should be helped to behave properly and not simply told how to avoid difficulty. Television, in particular, should afford suitable models for demonstrating prosocial behaviors and specific ways of dealing with situations (Liebert & Poulos, 1976). Moreover, parents, teachers, and other adult models should practice what they preach (Burton, 1977). Growing individuals should also be helped to understand principles that govern moral situations in order to achieve an integrated moral functioning. Otherwise, there is the danger of creating many options without knowing how to arrive at proper choices. As a result, youth may have difficulty deciding what they are committed to (Yankelovich, 1983).

VALUES AND IDEALS: THE OUTCOMES OF MORAL DEVELOPMENT

Appraisal of Youth's Morals and Values

Throughout history, ad hoc critics have wagged their heads over youth, often branding their value systems a witch's brew of amorality and recklessness. Meantime, their defendants applaud youth for being in fact so honest that they seem fake. There is considerable disagreement and confusion over what youth's values are, what they ideally should be, whether they are improving or declining, and what direction they should assume.

Adams and Looft (1977) perceive youth as idealistically attempting to develop social values. As a result of events in recent history, such as American hostages in Iran, Russian troops in Afghanistan, Israeli-Arab conflicts, Vietnam, Watergate, inflation, employment, and energy crises, youth are raising questions and asking of what worth their own life commitment is. They want to find a place somewhere for themselves, somehow, and to devise a better life style than that modeled for them by their elders.

Others observe that a changing morality is not necessarily a declining morality. Certainly girls have a healthier sexuality than in days when women believed that acknowledging sex as pleasurable was wrong, at least for their sex.

The sexes, more often than formerly, see sex as a way of communicating between individuals who possess a mutual respect (A new generation, 1976).

Still others assume a less sanguine view of youth's values. Vincent (1972) feels that youth brought up on a philosophy of "fun morality" lack a sense of history and focus too much on the here and now.

Changes in Values and Views
Over Time

Certain of youth's values and views change subtly over the years. There was little change in religious views from 1924 to 1977, but the later adolescents were less disposed to impose religious views on others. (Caplow & Bahr, 1979) They also expressed a little more tolerance on civil rights issues. Fewer of the recent students would prosecute pacifists or conscientious objectors; and more, but not a majority, favored unlimited free speech. There was scarcely any trace of disintegration of traditional social values. In 1977 young people were as strongly endowed with patriotism, religion, and the Protestant ethic as their grandparents had been at their age. It cannot be assumed that values expressed in Middletown are typical of adolescents throughout the United States, although Middletown was originally chosen for its typicality.

In other research the longitudinal perspective also demonstrated the influence of the times on personal values. Youth who experienced the civil rights movement of the 1960s dwelled in a quite different environment and experienced different concepts of justice from those of either earlier or later times. Youth of the 1980s are less willing to endorse society's values without questioning

Some researchers perceive ecology as a main focus for today's youth. (Courtesy of Community Relations Office, State University of New York at Oswego)

them than were the youth of the 1950s. They are more concerned now about self-fulfillment and personal privacy (Youth on the move, 1980).

Logan (1980) perceives ecology as the main focus today, perhaps because it symbolizes the "real world, unaltered by human activity" (p. 412). He sees people as searching for the natural, "the enduring," "the unpolluted," and rejecting qualities that contribute to pollution. He denies suggesting that concern about matters of environmental pollution are simply "an illusion" or "an obsession of those seeking their peer identity."

Young people today have a greater task than did their elders in defining and practicing their values because of the greater tolerance allowed them and the more fluid concepts involved. The new values "encourage greater tolerance, permit more sexual freedom and put less emphasis on sacrifice for its own sake" (Yankelovich, 1983, p. 36). In contrast to the early American ethic of self-denial, youth now learn that they have a duty to themselves. Even those young people who may have achieved relative stability of values will constantly rub shoulders of those who have not.

Meantime, research is showing the "giant plates of American culture shifting relentlessly beneath us [creating] huge dislocations in our lives;" and although those persons "closest to society's fault lines are the first to be thrown into new predicaments . . . even those at a distance feel the tremors" (p. 39).

Generational Differences

In Yankelovich's national sampling, attitudes of young people and their parents were compared on certain traditional American values: saving money, hard work, competition, self-control, compromise, legal authority, private property, and organized religion (Etzioni, 1978). On seven of the eight issues differences between the generations were 9 percent or less; the only significant difference was in attitudes toward religion. Two thirds of the young people believed religion to be important to an individual, compared to 89 percent of their elders—a difference of 23 percent. The difference between college and noncollege youth was far greater than that between young people and their parents.

Values also differ cross-culturally, even in the western world (Western world's "silent revolution," 1978). A study at the University of Michigan Institute for Social Research, embracing the United States and ten western European nations over the past decade, indicated a dramatic change in material values and political awareness. The change in focus has been away from materialism—physical security and material values—and toward postmaterialism—concern with self-expression and quality of life. These changing values have been accompanied by a rise in political skills that permit the masses to participate more directly in making significant political decisions. This value change is gradual but fundamental, effecting important changes in the political scene throughout the western world.

The postmaterialistic culture is making more rapid gains in affluent societies than in poorer ones, such as Italy and Ireland, with histories of foreign invasion and civil disorder. Other factors determining the pace of change in individuals are age, education, communication patterns, religion, political affiliation, labor union membership, sex, and nationality. The strongest predictor of value type in most of the countries is educational level. Postmaterialism is twice as common among the university educated as among those with only a primary school education. Higher education is an especially strong predictor because it relates to a family's affluence in pre-adult years and is thus linked with communication patterns.

Individual Values

Ordinarily values, like morals, arise from people's experience. Since the pace of change is so rapid, values and morals relating to particular experiences hardly have time to mature before situations change. The result has been a decline in universal values and a growing use of situation ethics in which individuals decide within the context of situations what is right or wrong. While certain behaviors may still be considered wrong, there is a growing acceptance of the individual's right to make personal decisions—for example, with regard to premarital pregnancy (Schippers, 1978).

Nature and Origin of Ideals

YOUTH'S IDEALS   Like values, ideals stem from the individual's moral code and reflect the self one wants to be. Ideals represent those aspects of an individual's code which serve as guideposts for behavior. Thus, ideals are personal, although rooted in culture in complex ways. For many youths the simple life has become an ideal—a reaction against what they consider to be pseudo-sophistication and ultramaterialism of the modern world. Wynne (1978) portrays youth as becoming increasingly alienated from society. He points to their increasing withdrawal from society despite an increasing dedication of economic resources to the young. Youth in the United States are more egoistic and privatistic but less altruistic, patriotic, and religious than those in other parts of the world; and such attitudes encompass not only college but noncollege students, who gradually absorb the college youth's patterns. Moreover, children and youth are becoming increasingly lonely and self-centered because of the tensions of life.

The question often arises: How idealistic, if at all, are modern youth in terms of serving others? As children emerge into adolescence they relinquish any dreams that they may have of truly dramatic human improvement (Adelson, 1980). They do not become cynical but simply more realistic, and true idealists are found only among the small number of more politicized youth.

When adolescents, ages 12 to 18, were asked, "If it were in your power to do whatever you wanted, what kind of society would you set up?", the typical 12-year-olds would say, "a nice one," and they would be sure that people obeyed laws and didn't rob banks. No truly Utopian idealism emerged until about age 18—but even then idealists were rare. Of 1000 adolescents, no more than ten displayed "a glimmer of Utopian thinking" (Adelson, 1980, p. 60).

Youths' focus on themselves is sometimes attributed to an affluent society where people no longer have to toil daily to achieve success. Complexities and competitive pressures of modern life, coupled with success symbols pursued by almost everyone, have produced an anomic condition which in turn encourages self-oriented activity. In consequence, youth possess little concern over the larger society since they feel helpless to control it and focus on themselves. In America's present mass society, youth's escapism and hedonism simply reflect having nothing to believe in;—"no wars, no causes, no villains, no heroes" (Leger, 1980, p. 283).

In contrast, Logan (1980) believes that youth, in their uncertain present state, seek for themselves some place in the "larger scheme of things," something idealistic to which to dedicate themselves. They seek especially those things that are "the genuine, the pure, the enduring" (p. 409). Such qualities afford "a solid anchoring point in the surrounding maelstrom of change and uncertainty" (p. 410). The more insecure individuals are about their identity status the more intensely they seek such qualities to give them a feeling of stability.

The truth is: some youth today do hold ideals of service, but the majority focus on their personal, private sphere. An individual's commitment relates to that individual's "sense of firmness or conviction about maintaining a belief or set of beliefs [or values]" (Thorbecke & Grotevant, 1982, p. 481). A relevant concern is: commitment to what—and is one's plan for discharging that commitment congruent with realities? (Menge, 1982).

Menge (1982) points out that adolescents are typically described as romantic but the romantic may be interpreted both positively and negatively. Negatively, it calls to mind such characteristics as "improbability, make-believe, and naivete." Constructively, it suggests "beauty, love, adventure, sensitivity and even charming innocence" (p. 419). Menge focuses on the positive aspect, that romantic thinking and active imagination are not time wasters but a positive aspect of one's life, leading the way to upgrading the human condition in socially significant ways. Menge endorses a process of planning for the future, employing both ideal and current reality.

In contrast, some youth become pessimistic regarding the realization of their ideals—"God is dead—humans are basically evil—we're modern dinosaurs" (p. 432). As a result they may escape into drugs, alcohol, and sex; yet such escape brings no solutions.

Nor is the typical problem-solving approach adequate—it is a "crisis orientation." This scientific method has indeed produced many dramatic developments in our society—in industry, medicine, and so forth; yet its failures are apparent because we still lack the values required to utilize dramatic advances in effective ways. More constructive, says Menge, is a model of problem-solving which combines romantic dreams with skills, systems, and knowledge that help to realize those dreams.

ADOLESCENTS AND RELIGION

Importance of Religion

As already noted, religion concerns the individual's conclusions about the most elemental issues of human life and his or her relation to a supernatural being. One's religion modifies and is in turn modified by morals, values, ideals, and personality characteristics.

Religion has always played an essential, though varying, role in human

Religion plays an essential, though varying, role in human affairs. (Photo by Margaret Hester)

affairs. In earlier centuries, before scientists gained sway as the most prestigious sources of authority, people depended more on religion than they do today to explain the universe. When monarchies were absolute and poverty was the fate of most of mankind, religion's promise of an afterlife, devoid of despotism and want, gave religion great significance.

Few would hold that religion has outlived its traditional role. Religion helps individuals to order what they can find out about the details of the universe into a meaningful pattern. It represents the basic orientation of a person's own values and gives meaning to one's existence. In Freudian terms, it powerfully reinforces the superego (conscience) in its struggle with the id (instinctual impulse that leads to immediate gratification of primitive needs).

Influences on Youth's Religious Attitudes and Practices

The research indicates how varied and complex influences on youth's religious views can be. For example, in interviews with 451 tenth graders, including Catholics, Southern Baptists, and Methodists, the Baptists indicated the greatest church commitment because of several critical factors. Baptist parents participated regularly in such activities themselves and talked with their children about religion. The Baptist youth had liked their past religious training and admired their religious leaders, believing them to be sincerely religious. Apparently churches strong in these critical determinants are most successful in socializing young people in their faith (Hoge & Petrillo, 1978).

Among the various influences on religion, three of the most important are family, sociocultural context, and the times. Family experience is an especially important factor in youth's religious beliefs. The vast majority of students share their parents' religious views, and only a small minority are atheists or religious cultists (A new generation, 1976). The more religion is stressed in the home, the more favorable are youth's attitudes toward religion, and the more youth are concerned about personal ethics. Those with less positive attitudes toward religion are more concerned with social ethics or improving life within the whole society. In general, a review of the research indicates that church-going youths identify with their parents more than do others, have a stronger sense of personhood, and are less likely to engage in premarital sex, drinking, or drug use (Hauser, 1981). A study of 16- to 18-year-olds in the state of Victoria, Australia (de Vaux, 1983) indicated that parents were more important than peers in determining their religious views. However, they were more important for shaping religious beliefs than for influencing religious activities. They were also more important regarding their children's value beliefs.

It is necessary, however, to make certain distinctions between religious belief and activity and between mother and father and close friends and the crowd. Whereas parents were more important than peers in determining adolescents' religious beliefs, religious activities, and self-concepts, the mother and close friends were more important in any of these matters than were the father and the crowd.

There was no evidence to indicate that there was any generation gap between these adolescents and their parents or of a distinctive youth subculture, with its own religious values. Although adolescents and parents might conflict on various matters they had not rejected their parents' religious views as out of date.

Another study, of 254 mother-father-youth triads from Catholic, Baptist, and Methodist churches, indicated that the young people were significantly less traditional in religious values than their mothers and on certain ones less than their fathers. With regard to sexual ethics the youth of both sexes were more tolerant of sexual freedom than their parents. On political issues there was a generation gap regarding some issues but not others. The largest gap in beliefs overall was in sexual ethics, relating to youth's trend toward greater sexual freedom during the 1970s.

A comparison of the impact of parental values on children's values with that of the children's denominational membership indicated the latter to be a bit stronger (Hogue, Petrillo & Smith, 1982). Overall the children had obtained their values from the culture outside the family as much as from their parents. Only one out of nine particular values reflected any real impact of family characteristics on the transmission of those values and that was creedal assent, or belief in traditional Christian religion. This transmission from parent to child was strongest where parents and children got along well, where parents were younger, had definite beliefs, agreed on them between themselves, and consciously conducted religious socialization in the home. Most significantly, parent-child correlations in values were somewhat weak and other influences more important, such as the denomination to which they belonged.

Inevitably youth's religious views vary with the times. In America's colonial period, youth looked on God with awe and fear and often felt like sinners. The whole system of social control was built around the authority of God and the Bible. The fear motive was used in an effort to keep children on the "straight-and-narrow" path. Judge Sewall, a pillar of Boston colonial society, wrote with great feeling of his daughter Betty, "It seems Betty Sewall had given some signs of dejection and sorrow; but a little while after dinner she burst out into an amazing cry, which caus'd all the family to cry too; her Mother ask'd the reason, she gave none; at last she said she was afraid she should go to Hell, her Sins were not pardon'd" (Bossard, 1954, p. 633).

Since the late 1970s youths' religious attitudes have reverted somewhat to the more traditional. In a northeast Texas high school, two-thirds white and one-third black, adolescent religious involvement declined steadily between 1964 and 1974, but reversed its trend between 1974 and 1979. The reversal was especially true for males, both black and white. The decline for females was "more subtle" and a bit less between 1964 and 1974; and it continued into 1979, thus narrowing the gap between the sexes (Dickinson, 1982).

Schneller (1982) points out the complexities that modern adolescents may experience with regard to perceived differences between their religious beliefs and doubts produced by modern science. At least among Israeli youth he identified seven main approaches in the literature regarding appropriate attitudes toward faith and science and their interrelationships. Schneller (1982) concluded that in dealing with youth no single approach is appropriate for all.

Current Status of Youth's Religious Practices and Beliefs

Apparently, youth today are somewhat more religious than those in the recent past. In a national sampling of the late 1970s, 45 percent of people under age 30 believed religion to be very important; 35 percent fairly important; and only 5 percent not at all important; compared to 58 percent of those 30 to 49 years old who believed it to be very important; 30 percent fairly important; and 5 percent, not at all important (Gallup, 1977). However, the fact that today's youth find religion important cannot be interpreted to mean that they practice it in the way their elders do. A Gallup survey May 13, 1981 showed that adolescents had a strong interest in religious affairs but that they had noticed considerable difference between adults' practice and teaching and therefore labeled them hypocrites (Schab, 1982). Another Gallup youth survey (June 2, 1981) indicated that 13- to 15-year-olds were somewhat ignorant of biblical teaching, although honor students and regular church attenders did better than the others. The adolescents, in general, could name just four of the ten commandments but still felt that all were valid.

A study at Russell Sage College sheds light on students' current religious attitudes and experiences and how such views have changed. Among these young women 72.7 percent felt they required some form of religious orientation or belief to achieve a fully mature life; 14.3 percent said they did not; and 13 percent were doubtful (McAllister, 1981). With regard to religious observance, about a half attended church weekly, a fourth prayed daily, and another 30 percent often. Almost 40 percent felt reverent daily or often; and fewer than 5 percent had not prayed the last half year.

In comparison with data from students in similar institutions these students felt more positive about religion than did students in the 1940s. During the interim period, from about the mid-50s through the early 70s, religiosity appeared to decline and then revive (McAllister, 1981). Perhaps the rapid development of religious television programming, the election of a born-again President, and other indicators of return to traditionalism are factors.

The study also showed that religious orientation continues to be encouraged in most families, for 37.3 percent said religion had been a significant aspect of their upbringing, 39 percent a moderate one, 13.2 percent slight, and just 0.4 percent no influence at all. The major factors influencing religious attitudes were parents and church teaching, despite the currently common view that such influence is weakening.

The religious experience itself varied considerably. Just 10.9 percent had experienced something mystical which contributed to their religiosity. Another 10.6 percent reported some definite crisis or distinct religious conversion. Of the others, 16 percent said their experience was an emotional stimulus awakening, and 73.4 percent said it was a gradual awakening, the median age for the experience being 15.4 years. In fact, half these individuals made their religious decisions by the ninth grade.

It is easy to over-generalize regarding adolescents' religious beliefs because they change with age. In a national probability sampling of American adolescents, ages 13 to 18 (Potvin & Lee, 1982), adolescents appeared to go through certain changes over time in their approach to religion. Up to ages 13 to 14, individuals of both sexes, whose families belonged to more conservative denominations, participated without question in the rituals of their religious group. At about ages 15 to 16 adolescents' peers began to influence their religious beliefs and experiences, often producing some internal conflict. In consequence, in middle adolescence, individuals may develop a "world view, a system of meanings" and a reinterpretation of their religious views. The process of rejecting or affirming earlier meanings is not a matter of rebellion but results from their interaction with their peers. In later adolescence, at ages 17 or 18, religious factors come to impact on their internal meanings and experience more than the reverse. Now they may confirm their traditional views and experiences or, if they are unable to do so, may acquire new beliefs and experiences. Even after this time, there may be further modifications of a lesser nature. Potvin and Lee conclude by saying that they do not imply that age itself dramatically triggers change, or that there are literally stages. Not all adolescents progress in the same manner nor at the same age.

Youth in particular faiths experience their religion in characteristic ways. For example, among a sampling of Jewish undergraduates at York University, Toronto, Davids (1982) found that Jewish identity functioned independently of Jewish religiosity. Five in six students reported a high sense of Jewish identity but fewer than one in ten were highly religious. Those individuals with more Jewish schooling and the highly religious had somewhat more traditional moral attitudes—for example, they had lower sex-liberation scores. More religious individuals tended toward the moral side of sex liberalism and the nonreligious toward the nontraditional regarding premarital sex. It appeared that the same might be said of Jewish college students in the United States.

A youth's denomination is usually one of a constellation of factors that relate to morality and religion. There are major differences among different categories of youth with regard to their participation in the youth revolution and tasting the forbidden fruit—for example, marijuana, alcohol, and premarital sex (Davids, 1982). In general, students who are from smaller communities, are more religious, and are Catholic tend to be more conservative, report lower rates of premarital coitus and cannabis consumption than do nonchurch-going, non-religious-affiliated big city students. Also, girls typically uphold traditional norms somewhat more than boys.

Youth's religious attitudes also vary by race and sex. In a study of eighth graders in Georgia 13 percent of the black boys said their faith was very important, compared with 62 percent of black girls, 43 percent of white girls, and 40 percent of the white boys. The rest thought it was somewhat important except for 5 percent of both white sexes who said it was not. A fourth of all the groups said that they seldom went to church. With regard to praying when not in church, all the black girls said they did, compared with 92 percent of the white girls, 91 percent of the black boys, and 75 percent of the white boys (Schab, 1982).

In the 1970s the small minority of youth who were interested in Eastern and mystic religions grew even less significant. Charles Coleman, Director of the Religious Affairs at Pennsylvania State University, attributes college youth's return to Western religion to a search for roots. The student movement toward non-Western religions of the late 1960s was partially a matter of students' rejection of their parents' culture. The current religious revival is not cognitive, involving study of religion, but experiential, as students are asking how religion can make them better people. Coleman perceives the new religious trend as personal, individual, focused on self-development, and not strongly supportive of social action (Students returning to Western form of worship, 1978).

Here are two college students' religious views:

FEMALE: I am a Catholic. Right now I don't believe it has much importance for me but it is still there. Later in life I will go back to it more seriously because I will probably need it more. I also know some adolescents or young adults who have turned their backs to religion because a death or something else happened. As for the majority on this campus I don't believe it has too much of an effect.

MALE: I am of the Jewish faith but do not participate in observing. I used to pray regularly and go to the synagogue on all the major holidays up until 13 years of age. At this time I began to see through my parents, that their beliefs were hypocritical. They would say one thing and do another. This caused doubts in myself. I was not getting anything out of attending services, so I decided it wasn't necessary and began to regard it as a waste of time. I have always doubted the validity of structural religion, but I do feel that belief in some spiritual force is a good idea, just because it is a unifying force.

NONTRADITIONAL RELIGIONS AND VIEWS   Although a large majority of youth belong to traditional religious denominations, a very small minority are attracted to cults. One of these cults, the Unification Church, claims 30,000 members in the United States, averaging 24 years of age. It was introduced into this country by Korean missionaries in 1961; and its members are called Moonies after its leader, the Rev. Sun Yung Moon. Dean (1982) found that Moonies recruit mainly college students from white middle class affluent backgrounds.

Among 237 unification members surveyed in California 89 percent were white and 91 percent unmarried.

These young people are attracted to the Moonies for several reasons. Many of them are very idealistic and wish to improve the world, and the Moonies' cult claims to provide its converts opportunities for helping to correct perceived weaknesses within society. For many young people, the more traditional churches lack the "ideological fervor necessary to inspire their commitment" (p. 569). "Truth," one Moonie said, "only has value if it is lived." Participating in an idealistic movement can also be exciting, and being committed to a significant moral cause romantic. One Moonie described the atmosphere of the group as having a sense of involvement in something very important—"You really got caught up in it" (p. 569).

In addition, adolescents are open to new ideas. They want something new to challenge them and when the cult presents itself, quite different from what they have known, they are curious about it. It is something of an adventure. Also recruiters may capitalize on adolescents' somewhat simplistic outlook and need for romantic and idealistic experience. One young Moonie said ". . . if you think there's one chance in a million that it will work, how can you not try . . . ?" (p. 570).

Many college students feel quite anxious and disillusioned with their environment. When they come to college they are separated from their parents and often feel somewhat lonely and alienated; and the Moonies provide a secure support system. They also may feel unhappy and insecure about making life decisions, including career choice, and the Moonie recruiter may be "an exceptionally friendly, sincere and tranquil cult member" (p. 570). The very fact that adolescence is a somewhat extended period allows young people to experiment with various alternative life styles before settling down. This, combined with their own immaturity, makes them highly susceptible to appeals by the Moonies. The Moonies' recruiters often seek out their young prospects "in bus stations, historical landmark sites and city parks, where numbers of wandering or aimless youths are likely to congregate" (p. 572).

Youth who have undergone some traumatic experience, such as death of a friend or family member, a broken romance, or other personal trauma, are also attracted to the Unification Church. Such events create a positive atmosphere for religious conversion. Devastated by their loss, youth may have guilt feelings, question their values, and welcome the outstretched arms of the Moonies. The Unification Church also appeals to romantics who visualize victories over suffering and inequities and to the alienated who seek some direction in their lives (Dean, 1982). One 26-year-old Moonie said "I wanted to be free—free of hassles, free of emotional problems, free of relationships" (p. 567).

Another cult, the Divine Light Mission, stresses updated versions of Hindu meditation, proselytizing, and servicing in hospitals and prisons. The International Society for Krishna Consciousness is based on Hindu scriptures and prohibits drinking alcohol, eating meat, and many sexual activities. These and similar cults share certain characteristics. They stress warmth and love among their members and rely on a spiritual father of their unified family. Such cults often ban drinking and drugs and occupy much of their time in lectures and prayers. Many of the members live in communes, sometimes taking up collections for their cult. From one to three million Americans, mostly in their 20s or late teens, are members of from 200 to 1000 such cults.

Opponents of the cults, especially parents, refer to their modes of indoctrination as "psychological kidnapping." They charge that cult members collect money that goes to the cult leader and that resistance to indoctrination is weakened by too little sleep and too much work. Discipline is often harsh and sometimes includes sexual abuse by the cult members.

Many parents have made serious efforts to rescue their children from the cults, usually by seizing them outside a commune and taking them away. The youth may be turned over to "deprogrammers" who are reputedly often successful in ridding them of their cultist views. In other cases, sympathetic judges help parents obtain a writ of habeas corpus ordering that cults produce their children in a court hearing to determine whether they are mentally competent. After hearing testimony regarding radical changes in the youth's behavior, the judge may grant parents a 15- to 30-day "conservatorship" (Galanter et al., 1979, p. 54). During this time the deprogrammers go to work, but the ex-members are free to return after the court order expires.

Overall, new religions are linked to recent countercultures rather than to the puritan ethic. A minority of college students disavow religion; others are uncertain. Still others return to the church after a period of doubt.

MALE: Ever since I have learned the different theories of man's origin I have begun to doubt religion. Darwin versus Adam and Eve just don't match. I always doubt religious beliefs when I look around and see poverty, suffering, starvation, and then hear people speak of a gracious, generous God.

MALE: I attended church for only about a year, ten years ago. I have attended maybe five times since then. Religion plays no role in my life. I feel I have gotten along pretty well without it. I have always been told I should have religion to fall back on when in trouble. I say, tell that to the Christians thrown to the lions, to the Jews during Nazi Germany, to the Irish Catholics and Protestants.

MALE: I had doubts about my religion but found later on that there is a God. I didn't want to get all hung up so I came to the conclusion that I can still believe without going into much depth.

Some counterculture youth have gone to the other extreme, adopting strictly fundamentalist views. Counterculture fundamentalists number about 400,000 members in the United States and 600,000 worldwide, not counting certain closely related groups. Mostly, they are youth in their late teens or early twenties and, like youth in the broader counterculture, they are from middle- to upper-class white families. Religion is the core of their lives. They interpret the Bible rather literally, lead somewhat ascetic lives and move in close-knit groups. Several fundamentalist groups are found on most college campuses.

FUTURE PERSPECTIVES

In contrast to the strong interest adolescents show in religion, the early 20s have been called the least religious period of life. Down-to-earth problems are too pressing at that time to permit much thought of such things. By then individuals have either resolved their doubts and settled for religious philosophies to which they will adhere the rest of their lives, or they have rejected organized religion as having little to offer. Not until several decades later will religion again achieve the importance it attained in adolescence. After having weathered some of the crises of life, a person may once more come to feel the need for a firm basis for life values in religion. Whatever the decision for or against religion may have been in youth, it will tend to persist.

Youth's religious experience relates to adult life in at least two important ways: First, they must arrive at decisions about whether to date and marry only persons of their own religion. Second, youth is a most important time for examining one's own and others' religions; the conclusions reached, often after periods of doubt, tend to persist through adulthood. Finally, it is mainly in high school and college that youth gain some appreciation of the diversity of religions, including their rationale and origins, which is so important to functioning in a religiously pluralistic society.

Whether youth, in the future, will become more actively involved in religion is uncertain. The polling expert Daniel Yankelovich (1983) sees in the years ahead a "quest for the sacred to intensify—from deeper religious beliefs and increased church going to a resurgence of patriotism" (p. A11). Meantime, churches will expand their roles, as places where people can come together, share interests, and discuss a broad range of problems; and organized religious denominations will realign along conservative and liberal lines. The more liberal denominations, including the main-line Protestants, Reformed Jews, and liberal Catholics will be "egalitarian, stressing the brotherhood of human beings around the world"; whereas the conservative sects, "such as Southern Baptist, the Church of God and Orthodox Jews" will meet the needs of those who seek simplicity, certainty, and security.

Values established in youth influence the way individuals relate to the adult world. In 1979 freshmen across the country expressed considerable optimism concerning their personal future (Bachman & Johnston, 1979). Will such optimism cause them, as adults, to assume a confident stance, or will it invite disillusion? Discussions of important issues in high school and college will help develop realistic values. Tackling such questions helps individuals find inner direction in a complex world.

Many authorities advise that today's youth be prepared to adapt their values to changing conditions. For example, young people will be moving into a society where four-fifths of Americans have shifted dramatically in their culture, the remaining fifth being mainly older persons living in rural areas (Yankelovich, 1983). Hence, they will be living in environments with less stable, more fluctuating values than their forebears experienced. They must also adapt to fast-paced changes wrought by technology and must be prepared, as citizens, to react to ethical issues in matters of public policy. Already, at Harvard University, enrollment in traditional ethics courses is rising swiftly after a long period of being in the doldrums (A search for life's meaning, 1983).

In short, as they emerge into adulthood, young people must somehow adapt their own value systems to reality if such values are to be effective guides for their own behaviors. Also, youth must somehow reconcile the values relating to duty, tradition, and work, as expressed in the Judeo-Christian ethic, with those of creativity and responsiveness, stressed in existentialist philosophy (Scanlon, 1979). Adolescents should also be helped to understand how values vary among peoples of the world. As they move from the protected environment of family and school "to the group, the tribe, the nation and the family of nations, they can no longer think in terms of a single set of values . . . and the problem of establishing priorities among values becomes almost insoluble" (Scanlon, 1979, pp. 106–107).

Society, in general, and educators in particular, should search for ways of insuring that adults continue to grow and develop in terms of moral and ethical judgment, in order to keep pace with change. Yet, such evidence as we have, stemming mainly from cross-sectional research, would indicate little change in level of moral judgment after youth (Pratt, Golding & Hunter, 1983). There does appear to be some increase after that time in "philosophical reflectiveness;" however, that might be expected as a result of life-long testing of one's experiences. It would seem, therefore, that a critical time for arriving at one's highest moral stage occurs in youth.

SUMMARY

Adolescents' relationships to their universe may be described in terms of morals, values, ideals, and religion, all of which overlap one another. Morals are standards of right and wrong, determined by the values of the culture. Values refer to the relative worth an individual attaches to objects and behaviors. Ideals represent standards toward which an individual strives. Religion is that aspect of an individual's philosophy that concerns the most elemental and universal issues of human existence; as conventionally defined, and consists of those attitudes, practices, ceremonies, and beliefs that define one's relationship to a supernatural force.

Of the foregoing concepts, morals have recently attracted special interest, particularly as they relate to developmental theory and are organized at successive age stages. That is, various authorities have defined moral development in terms of stages through which most individuals presumably pass. The best known of such theories are those of Piaget and Kohlberg, neither of whom argues that moral judgments are always age-related. Rather, they suggest that concepts are developed according to a specific sequence, and that an individual can become fixated at any level of moral development. Some critics question the ordering of Kohlberg's stages; others object that his theory is derived from faulty research methodology.

The adolescent's own morals are shaped by numerous factors, especially family experience. Another important influence is college experience, its impact varying with the college and subject areas involved. However, college may have less effect than is commonly supposed, for, in general, students become increasingly entrenched in whatever beliefs they held as freshmen.

Another important factor in moral development is sex role. Girls are more precocious than boys in acquiring adult-approved standards. However, boys' morality is probably of a more independent type. The girl is socialized to comply, while boys are encouraged to test concepts in the process of defining their own moral codes. During the teens, the impact of peers on a youth's moral decisions becomes increasingly important. However, parental influence remains more significant on basic issues. An individual's morals also relate to personal characteristics, including mental abilities, social traits, and emotional adjustment. Sociocultural factors are important, too, accounting for variations in moral codes from one historical epoch and culture to another. Hence, youth's views are in process of continuous change, producing the so-called "generations effect."

Many writers have prescribed formulas for moral education. Kohlberg, for one, believes such programs should be cognitively challenging and geared to the individual's progressive development. Moral education, in order to be effective, must result in intelligent discrimination in moral issues and the translation of theory into intelligent action. While theorists differ in particulars, they generally agree on certain broad principles of moral socialization.

An important outcome of moral development is the acquisition of values and ideals. But how satisfactory modern youth's values and ideals may be is a matter of debate. Some research suggests that present-day youth still strongly endorse patriotism, religion, and the protestant ethic. Some critics believe that generalizations are unjustified and that values vary according to subcategories of youth, sex, individual, the culture, and the times.

Like values, ideals are quite personal, reflecting the self an individual wants to be. Often, individuals' ideals are modified by identification figures, or persons whom they especially admire. Such individuals may include teachers, public figures, friends, or characters in books, movies, or television. Factors that relate to an individual's choice of identification figures are sex, culture, and the times, as well as personal characteristics and needs. In the formation of ideals, the adolescent does not unselectively embrace the identification figure's value system. Individuals may copy different traits from each of several models, or they may negatively identify, seeking to avoid the characteristics of a particular person.

Somewhat neglected in research in recent years are adolescents' religious beliefs, or their relation to the supernatural. Although youth tend, increasingly, to assume more modern views in this area, few would argue that religion has outlived its traditional role. Nevertheless, some authorities believe that teenagers' religious commitment is somewhat shallow, despite youth's own testimony to its importance. Indeed, most young people retain remnants, or even large segments, of traditional religious beliefs. The residual effect is a considerable ambivalence and a wide diversity of religious views among different groups of youth. Such differences reflect a wide diversity of influences, including family experience, formal religious training, socioeconomic status, sociocultural context, and the times. In America, in particular, youth's views tend roughly to fall into three categories of belief, depending on whether they are Christians, Jews, or students with no formal religion. A small minority of youth become attracted to mystical Eastern religions and others to fundamentalist sects and cults, such as the Unification Church and the Divine Light Mission. Opponents of the cults brand their modes of indoctrination as "psychological kidnapping" and may attempt to "rescue" them from their involvement. At the other extreme, very few youths are agnostic or atheistic, but most youth are tolerant of others' disaffection from religion.

An individual ordinarily shows more interest in religion during adolescence than in young adulthood. By adolescence, individuals are sufficiently mature to handle the abstractions involved in religious concepts and they have not yet become so submerged in problems of society that they have no time to ponder these concepts. All products of moral development—values, ideals, and religion—become part of an individual's philosophy of life, a blueprint of what life is all about. Whatever conclusions they reach at this stage tend to persist through life.

DISCUSSION QUESTIONS AND ACTIVITIES

1. Attempt to account for prevalent adolescent attitudes toward sex, drugs, and religion.
2. The following questions may provide subjects for panel discussion: (a) To what extent is religious instruction justified in public education? (b) What are the greatest moral issues facing teenagers today? (c) What type of guidance should adults provide concerning these issues? (d) Where peer groups and parents differ, whose direction should the teenager follow?
3. What are the most significant changes currently occurring in adolescents' ideals and their attitudes toward religion? Discuss each area separately.
4. Write down names of personal acquaintances or of persons in public life who have significantly affected your ideals, and explain how these persons have influenced you. Answers of all the members of the class may be compiled and discussed.
5. Discuss possible effects on adolescents' moral codes of various contemporary developments, including accelerated scientific advancement, television, racketeering, urbanization, and rapidity of world change.
6. Discuss under what circumstances it may or may not be wise to marry someone of another religion.
7. A panel of students—one each from the Jewish, Protestant, Catholic, and some fundamentalist religion as well as an atheist or agnostic—may discuss the role of their respective religious views on youth's life style and personal development.

SUGGESTED READINGS

Colby, A., Kohlberg, L., Gibbs, J., & Lieberman, M. (1983). A longitudinal study of moral judgment. *Monographs of the Society for Research in Child Development, 48*(1–2), 124. A study which involved 10-, 13-, and 16-year-old males supported Kohlberg's stage theory and disclosed a positive relationship between moral judgment and socioeconomic class, IQ, and education.

Dean, R. A. (1982). Youth: Moonies' target population. *Adolescence, 17*(67), 567–574. An analysis is made of reasons that youth may be attracted to join cults—in particular, the Moonies.

DeVaus, D. A. (1983). The relative importance of parents and peers for adolescent religious orientation: An Australian study. *Adolescence, 18*(69), 147–158. A study of Australian adolescents indicated that peers were important for their self-concepts but that parents had more effect on their religious views.

Dien, D. S. (1982). A Chinese perspective on Kohlberg's theory of moral development. *Developmental Review, 2*(4), 331–341. This analysis resulted in the conclusion that Kohlberg's theory of moral development, which is based on Western views of rational choices, is inappropriate for the Chinese because of their different culture.

Glenn, N. D. (1982). Interreligious marriage in the United States: Patterns and recent trends. *Journal of Marriage and the Family, 44*(3), 555–566. The study of patterns of interreligious marriage since 1957 indicates a considerable increase in numbers of religiously mixed couples, and that mothers exert greater control over their childrens' religious socialization than do fathers.

Guttmann, J. (1982). Israeli children's reactions to moral judgment dilemmas as a function of pressures from adults and peers: A developmental study. *Journal of Genetic Psychology, 140*(2), 161–168. Israeli children of three age groups—8–9 years, 11–12, and 14–15 years—were administered a morality test which indicated differences in moral judgment according to age and sex.

Hauser, J. (1981). Adolescents and religion. *Adolescence, 16*(62), 309–320. The author discusses youth's attitudes toward religion, the needs that cults fulfill, and alternatives to cults.

Hoge, D. R., Petrillo, G. H., & Smith, E. I. (1982). Transmission of religious and social values from parents to teenage children. *Journal of Marriage and the Family, 44*(3), 569–580. A study of 254 mother-father-youth triads from Catholic, Baptist, and Methodist churches indicated that several factors related to enhanced transmission of religious values to the young—younger age of parents, parental agreement about religion, and good parent-child relationships.

Loevinger, J. & Knoll, E. (1983). Personality: Stages, traits, and the self. *Annual Review of Psychology, 34* 195–222. Certain stage theories are studied in relation to personality development.

McMahon, R. C., Pulvino, C., & Sanborn, M. (1982). Value consistency of superior achievers. *Adolescence, 17*(68), 801–813. A study which explored patterns of change or stability in values of superior students over a period of seven years indicated a trend toward greater concern for individual development and less for recognition.

Nisan, M. & Kohlberg, L. (1982). Universality and variation in moral judgment: A longitudinal and cross-sectional study in Turkey. *Child Development, 53*(4), 865–876. This interview study of individuals ages 10 to 28, in Turkey, regarding Kohlberg's moral dilemmas supported claims for structural universality in stages of moral development, as well as some variations according to age and background (whether urban or rural).

Norcini, J. J. & Snyder, S. S. (1983). The effects of modeling and cognitive induction on the moral reasoning of adolescents. *Journal of Youth and Adolescence, 12*(2), 101–115. This study among junior high school students supports the role of conflict, or disequilibrium, as a medium of change in moral reasoning and underscores the significance of role modeling.

Potvin, R. H. & Lee, C. (1982). Adolescent religion: A developmental approach. *Sociological Analysis, 43*(2), 131–144. An analysis is made of the relationship between practice and internal religiousness (experience and belief) among adolescents, ages 13 to 18; and the results are interpreted within the context of a theory of religious development.

Pratt, M. W., Golding, G., & Hunter, W. J. (1983). Aging as ripening: Character and consistency of moral judgment in young, mature, and older adults. *Human Development, 26*, 277–288. The results of a study of young, middle-aged, and older adults supported the hypothesis that moral judgments become more consistent, organized, and philosophically reflective after maturity.

Schneller, R. (1982). The science-religion problem: Attitudes of religious Israeli youth. *Youth and Society, 13*(3), 251–282. On the basis of studies of Israeli youth strategies are examined for helping them resolve conflicts between scientific theories and basic beliefs of Orthodox Jews.

Shafii, M. & Shafii, S. L. (1982). *Pathways of human development: Normal growth and emotional disorders in infancy, childhood, and adolescence.* New York: Thieme Stratton, Inc. Stages of human development are discussed from varied perspectives; and the assessment and treatment of emotional disorders are considered from an integrated developmental perspective.

Stipek, D. J. (1983). A developmental analysis of pride and shame. *Human Development, 26*(1), 42–54. Theoretical and practical questions are discussed regarding the development of pride and shame in children and adolescents.

Chapter Seven

Psychobiological Sex Roles

This chapter concerns adolescents' psychosexual development—how male and female sex roles emerge as the psychobiological consequences of sex drive, sexual awareness, and sexual interests, as distinct from the broader social and economic roles of men and women, which will be treated in a later chapter. Within the context of this discussion, **sex roles** refer to the patterns of behavior considered appropriate for each sex, and **sex drive** is the psychological condition that causes the organism to desire and be selectively receptive to sex experience.

SOCIAL SIGNIFICANCE OF THE SEX DRIVE

The consequences of sexual behaviors involve some of the fundamentals of group living, such as marriage, parenthood, inheritance, and property laws. At the same time, the physiology of the organism is such that it is possible to frustrate sex drive to an extent not possible with other basic drives. Hence, society has been able to regulate the expression of sex drive to a much greater extent than other drives.

Every culture has its own codes concerning sexual behaviors. For example, the Nama Hottenhots of South Africa permit the practice of masturbation, of which our own culture disapproves. Whatever the local custom, rules for sexual conduct are enforced with such vigor that the individual is prone to feel that the practices within one's own culture are the only "natural" ones. Nevertheless, the existence of wide variations makes it clear that sexual practices are mostly culturally determined.

The private sphere of intimacy takes on new meaning in a complex, impersonal, automated technocracy. Active sharing and loving between persons becomes the antidote to dehumanization. If intimacy becomes the basis for establishing identity of marriage partners—and such a trend has appeared—adolescent sexual experiences may become a means of experimentation with intimate relationships (Maddock, 1973a).

In recent years the significance of sexual activity for youth has been redefined as a corollary to changing sex roles. Since reproduction is less often a requirement of sex activity, sexuality is increasingly perceived as a means of pleasure and communication between two loving individuals (Skovholt, 1978). Adolescents no longer regard sex as simply a way to express intimacy (Rossi, 1977). Nevertheless, males are still two or three times more likely than females to display somewhat casual attitudes toward sexuality (American Council on Education, 1976).

NORMAL SEXUAL DEVELOPMENT

Origin of Sexual Feelings

The human being is not born with sexual emotions, but with a capacity to develop them. Sex hormones are physiological secretions with powerful effects. The relationship between hormones and sex drive in subprimate mammalian species is relatively constant. Even in these species, sexual behavior is to some extent learned, although its built-in structural features set certain limits. In primates, too, sex drive is initially dependent on hormones. When humans or animals are surgically deprived of sex glands before puberty, sexual interests fail to develop. Furthermore, if the human culture fails to provide stimuli, one's urge for sexual activity remains latent throughout life. Once generated, however, sex drive can become extremely insistent.

Since the hormonal substrate itself selects no goal objects and since the structures of primates permit wide variation, the sex drive can be conditioned to be satisfied in many ways. In other words, the satisfaction of sex drive may become associated with a wide variety of persons or objects.

SEX-ROLE DEVELOPMENT

Biological Sex Roles

STAGES IN PSYCHOSEXUAL DEVELOPMENT   Children's sexual behavior can be thought of in terms of biological sex roles and social sex roles. On the one hand, feminine and masculine attitudes emerge as biological consequences of sex awareness, sex interests, and sex drive. Social sex roles, on the other hand, involve patterns of behavior judged appropriate for each sex.

According to Freud and his followers, cultural patterns are so organized that most individuals follow the same general stages in psychosexual development. In the first of four stages—birth to age 3—the child is narcissistic. Sensual satisfaction is derived from the infant's own body: from the mouth (nursing), from the anus (bowel movements), and from the sex organs (masturbation). Most children arrive at the point where they prolong the toilet experience, presumably for sexual pleasure. Babies also discover pleasant sensations when handling their sexual organs.

According to a contrasting view, infantile sexuality is mainly erogenous, with sensuality indulged in for its own sake. Sensual pleasures relating to anal and bladder evacuation, sometimes perceived as having erotic significance, play no role in adult sexual expression. When genital activities do gain greater significance in later years, adults retrospectively superimpose sensual interpretations onto infants' anal and urethral sensuality.

From ages 3 to 5 comes the phallic stage, when the child's interest focuses on his or her own genital organs. At this stage the child presumably becomes jealous of the same-sex parent while focusing attention on the opposite-sex one. The boy focuses sexual feeling on his mother while envying his father—the so-called **Oedipus complex.** Conversely, the girl identifies with her mother, though blaming the mother for her lack of external genitals, an emotion termed penis envy; collectively, these feelings are called the **Electra complex.**

During the third, or homosexual, period, in accordance with society's demands, children are weaned away from dependence upon their parents and from an exclusive interest in the parents' responses to them. The children are sent to school and are expected to spend their out-of-school hours at play. During middle and late childhood, therefore, boys and girls come to find greater satisfactions within their peer groups. Culturally prescribed differences in play patterns cause children to associate with their own sex, but their interest is not sexual in the usual sense. Nor is the hormonal substrate yet functioning to produce strong erotic feelings. It is therefore somewhat misleading that this period is labeled "homosexual."

The final, or heterosexual, stage normally begins at puberty and continues through life. Having been continuously conditioned to living in a sexually dichotomous society, the individual easily turns to the other sex when pubertal changes occur. Heterosexual adaptation is deemed essential for satisfactory adjustment in a sexually dichotomous society, especially within the family.

Critics of this theory point out that not all individuals go through all these stages, or in this order. Also, they may become arrested at a particular level, or even settle for various blends of such behaviors at any stage.

ADOLESCENTS' SEXUAL ATTITUDES AND PRACTICES

Sexual Practices in America Today

Over the years in America, changes in sexual behaviors and attitudes have occurred. Before World War I, unsupervised dating was unknown. After the war, casual dating and petting became widespread, but relatively few young women lost their virginity before marriage. During the next forty years, until the mid-1960s, early marriages increased but premarital sex among adolescents did not. Even in the mid-1960s, authorities were declaring that teenage female virginity remained unchanged (Bell, 1966). Then came the birth control pill's dramatic entry on the scene in the late 1960s. Since that time, a new and sensational revolution is often presumed to have occurred, but let us examine the evidence.

On the basis of studies at the Institute for Sex Research at Indiana University, Elias (1978) concluded that there had been no sex revolution among youth. Today's adolescents are more permissive in sexual behaviors and discuss sexuality more freely and naturally; they enjoy sex more and feel less guilty about it than their parents did. However, such changes merely represent a healthy trend and do not constitute a sexual revolution.

Other evidence indicates that a sexual revolution has taken place. Adolescents of both sexes are having earlier sex experience than formerly (Hopkins, 1977). This increase in sexual permissiveness is part of a generally liberal trend in adolescents' behaviors and does not mean a complete disavowal of established standards (p. 83). But let us review several studies to determine what forms youths' sexual attitudes and practices have assumed. It is estimated that over half of America's 20 million young people between 15 and 19 years old have had sexual intercourse, as well as a fifth of the 8 million between 13 and 15 (Kapp, Taylor & Edwards, 1980). Moreover, 25 percent of the one million reported cases of gonorrhea each year are teenagers' (Gelman, 1980).

In other research, at Michigan State University, undergraduates (Kallen & Stephenson, 1982) indicated standards controlling intercourse had changed significantly over the past 15 years. In 1967 it was assumed that intercourse would occur only if a couple was in love; but it was also implicit that the progression would be toward marriage (Carns, 1973). It is still assumed that intercourse will take place if couples are in love but not that marriage will follow. There is also support for intercourse in nonlove relationships if they are not exploitative. Even in the late 1960s, young people felt they had to pretend they were in love, to ask for, or to allow, sexual intercourse; whereas standards today "support an honest, undeceptive statement of relationship—friendship, 'being turned on,' etc.—and disapprove the false expression of emotional attachment" (p. 19).

Now let's look at college students' sexual activities. Among college students in a midwestern university (Darling & Hicks, 1982) "64.2% of the males had been involved in intercourse, 14.9% in heavy petting, 16.3% in light petting. Of the females 56.8% had engaged in intercourse, 19.5% heavy petting and 21.9% light petting" (p. 239). There was no important difference in sexual involvement of females and males. Overall, 40.5 percent of the males and 27 percent of the females had engaged in coitus in high school.

Another study at the University of Northern Iowa in 1974 and 1980, comparing their experience with various sexual outlets, indicated that the more recent class had experienced fewer of the less socially approved sexual outlets, such as group sex, sexual contacts with animals, and adult homosexuality. There was no difference in religious and political affiliations of the two groupings (Story, 1982). Apparently, the more conservative social mores of the 1980s curtail the number of students who experience the less approved sexual outlets, although the students did not call themselves conservatives. By 1980 the number of students giving oral-genital stimulation had increased, although there was no change in the number receiving it.

There were certain sex differences in sexual behavior and attitudes. More of the 1980s males than females practiced masturbation and premarital intercourse with other than the intended marriage partner; and of course such outlets have long been socially sanctioned more for males than for females. More females than males had experienced anal intercourse as a passive partner, or had been a victim of rape or attempted rape, which also reflect societal norms. In general, sexual behaviors were more traditional in 1980 than 6 years earlier. Other research regarding college students' sexual behaviors reported that males have more experience than females in various sexual behaviors (Medora & Burton, 1981).

Youth today are also less inhibited by internalized anxieties and fears regarding sex. Formerly, a major problem of college students, with regard to sex, was a feeling of guilt instilled by their parents. However, these days two thirds (63 percent) condone premarital sex—that is, if those involved love each other (Yankelovich, 1983).

Fewer young women feel that they will risk masculine rejection if they are not virgins when they marry; 57 percent reported that the woman should be a virgin when she gets married. Moreover, most Americans now reject the old double standard that husbands may play around a bit but wives should not.

Various reasons have been given for the increase in teenagers' sexual activities. First, teenagers have much less fear of pregnancy these days. Second, the average age of menarche over the past century has fallen from 17 years to $12^{1}/_{2}$ years; and for boys puberty ordinarily begins about age 14. And finally, when authority over teenagers was reduced in the 1960s, this reduction extended to the area of sex.

Today's youth are less inhibited by internalized anxieties and fears regarding sex. (Courtesy of Public Relations Office, State University of New York at Oswego)

Changes in sexual attitudes are not always a simple progression from less to more permissiveness, but involve complex changes over time. Robinson and Jedlicka (1982) report the results of a study of college students' sexual attitudes which employed the same survey in 1965, 1970, 1975, and 1980. In the first decade, 1965–1970, there was a decrease in numbers of those who agreed with the statement, "I feel that premarital sexual intercourse is immoral," with far more males than females agreeing. By 1975 the differences between the sexes had practically disappeared, with 20.7 percent of the females and 19.5 percent of the males agreeing, indicating that the double standard had practically vanished. Both sexes were less likely in 1975 than in 1970 to look upon a woman who had coitus with many men as immoral.

In 1980, however, a change occurred, among females at least. Females began to see premarital sexual intercourse as somewhat more immoral. During the decade from 1965 to 1975 the trend was toward a decreasing influence of the Judeo-Christian ethic and double standard; whereas from 1975 to 1980 the trend reversed, especially for females. By 1980 the number of women perceiving premarital coitus for both sexes as immoral and sinful had increased; for males, too, there was increased agreement that this was true. Recent figures suggest the formation of a new standard in which men require stricter morality of women and women want a stricter morality in men. It is somewhat different from the old double standard, in that women now expect better behavior both from themselves and from men.

In general, the trend since 1975 has been a return to traditional attitudes such as existed before the sexual revolution. There is a tendency for both sexes to have less permissive attitudes, regardless of the extent of their sexual experience. Even though more people are engaging in sexual intercourse with increasing numbers of partners these days, they are more likely to perceive it as immoral and sinful.

Perhaps these apparently contradictory findings can be explained in this manner. Women expect better behavior both from males and from themselves because they are respecting themselves more, perceiving themselves less as sex objects, and expecting males to treat them as equal persons. They are continuing to have more sex partners for several reasons, one being the increasing effectiveness of birth control methods, another the sheer momentum created during the early 1970s. Women, like men, are also coming to accept as valid their own sexual needs. On the other hand, there is some trend toward viewing such behaviors as immoral and sinful, reflecting the influence of such groups as the Moral Majority. In other words, there has not been time yet to sift out these conflicting trends and to arrive at some basic integration of views.

Damon (1983) concludes that "there is no evidence whatsoever that the vast majority of today's teenagers have revolted against early generations' mores by seeking promiscuity rather than stable relationships." Despite a trend over the past several decades toward more premarital sexual intercourse, a large majority still want to marry and to be true to their marital partners; and they hold somewhat traditional ideals regarding monogamy, the family, and marital fidelity (p. 263).

The development of sexual relationships has been viewed too simplistically. Rather, sexual expression "is a complex achievement that requires a coordination of many types of social and physical competencies, including communicative skills, empathy and a firm sense of self (Damon, 1983, p. 264). Rutter (1980) observes that sexual competence does not, as commonly believed, simply come natural to an individual, nor is it somehow made pleasurable by some inborn mechanism. Earlier experiences with intercourse may importantly impact on later ones (Rutter, 1980).

THE PILL A new element unavailable two generations ago—the pill—has had tremendous impact on youth's concepts of the proper function of sex. Historically, a girl felt that her primary adult responsibility would consist in bearing and rearing children; now she is coming to assume that she must limit childbearing. Moreover, girls, formerly charged with guarding the morals of both sexes, have been stripped of this burden by the pill without the built-in, deep-rooted sexual restraints that prepill sexuality imposed on their mothers.

Evaluation of Youth's Sexual Attitudes

It is generally and wrongly assumed that trends will continue in the same direction. Consider the trend toward the decline of the nuclear family as reflected in growing divorce rates and the rapid increase in single households. Those individuals who were in their mid-30s in the late 1970s were just arriving at sexual maturity when the pill appeared on the scene. People over that age had been reared in traditional views of marriage, family, and career. In contrast, those individuals now just emerging from young adulthood may be called the laboratory generation, being the first to have tested the pill in terms of its effects on their attitudes and life styles. This generation, brought up as children in the old traditions, proceeded with the sexual revolution, often getting divorced, moving, running households alone while holding full-time jobs, and returning to school in their 30s to learn a career. Their children, the youth of the later 1970s, had come to perceive such behaviors more as norms than as deviations.

It is inconclusive at this stage to what extent these changes, wrought by the sexual revolution and women's liberation, are temporary or more lasting. Research in the late 1970s involving high school and college students suggests that their concerns for marriage and family are more like those of their grandparents than of their parents (London, 1978). The question arises whether these new attitudes foretell a reversion to traditional norms or whether they are something different.

The laboratory generation itself does not know yet where its new patterns of intimacies may lead them. As they move into older adulthood they may grow weary of frequently changing affections and relationships and, like former generations, become concerned about being lonely in old age and yearning for commitment. Only time can tell what the result will be.

The Double Standard

The liberalization of attitudes toward sexual behavior raises a related question: Is the double standard, whereby the sexes are judged by different codes of sexual morality, fading? It is generally agreed that it is, at least among youth, in terms of sexual intercourse. A comparison of data obtained in 1965, 1970, and 1975 among students attending a southern university indicated that the premarital sex revolution which began in the late 1960s had quickened in pace. In the early 1970s the sexes gradually converged upon a single standard of behavior. Both sexes were more likely in 1975 than in 1970 to view a man who has cohabited with many women as immoral, but less likely in 1975 than in 1970 to view such a woman as immoral. There was a significant decrease among both sexes in the degree that they viewed older women who had had sexual intercourse with many partners as sinful (Bower & Christopherson, 1977). Also evident was a general liberalization in premarital sex behaviors and attitudes, beginning in the 1960s and increasing in the early 1970s.

College students' attitudes toward the proposed Equal Rights Amend-

The double standard is fading among youth. (Courtesy of Public Relations Office, State University of New York at Oswego)

ment reflects a weakened double standard. Seventy-five percent of the author's students in 1980 strongly approved it, another 15.7 percent approved somewhat, and only 9.3 percent opposed it outright.

> FEMALE: I approve of the Equal Rights Amendment. It's about time women and men were considered equal. Unfortunately, this is not recognized by all. Of course, they aren't equal in all aspects, but in those that they are, they should be treated as such.
>
> MALE: I don't approve of ERA because I don't believe women are equal in all respects. Woman's new role in society has contributed to the downfall of our society. If the traditional family were commonplace, our country would be much better off.
>
> MALE: I'm one who would like to believe that the ERA is unnecessary, but I can't because I know that it is. I hate the way people are discriminated against in general (whether it be racial, religious, ethnic, or sexual in nature); and I welcome the attempt at "forced" (if no other) change.

INFLUENCES ON ADOLESCENT SEXUAL DEVELOPMENT

Parental Influence

Parents—the same-sex parent especially—play an important role in their children's sexual development. Fox (1980) observes that adolescent daughters and their mothers are joined together through "their common female sexuality." The physical events of menarche, menstruation, birth, and menopause constitute a "universal experiential link among women. . . . mothers and their daughters are bound together in a time-lagged mutuality of shared sexual experience, a bond that is nonetheless potent for all its unspokenness" (p. 21).

The question might arise: does maternal employment diminish the worth of their relationship? In one study (Hansson, O'Connor, Jones & Blocker, 1981), girls whose mothers were employed outside the home during high school age were more likely to begin sexual relations before age 19, express less concern about the risk of becoming pregnant, and possess less practical knowledge of contraception. The daughters of working mothers were more sexually active and expressed greater willingness to risk pregnancy, despite their lesser knowledge of birth control.

On the other hand, recent research indicates that maternal employment is generally positive regarding adolescent outcomes. Well-adjusted mothers who demonstrate flexibility and competence across a variety of roles, including working, apparently develop adaptability and competence in their adolescent children (Hansson, O'Connor, Jones & Blocker, 1981).

Nevertheless, parents and their children disagree in certain areas which represent potential sources of misunderstanding between them. Parents underestimate the importance of their children's having a girl friend or boy friend and of enjoying dirty jokes, but overestimate their children's physical attractiveness. Rather, they appear to view their children as "presexual and attractive in a childlike way," apparently unwilling to perceive their children as growing up socially and sexually (Offer, Ostrov & Howard, 1981, p. 289). Note this testimony:

> FEMALE: I have many questions in my mind, but if I even mentioned the word sex, mother would warn that we shouldn't talk about such things. I grew up afraid of boys and of life. I was labeled "The Deep Freeze."
>
> MALE: At the age of 14, I became disturbed to learn that many things I had been told about sex were simply "old wive's tales"—such as the baby's being marked if the mother is frightened during pregnancy. When I confronted my mother she still refused to accept what I knew to be true.

A review of the research indicates that mothers and fathers often assume one or both of two responses to their adolescent children's sexuality. On the one hand, they may assume the "ostrich response," evading thought of their children's sexual behaviors. On the other hand, they may become unduly solicitous, especially of their daughters (Fox, 1980, p. 26).

Parents inevitably convey to their children sexual communications, both verbal and nonverbal, both positive and negative in nature. Positive sexual messages include frequency of parents' discussion of sex, liberality of parents' sexual views, and the message that sex is a positive experience; whereas negative sexual messages include indications that sex is a dangerous or dirty experience. Darling and Hicks (1982) found that parents communicated both positive and negative sexual communication to their children, the most frequent one being that sex is a dangerous experience, especially for females.

Parents transmit quite different sexual messages to their sons and daughters. Both sexes receive the message that pregnancy may lead to terrible things, the daughters more often than sons. Daughters learn more frequently that no nice person has sex before marriage and that petting can easily lead to intercourse. Both sexes receive a double message about sex, that it should be satisfying and that it poses dangers. Positive sexual messages constitute a relatively small proportion of those transmitted by the parents and tend to be "overlaid with negative ones that can produce ambivalence at best and guilt and fear at first" (Darling & Hicks, 1982, p. 241).

Females' reports of low satisfaction in sex can be explained in terms of cultural inhibitions placed on them which, combined with the negative messages from parents, tend to obscure the very weak positive messages. Today the culture still sends strong messages to females against sexual experience; and though they are told that sex should be pleasant, the messages are strongly weighted on the negative side both by parents and the culture.

Even within the same culture individual adolescents react differently to the sexual communications that parents convey. For example, in Nigeria, where parents strongly uphold a code of purity in marriage, those adolescents who identify more closely with their parents tend to avoid sexual activity, whereas those more dependent on their peers look on sex more as a matter of pleasure and associate it less with childbearing and marriage. Among a group of young Nigerians studied, 68 percent reported that peers encouraged their sexual activity, whereas 56 percent of those who engaged in no form of sexual activity indicated that they refrained because of their parents (Owuamanan, 1983).

Other Influences

Apparently, the black and white subcultures in America tend to foster somewhat different sexual attitudes. Among 1,015 undergraduates at Rutgers University, females gave more romantic responses and males more erotic responses, but the differences between black males and females were bigger than those between the white sexes. The wide discrepancies between black males and females suggested that there would be considerable conflict between the sexes among blacks in dating situations. The black male was more erotic than the white male, but there was no clear distinction in responses of black and white females. It is possible that black males' greater eroticism may relate to their having historically had less access to other manifestations of manhood or ways of proving masculinity, especially self-assertion. That is, black males have employed sex-role activities as a safe means of proving their masculinity (Houston, 1981).

In a study of undergraduates at the University of Nebraska at Lincoln, Medora and Woodward (1982) determined other factors associated with variations in sexual views. They found, for one thing, that sorority and fraternity membership made no difference, despite the long-held view that members of such organizations were more the "party type" and sexually permissive. Nor was there any difference in replies of subjects born in rural and urban areas or those in upper, upper-middle, or middle social economic groups. However, differences reported with regard to social class have typically not been between segments of the middle class but rather between the working class and the middle class. Those who attended church regularly were more religious, and were also more conservative with regard to views about sex, confirming many other studies, although a few recent ones have found no such differences. With regard to sex the males were much more permissive than the females regarding premarital sex, despite the woman's movement. Note also that although Nebraska is in a more conservative part of the country the findings overall confirmed results of other studies.

Other research, at a southern university, disclosed similar attitudes. A majority of both males and females disapproved of extramarital sex, females more than males, with 39 percent of males and 22 percent of females being permissive. However, the researchers, Medora and Burton (1981), believe that the males' greater approval of extramarital sex did not prove that a double standard of behavioral sex-role norms prevails. They hypothesize that males might give permission to both sexes and that females might expect marital fidelity from both marriage partners.

The general concern over exposure to sexuality, pornography, and sex education in the schools, as they affect premarital sex relations, is without foundation. At least they seem not to contribute to sexual promiscuity. Basic attitudes on sex are acquired from "significant others"—people whose opinion one considers especially important and whose approval one desires (Spanier, 1975).

To a considerable extent, youth's changing sexual practices also reflect modifications in societal values regarding sex. Today a distinction is made between sexual behavior for its own intrinsic value and for procreation. In consequence, the use of contraceptives is widespread (Sussman, 1978).

Sex Education

It is generally agreed that youth need sex education. However, whatever help they obtain comes mostly from peers. In studies of high school students in the same Texas high schools in 1962 and 1974, peers proved the most frequent source of sex information, followed by parents of the same sex, both parents, and books and pamphlets, in that order. Courses, parents, and books and pamphlets declined in importance during that period.

Youth's ignorance about sexual matters reflects this haphazard sex education (Dickinson, 1978). In a survey of 421 high school boys, ages 12 to 19, one third white, one third Hispanic, and one third black, only 50 percent of the questions asked regarding venereal disease and pregnancy were answered correctly. Their mean age for first coitus was 12.8 years, although their sexual activity was erratic—about three times a month with one or two partners. Over half of them depended on unreliable techniques of withdrawal, douche, or no contraception at all (Connolly, 1978).

All categories of youth need more adequate sex education, both in home and school. Most children receive little such teaching from their mothers, but that which exists, even if inaccurate, relates to postponing the child's sexual activity and to providing adequate contraceptive protection for the child (Fox, 1980). In the absence of a healthy relationship between parent and child, however, such education might more effectively be imparted by persons outside the family unit.

Darling and Hicks (1982) believe that sex education for school sex educators and parents is "critical." Parents need to understand "the full range of sexuality including biological, physiological, psychological, emotional and cultural issues" (p. 243). They also need to understand the kind of verbal and nonverbal messages that they are sending to their children. They need more information about the biology and psychology of sex so they can be more accurate and explicit in what they communicate. As for sex educators, they should realize that different messages are being sent to males and females and that somewhere in the developmental process both sexes in different age groups should communicate and explore with each other "where they're at" (p. 243). In this way, perhaps relationships between the sexes will be improved.

Sex education programs, of any caliber, are still exceptions in most schools. Only three states require them and fewer than 10 percent of all students participate in such programs. Most are taught at high school level even though individuals under age 16 are at highest risk for problems associated wtih pregnancy (Rienzo, 1981).

Many suggestions have been made for improving sex education. For example, Thomson (1982) discusses two strategies for preventing pregnancy among unmarried adolescents, based on quite different principles. First, a morality of absolutes portrays premarital sex behavior as wrong, regardless of the consequences. The second morality, of relative consequences, views rightness or wrongness of premarital sex in terms of its consequences for adolescents and society, such as venereal disease and pregnancy.

The moral-absolutes strategy, which encourages unmarried adolescents to abstain from all sexual intercourse, has at least some validity. Adolescents who are closer to their parents are less likely to be sexually active (Inazu & Fox, 1980). However, males are more likely to be influenced by adults outside the family. The relative-consequences strategy simply recognizes that many unmarried adolescents will be sexually active and is concerned about the ineffective or infrequent use of contraceptives. Reasons for nonuse may be either carelessness, lack of information, lack of contraceptive accessibility, or adolescents' belief that it can't happen to them.

The absolute morality, in certain ways, can endanger sexually active teenagers. For one thing, it may inhibit their contraceptive use, for adolescents brought up by moral-absolutists are less likely to find out about or to purchase contraceptives; and they are less willing to use them. Such an upbringing may also close channels of communication in which contraception would be discussed. Thomson (1982) suggests that both strategies may have value for preventing premarital pregnancy, if used in conjunction with each other instead of in conflict with each other. Parents may provide contraceptive information, while maintaining "an ongoing dialogue regarding the morality of particular sexual relationships" (p. 124).

De Anda (1983) observes that the recommendation for early instruction regarding reproduction and birth control is "a rather simplistic approach to a complex social problem" (p. 41). Since sexual activity leading to adolescent pregnancy most often happens in steady relationships, such information should proceed within the general context of interpersonal relations. Thus, young adolescents would come to perceive sexual behaviors as they relate to total personal and interpersonal experiences. Also, since parents' efforts to forbid early steady dating are likely to fail, adolescents should become aware of the possible risks

Sex education is still inadequate and youths' knowledge of sex is highly variable. (Photo by William J. Butcher)

involved, and of precautions that should be taken. It is important that the total focus not be on the adolescent girl, but on the sexes mutually.

Sex education is still woefully inadequate and youths' knowledge of sex highly variable. A study of 288 students, ranging in age from 11 through 18, indicated important differences in sex knowledge and interest according to sex, age, ethnicity, and residence, whether urban or rural. In general, the girls had more knowledge of sexual facts than did the males and were more interested in them—except for two terms, homosexual and pornography. Females were also more interested in control over sex and pregnancy. Finally, they received more information regarding sex from their parents and less from movies than did the males. The older youths were more interested in such terms as pregnancy, birth control, and birth control pills than younger ones, reflecting the influence of having to cope with such matters. Urban, as compared with rural, students were more knowledgeable about sexual terms probably because of urban students' greater exposure to such topics. Among the three ethnic groupings, Anglo students were most knowledgeable, native Americans least, with Hispanics in between (Davis & Harris, 1982).

SPECIAL PROBLEMS OF PSYCHOSEXUAL DEVELOPMENT

Problems of Puberty

Both sexes experience certain "problems of puberty," but in different ways. In puberty, spontaneous erections call a boy's attention to his genitals which, being easily accessible, encourage manipulation. For girls, the most significant biological occurrence, menarche, has a reproductive rather than a sexual meaning. Other anxieties center upon masturbation, petting, intercourse, and the possibility of impregnation.

Most girls are concerned about menarche, which is especially important for their sexual identification. Autobiographical accounts indicate that it is the one overwhelming evidence of femininity, and it seems to mark the final crystallization of sexual identity. Let us examine the evidence.

Until recently little was known about menstruation or how attitudes develop towards it. It appears to be an important event for most adolescents, one associated with physical discomfort, increased emotionality and mood change, as well as disruption of activities (Clarke & Ruble, 1978).

Apparently, girls' own feelings about menstruation are considerably influenced by negative views portrayed to them, such as advertisements for sanitary products which tend to represent menstruation as a "hygenic crisis" (p. 53). Indeed, sociocultural and emotional factors appear to be just as important as biological ones in limiting one's attitudes and experiences with menstruation. Yet, to this date, there has been no truly reliable evidence that connects menstruation with either emotional state or particular behaviors.

It has also been found that feelings about menstruation vary greatly between cultures and subcultures, in terms of religion, and in terms of self-concepts about one's own body, sex, femininity, and illness. In general, views about menstrual effects are determined mostly by beliefs deriving from cultural attitudes and expectations relative to menstruation—and these beliefs are still negative (Stubbs, 1982).

Transitions in the sexual life of males are less dramatic than those in females because sexual maturing proceeds more gradually and both originates and diminishes at a much slower pace. Nevertheless, these transitions are significant for men (Crites, 1978). Indeed, biographical materials indicate that the boy's first ejaculation is a profound experience for him. Slightly over 50 percent experience it after a nocturnal dream, the rest from masturbation. The incidence of fright when the first ejaculation accompanies a dream is 15 percent; from masturbation, 20 percent. Among boys' reactions were these: "It scared the hell out of me"; "I thought I was ill"; "I thought I had hurt myself"; "I thought I had regressed to the age of four and had wet the bed." Only 15 percent of the boys understood the phenomenon at the time of its occurrence, and only 6 percent felt they had been adequately prepared for it by their parents. Although overcome with curiosity, the boys reported considerable embarrassment at the experience and tried to hide the stains on sheets and pajamas.

Little attention has been paid the boy's transition from virginity to non-virginity (Lewis et al., 1978). There is considerable question of what is meant by loss of male virginity: whether it is lost when boys have any kind of intimate sexual contact, or whether it depends upon ejaculation—through female contact, through self-manipulation, or through bringing a female to climax.

Masturbation

FREQUENCY   Masturbation is even more poorly treated than most other sex problems. Masturbation refers to the satisfaction of sexual desire through manipulation of one's own genitals. Frequency varies according to social class, sex, and marital status; and is higher among the better educated (95 percent of college males report having masturbated), compared to 89 percent for those who never went beyond the first eight grades. As for sex differences, "most males masturbate and masturbation results in orgasm for the vast majority of males by age 16. Only about two thirds of all women ever masturbate, and half of this number do it after they have experienced orgasm in petting or coitus" (Gagnon & Simon, 1969, p. 47). Since such data depend on self-report, the true figures are probably higher.

Many boys learn about the practice before they attempt it themselves. Introduction by an older boy or group masturbation is not uncommon among boys in early and middle adolescence. Girls more often discover masturbation themselves; they rarely discuss it and almost never practice it in groups.

Differences in masturbatory experience of the sexes impact upon their sexual adjustment in general. First, note that girls may have sex before they understand their own sexual responses or have achieved genital priority (Darling & Hicks, 1982). In contrast, males, through early masturbation, develop genital priority far earlier and learn about the body sexually in ways that females do not. The male masturbates to orgasm over 1,500 times before he marries, whereas females masturbate an average of 220 times before they marry. Masturbation is important for creating genital priority by focusing sexual feelings on the genitals.

The sparse amount of masturbation among young females produces a nonsexual period before their genitals become their chief source of sexual pleasure. Indeed, early intercourse precedes genital priority for many females—hence, may produce lower satisfaction. In contrast, the practically universal practice of masturbation among males produces a feeling that sex is both all right and essential. Masturbation also provides males with a certain sexual independence, whereas females, without masturbation as a recourse, lack the same degree of sexual autonomy.

Males' masturbation experience may also contribute to their approach to sexual intercourse as adults, when they focus almost exclusively on "penile sensations." The fact that females are more concerned with feelings over their whole bodies may contribute to lack of satisfaction in their sexual contacts with males.

EFFECTS ON ADOLESCENTS   In the early part of this century, boys, especially, were warned of the presumed severe effects of masturbation and of those who might encourage such a practice. In 1905, Hall advised youth as follows:

> If a boy in an unguarded moment tries to entice you to masturbatic experiments, he insults you. Strike him at once and beat him as long as you can stand, etc. Forgive him in your mind, but never speak to him again. If he is the best fighter and beats you, take it as in a good cause. If a man scoundrel suggests indecent things, slug him with a stick or a stone or anything else at hand. Give him a scar that all may see; and if you are arrested, tell the judge all, and he will approve your act, even if it is not lawful. If a villain shows you a filthy book or picture, snatch it; and give it to the first policeman you meet, and help him to find the wretch. If a vile woman invites you, and perhaps tells a plausible story of her downfall, you cannot strike her; but think of a glittering, poisonous snake. She is a degenerate and probably diseased, and even a touch may poison you and your children (p. 470).

The question is: Does masturbation deserve its bad name? Even compulsive masturbation is of concern only in terms of the anxiety it generates or what it suggests about the individual's adjustment. Lonely, insecure adolescents may become so wrapped up in pleasant sexual fantasies that they withdraw into themselves and cease to make adjustments to other people. Some writers even suggest that masturbation, as normally practiced, is desirable. For one thing it centralizes sexual impulses in the genitals. For another, it permits safe catharsis for sexual feelings, without involving exploitation of another. Finally, it is one aspect of self-discovery and of coming to know one's own body and feelings (Hettlinger, 1970).

Homosexuality

INCIDENCE   Confused thinking concerning masturbation is equalled, or even exceeded, by that relating to homosexuality. In 1974, 20 to 25 percent of males reported at least one homosexual experience, and 2 to 4 percent had remained primarily homosexual (Hunt, 1974). Where a single homosexual experience occurs it is usually in early adolescence. Over half reported no homosexual experiences after age 16. Apparently homosexuality is about three times as common in males as females. Indeed, almost all sexual deviations are far more common among males (Katchadourian & Lunde, 1975). [Some researchers, among them Money and Ehrhardt (1972), suggest that the male's sexual identity is more uncertain and fragile than is the female's.]

CURRENT ATTITUDES TOWARD HOMOSEXUALS Young homosexuals today may be less self-rejecting because they do not face such strong social sanctions against them. Only a minority of adults feel discomfort with having friends who are acknowledged homosexuals, although a small majority still believe such relations are morally wrong (Yankelovich, 1983). On the other hand, homosexuals still suffer from considerable negative reaction, even among presumably more enlightened university students. In one experiment half a group of interviewers wore "gay and proud" buttons and mentioned their affiliation with the Association of Gay Psychologists and the other half wore no buttons and simply said that they were graduate students working on their theses. Without letting the students being interviewed become aware of it, the distance they placed their chairs from the interviewers was measured. Though interviewers and students were of the same sex, students pushed their chairs almost a foot farther away from the interviewers perceived as gays.

A comparison of lesbian and heterosexual women indicated that lesbian feminists, compared to heterosexual feminists, reported that during high school their fathers were somewhat repressive and would not tolerate expression of anger (Johnson, Stockard, Acker & Naffziger, 1975). It appears that the lesbian woman's image of the father, but not of the mother, differs from the images that heterosexual women have of their fathers.

MYTHS REGARDING HOMOSEXUALITY Many common views about homosexuality are false. A comparison of homosexuals with nonhomosexual controls in the San Francisco Bay area, commissioned by the National Institute of Mental Health and conducted by Bell and Weinberg, indicates that homosexuals do not resemble the stereotype that people hold of them. They differ little from others except in their sexual preference. They engage in sexual violence, seduction, and rape less than heterosexuals do; and they are less likely to make objectionable sexual advances. The males appear more interested in impersonal sexual encounters while the women prefer lasting relationships. The men's sexuality relates to males' greater tendency to divorce sex from affection, to validate their masculinity in terms of sexual activity, and to perceive fidelity as an undue restriction of their independence. The male's greater promiscuity may also derive from his lack of opportunity to meet other males on anything more than a social basis. The researchers concluded that the relative instability of homosexual relationships derives from society's oppression of them. Steady relationships with a partner are meaningful for homosexuals of both sexes. The majority of homosexuals are satisfied with being what they are; and lesbians are more contented than gay men. In general, both sexes are about as well adjusted as heterosexuals (Montagu, 1978).

Such limited evidence as we have confirms that lesbians feel positively about their lives. In a survey of 140 lesbians, Marilyn Fleener of California State

University found that they were not the products of any particular kind of family situation. Most of them had acquired their present sexual orientation by their early teens, despite pressures on them to be heterosexual. About four in five had been tomboys as children but few wanted to be men and those few only because of male privileges in society. Most of them were faithful to their partners and 98 percent denied playing butch-fem roles. A full 80 percent experienced orgasm every time or most of the time and only 7 percent, compared with far greater numbers of heterosexual women, rarely or never experienced orgasm. However, lesbians perceive sexual activity as only one aspect of a generally rewarding life style and object to society's focus on the sexual activities of their lives (Lesbian life styles, 1977).

Another myth is that most homosexuals are poorly adjusted sexually. After a monumental study of homosexuals, Masters and Johnson, of the sex research institute in St. Louis, reported that homosexuals who are committed to each other, as distinct from the cruising variety, appear well adjusted sexually. They spend much time in preliminaries to orgasm, in contrast to married couples who seem to be mostly goal-oriented, moving rapidly from foreplay to intercourse (Sex and the homosexual, 1979, p. 82). The cruising variety move as quickly to the final goal as do the heterosexuals. Among the homosexuals who had sex problems, the males' most common one was impotence and the lesbians' was failure to reach orgasm.

Early Love

Certain problems for which we lack definite answers relate to early love. Some adolescents fall in and out of love with the agility of circus acrobats. Such a perennial characteristic of young adolescents, described in biographical excerpts of the early 1900s, is familiar to young adolescents today:

> Beth's first love affair was with a bright, fair-haired, fat-faced boy, who sat near her pew on Sundays. They looked at each other during services, and she felt a glad glow in her chest spread over her, dwelt on his image, smiled, and even the next day felt a new desire to please. She watched for him to pass from school. When he appeared, "she felt a most delightful thrill shoot through her." The first impulse to fly was conquered; she never thought a boy beautiful before. (Hall, 1905, p. 553)

> Jacob Riis "fell head over heels in love with sweet Elizabeth" when he was 15 and she was 13. His "courtship proceeded at a tumultuous pace, which first made the town laugh, then put it out of patience and made some staid matrons express the desire to box my ears soundly." She played among the lumber where he worked, and he watched her so intently that he scarred his shinbone with an adze he should have been minding. He cut his forefinger with an ax when she was dancing on a beam nearby, and once fell off a roof when craning his neck to see her go round a corner. (Hall, 1905, p. 586)

The usual pattern involves a somewhat wary emergence of sexual behaviors in midadolescence, which involves some hesitant experimentation, developing in time into more lasting and intimate sexual relationships (Miller & Simon, 1980). Teenage sexual partners often do not share the same values, or communicate about the difference. They interact somewhat egocentrically and in a somewhat "parallel" way, demonstrating little interest in the other's understanding of the relationship.

A second problem at this stage is establishing an appropriate level of intimacy. First, note that early pregnancies among adolescents result in premature commitment. That is, adolescence itself requires the postponement of any long-term commitment that might restrict the growth of one's self-identity and life style. On the other hand, true intimacy cannot be completely without commitment, because sexual expression with no commitment lacks significance and encourages exploitation.

Erikson (1968) considers intimacy the major task of young adults and he obviously has heterosexual relationships in mind. Nevertheless, competencies in the task of intimacy have their roots in skills acquired at earlier stages, often with the same sex. Males' uninvolved manner of relating to each other may interfere with their ability successfully to cope with the intimacy task of young adulthood when opposite-sex relationships become significant. Those who do make such a transition may owe it to females who socialize them for heterosexual relations on the basis of their own prior experiences with same-sex intimacy (Fischer, 1981).

Yankelovich (1983) sees persons so committed to self-fulfillment that they focus on their own needs instead of developing intimate relationships that they need; and they become separate from others. Although "their goal is to expand their lives by reaching beyond the self," the strategy they use has the effect of "drawing them inward toward an ever-narrowing closed-off 'I' " (p. 40).

Contraception

Contraception is of growing significance, partly because 20 percent of babies born in the United States are to teenagers (Finkel & Finkel, 1978). Five in six infants are born to girls age 14 and younger; and over one in three born to 14- to 19-year-olds are born out of wedlock. Early chidbearing is associated with higher maternal mortality rate, toxemia, prolonged labor, and iron deficiency anemia. Teenage mothers' infants also experience a high incidence of death, prematurity, cerebral palsy, mental retardation, and increased risk of epilepsy (pp. 443–444). Despite this situation, sexually experienced teenage boys do not take effective precautions to avoid impregnating their partners during coitus. Among a sampling of urban high school boys, only 28 percent had used a condom at last coitus, the whites more consistently than the blacks and the Hispanics, and older adolescents more than the younger ones.

Various reasons may exist for not taking adequate precautions. A plurality of the boys said they did not use a condom at last coitus because they did not have one with them. A quarter said that using condoms was simply unimportant to them and a matter of little concern.

One study indicated that adolescent girls who do not employ birth control techniques despite being sexually active may be placed in three groups; those who: (1) lack accurate contraceptive information, (2) have such information but lack motivation to use it, and (3) desire a baby as a means of fulfilling the only adult role which seems important to them (Ross, 1979).

Several other factors may account for adolescents' ineffective and inconsistent use of contraceptive techniques. Sex encounters may be infrequent and spontaneous; the adolescents may have poor access to contraceptive services; or they may be misinformed about contraception. Most teenagers use contraceptives occasionally and their use "is influenced by the availability of birth control devices, by the level of communication between the sexual partners, by their understanding of cyclic fertility and risk factors and by the effects on their behavior of drug and alcohol use" (Rienzo, 1981, p. 192).

Herold (1981) reported that female adolescents and youth may not purchase contraceptives because of embarrassment, depending somewhat on the device employed. In general, they felt more at ease when buying birth control pills than other contraceptive devices. They were especially embarrassed asking for condoms, perhaps because they view it as a male's responsibility and are anxious lest others consider them sexually aggressive. They might also associate condoms with sexual promiscuity. Perhaps buying birth control pills is less embarrassing because the pill is sometimes used to regulate menstrual cycles.

Among factors associated with contraceptive embarrassment, feelings of guilt about sex were particularly strong and strongly affected the use of contraceptives. Other factors influencing such embarrassment were attitudes of peers and parents, especially parents' feelings about premarital sexual intercourse. When buying contraceptives close to their parents' home, young females were more aware of the parents' attitudes, possibly because they were afraid the parents might find out. In distant locations they were more concerned about their peers' attitudes.

Herold (1981) believes that counselors and family-planning educators should be aware of the factor of contraceptive embarrassment and its deterrence to contraceptive use. Sex education courses should present not only information regarding birth control, but also those factors, including contraceptive embarrassment, which diminish contraceptive use. Moreover, young people should be able to buy contraceptives in locations which are "non-judgmental and anonymous" (p. 241).

In contrast, Kallen and Stephenson (1980) believe that college students, at least, encounter no real barriers, internally or externally, in purchasing contraceptives. Males chiefly buy condoms and females the pill, and neither experience any difficulties in purchasing them. The major factor determining where they purchase them is convenience, which encourages college students to rely less on such ineffective techniques as the rhythm and early withdrawal (Kallen & Stephenson, 1980).

For high school students, especially, Fisher (1983) suggests certain techniques in sex education courses to prevent pregnancy. One is to have them "walk through," in fantasy, steps in the contraceptive process, including "learning about birth control, anticipating intercourse and obtaining contraceptives" (p. 71). When they feel comfortable about the fantasy procedures, they might proceed through them in reality, telephoning for an appointment at a birth control clinic, for example, or "role playing a pre-sex discussion of contraception with a partner" (p. 71). Fisher also suggests that adolescents habituate the inclusion of contraception in their preparation for dates, for example, deciding what movie to attend and picking up "a three-pack of condoms" (p. 71).

Abortion

A review of research on adolescent girls' abortion reactions (Horowitz, 1978) discloses few psychiatric complications, with girls under age 16 being at somewhat greater emotional risk. In a study of pregnant teenagers from low-income families, all of whom had had a previous induced or spontaneous abortion or other infant or fetal loss, fewer than a fourth had pursued "a sequence of adaptive responses" (p. 555). They had expressed little sorrow, anger, or mourning although those who had deliberately induced abortions avoided talking or thinking about terminating the second pregnancy. Even this difficulty passed with time. In many cases their boyfriends had been angry at them for having an abortion; and some of the boyfriends learned of the abortion only after it occurred. Few of the young women had decided upon the abortion themselves and complied only after being convinced they had no choice. Fewer than a quarter approved it afterward, chiefly because they judged abortion the same as killing the child. Those supporting abortion believed it advisable in cases when the woman was too young or not ready to have a child. The young women were concerned about the effects of abortion or stillbirth on their bodies; and some became pregnant again soon after an abortion to prove to themselves that they could conceive again. Such girls get little support from their parents, who are usually relieved that the pregnancy has been terminated.

A comparison of pregnant black girls who had chosen abortion with girls who planned to have their babies, and also with nonpregnant controls, disclosed interesting findings (Falk, Gispert & Baucom, 1981). The nonpregnant controls appeared to be the best socialized, followed by those requesting abortion, and finally by those planning to have the child. Apparently those planning to go through term felt some void which they hoped to fill by having the child; and becoming a mother was a significant step toward achieving an adult female role. It was hardly surprising that those girls who had been seriously involved with their boy friends had fewer problems, were better socialized, and seemed to think more clearly than those who had become pregnant through casual relationships. The researchers had desired that the girls who planned to have their babies would be the most mature and thus best prepared to become mothers; however, their findings did not support this wish.

Most college students approve abortion, at least in certain cases. Of 118 undergraduates at SUNY Fredonia, 18 would deny abortion for any reason; 41 would grant every abortion request; and 59 would recommend abortion in some cases but not others. The antiabortion group was more likely than the others to agree with statements that "abortion is murder" and "premarital sex is immoral"; and they attended church twice as often as the mixed group and three times as much as the prochoice group. The antiabortion group had been reared in generally more sex-restrictive environments, at least with regard to premarital sex. The prochoice adolescents had been socialized in less guilt-inducing climates; and they accorded the potential mother's choice priority in making abortion decisions. The researchers, Allgeier and Rywick (1981) suggested that a procedure proposed by Nathanson (1979) might provide a way out of the dilemma. This remarkable physician, Nathanson, who reported 75,000 abortions performed under his administration, suggests a transplant procedure. When a woman finds that she is carrying a fetus which she does not desire to have, the fetus might be transplanted into the womb of a woman who has been unable to conceive but wants a child. Thus, both fetal rights and the rights of women desiring to terminate their pregnancies would be protected.

Another study, of undergraduates in a large southern university, indicated that quite different factors related to differences between male and female attitudes toward abortion. The single factor relating most significantly to the males' attitude was general conventionality—that is, the more conventional they were the more they opposed abortion. Women were likely to consider both the welfare and rights of the fetus—thinking of it as a potential child—but also the rights and welfare of the woman who becomes involved in a pregnancy that she does not desire (Finlay, 1981).

Sexual Assault

A commonly neglected topic among normal youths is that of sexual assault, which is far more common than generally realized. Among a sampling of 42 white females, ages 13 to 17, involved in a residential delinquency intervention program, half reported at least one sexual molestation experience, most often forceable rape, and a majority were affected adversely by the experience. However, the disturbances were not of the severe type often reported in child sexual-assault literature. Rather, they reported reactions more characteristic of adult victims. Twenty-one of the 42 who had been molested had been victimized at ages ranging from 4 to 17, most often between ages 13 and 14. Most of the assailants were friends; 6 were family members or relatives; only 3 were strangers. Although the majority told no one, those who did tell most often confided in friends. Fewer than a third told a parent or guardian (23%) or a helping professional (12%). Overall, few suffered "intense traumatic reactions" from the assault (p. 548).

Youth and adult reactions are interpreted somewhat differently. Adult victims are allowed to take absences from work or school, to travel, and to regulate their own use of drugs. In contrast, the same behaviors shown by youth after sexual assault are labeled truancy, running away, acting out, and substance abuse (Gruber, Jones & Freeman, 1982).

A special form of assault is incest, in which an adult sexually victimizes a child. Incest is interpreted as "all forms of sexual contact, sexual exploitations through pornography, etc. and sexual overtures initiated by an adult who is related to the child by family ties or through surrogate family ties" (p. 730). Researchers consistently report that most incest victims are females younger than 17 years old; the perpetrator of incest is most often the biological father; and incest ordinarily is a long-term matter beginning before the child reaches puberty. It most often occurs in unbroken homes where there has been no divorce, separation, or death of spouse; and first-born daughters are more often involved than later-borns. Other factors associated with incest are "alcoholism on the part of fathers, authoritarian fathers, indifferent or intimidated mothers, the wife's rejection or refusal of sexual intercourse, social isolation of the family and role disorganization in the family. . . ." (p. 731).

Various means have been suggested to prevent, treat, or thwart incest, including sex education and counseling. Although such methods are believed to be helpful, rigorous evaluation of their outcomes are lacking. In addition, there is need for larger research samples and more and better measurements (Vander Mey & Neff, 1982).

Teenage Prostitution

Baizerman, Thompson, Stafford-White, and "an old-young friend" (a former teenage prostitute) (1979) discuss the growing practice of adolescent prostitution, on the basis of field work with young prostitutes in the twin-cities area in Minnesota. In this area the girl prostitutes range in age from 13 to 18; some have a male pimp, others do not. Many begin working independently and then transfer to working for a pimp. Most of them work the street—city blocks and particular locations such as shopping malls or areas near bars and after-hours clubs. Sex acts most often take place in cars, sometimes in apartments, and occasionally in motel and hotel rooms. Many of the prostitutes practice birth control—pills first and the IUD second. The girls have gained whatever information they know about venereal disease from "the street." Pimps tend to discourage the girls from using hard drugs because its use increases risk of arrest and endangers their operation. The pimps are male and most of the younger ones are black. Neighborhood pimps are 17, 18, and 19 years old; those from outside the state are older, having moved up from being neighborhood pimp to small businessman. The younger pimps are mostly disadvantaged and many of them will give up pimping if they find other work opportunities. Younger ones may use force to hold the girls, but older ones rarely do, generally employing psychological and emotional techniques to make the girls dependent upon them. Much of "the action" occurs in the afternoon and late in the evening. The afternoon works well with married men who must be at home in time for dinner.

Another study, of 200 street prostitutes, throws additional light on this relatively unknown group. Their average age was 22, 70 percent being under 21, 60 percent 16 and under, and many 10, 11, and 12 years old. Over two-thirds of the sample (68%) were from families with average or higher income, but at the time of study 88 percent were either very poor or just making it. A majority reported having had serious home problems, 70 percent having experienced emotional abuse, 62 percent physical abuse, and 60 percent sexual abuse. When asked how they found out about prostitution 32 percent mentioned movies, books, and magazines, 14 percent friends, 7 percent the kids at school, 6 percent a neighbor, and 13 percent a family member. On the average they were working regularly as prostitutes by age 16. The majority (55%) had become involved in prostitution through someone active in the business—by pimps, madams, or women recruiting for pimps. Often the pimps and madams had "sweet talked" them into becoming prostitutes or made threats.

Among reasons given for becoming prostitutes three-fourths said they had no other options if they were to survive economically. Some felt they might have survived by dealing drugs or going on welfare. Although they had had good friends in high school, after leaving school and beginning prostitution a third of them had no friends. A large number had run away from home and had no other means of support. Not surprisingly, 94 percent felt quite negatively toward themselves (Silbert & Pines, 1982).

In recent years girls have been more likely to go into prostitution and stay there because they believe that they are in love with their pimp. He makes them feel cared for and paid attention to. Girls in the pimp's "stable" compete with their sisters to become the pimp's main woman. Thus prostitution in such cases is not so much a matter of immorality as a distortion of affectional needs.

It is very difficult to deal with those girls already engaged in adolescent prostitution, but those not already inducted may be educated by regarding how pimps operate, especially in high-risk neighborhoods.

Unwed Teenage Parents

EXTENT OF THE PROBLEM   The incidence of teenage out-of-wedlock pregnancies is growing at an alarming rate. Over a million of such pregnancies occur each year, accounting for about half of all out-of-wedlock births in the United States.

THE UNWED FATHER   The unwed teenage father has been a missing person in most adolescence texts. Here, two unwed fathers tell what they feel they have learned from their experience.

> AGE 19: I regret what I have done but feel that I must make the best of what has happened. I know now that no matter how much in love you may think you are, you are still responsible for your emotions and must control them and aid the girl in controlling hers.
>
> AGE 20: To be more careful. However, I would take the same chance again, but not with just any girl.

A study of young unmarried fathers, chosen from the heavily populated black areas of Tulsa and Chicago, indicated that 70 percent of the Tulsa fathers and 89 percent of the Chicago fathers saw nothing wrong with having a child out of wedlock. Almost all of the Tulsa and Chicago fathers were concerned about the child's future. Both groups were accepting of their young fatherhood and concerned about the child and the young mother, whom most of them said they loved. However, it is uncertain whether their profession of love also carried with it any feeling of commitment and long-term involvement. Note, too, that these young fathers had volunteered to take part in the research; and it is uncertain to what extent their views could be generalized to all young black fathers (Hendricks & Montgomery, 1983).

In general, the unwed father gets less support than the unwed mother. He obtains no help from his peers, partly because boys do not form the intimate kinds of friendships girls do. Besides, young fathers feel that anybody desiring to contact them is seeking them for some punitive reason (Connolly, 1978).

The number of young unwed mothers is growing rapidly as is the number who choose to keep their babies. (Photo by William J. Butcher)

THE UNWED MOTHER   The teenage mother also has problems, one being a false stereotype of her as promiscuous and immoral. In reality, she can be any girl; there is little hard evidence that girls who become pregnant are either different from others or desire to be pregnant. Before the pregnancy most of the girls had gone with their partners at least six months and felt committed to and in love with them.

The number of young unwed mothers is growing rapidly. Although the birth rate in the country is going down, that for teenagers, age 17 years and younger, is rising (Held, 1981). Note, too, that younger teenagers are at greater risk than older mothers with regard to infant mortality, and such defects as mental retardation, blindness, and epilepsy; and their prenatal care is also not as adequate. Pregnant teenagers are also less likely to complete high school although many programs exist today to help them, at least during the pregnancy period. After the child's birth there is little help with transportation, day care, and other matters that would make it possible for them to continue in school (Held, 1981).

Ninety-five percent of teen mothers keep their babies today, compared to 10 or 12 percent years ago (Connolly, 1978); and those mothers who give up their children differ in certain ways from those who keep them (Juhasz, 1974). Those who give them up more often identify with adults and possess strongly traditional sex norms, including intolerance for illegitimacy. Girls who keep their babies tend to be better educated, more independent, more intelligent, and more emotionally stable. Many couples marry merely to make the child legitimate—no wonder that teenagers' divorce rate is five times that of adults.

A study of low-income pregnant adolescents (Smith, Nenney, Weinman & Mumford, 1982) pointed to the need for helping adolescents to perceive individual risk. Apparently most adolescents simply lack adequate biological knowledge about pregnancy. Researchers recommend various alternatives for helping teens to sense their own risk. The common technique has been to encourage girls to mark the dates of their menses on charts or calendars. However, such timing is poorly comprehended by adolescents and often proves meaningless. Effective approaches might include such creative teaching tools as educational comic books or even games of chance which focus risk-taking on reproductive issues.

However, until adolescents have both the motivation and maturity to employ contraceptive methods effectively, this knowledge will not be used (Peabody, McHenry & Cordero, 1981). Adolescents vary in degree of motivation. For example, a study of teenagers, age 17 and under, in the Houston area—including Caucasians, Mexican-Americans, and blacks—indicated that the black mothers keeping their babies had the highest self esteem. The Mexican-Americans were most approving of the pregnancy itself, which makes prevention of pregnancy difficult. Blacks perceived the pregnancy as disadvantageous; the Caucasians rated it more highly; and the Mexican-Americans highest of all (Held, 1981).

Young Marrieds

Most jurisdictions recognize the right to marry at ages that coincide with, or even antedate, the age for completing secondary education. But psychologies of adolescence neglect young marrieds because they have, in effect, entered adult society. Besides, married adolescents constitute only a small portion of the total youth population.

In recent years, especially, young marrieds have tended to remain in school. Formerly, their determination to stay in high school met with stiff resistance from school authorities. Although policies varied widely, most married youth suffered a wide variety of restrictions. Nowadays, the most general reaction is to permit students to continue in school after they marry if they wish to do so. The legal picture is confusing, with few guidelines established. However, no constitutional justification exists for restriction, especially for expulsion or lengthy suspension. The more common practice of restricting participation in extracurricular activities has also been challenged. Many school officials still prefer not having pregnant or married students enrolled. A more positive policy toward married students is slowly emerging but still has a long way to go.

The frustrations of young marrieds with children are especially acute. In a study of young mothers, about half reported greater responsibility and less freedom after they had the child. A few did report that they had more fun after the child came. Many problems connected with motherhood are enhanced by the young mothers' youthfulness and lack of skills. Certain of their "life choices" are terminated or greatly limited after pregnancy and childbirth (Cannon-Bonventre & Kahn, 1979). The most common problem is lack of financial resources. The parents often have very poor and undependable resources and many of them depend almost wholly on public welfare.

Young parents express strong need for concrete assistance in obtaining clothing, child care, housing, food, medical care, and job training. Most often they are provided counseling services with little concrete help. Also there is "almost universal fragmentation" of such services so that there is little integration of programs (p. 19).

FUTURE PERSPECTIVES

Whatever is written about youth and sex may be outdated before the ink has dried on the page. Convictions about what youth should or should not do in this area are often firmer than the facts that support them. Are youth's attitudes the harbingers of demoralization and decay or simply a response to changing needs and times? What sorts of philosophies, attitudes, or practices might be appropriate, on a continuing modified basis, to prepare youth to achieve satisfying yet realistic adaptations in the years ahead?

Adolescent sexual attitudes and experience influence later adjustment in several ways. Some adolescents fail to arrive at the stage of normal heterosexual adjustment and hence have little prospect of a successful marriage. For other adolescents, strong sexual attraction or involvement leads to early marriage, before they have achieved psychological or physical maturity, in effect denying themselves the chance to prepare for adulthood. Once married, they will find it difficult to pursue the patterns of personal development normally expected of adults. Interviews conducted with a national sampling of 30-year-olds who had parented a child during adolescence indicated that the experience had significant effects on their young adult lives. Such parenting occurs most often among low-ability and low-socioeconomic groups. The most immediate result, especially for girls, was the termination of their schooling. Their lower level of education, in turn, restricted most of them to low-level low-paying positions. About twice as many of them had been separated or divorced, compared with the average for all young adult parents (21 percent versus 11 percent). They had children at an earlier age and more children than did the average; however, they attached just as much importance to relationships with their children (Russ-Eft, Sprenger & Beever, 1979).

The Conference on Major Transitions in the Human Life Cycle (Scanlon, 1979) emphasizes the need for better genetic education and counselling to make young adults become aware of genetic defects and susceptibilities that might be transmitted to their offspring. Youth should be informed that for certain conditions, such as cleft palate, cleft lip, congenitally dislocated hips, and arteriosclerosis, a genetic susceptibility has been established. They should be advised about precautions to be exercised by people with a family history of breast or lung cancer and to dangers of smoking and drinking during pregnancy. Young people should also examine such questions as the morality of allowing a preventable birth of an extremely defective child.

They may have to examine issues relating to sperm banks, perhaps designed to upgrade the human race. As the population proliferates, the question will arise, Who will have the right to reproduce? The author has found that such questions upset her classes of mostly college seniors, because their views are rooted in the tradition that any adult has the right to reproduce.

College-age youth, especially, are keenly interested in how such matters

In general, the sexual attitudes and behaviors of today's youth hold good prospects for future sexual relationships. (Courtesy of Public Relations Office, State University of New York at Oswego)

will affect their own futures. In one study (Chico & Hartley, 1981) they displayed great interest in reproductive engineering and expanded choices in methods of procreation, such as sex predetermination of offspring, sperm banking, test-tube conception with embryo transplant, development of artificial wombs, and human cloning. A large majority (83%) felt that "the general public should be included in discussions and decision-making regarding genetic engineering" (p. 15).

In general, the sexual attitudes and behaviors of today's youth hold good prospects for future sexual relationships. They talk about sex more openly and are more accepting of themselves sexually than were former generations. Also, instead of the sexes exploiting each other or males looking on females primarily as sex objects, most young people have come to utilize sex as a means of communication between mutually respecting persons. The result should be healthier and more satisfying marriages.

SUMMARY

An individual's psychobiological sex role involves the consequences of sex drive, sexual awareness, and sexual interests, as distinct from the broader social roles of the sexes. The consequences of sexual behavior are important because they relate to the fundamentals of group living, including marriage and property laws. For the individual, the sex role is important for all his or her heterosexual relationships, and integrally affects both self-concept and personality development. Sexual intimacy becomes especially important in today's complex technocracies, as an antidote to dehumanization. Indeed, sexuality is increasingly perceived by youth as a means of pleasure and communication between loving individuals, and not simply as a process of sensual gratification.

Because of either common biological or sociocultural factors, most individuals proceed through similar stages of sexual development, the first stage being the narcissistic period when an individual presumably derives genital satisfaction from his or her own body. In the next, or phallic stage, the boy presumably becomes emotionally attached to his mother and the girl to her father. In late childhood, or the so-called homosexual stage, an individual is supposed to derive sexual satisfaction from like-sex peers. In the final or heterosexual stage, which begins at puberty and continues throughout life, the individual seeks such satisfaction from members of the other sex.

Despite some evidence to the contrary, most studies, with a few exceptions, indicate that large changes in youth's sex attitudes and practices have occurred, in a more permissive direction. Also, the data suggest that more liberal behaviors are following in the wake of increasingly liberalized attitudes. One element was the pill, which set the stage for a new level of permissiveness, especially among females. Meantime, the double sexual standard, whereby the sexes are judged by different codes of sexual morality, is fading. Even males, at least in the middle class, who stand to lose some of their erstwhile sexual advantage, no longer favor the double standard. Blue-collar and lower-class males still support it, though not as firmly as before. The older generation is also becoming more liberal in sexual attitudes; however, the gap between the generations, on matters of sex, is wide. Youth themselves can hardly grasp the realities of their parents' own sexuality, reflecting a common notion that sex behaviors are somehow less desirable in later years.

Of the various influences on children's sex development the family is perhaps most important, although peers and mass media have a strong impact also. By contrast, the influence of pornography is probably slight, even superficial, by comparison. Such influences have not been wholly satisfactory, as youth's sex problems bear witness.

Some problems, perhaps inherent in adolescence itself, at least in this culture, relate to early love, petting, and the sometimes unfortunate consequences of pregnancy. It is difficult for adolescents to determine proper levels of intimacy or to cope with their sexual impulses. Most of them lack much basic information about sexual behavior and its consequences. Although they have access to far more effective contraception techniques than any previous generation, they are often uninformed or simply careless. For one thing, sexual instruction is completely inadequate even in as sophisticated an age and society as ours. While many parents and educators favor sex instruction in schools, authorities disagree on how it should proceed and exactly what its content should be. Other issues derive from the discrepancy between traditional morality and new morality and what constitutes the most functional sexual behavior for modern times.

Other problems of psychosexual development relate especially to physical maturation and puberty—for example, the girl's first menstruation, the boy's first ejaculation, and transitions to sexual awareness and nonvirginity for both sexes. Also anxiety producing is the practice of masturbation, which refers to satisfaction of sexual craving through manipulation of one's own genitals. Actually, the only danger from masturbation, as normally practiced, arises from the adolescent's own feelings of fear and self-disgust, caused by adults' misinformed teaching. Neither is compulsive masturbation of concern, except in terms of the anxiety generated or what it suggests about the individual's adjustment.

Confused thinking also exists concerning homosexuality, which signifies primary sexual orientation toward members of one's own sex. While many young people have become increasingly accepting of homosexuality, others strongly condemn the practice and believe the many myths surrounding the subject. Various questions relating to homosexuality are still unresolved; among them, to what extent homosexuality or heterosexuality may be genetically based or socioculturally induced. The majority of authorities today recommend that confirmed homosexuals be assisted to accept their condition and learn how most effectively to adapt to a heterosexual society. Still other problems at the adolescent stage relate to establishment of appropriate levels of intimacy—especially in early love, contraception, and, when unwanted pregnancies occur, abortion. A largely ignored problem is the growing practice of teenage prostitution.

Another increasingly frequent problem is that of the unwed parent. The father, especially, has been ignored, although some welfare agencies are beginning to show concern about him. At least in many larger cities, unwed mothers nowadays receive guidance both during pregnancy and after childbirth, both for themselves and for their babies. Far more often today, girls are electing to keep the children despite the great problems involved. While such pregnancies should be avoided, sympathetic, informed assistance should be available when they occur.

Teenage married couples have likewise been neglected, partly because they have already entered the adult society. Probably premarital pregnancy is the single factor most often precipitating early marriage, although a complex of factors may be operative in particular cases. Most often, young marrieds stay in school; however, teenage mothers will incur considerable antagonism from school administrators. Although a more enlightened attitude toward teenage parents is emerging, antiquated attitudes and practices are still common. Especially needed is better research on which to base programs for assisting them with their problems.

DISCUSSION QUESTIONS AND ACTIVITIES

1. Clip from newspapers or magazines advertisements that utilize sex drive as a means of arousing interest, and discuss the probable extent of their influence, if any, on adolescents.
2. Analyze popular songs and TV shows in terms of their possible effects on teenagers' psychosexual attitudes and behaviors.
3. Criticize a current book, article, or pamphlet giving sexual advice to teenagers. What are its strong and weak features?
4. Compare the book, article, or pamphlet used in Question 3 with similar material written a generation or more ago.
5. Straightforwardly, and anonymously, provide class discussion information on the following: (a) how you obtained sex information; (b) your chief worries over sexual problems during adolescence; (c) an estimate of your own sexual adjustment and of factors contributing to it.
6. Be prepared to participate in panel discussions of these topics: (a) What should be the school's function in sex education? (b) What is the teenager's best solution concerning petting? (c) Should there be a single standard for judging sexual behaviors of male and

female? (d) Would government subsidies of early marriage be advisable? Give arguments to support your answers.

7. In what ways can the new morality be defended as being more functional than traditional sex mores in modern society?

8. Should laws be passed that provide full societal support of unwed parenthood, homosexuality, and abortion at the adolescent-youth stage? Support your position, whether pro or con.

9. Discuss the current status and trends of sexual mores, attitudes, and behaviors on campus.

10. Discuss the status of, and youth's attitudes toward, unwed adolescent mothers and fathers.

11. Under what circumstances should or should not an unwed mother keep her baby?

12. What should be the rights of unwed fathers?

13. What are the most common anxieties about sex of present-day adolescents and youth? Are they as blasé about the topic as adults often assume?

SUGGESTED READINGS

Allgeier, A. R., Allgeier, E. R., & Rywick, T. (1981). Orientations toward abortion: Guilt or knowledge? *Adolescence, 16*(62), 273–280. The results of a study of youth's attitudes toward abortion are discussed within the context of the public controversy over the topic.

Andres, D., Gold, D., Berger, C., Kinch, R., & Gillett, P. (1983). Selected psychosocial characteristics of males: Their relationship to contraceptive use and abortion. *Personality and Social Psychology Bulletin, 9*(3), 387–396. A study of young adult men whose partners were either receiving an abortion or obtaining contraception indicated that the males in the contraceptive category had more liberal attitudes toward sex as well as a higher frequency of coitus than those in the abortion group suggesting the importance of attitudes in influencing contraceptive behaviors.

Darling, C. A. & Hicks, M. W. (1982). Parental influence on adolescent sexuality: Implications for parents as educators. *Journal of Youth and Adolescence, 11*(3), 231–245. The results of this study indicated that the effect of parental messages on their son's sexuality appears straightforward but more complex for daughters, and it suggests the need for modifying such messages.

Davis, S. M. & Harris, M. B. (1982). Sexual knowledge, sexual interests, and sources of sexual information on rural and urban adolescents from three cultures. *Adolescence, 17*(66), 471–492. This survey of 288 adolescents related their sexual information and knowledge to their sex, age, ethnicity, and urban or rural residence.

Emans, S. J. (1983). The sexually active teenager. *Journal of Developmental & Behavioral Pediatrics, 4*(1), 37–42. Adolescent sexual behaviors are discussed in terms of developmental issues, contraception, pregnancy, and sex education.

Goldman, R. J. & Goldman, J. D. (1982). How children perceive the origin of babies and the roles of mothers and fathers in procreation: A cross-national study. *Child Development, 53*(2), 491–504. Interviews of 838 5- to 16-year-olds in Australia, England, North America, and Sweden regarding physical and sexual development, including reproduction, disclosed cross-national differences in their views and in their access to sex education.

Goldsmith, H. H. (1983). Genetic influences on personality from infancy to adulthood. *Child Development, 54*(2), 331–355. A review of behavior-genetic studies of personality documents points of general agreement and continuing controversy.

Gruber, K. J., Jones, R. J., & Freeman, M. H. (1982). Youth reactions to sexual assault. *Adolescence, 17*(67), 541–551. A study was conducted of females, ages 13 to 17, in a delinquency intervention program with regard to the incidence, nature, and effects of sexual assaults which they had previously experienced.

Hansson, R. O., O'Connor, M. E., Jones, W. H., & Blocker, T. J. (1981). Maternal employment and adolescent sexual behavior. *Journal of Youth and Adolescence, 10*(1), 55–60. Female subjects whose mothers were employed outside the home, compared with those whose mothers were not thus employed, began sex relations earlier, felt less concern about the risk of pregnancy, and scored lower on knowledge about conception.

Kallen, D. J. & Stephenson, J. J. (1982). Talking about sex revisited. *Journal of Youth and Adolescence, 11*(1), 11–23. A retrospective comparison of means of reporting first intercourse by college students studied in 1967 and 1976 indicated a change from wide gender differences to a single standard of such behavior.

Medora, N. & Woodward, J. C. (1982). Premarital sexual opinions of undergraduate students at a midwestern university. *Adolescence, 17*(65), 213–224. In this study undergraduates' sexual views differed by sex and religion, but not according to fraternity or sorority membership, place of residence, or socioeconomic status.

Roosa, M. W., Fitzgerald, H. E., & Carson, N. A. (1982). Teenage and older mothers and their infants: A descriptive comparison. *Adolescence, 17*(65), 1–17. A comparison of childbearing and childrearing experiences of teenage and older mothers indicated similarity on most variables except for socioeconomic status, thus tending to refute much of the literature on teenage pregnancy.

Story, M. D. (1982). A comparison of university student experience with various sexual outlets in 1974 and 1980. *Adolescence, 17*(68), 737–747. This study compared university students for the years 1974 and 1980 with regard to their experiences with various sex outlets, by year groups and by sex.

Thomson, E. (1982). Socialization for sexual and contraceptive behavior: Moral absolutes versus relative consequences. *Youth and Society, 14*(1), 103–128. This study concerns the relatively different effects on adolescents' of two major socialization strategies for preventing premarital pregnancy.

Urberg, K. A. (1982). A theoretical framework for studying adolescent contraceptive use. *Adolescence, 17*(67), 527–540. The various aspects of contraceptive use are discussed with regard to such aspects as adolescent attitudes, usage, effectiveness, and types employed.

Chapter 8

The Adolescent In The Family

THE IMPORTANCE
OF THE FAMILY
IN HUMAN DEVELOPMENT

Functions of the Home

Whether a particular household is a matriarchy, patriarchy, oligarchy, or anarchy, the chances are that it will have an important effect on the growing child. Firm links have been established between parental childrearing practices and children's behavioral traits. The home is also the reservoir of strength upon which children draw to meet their physical and emotional needs; its warm, intimate contacts contribute to their feelings of security and belonging. When parents make much of them, chlidren decide that they have worth. Harmonious family relationships relate to high self-regard and effective social function in adolescence (Rutter, 1980). Conversely, unhealthy family relationships relate to conduct disorders and poor social relationships in adulthood (De Wuffel, 1982).

Parents also assist children in learning their different roles—as boy or girl, leader or follower, helper or planner, member of the group, or future parent. Society provides adolescents little training for parenthood; their ideas on this topic are obtained in the home. The way parents teach these roles is not capricious, for the societal pattern provides guidelines. However, this pattern does permit a degree of latitude, and its specific shape will be determined by the parent.

Through helping in the family adolescents also learn domestic roles of significance for both sexes in dual-worker families. A study of 790 Nebraska parents with children under 18 (White & Brinkerhoff, 1981) concerned the work that their children performed in the household and the meanings that they themselves attached to it. By the time the children were 9 or 10 over 90 percent were involved in some kind of chores, though such work tended to diminish slightly in the late teens as adolescents reduced family, in favor of peer, activities. Such chores are still almost universally performed; however, the children did not put in "hardship hours," the median number was 4.0 hours a week. For the hardest-working group, the older girls, the median is just 6 hours a week. In addition to school work and extracurricular activities such work may constitute considerable demand on a minority of children. Also, by the age of 10 most children have moved away from exclusively self-centered work (making your own bed, picking up your own toys) to doing things for the family, such as setting the table. When asked why they make their children work, the key word of parents was "responsibility" (p. 792).

In looking ahead over their future life course, adolescents also gain value from living in the family because of its multigenerational character. That is, members of the family move through life at different stages—hence, gain a closer view of developmental tasks at future life stages. Thus, observes Fox (1980), the family "provides an experiential laboratory for transcending the temporal dimension of human life through involvement in the continual changes in the lives of loved ones" (p. 25). The same factor may introduce certain problems, one being that all life transactions occur within a temporal context; and by the time adolescents reach their parents' age that context will have dramatically changed. In addition, developmental changes in parents and their children may work out so that they impinge negatively on each other—for example, at the same time that adolescent children are pursuing the developmental tasks of gaining greater independence and establishing an identity, the parents may be undergoing a midlife crisis (Fox, 1980).

The dwelling itself is also important, as these teenagers' statements indicate:

> My house was always neat and represented order. Its spaciousness made me feel free to move; and its many windows made it bright and cheerful. I loved the house and gave my parents a hard time when they decided to move into an apartment.

> We live in a duplex whose two sides are identical. The rooms are large and square, with tall ceilings. Their openness offers no privacy. I used to spend much time in my bedroom closet or the attic stairway, having made these areas into something of an office—just to gain some feeling of privacy. The house must have been built by a mathematician who liked the shape of squares. I would not live there if I had any choice.

Changing Significance of the Family

In certain ways and situations, family influence may be growing stronger. In mobile families, the family becomes the one constant for its members. Furthermore, since parents are freed from much of the drudgery of former times, they can devote more time to social and psychological aspects of their children's upbringing. Gordon (1977) predicts that the family will remain strong, although alternative family forms may constitute important laboratories for social reform.

Neither alternative life styles nor divorce are proof of the family's decline. Sussman (1978) points out that, although the divorce rate is high, the rate of remarriage is just as high. Thus marriage as an institution is not being rejected, but unhappy marriage relationships are. The common assumption that almost all children in colonial times lived with both their parents is a myth. Because of high death rates and mobility of the breadwinner, more children in those times had fewer parent surrogates than they do today. Most children now have at least one parent living with them; besides, there are no hard data to prove that two parents are better than one at socializing children into becoming "vital, creative, persons" (p. 34).

In some ways the home's influence may have weakened. For one thing more of the younger generation are college-educated, and hence more prone to do their own thinking. Of course, these young people's attitudes may not be as liberal after they marry, have families, and become responsible for their own children's morality. Or will they become a new breed of parent?

Another factor tending to weaken the family's influence is youth's expanded interpersonal world. In times past, growing children associated mostly with members of their families and people in their own neighborhoods. Now families have less to do with defining their children's particular social status; instead, adolescents are left to work out their destinies among their peers. The proportionate increase in their secondary-group relationships may also have the effect of creating a more superficial personality because such contacts become more casual. Young people are exposed to a diffusion of basic values, standards, and goals, instead of a single, well-integrated standard.

Alternatives Among
Family Life Styles

Levine (1978) believes that we should discard the myth of the average American family and acknowledge in classrooms, children's books, and on television shows "the existence, strength, and variety of the many families in which children actually live" (p. 15). Among the traditional alternatives are extended families, where grandparents and relatives share the same roof with a couple and their children, and the single-parent household, which is headed by an unwed parent or one whose mate is not present because of death, divorce, or some other reason. One in six children lives in a single-parent household; and 45 percent will do so before age 18 (Cornish, 1979). It has been predicted that almost half of the children born in 1977 will live in single-parent families sometime before age 18. In over half of all families mothers are employed outside of the home—the majority, full time. Moreover, in a growing number of families children are being reared in homes where the father stays home full or part time.

DIVORCE   Many children must adapt to changing family climates and relationships as they progress toward adulthood. In particular it is important to consider the impact of parental divorce on adolescent children because of its vastly increasing rate. In the past half-century the divorce rate has increased 700 percent in this country, and in 1976 alone, although there were over 2 million marriages, there were also a million divorces. It is predicted that by 1990 a third of our nation's children will have experienced a parent's divorce before they are 18 years of age (Glick, 1979). Many factors affect children's experience of parents' divorce, one being belief systems and ideologies regarding family life.

Until the 1920s, the father, as head of the family, was granted child custody; however, as mothers came to be perceived as critical in childrearing, courts began rewarding them sole custody (One child, two homes, 1979). Even today nine in ten children are awarded to the mother, though joint arrangements are increasing. Christine Rosenthal, a sociologist, reports that most joint custody arrangements work well, even after the parents remarry. Psychiatric social worker Judith Brown Greif reported that in joint arrangements fathers are closer to their children and have better relations with their ex-wives than do noncustodial fathers, with success dependent chiefly on "a spirit of give and take." By the end of the 1980s, joint custody may become the rule and not the exception.

Various factors tend to reduce whatever negative effects may result from divorce. For one thing changes with regard to the family, children's rights, and social views of divorce provide a more supportive context within which children may experience divorce and thus reduce the more negative effects. Divorce is becoming increasingly viewed as acceptable in cases of unhappy marriages; and the increase in divorce rate is one indication that the social barriers to it have diminished (Levinger, 1979). Also the encouragement of androgynous sex roles may help to reduce stresses associated with divorce in the absence of parents who traditionally performed "sex-role specific behaviors" (Kurdek, 1981, p. 858).

In consequence single parents feel more adequate and thus provide a less anxious environment for their children. In addition, women who are economically independent and androgynous more often get divorced. They also achieve a better adjustment after the divorce (Scanzoni, 1979). Again, the emotional climate for the children is correspondingly healthier.

A new trend is to accord greater consideration of children's rights in such matters (Kurdek, 1981). There is still considerable reluctance to intrude on parent-child relationships; however, the child's right to psychological health is viewed as having priority over the right of parents to rear their child in any manner they see fit (Goldstein, Freud & Solnit, 1979). With regard to divorce, specifically, there is considerable feeling that children should have access to legal counsel in matters regarding custody (Kargman, 1979).

In certain ways divorce, at least in the long run, contributes to the children's emotional health. Some parents say that their children have experienced positive changes after the divorce including greater feelings of responsibility, independence, and maturity (Fulton, 1979). Contributing to this outcome is the child's assumption of greater initiative and responsibility in the single-parent household. Wallerstein and Kelly (1980) point out the decrease in divorced parents' confidence resulting from their emotional stress; and Weiss (1979) notes that in two-parent families both parents share decision making and children are then expected to accept the decision. When the second "buffer parent" is absent, the single parent often brings the children into the decision-making process—such "parent-child relationships often lead to close ties between the child and the custodial parent, resulting in the enactment of a reciprocal friend/confidant role" (Kurdek, 1981, p. 859).

Certain factors, if present, collectively minimize children's problems stemming from their parents' divorce (Kurdek, 1981). These include minimal depletion of financial resources (Wallerstein & Kelly, 1980); minimal conflict and hostility between parents after divorce (Porter & O'Leary, 1980); agreement between the parents regarding discipline and childrearing and being approved and loved by both parents (Wallerstein & Kelly, 1980); authoritative discipline from the custodial parent (Santrock & Warshak, 1979); good relations between the ex-spouses; and regular visits by the noncustodial parent (Wallerstein & Kelly, 1980).

On the other hand, there are still certain negative factors surrounding divorce (Kurdek, 1980). It is still considered by some to be something of a social stigma; and the single-parent family is viewed as less favorable than the two-parent family (Hancock, 1980; M. J. Smith, 1980). Children may also suffer in custody battles (Kargman, 1979). Especially affecting children are problems relating to diminished financial resources (Colletta, 1979). Adolescents from broken families like school less, perform less well academically, and expect not to be as far along in their studies. However, this lesser optimism stems, not from the parental divorce or widowhood, as much as from reduced socioeconomic advantage. When mothers have custody, downward social mobility occurs, so that the children live below the father's socioeconomic level. Thus, adolescents' more pessimistic views of the future may simply reflect a realistic appraisal and a healthy adjustment to reality.

In second marriages, the children often maintain a link to the divorced parent, thus creating a conflict within the new marriage, with consequent emotional turmoil for the children. The children find themselves confronted with a somewhat different life style and a comparatively strange adult who abruptly assumes an authority role over them. The children are caught up in conflict as marital partners attempt to compromise between efforts to satisfy their children and to please the new spouse. Sometimes, too, there is the question of adapting to a new set of siblings, which may introduce elements of jealousy and rivalry.

Little is known about support systems available to children after the divorce (Kurdek, 1981). They may include friends, siblings, classmates, teachers, neighbors, and relatives. The tendency to seek help is a generalized characteristic, and children who turn to parents for help are also most likely to turn to teachers and friends. Thus, children who ordinarily seek help avail themselves of varied resources, whereas those who do not become "psychologically stranded" (p. 860). Another problem is that children sometimes lose the support system of kins-people of the noncustodial parents. On the other hand, they gain a new support system in a stepkin network.

Sometimes adolescents are portrayed as being sufficiently mature to understand the dynamics of separation and divorce; however, authorities disagree on the nature of their emotional response (Kurdek, 1981). Some believe that disturbance to adolescents is minimal because they can turn to people outside the home for advice and security. Others believe that they are "maximally affected" because they were exposed to longer periods of their parents' conflict before the divorce (Wallerstein & Kelly, 1980).

Sex is a factor also; sons apparently experience more problems after the divorce (Hetherington et al., 1979a). Perhaps girls receive more support from their mothers and teachers; or they are more "psychologically resilient"; or the mother, who is usually the custodial parent, may not give sons the same feeling of security as the same-sex custodial parent would (Santrock & Warshak, 1979).

Divorce does not appear to negatively affect the self-concepts of offsprings. However, to what degree it affects their opinions of parents is controversial, with considerable variation from one study to another. Among college students Parish (1981) found that children from divorced families, regardless of whether the mother had remarried, view their parents more negatively than parents in intact families or those where the father had died. Parish (1981) theorizes that since adolescents view parents as the ones responsible for getting the divorce *they*, and not the children, are responsible for problems relating to it—explaining why the children's self-concepts do not suffer.

It has been widely assumed that socialization about marriage and family life proceeds mainly in the family itself; however, attitudes toward marriage and family life differ but little among adolescents who live either in intact, reconstituted, or single-parent families. In spite of their different personal family backgrounds both sexes' views reflect the stereotypic notion of ideal family life. That is, adolescents seem to absorb "societal myths" regarding marriage and family, despite their own contrary family experience and widely circulated statistics concerning modern families and marriage. These social myths are, in part, maintained by political institutions, the media, schools, and religious groups.

It is important to look at the divorce from the adolescent's perspective and not just that of the adult (Kurdek, 1981). Assumptions made by the parents regarding their children's adjustment may be more a reflection of their own disturbance than of the child's. One factor in adaptation is the child's own temperament and general adjustment.

Reactions in the period immediately after the divorce may not be the same as later on, for several reasons. The adolescent children's view of the divorce may change; the parent may become increasingly competent in the single-parent role; and relations with siblings may change. That is, reactions after the divorce are not static but constantly change, along with the general situation within the family (Lerner, Skinner & Sorell, 1980).

Tiger (1978) calls attention to **omnigamy,** a new kinship system produced by the high divorce and remarriage rate. The divorce rate increased 250 percent in the past two decades, and 80 percent of divorcees remarry. With each new marriage, both parents and children gain a new set of friends, relatives, and associates, thus expanding their kinship system. In this way "many people are married to people who have been married to other people who are now married to still others to whom the first parties may not have been married . . ." (p. 14). The kinship relationships among families of divorce are complex and extensive. The effect on children is still uncertain. We do not yet know how the example set by their parents is affecting them. It would seem that it would "increase the child's sense of tentativeness in all relations that the new system reflects" (p. 17).

Alternative family forms, which include communes, single-parent families, and social-contract marriages, have developed in reaction to new values of "individualism, humanism, self actualization," and others (Kurdek, 1981). Regardless of family form, functions have shifted. Much of the family's impact on economic, religious, and educational matters is now delegated to social institutions; yet families are now expected to foster their children's happiness and emotional adjustment as well as their physical health and safety (Gadlin, 1980). Another trend, where both parents work, is toward a more androgynous life style. Such a life style will change the kinds of behaviors in which children are socialized and the parental models to which children are exposed (Kaplan & Sedney, 1980).

Family alternatives may affect adolescents in at least three ways. First, some youth themselves are the products of such families. Second, more traditional families are incorporating some of the behaviors demonstrated in newer life styles; hence, conventional youth may somehow feel their effect. Finally, some young people look forward to trying out alternative family styles themselves, on either a temporary or a more enduring basis. Their conclusions can have important implications for the total society in years ahead.

Eventually adults may even have to justify their right to achieve the parent role. To date, they have simply reproduced children at will, without any formal training for parenthood. They may have done reasonably well without sophisticated preparation for this task, but today's complex world suggests that more advanced training may be required. We are confronted constantly with the negative effects of amateur parenthood.

THE ADOLESCENT'S ROLE
IN THE FAMILY

Family experience is a product of the interactions of all family members who, as a result, come to assume special roles. Each member helps establish every other member's role, and one's own role is in turn affected by those adapting to such changes; and in parents' continuing desire to understand their children, they may model after their children's behavior.

Sex as a Factor in Family Role

Role modifications are partially determined by sex. The adolescent boy's family role diminishes as his orbit of activity expands beyond the home. However, his personal role becomes more dominant because an older male acquires heightened prestige and greater prerogatives. The boy once teased by an older sister now flaunts before her his greater privileges.

Such situations reflect persistent though weakening distinctions in parental concepts of sex roles. In a study of family roles (Larson, 1974), the fathers and mothers, on being questioned, approved traditional sex-role patterns. Two-thirds of the husbands and wives agreed that the mother alone was responsible for housework. The least agreement (57 percent) occurred with regard to lawn mowing and snow shoveling. Twenty-eight percent of the husbands and wives perceived these tasks as being carried out by the husband and their sons, and 17 percent, by all family members. In general, odd jobs and chores were perceived as appropriate for fathers and sons, while mothers and daughters were perceived as being responsible for child care, housework, and meals.

Parental authority patterns have important consequences for children. When parents make decisions about household affairs, economic activities, and discipline, they distinguish more between the roles of boy and girl. They make clearer-cut distinctions between what they perceive as desirable personality traits, skills, and activities for sons and daughters if their own roles are highly differentiated. In such families, the children are less democratic among themselves and less open in expressing affection than in families where the parents share activities.

PARENT-ADOLESCENT RELATIONSHIPS

Parent-Adolescent Interaction

For clearer perspective on parental attitudes, consider these observations. Most parents unconsciously project their own conflicts onto their children. For example, in a culture that places a premium on youth, the mother who fears aging may resent her daughter's clear skin. Or selfish parents may feel their children owe them a debt. At one time adults considered adolescents as an economic asset, useful in performing numerous household chores or in earning their keep. However, household appliances, urbanization, and labor laws have taken away most of the tasks that children used to perform, and some parents find children an economic burden.

Youthful revolt against parents does not always mean rejection. A certain amount of rebellion is normal; it is an essential preliminary to attaining the independence required for establishing one's own family. Besides, the overt expression of conflict serves as catharsis which, if repressed, takes the form of anxiety. In any event, adolescent revolt may not be so much against parents as against one's baby or small-child self, an outgrown role of which parental authority is a reminder. Hence, parents should treat their teenagers not as children but as adults-in-the-making. They should guard them from unduly traumatic experiences but avoid assuming too active a role in helping them cope with normal problems.

Youthful revolt against parents does not always mean rejection and a certain amount of rebellion is normal. (Photo by Sybil Shelton, Monkmeyer)

Parent-child influences are not unidirectional. Just as the parent affects the adolescent, so does the adolescent influence the parent. Young adult children apparently act as important mediators of broad sociocultural change to their mothers (Hagestad, 1977). They help their parents make "sense out of what may otherwise seem alien to a parent" (p. 11). Children become bridges to such extrafamilial areas as work, education, and leisure.

The Role of the Parent in the Life of the Adolescent

PARENTAL ROLES AND FUNCTIONS   Though parents are many things to their children, perhaps their most important role is as a source of affection. It seems unnecessary to go the full length of Oedipal theory to explain the teenager's devotion. Attachment to either parent is "natural." Both sexes, buffeted by experiences in the world, rely heavily at times on support from their parents. Girls who are constantly thwarted by their mothers in conflicts over emancipation may depend more than usual on their fathers. Boys, weary of proving themselves men outside the home that does not yet accept them as such, may regress to clinging to their mothers. These frustrations suggest the importance of parents as a source of approval. Adolescents derive status in their own eyes from the recognition that they please their parents. Such feelings of self-worth must be reinforced again and again.

Elkind (1979) speaks of "three basic contracts" between parents and their children, one being freedom and responsibility. Parents give their children freedom to the degree that children show responsibility. Adolescent children can have friends over for the night if they constitute no disturbance in the house. Another contract concerns loyalty and commitment. Parents will take much time with their children, being loyal and committed to them, if the children in turn show respect for the parents' values and beliefs and care more for them than they do for other adults. The third contract is between achievement and support. Parents will support their children in various endeavors, provided that the children achieve goals that the parents see as worthwhile. They will pay for their children to go away to college if the children achieve acceptable grades.

At times a disturbance or disequilibrium may arise in the parental-child contract. The adolescent may resent parents who insist that they achieve but are not supportive and show no interest in their work. Youth brought up in the belief that they should be loyal to their parents have difficulty establishing commitment to adult goals that seem worthless or harmful to them. For example, they perceive adults as polluting the environment—hence revolt against this and other values that their parents represent.

DIFFERENTIATION BETWEEN FATHER AND MOTHER ROLES   Despite their shared functions, each parent's role is carried out somewhat differently. In a study of high school juniors (Wright & Keple, 1981) the girls' reactions to their fathers was one of "personal noninvolvement," whereas the boys often reacted toward their fathers with "ambivalence and conflict" (p. 569). Often fathers feel inadequate about dealing with their daughters' problems because they feel they just don't understand girls in emotional matters. They are more comfortable about relating to their adolescent sons, with whom they identify more closely and feel they have a greater stake in their growth into manhood. Yet the son may perceive the father's concern as an effort to keep control over him at the very time that the son is trying to become independent—hence the conflict.

FATHERS   Conflicts between sons and their fathers are so common as often to be judged inevitable. In Daniel Levinson's (1978) study of men during their twenties, four-fifths had experienced considerable conflict with their parents, ordinarily the father, and had moved away either socially or geographically. Most of them said their relationships with their parents diminished steadily during their twenties.

Though considerable attention has been paid to the effect on youth of absent fathers, little has been said about present fathers. Most research of any kind relates to the fathering of babies and young children.

Rubin (1982) cites a study by Mirra Komarovsky regarding college seniors and their fathers. These young Ivy League men reported that they were closer to their mothers than their fathers and often they complained that their fathers simply remained distant and somewhat cold.

Rubin advises that if father-son relationships are to improve or to remain healthy they must change over time. The child's relationship, which is characterized by the father's authority and the son's dependence, must become an adult relationship between two independent individuals. The father must view his own role differently, in ceasing to think of himself as the great authority and the protector of his sons. On the other hand, the father should not surrender these roles too soon through simply abdicating his obligation to maintain certain standards for his growing sons. Nevertheless, some of the worst disagreements between sons and their fathers develop when the father attempts to preserve such behaviors too long. As the adolescent son moves toward adulthood the father must come to acknowledge that he cannot now be the "guardian" of his son's "beliefs and values" (p. 28). Meantime, as fathers set aside their former roles as "authorities, providers and moral guardians" the sons often wish that their fathers would become closer to them. Their sons may desire freer expressions of love and affection, partly to make up for former years in which the father's love was not overt (p. 28). This need, on the part of these young adult sons to get closer to their fathers, is much more common today than formerly—hence, we have a generation gap. For their part the fathers, rather than desiring more intimate relationships with their growing sons, want a different form of closeness—"the bond that comes from the sharing of values or interests" (p. 29).

Fathers often hope that their sons will follow their own occupations, for several reasons. First, if they have enjoyed their work they may truly believe it is an area in which the son will find his greatest satisfaction. Second, fathers may believe that it is testimony to the father's worth if the son follows his vocation. Third, the son who chooses his father's vocation "helps to preserve the father's stake in the continuity of the generations." Also the sharing of their occupation can mean that the father and son have common interests about which to converse.

Some sons feel that there is no chance of developing more than a superficial relationship with their fathers; however, various factors may ultimately bring them together. The son may come to appreciate his father's interest in him as a child; or they may have developed common interests that constitute a lasting bond. Much depends on whether they have sufficient sensitivity to understand each other.

MOTHERS   The mother's impact, like the father's, is different for sons and daughters. In a study of lower-class black children, ages 10 to 13, girls more often perceived their mothers' behaviors toward them as monitoring them than did boys. Although girls may be encouraged to be independent the range of their behavior is more limited. The data also showed that girls saw their mothers behavior as more affectionate, as one of companionship and encouraging dependence. Such perceptions had an even greater influence on the boys. It may well be that although sons' activities are monitored by mothers, the boys do not

Although girls may be encouraged to be independent, they are more often closely monitored by their mothers and spend more time with them. (© Ann Zane Shank, Photo Researchers, Inc.)

perceive it as overprotectiveness but as a sign of their mothers' interest. Somewhat surprisingly, no relationship was found between the children's perceptions of their mothers' affection and their own self-evaluation (Fields, 1981).

In recent years the main concern about mother-child relationships has been the potential impact of the entry of large numbers of women into the workplace. Adolescents, at least, rarely suffer ill effects and may instead benefit. Nor are they more likely to be delinquent or to do any worse in school. Rather, maternal employment is associated with the daughter's having more ambitious career goals; and both sexes profit from the working mother's broader outlook (Hoffman, 1974).

PARENTAL POWER   Relationships change with parents as children move into adolescence (Montemayor, 1982). Mothers spend more time with preadolescent children than do fathers; however, in adolescence, fathers and mothers may spend equal time with their children, but mostly with the same-sex child.

In adolescence fathers' involvement remains about the same for their daughters but grows a bit for their sons. In addition, during this time, sons appear to acquire power at expense of their mothers, whereas the father-son relationship remains unchanged (Steinberg, 1981). That is, the mother feels that she can no longer dictate rules to her son, although she continues to do so to her daughter. In addition, since males have a higher status in society, in general, this status diminishes to some extent the greater power that adults otherwise might have over them.

As adolescents strive to become independent it can be expected that they will sometimes take issue with their parents and spend increasing amounts of time away from home. Hence, Matthews and Serrano (1981) warn that parents should be able to tolerate some negative behaviors and distance on the part of adolescent children. Nor should parents assume that such behaviors place irreversible distances between them. When they permit such movement adolescents continue to return and to maintain a link with their parents.

Students' descriptions of their parents' roles in their lives suggest how personal such relationships are:

> FEMALE: I live alone with my mother; and even though I do not feel free to talk to her about many things, there is an understanding between us. She consults me about decisions rather than the other way around.
>
> MALE: During middle adolescence, school, work, and sports were my major interests. My parents showed they were only interested in my getting through school. This made me feel that my other interests they wanted no part of.
>
> FEMALE: Everything I do is with my father in mind and to make him proud of me; I have his features, temper, ways of action, and feeling. I am a great deal closer to him than to my mother and brother. I feel I unconsciously relived his childhood even though our physical environment differed.

McDonald (1982) sought to discover those factors which impact on adolescents' perceptions of the relative power of their fathers and mothers. In general, females perceived the mother as having more power than the father and the males the father. Only in the area of economic factors did both sexes perceive the father as having more control. Religiosity was also a factor; religious youths attributed more power to their parents and more to the father than the mother. Older adolescents attributed less power to the parents because they had more alternative resources than did younger ones. In general, the larger the number of siblings the less adolescents turned to the father, possibly because they had more siblings to whom to turn. In general, adolescents tend to identify more with the parent who is perceived as having more power, in contrast to sex-role identification theories that portray children as identifying more with the same-sex parent.

Often for the first time adolescents establish a comparatively close relationship to the father who may have focused too much on his work to notice them. A father may have grown disillusioned with the vocational rat race and seek to strengthen his relationship with the family. This relationship is one of almost equals since the children are now almost grown. Children are in "input" positions within the family in the role of receiving care for their needs; the adolescent's position is marginal, with one foot in childhood and the other in adulthood. At this age, adolescents begin to feel pressures to shift to an "output" or giving role with reference to others (McIntire, Nass & Battistone, 1974). At such points, when individuals occupy certain marginal roles and seek direction, they are especially susceptible to the influence of others. The father, as representative of the outside world, is in a position to exert unusual influence at this time.

Various authorities have reported that father absence produced certain negative effects on adolescents, which may, in fact, stem from other causes. Hetherington (1972) concluded that father absence in a girl's childhood may provide a sleeper effect, having significant effects in adolescence when heterosexual interactions increase. However, among college-age women who had lost their fathers through death or divorce at an early age there were no significant differences from father-present controls in such matters as sex-role traditionalism, romantic love, or anxiety. While the daughters of widows were somewhat less accepting of premarital sexual behaviors, they participated in approximately the same amount as did the controls. It should be noted that the effects of "father absence" on developing children, as in one-parent families headed by females, include such correlates as economic pressures and the necessity of the mother's working outside the home (Hainline & Feig, 1978). It should be added that single parents of either sex do a very creditable job of childrearing.

Apparently similar paternal behaviors are experienced quite differently by the children. Interviews conducted with 40 young men, 20 of whom had earlier indicated feelings of being understood and 20 as being misunderstood by their fathers, indicated that the fathers of the two categories were not extremely different. Both groups of fathers were somewhat strict and spent time with their sons but aroused contrasting perceptions in their sons. The admittedly strict fathers were perceived by the understood sons as reasonable and by the misunderstood sons as irrational in their use of punishment. Time spent with their fathers was perceived as pleasant by the understood sons but tension-producing by the misunderstood sons. Both groups of sons perceived themselves as resembling their fathers, but the understood sons deliberately patterned them-selves after their fathers while the misunderstood ones tried to erase similarities between the fathers and themselves. It is unclear why two similar groups of fathers had had such contrasting effects on their sons (Roll & Millen, 1978).

Basically, most adolescents love their parents, seek and welcome their advice, and hold their standards in esteem. Nevertheless, for various reasons they may be critical of them. For one thing, teenagers may question their parents' competence for decision-making simply because they belong to an older gen-eration. For another, wider contact with adults leads them to make comparisons. The effect is sometimes disillusioning. The children are brought up to believe that parents are always right; this erstwhile overidealization of them brings parents' faults more sharply into focus. Adolescents may even become ashamed of their parents and avoid introducing them to their friends. Note this girl's dilemma:

> Vera's mother wore old-fashioned clothes, twisted her stringy hair into a tight knot, and "murdered the King's English." Through her own efforts, Vera herself had acquired considerable polish. When her out-of-town beau was to come to call, she dressed up her mother and in-structed her in what to say and how to say it. However, [the mother] could not shed her background that easily. During the meal the mother remarked, "If y'all will excuse me, I'll go to the kitchen to see if the water ain't het yet."

Baranowski (1978) interviewed high school students and their parents in order to determine how actively and in what way adolescents attempt to influence their parents' behaviors. Those students who had greatest autonomy needs reported more areas of influence on their parents than those having less autonomy. They attempted to influence their mothers more than their fathers, perhaps because fathers have greater need for dominance and are less likely to yield to adolescents' efforts to influence them. Fathers are usually perceived as more authoritarian and formal, hence less responsive to their children's de-mands. They attempted to influence their fathers more than the mothers in just three areas: purchase or sale of a car, use of tobacco products, and use of alcohol, all traditionally male-dominated behaviors. Mothers were subject to more pres-sure regarding household chores and day-to-day activities. The girls attempted to influence the parents more than the boys did, perhaps because they are becoming more assertive and autonomous in recent years. Girls are also more homebound and in closer contact with the parents than are the boys, who or-dinarily spend more time away from home. The adolescents made greatest attempts at influence in areas of special concern to them, such as personal appearance, preparation of meals, or decorating the house. They made little effort to influence parents with regard to religion, politics, and civic activities. These areas have less relevance to adolescents' immediate needs and status sys-tem. Besides, they realize that their parents are less receptive to influence re-garding basic values.

IMPACT OF LEAVING HOME   Especially critical in family-child relation-ships is when the time for the adolescent's leaving home arrives. Goleman (1980) cites a study by Kenneth and Anna Sullivan regarding relationships between parents and sons who were leaving for college. The Sullivans compared male students from high schools in the Northeast who lived at home and commuted to college with those who went away to school. The results showed significant differences between the two groups—those who had left home believed that they now communicated more effectively with their parents and felt more affectionate toward them than did those who stayed at home. Those at college felt more independent and were better satisfied with their lives.

In another study Cheryl Kurash (cited in Goleman, 1980) followed incoming freshmen shortly before they entered college, two weeks after their arrival, and during their second semester. Typically they expressed considerable anxiety about leaving home, the women more than the men. However, as they adjusted to college life their attachment to their parents increased. Goleman also cites work by Jay Haley who recently published a book called *Leaving Home*. Haley believes there is nothing wrong about those children who remain in their homes well into adulthood, if satisfactory arrangements can be made for all concerned. Anyhow, observes Haley, youth can leave home and still be dependent. And leaving home does not necessarily mean remaining away from home: a girl may marry and, after a divorce, return home.

A major difficulty for the young person is the parent, often the mother, who becomes upset at her child's leaving. If she does not work, she may feel left without anything when the child leaves; and she either voluntarily or involuntarily communicates this feeling to the child, who then has greater difficulty letting go.

Goleman points out that leaving home has a dual meaning, as the process is physical and internal. In adolescence one leaves home "in the symbolic sense of finding an autonomous identity." Without this "inner sense" of leaving home an individual does not become fully mature (p. 61).

IMPACT OF FAMILY MEMBERS IN GENERAL   Not only parents, but all family members, including grandparents, impact on adolescents. Today, most adolescents do not live in the same household as their grandparents and many families are quite mobile—hence, adolescents relate far more to the nuclear than to the extended family. There also exists a new "social contract" between grandparents and their adult children that neither will interfere with the other (Kornhaber & Woodward, 1981). And adolescents, in attempting to define their own identities, may unconsciously underestimate the influence of both their grandparents. On the other hand, several factors operate to make grandparents influential on their adolescent grandchildren.

Contacts with grandparents may have several effects on adolescents' development. A sense of continuity of the generations may contribute to an individual's feeling of identity. Especially in times of rapid technological and social change, awareness of one's family history creates links between past, present, and future. In other words grandparents may provide a continuity between generations through their discussion of the times they have lived through as well as the personal family history. Grandparents may also improve parent-adolescent relations through helping adolescents to understand their parents. Or adolescents may turn to their grandparents as confidants or arbitrators when they are having difficulties with their parents. Adolescents' attachments to their grandparents also allow them, in some measure, to "circumvent the intense emotional environment of the isolated nuclear family" (Kornhaber & Woodward,

Not only parents, but all family members, including grandparents, impact on adolescents. (© Suzanne Szasz, 1981, Photo Researchers, Inc.)

1981, p. 185). In one study of young people, ages 5 to 18, those who had a close relationship with one or more grandparents viewed older people in general more favorably, which is important for at least two reasons. First, young people who view older adults positively have a more favorable environment in which to live; and second, adolescents may themselves preserve a healthier self-concept when they become older adults (Baranowski, 1982).

DEGREE OF FAMILY INFLUENCE Among samplings of the author's college students, ranging in number from 77 to 97, 91.6 percent said they had been strongly influenced by their fathers, 95.8 percent by their mothers, 64.9 percent by an older sibling, 37.3 percent by a younger sibling, 20.4 percent by an aunt, 21.5 percent by an uncle, 33.7 percent by a grandfather, and 41.9 percent by a grandmother.

Father

FEMALE: My father had a lot of influence on me. Since I'm the sixth child out of six, I always received a lot of attention, including from my Dad. He always spent time with me, especially in the area of athletics. I was the most athletic in the family, my father's favorite for that reason. He always spent time after dinner playing catch or anything. When I left for college, it was my Dad I missed the most. I missed the talks we had every night before dinner. I missed him at athletic events. He and I talked about everything from guys to politics. My relationship with my Dad is unique—at least I think it is, and it's something I treasure highly.

MALE: The most important person in my life is my father. He has set an example, and if I do exactly as he has done I will be very, very happy. My father started out at IBM as a janitor with just a high school degree. Now he is senior associate engineer designing machines.

Mother

FEMALE: My mother has had a very strong influence on me. She has never said "no" to me—just made me realize different alternatives. Her sense of humor and outlook on life are very admirable. I really love her—she has taught me a lot.

MALE: My mom has had a tremendous positive influence on me. Although we don't always agree on goals, she has taught me how to pursue and realize them. Both she and my dad have brought me up in a positive nurturing environment, with guidance, not control, to shape my later life.

Older Sibling

FEMALE: My older brother (11 years older) was very influential on my life. He always showed a special interest in me. He took me places with his friends, taught me how to write, tie my shoes, and was always there if I had the slightest problem. He always treated it like it was important, even if it was the smallest problem in the world. He knows every aspect of my life . . . I could and have turned to him for every reason, and for everything. When I'm down, my brother can always be counted on to pull me up.

Younger Sibling

FEMALE: My younger brother has had a negative influence on my life. My parents devoted more attention to him because of his unstable state of health. I was jealous of him and this resulted in damaging my relationship with him. It also caused conflicts between myself and my parents.

Aunt

FEMALE: My great aunt is very important to me because I have never had any grandparents, and she has served as a substitute for our family. She tells us the stories and historical events of our family's history that without her we wouldn't have known.

MALE: I had a very influential aunt who was a great help to my family while I was growing up. The reason that she played such an important role is that she lived with my family. My mother and she complemented each other well and at times it seemed as if we had two mothers.

Uncle

MALE: My uncle had a great influence on me because when I was young my father had a heart attack. My uncle came over every day to play sports with me and teach me things like gardening, lawn care, shrubbery, and things like that. After we mowed the lawn, we would have a tennis match or play basketball.

MALE: I have an uncle who has an influence on me in that I don't want to turn out like him. He is a no-good drunk all the time.

Grandfather

MALE: There is wisdom in years, and the wisdom my grandfather passed down to me will always be part of me. Whether we were out fishing or I was playing in some tennis or golf tournament, I always knew that I would have his support. I am also proud to be able to carry on the family name and the tradition my grandfather and his grandfather before him has put in it.

Grandmother

FEMALE: My grandmother was 80 in February and has led a very active life. She is my only grandmother and lives four houses down the road from our family in a small town. She has been a real strong influence on my life, and I think most anyone could learn a lot from her. She doesn't worry about things as many older people do. She doesn't sit around and complain but has lots of hobbies, such as baking, oil painting, crocheting, growing African violets, making shell jewelry, playing the piano and painting her own Christmas cards. She also reads a lot, which is how she taught herself so much since she only went to the 6th grade in school. She's always been very close to me, interested in whatever I do.

PARENT-ADOLESCENT CONFLICT

Discipline and Punishment

CURRENT PRACTICES   An important aspect of the authority-submission question is how parents should exercise discipline. While parents vary greatly in this regard, the trend is toward some relaxation of control, which results in less adolescent rebelliousness than is ordinarily expected. Among undergraduates in a midwestern university (Frankel & Dullaert, 1977) the 25 percent judged highest in rebellion were from homes either high or moderate in control. Even in this fraction the rebelliousness was quiet and not dramatic. Three-fourths expressed little or no rebellion and reported every style of parental discipline from high to low. It might be speculated that in some cases the rebellion had not yet begun or that the high percent of females among the subjects made it less obvious. Even among those parents described as authoritarian, control was often less rigid than was expected. The students felt little guilt and had received little punishment since childhood.

Where control was high they had simply adapted to parental demands and toed the mark. Eighty percent of the students judged their homes high in control but the parents seemed less demanding than the researchers had anticipated. Parents are changing along with society, and society is accepting a broader range of adolescent behaviors now than formerly.

In general, parents are less restrictive of their sons than of their daughters. Hart (1978) points out that boys have more special privileges and more room for negotiation because their rules are more flexible. Parents are also more tolerant of boys' misbehaviors ("boys will be boys"), while according their daughters less privacy and independent action (Duke, 1978). The girl's only alternative is to run away from home, an act usually construed as negative; nevertheless, when the home situation is intolerable it may be constructive in motivation and effect. Despite this situation, mothers hardly seem aware that they employ a double standard. In regard to both sexes, many adults have concluded that youth have been treated too permissively, especially at home—"a makeshift response to social and economic changes of the postwar decades—and disastrous in its effects" (Permissiveness, 1976, p. 54).

Apparently severe punishment is relatively rare among middle-class parents. A study of undergraduates in a large midwestern university, mostly freshmen and sophomores, disclosed only weak support for the hypothesis that only-children would be given more autonomy and be punished less severely by the parents than those with siblings. Instead, the data indicated that most of these young people, regardless of family size, had been given considerable freedom in the areas investigated (academic achievement, alcohol consumption, cigarette smoking, dating, driving privileges, athletic participation, money saving and spending, movie attendance, and worship-service attendance). In addition, regardless of family size, most of these students had rarely or never been punished physically by their parents or punished by withdrawal of financial support (Kloepper, Leonard & Huang, 1981).

Patterns of discipline vary according to subculture, sex, race, and other factors. A study of eighth graders in Georgia middle schools indicated that the father was more often named as the stricter parent by whites and the mother by blacks (Schab, 1982). As for reporting their whereabouts to their parents, 65 percent of the white girls had to report at all times compared with 51 percent of the white boys, 38 percent of the black girls, and 55 percent of the black boys (Schab, 1982). Perhaps, for black girls, it was simply assumed that they would be at home more.

With regard to mode of punishment the boys of both races most frequently reported being grounded, followed by removal of privileges, being whipped, and made to feel guilty. The white girls reported, in descending order, privileges being taken away, being grounded, made to feel guilty, whipped, and made to do housework. The black girls were required to do housework, be grounded, have privileges taken away, be whipped, or made to feel guilty, in that order. More blacks of both sexes said they had never been punished.

PERMISSIVE VERSUS STRICT PUNISHMENT   Severe punishment has devastating effects; the case against it is clear-cut. In a study of 417 college students, adolescent rebellion was found to be the product of homes that were patriarchal and unhappy, patriarchal and very restrictive, or patriarchal and very permissive (Balswick & Macrides, 1975). Whether parents are permissive or restrictive is not as important as the extent of their permissiveness or restrictiveness. In the very strict home, youth feel frustrated and become aggressive. In the very permissive home, they are frustrated because they do not know what their parents expect; hence, they too become aggressive. Their only option is to behave in increasingly extreme ways in order to discover what the limitations are. Similarly, in the larger society, standards are often so ambiguous that youth may be defined as rebellious when they may be testing the environment in search of norms.

A study of community college students, 84 percent of whom were between ages 18 to 23, indicated that 95 percent had received corporal punishment when growing up (Bryan & Freed, 1982). Note, too, that people tend to underreport negative behaviors; this figure is higher than that commonly reported by parents themselves regarding their use of physical punishment. This writer conjectures that a cause for the discrepancy may be that parents' memories screen out realities which they do not desire to confront. Also males reported receiving more abuse than did females, perhaps because society perceives aggression as more appropriate for boys or because males themselves are more aggressive. This writer suggests that since boys behave more aggressively and commit infractions of rules far more commonly than girls they may receive even less abuse for each infraction involved. Also Bryan and Freed found that males are hit more often by their fathers than their mothers. They found, too, that parents with significantly less income abused their children more often because they are under greater stress.

The study further supported the theory that corporal punishment relates to long-lasting psychological and behavioral outcomes. Students reporting most corporal punishment also reported having received lower grades, although their transcripts did not reveal lower grades. They recalled more negative social interactions, including having fewer friends, committing more aggression, and being more delinquent, as well as experiencing more anxiety and depression.

In addition, conclude Bryan and Freed, exposure to adult aggression results in long-term aggressive behaviors by the child; and the more a girl is struck by her parents the more likely she is to remain with an abusing spouse as she grows up. The more often children are abused the more they themselves favor violence as adults in political and interpersonal situations. Thus parental modeling in this area appears to be highly significant in their children's future adult behaviors. Consider, too, that parents who employ less corporal punishment are those who use more discussion, reasoning, and compromise with their children.

Of course, this matter is quite complex—for example, lower-class parents abuse their children more frequently and reason with them less. Such parents are typically less well educated—hence may employ abuse because they are simply unskilled in using reasoning and discussion. It should be pointed out that physical abuse does not necessarily mean an attempt on the part of the parent to be abusive to the child. Many times parents who engage in such abuse feel that they are doing the right thing.

It is difficult to appraise research concerning discipline properly. Although most methods used are blends, most researchers study polarized approaches to child socialization. Probably the extremes of any technique would have unfortunate results. Extreme authoritarian treatment would probably provoke negative reactions; however, a measure of openly expressed hostility between parent and child might strengthen a child's developing capacity to cope with social realities.

At the other extreme, when love-oriented methods are used, positive methods, coupled with praise for good behavior and reasons for rejecting the disapproved behavior, apparently have the desired consequences. However, threats of withdrawal of love may undermine feelings of security and independence. Instead, plentiful reinforcement of socially approved behaviors should be employed, reserving power-oriented techniques for emergencies when instant obedience may be required.

Outcomes of particular disciplinary techniques are difficult to assess, partly because parents and teachers use complex blends of methods instead of easily identifiable techniques. Most authority figures use characteristic patterns representing a generally consistent approach, at least with particular children or adolescents. Undoubtedly, the best method of control for a particular circumstance is no clear-cut, either-or proposition. That is, the method chosen must be modified to suit the particular situation and personalities involved.

INDIVIDUAL DIFFERENCES IN RESPONSE TO PUNISHMENT   Reaction to punishment is also individual, depending both on specific parent-child relationships and on the child's personality, as these illustrations show:

> MALE: When I felt I had been treated wrongly, I never felt free to explain my position. I would be "talking back." I found passive resistance best.
>
> FEMALE: My junior high school clique broke some windows with snowballs, and my parents would not believe me when I said I had not taken part. Our parents would not let us go out together for some time. The clique dissolved forever. I was resentful and refused to go anywhere with my family and just sulked around.
>
> MALE: During my early teens I was severely punished for taking money from my mother's purse. I was restricted from my main love, swimming, for a week and from social functions for a month. I deemed it fair because I was disgusted with myself. I even enjoyed adding to the punishment by restricting my other activities. As I look back, however, I feel a great anger toward my parents, especially when I quarrel with them.

Abuse

The preceding discussion concerns discipline within the normal range. Even with this range, unwise discipline can be damaging; it can be traumatic when it becomes abuse. Child abuse refers to physical and mental injury, sexual abuse, or negligence of any individual under age 18, by people responsible for his or her welfare. It may take such forms as "actual physical assault, permanent confinement in a small enclosure, sexual molestation, or denial of food, clothing, and shelter" (Dudley, 1979, p. 28). Boys more often than girls are victims, and fathers more often beat their children than mothers do. The most frequently abused children are 3- to 5-year-olds and 15- to 17-year-olds.

The Society for the Prevention of Cruelty to Animals was significant in developing the children's rights movement. It intervened in the first reported case of child abuse in this country because other organizations were either unwilling or not organized in such manner as to aid abused children. Another 75 years passed before anything approaching effective medical and social intervention was developed (Matthews & Serrano, 1981).

Various studies of child abuse reveal estimates from 6,000 cases a year to over a million annually (Conger, 1980, p. 36). This wide variation may stem from differences in definition of abuse, modes of reporting, and attempts to extrapolate from particular data sources. In a study of 181 high school students in a southern Appalachian city parental abuse was reported by 87 percent, 52 percent saying it was done with regularity, or more than five times. Almost a third (30%) said they had been struck in ways other than by spanking; 7 percent with some regularity. About one in four (27%) reported being called names and 18 percent said they had received bruises when punished (Brown, Whitehead & Braswell, 1981).

It is estimated that acts of violence occur in over half of American households. Annually, over 50 million people become physical victims at the hands of other family members. Six and a half million children are harmed by other family members and 8 million children—18 out of every 100, most of them teenagers—assault their parents (Battered families, 1979). About 98 percent of parents employ some physical punishment on their children, including some adolescents. One father, accustomed to being instantly obeyed, struck his daughter because she refused to quit dating a young man who, in fact, held the highest credentials. Although parental abuse of teenagers is far more often psychological than physical, it can be just as cruel.

It has often been reported that child abuse is more common in the lower social classes; however, maltreatment is less likely to be detected or reported at higher social levels. In the study cited above, abuse was modestly greater among the working class. The reasons may be that lower-class persons value toughness more, are more impulsive, or more violent. This writer suggests that ordinarily the lower classes are less well educated, hence less knowledgeable about other means of child control, such as reasoning.

The picture of psychological damage can be devastating in such cases. A study of adolescents thus abused (Hjorth & Ostrov, 1982) indicated that they had developed quite negative self-images, were emotionally unstable, and had special difficulty with family relationships. They reported poorer impulse control and coping skills and greater psychopathology. They also had more difficulty establishing vocational and educational goals. They did better in the area of peer relations, perhaps because they sought compensation in this area for their unhappy family life (Bryan & Freed, 1982).

Also they frequently reported an association between maltreatment and behavioral problems such as aggression and delinquency (Conger, 1980); and again this study supported that conclusion. It is possible that being abused produces personality disorders which "predispose" youths to employ deviant behaviors; or it may be that victims are more likely to be judged delinquent (Smith, Berkman & Fraser, 1980). For instance, very often juvenile courts may "adjudicate neglected children as status offenders . . . similarly, victims of maltreatment comprise a large number portion of runaways" (p. 85). A few may be judged status offenders, regardless of why they had run away from home. Also, it is sometimes suggested that delinquency may produce the maltreatment rather than reverse. That is, the incorrigible child may be so difficult to deal with that the parent loses control; or, alternately, both delinquency and maltreatment may be viewed within a broader context of socioeconomic factors (Brown, Whitehead & Braswell, 1981).

While much attention has been paid to problems of battered wives and children, little has been paid to problems of adolescent abuse. When abused girls run away, they are treated as offenders and judged incorrigible, though their parents are the true offenders. Even less attention has been paid to brothers' and sisters' assaults on each other or teenagers' on their parents. In one case, a 15-year-old boy was charged with involuntary manslaughter for killing a 12-year-old brother. In another case, a 16-year-old had been beating his sick elderly father for at least four years. A child whose parents are either too lenient or too harsh may turn on them, and in effect become the disciplinarian. Among all children, 78 percent report having pushed a brother or sister; 47 percent have struck another with an object; and 20 percent have beaten up a sibling. Also,

10 percent of children, mostly teenagers, had hit their parents, and 7 percent had struck them with objects. One percent had beat the parent severely and another 1 percent had used a lethal weapon.

Unfortunately, the average citizen takes little direct interest in matters of child abuse. Most people are only remotely concerned about other peoples' children and share the social attitude that it is best to keep hands off other peoples' private affairs. Minors themselves have no political savvy or power, and public policies are ordinarily framed by individuals who have little real knowledge of minor's welfare.

Youth's Rights

Youth's, relative to parents', rights are being recognized increasingly in the courts. In certain states and in certain cases, court decisions have allowed minors to obtain medical help without their parents' knowledge or consent. Forty-eight of the states grant such freedom to teenagers who have venereal disease. Some states relate this concept to abortion, conception, drug addiction, pregnancy, mental disorders, and severely contagious diseases.

One development is that now the family may be said to exist for the benefit of individuals instead of individuals existing for the benefit of their families (Sussman, 1978). Another change is the view that parents, and not only children, have a right to a full life and that the parents' mental health is important. Hence, parents no longer expect to sacrifice all for their children but to retain benefits for themselves. While this change may be viewed as threatening to children's mental health, the opposite may well be true: parents who find life satisfying and growth-producing may provide a more wholesome family environment in which their children may develop.

Adolescents' conflicts with their parents typically focus on details of daily family life such as home chores, disobedience, school work or "general irritation" (Montemayor, 1982, p. 1518). These conflicts, generally about family matters, involve mothers more than fathers, since mothers are still charged with running the household and socializing the children. For the same reason, there are more arguments between mothers and daughters than between mothers and their sons. Montemayor suggests that they may be in direct competition for establishing dominance in the home. This writer doubts that adolescent girls care about establishing dominance there because they are more oriented to life outside the home at this period. Arguments arise because daughters resent the infringement of home duties on time they would like to spend with their peers. Also, they are growing up and wish to establish some independence; yet mothers are more likely to overprotect daughters than sons.

In common causes of parent-youth conflict there is no clear social consensus about who is right. When a thousand residents of Los Angeles, ages 17 to 94, 42 percent of them parents, were asked whether they would back adolescent child or parent in certain hypothetical situations, 84 percent supported the parent who required that a 15-year-old boy leave his door open when his girl friend was in his bedroom. Almost all (90%) agreed with the mother who refused to discuss the matter when her 15-year-old daughter, after just two dates with a college boy, says she is going to spend the weekend with him. A large majority (86%) believed that parents should insist that the 14-year-old boy report to the principal that a man teacher had made sexual advances to him, although the boy insisted that it would embarrass him in front of his classmates; and 71 percent would support parents who would not let a 14-year-old girl go to school if she doesn't wear a bra. However, only 42 percent would back the parent who wanted their 12-year-old son to cut his hair the length they desired. A considerable majority (71%) backed parents who wouldn't let their 12-year-old boy read best sellers with sexual references, or attend a movie with nude scenes. The adults were divided almost equally on whether a father might insist on accompanying his 14-year-old son to the doctor when he believes he has contracted VD. However, 70 percent would take sides with the 14-year-old girl whose parents found out that she had asked a doctor for advice on birth control and forbade the doctor to see her.

The adults in the study were sympathetic with some, but certainly not all of the parents' fears regarding their children's religious decisions. Over three-fourths (78%) supported parents who would not let a 14-year-old daughter attend a private school run by a group from an oriental religion; and 71 percent would back parents who insisted that their 10-year-old son go to church even though he said he didn't believe in God. Yet 64 percent would back the 14-year-old Protestant boy who desired to convert to Catholicism; and 65 percent would allow a 10-year-old Jewish girl, disinterested in her own faith, to go to services in various other churches. Over half the adults (69%) would support the 12-year-old girl who wanted to stop after-school music lessons so she could join the basketball team.

CURRENT STATUS OF FAMILY-ADOLESCENT RELATIONSHIPS

Authorities believe that research justifies at least some conclusions about child-rearing. Baumrind (1978) believes that certain parental and familial orientations have varying effects on adolescent development. Those youth from traditional families, who have internalized traditional values, experience less turbulent development. Parents with strong belief systems have children who conform and often bypass adolescent crises altogether. Parents who exploit their children turn their adolescent children against them and produce a rejection of their own authority. Parents who are punitive have adolescent children who are noncompliant and often transgress. The best overall approach is firm discipline by parents who are authoritative but not authoritarian.

In other research, a Harvard team did follow-up interviews of individuals in their early 30s who had been studied twenty-five years before by Robert Sears, Eleanor Maccoby, and Harry Levin in order to determine the relationship between specific childrearing practices and maturity levels achieved by young adults reared by various methods (McClelland, Constantian, Regalado & Stone, 1978). It was determined that what people do as adults does not relate to specific techniques of early childrearing, but how parents feel about their children has considerable impact. When parents, especially the mothers, genuinely loved their children, the children were more likely to achieve the highest levels of moral

Authorities believe that certain parental and familial orientations have varying effects on adolescent development. (© 1983 Nancy J. Pierce, Photo Researchers, Inc.)

and social maturity. The other main dimension of importance for later maturity was how "strictly the parents controlled their children's expressive behavior. A child was less apt to become socially and morally mature when the parents tolerated no noise, mess, or rough-housing in the home [or] when they reacted unkindly to the child's aggressiveness toward them, sex play, or expressions of dependency needs" (p. 45). The relationship between punitiveness in childhood and later functioning was negative but slight. Strictness, where parents tried to put down children's tendency to act out their feelings, was far more inhibiting. There was no relationship between reasoning with children or withdrawal of love and children's later maturity. The most important factor in later maturity turned out to be mother's warmth; however, extreme mother's warmth bore a negative relation with the mutual give-and-take related to highest-thinking maturity. That is, strong mother love develops in children conscious values of sharing, understanding, and tolerance but inhibits development of thinking at this level. In contrast, father love relates positively to thinking and functioning at the highest level, possibly because fathers are at home less and therefore less easily smother their children with love. Parents stress self-reliance and doing well, but at the highest stage of moral maturity some self-orientation must yield to the common good.

The research needs supplementing and continuous updating. We have few good phenomenological studies of parent-child relationships, especially longitudinal ones. Also needed is an adequate psychology of parents themselves. Since adults control youth's environment, only through understanding adults' behaviors can youth be understood. A possible reason for the neglect of adults is our "youth-bound" social science.

FUTURE PERSPECTIVES

Adolescents' family experience significantly influences their preparation for adulthood and their family adjustment as adults. When youth are engaged in skirmishes with their world in an attempt to establish their own mature identities, the home becomes an important base of security, a safe place to which they can retreat. Individuals lacking such support may have difficulty establishing themselves as adults. Future performance as parents reflects earlier experience with one's own parents. Such relations today are generally harmonious—a good omen for young parents-soon-to-be. Youths who feel abused within their homes typically become abusers of their children when they become parents.

Longitudinal research is beginning to yield some generalizations about the long-term outcomes of earlier family experiences. In the Terman study, the men's marital stability and good mental health in late middle age related to good attitudes in youth toward their own parents, especially toward their mothers (Goleman, 1980a). Among the women in the study, married women with children were more likely to be happy if their own parents' marriage had been good and if, as young women, they had had a warm, affectionate relationship with their parents (Goleman, 1980b). However, early family experience was a poor predictor of happiness among single women.

In one important area, decisions about marriage and fertility, the roots are traceable to youth; therefore, that period should be the point at which to provide intervention programs dealing with fertility control. In general, young adults' fertility and marital behaviors are strongly influenced by social background and adolescent attitudes. The development of familial and status aspirations during the adolescent period plays a focal part in the process. Young adult women who as adolescents had expressed a desire to marry young tended both to marry and to bear children early. Those who as adolescents had expressed a desire for more education tended to delay both marriage and childbearing (Marshall & Cosby, 1977).

The current generation of youth expect to limit the size of their families. Indeed, over the last decade or so the family size favored by youth has steadily declined (Juhasz, 1980). Of 287 college students questioned, 59.5 percent had decided to have children, 8.5 percent never intended having children, and the rest were undecided. About half (49 percent) wanted two children, 26 percent, three children, and 17 percent four children. Given present trends, the goal of a two-child family can be reached by voluntary means, thus halting the threat of overpopulation.

Youth must become aware of appropriate adult tasks at different life stages and how such tasks evolve with changing times (Scanlon, 1979). The typical model of the adult in the family emphasizes parenting tasks and overlooks the continuing developmental needs and tasks of that adult. Such a view may have reflected the child-oriented society of the 1960s, but it has little relevance to the increasingly adult-oriented one of the present.

In former times it was assumed that young people would learn by observing their parents how to run their future families. However, the traditional nuclear family composed of the father-who-works, the mother-homemaker, and the children is now one form among many. Although it is still the most common form, it is not even in the majority at present. The important alternatives today are single-parent families, working-parent families, and reconstituted (after divorce or death of parents) families. Therefore, during their high school and college careers, young people should study such variations, their significance for society, and how individuals may adapt to them most effectively (Scanlon, 1979).

Youth will be more independent since their parents work and they themselves belong to more than one family group. Joint-custody arrangements will increase in number and children will make more of their own decisions about their life styles. Perhaps, even as young as age 12, children may choose the parents they will live with after divorce.

Overall, families of the next century will be as different from those now as the patriarchies of "old testament times"—and the concept of husband as breadwinner and wife as homemaker will simply be "an historical curiosity," says Emory University Professor Levinson (When "family" will have a new definition, 1983).

It is also widely predicted that the family will remain strong, despite "sprouting some odd branches" (p. A3). As people live longer and change mates "to suit the seasons of their lives," serial marriages will grow common and children will have successive sets of parents and assorted half- and stepsiblings. In consequence youth's home life experience will be uncertain because so many will spend part of their childhood and adolescence in stepfamilies. However, as divorce grows so common society will probably develop more adequate ways of dealing with it. Besides, such individuals will have the advantage, in effect, of growing up in an extended family. Thus, they will have more significant figures and role models in their lives, and a larger support system. To date, children of divorce have seemed to experience negative consequences in cases of economic stress, but otherwise no long-term deficiencies. For many growing individuals pain relating to their parents' divorce is offset by the maturing involved.

Even today young people attach much importance to choosing a suitable marriage partner, indeed a realistic concern (When "family" will have a new definition, 1983).

It is also predicted that "new technologies will allow families to spend far more time together as they use computers for pursuing their careers at home, becoming educated or for shopping. Extended longevity plus the increasing time families spend together may well create friction and hitherto unknown generation gaps" (When "family" will have a new definition, 1983, p. A3). However, the reverse may well be true, as the generations share more common experiences. Besides, older generations now are better educated than formerly and keep up with current trends. The current emphasis on continuous renewal through adulthood should greatly reduce the gap between youth, parents, and grandparents.

SUMMARY

Although the functions of the family have changed somewhat over the years, its influence on the individual remains highly significant in early childhood and hardly less so in adolescence. It is true that peer-group standards influence adolescents in many ways; however, parental influence remains paramount in most basic matters. It is also true that family influence is changing, in some ways growing stronger, and in some ways diminishing.

Since the average family is smaller today, the impact of individual family members on each other is correspondingly greater. On the other hand, institutions outside the home have taken over many functions that the family formerly filled. Nevertheless, parents have assumed greater responsibility than formerly in their children's emotional development, and they have become highly self-conscious of their inadequacy in this area. Another growing emphasis in family life has been on mutual assistance in personal growth.

Families have come to assume increasingly diverse forms, including single-parent families, reconstituted families, and counterculture families—as in communes. Even nuclear families may undergo significant changes in the future. Indeed, it is increasingly apparent that youth's experiences in the family will be widely varied and changing over the years.

Each member of the family—whatever its form—plays a special role, and his or her own functioning is influenced by every other member's role. During adolescence, an individual's family role becomes somewhat modified. For example, the boy's influence increases, reflecting the generally higher status of the mature male in the society. More specifically, sex-role assignments vary somewhat with parental authority patterns in particular homes and according to which parent is dominant. Another important influence on family role is the characteristics of the youth concerned. Children who are unusually bright and dependable may be accorded unusual influence, regardless of their order in the sibling lineup. Siblings' relations to each other are also vital in defining such roles. These relations, in turn, depend somewhat on birth order.

The dimensions of the parent-child relationship, such as patterns of acceptance-rejection, have been studied extensively. Rejection by the parent may take the form of active rejection, passive rejection, or indifference, and it may also be conscious or unconscious. The effects of rejection differ according to the sex of the child, which parent does the rejecting, and the form the rejection takes. The polar opposite of rejection—acceptance or nurturance—suggests parental attitudes of warmth and helpfulness toward the child. In general, healthy acceptance has a positive effect. However, overindulgence may cause infantile and withdrawing behaviors and overdependency. Children and adolescents profit most from nurturance that is warmly supportive but not overly possessive.

Parents play several important roles in the lives of their adolescent children, especially as sources of affection and approval and as identification figures and advisors. Nevertheless, the father's and mother's roles are somewhat different, the father's being effective, representing the ego ideal or reality principle, and the mother's being affective, emotional, and expressive. Traditionally, the mother has been chief custodian of the child's socialization, and she has sometimes pursued this role overzealously. However, most mothers probably do a pretty fair job on the whole. The father, too, is beginning to come into his own and today is accorded an influence of considerable significance. Teenage youth, especially, come to appreciate the guidance of their fathers, and considerable research testifies to the fathers' critical influence. However, this influence varies in quality and degree according to race, social class, and personality. Indeed, the relationship of all adolescent children to their parents is complex and not easily understood.

Parent-adolescent child influence is not unidirectional. Adolescents react strongly to, and try to influence, both parents as people, sometimes positively, sometimes negatively. At this age adolescents have ceased to look upon their parents as all-powerful beings, as they did when younger. They also are beginning to criticize and compare their own parents with those of their friends. Sometimes such reactions result in conflict between the generations, a condition much publicized in recent years. Conflict arises in such matters as emancipation, discipline, and punishment, and it is always the parents' difficult task to decide upon just the right blend of authority versus emancipation and permissiveness versus discipline. Most authorities favor a program of preparing the growing child for emancipation from the earliest years and loosening the reins as rapidly as the child proves capable of handling freedom. Concerning matters of discipline, it is difficult to interpret available research properly; in general, a mixture of firmness and warmth produces the best results for both child and parent. Parents are coming to believe that they have rights, too, which children must learn to respect.

In some cases, the fallout from severe or unusually strict discipline is very harmful to children, sometimes resulting in overdependency and unhealthy submission on one hand, or outright hostility and delinquent behaviors on the other. As a result of the civil rights movement and the child advocacy programs that emerged from it, minors' rights are being recognized. A concurrent trend is toward recognition of all family members' rights and their mutual obligations. When minors' rights are abused, the structure of the nuclear family and the traditions that support it create almost insurmountable obstacles to those who work on behalf of children and youth.

Considerable confusion surrounds the question of parental guidance of youth. There is much debate on what methods constitute optimal childrearing. Fortunately, longitudinal studies are yielding results that may help to clarify questions still at issue. It is already apparent that the family experiences of youth exert a strong influence on personal and family adjustment in adulthood.

DISCUSSION QUESTIONS
AND ACTIVITIES

1. Read an autobiography and analyze the effect of the author's home environment and family on his or her development. Be sure that the selection you choose is adequate for analysis of this type.

2. Write an analysis of how your own family life has affected your development.

3. Interview one or more parents about their chief problems in rearing teenagers, their feelings toward today's youth, and how their teenage children have influenced them. Present your report to the class for general discussion.

4. Interview your brothers and sisters separately to determine in what respects each may have experienced family life differently.

5. Be prepared to suggest a conflict situation, involving teenagers and their parents or their siblings, that may be acted out by members of your class.

6. Make a list of major family problems you faced, or are facing, during your teens. Your list and those of the rest of the class may be sorted according to sex and discussed by the class.

7. Interview parents concerning restrictions placed on them when they were teenagers. Compare those restrictions with practices current today. Discuss the relative merits of the practices of the two generations.

8. Be prepared to participate in panel discussions of these topics: (a) What should teenagers do when they believe their parents' regulations are unreasonable? (b) What differences, if any, should there be in the regulations made by parents for their sons and for their daughters? (c) What are the major ways in which today's parents are helping or failing teenage boys and girls? (d) Are parental attitudes toward today's teenagers too lax?

9. Write two paragraphs, one analyzing a specific home situation which you believe to be ideal, and another describing a situation which you believe to be extremely unfavorable. Some of the paragraphs may be read to the class and discussed.

10. A class panel may discuss the special situation of adolescents whose families are of the communal, stepparent, or single-parent type.

11. Discuss, as a class, the way you and your classmates attempt to influence your parents and with what success.

SUGGESTED READINGS

Baranowski, M. C. (1982). Grandparent-adolescent relations: Beyond the nuclear family. *Adolescence, 17*(67), 575–584. The adolescent-grandparent relationship is explored in terms of its nature, quality, and factors which modify it.

Benalcazar, B. (1982). Study of fifteen runaway patients. *Adolescence, 17*(67), 553–566. This year-long study of adolescent runaways throws light on causes, effects, and modes of approaching this problem.

Blyth, D. A., Hill, J. P., & Thiel, K. S. (1982). Early adolescents' significant others: Grade and gender differences in perceived relationships with familial and nonfamilial adults and young people. *Journal of Youth and Adolescence, 11*(6), 425–450. In a study of almost 3,000 seventh through tenth graders almost all listed parents and siblings as significant others, and a majority also named some extended family adult and nonrelated adult as being significant in their lives.

Bryan, J. W., & Freed, F. W. (1982). Corporal punishment: Normative data and sociological and psychological correlates in a community college population. *Journal of Youth and Adolescence, 11*(2), 77–87. A survey of college students disclosed factors relating to the frequency and intensity of corporal punishment which they had experienced while growing up.

Covell, K., & Turnbull, W. (1982). The long-term effects of father absence in childhood on male university students' sex-role identity and personal adjustment. *Journal of Genetic Psychology, 141*(2), 271–276. This investigation of long-term effects of father absence on male children's and adolescents' sex-role development indicates the importance of the mother on the son's self-esteem and of father absence on later heterosexual relationships.

Guidubaldi, J., Gullo, D., & McLoughlin, C. (1982). The psychological rights of the child and the family. *Viewpoints in Teaching and Learning, 58*(1), 23–35. The psychological rights of minors are considered within the context of the family including parents' views of children relations between the parents, and childrearing methods.

Krementz, H. (1982). *How it feels to be adopted.* New York: Alfred A. Knopf. Nineteen individuals, ages 8 to 16, discuss their adoption in terms of their feelings about their adoptive status, their relationships to their foster families, and other matters.

McDonald, G. W. (1982). Parental power perceptions in the family: The influence of adolescent characteristics. *Youth and Society, 14*(1), 3–31. Adolescent's perceptions of the differential power of their parents is examined according to their nature and significance as well as sex, religiosity, age, and birth order of the adolescents themselves.

McMillan, D. W., & Hiltonsmith, R. W. (1982). Adolescents at home: An exploratory study of the relationship between perception of family social climate, general well-being and actual behavior in the home setting. *Journal of Youth and Adolescence, 11*(4), 301–315. A study of eighth grade students who gave information about how they utilized the home environment indicated a strong positive relationship between sense of well-being and time spent with adults in leisure and recreational activities in the home.

Montemayor, R. (1982). The relationship between parent-adolescent conflict and the amount of time adolescents spend alone and with parents and peers. *Child Development, 53*, 1512–1519. The time that adolescents spend with peers and parents is compared in terms of quantity and activities involved, and is related to amount of parent-adolescent conflict.

Montemayor, R., & Clayton, M. D. (1983). Maternal employment and adolescent development. *Theory into Practice, 22*, 112–118. This review of the research regarding the relationship between maternal employment and adolescent development on such matters as sex roles, academic performance, parent and peer relations, and adjustment indicates this relationship to be so complex as to make simple generalizations impossible.

Offer, D., Ostrov, E., & Howard, K. I. (1982). Family perceptions of adolescent self-image. *Journal of Youth and Adolescence, 11*(4), 281–291. In general, this study supported the hypothesis that parents somewhat accurately perceive their adolescent children's self-image and that greater congruence between parents and children relates to a better adolescent self-image.

Saucier, J., & Ambert, A. (1982). Parental marital status and adolescents' optimism about their future. *Journal of Youth and Adolescence, 11*(5), 345–354. A sampling of all French-speaking adolescents in Montreal, including those from legally intact homes,

separated or divorced homes, or homes in which a parent was deceased, indicated that those from both types of broken homes were less optimistic about their futures than were those from intact homes.

Walker, A. J., & Thompson, L. (1983). Intimacy and intergenerational aid and contact among mothers and daughters. *Journal of Marriage and the Family, 75*(4), 841–849. Mother-daughter relationships were analyzed in terms of such variables as modes of contact, degree of intimacy, difference in ages between mother-daughter pairs, positive or negative effect, and type of aid given by each to the other.

York, P., York, D., & Wachtel, T. (1982). *Toughlove.* New York: Doubleday & Co. The program described here, now a nationwide movement, is a means by which parents form a support system within the community for dealing with their teenage children.

Chapter Nine

The Adolescent In The Peer Group

THE SIGNIFICANCE OF SOCIAL
RELATIONSHIPS

General Importance

Group relationships perform certain essential functions both for the individual and for society. Primarily, they satisfy what Slavson (1947) calls "group hunger," or the drive to escape loneliness, considered by some to be the most basic of human problems. In addition, a group clarifies the self each person sees in the looking glass—the "social self," or the self that others see. Helen Keller reported that she was unable to acquire a real sense of self until she learned how to communicate with others. People's attitudes toward themselves are modified as they look at themselves through others' eyes. When they evoke praise or criticism they unconsciously develop self-attitudes that range from self-love to self-abnegation.

In one sense, the individual's socialization takes on the characteristics of radar (Riesman, 1950). Individuals learn to send out signals, to bounce them against targets—their peers—and, by the way the signals are reflected, they judge how acceptable they are to those to whom they were sent. The reactions of other people tell the individual whether or not they are "on the beam." Thus the development of sensitivity to others is an essential ingredient in the process of each person's socialization.

Society is becoming increasingly peer oriented. As the gap between generations increases, age groups are drawn more toward each other. Thus the peer group has not so much won out in competition with the family as it has moved into a vacuum. Young believes that the waning of parental influence could have highly negative results. Lacking strong adult-child bonds, children will simply become impersonal, destructive, empty, violent, and even psychotic (Peer group replacing family?, 1979).

What constitutes a peer is rarely specified. Peers may mean all other adolescents as distinct from adults. The differential impact of different categories of peers—for example in terms of age—are rarely studied. Also peers are ordinarily defined in terms of school settings, perhaps because school associations are easier to research. But neighborhood and other associations are equally important for developing adolescent relationships (Blyth, Hill & Thiel, 1982).

Unpopularity in childhood suggests a poor prognosis for personal adjustment later on. When teacher ratings of 187 children seen at a guidance clinic were compared to social adjustment of the same individuals 9 to 15 years later, those individuals having poor peer relationships as children had the poorest adult adjustment. Girls who withdrew from their peers and had temper displays, and boys who became involved in fights, were selfish; preferred younger children proved more maladjusted in adulthood than those not thus characterized (Janes & Hesselbrock, 1978). It is essential, therefore, for adolescents to develop meaningful peer relationships. With regard to this ideal, consider the contrast in these adolescents' reactions to social situations:

MALE: I never had a brother and I grew up in the country. I was poor in sports and disliked by all the members of the class. I find it hard to adjust to groups, especially in the Navy.

MALE: I intensely hate crowds; they clutter up the place and make noise. I lose intimacy and individuality in a large party or meeting. You make small talk and try to block your ears from the rumbling around you. I cannot sit still long in a crowded room; I simply have to leave. I prefer a small group—three or four couples—with room to move about freely.

FEMALE: I much prefer being among other people to being alone. I find the presence of others exhilarating and fun. Part of the reason is that I never developed any real hobbies and rely on other people for my entertainment. Besides, certain features of my living situation are unsatisfactory and being with others takes my mind off myself.

Special Significance During Adolescence

Peer adjustment is also important because society is coming to encourage team play instead of rugged individualism. For example, in industry and government teams of researchers and administrators work together because social issues and technologies are so complex that no one person has the expertise to deal with an entire operation. For another, consider how childrearing is becoming an increasingly greater cooperative enterprise (What the next 50 years will bring, 1983).

Peer relations allow an individual to find role models appropriate for the times. For example, an individual with a nontraditional identity is more likely to validate his or her identification among similar-aged rather than older persons (Morgan & Farber, 1982).

Adolescents' peers constitute significant reference groups which modify the attitudes and behaviors of their members by constituting an "interim framework" between childhood and adulthood (Seltzer, 1982). In general, this framework does not conflict with adult society, but is a mixture of present adolescent and future adult meanings (Peterson & Peters, 1983).

Peer relations are especially important when adolescents are seeking to establish their independence, at a time when they are in between their two major sources of emotional support. As adolescents begin seeking independence from the family their former source of support is weakened, partly because they perceive a weakness in seeking such support. At the same time they have not yet developed sources of support outside the family. As a result their self-esteem wavers, and they employ strategic social interactions to boost their self-esteem in relation to their peers (Elkind, 1980).

Such strategies assume a variety of forms. The group leader temporarily replaces the repudiated, yet needed, father figure; and the group itself provides support when the youth rebels against parental authority. If a boy insists on his right to smoke, his guilt feelings are alleviated by his friends' assurance that he is within his rights. Also, the fact that many different homes are represented in the peer group helps adolescents keep their own families in perspective: Kate comes to realize that her family's insistence on no dates until she reaches age 17 is simply too old-fashioned to be respected.

The separation process is not a single event or confined to a quite limited period (Lipsitz, 1979). Adolescents begin to detach themselves from their parents through associating with peers and developing their own preference for dress, language, and music. Not until later adolescence have they pretty well developed their own value systems and emotional independence. Adolescents' "lifeline" is the peer group as they try out different roles and relationships, but adults are also lifelines. Thus there is a need for both detachment and continuing adult support.

The peer group influence is also important because of the large number of hours adolescents devote to its activities. Indeed, they spend more time with peers now than formerly for several reasons. They spend more time away from home on school days and on weekends; more extracurricular activities and commercial recreational activities are available to them; and both parents are away from home much of the time in connection with their employment (Glaser, 1979).

Variations in Peer Relationships

It is often, but incorrectly, assumed that adolescents' significant relationships exist only within same-age peer groups. Montemayor and Van Komen (1980) observed adolescents in three high schools as well as seven out-of-school settings and found greater age differences among those associating together in out-of-school than in-school settings and in mixed-sex than in same-sex groups. Of those studied over a third (37%) of their companions in out-of-school settings were adults, a high figure in view of the age segregation presumed to prevail in adolescence.

In their study of seventh through tenth grade students in a midwestern suburban school Blyth, Hill, and Thiel (1982) identified the significant others in their lives. They named more same-sex nonrelated young people than those in any other category. However, parents were listed by both sexes at all grade levels; and 77 percent of the students listed siblings as significant others. Over three-fourths listed at least one extended family member—that is, not just a parent or a sibling; and 60 percent of the males and 75 percent of the females listed as least one nonrelated adult as significant.

Thus the results indicated that adolescents are not as age-segregated as commonly believed. Although same-sex unrelated young persons were the most frequently listed, respondents of all grades studied continued to list their parents, older siblings, extended family adults, and unrelated adults.

There were several gender differences. Girls listed more significant others than did boys. Also, girls mentioned opposite-sex peers as significant at an earlier age, because they mature earlier and become sexually involved at an earlier age. In no category did boys list significantly more persons than did females because females develop a greater ability for intimate associations. Although young people turn increasingly to their peers in adolescence, there was more growth in number of significant same-sex peers from grades 7 through 10.

THE IMPACT OF THE PEER GROUP

The Cult of Conformity

The peer group's influence, although vital, is often portrayed as strangling the individual's personality. Adolescents may find themselves enmeshed in unpleasant networks of reciprocity and learn that the relationship between privilege and responsibility restricts freedom. They learn, in essence, that it hurts more than a little to grow up and that the privileges of adult life are paid for by assuming responsibility. In high school they create a new and, to them, better society of their own where conformity is the rule. College students are more independent and inclined to "do their own thing."

Gelman (1980) notes the paradox that "while adolescents are traditionally rebellious within their own circles they tend to be fiercely conformist" (p. 48). Indeed, many adolescents swim with the social stream largely from habit—a habit so ingrained that they feel uncomfortable when they do the slightest original thing. Note this teenager's experience when attending a jazz concert:

> FEMALE: The auditorium became alive with foot-tapping and finger-drumming. A boy in my immediate vicinity seemed to be doing a rock 'n' roll sitting down, punctuating the jazz band's performance with cries of "Go, man!" and "Crazy beat!" . . . I was sitting there excited, enjoying the rhythm, until I suddenly noticed with horror that my feet were not tapping, my head wasn't swaying, my little finger wasn't even quivering. This discovery had a strong psychological effect on me. Was I a musical blockhead? Was I mentally deficient? I was mortified! I glanced self-consciously to right and left and then began tapping my foot furiously, hoping no one had noticed what an odd duck I had been. . . . I live in a conformist society and alas, I live by its rules.

Adolescents often learn the relationship between privilege and responsibility can restrict freedom. (Photo by William J. Butcher)

It is difficult to determine to what extent adolescents truly have an inner need to conform or simply feel pressured to, while covertly wishing to be independent. The common view, that the self-preoccupation and indulgence of the 1960s are over and the conservatism of the 1950s has returned, received a jolt in research by sociologist David A. Snow and Cynthia L. Phillips at the University of Texas. Over the period 1976–1980, 80 percent of the students they studied perceived themselves as guided primarily by their own feelings, thoughts, and experiences; only 20 percent felt guided mainly by institutional statuses and goals.

Other research suggests that youth conform largely because of peer pressures. When asked in an open-ended question to name the most difficult task they had experienced as teenagers, an equal proportion of both sexes (35 %) named something relating to peer pressure (Brown, 1982). Females felt far greater peer pressure than did males, especially regarding grooming and dress, having steady opposite-sex relations, being active socially—such as dating and going to parties—and smoking cigarettes. Both sexes felt that peers were especially insistent that they participate socially. Pressure to use alcohol and drugs came second for boys, and boys felt slightly more pressure to engage in intercourse, although not that much. Both sexes reported little pressure regarding smoking cigarettes or parent-teen relations.

The strongest, most consistent finding was that peer pressure is more influential on girls than boys in their high school years. For girls these pressures were intense and influenced their behaviors more. The results also supported the traditional image of women as responding more to interpersonal relationships and being more subject to others' influence than are males. Males were influenced by peer pressures but considerably less.

Despite such evidence, C. R. Snyder (1980a) casts some doubt on the popular theory that human beings, including youth, are rarely willing to risk their social acceptability by seeming too different. The literature indicates that people are happier if they are more like other people—hence, there is much pressure to go along with the crowd. However, Snyder believes that there is a persistent "uniqueness-seeking as a counterpoint to the psychology of sameness" (p. 86). He cites various advertisements that cater to this need for uniqueness, including a Winston cigarette ad that shows a young man gazing at the reader and saying, "I don't smoke to be like everybody else" (p. 87). Traditionally, it has been assumed that people are happiest being considerably like others, while feeling a little different. However, Snyder found that those individuals had the most positive emotional reactions who were neither a little different nor extremely different but who felt moderately different, and that people who felt just a little unique or not at all unique were uncomfortable with themselves.

Perhaps youth's conformist-appearing behaviors represent a compromise between their needs to be accepted and to preserve their individuality. Teenagers have felt a great concern about their popularity with their peers, girls even more than boys (Sebald, 1981); and even though contemporary teenagers believe in the importance of being an individual, at the same time they find it necessary to conform to their peers in order to be popular (Sebald, 1981).

PEER VERSUS PARENT IMPACT   The relative extent of peers and parents' influence is controversial, partly because our present comprehension of the adolescent's social world is limited (Blyth, Hill & Thiel, 1982). Adults other than parents have mostly been ignored, as well as siblings and extended family members. Also neglected has been the influence of youth leaders and teachers in such areas as drug use, youths' work experience, and nonfamilial modeling. Siblings also constitute important sources of information with regard to support, advice, and supply of liquor, cigarettes, and drugs to adolescents, directly or indirectly.

Let us have a look at a sampling of relevant research. A study of 170 high school juniors disclosed interesting data regarding the relative strength of their interpersonal relationships with their parents, same-sex, and opposite-sex friends (Wright & Keple, 1981). The girls attached more importance to their friends than their parents, whereas the boys attached almost equal significance to the four target persons: mother, father, best same-sex, and best opposite-sex friends. One reason may be that, compared to the boys, these 16-and 17-year-old girls had matured faster and were now relatively more independent of their parents.

Other research shows the relationship between child and child and parent and child to be somewhat different. The parent-child relationship is complementary, in which children exchange obedience for parent's parental care, whereas peer relations are egalitarian, based on mutual assistance and solutions. Youniss (1980) concludes that parent-child relationships form the basis of children's respect for rules of the social order, and child-child relationships for children's concern for mutuality and fairness.

As children move into adolescence the relationship changes somewhat. Although adolescents continue to recognize and accept parental authority to some extent, they now bring to the relationship more of a peer-like orientation, deriving from the parents' growing respect for their almost grown children's views. The common view is that adults role-model social behaviors for children, which their children then apply to extrafamilial relationships. Youniss portrays the social relations process as proceeding in the opposite direction—that is, teenage children bring to relationships with their parents insights about mutuality and equality gained from peer interaction. This writer would prefer an interactional view—that adults, from the vantage point of their own greater experience, bring important insights to their interaction with their own children, but that their adolescent children also bring to the relationship what they have learned from their peers.

Parent-peer relations vary greatly among cultures. Comparative data obtained on youth in France, Israel, and the United States indicate that adolescent drug involvement relates to the overall use of the substance in a particular culture. However, the situation is not as simplistic as that observation would imply. Parents and peers exert an important influence in all three countries but most in Israel and least in the United States. The three countries also differed with regard to peer pressures and peer orientation of adolescents, with peer orientation highest in the United States and least in Israel. Usually, in Israel, adolescent alcohol use is not an expression of rebellion, nor does it indicate any rejection of norms and values of the adult culture. Rather, the family environment constitutes a model for alcohol use, because adolescents are used to wine and alcohol in family situations, chiefly for ritual religious purposes (Adler & Kandel, 1982).

INDIVIDUAL SOCIAL ADJUSTMENT

With so many complex and often conflicting social influences pulling and tugging them this way and that, adolescents' adjustments to society vary considerably. In the following statements adolescents tell how well adjusted they think they are socially and why:

> FEMALE: A strong inferiority complex about my looks—I am ugly—has caused me to be self-conscious around people. I am quiet because I fear I won't say the right thing.
>
> FEMALE: I am well adjusted socially. There is nothing I like better than meeting people and making friends. Growing up in a large family and participating in high school activities have favored my adjustment.
>
> MALE: My folks worried so much that I took refuge in a world of daydreams. I couldn't seem to snap out of it even at school. I was an onlooker. For another thing, I was small and disinterested in athletics. Outsiders rarely attempted to penetrate the daydream world where I was undisputed king.

Individual adolescents' popularity with their peers depends on a combination of personality and physical characteristics. Adolescents themselves associate with pupil popularity such physical characteristics as strong, handsome, and sporting for boys; and pretty, shapely, big breasted for girls (Hendry & Jamie, 1977).

Other Factors that Affect
Peer Group Influence

Minority group membership also modifies an individual's susceptibility to peer-group influence. The group's status-giving function, mentioned earlier, is especially significant for members of a minority group. Their crowd becomes a means of obtaining not only the status refused them by society but also the sense of belonging denied them by other adolescent groups. Even under the most favorable circumstances, youth tend to associate mostly with their own race, at least partly because they feel more comfortable in culturally homogeneous subgroups. Even over a period of time, in the face of the most positive circumstances, they tend to affiliate strictly with their own racial group (O'Mara, 1978).

Julius Tanner (1978) portrays the working-class youth subcultures of Britain as derived from the economic situation. The mods, typical of the skilled working-class youth, had come to doubt that they could ever realize the social mobility they desired. Their style was a "parody of the upward mobile worker." The mods superimposed on the commercial symbols of youth culture the fashion, and music, London's West End, the gesture and argot of their local working-class community. The skin heads (another group which emerged in the late 1960s and early 1970s) were recruited from the unskilled working class and more passively accepted their lot in society. Their style (industrial jeans, boots, and braces) derived more from traditional working-class concerns than from modern youth culture. In contrast, the mod's style focused more on age-specific fashions and music. Thus, concludes Tanner, particular subculture groups within the society "extract core components of style—clothes, music, hair styles, and so on [from the larger youth culture] and rework them to signify and reflect key themes of their group" (p. 361).

Peer-group influence also varies by sex. The sexes follow somewhat different patterns in their social development. Males display a greater peer orientation than females before puberty because they are allowed to range more freely from home. Peer acceptance must be distinguished from peer orientation in assessing social behaviors. Massad (1981) reported that among males high masculinity related to overall peer acceptance; however, for females high peer acceptance was associated with higher levels of both femininity and masculinity.

Popularity also relates to emotional maturity. A study of social competence as measured by social knowledge indicated that "knowledge of appropriate emotions for specific contexts" is important (Adams, 1983, p. 205). At least in high school popularity relates to following the traditional sex roles. It has been speculated that androgynous individuals are more socially competent, since they manage to integrate the "agency and communion" authorities in their "social interactions style" (Baumrind, 1982). However, Adams' study suggests that traditional sex roles are associated with peer popularity. Despite the women's movement, the American high school scene appears strongly influenced by traditional sex-role differences. The validity of popularity as a goal should be questioned.

Popularity in high school is often seen as a goal for adolescence but its validity should be questioned. (Courtesy of Public Relations Office, State University of New York at Oswego)

Very popular adolescents may become unduly manipulated by others or spend a relatively too large amount of time socializing. Hence, judging the worth of popularity would also require looking at other factors associated with attainment of that status.

Another characteristic which relates positively to social acceptance is trust. When 250 sorority and fraternity members at the University of Connecticut rated themselves and their peers on the characteristic of trust, those individuals high on trust were better liked and better adjusted psychologically (Rotter, 1980). Although the low trusters might say that high trusters were "just plain dumb," high trusters did equally well on scholastic aptitude tests (p. 38). Nor were high trusters more easily taken in by other people. On the other hand, high trusters were more "conventional and moralistic," viewed today as not entirely positive. Their ethical code was based more on conventional morality than on personal moral principles. High trusters were more often involved in do-good activities, such as the Eagle Scouts. High and low trusters also differed in their reactions to strangers. High trusters would trust others until they had proof to the contrary; low trusters would distrust strangers until they had evidence that they could be trusted.

Also affecting social adjustment are communication skills. Critical components are mutual respect and cooperation which enable friends to share common thoughts. Yet free and open communication, unless tempered with good judgment, means that very personal revelations are made public, often to the individual's disadvantage.

A follow-up of individuals who had participated in a communications skills training program, showed significant increases in their abilities to use self-control and to respond with empathy to their peers, in comparison with a control group. These dimensions were employed because of their general acceptance as important components of satisfactory interpersonal relationships. Empathy was defined as "ability to recognize and understand another person's perceptions and feelings . . ." and self disclosure as "the process whereby individuals allow themselves to be known to another through open, honest expression of feeling, thoughts and ideas" (Avery, Rider & Haynes-Clements, 1981). The experimental groups significantly improved their abilities to self-disclose and to respond with empathy from the first test to the follow-up five months later and their post-training empathy level lasted at least for this period of time. This writer would question the value of improving self-disclosure skills without parallel training in judging when and how much to disclose. Otherwise, increased disclosure might have unfavorable outcomes. One might ask at what level does amount of disclosure become negative in its effect.

It is commonly assumed that strong individualism interferes with healthy adjustment. Some individuals define individualism "in terms of unscrupulous competition, atomistic self containment and alienation . . ." and they view individualism as the antithesis to cooperation (Waterman, 1981, p. 768). Others believe that independence and self-interest need not "preclude acting for the benefit of the partner" (p. 768). The ideal would be a reciprocal relationship in which one identifies the interests of others with one's own. Meantime, achieving sound mutual relationships would undoubtedly raise feelings of self-respect. Waterman points out that research studies have been consistent in showing a relationship between self-esteem and concern for others.

Sex and age also relate to social adjustment; just how these factors relate is uncertain. Kurdek and Krile (1982) found that more girls than boys, and more older than younger children, had higher levels of social competence and interpersonal understandings. It has been commonly assumed that gifted children of either sex would have more problems than others in making friends, because popular children are often peer dependent, bound by peer rules and routines which are characteristics untrue of most gifted children (Coleman, 1980).

The research on this matter is mixed and somewhat ambiguous. Freeman (1979) found among 5- to 16-year-olds that high IQ children had fewer friends, more often felt different from other children, and were rated by their teachers as more hostile and maladaptive. However, in Freeman's research it wasn't merely IQ difference that predicted fewer relations—and the measures were not sufficiently refined to decide whether gifted children were really rejected by their classmates or merely viewed with indifference. The gifted children not only felt no anxiety in their peer relations but had older, though fewer, friends than those with average IQs, partly because the high achievement students were younger than the others by a grade or two. They may be at some physical disadvantage in school; however, as they become older or move into adulthood, physical stature becomes less important. Overall, peer relations are not a good criterion for predicting future social adaptations, partly because of the difficulty of interpreting adolescent self-reports (Monks & Ferguson, 1983).

Among environmental factors that influence social development, happy family experience is especially important. If their family is a closed world, having little to do with others, or if their parents, as role models, frequently derogate others, children may feel uneasy with others and distrustful of them. If they have poor relationships with members of their family, being constantly belittled or manipulated by them, they come to perceive themselves as socially inept and incapable of effective group membership. Finally, parents who restrict their children's social contacts hamper their peer relationships, in contrast to those who send their children away to camp or who open their homes freely to their children's friends.

School experience is also significant in peer relations. Where students sit in the classroom, especially when seats are assigned, subtly modifies relationships. Cross-sectional and sociometric data from the sixth, seventh, and eighth grades and longitudinal data from grades 4 through 6 disclosed that classroom characteristics influence individual popularity and friendship, the number of isolates in the class, and the incidence of cross-sex friendships. They also affect the numbers or size of cliques, clique stability, and the number of students having no membership in cliques. Among these classes, 61 percent contained no social isolates; 25 percent, one; 8 percent, two; and 6 percent, three. Every class had at least one social isolate at some time over the school year. More social isolates were found in open classes than in traditional ones. In such classes students are more on their own. The eighth grade had most isolates and the sixth grade had least; and the sixth graders were better integrated into the social structure of the classroom (Hallinan, 1979).

Viewing television can be a positive factor in social development. In the process, adolescents experience a sort of "intimacy at a distance," creating for themselves an illusion of personally reacting with television characters (p. 75). By defining televised characters as their own significant others, they evaluate in fantasy their own actions. Or they may try out televised role behaviors in their peer groups and then evaluate their peers' responsiveness to these behaviors (Peterson & Peters, 1983).

In the process of vicarious role-taking adolescents may mentally rehearse role expectations from the vantage point of relationships in which they themselves are not actual participants (Ellis, Streeter & Englebrecht, 1983). For instance, they may view a televised portrayal such as a couple dating, and then speculate regarding the adequacy of each of the two dating partners' performance. In other words, they mentally rehearse televised role behaviors which they may later incorporate into their own group behaviors (Peterson & Peters, 1983).

Youth do not necessarily perceive television images as portraying an objective reality (Peterson & Peters, 1983). Television portrayals become real to the extent that youth relate them to real-life situations. Adolescents react to televised images selectively, in terms of their own experience. Thus, televiewing becomes a means of gaining impressions of peer issues such as heterosexual relations, independence of parents, and life styles—including hair styles and clothing—as ways of presenting one's identity. Moreover, televiewing becomes increasingly selective as individuals move from childhood into and through adolescence (Murray, 1980).

THE DYNAMICS OF PEER GROUPS

In the following, the peer groups to be examined are composed of adolescents of approximately the same age, with similar interests and ideas. Some groups are only slightly cohesive; others are close-knit. They may be social or antisocial, creative or commonplace.

Adults are relatively indifferent to the existence of these peer societies, probably because they are hardly aware of the dual social system within which adults and adolescents live. They expect adolescents to follow the rules of their peer group without violating those of the adult world, but such conflicting demands often place them in dilemmas: Instructors demand long hours of study; the fraternity involves heavy social obligations. If adults are to lay claim to understanding adolescents, they must accept the reality of this kind of culture within a culture.

Developmental History of
Peer Groups

In our society, there are characteristic forms of groups according to age levels of the individuals comprising them. First, there is the play group, beginning at about age 2. Then at ages 8 to 10 the gang age begins; it may continue through a decade. The gang is almost always unisexual in composition and focuses on activities and role models appropriate to the particular sex. The gang generally declines with the onset of adolescence, when the clique emerges, followed a little later by the crowd.

Adolescent groups may be either *formal*—those with a reasonably permanent structure like clubs and fraternities—or *informal*—those which tend to

Participation in organized clubs is important to adolescents. (Courtesy of Public Relations Office, State University of New York at Oswego)

appear and disappear, assemble or dissolve, depending upon the occasion. Participation in organized clubs is important to adolescents for several reasons. Students gain experience in cooperatively and intelligently planning goals, programs, and activities. They have opportunities for sharing special interests and skills like hobbies and sports. They learn group roles, such as constructive leadership and followership.

Informal Social Groupings

The most common informal adolescent groups are **friendships, cliques,** and **crowds.** There are also *networks*, a term used to describe the relationships between groups. Some groups dominate or oppose others; some regularly work with other groups. The typical late-childhood peer group, the **gang,** has generally disappeared by adolescence. But adolescent gangs do exist, and their activities vary, running the gamut from nondelinquent athletic competition to crime.

FRIENDSHIP   Friendships should be distinguished from popularity. A friendship denotes "ongoing reciprocal liking and behavioral involvement between two individuals"; whereas "popularity typically means being liked and regarded as a friend by a relatively large number of peers" (McGuire & Weisz, 1982, p. 1479). An individual may be popular without having any close friends or have good friends without being popular.

In a sampling of the author's college students, 87.3 percent of 95 youths said close friends were very important to them, and the rest somewhat; 79.5 percent of 98 said friends in general were very important, and the rest somewhat important.

FEMALE: Friends are very important to me at this stage in my life. I have friends, but only a few very close friends that I can share personal things with. Friends are more important now than ever before because I'm away from my family and boyfriend. I think this is true for almost every college student.

MALE: I don't know if my friends have had strong influences on me. I've usually been an introverted person, although I've become more outgoing at college. Friends have not influenced me very much.

Friendships fulfill certain important functions for youth. Friendship constitutes an egalitarian relationship, in contrast to the hierarchical relationship between parents and their children, or siblings with each other because of their age differences. Thus, friendships are presumed to provide foundations for later egalitarian relationships with spouse, neighbors, and colleagues (Youniss, 1980).

There is also evidence that friends influence each others' social behaviors, academic achievements, and attitudes, and that close friendships increase self-esteem. However, there is almost no evidence that adolescent friendships improve social adjustment either in adolescence or later life (Berndt, 1982).

On the basis of interviews with children and adolescents, Youniss (1980) analyzed how young adolescents acquire their interpersonal concept and concluded that there are two main characteristics of emerging adolescent friendships: mutual understanding, including loyalty, and intimacy. *Mutual understanding* means appreciation that friends' personalities and activities are reciprocal in nature and that individuals can relate to each other in mutually beneficial ways. Understanding others' personhood means appreciating each other's distinctive interests, abilities, and experiences. That is, one recognizes oneself and one's friends as unique, yet sharing complementary relationships.

Critical to adolescent friendship is *intimacy*, which has three elements. First, friendship affords a mode of self-revelation in which one reveals one's innermost feelings and views to a friend. The second element, confidence, is the conviction that these self-revelations will be respected and in no way used against oneself; this confidence is rooted in a context of mutual trust. A third element, exclusivity, suggests that intimacies are limited to specially valued friendships. Thus, adolescents do not share their inner feelings with people generally but limit their confidence to a very few trusted individuals. They are encouraged in such expression by the belief that each understands the other and accepts what one is.

A study of five age groups of women, embracing ages 14 to 80, revealed that friendship fulfills several highly significant needs: intimacy-assistance, power, and status. The need for *intimacy-assistance*—that is the sharing of secrets along with helping or receiving help—is constant over all age groups. Intimacy appears to be a critical and instinctual factor, found from infancy on. There is an overpowering need for having a confidant or friend, someone with whom one can have a helping, understanding relationship. However, friends are probably more important to women than men because they are normally more intimate with their friends. In this study the *status* need—to have friends who will increase one's self-esteem—was greatest in adolescence, declined thereafter, and became more important again for women over 60. The need to have friends for *power*—to help in controlling others' behaviors—was high in adolescence and less so from then on (Candy, Troll & Levy, 1981).

A study of friendships among college women indicated that they have a highly therapeutic value; women valued both giving to and receiving help from their friends. They said their closeness "freed them up and produced a unique shared feeling" (p. 506). Also rating consistently high was the opportunity for expression of feelings which helped them to cope with their own difficult emotions besides providing someone with whom they might express joyful ones. The possibility for modeling ranked low, possibly because imitation of another individual's behavior threatens one's own individuality. This confirmation of the importance of friendship contrasts with a long-held point of view that women attach little importance to friendship with other women. Friendships between women are less visible than the more "overt camaraderie of men, nevertheless [they] have a special and highly valued quality (Davidson & Packard, 1981).

In adolescence individuals typically become increasingly detached from their family as their peer relations grow stronger and, at the same time, friendship relations become more restricted, intimate, and intensive. That is, the number of friendship relationships actually decreases after the age of about 15 (Selman, 1980). Also, friendships of early adolescents, as compared with those of younger children, involve more intimate self-disclosure and information about each other, and they become even more intimate in later adolescence (Youniss, 1980). However, the hypothesis that same-sex friendships decrease in intimacy as heterosexual relationships develop does not hold up. Both intimate same-sex and cross-sex relationships increase simultaneously during adolescence (Sharabany, Gershoni & Hoffman, 1981).

At the stage of adolescence and youth, individuals are somewhat open to others—they have not defined the boundaries of their own personalities. As they seek to determine who and what they are, they gain from their peers feedback concerning their strengths and weaknesses. Because of this lack of boundaries and the anxieties of their situation, they form deep commitment to their friends, and for this reason the friendship tends to last. In later stages, in young adulthood and beyond, it becomes more difficult to admit others to the "inner core" of one's personality (Bensman & Lilienfeld, 1979, p. 60). By young adulthood, individuals have become clearer about their identity and their commitments, and possibilities for deep friendships have become more limited.

Berndt (1982) points out that unstable friendships may not be especially damaging to adolescents if they form new friendships to take their place. This writer would like to add that, as an individual develops, successive new friendships may simply be evidence of growth and of exploring new aspects of one's personality. As individuals test themselves in more environments these environments will involve diverse contacts with different individuals.

The sexes experience friendship in different ways. Yoon (1978) found that females' friendships are "more intense, physically more demonstrative, more nurturant and ego supportive than those between men. Females must often choose their best friends as confidants; and their conversations are often on personal topics, which helps them to grow as persons." In addition, female friendships provide "a vast new spectrum of anchorages with validation and identification potential for those women who reject their parents' norms and values" (Bardwick, 1979, p. 150).

In considerable measure female/female friendships parallel the mother-daughter relationship in terms of their "coincident emphases on intensity, nurturance, exclusivity and ego support"; and they exert a significant influence on women through identification (Morgan & Farber, 1982, p. 209).

Sex distinction becomes even greater in close or intimate friendships. Intimacy may be defined as the joint sharing of one's concerns, accepting and caring for another individual, and exchanging help and assistance. It is a relationship to another individual to whom one feels very closely attached, whether of the same or of the other sex. A study of undergraduates indicated that androgynous individuals have highest intimacy scores, the sex-typed the next highest—a little below; and the undifferentiated the least. Females, both sex-typed and androgynous, were higher on intimacy than were males. In particular dyads, or twosomes, female relationships achieved the highest intimacy scores and male relationships the least. The currently higher scores of intimacy of female-female relationships may derive partly from the femininity of women—women have always been more intimate than men—as well as the women's movement, which brought women closer together. Men may not lack intimacy, however, they fail to develop intimate relationships as do women (Fischer & Narus, 1981).

Still other research suggests that females' friendships may not be more intimate than males', but different. Berndt (1982) found that girls more often than boys mention sharing their intimate thoughts and feelings with their friends; and girls share theirs more with close friends than with other classmates, whereas boys treat classmates more alike. Girls also are less willing than boys to make new friends when they already have close ones, suggesting that girls' friendships are more exclusive. However, boys rate their own friendships as intimate as girls do, and they apparently have as intimate a knowledge of their close friends. Berndt (1981) concluded that girls do not have closer or more intimate friendships than boys, but that their patterns of friendship are different.

On the other hand, observes Tognoli (1980), men may often prefer the company of other men to women but their level of intimacy is typically shallow. Most male friendships are limited to such "formalized settings . . ." as "teenage gangs, school, college, work, sports and the military" (p. 273). Various social factors mitigate against their establishing such friendships including taboos against male intimacy, competitiveness, and homophobia.

Tognoli suggests three solutions for reversing men's alienation from each other. First, there should be men's movements to provide consciousness-raising groups among them to encourage open communication. Second, fathers should become more involved with their children in the home to constitute models of the nurturant male. Third, men must learn to "defy the myths in our culture" that have inhibited the male's sex roles such as competition, homophobia, and inexpressiveness, all being factors that divide men from each other.

CLIQUES   The clique is a small, exclusive group made up of three or more individuals who possess similar interests and sometimes a strong affection for each other. In a clique, menbers find refuge from the conflicting demands of their other worlds. A clique is also a particular type of friendship group, marked chiefly by "the goal of sharing information and decision making. It tends to be less primary than friendships (held together primarily by emotional ties), more institutionalized (for example, like a group of friends who regularly meet for a game of bridge), more 'in' (because of their information sharing)" (Loeb, 1972, p. 19). To a certain extent, cliques institutionalize friendship patterns.

Strategic interactions may be employed also with regard to cliques. Adolescents may prove their self-worth by belonging to high status (in their own eyes) cliques, having many friends, and rejecting approaches from outsiders. Also they attain a feeling of higher status by being seen with the right people in public places and simply not recognizing those of lower status, a tactic called *cutting* (Elkind, 1980).

As early as age eight, one-sex, close-knit cliques may take shape, especially among girls. During the teens, most members of both sexes become involved in cliques and in pursuing heterosexual goals. Some cliques may be due not so much to affection as to the bond of feeling produced by being excluded elsewhere. A clique's members are usually of similar social status, although individuals with a different background may be admitted if they can contribute to the clique's activities.

THE CROWD   The crowd is a larger, less closely knit, and more impersonal group than the clique. There may be several cliques within the crowd, and these subgroups may cooperate with each other or may retain a considerable degree of autonomy.

Crowd members are usually carefully chosen; and crowd membership presents a closed door to outsiders. A nonmember cannot simply decide to join but must be invited to do so. Membership is usually quite evenly divided between the sexes, but extra boys are more welcome as members than are extra girls. Crowd activities are usually social in nature and relatively harmless—such a group rarely is involved in trouble.

THE GANG   The adolescent gang is treated separately here because it possesses some of the characteristics of both formal and informal groups. Gangs differ from cliques in several important ways. Members of cliques have mutual affection and spend more time interacting with each other as individuals, whereas gang members focus more on group activities. The gang member is more likely to play a well-defined role than is the clique member.

The gang maintains a degree of structure which, from the frame of reference of social systems, tends to institutionalize aspects of delinquency. Gang activity is intense and its rules are rigidly enforced. In authoritarian gangs, a few individuals will take on the role of demanding compliance with the gang code. On the informal-formal continuum, the gang's status is somewhat formal; such matters as decision-making within the group are predictable.

Gangs vary greatly among themselves, in both type of activity and organization; hence, making firm generalizations is difficult. The most common type is an action group, usually of one sex only, with concrete goals and a structured organization. When it comes into conflict with the law, its defenses are group solidarity, loyalty, secrecy, and physical strength. Within a given gang, a characteristic type of activity may predominate, with a more or less fixed routine. To avoid conflicting interests, a gang's operations are often restricted to its own sphere of influence, the violation of which may lead to conflict with other gangs. As for the leader, such assets as physical prowess, fearlessness, and fighting ability are requisite, as are ingenuity and cleverness. The leader has great power, and no decisions are made without his consent. At the same time,when he deals with gang members he must be fair, loyal, and generous.

THE PEER CULTURE

Functions of Peer Culture

All the adolescent groups discussed constitute the so-called peer culture which arose in the 1930s and 1940s, as a distinctive pattern of life in the high school, with its own dating styles, cars, and clothes.

The peer culture is presumed to perform certain official functions for its members. For example, social fraternities and sororities become ways of sorting people out, although these groups are not as important now as in former years. The peer society also helps individuals to sort out demands and to determine which they must meet and which they can ignore. Peer society also helps youth to define values and behaviors. Most youth today cannot merely follow in the footsteps of their parents; they face many alternatives concerning moral codes and life styles. As a result, they take refuge in their own culture until they have, in a sense, sorted themselves out.

Adolescent peer groups assume more importance in some societies than in others, being most important in cultures where the kinship unit fails to provide youth full social status or adequately to meet their social needs. In Western society, parents are often preoccupied with their own special interests and are relieved to be rid of the all-family activities of former days. Also, in Western society, individuals become biologically mature long before they are ready to play adult roles in their culture. To fill the vacuum thus created and to make up for the resultant feelings of inadequacy, teenagers band themselves together.

Is There a Youth Culture?

THE AFFIRMATIVE VIEW   The concept of youth culture involves certain issues, the most essential being whether the concept itself is justified and whether the youth culture is a coherent entity. Most social scientists agree that a youth culture exists (particularly in the absence of puberty rites) in order to signal maturation. Modern society has produced among youth an increasingly confused and lengthy struggle to win adult status. Moreover, because a technological society requires increasingly complex adult roles, the adolescent period of preparation becomes correspondingly prolonged and more cohesive. In addition, the youth culture concept is supported by the existence of adolescents' own social system, its supportive activities, and their distinctive norms regarding schoolwork, sex relations, music, clothes, and other matters (Coleman, 1974). Finally, youth are segregated in their high schools and colleges, and information circulates there by various routes, including nationally affiliated chapters of students' organization, campus newspapers, campus radio stations, and campus speaker circuits for controversial figures.

THE NEGATIVE VIEW   Some people believe that the youth culture may be more of a theoretical construct than a factual entity. Davis (1971) notes the "tremendous fluidity of movement by young people among and between subcultures"; the subcultures are "fluid systems of norms which come and go, wax and wane, emerge and recede," in response to broader social changes (p. 76). Since student subcultures are relatively amorphous, they are hard to define as entities.

Kandel (1978) stresses the need to differentiate among various adolescent subcultures, in particular between subcultures that do or do not use drugs. The marijuana-using groups, as compared with nonusers, were not as close to their parents, were more likely to stay away from school, spent less time on school work, and less often got good grades. Also, they were less likely to attend religious services, more likely to hold radical political beliefs, and more likely to participate in both major and minor forms of delinquent activity. They were more often depressed and more likely to be dissatisfied with themselves.

Characteristics of Teen and Youth Cultures

The traditional youth culture has not been a counterculture. Although encouraging autonomy from adult society, it has socialized the young adult into it. Thus, we find that the hot-rod and motorcycle groups became the mechanics and technicians, and the "apathetic, athletic, dating" youth emerged as the "apolitical organization men who married the cheerleaders and moved to the suburbs, to become more concerned with crabgrass than with social justice" (Block & Langman, 1974, p. 416).

Among material aspects of the teen culture are clothes. Teenagers dress as their peers do but strive for a touch of individuality. In one study about 80 percent of the females and 60 percent of the males cared very much or somewhat about the latest clothes, records, and leisure activities (Youth on the move, 1981).

Another basic characteristic in the material culture is the automobile. Except in big cities, it is taken for granted that every teenager will learn to drive or at least have access to a car. Other material aspects are athletic equipment, popular records, stereo equipment, and cosmetics. Teenagers also spend their money on a bewildering variety of periodicals concerning photography, sports, athletics, and even pornography. In teen magazines, the key subjects are fun and popularity—how to be attractive in order to be popular.

Television commercials encourage youth to purchase life-style items such as music recordings, video games, electronic equipment, and clothing. These items give status in the peer group, partly because of their association with certain television characters. Thus, clothing becomes "a visual means of portraying social roles or images that adolescents wish to present to their age mates—for instance, the black leather jacket of the delinquent, the business-like look of the serious student, and the unorthodox dress of punk rock fans" (Peterson & Peters, 1983, p. 80). On the other hand, sleek-looking automobiles evoke images of glamour, power, and status.

Television and music are associated with relatively different kinds of life styles (Larson & Kubey, 1983). Television is geared more to adults, and more often watched by adolescents who earn better grades and spend more time with

The telephone is a highly prized item in the youth culture. (Photo by William J. Butcher)

their families. Thus television, to a certain extent, may reinforce adult goals. In contrast, listening to music harmonizes more with life in the peer group and is an important part of the time that they spend with their friends.

In college years as televiewing declines, music listening increases. Since much popular music is intended for youth it relates to their own concerns, life styles, and emotions, and it becomes an important part of their activities including parties, dancing, and dating (Larson & Kubey, 1983).

Another highly prized item in the youth culture is the telephone. Elkind (1980) mentions several types of strategic social interaction that American teen-agers apply, one by phoning and being phoned. In order to prove popularity to themselves and to others they make numerous telephone calls.

The youth culture also has its nonmaterial aspects, including its own language—a blend of accepted usage and special jargon, with constantly changing modifications. This language serves to demark adolescents from adults and provides separate identities to different youth subcultures (Leona, 1978). It reflects their various life styles and standards as being distinct from those of others and the larger society. Even "recent alumni" of the teen culture have trouble understanding their successors. Teen songs are also distinctive, and they provide insight into teen life. Songs that fail to capture the current mood simply never catch on.

Other nonmaterial aspects of teen culture include its own special codes of honor and sex, its norms and values, styles and self-imposed rules. There are norms for dating and petting and for relating to adults, especially to parents and teachers. Characteristic values are attached to all the material and non-material features of their lives, including studies, cosmetics, smoking, religion, abortion, and war.

Aspects of the youth culture vary according to the age, marital status, and social class of the youth involved. College youth's activities differ from those of their younger siblings in high school. Married teens are hardly part of the teen culture at all. As for social class, the middle and upper classes formerly set the tone for the teen culture, while lower-class youth often had to go to work and hence were hardly involved in teen activities. Of late, lower-class youth are practicing their own version of the teen culture and are contributing to, as well as borrowing from, patterns of higher status peers.

Indeed, the new youth culture lacks specific social-class connotations and is neither "rooted in traditional class values" nor related to class consciousness; instead, it has arisen from attitudes associated with "the more prosperous segments of the working class" (Horowitz, 1982, p. 635). These youth, in turn, have influenced teenagers from middle-class backgrounds. Furthermore, the greater stress on "nonutilitarian" consumption motives is suggestive of a basic change in the culture.

More transient features of youth subculture are somewhat specific to an area or to the times. In the 1960s Americans began doing their own thing, and in the 70s people in masses were devoting themselves to the simple life trying to do more with less. In the 1980s both high fashion and "doing your own thing" are in style. The country is becoming "demassified," as demonstrated by "segmented markets" in consumption, various family life styles, more different type audiences for television, and the proliferation of special interest groups (p. 45). One concern of all ages and all people appeared to be physical fitness. It was an "in thing" to stay fit, not according to any particular pattern. Jogging, tennis, and racquetball all successively peaked as fads, however, many people still engage in these activities.

Some items of youth subculture have but limited life. In 1982 American adolescents were caught up in styles with terms that adults didn't understand: "valley girl," "punk," and "new wave"; but in 1983 they were dispersing in all directions, getting rid of last year's fads but not having settled upon new ones.

In Houston and San Francisco adolescents were flaunting the Marilyn Monroe look of the 1950s, including "strapless dresses with billowy skirts, colorful plastic earrings and tight pants—or were donning leather jackets á la James Dean. They wore red or white sunglasses" (p. 48). In New York and Washington, D.C., adolescents liked "safari and military style clothes, especially surplus army jackets" (p. 48). New wave music was giving way, at least in Atlanta, to a mellow type of disco and in the midwest to "rockabilly, or rock with simple guitar chords" (p. 48). In many parts of the country teenagers and young adults flocked to video bars where they watched artists performing on video cassettes.

One teenage clothing expert observed that "technology has broadened kids' tastes. The more images they see the more creative they become and in turn the more markets they create" (p. 48).

In general youth in the early 1980s were blending the traditional with the new, while cautiously "feeling their way, seeking quality of life; but sometimes [taking] chances. . . ." (p. 48).

Activities of Peer Groups

Leisure activities vary in significance at all life stages, including youth. Babies' play involves body movements that provide pleasant sensations and gratification. As they gain greater control over their senses and muscles, their play becomes correspondingly more varied. In childhood, play activities become further diversified and more socially interacting. As girls move into later childhood and early adolescence, they have a tendency to prefer so-called boys' games. Adolescents choose leisure activities that promote peer participation and autonomy from their parents, while televiewing affords escape from school work and boredom. However, adolescents' activities help them to relate to others.

Kelly (1979) reports a study of peer culture in a white middle-class suburb of Detroit. Boys from two schools were asked where they would go if they could go anywhere they wished during the school day. Fifty-four percent said they would seek a place on the school grounds, and 29 percent would go off grounds, but 17 percent said there was nowhere they wished to go. Of the 83 percent who did wish to go, 70 percent said they would go there to be with friends; 17 percent, to be alone; and 13 percent, to engage in some other activity.

Among the boys, two main groupings existed; citizens and tribes. The citizens were active participants in school activities; and they generally conformed with the school's rules, functions, and activities. The tribes' members took little part in school activities and often took issue with school rules and authorities. Members of the tribe were distinct from the hard guys or greasers, who were somewhat destructive and disruptive, as well as from deviants, such as drug users and political activists. Tribe members employed school settings to carry on considerable informal interaction. The citizens participated more directly in academic and extracurricular activities, while tribe members were involved in more active informal behaviors.

The citizens' extracurricular activities prepared them for future college roles, while tribe boys' behaviors were better prepared for military or semi-skilled work which focused on peer interaction, both on the job and in leisure time. The tribe boys did not seek satisfaction in activities valued in the larger culture, even though they had few alternative outlets for rewarding experience. Some of the boys in the citizens' group fared poorly, too. Such boys might do poorly in academic work and school activities—hence would be withdrawn and low in self-esteem.

A perennial, and especially healthful, activity of peer culture has been camping. Groves (1981) points out its advantages and potential influence of adolescent development. While camping, individuals have a chance to develop their identities in relation to their peers in a relaxing outdoor environment where there is tranquility and peace. They can develop their relations with their peers while exploring the natural environment. A problem is that when they return to their usual environment they generally revert to former patterns of behavior. The problem becomes one of integrating the camping experience with other sectors of their lives. Since camps are interested in developing year-round programs, and since schools desire to expand their programs into new areas, they might well develop joint programs. It might be added that across the country there are camps designed especially for helping individuals develop the basics of computer skills.

American Teen Cultures

IN THE SCHOOLS   A study of a middle-income suburb in Massachusetts (Leona, 1978) disclosed an intriguing picture of the peer culture's components within the schools. There were several small cliques, such as the "chewers." These eight to ten boys, who chewed tobacco both inside and outside school, were mainly interested in popular sporting events, citizens' band radios, and country-western music. They called women of disputed reputation "scumbags" or "scuzbags." Students with no specially distinctive life styles or speech were called the "normals." They had no distinctive dating habits, extracurricular activities, or speech. Anyone not assigned to a distinctive clique was called a "normal."

There were three main cliques in the school, all with a considerable number of members and certain distinctive expressions—the "jocks," the "motorheads," and the "fleabags." The jocks were mostly males, but included some females who participated in sports. They were friendly to everyone, clean-cut, self-confident, and admired by their classmates. They spent their free time in weekend practice and games, attending sports events, and going to group parties. They drank alcoholic beverages at the parties and sometimes smoked marijuana. Their grades were above average; they wore sneakers to class; and all participated in one or two sports in the school year. They called each other by their last names and by nicknames indicating their athletic performance, such as Speedy or The Jumping Machine. Someone who ran quickly was "really moving," and getting excited prior to a sporting event was "becoming psyched." Someone who made a mistake in a game was "a flake" and someone with smelly feet was warned, "Your socks are on fire."

The motorheads, all males, devoted their time to working on cars and talking about them. They made below average academic grades and took automotive shop courses. They looked like other students except for their grease-stained clothes and often dirty hands. In their own group there was a status hierarchy. High-status motorheads had fast racing cars, knew a lot about car engines, and were regarded as cool. Their clique language referred to cars: Toyotas were called "toilet odors"; Fiats were "farts"; and a General Motors car was a "Detroit." An undesirable car was called a "shit box." The motorheads raced their cars against each other to gain status, and when two cars raced down the road trying to pass each other it was a "rat race." Students differed in their opinions of the motorheads, some regarding them somewhat negatively, others saying they were okay. Since many of the motorheads feared the students, they were cautious in their behaviors toward them. Some of the students called them ass holes and declared that they had motors for brains.

A third clique, the fleabags, took drugs regularly—mostly marijuana, but sometimes other drugs. In appearance, they resembled the hippies of the 1960s, having long hair and wearing denim clothes. They went to school mainly to make friends and to maintain drug connections. The fleabags, like the motorheads, sat in their own section of the cafeteria. Often they simply skipped school to go to someone's house to smoke marijuana cigarettes, called "joints" or "bones." A large marijuana cigarette was called a "stogie." Smoking marijuana was termed "taking a hit" or "smoking a bone." Someone high on marijuana was called "baked," "wasted," "spaced," "tripped out," or "stoned." The remains of marijuana cigarettes were known as "roaches" and many fleabags carried small tweezers called "roach clips" to smoke the remnants of the cigarettes. The fleabags were not well liked by the other students, who called them weirdos and jerks.

The school cliques afforded the adolescents well-defined identity roles, with their own special conversations, activities, and philosophies of life. They defined for the adolescents what they should do with their free time, what to say and when, and how to react to school and to the students. Many students would not admit to being a fleabag, motorhead, or jock. They claimed they were individuals but might admit that they were judged as belonging to a particular group.

THE VIDEO GAME SUBCULTURE   Through most of the century teen-agers, mostly males, have met in commercial establishments such as pinball arcades, soda shops, and pool halls, which allow them at least some free social space (Panelas, 1983). In such places they "can meet peers, relieve boredom, act on their emerging sex-role identities and institute cultural practices that build peers into a stable, temporary form of social organization" (p. 62). Often peer interaction at such places involves some form of competition, such as games, which become a means of forming hierarchies of performance and of vying for leadership.

In this sense video games are an extension of pinball parlors. Thus, video games involved "familiar cultural genres" with "such themes as invaders from outer space, grand prix racing . . . and escape from various dangerous situations" (p. 62). Adults tend to look with some suspicion on video game arcades, as they did on pool halls and pinball arcades, believing that they foster delinquency.

THE ATHLETIC SUBCULTURE   One of the most widespread and endur-ing of youth groupings is the athletic subculture. For better perspective on this category, first consider the status of sports in high schools. After studying the status systems in certain Illinois high schools in the late 1950s, James Coleman (1961) reported that athletic prowess was the single most important criterion for status. In a replication of this study, Eitzen (1975) found that there is still widespread acceptance of sports among teenage boys. Nevertheless, certain vari-ables affect each boy's attitude toward sports. Sports are most strongly supported by sons of the less well educated, by students in small schools and in schools with strict authority structures, and by those at the very center of the school's activities. The sons of college-educated fathers, and students from suburban and large urban schools or from more affluent and permissive schools, are less en-thusiastic about sports. They like sports, but to a lesser degree. Some categories of adolescents are even becoming apathetic toward sports. Certain factors, in-cluding the increasing size of schools, the larger portion of adolescents attending suburban schools, and the increasing improvement of education with each suc-ceeding generation, indicate that enthusiasm for sports may wane in the future.

THE GREEKS   On the college level, fraternities and sororities have been conspicuous manifestations of peer subcultures. Over the years, Greek letter organizations, sororities and fraternities, have had both their defenders and their detractors (Fraternities bounce back—with big changes, 1979). The critics have called them elitist and anti-intellectual. Fraternity group members have often been accused of such infractions as drunkenness, vulgarity, and cruel or even dangerous hazing of members during the process of initiation. Defenders say that Greek organizations afford their members a large circle of close friends and help them to learn social skills and to cope with the impersonality of large institutions. In the 1960s, sororities and fraternities were becoming increasingly unpopular on college campuses, partly because many had been branded as racially and ethnically prejudiced. Of late, however, the Greek organizations have been making a comeback, with some differences. A few of the men's fraternities have admitted women members, although sororities rarely admit men to their membership. Stronger emphasis than formerly is placed on matters of community service and scholarship, and large sums are raised by members for many worthy causes. Some critics claim that the Greeks have not yet set their house in order and that undesirable practices persist, such as sadistic initiation activities, and undesirable behaviors.

An Evaluation of the Peer Culture

The question is often asked: How sound are the values of the teen cultures? Is youth's propensity for pornography, pin-ups, and beer a sign of simple fun or sheer frivolity? Are blue jeans a commendable symbol of simplicity or a sort of snobbism in reverse?

Many observers perceive in youth cultures certain positive values and contributions. According to Havighurst (1975), youth constitute the chief agents in the change toward postindustrial society. They are more sensitive to change than their elders are, and they are forming life styles appropriate to contemporary society. Block and Langman (1974) commend youth's concern with warm

Youth cultures have certain positive values and contributions but they also have detractors. (Courtesy of Public Relations Office, State University of New York at Oswego)

interrelationships, openness to new experiences, and expressive freedom. Individual freedom refers to the self-determination of one's actions, the do-your-own thing attitude, and self-realization, as distinct from a competitive individualism which is rewarded from without and depends on opportunism. By contrast with the impersonality of urban industrialism, youth's concern for community accords great importance to having close and meaningful interrelationships with others.

The youth culture also has its detractors. Gutmann (1973) laments a culture given to "narcissism and even madness" (p. 148). However, he understands why it appeals to youth, for "why should they resist cultural messages that ratify their fantasies of omnipotence, and that urge them to eat their cake and have it, too?" (p. 148).

FUTURE PERSPECTIVES

In many ways youth's peer experience relates to adult adjustment. Their experience in relating to and coming to trust each other prepares them for the intimacy that marriage demands. In addition, the adolescent's experience in cliques, gangs, and clubs constitutes practice for social relationships in the larger community of adults. People who can both accept and give friendship in constructive fashion are in a much better position to establish sound support systems in later stages of their life cycle, especially in such circumstances as widowhood or confinement in nursing homes. Children working and playing together focus on mutual activities, but youth concentrate on each other and provide important support for each other's personal development.

Effective peer relationships are especially important in a society that carries on its business largely through group activity. Institutions and technologies today have become so complex and sophisticated that their efficiency depends on groups operating together in order to capitalize on collective expertise. The peer-oriented relations of youth would seem to be significantly relevant to these group-conducted tasks.

Longitudinal research is yielding evidence of the long-term importance of early peer relations. In the Terman study, good marriages and satisfaction with family life of men in their late sixties related to such early experiences as good social adjustment and extracurricular activities in high school and college (Goleman, 1980b). Successful individuals in early adulthood were often leaders or had good friends; in contrast, as children they had felt different from others and had trouble making friends or entering into social activities (Goleman, 1980a). Individuals who have poor peer relationships as children have the poorest adult adjustment (Janes & Hesselbrock. 1978). On the other hand, individuals who are sociable in high school and date heavily are more likely to occupy lower-status jobs in later life than the less sociable ones who are more attentive to their studies (Jencks, 1979).

There is considerable controversy over whether, or to what extent, youth should mingle with adults as preparation for adulthood. It may be argued that youth culture is too isolated from adult society; on the other hand, their withdrawal from the mainstream of society gives them a certain perspective they would not have if they were totally involved. To date, most authorities have limited themselves to analyzing youth subcultures and have done little about making them functional in terms of their influence on peer relations in succeeding life stages. Society might well contribute to the wholesome dynamics of peer groups through encouraging their participation in various projects under the direction of adults who understand and care about youth.

SUMMARY

Group relationships perform essential functions, both for society and for the individual. Such relationships attain special significance at adolescence, for at this age individuals are strongly influenced by group pressures. They are also establishing ways of relating to groups broader in scope and more heterogeneous in type than their own families. Their peer groups, in particular, help them to attain independence from the family and to define relationships to themselves and society. Unpopularity as a child or adolescent suggests a poor prognosis for adjustment later on.

The influence of the peer group has been variously portrayed as harmful, helpful, or both. On the negative side, it is criticized for stifling individuality. On the positive side, it is perceived as providing adolescents with support during the process of establishing autonomy and a haven of security during their initial sorties into the larger world. The peer group is also important because of the larger amount of time youth devote to its activities. Such involvement may range from deep commitment to superficial; moreover, each individual reacts to peer group experience differently. The specific quality or content of peer group influence depends on the values, activities, and composition of groups with whom a youth interacts.

Many factors, such as minority-group membership, modify the individual's susceptibility to peer-group influence. Peer-group influence also varies by sex: girls are more dependent on such relationships than are boys. Males' friendships are less intimate; hence, they do not fare as well in terms of satisfying affiliative needs, in both adolescence and adulthood.

Many factors operate simultaneously and complexly to explain the wide variations in adolescent's peer interaction and adjustment. These factors include the differential socialization of the sexes, current philosophies of personal interaction, family and school experience, and the adolescent role in society.

Peer groups have their own dynamics, and members have their respective roles. The nature of their roles depends on the composition of the group and on adolescents' special needs, as well as on their own personalities. Roles also depend on the parts individuals played within their families from earliest childhood. In other words, the role that an individual plays in one group tends to transfer to other groups.

The peer groups in which adolescents transact their roles are composed of persons of approximately the same age with similar interests and ideals. Adults are relatively indifferent to and ignorant of the nature of these peer societies, which have their origin in the play groups of very early childhood. The gang age begins at ages 8 to 10 and may continue for certain individuals into or even through adolescence. However, the most common adolescent relationships consist of friendships, cliques, crowds, and group networks. The intimate friendship is particularly important in adolescence, although many apparently close relationships are superficial. Genuinely intimate ones, however, perform several important functions. They help individuals to explore their own personalities and to define their own identities. They provide opportunities for catharsis and expression of problems that might otherwise be repressed.

The nature and function of friendships vary over the life cycle. At adolescence they are intimate and intense, especially among girls. They help to counterbalance the depersonalization of modern society. A group of close friends often forms a clique, or especially close-knit group, usually all of the same sex. Several cliques, in turn, may constitute a crowd, which is somewhat more loose-knit and less rigid in its membership. The gang may be either formal or informal in organization, and large or small. Ordinarily, roles within the gang are well defined and rules are somewhat rigidly enforced. Nevertheless, there are many kinds of gangs, and no one stereotype can adequately describe them all.

All these groups collectively constitute the peer culture, or adolescent society. Peer culture is relatively independent of the larger society and has its own distinctive behaviors and values. Considerable controversy surrounds the concept of youth culture—for example, whether such a culture in fact exists, or is even justified. Most behavioral scientists agree that such a culture does exist, and that whether or not it exists, it is a useful concept. Some argue that the youth culture concept is perhaps invalid and certainly unnecessary. They point out that the high visibility of minority groups creates an illusion of distinctiveness that hardly applies to youth in general. Besides, they claim that no real conflict exists between adult and adolescent cultures, and that few basic differences are involved. Others stress the need of thinking in terms of particular peer cultures instead of some overall culture. Peer cultures also have their distinctive patterns of activities, or life styles.

Assuming that a peer culture does exist, its existence may be accounted for by various factors, which include the current nonfamilial division of labor, the recent affluence that supports adolescent activities and the rapid pace of change that tends to create a gap between generations. Also contributing to youthful group consciousness has been the discovery of modes of repression that adolescents discern as being pointed especially at them.

Teen cultures, at least in Western society, have certain distinguishing characteristics. For one thing, they cater to certain types of youth but not to others. The culture itself has both material and nonmaterial aspects. Among the material aspects are clothing that identifies members of a particular group, athletic equipment, popular records, stereo equipment, and cosmetics. Among nonmaterial aspects are group norms pertaining to dating and petting, teen values, and teen speech. Peer cultures also have their distinctive patterns of activities, or life styles. Youth cultures that incorporate unmarried individuals in their late teens and early twenties should be distinguished from those of the early and middle teens.

Despite certain characteristics shared by teen cultures generally, they vary greatly in diversity and according to social class, sex, and the times. Examples are high school groups, the athletic culture, and fraternities or sororities. Once married, couples share only peripherally in the teen culture. Whether or not they practiced premarital cohabitation apparently makes no real difference in their postmarital adjustment. Youth cultures also vary widely in different countries, as exemplified in Britain and Nigeria.

Whether peer cultures in general have sound values is a matter of concern and dispute. Some studies reveal peer cultures to be somewhat shallow in their orientation; others disclose more mature values. Perhaps these differences are partly a function of the particular subjects employed and partly a reflection of rapidly changing times.

DISCUSSION QUESTIONS
AND ACTIVITIES

1. Bring to class newspaper columns giving social advice to teenagers, and criticize them in terms of psychological principles.
2. Observe teenagers participating in some social situation, and analyze their behavior in terms of the factors that seem to determine individual roles; (a) evidence of insecurity and (b) the stratagems, conscious or unconscious, that individuals use to make themselves acceptable to the group.
3. Write descriptions of adolescents you have known who have played the following roles: leader, isolate, devoted follower, servant, clown, and other roles. Descriptions written by class members may be collected and compiled to determine the characteristics believed most generally to accompany each role.
4. Analyze an adolescent crowd of which you are, or have been, a member as to its size, the proportion of each sex among its members, members' roles and activities in the group, and the group's worth or harm to its members.
5. Record subjects of teenagers' conversations overheard for several days. Analyze them as to content.
6. Cut out and bring to class advertisements that are intended to appeal to adolescents' needs to adjust to their peer groups.
7. Interview guidance counselors concerning the chief social difficulties encountered by adolescents.
8. List anonymously the major social problems you experienced during adolescence. The class lists may be collected and analyzed.
9. Contrast the dynamics of two adolescent groups of which you have been a member—one which you judge to have been successful, the other unsuccessful.
10. Analyze your own social adjustment during adolescence, specifying the traits you feel helped or interfered with your adjustment, and how you think others felt toward you. The class statements may be collected and analyzed to determine how people generally feel about their own adjustment.
11. Recall several especially popular or unpopular individuals from your high school and college days and list reasons for their status.
12. Analyze friendships experienced during your adolescence, including reasons for the close association, what it contributed to each party, and how it changed over time.

SUGGESTED READINGS

Adams, G. R. (1983). Social competence during adolescence: Social sensitivity, locus of control, empathy, and peer popularity. *Journal of Youth and Adolescence, 12*(3), 203–211. Among adolescents, ages 14 to 18, the predicted relationship between social competency and peer popularity were found, but with some differences according to sex.

Berndt, T. J. (1982). The features of and effects of friendship in early adolescence. *Child Development, 53*, 1447–1460. Early adolescent friendships are examined in terms of their patterns, characteristics, relation to developmental features of this stage of life, as well as the impact of such friendships on social and personality development.

Brown, B. B. (1982). The extent and effects of peer pressure among high school students: A retrospective analysis. *Journal of Youth and Adolescence, 11*(2), 121–133. Retrospective accounts by college students were employed to determine the nature, extent, and effects of peer pressures experienced in various areas of high school life.

Burleson, B. R. (1982). The development of comforting communication skills in childhood and adolescence. *Child Development, 53*, 1578–1588. A study among individuals in grades 1 through 12, which measured comforting communication skills in hypothetical situations, indicated increasing sensitivity and skills with age and differences according to sex of subject and nature of the situation concerned.

Cohn, N. B. (1983). Self-disclosure reciprocity among preadolescents. *Personality and Social Psychology Bulletin, 9*(1), 97–102. In grades three and six preadolescent girls spent more time than boys in intimate self-disclosure after receiving intimate input.

Collins, W. A., & Korać, N. (1982). Recent progress in the study of the effects of television viewing on social development. *International Journal of Behavioral Development, 5*(2), 171–193. The effect of television viewing on social development is examined in terms of its adequacy and future directions.

Eisert, D. C., & Kahle, L. R. (1983). Self-evaluation and social comparison of physical and role change during adolescence: A longitudinal analysis.*Child Development, 53*, 98–104. A comparison of two competing theories about the relationship between self-evaluation and social comparison in late adolescence indicated greater consistency with self-adaptation theory than social adaptation theory.

Fischer, C. S., & Oliker, S. J. (1983). A research note on friendship, gender, and the life cycle. *Social Forces, 62*(1), 124–152. Friendships are analyzed over the life cycle as they vary according to stage of life and sex.

Horowitz, T. (1982). Excitement vs. economy: Fashion and youth culture in Britain. *Adolescence, 17*(67), 627–636. A study of 600 British consumers indicated that youth's purchasing power is devoted to goods and services affected by fashion, with a preference for an excitement over an economy motif.

Hunter, F. T., & Youniss, J. (1982). Changes in functions of three relations during adolescence. *Developmental Psychology, 18*(6), 806–811. Certain functions of interpersonal relations (intimacy, nurture, and attempt at behavior control) were assessed in terms of adolescents' friendship, father-child, and mother-child relationships, as well as their consistency with Piaget's framework of social development.

Larson, R. W. (1983). Adolescents' daily experience with family and friends: Contrasting opportunity systems. *Journal of Marriage and the Family, 45*(4), 739–756. This comparison of adolescents' daily interactions with family and friends indicates that friendship interactions have positive feedback but often lack stability, whereas family interactions involve more negative feedback, being constrained by the requirements of socialization.

Lewin, B. (1983). Attitudes among adolescents in a Swedish city toward some sexual crimes. *Adolescence, 17*(69), 159–168. A study of Swedish adolescents in 1969 and a decade later indicated a general trend toward more liberal views regarding sexual behaviors.

Muuss, R. E. (1982). Social cognition: Robert Selman's theory of role taking. *Adolescence, 17*(67), 499–525. Social, or interpersonal, cognition is discussed in terms of definition, earlier and more recent theroies, stages and concepts, and educational implications.

Parke, R. D., & Asher, S. R. (1983). Social and personality development. *Annual Review of Psychology, 34*, 465–509. A review of the literature of the last five years regarding social-personality development discloses particular themes, issues, and methodological changes and advances.

Schlecter, T. M., & Gump, P. V. (1983). Car availability and the daily life of the teenage male. *Adolescence, 18*(69), 101–113. This study indicated that car ownership by adolescent males is associated with more freedom from parental control, more time with friends, and positive effects in general.

Tesch, S. A. (1983). Review of friendship development across the life span. *Human Development, 26,* 266–276. Characteristics of friendship are considered from the long-term developmental perspective and further research needs are suggested.

Thorbecke, W., & Grotevant, H. D. (1982). Gender differences in adolescent interpersonal identity formation. *Journal of Youth and Adolescence, 11*(6), 479–492. This investigation of gender differences in adolescent interpersonal identity formation involved assessment of the progress of 83 high school students toward interpersonal identity achievement in friendship and dating relationships.

Weisfeld, G. E., Bloch, S. A., & Ivers, J. W. (1983). A factor analytic study of peer-perceived dominance in adolescent boys. *Adolescence, 18*(70), 229–244. In this study of boys, ages 15 to 18, athletic ability and attractiveness correlated more highly with dominance status than did intelligence and other factors.

Williams, J. M., & White, K. A., (1983). Adolescent status systems for males and females at three age levels. *Adolescence, 18*(70), 381–390. In this study, designed to identify the primary determinants of male and female status at high school age, students were asked how they most wanted to be remembered—as a brilliant student, a popular one, an athletic star, or activity leader.

Zeldin, R. S., Small, S. A., & Savin-Williams, R. C. (1982). Prosocial interactions in two mixed-sex adolescent groups. *Child Development, 53,* 1492–1498. Through the use of participant observers adolescent's prosocial behaviors were studied in a camp situation and analyzed according to type of activity displayed as well as individual and sex.

Chapter Ten

Alienated Youth

BACKGROUND OF YOUTH'S ALIENATION

Alienation in History

In times when the vast majority of youth claim to share the basic values of their society, it might seem inappropriate to devote this chapter to alienated youth. However, periods of dissent, albeit by a small minority of youth, surface from time to time, and we have no way of knowing when the next such period will be. Even in conservative times, such as the late 70s and early 80s, there are always small numbers of youth who disagree with the mainstream of their culture or who create minicultures of their own. Besides, there persists a tendency by many adults to think of youth as more disaffected from society than they are—hence, the need to take a realistic view of the topic. The term **alienated youth** itself encompasses all those young people who, for one reason or another, feel somewhat estranged from the larger society in which they live. They feel isolated or socially withdrawn from their peers, neither career-oriented nor ready to join the work world, and they believe that there is something significantly wrong with society (Wynne, 1978). Such feelings are not the monopoly of youth but are shared by many adults. In the 1970s, college students testified to a need for privacy and freedom but felt little loyalty to country, religion, or society. Alienated youth collectively constitute an oppositional or countercultural role to the main culture. As members of the alienated minority, their role is similar to that of the party out of power in a two-party system, serving as critic of those currently in charge.

Nevertheless, all too often a tiny percentage of youth tend to account for the image of a whole generation, perhaps because they are more vocal and different. When we speak of youthful crime we tend to forget that the overwhelming majority are law-abiding. Indeed, across the years, and now perhaps more than ever, most youth feel close to their parents and share their basic values.

Thus, countercultures, as alienated groups are called, are a perennial breed with roots in the distant past. Student youth, in particular, have tended to constitute a sort of institutionalized underground. For example, at Die in England in 1649, the masters barricaded themselves inside the college to prevent the masters and pupils of other classes from entering. They fouled the rostra in certain classrooms, fired cannon shots, threw classroom desks out the windows, tore up books, and finally climbed out the windows of the classrooms, scandalizing the public. Sometimes they even attacked passers-by with their swords, and at other times with traditional fireworks (Ariès, 1962).

In the eighteenth century youth were castigated for disobedience, boasting, breaking the Sabbath, sexual promiscuity and rebellion in general (Manning, 1983). In the nineteenth century the literature about youth often referred to their licentiousness and indulgence.

At Winchester at the end of the eighteenth century, boys occupied the school for two days and hoisted a red flag; in 1818, two companies of troops with fixed bayonets were called in to suppress an uprising of the pupils (Ariès, 1962). At Rugberg, pupils burned the books and desks and took refuge on an island, where they had to be conquered by assault from the army. Other incidents followed, and in 1768 the monitors, or good pupils, seceded and left the school. In 1783 students revolted against the headmaster, rooms were pillaged, and windows broken. In 1818, after the gate was locked to prevent the boys from going hunting, they pelted their master with rotten eggs, knocked down part of the wall, and had to be overcome by force. The last insurrection at Eton, which resulted in the flogging of 80 boys, occurred about 1832, but the final important school mutiny in England happened at Marlborough as late as 1851.

In America the industrial revolution became a factor in increasing youth's defection from society. After the Civil War the growing number of immigrants placed greater pressure on the job market and increasingly mechanized manufacturing required more mature workers. As youth unemployment increased so did crimes by juveniles—hence, came a movement to separate younger from older offenders. The idea was to employ corrective rather than punitive treatment and the first juvenile court was established in Illinois in 1899. Hearings were supposed to be confidential and informal; however, the results were not ideal, for adolescents became reduced to dependence on the court systems without full rights of citizens. Their procedures did not guarantee youthful dependents the right to "hear the charges, be allowed to face accusers, be represented by counsel, or be tried by a jury" (Starr, 1982, p. 198).

In just recent years about "23 percent of the boys and 70 percent of the girls held in juvenile correctional facilities were not guilty of any crime for which an adult could be arrested and prosecuted" (p. 198). Note, especially, the difference between girls and boys because even though boys mature later physically, girls are treated as though they are more immature. These so-called status offenses may include transient running away and disobedience. Meantime, adolescents' efforts to claim rights traditionally accorded those of their age became viewed as delinquent. Hence, these modes of resistance against authorities brought on by policies dictated by the government to forcibly subordinate the young represent, in fact, a struggle "between age strata over social goods in modern society" (Starr, 1982, p. 191).

Thus juvenile delinquency was a legal creation which imposed certain social norms on the new social state of adolescence. Adolescents were encouraged to be conformist instead of independent of adult authority. They were expected to accept their subordination and to defer to authority. Otherwise, they would be labeled juvenile delinquent. Meanwhile, various adult-sponsored youth organizations, such as the Boy Scouts and the YMCA, were established, mainly between 1890 and 1920, to assist family and school in disciplining young people, especially boys. These organizations were mainly controlled by middle-aged "morally conservative" adults "tinged by a mixture of altruism and authoritarianism" (Starr, 1982, p. 199).

Causes of Alienation

In all areas alienation often has resulted from society's own failures—for example, to develop sufficient alternatives for youth, from poor communication with youth and from certain current social deficiencies such as increasing impersonality, materialism, and pseudosophistication (Rogers, 1982). In other cases alienation may simply reflect growing up and trying out different cultural values before arriving at one's own. Meantime, youth are mostly insulated from adults within their own groups. They have far more autonomy than former generations and they live in a highly complex society; therefore they may experience more problems in assessing and committing themselves to values.

A potential source of disaffection, and a reversal of the recently more passive acceptance by youth of their society, is their growing perception of a decline in the quality of American life (Tolor, 1983). Although Americans have generally perceived their quality of life as better than that in developing nations, the current trend may eventually dissipate this view.

Youth may feel alienated for reasons that they only superficially comprehend. Philosophy professor Michael Zimmerman believes that college protestors of the late 1960s did not understand their own protest (Technology's effect, 1978). They attacked all technologies, including the technology of war, the polluting technology of industry, and the wasteful technology of consumers, but their attacks were launched at technological hardware. Technology is a way of viewing the universe as raw material, ready for exploitation, observes Zimmerman. Since human beings are a part of nature, such a view even leads them to manipulate themselves through social engineering, as in behavioristic psychology. Thus, technology becomes a means of interpreting reality. Alternatively, it is possible for nature to be viewed as a partner and not something to be dominated. According to this view, technological hardware, though used, would not be employed wastefully and ruthlessly. People exploit their environment because the social costs may be hidden, at least for a time. The breakdown comes when the social costs begin to break through, forcing humans to come to grips with the problems created. For example, consider the pollution caused by chemical wastes in a culture built on transportation and requiring energy that sometimes is in short supply.

Much has also been made of social class as a factor in determining youths' approval of, or disaffection from, society. However, it appears that youth's politics and reactions to their society relate even more to their projected or anticipated social class, the one they believe they will belong to in the future, than to their class of origin (Goodman, 1983).

Sex is another factor in alienation, although the woman's movement has perhaps narrowed the gap. In general, more males than females have displayed a disaffection from their society, perhaps because of differences in their earlier socialization (Ullian, 1984). From earliest years girls are taught care-taking responsibilities and to be concerned about the welfare of others. While the female's tendencies toward docility and nonaggression may resemble, and be confused with, patterns of nurturance and social sensitivity, they might derive even more from her feelings of "physical vulnerability" and "related anxieties and inhibitions." In other words, she is less likely to protest what might be perceived as shortcomings of society because she feels little self-assurance and considerable vulnerability. She isn't ready to challenge the status quo because she believes she would be defeated.

Recent Alienation

Many authorities have tried to account for youth's intermittent alienation, most importantly through characteristics inherent in youth itself. Youth are conscious of themselves as a group, and that consciousness may be enhanced by force of various circumstances: youth unemployment, problems in the university setting, and regulations on the use of marijuana. Consider, too, youth's idealism and confidence, not yet tempered by the hard realities of life. They are experimenters, seeking fresh solutions; hence, "more or less anti-Establishment."

Just how much adults have accounted for youth's protest is in question. Robert Coles of Harvard attributes youth's protest movement to tensions arising between "the elements of change and the elements of stability—tension that often pits young against old" (For American youth, 1976, p. 59). On the other hand, he thinks that youth and their elders have made accommodations to each other. Youth are no longer pressured prematurely into assumption of adult responsibilities. Because of the availability of legalized abortion and contraceptive devices, children are more likely to be wanted. The older generation has come, within a surprisingly short length of time, to accept young people's sexual experimentation, dress styles, and milder drugs like marijuana. As American society has become more accepting of new trends and ideas, youth find less and less to fight against (U.S. News, 1976). Some adults have even adopted counterculture values of their own.

Agrawal (1978) portrays adolescence as a "subculture of negation in which the positive valence of prevailing culture is distorted to a philosophy of youthful dissidence and protest—sometimes to the point of extreme radicalism" (p. 108). Wynne (1978), in effect, agrees, judging youth to be increasingly individualistic, even selfish. They destroy public property and they are selfish in becoming pregnant and bringing children into the world without proper economic or emotional support.

Several factors have produced increasing alienation over the past two or three decades. Schools have become larger, more bureaucratic, more departmentalized, and more focused on subject matter. Teachers have only brief contacts with many groups and only transitory relationships with most students. Thus, the current school "seems scientifically designed to teach students how not to handle intimacy and, consequently, how to flee from it. But establishing intimacy is essential to a satisfying life" (Wynne, 1978, p. 313).

Values and Life Styles of
Recent Countercultures

An essential ingredient in movements of alienation and "collective rebellion such as illustrated by the skinheads, teddy boys and punks of Great Britain is music" (Hebdige, 1979). The rock music of the 1960s was one element which united the youth generation's rebellion against adult values; and rock groups transmitted through the world youth's common concerns with drugs, sex, religion, politics, and love. In the 1970s punk rock performed a similar role for smaller but even more alienated groups (Hebdige, 1979).

The words and sounds of youth's music "mirror the intensity and turbulence" of their experience. Its sounds may be "frenzied and hard driving, euphoric, melancholy or seductive. The lyrics speak of loneliness, misunderstanding, adoration, desire, rejection, independence, bliss, remorse and confusion" (Larson & Kubey, 1983).

Certain rock music presents the message that youth music is better than, and distinct from, that of the adult world; and though fewer in number than

Counterculture members share certain cultural symbols, including hair and clothing, which represents their ideals of identity and freedom. (Photo by Paul S. Conklin, Monkmeyer)

former "cohorts of alienated youth, the very existence of today's punk rockers and new wavers—named for their music of preference—demonstrates music's power to arouse the collective experience of young people" (Larson & Kubey, 1983, p. 28).

Members of the counterculture share certain cultural interests and symbols, including styles in hair, clothing, and language, which represent not only who they are but what they intend to become. Their symbols are intended to represent their ideals of identity, freedom, naturalness, sexual equality, openness of relationships, and experimentation with life styles. These symbols also imply rejection of establishment values, including status distinctions, occupational prestige, worship of technology, dishonesty in relationships, and hypocrisy. They place special value on feelings and experience, in contrast with self-discipline, logic, and rationalism—the core Protestant ethic values. They see bureaucracy as "a form of organization designed to accomplish specific purposes in the most efficient way possible (ideally speaking, that is)" (Carroll, 1973, p. 362). In the interest of efficiency, bureaucracies are typically organized along rational, utilitarian, hierarchical lines, with formal rules for the performance of particular roles; these principles are antithetical to the values cherished by the counterculture.

Countercultures are a perennial phenomenon. In the 1960s certain youth countercultures, especially students and racial minorities, assumed a somewhat hostile stance toward the Establishment. Black high school youths often assumed an aggressive stance toward the school, and they initiated many Afro-American organizations which were militant and political in nature. Across the country there were many sit-ins and class boycotts, involving hordes of students. As a result, in June 1970, a majority of people polled by Gallup named student unrest as the nation's leading problem, above the Vietnam War or inflation. There also sprang up high school chapters of Students for a Democratic Society (SDS), the Student Nonviolent Coordinating Committee (SNCC), and other new left groups (Starr, 1981). For the first time in many years there is a "significant non-liberal non-left cadre of intellectuals in America" (Adelson, 1980, p. 60). Theirs is a "counterculture . . . of intellectual depth, vigor, tenacity, and subtlety. . . ." and these "neo-conservatives" are children patterning after their fathers.

In the 1980s only traces of the highly publicized youth counterculture of the 1960s persist; however, they have left their mark on the current generation. Smith (1983) sees present-day youth as still living with the heritage of the countercultures of the 1960s, with their emphasis on the "here and now" and their "hedonistic impulses (if it feels good do it) and its wariness of bonding human commitments" (p. 393). National surveys (Yankelovich, 1981) show that "mainstream youth have selectively simulated certain counterculture values to a considerable extent," those of hedonism and impulsiveness. Hence, we have a "me generation," an age of sensation, and a culture of narcissism. In addition, young people are sexually permissive without having the emotional link between them that their counterparts of the 1960s had. Although permissive sexual standards are the norm, the emotional bond is gone (Leger, 1980).

Alienation Today

Typically, adolescents have been portrayed as having special needs not being met by the prevailing society, which induces them to create their own culture. From the vantage point of their resultant isolation, presumably they have a clearer view of the larger culture and a better chance to produce "a brave new world" (Emihovich, 1983). Thus, in the late 60s and early 70s a "liberated generation" of youth was perceived as ready to revive a decaying culture.

However, research has contradicted this romantic myth. For one thing, only a small minority of youth were activists during that period, and upon entering the adult society and having children of their own, even this minority tended to merge with the majority, in practice if not wholly in spirit. Then, as a more conservative social and political order returned, and jobs became hard to get, the youth revolt ended. In effect, in any era, youth are not typically alienated from their society but are part of it. While alienated youth are present in any society, they usually constitute an insignificant minority varying in number according to the prevailing economic and social trends. In order to assess the current situation regarding youthful alienation, the writer submitted a questionnaire to her junior and senior students in three psychology classes at the State University College, Oswego, New York. The results indicate that the pervasive alienation of the youth of the late 1960s has dramatically subsided.

> FEMALE: I do feel pretty much in the mainstream, although I also think of myself as somewhat more radical than most others. I am a very firm believer in equal rights for all—minority groups, i.e., races, women, gays, etc. I'm especially concerned with women's rights. I would be more active, especially concerning ERA, if I had more time.

> FEMALE: I feel pretty much a part of this society. I think it's getting a little too conservative lately, though.

MALE: I would not be an activist because I think it is a waste of time. No matter how much you protest or are against something, politicians make the final decisions—you can't change their minds.

FEMALE: I feel very much out of the mainstream but I prefer it that way. I think I would be an activist depending on the cause and situational circumstances.

MALE: I feel pretty much in the mainstream of today's society. I do feel that if a major issue came up that I felt very strongly for, I would or could be an activist for that cause.

Most of the students named something they did not like about modern society, but there was no real consensus about what the big problems were. In the late 1960s there were focal points of student unrest, but these students' dislikes were more varied and less intense, not strong enough to reflect outright alienation from society.

FEMALE: I do not like how competitive society is. It makes me very nervous.

MALE: Society isolates many individuals because of the present-day high cost of living. Plus, I really don't feel that today's society is living for tomorrow, which will hurt our future generations.

MALE: I hate the constant emphasis on the economy. Everyone concentrates on making money. Everything seems geared toward career.

FEMALE: I am discontented about the quality (more truly, lack of quality) and the influence of television programming. It is appalling, this drivel produced as entertainment. It also disturbs me how much time is spent watching TV in the home.

MALE: I don't like the way that people in society (especially the U.S.) seem very concerned with impressing other people, and "fitting in," at the risk of doing things that they are against.

MALE: I don't like the way society has depersonalized people. At times it seems that everyone is a number or punch card.

Most of the students felt reasonably content with modern society. A large majority felt pride in being an American. Things they especially liked about society were as varied as those they disliked.

MALE: Today's society has many groups that individuals can belong to. This takes away the aspect of loneliness for many people, especially the elderly.

FEMALE: Women have more freedom and opportunities in many areas than previously—socially, sexually, and economically.

FEMALE: There are a lot of good things about our society. We're always complaining about the education system, but it beats a lot of other places. In some countries it's so expensive to go to school that few people can go at all.

MALE: What I like about modern society is its abilities in mass transport and mass communication. These two aspects help to make the world more an international society.

Views about government and social issues were also diverse. Almost half the students favored capitalism; yet a majority felt that labor unions and corporations held too much power. Most of the students felt strongly about some social issue; and a majority would contribute time and money to help do something about it, thus refuting the common view that today's youth are disinterested in social issues. Few would favor illegal activity to support their side of the issue. Nor did they, except for a very few, belong to activist groups or assume an activist role themselves.

FEMALE: Haven't recently belonged to a group out of the mainstream. But when I was 13 or 14 I hung out with a group who got high a lot and did other drugs, too, when most of my friends in school wouldn't even think of it. We smoked a lot of pot or did other types of drugs and hung out in a park or anywhere else we could.

MALE: I am committed to associate myself with the program for peaceful change as proposed by the Socialist Labor Party of America.

The general picture was of relatively contented students who, nevertheless, would like some changes made. There were no major causes that unified students, such as those that had rallied youth in the late 1960s. The recent students showed concern and would be supportive of those who tackle important issues, but few would take direct part themselves. Few of these youth could be called alienated from their society; however, because youth's mood reflects changes in the larger society, symptoms of alienation wax and wane.

A Perspective on Counterculture Values

Certain considerations are essential if counterculture values are to be judged fairly. First, publicity about delinquency should not blind us to the fact that most counterculture youth's activities are somewhat harmless, though they seem strange and often pointless to adults. The serious disrupters and law breakers embrace only a small minority; nevertheless, they are a serious hazard to society. A Los Angeles school principal observes that "only two or three percent are the real donkeys, the gang kids" (Getting young people to learn, 1976, p. 53). In the second place, many people overgeneralize about youth, speaking of their anti-intellectualism and of teenage tyranny (Tyack, 1978). They tend to ignore class and cultural differences, thus obscuring the root issues of what may be involved.

Often adults read into youth's behaviors deeper, more complex implications than may be justified. Riemer (1981) points out that social scientists have consistently ignored deviant behavior as a purely fun activity, as "frivolous, flippant" (p. 39). Rather, they persist in limiting themselves to "more sober, social, psychological and sociological explanations. . . ." (p. 39). Yet many youth

Counterculture youth's activities are usually harmless and the serious disruptures and law breakers embrace a small minority. (Photo by UPI/Bettmann Archive)

activities appear to be "spontaneous, just for the hell of it," engaged in purely for the fun that it may afford (p. 39).

TYPES OF ALIENATED YOUTH

The Silent Majority

The vast majority of youth are not alienated, in the broad sense, although they may dislike specific features of the larger society. In general, they accept and agree with the major values of their elders. The image of youth, as portrayed in *Who's Who Among American High School Students*, is somewhat conservative. Half the students surveyed did not drink; eight in ten anticipated a traditional marriage; and 89 percent never used drugs. Two thirds (68 percent) approved passage of the Equal Rights Amendment, but a mere 1 percent thought that women's rights topics warranted national attention. Although about a half perceived women's role as having changed, 58 percent believed that women could become completely fulfilled by a full-time role as homemaker (Nation's teenagers, 1977).

Some individuals within this silent majority do play a role with regard to alienation. While not actively involved in resistance, they may extend silent support to their more vocal age mates. Their members are indeterminate, but their support is apparent in their failure to report transgressions of activists and in sympathetic attitudes when questioned.

Activists

CHARACTERISTICS OF YOUTHFUL ACTIVISTS   Recent activists, as compared with those of the late 1960s have values that are not nihilistic, but congruent with accepted concepts of social organization. They are interested in interpersonal relationships and feelings, as well as in political arrangements, but translate these values into plans for society (Hagestad, 1977). For example, many of them join with adults in protests over nuclear power and environmental issues.

Still, on certain issues there remains a generation gap—for example, regarding students' rights. Many students, and also adults, have initiated legal challenges to school authorities with regard to regulating students' political and cultural expression. This "age-based rebellion" against school authority and compulsory schooling produced a broad gap between students and adults over the student rights issue. Youth, to a far greater extent than adults, felt they should have more to say about curriculum, teacher evaluation, schools, and school dress (Starr, 1981). Such issues are far less prominent than formerly because youth have achieved so much regarding them. However, students continue to assert themselves though in institutionalized ways, when they feel their rights and interests are being violated.

INTERPRETATIONS OF ACTIVISM AS A GENERATIONAL CHARACTERISTIC   Other researchers focus on activism itself and factors that contribute to it. Wright (1975) identifies a tradition of student radicalism in the United States and only in comparison with the "silent generation" of the 1950s did the generation of the late 1960s seem especially activist. The 1950s were the "years of loyalty oaths . . . of Joe McCarthy . . . and the rest of the redbaiters of the era, definitely not an era conducive to radical protest" (p. 290).

An analysis of the causes for activism helps account for such change. For one thing, activism derives not so much from something within youth, compelling them to act, as from a lifting of restraints imposed on earlier generations that make recent ones seem more activistic. In earlier times, social circumstances were not conducive to radical behaviors. Today, youth are the only ones, except for the very rich, who can take time off to participate in such movements. The price they must pay for such activities is slight. Finally, note the rather particularistic nature of much recent protest. Observers have often overlooked that "no activist worth his stripes would ever schedule a rally in the dead of the winter or before 11 a.m. or on a rainy day" (p. 292).

Wright prophesied accurately that these youth would become less distinct as a generation as they settled down "into comfortable jobs, families, and the rest of the necessarily deradicalizing experiences of young adulthood and middle age. Like good liberals everywhere, they could be expected to live out their political lives in the classic manner established by their own liberal parents; mild activism on behalf of social welfare causes and candidates, allegiance to the liberal wing of the Democratic party, fastidious donations to liberal causes, and little else" (p. 293).

CONSEQUENCES FOR SOCIETY   It is unclear how much student activists achieve. Because of their visibility and vigor, they may have had an impact disproportionate to their numbers. Both major political parties are now concerned with personalistic ideas. Reform movements launched by youth are reflected in related movements in various professions. Thus, "the themes of the counterculture and radical humanism have become fashionable for a significant segment of their elders" (Bengtson & Starr, 1975, p. 265).

In contrast, Keniston believes that campus protestors have had little real impact socially. Neither did they drop out. They came to realize that changing things is difficult, yet they had not abandoned the idea that the country can be made better (Student apathy and cynicism, 1974).

One consequence for society, since society is largely run by middle-age adults, is what sort of citizens young activists later become. A study of Michigan University alumni throws light on this question: To what degree does activism in college relate to later life behaviors and values? (Hoge & Ankney, 1982). Activists were divided into two categories: the demonstration activist who became actively involved in protest and politically involved students who participated in politically involved organizations but not in protest. By 1979 both groups had moved somewhat to the majority, but were still distinctive in certain ways. The demonstration activists were still very interested in political affairs, suspicious of free enterprise ideologies, and doubted the worthwhileness of serving in the Armed Forces. The organization activists were also still distinctive, being disproportionately unmarried and involved in business. They were more likely to be unmarried, absent from business, and working in human service areas. They were also more politically interested and more suspicious of free enterprise than nonactivists. Both types had shifted away from involvement in national affairs to community affairs. Both groups had shifted in the direction of nonactivists in terms of becoming "more family oriented, less critical of college and organized labor, more open to traditional religion and less alarmed about the inevitability of future wars" (p. 370). Thus, it seems that activism is not transitory in its impact but relates to long-term values. The question may arise: Did the activist experiences impact on longer term values or would such individuals, regardless of involvement, maintain such values over time?

To the degree that alienated youth do affect society, Wynne (1978) believes their potential impact may be dangerous. He asks how a society can survive unless youth are committed to continuing its major traditions—traditions that produce goods and services for all segments of society, that sponsor an adequate level of public orderliness, and that commit citizens to constructive community activities. Such traditions can thrive only in a society where people work for others and not just for themselves.

THE PUNKS AND OTHER YOUTH SUBCULTURES   In the later 1970s emerged an alienated youth category who labeled themselves "punks." Punk rock debuted in London in 1976 and early punks' appearance was characterized by "short and spiky, brightly colored hair, torn T-shirts and the use of razor blades and safety pins as jewelry. Some wore symbols associated with fascism, such as swastikas and iron crosses" (Levine & Stumpf, 1983, p. 422). The punk movement got underway in Los Angeles in fall 1977 with several home-grown bands, a club in a dingy basement, and an insider's magazine *Slash*. For their hair they rejected the bright colors of the London punks and chose instead "jet black and platinum blonde. Loud tattered clothes gave way to black and red thrift shop fare. Dirty tennis shoes were replaced by heavy black leather biker boots wrapped in padlocked steel chains" (p. 423).

Punk rock is one of the most recent of a series of music subcultures. Its music is described as "the frantic music of zombies with the high-speed drumming and machine-gun clatter of guitars" (p. 423). It is designed "to repel" and characterized by "a calculated outlandishness" (p. 423). Punk rock's most common theme is death, involving death symbols as The Skull and Dead Skin, agents of death such as Black Flag, Agent Orange, and killers, such as Assassins, Maus, Gun Club. An allied theme is the notion of danger—whether dangerous substances Black Flag, Agent Orange, or people Red Army, Castration Squad. The theme of victimization also appears—for example Nervous Gender, Sex Sick, Sexually Frustrated (p. 430).

The punks themselves are completely aware of the images that they project. They prefer to be viewed "as society's misfits or outcasts . . . one member of the Circle Jerks claimed to have chosen the name for his band because it was disgusting" (p. 431). It seems that "punks want to repel those in the mainstream culture and to challenge them with what the latter would regard as negative," including symbols, "repulsive band names, iron crosses, swastikas, bikers' clothes and the like" (p. 431). Punks are also concerned about genuineness and constantly criticize themselves. Another focus is fear and various punk rock bands attempt to incite it in an entertaining manner.

The punk movement embraces the elements by which subcultures may be defined: a characteristic style that distinguishes its members from the mainstream, "focal concerns" that give their style its significance, and their own code through which their style and focal concerns are expressed (p. 430). With regard to its relation to the mainstream culture it addresses the issue of self-preservation which insulates it from the dominant culture. Its techniques of self-preservation include "such mechanisms as formalized secrecy and indoctrination" (p. 433). The punks also stress fears which are everywhere in the larger culture, such as nuclear threats and urban violence. Through emphasizing the theme of fear in their music and dress they reflect the perception of their fears in the wide world of culture. Thus the punk culture serves the function of highlighting the main features of the major culture. Hence, Levine and Stumpf call this a reflective subculture.

The motorcycle gang provides a family for its members and is considered an outlaw culture. (Photo by Pat Caulfield, Photo Researchers, Inc.)

Other subcultures serve different functional roles with regard to the larger society. For example the motor cycle gang provides "a family for its members, exists outside the mainstream and is seemingly uninterested in remaining part of it" (p. 433). It is an outlaw culture. A third type is the alternative subculture—for example, the hippie movement existed within the dominant culture yet was disinterested in it and provided its own life style as an option. Levine and Stumpf conclude that much could be learned about the mainstream culture by studying "its underside" in terms of its "reflective subcultures" (p. 434).

Since the early 1920s youth's subcultures have been studied in terms of various frames of reference. Especially in the late 1950s and 1960s youth subcultures were simply equated with delinquency and gangs, and analyzed in terms of crime and deviance. Atypical groups were perceived as failures to conform or to assume the desired middle-class values and goals.

In contrast, in the transaction approach such subcultures are perceived as "outcomes of a complex interactive process between groups with differential access to power" (p. 419). In this sense deviance is a term simply ascribed to power-status groups by those having greater power and authority.

Runaways

A neglected category of youthful escapists is the runaways. About a million minors run away from home each year—in recent years, more girls than boys and at an earlier age (Shore, 1981). The typical runaway is a 13- to 14-year-old, most often a girl from a white, middle-class suburb. Only one in ten lives with both biological parents. Runaways have displaced the adventure-seeking flower children of the 1960s. Instead of hitchhiking across the country they may go to a friend's house or to a nearby runaway shelter. Growing numbers are "trashed" kids, throwaways, or pushouts. Some shelters say that most of them are throwaways—rejected by parents and forced into the street.

Over the past two decades the number of teenage runaways has increased dramatically, one estimate being 600,000 a year (Johnson & Carter, 1980). A much greater number are potential runaways. Among eighth graders in Georgia among those reporting that they had run away from home the highest number was among black girls (25 percent) followed by white girls (18 percent), white boys (17 percent) and black boys (9 percent). However, many more had thought about leaving—82 percent of the black boys, 81 percent of the black girls, 62 percent of the white boys, and 50 percent of the white girls (Schab, 1982).

Roberts (1982) employs a five-point continuum in describing degree of parent-youth conflict for runaways. At the zero or minimum conflict level between parents and their adolescent children, whatever conflicts develop would be resolved without the use of running away. Level 1 included two types, runaway explorers and runaway social pleasure seekers. The explorers had a desire to travel alone and to be independent and only ran away after their parents would refuse permission on the basis that they were too young. The social pleasure seekers were those who had some conflict with their parents, although ordinarily they got along well enough with them. They might leave because of some restriction, say over an early evening curfew or grounding that kept them from going to some social event. The youth would go anyhow and sometimes manage to return without having been discovered. At level 2, after frequent conflicts between themselves and their parents, adolescents might run away, hoping that parents would become worried about them and accept them back on their own terms. At the next higher level, the runaway retreatist would impulsively run away after a serious situation of conflict and tension. These individuals often had school problems as well and indulged in retreatist behaviors, such as getting drunk or wasted on pot. At the highest level, the endangered runaways would have had frequent conflicts with their parents, including repeated incidents of physical or sexual abuse by them, often while the parents were drunk. Such youths typically use a variety of drugs and half of them have drinking problems. They all have been physically abused and occasionally sexually abused. Often running away was precipitated by being beaten and threats of future beatings.

A study of former runaways, since then reconciled with their parents, suggests that emotional stress, self-doubt and personal guilt are more common among girls than boys (Gottlieb & Chafetz, 1977). Parents generally accord boys far more freedom and flexible behaviors than girls. Neither the parent nor the runaway child had any conscious desire to hurt the other. When their children run away, less affluent parents either impose severe restrictions or seek help from the clergy or police, while affluent parents seek professional help. Ultimately, both parents and their reconciled children become more responsive to the others' needs, the parents being more flexible than their children. Neither parents nor their children had expected their conflicts to become so strong as to precipitate the child's leaving home.

After the runaway experience, boys more often than girls reported improved relations with their fathers. Two thirds of the group believed, in retrospect, that running away had been a growing experience. The majority believed that their lives, after running away, were better than before, although still not trouble-free. However, even those who reported a positive experience hesitated to recommend the same action for others, because of the struggles involved. They were concerned about their parents' welfare but found traditional life styles unpalatable.

The Disadvantaged

Youths who are disadvantaged—that is, barred by socioeconomic factors from usual participation in the benefits of the larger society—may be ignored simply because their problem has so long been with us.

Simply being poor in an affluent society is a real handicap. Poor families feel poorer still when the great majority of people have so much more than they do. The parents may come to find their children a real burden and welcome their leaving home. Such throwaway children often leave home during a quarrel. Also, older children may be shoved out to make way for younger ones. In more affluent homes family breakdown is more often the cause (Dudley, 1979). Often they drop out of school which tends to produce both a rise in self-esteem and also in delinquency because such individuals are most likely to be those who are not successful in school and who resent authority. These mostly poorer and working-class youths become stereotyped as "leather-jacketed, poor, sinister and amoral" (p. 214). The "prototype here is the wild and untamed juvenile delinquent, clearly lower class in appearance and manner . . . [he] is beyond the pale of adult intimidation, manipulation or moral appeal, a figure to be feared and ridiculed" (Starr, 1981, p. 214).

A study of lower-class black adolescents indicated that both sexes felt alienated from school as well as from society. It had been hypothesized that females would be less alienated because of the presumed matriarchy in the black lower class; however, even though female-headed families are more common among blacks than whites, the predominant role is occupied by black males. Indeed black lower-class intact families are more patriarchal than their white counterparts.

Overall, some poor youth "make it"—that is, find a reasonably confortable niche in society—while others remain maladjusted and unhappy. The difficulty is not that a lower-class value system contains elements in conflict with middle-class ones. Nor is it generally that lower-class youth who fail to make the grade oppose middle-class life styles. In fact, their ideals seem much like those of the very society that poses so many obstacles for them. Instead, poor adolescents find themselves forcibly alienated because they lack both the resources and referents required to attain the goals of the society. Nor do they receive support within their own homes. Yet when poor youth turn to people on the outside, they find little help there, either. Few of their peers and relatives can help; nor does a ghetto school provide the resources or environment that convinces students that they will be meaningfully rewarded for their efforts. Such young people may also lack adult referents with the power or will to demonstrate or explain what the benefits of education might be. Thus, their deprivation is global, limiting occupational, social, and intellectual resources, as well as medical and dental care.

Juvenile Delinquents

JUVENILE DELINQUENCY DEFINED   Another form of disaffection from society, different from the foregoing types, is juvenile delinquency. Juvenile delinquents are individuals, not yet adult, who have broken the law. The concept of delinquency itself is flexible. It may be defined by society through its laws, rather than by psychology and medicine. As defined by psychologists, delinquency would be determined to mean intentional noncompliance with the dictates of constituted authority. Note that delinquency is not an either-or condition. Youth may not easily be classified merely as delinquents or nondelinquents but should be judged in relative terms as more or less delinquent.

INCIDENCE AND TYPES OF DELINQUENCY   Let us now look at the record. From 1968 to 1977 serious crime (murder, rape, robbery, burglary, larceny, auto theft, and aggravated assault) arose at its fastest pace ever. Since 1970 juvenile arrests and violent crimes by females under 18 have grown a dramatic 16.3 percent (Burquest, 1981). However, after 1975, there was some decrease in most categories for both sexes. That is, there was a dramatic increase between 1970 to 1975 and a small decrease thereafter. Looking ahead, there appear no signs of lessening youth crime. Since 1969 juvenile arrests for violent crimes have grown by 246 percent, over twice that for adults. Whereas youth, ages 10 through 17, comprise just 16 percent of the population they account for almost half of all property crime (Starr, 1981).

Acts of vandalism include destroying or injuring animals and personal property; breaking and entering buildings; breaking down or entering fences and gates; destroying trees, boundary markers, lightbulbs, telephone poles, and billboards; damaging memorials to the dead; damaging library books; and throwing missiles at trains and cars (Tobias & LaBlanc, 1977). Usually the acts are committed by two or more youths, and a car is involved for mobility or as a weapon of destruction.

The offenders follow typical patterns and possess characteristic motives. They commit multiple acts, not vandalizing just a single piece of property. They have neither malice toward or concern for the victim but usually consider their activity as a matter of fun and games and employ their own special "slanguage" to describe their behaviors. Driving over a suburban lawn and spinning tires to create a road is "jungle patching." "Car stomping" is walking on top of, or kicking in, a parked vehicle. "Bombing" or "blasting" refers to blowing up suburban mailboxes or school toilets with firecrackers. The "academic hot seat" refers to burning plastic toilet seats in school lavatories by placing pieces of Kotex between the seat and the bowl and igniting them.

CAUSES OF DELINQUENCY   The causes of youth crime are not easy to determine. The common assumption that youthful crime derives mostly from breakdown in the family is open to question. The quality of family life apparently has more impact on less serious forms of norm violation than on hard-core crime. Family disruption may play its most significant role in benign social environments, whereas in deteriorated neighborhoods, poverty and unhealthy street influences may very well be a more important influence than the home (Johnstone, 1978).

However, family influences on delinquency are undoubtedly significant. Farrington (1982) found that chronically delinquent youth—those with six or more convictions—were characterized by poor parenting, prolonged separation from a parent, and being from large families and deprived households. Covert antisocial behaviors are mainly associated with parents' lack of monitoring, whereas overt antisocial behaviors relate to disruptions in parental discipline—for example, failing to match children's behaviors with appropriate consequences (Patterson, 1982). Though we know little about how children's antisocial behaviors modify parents' management behaviors, it has been assumed that antisocial children succeed in manipulating their parents into giving up efforts to control them.

When parents are simply "chronically unable to apply discipline and monitor the child's whereabouts, the chances are much higher of both covert and overt antisocial behaviors." Certainly, the parents of recidivists—that is, youth who are repeated offenders—usually have inadequate family management skills. In her study of 10- to 17-year-old boys Wilson (1980) found that none of the parents of the recidivist boys were strict supervisors. Rather, 7 percent of the recidivists had received intermediate supervision and 63 percent quite lax supervision.

Family experience may also contribute to youth's delinquency in quite subtle ways. For example, a parent may model aggression, but not criminal behaviors. A sampling of high school males from a mid-southern high school whose mean age was 16.2 years, with a range of 14 to 19, tended to pattern aggressive behaviors after their fathers but not their mothers. The individual identifying with an aggressive father may perceive aggression as part of being male; whereas he may simply perceive his modeling after his mother as a non-desirable thing to do (Neapolitan, 1981).

Also contributing to delinquency is personality, though in poorly understood ways. For a long time deviant adolescents have been viewed as having immature self-concepts, with younger children thinking of themselves in concrete ways (physical characteristics and material possessions) and older ones in more abstract interpersonal psychological terms; however such may not be the case. A comparison of law abiding high school students and delinquents, which involved giving five answers to the question "Who am I?", revealed no cognitive immaturities in self-concepts. On the other hand, the delinquents defined their self-concept in terms of deviant social status. In comparison with controls they saw themselves less often in social roles such as kinship and student roles and more often in terms of criminal, deviant, and antisocial roles (Chassin & Young, 1981).

Sex has long been recognized as a major factor in delinquency. The greater degree of male delinquency is sometimes attributed, at least partly, to "male sex hormones, particularly testosterone, which have been demonstrated to be the most important hormones influencing aggressivity" (Burquest, 1981, p. 753). Presumably these hormones plus modes of male childrearing and their role in society produce the so-called masculine traits of aggressiveness, competitiveness, and nonemotionality relating to patterns of delinquency, whereas female characteristics of passivity, emotionality, and noncompetitiveness are presumed to inhibit delinquency (Thornton, 1982). Hence, the recent increase in women's crime rate has been explained by their assumption of more masculine traits. However, a study among eight twelfth graders in a northwestern city cast doubt on these assumptions. Neither male or female gender traits related to

Sex is a major factor in delinquency. (Photo by Sibil Shelton, Monkmeyer)

frequency of delinquency for either sex except for a slight relationship between masculinity and property types of delinquency. There was some suggestion that stealing may constitute a "form of masculinity verification." Overall the relationship between gender traits and aggressive delinquencies was quite weak, although masculine males and females tend to become slightly more involved in delinquent aggressions than do more feminine individuals of either sex. Thus, it seems that the relationship between delinquency and gender traits is weaker and more complex than commonly believed (Thornton, 1982).

Juvenile delinquency has long been associated with poorer sections of big cities. Violence in such areas is still much higher than in suburban and rural areas, although in recent years the rate in suburban areas has increased faster than in urban ones (Burquest, 1981). However, much of the increase in the largely middle-class suburbs has been in less serious offenses.

Segrave and Hastad (1982) concluded that lower socioeconomic status relates especially to more serious offenses. They studied causes of delinquency in high schools in a major east coast city, with regard to socioeconomic status, perception of opportunities, and value orientations. These orientations were defined as conventional—that is, "defined by adherence to such overt, and formed official values as deferred gratification, hard work, practicality, the worth of formal education and the like"—and subterranean—that is, commitment to "such covert, informal and unofficial values as short-run hedonism, excitement, trouble, the ability to make a fast buck, the ability to con others and the like" (Cernkovich, 1978, p. 342). Delinquency was treated as involvement in acts for which both juveniles and adults might be legally prosecuted. The results indicated that adherence to conventional norms tended to insulate an individual against delinquency; whereas delinquent behavior was associated with perception of limited opportunity and subterranean values tended to allow delinquency involvement.

Surprisingly, the perception of limited opportunities played a more important role in the ideology of delinquency among females. It may be that girls find it more difficult psychologically to perform unacceptable acts than do boys, yet may finally be driven to it by economic hardship. Other motivators might be insufficient to break through their controls, but this one becomes the trigger.

Some persons have suggested that there is no social relationship between social class and delinquency, but there appears to be a consistent one, although not very large. One reason for the difference in this and other studies in this regard is that the present study dealt with chargeable criminal offenses rather than trivial and non-serious ones which may mask differences (Segrave & Hastad, 1982).

It has also been suggested that computer games, directly or indirectly, contribute to aggression and presumably to delinquency. Indirectly, such games may simply displace time that would be spent doing other things. The direct effect of aggressive video games may conceivably be the same as that of violent shows on television. The effect may be even greater since video games are more ego involved and active than the relatively passive matter of sitting in front of a television set. Certainly, many video games have relatively violent themes—for instance, one in which a player takes the role of an arsonist trying to burn down a building, and another in which the player tries to run down pedestrians on the highway. On the other hand, with a few exceptions like those above, video games do not have aggressive themes toward other humans. Ordinarily the contest is against "alien robots, malevolent spaceships, technomonsters and beasts" (Condry & Keiths, 1983, p. 105). Note too, in considering the effects of such media that males who are involved in far more delinquent acts than females are also those who throng the arcades.

After reviewing the research Loeber (1982) concludes that high-risk youth can be identified with a minimum number of errors, and treatment is most successful when children are relatively young and delinquent behavior patterns not yet firmly established.

TREATMENT AND PREVENTION OF DELINQUENCY   Several methods have been used for reducing school-related norm-violating behaviors. Structural adjustments have been made in school systems, such as using television cameras, radar systems, intercom systems, and flood lights. Preventive programs have taken forms of psychological intervention (behavior modification techniques, and group guidance meetings) and restructuring youth's social environments. Adolescents may hold meetings for discussing their various problems, with group leaders available on call. Thus, the peer culture comes to assume more positive values and the group becomes responsible for its members. Still another approach is through curriculum intervention, by providing content that is more meaningful to the student, especially career education and content geared toward improving interpersonal relationships, such as those within the marriage and the family (Sabatino, Heald, Rothman & Miller, 1978).

One common approach is for schools to allow disadvantaged and otherwise potentially delinquent youth to play on sports teams despite weak academic performance. After reviewing the research Donnelly (1981) concluded that sports may not always be effectively substituted for delinquent behavior. Much depends on the type of individual involved and why a particular youth rebels against the system. On the other hand, for individuals who are nonconforming and enjoy risk-taking, challenging sport and adventure programs may be successful. However, one might question the integrity of school systems that trade diplomas either for winning teams (the more probable reason) or for reducing crime.

There is little evidence of the value or the long-term effects of programs designed to reduce delinquency, and that which does exist is often discouraging. Psychologist Joan McCord compared men who had been in treatment programs designed to prevent delinquency four decades earlier with a matched group of men who had not been thus treated. In the treatment process, the so-called Cambridge-Somerville Youth Study, boys ages 5 to 13 had been divided into two groups as closely matched as possible. The boys in one group received no treatment, while those in the other saw counselors twice a month for about five years. In many instances, the boys were tutored in school, received medical and psychiatric help, and were involved in Boy Scouts, YMCA, or other groups. The follow-up indicated that, of the treated group, 119 had committed minor offenses, and 49, serious ones. In the untreated group, 126 had committed minor crimes, and 42, major ones. A higher percentage of the untreated men had become white-collar workers or professionals and more of them were satisfied with their jobs. McCord believes that social action programs should be tested first in order to estimate any hazards for the people they are presumed to help (Bush, 1978).

THE COURTS AND JUVENILE OFFENDERS   What happens to juveniles suspected of antisocial behaviors varies greatly according to their socioeconomic status. Typically the upper classes deal with such matters through their personal attorneys (Burquest, 1981).

Vinter (1979) reported that 71 percent of institutionalized females had been committed there for status offenses, misdemeanors, or violations of probation or parole. However, many such girls admit to having been involved in felonies and sometimes violent crimes. That is, many of them are criminally delinquent and not merely status offenders. Thus, in such facilities one finds genuine status offenders housed with criminally delinquent girls, thereby diluting efforts to help the more serious offenders and placing the status offenders at risk.

The chances of a juvenile's being arrested and being placed in a correctional institution are ninety-one times as great in some states as in others. Those states with high crime rates detain greater numbers of youths than those with low crime rates; however, they generally retain them locally without sending them to other residential facilities.

There is some conflict between the goals of rehabilitating delinquent youth and segregating them from society so that people will feel more secure. Lately, increasing juvenile crime rates and the widespread publicity given them, especially violent crimes, have placed greater pressure on trying such offenders in adult courts (Malmquist, 1979). In the past decade a trend has developed toward deinstitutionalization of deviant populations (Starr, 1981). For example, in some states, notably Massachusetts, youth training schools and extension schools are being opposed in favor of group homes, private schools, foster homes, alternative schools, and community programs. At the same time, there has been a movement to provide legal safeguards in dealing with juvenile delinquents. Such developments raise the question: to what extent do they reflect a change in attitudes toward the young, that perhaps they should be given greater independence?

The juvenile court system in the United States has operated in the main on the principal that minors, those below the age of majority, lack mature motivation and that their behaviors call for guidance and understanding rather than punishment in cases of antisocial behavior because associating them with criminality will merely stigmatize the youths concerned (Rich, 1982). Courts have felt that procedures designed especially for juveniles and protecting them from stigma and punishment are significant for the well-being of both society and the juveniles themselves. The courts concern themselves not so much with matters of guilt or innocence as with attempts to save juveniles from future criminal activities. However, these courts have not succeeded in reducing juvenile crime nor repeat of crime—that is, recidivism—perhaps for several reasons. First, juveniles have not been granted all the rights that the Constitution provides for its citizens. Also, laws relating to juvenile delinquency vary greatly, and almost any minor might be declared delinquent depending on interpretations placed on particular activities. Indeed, delinquent acts are committed by large numbers of young people and not simply juvenile delinquents. In addition, the apprehending officer and the judges involved have tremendous discretion, and they often place the emphasis on the nature of the offender rather than the offense itself. Many factors—including prior record, sex, age, appearance, demeanor, and family status—play an important role in the way apprehended juveniles are treated. As a result, one finds in institutions many juveniles who have been committed there for conduct that would not have been considered criminal for adults, along with others who have committed truly serious offenses. Overall, it appears that the juvenile justice system is characterized by lack of definition and coordination, defective delivery of service, and confusion of roles and responsibilities of all persons involved, including judges, social workers, police, and community agencies.

Another problem is in determining whether juvenile offenders should be tried as adults. Juvenile courts typically assess a youth's degree of maturity, aggressiveness, sophistication, and relative potential for rehabilitation in the adult or juvenile systems. Other considerations are the juvenile's ability to help in his own defense and his or her capacity for rational judgment (Solway & Hays, 1978). Even when juvenile courts are the choice, there are few specialized ones, and these few rarely have adequate probation and clinical services. Yet many juvenile offenders are guilty of hard-drug use, murder, stealing, excessive drinking, and gang involvement. They are not simply truants or disobedient children whom parents were unwilling or unable to discipline.

Various proposals have been set forth for improving what research shows to be a highly ineffective juvenile court system (Rich, 1982). It has been suggested that all juvenile status offenders be removed from detention—that is, those who commit offenses for which adults would not be apprehended. Other suggestions include basing sentences on the seriousness of the offense and not on the court's view of the juvenile, thus getting rid of the vague subjective criteria; giving fixed rather than open-ended sentences; employing the least restrictive alternative for intervention; making court proceedings visible and accountable; providing council at all critical stages of the proceedings; and defining the role of parents in such proceedings (Rich, 1982).

Considerable progress is being made regarding legal rights of minors. The American Civil Liberties Union has investigated many cases, publicized the plight of minors, and acted as their advocate. The Supreme Court, too, has made significant decisions on their behalf, notably the Gault decision, in which the Court ruled that juvenile suspects are entitled to a lawyer, to cross-examine witnesses, and to have other safeguards guaranteed to adult defendants by the Constitution. In effect, the Court for the first time recognized that minors are citizens entitled to the same protection that the Constitution affords adults.

SUGGESTIONS FOR DEALING WITH ALIENATION

The many recipes for dealing with youth's alienation would rival the variety in any cookbook. Some authorities believe that adults who humor youth and who fail to establish firm boundaries or require that they be fully responsible for their acts are abdicating their proper role. We pamper youth, observes Baumrind (1974), and we "reinforce the antisocial choices of disadvantaged or affluent youth by providing free clinics, runaway centers, and counterculture high schools" (p. 81). Instead, youth's obligation should be clearly stated and firmly enforced. Crimes committed in the school setting should be punished just as surely as those committed in the larger society. If authorities simply "look the other way" when youth commit crimes, they are, in effect, strengthening their tendencies to aggression.

On the other hand, more viable solutions to the problem may be devised. Coleman (1978) believes that alienation can be reduced by changes in the family. He suggests that the family has become a mere "convenience institution" for husband and wife (p. 319). One result has been the rapidly increasing number of runaway children, ages 12 and up. Wynne (1978) suggests that all social institutions should participate in curing youth's alienation. A single agency, such as the school, cannot do it alone. Schools must alter those phenomena which produce interpersonal isolation and loneliness. Different patterns of change will be dictated in different communities and schools. Tyack (1978) suggests that society should be challenged to create a meaningful niche in its economy for youth and to capitalize on youth's idealism. In other words, help for youth rests in the larger society. A guaranteed job is as important as free-lunch programs were for earlier generations. High school students who see their older friends without jobs are not motivated to do well in school.

Finally, it should be recognized that alienation is "the tip of the iceberg" in the sense that its roots lie in the structure of society. Hence alienation must basically be treated in terms of that society. While youth may be called upon to internalize societal norms, at the same time traditions and their place in the structure of society should be examined (Pacheco, 1978, p. 318).

FUTURE PERSPECTIVES

Alienated youth may be a significant segment of society, both at their present stage and in adulthood, depending on how they are treated. Among them are many thinkers and doers whose criticisms of society should be taken seriously. Such individuals typically achieve a relatively good, often superior, adjustment as adults. Alienated youth may find adjustment as adults easier in today's society, with its acceptance, even encouragement, of pluralism than formerly, when the old melting-pot concept prevailed and alternative life styles were discouraged. After becoming parents, they usually become concerned about their children's welfare and prefer a more secure, traditionally constructed world.

With regard to delinquents, the majority eventually marry, have children, and become law-abiding; however, some of them remain troublemakers. Adelson (1979) observes that "many forms of social and personal pathology usually make their first appearance during adolescence: alcoholism and other addictions, delinquency, out-of-wedlock pregnancies, depression, and schizophrenia, to name just a few" (p. 34). A follow-up study of children first seen in a child guidance clinic as preadolescents indicated that the item, "fails to get along with other children," related to a wide range of adult behaviors. Moreover, composite scores indicated that bad conduct in early years related significantly to bad conduct in adult life (Janes, Hesselbrock, Myers & Penniman, 1979).

On the other hand, it should be determined which new behaviors merely represent needed adaptations (Alexander & Cohen, 1981). Dramatic changes in social customs and values make it difficult to differentiate behaviors which represent healthy ways of coping with social change from those that are unhealthy and simply disguised by social change. The common tendency is simply to label changed values as deviant.

Finally, all youth at risk should be helped, in whatever ways possible, to realize their potential and establish desirable but realistic goals. An older youth or teacher-mentor would prove useful here. Only those youth who have some confidence in what the future holds will be prepared to make commitments and to control their impulses in order to obtain long-term benefits (Smith, 1983).

SUMMARY

In recent years, a great deal of interest has focused on alienated youth—those who, for various reasons, feel estranged from the larger society in which they live. Such youth collectively constitute the counterculture, or oppositional culture. The problem of estrangement is both perennial and universal. In general, youth demonstrate considerable alienation intermittently, and subgroups or individual youth demonstrate it constantly.

Theories devised to explain the alienation phenomenon are varied, representing views from many disciplines. Perhaps the most basic cause of alienation is cultural lag, or the failure of society to adapt with sufficient insight and flexibility to youth's current needs. Moreover, the gap between generations obstructs the sort of communication that might define precisely what those needs may be. Other factors contributing to youth's estrangement include outmoded curricula, society's failure to involve young people in meaningful tasks of citizenship, and the materialism and impersonality produced by technology. Youth may also feel alienated in ways that they only superficially comprehend, as in their attacks on technology.

Countercultures are variously interpreted in terms of their basic emphases, values, and life styles. Some observers accuse them of radicalism, bohemianism, communalism, and revivalism; others perceive in their values and life style a concern for transcendence, mystery, antimaterialism, cooperativeness, openness, naturalness, and quality. Youth, in the main, find some things they do not like in today's society, but most of them feel reasonably satisfied with it.

Not all youth can be categorized as alienated or as representing the same brand of alienation. The vast majority of young people maintain a reasonably good working relationship with their elders. However, most of these individuals silently support certain of their less conventional age mates. The more alienated youth, at least in recent years, became subdivided into various categories, including political activists, hippies, runaways, the disadvantaged, minority group members, and juvenile delinquents. Each of these groups has its distinctive characteristics: Some are active; others are passive. Some seek to take over society and redeem it; others turn their backs on the larger society and form relatively independent subcultures of their own. All share the feeling that their elders have failed to provide for them the sort of world they would like, and they seek alternative ways to achieve their own destinies.

Members of the older generation differ sharply in their attitudes toward youth's alienation and how to deal with it. Some authorities praise youthful critics for their concern and hail them as the harbingers of a new and perhaps better social order. They believe society should identify and preserve whatever is good in alienated youth's philosophies. Others feel that only adults have the expertise and maturity required to guide the world. According to the latter point of view, adults should provide the kind but firm leadership that a confused younger generation perhaps unconsciously seeks. Still others believe youth pose a threat to society and that its roots lie deep in defective social values and structures that deserve careful examination. A fourth group of authorities views alienation merely as an inevitable symptom of growing up, a natural concomitant of resolving personal and social conflicts.

DISCUSSION QUESTIONS AND ACTIVITIES

1. In what ways, if any, do you believe youth's recent alienation was a new form, different from historic representations of this phenomenon?

2. What forms, if any, does youthful alienation take on your campus? What forms did it take in your high school? In what ways does your school serve to intensify or reduce such alienation?

3. Interview one or more individuals who represent some type of alienation, concerning factors they believe led to their current attitudes, their reasons for protest, and how they feel protest activities have influenced their own lives and personalities. Compare notes in class on your findings.

4. Clip from current newspapers, journals, and teen magazines items relating to alienation. Analyze them and report to the class your conclusions about the causes of present-day youth's alienation.

5. Be prepared to debate the topic in class: Resolved, that, on balance, alienated youth make a positive contribution to our society.

6. Have you ever known a young person who became a juvenile delinquent? What factors do you believe contributed to his or her delinquency? Can you recall someone else who seemed destined for delinquency but turned out well? If so, can you explain this reversal in his or her behavior?

7. Collect newspaper items reporting crimes or antisocial activities involving juveniles. Discuss these items in class in terms of the nature of, and probable reasons for, these offenses.

8. List anonymously any of your own feelings of alienation. Indicate to what degree you feel inside or outside the mainstream of society and why. These may be collected and analyzed.

9. Briefly interview several adults of various ages regarding causes and modes of alienation when they were in high school and college. What measures might be taken by the government, schools, or other institutions to effectively reduce youth's alienation?

10. Debate pros and cons of the issue: A tough rather than a soft approach is more effective in dealing with delinquent youth.

SUGGESTED READINGS

Covington, J. (1982). Adolescent deviation and age. *Journal of Youth and Adolescence, 11*(4), 329–344. In this study, an age-based theory of delinquency is developed which identifies role transitions most likely to produce the anomic status conducive to deviant behaviors.

Ellis, P. L. (1982). Empathy: A factor in antisocial behavior. *Journal of Abnormal Child Psychology, 10*(1), 123–133. A comparison of 12- to 18-year-old institutionalized delinquents and nondelinquent controls helped to clarify the role of empathy in the development of antisocial behaviors.

Hoge, D. R., & Ankney, T. L. (1982). Occupations and attitudes of former student activists 10 years later. *Journal of Youth and Adolescence, 11*(5), 355–371.

Kramer, D. A. (1983). Post-formal operations? A need for further conceptualization. *Human Development, 26*, 91–105. Piaget's theory of cognitive development is discussed in terms of alternative conceptualizations and the need, if any, of postulating post-formal stages.

Kulka, R. A., Kahle, L. R., & Klingel, D. M. (1982). Aggression, deviance, and personality adaptation as antecedents and consequences of alienation and involvement in high school. *Journal of Youth and Adolescence, 11*(3), 261–279.

Levine, H. G., & Stumpf, S. H. (1983). Statements of fear through cultural symbols: Punk rock as a reflective subculture. *Youth and Society, 14*(4), 417–435. The punk rock culture is analyzed in terms of its origins, characteristics, and significance and its relationship to the wider culture.

Loeber, R. (1982). The stability of antisocial and delinquent child behavior: A review. *Child Development, 53*, 1431–1446. A review of the research indicates that chronic, compared with nonchronic, delinquents tend to have engaged in more varied antisocial behaviors as children, and at earlier ages.

Penner, M. J. (1982). The role of selected health problems in the causation of juvenile delinquency. *Adolescence, 17*(66), 347–368. This analysis of the role of selected health problems in the causation of delinquency suggests a direct and consistent relationship but not necessarily a causal one.

Realmuto, G. M., Shenehon, D. L., & Erickson, W. D. (1983). Deviant adolescents: Social rejection and psychiatric diagnosis. *Adolescence, 18*(70), 259–268. A study of adolescent inpatients indicated that deviant adolescents themselves tend to reject non-compliant adolescents, and to accept more open, trustworthy individuals.

Rich, P. (1982). The juvenile justice system and its treatment of the juvenile: An overview. *Adolescence, 17*(65), 141–152. A review of the history and philosophy of the American juvenile court system suggests the need for more adequate procedures.

Roberts, A. R. (1982). Adolescent runaways in suburbia: A new typology. *Adolescence, 17*(66), 387–396. Research is reviewed regarding the characteristics of runaways and a five-point continuum is proposed for judging the degree of seriousness of parent-youth conflict.

Segrave, J. O., & Hastad, D. N. (1983). Evaluating structural and control models of delinquency causation: A replication and extension. *Youth and Society, 14*(4), 437–456. This investigation into the etiology of delinquent behaviors showed social class to be a factor in delinquency and that theories of delinquency developed largely from male populations are equally applicable to females.

Tannenbaum, S. (1982). The self and youthful deviance: Some comparative notes. *Youth and Society, 14*(2), 235–254. This analysis of studies of relationships between the self and youthful deviance reported in the preceding articles discloses wide disagreements among the researchers concerned as well as certain common "parochialisms" or unfounded assumptions.

Thornton, W. E. (1982). Gender traits and delinquency involvement of boys and girls. *Adolescence, 17*(68), 749–768. This study, designed to determine how gender traits relate to delinquency, indicated a lack of such relationship as measured by frequency and type of offense.

Wilkerson, J., Protinsky, H. O., Mazwell, J. W., & Lentner, M. (1982). Alienation and ego identity in adolescents. *Adolescence, 17*(65), 133–139. A study of high school students indicated that as ego identity increases alienation moderately decreases, and that adolescents who successfully resolve identity crises will feel control over their destiny.

Chapter Eleven

Sex Roles
Of The Adolescent

The social sex role is a composite portrait of behavior patterns deemed proper for each sex. It is an ascribed status that distinguishes male and female behaviors from birth to death. The role carries with it a whole array of attitudes, feelings, and activities, as well as privileges, discriminations, and limitations. It may involve anything and everything associated with being a male or a female within a particular culture. For the sake of making this point vividly, let the reader imagine spending an entire day doing everything exactly as the other sex would do it!

In general, characteristics are labeled as masculine or feminine according to differential perceptions of the sexes within a particular society. Thus, in the United States, the Bem Sex Role Inventory categorizes the characteristics of ambition, self-reliance, independence, and assertiveness as masculine, while gentleness, compassion, affection, and sensitivity to others' needs as feminine. To the degree that individuals describe themselves in terms of both feminine and masculine characteristics, they are called androgynous.

Research regarding sex roles has zoomed from a near-zero baseline; nevertheless, certain common distortions persist. The vast majority of such research has involved middle-class subjects, which conveys the impression that changes in sex role have been more sweeping than they are. Also, studies of sex role are "culturally contaminated" because they are conducted by persons with their own special biases on the subject. Finally, findings may not be replicated in longitudinal samples that may originate today, because of the woman's movement and rapidly changing sex roles.

SIGNIFICANCE OF SOCIAL SEX ROLE

General Significance

With the foregoing caveat in mind, let us consider the significance of sex role, because it importantly influences the way individuals relate to themselves and to others. Sex role also determines how members of each sex behave toward others of their own and of the opposite sex: Mona acts almost as if she had two personalities, one for Tom, Dick, and Harry, and another for Sue, Sally, and Sherry.

The way individuals play sex roles subtly affects their reactions to all sorts of situations. For example, in a study of college students in four sex-role categories (masculine type, feminine types, androgynous, and undifferentiated) role-playing situations required appropriate expressions of either commendatory or refusal assertiveness. The androgynous subjects proved best in skills components for both kinds of situations; whereas the undifferentiated individuals were least effective. Surprisingly, the feminine-type persons did not compliment more effectively than did the masculine-type persons; nor were the masculine-type individuals better than the feminine-type in displaying convincing refusal assertion. Apparently "complex interpersonal situations require the use of well integrated masculine and feminine social skills" (Kelly, O'Brien &

Hosford, 1981). Friction arises from infringements on sex roles by individuals who defy the prevailing patterns. For example, many men disapprove of women's being assigned to serve on naval vessels.

Special Significance
During Adolescence

In adolescence, sex role and its accompanying problems spring into bold relief. Bodily changes that signal arrival of pubescence force a more rigid role definition. The girl stops playing football, and Tommy's all-boy gang is kid stuff now. From now on, boys and girls will be constantly and insistently reminded that they are male or female and that they must behave as such if they are to escape social penalties. The complementary relationship of the sexes is reflected throughout the organization of teenage society. At dances, the boy leads; the girl follows. In short, writes Adelson (1980), adolescence is that period in the life cycle when sex differences are the greatest. He says "it's an age when children become caricatures of male and female roles" (p. 68).

ACQUIRING A SOCIAL SEX ROLE

Biological Factors

Those who believe that sex-role distinctions are preordained by nature point to the historically and cross-cultural practice of assigning instrumental roles to males and nurturant ones to females. For example, with regard to physical initiation into sexual activity males in all the years studied have made first physical contact twice as often as females (Toffler, 1980). Moreover, a cross-cultural study of nurturant behaviors, in which an individual offers services or help to others, among children and preadolescents in India, Kenya, and Liberia (Edwards & Whiting, 1980) disclosed that, overall, girls behave more nurturantly than boys. Such differences in nurturance were most consistent in behaviors relating to very young children and least common in relation to mothers and older children; but in no dyadic interactions—that is involving two individuals—were boys more nurturant than girls. This finding is hardly surprising considering the female's traditional role in childbearing and childrearing, as well as the secondary role accorded her of rearing the family while the male deals with external affairs.

In contrast, John Money (1977) believes that biological bases for differentiating sex roles are relatively insignificant and that the focus should be on encouraging both sexes to realize their best potential and to dispense with artificial sex-role barriers. Hoffman (1978) concludes that sex roles may be based on biology but are not unalterable. They derive from women's inevitable role as childbearers, for until recently most women spent much of their lives in nursing and rearing children. However, because of their increased longevity, improved birth control, and smaller families, women devote a much smaller fraction of their lives to mothering than they formerly did. Women also return to work when their children are quite young.

Early Experience

Studies of how behaviors vary according to the perceived sex of an infant suggest that sex socialization begins early. When young women handled six-month old babies, two boys and two girls presented equally often as their own or the other sex, with sex-appropriate and cross-sex clothes and names, the women typically handed the toy hammer to the perceived boy and the toy doll to the perceived girl. They more often encouraged the perceived boy to crawl, walk, and engage in large-scale, vigorous, coordinated physical activities (Smith & Lloyd, 1978).

Thus, a child's views are shaped by parents, older siblings, and other significant adults through the selection of toys, stories, and clothes, and through manipulations of their early experiences. For example, toys commonly selected for boys are wheel toys, guns, building blocks, footballs, and the like, which encourage boys to be active and assertive (Chapman, 1978, p. 37). Fathers, especially, play masculine games with sons, but not with daughters, and handle them more roughly. Meantime, these same rough behaviors are frowned upon at school.

Boys are constantly exposed to models of males who value "material success, physical and psychological strength, leadership, and invulnerability; who suppress their fear, control their emotions; who are pragmatic, know all the answers, never seek help, are tough and independent" (Farrell, 1978, p. 22).

Once established, sex role is very persistent and resistant to change. By the age of 5 or 6, boys have introjected the notion that they should not act afraid or cry or behave in any way like girls. They come to reject in themselves any so-called feminine feelings of doubt or disappointment or the need for tenderness or love.

Boys are encouraged to be tough and aggressive. Through the centuries, young males have been the warriors—thus, society has capitalized on their aggression and toughness. "If universal conscription should be at 50 instead of 17," observes Skovholt (1978), "negotiations instead of combat would solve territorial disputes" (p. 6). Athletics is the counterpart of combat for most young American boys. By contrast, adults require that girls be more orderly and obedient; they tolerate more physical aggression from boys.

Sex-role Models

Both parents influence their children's sex-role development, the father more than the mother (Johnson, 1981). Especially during earliest years, he distinguishes more sharply than the mother between the way he treats the daughter and son. He maintains this distinction between them through adolescence.

In a study of 36 pairs of late-adolescent siblings it seemed that fathers, but not mothers, varied their sex-role behaviors in relating to their sons and daughters, constituting different sex role models for each (Heilbrun & Landauer, 1977). Thus, girls may acquire a feminine identity and boys a masculine identity, even if both identify primarily with the same father. That is, the father becomes the first to reinforce conventional sex-role behaviors in both sons and daughters.

Authorities differ regarding parental influence on their children's sex roles in adolescence. Some authorities believe that a clear distinction in sex-role behaviors is not developed until the teenage years (Frank, Athey, Coulston &

Parsons, 1982). Meantime, parents pressure their sons to be relatively more masculine—"that is, more assertive, dominant and achievement-oriented and daughters to be more feminine, that is sociable, submissive and nurturant" as they mature. Such pressures are further reinforced by their peers, counselors, and teachers (Baumrind, 1980; Schaffer, 1980). Moreover, parents still subscribe to and model the traditional sex roles (Baumrind, 1980).

In contrast, a study of undergraduates and their parents indicated that neither their fathers nor mothers stressed traditional sex-role expectations (Frank, Athey, Coulston & Parsons, 1982). Rather, the fathers had androgynous goals for their sons and the mothers emphasized more masculine expectations for their daughters. Thus their expectations for their children seemed well suited for making the most of their college experience.

Especially important is the way that parents define their marital roles and relationships. Those children display more socially appropriate masculinity and femininity when their parents as a couple play an appropriate model of masculinity-femininity or have a good marital adjustment (Klein & Schulman, 1981). Those children have most problems whose parents have poor marital adjustment and whose gender-linked roles are reversed, with the father assuming an expressive role and the mother a somewhat instrumental role.

Boys and girls are fully aware that their parents expect them to follow sex-typed activities, and by mid-childhood, the traditional roles are thoroughly rooted in most children. In Charlotte Zolotow's story, *William's Doll,* a small boy wants a doll. Estelle Nisenson asked her fourth, fifth, and sixth grade classes to comment on the theme of this story, and several of the answers follow (Shapiro, 1974, p. 43):

> GIRL: Boys should not have a doll. They will break it up. . . . They don't know how to take care of a doll.
>
> BOY: I think it was a very dumb idea about William buying a doll. A father shouldn't have to take care of a baby. A mother should. I think William is a sissy. Sissy and a queer.
>
> BOY: I don't think a boy should have a doll because it can send him on the wrong road to be a man.
>
> GIRL: Girls play boys' sports. We even have girl rabbis. So why shouldn't boys have dolls? I think it's cute.

In comparing the influence of parents and peers on adolescents' gender expectations males apparently experience greater parental influence than do females. One reason is that females closely affiliate with other females at this stage, and are simply more conforming to them (Loy & Norland, 1981).

Television is another source of learning gender roles and, though television's portrayal of these roles has become increasing nontraditional, the great majority are still stereotyped, according to traditional feminine and masculine roles (Petersen & Petersen, 1983). Men continue to control the world of work on television (Greenberg, 1982) whereas women are overly concerned with family life, romance, and marriage (U.S. Department of Health & Human Services, 1982). Often males are stereotyped as smart, rational, competitive, stable, powerful, ambitious, dominant, whereas women are seen as warm, romantic, sociable, attractive, sensitive, fair, peaceful, and submissive (Greenberg, 1982).

Petersen and Peters (1983) believe that television may contribute to distortions of sex roles by treating the topic mainly through "innuendo and humorous contexts, as in situation comedies, rather than realistic portrayals" (p. 80).

Haskell (1983) perceives in portrayals of leading women on television and movie screens reflections of changes in the women's movement. Already we have seen women in the movies being referred to as "post-feminists. This means big, beautiful, strong, but not—you know 'women's lib'" (p. 18). Haskell also notes a "built-in reflex to take elitist woman down a peg or two. That reflex, sadly, is stronger today than it was in the 30s and 40s probably because there are more of us who want to 'do it all' or 'have it all' and more areas in which to feel anxious and inadequate" (p. 20). She notes that the male is allowed to "have it all—a Harvard education, looks, glamour, wealth, well-shaped thighs—and no one resents him but bring on a female Warren Beatty and you will have the audience hissing" (p. 20).

Thus Haskell has become "leary of so-called breakthroughs in women's roles" (p. 20). In conflicts between career and marriage, women are often placed in "a no-win situation of stark contrast, in which the usual covert theme is chronic inadequacy" (p. 20). Formerly women actors actually had greater economic opportunities and more and better parts than in the so-called "enlightened '60s and '70s" (p. 23). Those actresses who wanted to build careers somewhat on their own terms found no writers to write appropriate scripts for them. No one knew how women should be portrayed—"truthfully—that is, as victims of a patriarchal and still heavily male-oriented society—or hopefully and progressively as vanquishers of mighty odds" (p. 23). "The trouble is," one writer-director said, "you can take a male star and make him a detective or lawyer or cop and get on with the picture. If you put a woman in the same role, you have to spend so much time explaining who she is and how she got there that the picture becomes that" (pp. 23–24).

Also, over the years, Hollywood has held its own "rigid idea of The Couples . . . young and beautiful men slightly older and slightly taller than the women, enshrined in images that we internalized as our ideal destiny . . ." (p. 24). Audiences simply reject endings of scripts in which the heroine "goes off into the sunset alone" (p. 24). Although the woman's movement and the fact that more women are working and going up the professional scale is requiring that movies react, they have not yet done so in effective ways. It is time for women to demand new versions of their movie roles. For example, do all rite-of-passage stories have to belong to men? Can we look forward to the time when "women who insist on seeing as well as being seen . . . will come to write, direct and act in stories that will illuminate our interior landscape, chart our passages . . . ?" (p. 27).

Despite such distortions, many adolescent females employ the media, including magazine fiction, to learn their cross-sexual scripts—indeed 6.5 million teenagers, mostly females, ages 13 to 19, read the magazine *Seventeen* (Reed & Coleman, 1981, p. 581).

To determine how role models of the sexes change over time, magazine fiction stories from *Seventeen* magazine were analyzed for the years 1961, 1967, and 1973. Stories were analyzed in terms of number of initiations of females or males in female-male interaction and they were scored female or male depending

Hollywood holds its own idea of "The Couple"—young and beautiful. (Photo by William J. Butcher)

on which sex spoke first in a particular sequence. For example, in one story a middle-aged man is strolling down the boardwalk checking out booths when Katie asks: "Try your luck, Sir?" This excerpt was scored as a female initiation. Physical initiations were scored, depending on which sex made first physical contact in such actions as kissing, reaching for the hand, or placing hand on arm. For example, the same girl, Katie, rushed over to a male and kissed him on the cheek, asking "Your birthday? That's for good luck." This was scored as a female initiation. Differences were also recorded in such sexual behaviors as kissing, petting, or coitus. In general, the stories indicated a trend away from passivity between 1967 and 1973 and a decline in that trend by 1979. In 1961 females initiated just 16 percent of narratives with males, whereas in 1967 and 1973 female initiations rose to 43 percent and 54 percent. However, in 1979 females initiated only 38 percent of the male-female interactions. Perhaps the trend back toward conservatism in 1979 reflects a more general picture in the country. Pressures to resume "the good old days" with regard to the nuclear family, sex roles, and morality have appeared in political campaigns and White House Conferences on the family.

AN ANALYSIS OF SOCIAL SEX ROLES

Several points must be kept in mind as orientation for the discussion that follows. First, it is applicable only to present-day culture in the Western world, especially in the United States. Second, the sex roles are discussed separately simply for the sake of clarity. The roles are interdependent, and whatever applies to one sex has implications for the other. Sex roles are not mutually exclusive or polar opposites; they are sometimes overlapping clusters in the same continuum. For example, boys are expected to be more aggressive than girls; yet girls may be aggressive under certain circumstances or in certain ways. With these points in mind, consider first the social sex role of females.

The Female Role in Our Society

The traditional American image of adult femininity is pretty consistently agreed upon and faithfully portrayed by the mass media. The image poses an attractive woman who jointly plays a number of roles (mother, wife, companion, and citizen) in the style and setting of a middle class suburban culture.

ADVANTAGES OF THE FEMALE ROLE   In certain ways, the female's traditional sex role puts less strain on her than the male's does on him. The girl is more sheltered as a child, and when she marries she may simply slip under the protection of her husband. There is less pressure on her to reach unrealistically high goals.

Many women construe the motherhood role as an advantage. They feel it a precious gift to be able to bear children. It is ego-strengthening to be the focal point of young children's existence. On the other hand, the modern woman may anchor her identity in work, basing her self-actualization on her individual talents. No longer, as in earlier times, need the woman simply nurture others, especially her husband and children.

Even the presumed disadvantages of woman's role have diminished. Douvan (1975) attributes the change in women's status chiefly to those factors having greatest impact on female socialization, such as improved education, vastly improved birth control technology, and the women's movement. The

Many women construe motherhood as an advantage and that it is a precious gift to bear children. (Courtesy of Public Relations Office, State University of New York at Oswego)

higher level of women's education today permits an intellectual companionship with the opposite sex. Education has also increased women's expectations of intrinsic satisfactions and intellectual stimulation. Meanwhile, birth control technology has separated sex and maternity from the core of feminine identity, permitting "a new integration in which the woman conceives of herself as fully developed, adult, sexual, and nonmaternal" (p. 33).

Girls who are satisfied with their sex roles give such reasons as these:

I am able to be flighty. When I want to relieve my tensions nothing much is thought of it.

I like to believe that the male sort of looks after me, brings me candy, and enjoys my company.

I like being the dominated sex; being respected and looked up to when I try to be a lady; being able to be a mother.

DISADVANTAGES OF THE FEMALE ROLE   Individual reactions vary greatly. Here several teenage-females tell what they dislike most about their sex role:

Not being able to do strenuous work simply because it is regarded as "mannish" or "tomboyish."

If you want to talk seriously, men won't accept it. Women have to rely too much on beauty.

While I sit at home, it is easy for boys to get dates.

FACTORS HARMFUL TO THE FEMALE PERSONALITY   The female sex culture has deprived girls from effectively developing a whole cluster of important abilities, including environmental mastery, problem solving, and achievement (Lee & Gropper, 1974). Nevertheless, many women have achieved according to male cultural standards without losing their basic identification with the female culture.

In dating, too, females are still expected to play a somewhat passive role. In one study Charlene Muehlenhard and Richard M. McFall asked male undergraduates how they would react if women asked them for a date, hinted for one, or simply waited to be asked. If the men liked the woman they said it would be all right for her to make the first move (Goodman, 1982). The young men rated intercourse against their date's wishes as more justifiable when the woman had initiated the date, if the couple had gone to the young man's apartment rather than to a religious function or movie, or if the man had paid for everything. Muehlenhard indicated that her findings should not be judged as supporting the view that women who are raped asked for it, but rather that women should realize that their behaviors are easily misinterpreted by men.

Those females are also disadvantaged who join the armed services. At the US Military Academy at West Point male cadets have a poor opinion of women's leadership ability and often resisted leadership attempts of female cadets (Adams, 1980). A major problem for these women is continuing to be women in a traditionally male situation. The Annapolis males were just out of high school upon arriving there; but women joining the Navy, at least before 1976, did so after college and after their identities as women had been set.

Women who entered the Academy often found themselves in "a no-win situation," and ways that they had of dealing with stress didn't seem to work here (p. 57). If they used traditional feminine means of coping with stress, such as crying or even smiling when somebody yelled at them, they were judged incompetent. If they behaved in more masculine ways they were viewed as "butch," and men didn't want to socialize with them. The men had norms for their behavior but the women as yet didn't have any.

The presumption that black female youth share a more favorable relationship with their men than white females with theirs is not true. They are mistreated more often than whites and they have more unfortunate experiences with their men. Perhaps the "popular but inaccurate view that black females have fared better, both educationally and economically than black males, has influenced negatively black male and female relationships . . ." (Smith, 1982).

The Male Role in Our Society

STATUS OF THE MALE ROLE   According to Fasteau (1975):

the male machine . . . is functional, designed mainly for work. He is programmed to tackle jobs, override obstacles, attack problems, overcome difficulties, and always take the offensive. He will take on any task that can be presented to him in a competitive framework. His most positive reinforcement is victory.

He has armor plating that is virtually impregnable. His circuits are never scrambled or overrun by irrelevant personal signals. He dominates and outperforms his fellows, though without excessive flashing of lights or clashing of gears. His relationship with other male machines is one of respect but not intimacy; it is difficult for him to connect his internal circuits to those of others. In fact, his internal circuitry is something of a mystery to him and he is maintained primarily by humans of the opposite sex. (p. 60)

The ideal role model of the complete male has changed over the centuries, with successive ages redefining its outlines and details according to current concepts of the image and proper duties of men (Crites & Fitzgerald, 1978). Among the most important of these models in Western thinking was that of the Renaissance man, which constituted a survival of the classical Greek model. This Renaissance ideal encompassed not merely rational aspects of the masculine model but affective characteristics, ordinarily labeled today as feminine. Thus, the Renaissance man was a complete individual liberated from the rigid confines of medieval times. One result was the production of some of the world's greatest all-time works of art, architecture, and literature.

In time, this Renaissance ideal became fractured as Reformation theologians attributed rational characteristics to men, turning them against affective feeling responses assigned to females. Such a duality was apparent some centuries later in the industrial revolution, which assigned men to the instrumental world of work and women to the home.

Even today the male is socialized to achieve characteristics associated with detective and adventure stories. He has purely instrumental characteristics and is lacking in emotional traits of nurturance, warmth and gentleness, and capacity for self-disclosure. Thus, "split off from half of his nature, a man restlessly seeks for it outside of himself" (p. 11). Although he unconsciously longs for this part of himself that he has been taught to hate, he has nevertheless been unable to develop nurturing, cooperative, intimate relationships with either sex. To achieve the goal of being a "competent male" he must be "half a human being" (p. 11).

ADVANTAGES OF THE MALE ROLE   The traditional male role has many well-recognized advantages. It is ego strengthening for males to live in a world that is ordered by males. Men usually are trained for the higher positions that carry the most power and prestige. Also ego strengthening is the male's sex advantage. The homely male can have a date while his unattractive sister sits at home. From adolescence onward, females outnumber males. In social situations, an extra male is an asset; an extra female is a liability. Besides, the unmarried man has a freedom of movement and action denied to the unmarried woman.

In addition, society attaches higher value to masculinity than femininity. Distinctions between the sexes that proved adaptive in less advanced societies may no longer be appropriate in fostering adjustment; however, within America male behaviors and characteristics are still highly valued and rewarded (Lerner, Sorell & Brachney, 1981). High self-esteem requires both femininity and masculinity, but greater emphasis on masculinity in both sexes. Lamke (1982) concluded that in early adolescence, late adolescence, and adulthood the degree of masculinity relates to self-esteem in both sexes.

Other writers disagree regarding the generally optimal proportion of masculinity, femininity, or androgyny (combining the best of an individual's potential for both roles). First, note the three main theoretical perspectives for predicting the relationship between sex-role orientation and adjustment in adolescence (Avery, 1982). Theories of sex-role development have emphasized the importance of establishing a traditional sex-role identity at this period. A second perspective emphasizes the need to develop an androgynous identity characterized by higher levels of both feminine and masculine characteristics. Androgyny presumably relates to psychological well-being since it allows individuals to employ both feminine and masculine capabilities and potential in social interaction. A third, and most recent view regarding adjustment in sex-role orientation, is that masculinity is most highly predictive of positive mental health (Lerner, Sorell & Brackney, 1981). It suggests that the masculinity-femininity dichotomy of the sexes, which may have proved adaptive in less technologically advanced eras, is no longer adaptive these days. It also suggests that in present-day America masculine behaviors and traits are highly valued. From this perspective both masculine (high masculine-low feminine) and androgynous (high masculine-high feminine) persons will adjust better than feminine (low masculine-high feminine) or undifferentiated (low masculine or low feminine) persons.

Males express general satisfaction with their role. Here several college youth say what they like about it:

> Greater freedom; being treated less strictly.
>
> Sports, outdoor life; man's role in general.
>
> I can do things that if done by the other sex would bring criticism—for example, staying out all night, going out drinking . . . or just taking off to another campus for a weekend.

DISADVANTAGES OF THE MALE ROLE   The male's role, however, has its drawbacks. Among them are problems relating to sex. Parents take for granted that their sons can take care of themselves sexually. The result is often an appalling ignorance, disguised by a pretense of knowing it all. Furthermore, the height of the male's sex drive comes in the late teens when he still lacks the resources and maturity to deal with it. Meantime, "the notion that [men] must be perfect Lotharios directing the sexual scene with cool dominance, locks [them] (and the women with whom [they] make love) into playing the same roles every time, [and discourages] spontaneity and variety" (Fasteau, 1975, p. 60).

The male's greatest handicap is inherent in the cultural concept of masculinity itself. Males are taught to be self-sufficient; hence, they are often awkward in human relationships. They are competitive and less comfortable about expressing warmth and support than females are. The man focuses on dealing with the outer world and ignores his inner world. Even if he rises to the pinnacle of success in middle age, he may face crises as he realizes that he has missed many of the significant experiences in life (Crites & Fitzgerald, 1978).

The Androgynous Sex Role

A review of the research (Frank, Athey, Coulston & Parsons, 1982) indicates that whether androgynous or masculine identity is most adaptive is uncertain; however, neither would appear to be superior to a feminine identity in furthering the undergraduate's psychological well-being. Rubenstein (1980) notes that recent research suggests that individuals who are traditionally masculine or feminine are handicapped, and that androgyny "became something of

Males are taught to be self-sufficient and are then often awkward in human relationships. (Courtesy of Public Relations Office, State University of New York at Oswego)

a buzz word" (p. 27). Androgynous individuals were portrayed as possessing the best of both masculine and feminine traits—hence, might engage flexibly and comfortably in both feminine and masculine behaviors.

Rubenstein cites commentary by Faye Crosby, a Yale psychologist, and Linda Nyquist, which raises questions about androgyny research. For one thing, scales employed to measure androgyny vary among themselves. Crosby and Nyquist also question whether flexible behaviors are always appropriate. For if the idea of flexibility is pushed to its extreme the bisexual individual, who is more flexible than either homosexuals or heterosexuals, might be considered psychologically healthier than either. They also suggest that adolescents who possess a broad range of both traditionally male and female characteristics might suffer from "ego identity diffusion"; or the young mother might be characterized as "ambivalent, even . . . the kind of schizophrenogenic [individual] who puts her children in a double bind" (p. 27).

They complain that the virtue of psychological androgyny was embraced before it was adequately researched, partly because it fitted the women's movement's goal of encouraging women to enter the "masculine domain of work," and men to help with the "expressive, feminine arena of home and child care" (p. 27).

This writer would like to point out that the concept of androgyny, as ordinarily defined, refers to characteristics in general and is not intended to apply to such specifically biological functioning as intercourse and, although studies of androgyny might vary, the sum total of such research—and it is research—is overwhelmingly on the side of the androgynous individual, especially after adolescence. Since adolescents have typically not been brought up in an androgynous fashion, even by androgynous parents who are hesitant about bringing up their children androgynously in a still mostly traditional world, any abrupt attempt to drag them immediately into androgyny might result in temporary ego identity diffusion. In the long run, however, research proves them better off. Anyhow, children brought up in an androgynous manner from birth on would suffer from no such diffusion. In almost any area one can name, one can find studies and instruments that yield somewhat different data. The challenge is to find those scales which are the most adequate.

Spence and Helmreich (1980) believe that concepts of sex-role differentiation are typically oversimplified. Currently men's and women's societal roles are not differentiated according to presumed temperamental differences, that is, instrumentality in males and expressiveness in females. Males are expected both to be assertive and to relate well to others. Females in the work world must be somewhat competitive if they are to advance, yet be nurturant at home. The truth is sex roles, as practiced, relate little to dichotomous, expressive, and instrumental traits dimensions. A whole complex of variables, including an individual's interests, attitudes, values, and changing situations account for particular sex-role attitudes and behaviors (Spence & Helmreich, 1980).

Current Sex Roles

To what extent has the women's liberation movement altered sex roles? It has undoubtedly influenced sex-role attitudes, though probably less than generally believed. Among sixth and seventh grade students the feminist ideology seemed to have had little impact on the girls' self-concepts or attitudes about their own sex (Bush, et al., 1977–1978). The girls had poorer self-concepts and devaluated their own sex roles more than boys did.

Among junior high school adolescents, ages 12 through 15, both sexes perceived differences in their sex role, directed chiefly toward traditional stereotypes. Surprisingly, both sexes perceived positive nonstereotyped words as being more typical of females and negative words more typical of males. They regarded words such as "nice" and "friendly" as feminine and words like "fights" and "stubborn" as masculine. Thus, it appears that both sexes are coming to perceive femininity as more desirable than before (Rust & Lloyd, 1982).

Parents underestimate the influence of traditional sex roles on their children's own attitudes and feelings. Perhaps because of the woman's movement they wrongly conclude that the world has become "as open" to their daughters as to their sons, and that their sons have become less macho and more open to their own feelings. In certain middle-class suburban high schools in the Chicago area the girls felt more conflict and fear regarding the competitive job market than their parents realized, whereas the boys were less open to emotions that might violate the macho image (Offer, Ostrov & Howard, 1981).

Especially in high school males and females have somewhat different ideals for the sexes. A study of high school students in a medium-sized southeastern city disclosed considerable sex difference in early adolescents' images of the ideal female and male. The early adolescent females stressed, in particular, two major dimensions of ideal masculinity more than the male adolescents did, these being emotional expression and altruistic understanding. Both sexes considered these traits to be descriptive of the ideal male; however, the females stressed it more. Both sexes named "gentleness, gratitude, emotional disclosure, kindness and understanding as characteristic of ideal males" (Curry & Hock, 1981, p. 787). The greatest sex difference in rating ideal masculinity concerned tender feeling, which was viewed as feminine by the boys but masculine by the girls.

With regard to the ideal female girls emphasized emotional expression and altruistic understanding more than did the boys. Both sexes judged competence and confidence important for the ideal female but adolescent females stressed it to a greater degree than did the males; and they were more likely to endorse self-assertion and mastery as feminine traits.

In addition, boys made significantly more discriminations between the sexes than did the girls. One reason may be the girls' lack of perceived differences derives from recent changes in sex-role stereotypes. Perceiving fewer differences between ideal femininity and masculinity is one aspect of stressing sex equality. Another reason is that for boys making more sex-role discrimination begins in childhood. Parents, especially the fathers, differentiate the children according to sex and emphasize masculinity in their sons. Boys are brought up to make greater sex-role differentiations than are girls.

Also, in comparing these sex-role ideals, girls are not stressing differences in agency traits such as assertiveness, leadership, and decision-making for the sexes but boys do make such a difference. Thus adolescent girls are now supporting task competence as a characteristic of ideal females and not differentiating the sexes on this dimension. In short, with regard to ideal sex-role discrimination girls make very little difference. Cultural changes are taking place in the agency roles of females and changing their ideals, but these changes are having less impact on young adolescent boys (Currey & Hock, 1981).

Even college students continue to support traditional sex roles, at least in their more fundamental aspects. While 40 percent of college-age subjects preferred no sex differences on 14 personality characteristics, another 60 percent favored such differences along traditional lines (Hamilton, 1977). These students believed it to be more appropriate for girls to display nurturance, deference, and abasement and for boys to be characterized by dominance, autonomy, exhibition, aggression, and achievement.

Nevertheless, most studies indicate some erosion of stereotypes, especially women's. A comparison of various sex-role studies indicates that college women recently are becoming more agentic in their sex-role attitudes. That is, they focus on activity and achievement, and this shift toward greater masculinity is supported by their mothers (Frank, Athey, Coulston & Parsons, 1982).

Similarly, a questionnaire administered to 430 students at Bradley University and again two years later indicated that attitudes toward women in general became more liberal for both sexes. Also for both sexes attitudes toward women's vocational and educational rights became more liberal than those concerning women's maternal and marital responsibilities. One may ponder to what extent this change reflected the differential dropout rate for more traditionally oriented students. Among those who had persisted through the two years about 25 percent, the same for both sexes, became more traditional. Perhaps this minority was influenced by the slight retreat in the country toward traditionalism (Etaugh & Spandikow, 1981).

Other research among undergraduates at the University of California at Berkeley indicated that women's work is, in general, not devalued, especially by women. There, as at other universities which have women's studies programs, the women's movement has received a great deal of support. There also has been much experimentation with alternative life styles. Indeed, both sexes have "ultramodern ideas" regarding the sexes' rights and roles (Isaacs, 1981).

Currently, the most common pattern for females to anticipate combining is marriage and career while placing more emphasis on their wife-mother role. Of 140 women at a small liberal arts college in Ohio, 90 percent wanted to have at least one child (Mash, 1978). About 81 percent of those who planned to have children also expected to work outside the home at some time, and a third had a sufficiently strong career commitment that they would continue to work even when their children were preschool age. Thus, young women no longer choose between career or family but intend to combine them. Yet they still give very high priority to motherhood. Their feelings about marrying and having children are as strong as in former generations.

FACTORS INFLUENCING CURRENT SEX-ROLE STATUS   Sex-role attitudes vary according to many factors, including the times. Comparison of data obtained in 1934 and 1974 disclosed a general trend toward equalitarian sex attitudes (Roper & Labeff, 1977). However, women university students remained more likely than men to approve equalitarian ideals as expressed by feminists. Both sexes persist in somewhat traditional views regarding sex-role division of labor in the home. Attitudes regarding speech, dress, and moral behaviors also remain somewhat traditional. At both periods, the higher the education level, the more feminist were the students' attitudes. Both generations of students were more favorable toward such feminist issues as economic and legal status than toward conduct and domestic matters.

In general children display more sex-role stereotyping than do youth, especially those in college. A comparision of 48 second and third graders with 48 college freshmen indicated that the children employed high stereotyping of sex roles, whereas the college students indicated little. The children disapproved manifestations of anger by women more than by men and they approved fearful behaviors more in women than in men. They disapproved helpfulness and poor sportsmanship demonstrated by males more than by females. Girls showed greater approval than did boys of both sexes showing independent behaviors, but boys gave both boys and girls greater approval than did the girls of domestic behaviors. In contrast, the college students demonstrated stereotyping of sex roles in only one case—that is, by disapproving fearful behaviors more in males than in females (Hensley & Borges, 1981).

A comparison of black and white females indicates that there is no difference between them in feminist outlook although there has been a tradition that black females have a tradition of being stronger. Historically, American plantation slavery distinguished between roles of the sexes, whereas white women were perceived as soft, weak, and delicate. It was also presumed that ghetto life required development of independence and self-reliance. Since then black women have been viewed as already liberated. On the other hand, in just recent years white women have been affected by the woman's movement; hence their relative status has greatly improved. Furthermore, recently many white women have come to experience less traditional sex-role training and work. It is also possible that the black female's self-sufficiency has been previously overstated.

Black males are more traditional than white males, especially in terms of expecting women to run the home and men to run the country. They believe that men are better suited emotionally for politics than women are. They don't object to their wives' working, but they do object to their having high political positions in the community. The black power emphasis has played up the assertiveness of black males and their occupation of positions of power and leadership (Ransford & Miller, 1983). For their part, black women are more likely than white women to rate men as economically untrustworthy.

Popular views of feminists on sex-role issues are distorted. In a study of midwestern female undergraduates the feminists and nonfeminists did not differ in how they evaluated male and female stereotyped traits. They rated both sets of characteristics neutrally to moderately positive, in contrast to previous research indicating more favorable evaluation of male characteristics. Perhaps there has been general reduction in positive evaluations of male characteristics and an increase in positive evaluations of female traits.

The data indicating feminists' similar evaluation of female and male characteristics suggest that feminists do not support women's "belittling" men and that they demonstrate a "key aspect of feminist ideology—that women and men are equally valuable" (p. 92). The nonfeminists, too, evaluated women's traits similarly instead of favoring men's characteristics, possibly because of the recent publicity given views of feminists. That is, it may be no longer acceptable to favor men over women. It may still be questioned whether reports such as these indicate genuine changes in students' attitudes or simply a recognition of presently fashionable views toward women (Rapin & Cooper, 1980).

Residual Status of Sex Roles

There is disagreement about the current status of sex roles today. For the second half of the 1970s, the original women's liberation movement lost its momentum, having been displaced by a "new feminism." The new feminism is not "an organized movement; nor does it hold meetings or press conferences. It is an all-pervasive rise in female awareness that has permeated virtually every level of womanhood in America, at all ages. Such feminists lack sympathy with the formal liberation movement. Their feminism applies to women who want to be women in the traditional sense but insist on their social and economic rights.

Nevertheless, Skovholt (1978) declares that the evolution in sex roles is the "most viable evolutionary-revolutionary movement" in the country today. Realignment of sex roles has produced all sorts of conflicting emotions: "hope and despair, fear and tranquility, anger and joy, resentment and appreciation. Most of all, the burning of old blueprints for our lives brings anxiety, the kind of anxiety which accompanies the hopeful traveler who goes forward without a map" (p. 3). The most obvious changes in sex role relate to women who are invading many activities formerly dominated by men, including weight lifting, ice hockey, and long-distance running.

The realignment of sex roles, believes Skovholt, derives from changing needs in the evolution of the species. The plasticity of roles has allowed societies to exact different characteristics and behaviors from the sexes in different periods in history and either play up or down the biological differences between them. The evolution to a technological society, in which major social functions place little premium on sexual differences, has tended to depolarize the sex roles.

ARE BASIC CHANGES POSSIBLE OR DESIRABLE?   The question arises whether sex roles should or can be modified. To what extent are they biologically decreed or negotiable? Is the liberated woman or the happy housewife the ideal? Those who urge conformity suggest that individuals who find it easy to go along with the prescribed roles are happier. In the area of sex role, as in any other, those who can accept the status quo are more comfortable than those who attempt reform.

Another argument against change is the tendency, already noted, to think of sex differences as being firmly rooted in biological fact. While it may be conceded that sex roles which harmonize with biological potential will function best, further research is needed to define that potential. Rossi (1977) believes that sex differences are firmly and permanently rooted in biology and that family systems depend upon the women's role in reproduction and childrearing. Current views of sexual equality and variant family forms do not take into account the biosocial fundamentals.

REASONS FOR MODIFYING SEX ROLES   In addition to reasons for altering sex roles implicit in the earlier discussion, there are others. Sex-role researcher Sandra Bem (1975) concludes that "we need a new standard of psychological health for the sexes, one that removes the burden of stereotype and allows people to feel free to express the best traits of men and women" (p. 59).

High scores in traditionally feminine traits consistently correlate with "high anxiety, low self-esteem, and low self-acceptance. And although high masculinity in males has been related to better psychological adjustment during adolescence, it is often accompanied during adulthood by high anxiety, high neuroticism, and low self-acceptance" (p. 59). Freeing people from rigid sex roles and permitting them to be androgynous (*andro* from the Greek for "male" and *gyne* from the Greek for "female") would produce more flexibility and fewer restrictions concerning what one can do. The ideal is not to produce masculinized females or feminized males but to let all persons be individuals.

The more negative aspects of each sex role should be resolved. For example, males should learn to relate to each other on a deeper, more human level. For their part, females should be emancipated from the almost total responsibility in matters of sexual expression including abortion, contraception, and adoption (Wagner, 1980).

Both individuals and society pay a penalty for strict dichotomization of sex roles—that is, the division of life tasks and privileges into mutually exclusive realms. Traditional male sex role traits may even endanger the species' survival because they are not adaptive. The more aggressive, competitive male is more likely to participate in the depletion of world-wide resources and the production of better technologies for destruction. It is obvious that deleting "lethal elements in male socialization [would] be a smart move" (Skovholt, 1978, p. 6). On the individual level, both sexes can best attain the good life if they develop all their gifts.

Programs designed to modify sex roles may fail if not carefully planned. Psychologist Thelma Jean Wortenberg compared two groups of middle-class seventh graders, one in which the boys took electrical wiring, woodworking, printing, and metalworking while the girls studied only cooking and sewing, and in the other, both sexes studied all six topics. At the end of the year the children in the sex-integrated classes had changed neither their vocational interests nor stereotyped views of the sexes, partly because of their parents' and teachers' attitudes (Adams, 1980). The parents typically down-played the importance of industrial arts for girls and expected them to be successful in women's jobs. The teachers' views were similar, and although they favored coeducational courses in practical arts they expressed sexual biases in class. A more effective way to reduce sex stereotype, says Wortenberg, would be to take children on field trips to see women carpenters and male nurses at work.

It should be added that a sizable and growing minority would oppose such programs and revert to traditional sex roles. Some people are saying that "opposing abortion or wiping out sex education or resisting feminism would glue the family back together again" and that women who are very independent are often called "defeminized, cold, tough, and—objective" (Toffler, 1980).

HETEROSEXUAL ADJUSTMENT

Thus far our discussion has concerned sex roles singly. Now we shall consider heterosexual adjustment—that is, social sex roles as they relate to each other or to interdependent activities. Achievement of this adjustment involves the capacity to love and to be loved in the fullest meaning of intimacy. It also means being able to be deeply fond of a person of the opposite sex as a friend. It connotes the capacity to find enjoyment in the various situations where men and women mingle socially and vocationally outside the home.

Feinstein and Ardon (1973) divide adolescent heterosexual development into four stages, the first being that of sexual awakening at ages 13 to 15. The frequently described antagonism between preadolescent boys and girls is interpreted as a mutual striving for sexual identity. Thereafter, hostility declines and is displaced by friendship with erotic overtones. Kissing and petting ("making out") are heterosexual, nonplatonic aspects of their relationships. During this period, many adolescents worry lest they are not attractive to the other sex. The second, or practicing stage, ages 14 to 17, is characterized by numerous short-term relationships. At this stage, dating is irregular and not perceived as all-important. Nondaters do not feel self-conscious or deviant. The only ones concerned may be parents, especially mothers. Dating in this stage may be on either a group or an individual basis. The third stage, ages 16 to 19, is marked by acceptance of the sexual role. At this point, adolescents face the task of establishing close relationships with others and settle down to a more regular dating pattern. They experiment with various dating models, date for longer terms, experiment increasingly with sex, and are more likely to engage in sexual intercourse. In the fourth stage, ages 18 to 25, the mature ego is capable of identifying with a love object. When this stage culminates in courtship, sex becomes a part of the traditional pattern, with progressively greater amounts of sexual intimacy traded for greater emotional commitment.

Dating

VALUES Heterosexual relationships prior to courtship may assume the form of dating. The rules are usually implicit instead of explicit, involving friendly relations with increasing sexual intimacy. The dating partners use various strategies within the limits of these unwritten rules to obtain their ultimate goal, a suitable marriage partner.

Dating serves four main functions, the first being to provide recreation. In one study, girls interviewed on the subject agreed that dating was a marvelous experience:

> It's the best. You just have more fun. You find more things to do. You have somebody to talk to. I love it. What would you do without boys?
>
> If I'm with someone I like, it's a lot of fun. It's nice to talk with a guy. It's different than with girls—something different to relate to. It makes me feel good. (Place, 1975, p. 173)

Second, dating is a form of socialization, permitting persons of the opposite sex to develop appropriate techniques of interaction. Third, dating is a means of status grading and status achievement. Through dating persons rated as desirable by one's peer group, individuals may raise their own prestige within the group.

While individuals have various reasons for dating each other, motives vary from one individual to another. One boy may date primarily in order to obtain sex favors more easily; another may do so because he needs an audience for tales of his strivings and exploits. One girl dates because she enjoys dinners, dances, and shows; another, because she gains status in the eyes of her friends.

DATING PRACTICES   Traditionally, dating has been a sexist affair with the male asking the female out, driving his car, deciding where to go, and paying the bills; however, the picture is gradually changing. Anne Petplau reported in a study of 200 student couples that 95 percent of the women and 87 percent of the men believed that dating partners should participate equally in determining the nature of the relationship. Fewer than half had achieved this goal in their own relationships, indicating a gap between ideals and reality (Akchin, 1978/79).

The frequency of dating varies according to age and sex. A study of eighth graders in Georgia indicated that 65 percent of the white boys, 35 percent of the white girls, 55 percent of the black boys, and 38 percent of the black girls were allowed to date (Schab, 1982).

Another survey of students attending junior and senior high schools in a large southeastern city indicated that the largest increase in dating frequency for females was between ages 15 to 16. From junior to senior high school the percentage not dating had fallen from 42 percent to 17 percent, and the fraction of those dating as often as two or three times a week had grown from 10 percent to 35 percent (Loy & Norland, 1981).

Among middle-class high school seniors in Texas there were apparently dangers involved in adolescents' beginning to date either too early or too late. Early dating related both to drug use and drug problems, perhaps because parents who allow early dating also provide less supervision and give greater freedom for experimenting with drugs. Also, over half the early daters used tobacco frequently, suggesting that parents who allow early dating are also more tolerant of their children's smoking. Early daters rated themselves as being more independent and confident, but also more tired than those dating later. Of the total population of ninety-five, seven of the nine subjects who reported serious suicidal thoughts had not been given permission to date until they were 16 or older, perhaps because their mothers were overly strict, thus creating a poorer parent-child relationship.

Three of the ninety-five said that parents let them date too early and twelve said that parents allowed them to date too late. All of these fifteen subjects had more than the average number of problems. The early daters reported drinking problems; and of the late daters, almost 60 percent said their childhood was unhappy. Also interesting was that four in five of the total ninety-five said that they had dated many times before obtaining their parents' permission. Dating without permission correlated highly with delinquency and illicit drug use (Wright, 1982).

Elkind (1980) believes that teenagers often date largely for the purpose of having an audience. In getting dates one proves to oneself one's own attractiveness just as refusing offers of dates from others does the same. Sexual activity, too, may be employed strategically, aside from other satisfactions involved, but the strategy is employed differently by the sexes. The male's strategy usually is to test the limits, trying to get as much from the girl as he can. The girl answers nonverbally, either moving toward or away from him in the process. The successes a boy achieves he can share with his friends, whereas girls are more uncertain about the self-esteem involved in giving in. Those who continue to utilize their social situations for ego gratification, says Elkind, are still at the adolescent level of maturity.

A long-held presumption that high school and college youth take prestige significantly into account in choosing dates is no longer valid (Gordon, 1981). Such values might have existed in the 20s, but not today when more humanistic values prevail. Relations between the sexes are more sincere, profound, and searching although popularity, good grooming, and good looks are still important.

Males still expect more sexual intimacy on dates and after a fewer number of dates than do women. Few daters believe their partners share their own feelings regarding sexual behaviors (Knox & Wilson, 1981). However, dating couples' disagreements are about the same as differences between people in other types of relationships. In a longitudinal study of 231 dating couples background factors did not relate to their different perceptions, and each partner interpreted these discrepancies somewhat differently (Hill, Peplau & Rubin, 1981).

A survey of over 500 students at East Carolina University disclosed how they first met their dates and what they did on dates, among other things (Knox & Wilson, 1981). About a third met their current dating partners through a friend, others at a party or at work or in school. The typical pattern was to go out to eat, to a ballgame, or to a party, and then back to his or her room; for those who didn't do all these things eating and going to his or her place were the common activities. The most common topic of discussion, reported by a third, was their relationship. School and friends were also discussed, but sex less than 5 percent of the time. With regard to sexual behaviors on dates 70 percent of the males and half the females felt that it was all right to kiss on the first date, and by the fourth date all the students, except 3 percent of the women, felt kissing was all right. With regard to petting (hands anywhere), three-fourths of the females and a third of the males believed that petting should be put off until after the first date, but a third of the males believed it was all right on the first date. As for intercourse, half the males compared with 25 percent of the females believed intercourse was appropriate by the fifth date. Only 15 percent of both sexes said that their dates shared their own views on the above matters. In general, the more involved they were, the more appropriate they considered greater levels of intimacy, the women more than the men. Only 1 percent of the women compared with 10 percent of the men felt intercourse without affection was all right.

The sexes differed little in ways that they encouraged or discouraged intimacy. A third of the females and a quarter of the males might encourage sexual intimacy, through saying something to that effect. Other ways included creating an atmosphere through music, candles, and so forth, by moving closer to the other or hinting. Although drugs were not mentioned as a means of encouraging intimacy over half had consumed alcohol on their last date and a quarter of the males and 20 percent of the females had smoked marijuana on their last date. Both partners simply told their partner to stop when they did not want sex.

Although most students believe they want an equal relationship with their romantic partner, fewer than half have achieved it. The majority succumb to the traditional pattern of masculine superiority, while only a tiny minority allow the female to be dominant. There is little difference in satisfaction between traditional and equalitarian couples, probably because couples settle for those relationships which they find personally acceptable. Female-dominated relationships work out least well because the rules of the game are as yet unclear about this pattern. Uncertain guidelines encourage anxiety because there is no generally agreed upon etiquette and ritual for such relationships (Akchin, 1978/79).

Current dating styles may be classified as formal, casual, or group. Informal dates are growing more egalitarian while formal dates are still somewhat traditional. The trend is toward more casual dating without much dressing up or spending. Some students avoid group situations, especially after an affair becomes serious, while many others prefer group outings. Still others like both formal and informal types of dating, reserving formal dates for encounters with a romantic flavor.

The coed dormitory has had considerable influence on such relations. Most dorms are fine for making friends but poor for developing romances. As one young woman undergraduate expressed it, "Going out with someone I'll be seeing for the next four years would be practically incestuous" (Akchin, 1978/79, p. 138).

RECENT TRENDS Youth's heterosexual relationships are taking new directions in dating practices and in other ways as well. The formal dating of the past has been replaced by informal, formless socializing. High school youth attend parties and dances in groups instead of as couples. After high school, groups shrink in size and more dating occurs. The male still does the asking and paying—certainly for the first few dates—and girls rarely ask boys for dates. However, dates are far less supervised than in former years, and less time elapses between the initiation of dates and entering sexual relationships. Couples more often share the expenses of dating, especially if they go steady. Several couples often go places together more often than formerly. Youth have became aware of the inadequacies of the mating-dating game and the abuse of purely sexual relationships. Accordingly increasing numbers of them are abandoning traditional practices and living together either as couples or as groups.

Premarital Cohabitation

Increasing minorities of young people are trying out alternative life styles and viewing them as viable options. Whether this trend will last and what its effects may be are uncertain. Such styles include extramarital sex relations with mutual consent, "marriage" between homosexual persons, group marriage, and communal and cohabitational living.

Over the past few decades cohabitation, the practice of unmarried persons living together, has greatly increased. It may be perceived "as an alternative to marriage, a type of trial marriage, or simply a variation in the courtship process . . ." (Bayer & McDonald, 1981, p. 387). Indeed, cohabitation is rapidly growing, not just among young adults, but among all age groupings in America.

The practice of cohabitation has not yet been fully legally defined, although scattered court cases may, after they reach sufficient number, set important precedents (Newcomb, 1979). These cases deal with such matters as oral contracts between cohabitants, the value of the woman's services for the purposes of property settlement after the couple separate, and the rights and support of illegitimate children.

Polansky, McDonald, and Martin (1978) reported little difference between marriage partners and cohabitants with regard to emotional closeness and stability. Olday (1977) reported that cohabitation was no more effective than traditional courtship for the purpose of finding an appropriate marital partner.

At Cornell University, over three-fourths of the students interviewed rated the cohabitation relationship as sexually satisfying. Almost all used contraception; over 80 percent used either the pill or the diaphragm. Many students listed parents as a major problem, saying that they disapproved of a boy or girl friend.

Problems relating to living situation, such as lack of privacy, lack of adequate space, and disagreements over money, were judged minor. Over half rated their relationship as successful, and over 80 percent believed that it was maturing and pleasant. They felt they had gained better understanding of themselves and of their own needs and expectations; more knowledge of such relationships and the problems of living with someone else; a clarification of their relations with the other sex; improved emotional maturity and self-confidence; and greater emotional security and companionship. A thread running through all their discussions of benefits was the belief that they had matured. Even those who had found the relationship painful felt that personal growth had occurred.

In a study of cohabitation which "was defined as sharing a bed for four or more nights a week for four months or longer" the significance of this practice proved somewhat different for the sexes (Abernathy, 1981, p. 792). For males cohabitation seemed little different from dating; for females it represented something quite different from the traditional stage of courtship between dating and marriage. Cohabiting females were far more negative than males in their definition of marriage and marital roles, to such an extent that their perceptions were more similar to those of males than of other females. Certainly, for adolescent females college cohabitation is quite different from either dating or marriage.

A review of the research indicates that sexual cohabitation derives from a number of factors: the introduction of birth control pills, changing attitudes regarding sex, adolescents' efforts to develop more meaningful relationships, and more relaxed residence regulations in the colleges (Abernathy, 1981). Personality also plays a role—in general those persons who practice cohabitation differ from those who do not. They are more liberal and far left and live in the northeast. Individuals are less likely to practice it who attend church regularly, are religious fundamentalists, and live outside the northeast (Bayer & McDonald, 1981).

Many young people are taking with them into adulthood a lifestyle of sexual cohabitation without marriage, although most of them marry eventually. In 1950, of all couples ages 25 to 40 who lived together, 85 percent were married; by 1970 that number had fallen to 80 percent (Scanlon, 1979).

Another trend, toward older age at marriage, will add a degree of stability because the marital partners will be more mature. Besides, more people will live together before marriage and, hence, have a better chance either of remaining together afterward or not marrying at all. Thus, there may be a larger number of more enduring marriages at the same time that the number of divorces arise (When "family," 1983). Both sexes, especially as they approach the 20s, attach a high value to future marriage; however, women place a higher premium on getting married than men do. Women often marry the first chance they have, the result being that they marry at a younger age than men. In addition, women are more likely than men to interrupt their education in order to get married (Marini, 1978).

Choosing a Mate

In former times, parents played an important part in arranging their children's marriages. Since daughters usually lived at home, parents were in a strategic position for getting rid of undesirable suitors. Parents also played a significant but lesser role in the son's search for a mate (Cornish, 1979).

Today's parents are still involved, but less than formerly. Although the mate selection system in this country has been described as self-selective on the part of youth, 60 percent of the females and 40 percent of the males said their parents tried to influence them in their dating choice. The females more often said that it was important for them to date people whom their parents approved. We might question, therefore, whether mate selection in America is as free as formerly believed. Despite the presumed generation gap, most of the students regarded their parents' involvement positively, with only 25 percent feeling quite negative about it (Knox & Wilson, 1981).

Most adolescents possess either a conscious or an unconscious image of their ideal mate, derived from many impressions, some of them originating in earliest childhood, and partially traceable to their parents. The boy whose mother personifies his ideal of womanhood may unconsciously choose a girl who reminds him of her. A once popular song contains this sentiment: "I want a girl just like the girl who married dear old Dad."

Early childhood experiences are not the whole story. Many things in a person's life experience, as well as personality needs, may shape the mate ideal. The male with unsatisfied cravings for power may desire a pliable girl whom he can control; or he may feel challenged to conquer a more aggressive female. Marital ambitions may also be modified by lack of confidence in what one has to offer. The girl who perceives herself as plain rarely aspires to a Prince Charming; she may welcome a proposal from any reasonably attractive male.

FUTURE PERSPECTIVES

There has been considerable conjecture about the impact of youths' changing sex roles on their later adjustment. It is untrue, as sometimes conjectured, that adolescents' cohabitation is a threat to their future marriage. Many youthful cohabitants take their life style with them when they cross the threshold into young adulthood, but in most cases they eventually marry. A comparison of young married adults who had or had not experienced cohabitation prior to marriage disclosed little difference in terms of communication, need satisfaction, closeness to marital partner, or physical intimacy (Jacques & Chason, 1979).

According to Yankelovich's (1983) surveys, at least half the major normative changes in America in recent years have to do with domestic norms.

Looking ahead, young people no longer feel they must marry, because society is far more accepting of the single individual. In the late 1950s four in five Americans viewed being unmarried as a somewhat unnatural status for either sex; however, a generation later almost the same number held the reverse position. In the future many young people will simply decide to live with someone of the other sex without getting married, at least for a time. Between 1960 and 1977, the number of unmarried couples living together more than doubled; and over half of all adults (52 percent) believed that it was not morally wrong. Hence, young people feel no pressure to get married, although many still prefer to do so. For those who do marry, predicts Andrew Cherlin, Associate Professor of Social Relations, a common pattern will be for parents to "divorce and remarry . . . leave home, cohabit, marry, divorce, live alone for a while and remarry" (A3). One reason is that, as life becomes more impersonal, the marital partner becomes more significant. Hence, "a so-so relationship" says sociologist Richard Levinson, "doesn't cut it" (When "family," 1983).

There is no evidence for the conjecture that youth's tendency toward more androgynous sex roles threatens a couple's adjustment in marriage. Individuals who assume a somewhat less polarized sex role may be better prepared than more traditional persons for adult life. As women move into the work world and as men assume more of the jobs at home, both sexes need to develop their fullest potential as persons. It might be added that, as the sexes moderate the traditional sex-role norms, concepts of what is typically masculine or feminine will change. Eventually, new interpretations of sex role will be perceived as natural, and not as violating what is appropriate for each sex.

The movement today toward a more pluralistic society allows and encourages more options in personality type than formerly. Formerly, variations from traditional norms were hardly tolerated; today, flexibility of sex roles reflects changing requirements of society. Alternative family forms call for different proportions of masculinity or femininity in the traditional sense. In the

As women move into the work world and as men assume more of the jobs at home, both sexes need to develop their fullest potential as persons. (Courtesy of Public Relations Office, State University of New York at Oswego)

many single-parent families headed by women, and increasingly by men, the parent must be both father and mother to the child.

To date, social institutions have provided youth with little help in modernizing their sex roles. On television, at school, and in most homes, nontraditional sex roles are neither exemplified nor encouraged. The male typically still initiates a date—although college women feel somewhat freer than formerly to ask men out or to pay their own way. Modifications of such practices might be appropriate for future adult roles in the work world, when both sexes are called upon to initiate activities. While it might be helpful to youth to have appropriate models of androgynous men and women, the author has never heard the question raised, in her experience on various committees for employing college instructors and administrators, about what sort of sex-role model an applicant might provide.

Both sexes tend to benefit from changing sex roles. Freed from the bondage of a spartan, hard-boiled, competitive masculine ideal, men should be able to enjoy interpersonal relationships more than formerly. Women should profit from being encouraged to become persons in their own right. In earlier times it was considered unessential for adolescent girls to develop individualities of their own. It was assumed that a woman's personal and intellectual development ended when she got married. Her choices were few and her roles well defined; her development was conceived chiefly in terms of family relationships. These days young women look forward to a quite different future in which they, like men, will strive for personality development for the rest of their lives (Scanlon, 1979).

Girls will be better prepared for an independent role as adults if, as boys have always done, they acquire experience in sports, vocational courses, and on the streets. Women in the work world today were poorly prepared for their recently won independence; as a result, they have experienced feelings reflecting their own "adolescent insecurity, loneliness, anxiety, chaos, and confusion . . ." (Gray, 1979, p. 449). If today's girls are given opportunities to define themselves as whole persons, later, as adults, they will be able to accept and capitalize on their strength and autonomy.

SUMMARY

Social sex roles—composite behavior patterns characteristic of each sex—hold considerable significance for both society and adolescents. For society, they serve as means of differentiating functions and activities. They are especially significant in countries where such roles are highly polarized, as in the United States. For individuals, social sex roles become the core of identity. They limit privileges and duties and, depending on how well or how poorly individuals adjust to their sex roles, influence mental health and define relationships with the other sex. At adolescence, sex role attains special significance because of complementary relations between the sexes in teen society. Sex-role patterns cannot be rigidly defined because each individual plays varying combinations of roles at different stages of life and never a single role in an isolated manner. In general, sex roles are most significant in societies where they are highly polarized.

Various principles govern the way sex-role patterning occurs. Authorities agree that sex roles derive, to some debatable extent, from genetic and biological factors, but that they are highly susceptible to sociocultural influences, such as television, school experience, and modes of socialization. Parents begin such teaching very early, assigning to their children those activities and objects considered appropriate to their sex. The father's role in such instruction may be even more important than the mother's because he tends to differentiate more clearly between the way he treats sons and daughters. Children of both sexes learn more of their social-expressive behaviors from the mother and more of their goal-oriented instrumental ones from the father.

The specific process of sex-role patterning is somewhat different for each sex, favoring girls in earlier years and boys later on. From birth, an individual begins to develop an idea that "I am a boy" or "I am a girl" and to perceive his or her sex role in a highly personal manner. Long before adolescence, sex identification has become thoroughly fixed, and is extremely resistant to change.

The larger culture also plays a significant role, as in the effects of the women's movement. Although the movement is perceived as having reduced sex-role polarization to some extent, specific effects are unclear and perhaps less than commonly believed. The "generations effect"—the time when such movements or other influences occur—is important but less so than sex in determining a particular individual's sex-role attitudes. Such attitudes also vary according to race, social class, and educational status.

Individuals of both sexes see certain advantages and disadvantages in their respective roles. Many females feel satisfaction that they can bear children; yet many girls are undecided whether to go the route of homemaker or of careerist primarily, or what proportion of each might be best. Whatever a girl's decision is, many aspects of her role are potentially damaging to her personality. She has to cope with the unfounded notion that women are less stable and less responsible than men. She is taught to be passive and to concede positions of greater authority and significance in society to males. She must deal with ambiguities in her role—how passively feminine or competently modern to appear. Girls vary widely in transactions of their sex role and its effects on them.

In contrast, the male's role is conductive to developing a strong ego. The world is ordered by males and is largely designed for their needs. Moreover, the male has a sex advantage, being accorded greater sexual freedom in dating and dominance within the home. Nevertheless, his role has certain disadvantages, the greatest being the unrealistic concept of masculinity itself. He is expected to be strong, a go-getter, the epitome of courage, independence, and success. He must deny his needs to be sensitive, warm, and dependent. The image of the male is quite narrow, and males who digress from the approved pattern face greater societal disapproval than do females who vary from their pattern.

There is some controversy surrounding the current status of sex roles, and the ways in which they should be modified. Even now young women still have poorer self-concepts, and the vast majority anticipate a stronger identification with the wife-mother role than with an achievement-oriented vocational role. College men are coming to appreciate their future parenting role and to be more expressive in their life styles, yet, in the main, they follow the traditional masculine role.

At least in the public mind, the sexes are becoming less polarized and more like each other. Nevertheless, whatever changes have occurred are probably more on the periphery than at the core of traditional concepts of masculinity and femininity. Some persons believe that this core will persist because sex roles are presumably rooted in biological sex differences. On the other hand, a wealth of evidence suggests that the majority of sex differences are cultural, and hence negotiable. For one thing, both sexes experience culturally generated handicaps and anxieties; their life's tasks and privileges are subdivided into mutually exclusive realms for each sex. Whatever modifications may be effected, sex roles should keep pace with the times, in order to accommodate future styles of family life, parenthood, and heterosexual relationships.

A significant aspect of social sex is heterosexual adjustment, which concerns social sex roles as they relate to each other in sexually interdependent activities. This articulation of social sex roles is especially important as adolescents make the transition to marriage and parenthood. In order to be effective in assuming these new roles, individuals must have established satisfactory adaptations to their own sex role and to that of their sex partner. Establishing heterosexual role relationships is neither automatic nor easy, for it involves certain essential adjustments. For one thing, individuals have become prepared for truly intimate relationships; for another, they must understand how each sex may function most effectively in a mutual relationship. Although both sexes support the goal of a more equalitarian relationship, this ideal is still far from achieved.

During adolescence, various behaviors may serve to promote individuals' normal heterosexual adjustment. Among the most important are the practices of dating and cohabitation. Although cohabitation presents various problems and has no clear legal status, most cohabitants believe its advantages outweigh its disadvantages. The dating practice was traditionally an exploitative relationship; however, at its best it provides valuable experience in relating to members of the other sex. Considerable controversy surrounds the status of American dating practices, which have changed in recent years. With regard to the choice of a mate, young people are pretty realistic, for they generally seek in their mates solid qualities rather than frivolous characteristics. In order better to judge their mates without too serious a commitment, a substantial minority live together without being married. Although women still place a greater premium on getting married than men do, the overwhelming majority of both sexes expect marriage and family to constitute a highly significant part of their lives.

DISCUSSION QUESTIONS
AND ACTIVITIES

1. Would equal vocational opportunities for the sexes make women discontented with their home roles, thus tending to disrupt family life?
2. If boundaries between behaviors prescribed for each sex become less rigid, how may this change affect, for good or ill, the relationship between the sexes?
3. Suggest ways in which sex roles of male and female may be improved.
4. Turn in an unsigned sheet of paper designating your sex and the features you like or dislike most about your own sex role. These papers may be read to the class for general discussion or compiled by a committee which will report to the class.
5. Be prepared to debate the statement, "At high school age going steady is better than random dating."

6. On an unsigned sheet of paper, list topics and questions relating to dating, courtship, and marriage on which you would like guidance. Your entire class may discuss how this guidance may best be given.

7. Clip cartoons and jokes that illustrate some form of tension between the sexes. What types of situations are portrayed? What basic problems seem to underlie these conflicts?

8. Analyze the respective roles of males and females in terms of traits commonly ascribed to each sex in literature and on television. What stereotypes of the sexes are found most often?

9. Analyze newspaper and magazine advertisements to show that advertisers use different approaches toward, and expect different reactions from, each of the sexes. How are advertisements slanted toward the trait differences that each sex is supposed to possess?

10. Discuss ways of improving practices in dating and courtship which would contribute toward greater happiness and better adjustment for both sexes.

11. Be ready to discuss in class the question, "Are problems of adjustment to one's sex role, as presented in this text, overemphasized and exaggerated?"

12. On an unsigned sheet of paper, list traits that you believe to be most characteristic of your own sex and of the other sex and what you perceive to be the greatest advantages and disadvantages of each sex. Lists may be collected, compiled, and analyzed by the class divided into groups.

SUGGESTED READINGS

Avery, A. W. (1982). Escaping loneliness in adolescence: The case for androgyny. *Journal of Youth and Adolescence, 11*(6), 451–459. This study of high school students indicated that androgynous individuals were less lonely than feminine, masculine or undifferentiated ones and that the impact of sex-role orientation was greater for males than females.

Carter, D. B., & Patterson, C. J. (1982). Sex roles as social conventions: The development of children's conceptions of sex-role stereotypes. *Developmental Psychology, 18*(6), 812–824. A study in which second, fourth, sixth, and eighth graders were interviewed regarding sex-role stereotypes of toys, adult occupations, and conventional table manners indicated that knowledge of sex-role stereotypes and beliefs in their flexibility increased with age.

Cutler, S. J. (1983). Aging and changes in attitudes about the women's liberation movement. *International Journal of Aging and Human Development, 16*(1), 43–51. The data from a four-year national study regarding changes in attitudinal support for the women's liberation movement indicated that all age groups became more favorable, with older persons changing more than younger ones, thus refuting the common view that social and political attitudes become more rigid with age.

Dickinson, G. E. (1982). Changing religious behavior of adolescents, 1964–1979. *Youth and Society, 13*(3), 283–288. An analysis is made of similarities and differences among three generations of women in their attitudes toward the female role in society.

Emilhovich, C. A., & Gaier, E. L. (1983). Women's liberation and pre-adolescent sex role stereotypes. *Adolescence, 18*(71), 637–648. The results of a study of androgynous conceptions of sex-role behaviors among pre-adolescents in grades 5 through 8, who had grown up during a period of renewed concern with women's issues are discussed in terms of viewing masculinity-femininity as a humanistic concept.

Erdwins, C. J., Tyer, Z. E., & Mellinger, J. C. (1983). A comparison of sex role and related personality in young, middle-aged and older women. *International Journal of Aging and Human Development, 17*(2), 141–155. In a comparison of younger with middle-aged and older women the former proved more likely to describe themselves as having masculine sex-role characteristics and to be less self-controlled, affiliative, and responsible, thus reflecting changes in societal attitudes toward sex role.

Fabes, R. A. (1983). Adolescents' judgments of the opposite sex. *Adolescence, 18*(71), 535–540. During an adolescent sexuality workshop high school males and females were asked to judge the advantages and disadvantages of being a member of the opposite sex, and this information was used to enhance their mutual understanding.

Flick, R. (1983). The new feminism and the world of work. *Public Inquiry,* Spring, *71,* 33–44. Problems and proposed policies associated with achievement of sex equality in the world of work are examined along with the possible impact on women's femininity.

Haskell, M. (1983). Women in the movies grow up. *Psychology Today, 17*(1), 18–27. This analysis of changes in roles and images of leading women in films suggests that some are better role models for female youth although there are still large deficiencies.

Korman, S. K. (1983). Nontraditional dating behavior: Data initiation and date expense-sharing. *Family Relations, 32,* 575–581. A study which involved 258 single undergraduate women indicated that the feminists, in comparison with the nonfeminists, were more likely to initiate dates and to share the costs of woman-initiated dates.

Macke, A. S. (1982). Using the national longitudinal surveys to examine changes in women's role behavior. *Journal of Social Issues, 38*(1), 17–38. Data from National Longitudinal Surveys are used to study certain women's issues including labor force behaviors, role conceptions, and family statuses.

Morgan, K. P. (1982). Androgyny: A conceptual critique. *Social Theory and Practice, 8*(3), 245–285. The author examines the concept of androgyny and its presumed advantages and concludes that it is an illusory ideal.

Overton, W. F., & Meehan, A. M. (1982). Individual differences in formal operational thought: Sex role and learned helplessness. *Child Development, 53,* 1536–1543. Contrary to expectations, this investigation of sex-role identity and learned helplessness as mediating factors affecting performance on formal operational tasks disclosed no significant differences between 13-year-olds with a feminine or masculine sex-role orientation; however, certain inconsistencies require explanation.

Puglisi, J. T. (1983). Self-perceived age changes in sex role self concept. *International Journal of Aging and Human Development, 16*(3), 183–191. A study of sex-role self concepts among persons in three age groups—17 to 29, 30 to 59, and 60 to 85—both sexes held high masculine self-concepts in middle age followed by a decrease in masculinity in later life.

Quarm, D. (1983). The effect of gender on sex-role attitudes. *Sociological Focus, 16*(4), 285–304. An effort to resolve contradictions in findings about gender differences resulted in conclusions that age and education are significant predictors of sex-role attitudes but for younger and older adults greater differences were found in matters regarding caring for children than for women's role in the public sphere.

Ramage, J. C., Rotherham, K. S., & Robinson, C. (1982). The psychological rights of the child and sexual identity. *Viewpoints in Teaching and Learning, 58*(1), 64–74. An exploration is made of components of sexual identity including biological sex, gender identity, sexual preference, and social sex role in relation to the rights of minors as they grow up.

Rekers, G. A., Mead, S. L., Rosen, A. C., & Brigham, S. L. (1983). Family correlates of male childhood gender disturbance. *Journal of Genetic Psychology, 142*(1), 31–42. A study of boys, ages 3 to 13, indicated a positive correlation between deviations in male role development and psychiatric problems in their parents.

Robinson, I. E., & Jedlicka, D. (1982). Change in sexual attitudes and behavior of college students from 1965 to 1980: A research note. *Journal of Marriage and the Family, 44*(1), 237–240. This third replication of a 1965 survey of premarital sexual behaviors among college students indicated an increase in such behaviors for both sexes, diminished differences between the sexes, and a new double standard, by which stricter standards are imposed on others than oneself.

Shornack, L. L., & Shornack, E. M. (1982). The new sex education and the sexual revolution: A critical view. *Family Relations, 31*(4), 531–544. Recent theories and practices in sex education are sharply criticized as inappropriate for adolescents and negative in outcome.

Taylor, M. C., & Hall, J. A. (1982). Psychological androgyny: Theories, methods, and conclusions. *Psychological Bulletin, 92*(2), 347–366. A review of the research indicates that masculinity rather than androgyny is associated with psychological well-being, and there seems to be no support for the traditional model that masculinity is best for men and femininity for women.

Tolor, A. (1983). Perception of quality of life of college students and their faculty. *Adolescence, 18*(71), 585–594. In a study of perceptions of quality of life at a particular university students expressed more dissatisfaction than faculty members and they differed in areas of chief dissatisfaction.

Chapter Twelve

The Adolescent In School

TODAY'S SCHOOLS

Goals of Schooling

The school is the one institution charged by society with its citizens' academic preparation, but for many students this mission has degenerated into a pursuit of degrees for career goals, rather than a quest for learning.

Educators themselves stress broad ideals for education and deplore the vocational focus. Norton (1970) advises that colleges open up options to adolescents by cutting across the spectrum of human possibilities. From such a broad perspective, adolescents come to appreciate life styles different from their own. They acquire not simply tolerance but the comprehension that different life styles involve distinctive modes of self-realization. Socrates pronounced this principle of varieties of value long ago: "Everyone chooses his love from the ranks of beauty according to his character." In short, the major aim of adolescent education is "to transcend the narrow confines of child identity in the discovery of the inner taste and texture of a wide variety of life styles . . ." (Norton, 1970, p. 37).

Others define the school's major function as socialization, but the question becomes "socialization toward what?" (Greenbaum, 1974, p. 431). Greenbaum calls for educational pluralism and recommends that schools make available more varied models than those provided by "the Anglo-Saxon, Western European, Anglo-American tradition." The best approach is to examine alternative values in order to "create new, self-respecting institutions and communities" (p. 440). In the process, majority group members will learn not only from minority members, who are nearest to the mainstream of society, but also from Third World people "at the margins where, throughout history, mankind's prophets have been found" (p. 440).

One school superintendent observed that "the classsroom has to be a place where you can come to learn and where you can't do your own thing . . ." (Three r's in schools now, 1976, p. 51). Most people would agree, as one nationwide survey proves. About three fourths of this sampling favored requiring students to pass reading and mathematic comprehension tests before being awarded high school diplomas; and three in four felt it was essential that they know how to read and write standard English (Nation's teenagers, 1977).

The School's Achievements

The school's contributions to society may easily be underrated. Today's youth are no less well educated than their predecessors. On the contrary, their efficiency in basic skills appears to be increasing. Moreover, recently there has been improvement in reading at earlier ages (Rodriguez, 1980). Most students do not lack basic skills, but they lack higher cognitive development, as in coherent writing and critical thinking. The highly publicized declines on the SAT (Scholastic Aptitude Tests) scores over recent years derive largely from a change in composition of individuals taking the SAT.

The data also showed that the education of most youth has improved greatly over the past several decades. The percent of the population, ages 25 to 34, completing four years of college has risen from "6% in 1940 to 11% in 1960

Most students do not lack basic skills and their efficiency in these appear to be increasing. (Courtesy of Public Relations Office, State University of New York at Oswego)

to 24% in 1976; even more dramatically the percentage of the population with four years of high school or more rose from 38% in 1940 to 61% in 1960 to 85% in 1976" (Steinberg, 1982, p. 201).

Certainly there is evidence that college attendance makes a difference. In his book, *The New Morality,* Yankelovich reports that a major factor that divides all Americans, including youth, is college attendance, which leaves a residual liberalizing effect. The gap between college-educated and non-college-educated individuals is as great as, and often greater than, gaps between the generations (America's youth, 1977).

The question might arise: Does college pay? The answer: Yes, but not as much as it used to, at least in monetary terms. In 1970 the median income of males with a college education was 32 percent greater than that of just high school graduates; however, by 1980 the college graduates' advantage had dropped to 24.9 percent. In 1970 college educated women earned 55.8 percent more than women high school graduates, but by 1980 the advantage had descended to 31.3 percent. Overall, female high school graduates had begun at lower wages than their male classmates ($3.70 compared with $4.63 an hour) and, after seven years, increases for women had been 12¢ compared with 35¢ for men (S. Guinzburg, 1983).

In any case, by 1985 18.1 percent of all jobs will require a college degree; and employment among young adults, ages 20 through 24, is twice as high among high school as college graduates (14.1 percent, compared to 6.1 percent) (American youth, 1977).

In addition, college graduates have certain nonmonetary benefits. They generally get the highest status jobs and are better satisfied with them than the less well-educated (Rumberger, 1983). Also, they develop, to a higher degree, those qualities of personality and mind that allow an individual to participate more broadly and deeply, cognitively and otherwise, in the life experience. College graduates participate more actively in civic and political organizations. They read more books, watch less television, and more often take advantage of adult education programs. In general, better educated people are more understanding of others and are better able to get along with other people. College-educated men more often help around the house, and college-educated parents devote more money and time to their children. College graduates are better able to cope with the growing complexities of modern life; and they have better health and live longer than nongraduates.

Most studies, including the two cited just below, indicate that most but not all, students view their school experience positively. In Rumberger's study (1982), the majority reported their high schools to be challenging, their teachers knowledgeable and helpful and their counselors at least adequate. On the other hand, about one in four students said they could get away with almost anything. Over a tenth did not feel safe at school and over half found classes boring. However, attitudes varied according to sex and race. More whites than minorities and more males than females found it easy to make friends at school. A higher fraction of females than minorities found schools unsafe; and whites more often reported their classes boring than did nonwhites. Whites more often than minorities felt they could get away with almost anything and whites were less challenged by school life than minorities.

In other research (Chase, 1982) obtained from 10,292 students in 24 school systems in 22 states produced a mainly favorable picture. The students felt in general quite positively about their school and thought teachers cared about them and helped them to learn. They thought that counselors treated them positively, that they were "learning a lot" and learning important things, and they were in general pleased with the school spirit. They expressed positive feelings about the school over twice as often as they did negative feelings. With regard to items with which they felt least pleased, they reported only moderate involvement in school administration, said they received little help from counselors on vocational and personal problems, had little control over the activity program, and that teachers spent little time encouraging individual students.

Student's Views on the Significance of School Experience

Among a sampling of the author's students at the State University College, Oswego, New York, two thirds (67.7 percent) said that they had at some time in their career been strongly influenced by some teacher, 29.2 percent somewhat, and just 3.1 percent never.

FEMALE: In high school I had an English teacher who had a great amount of influence on me, for one basic reason. She looked at me for what I was, what I was capable of doing, not how I acted (like a perfect female) or how I dressed. She showed interest in me, and she attended athletic events. She sort of gave me a role model. She was intelligent, witty, tender, single, and full of life. We had a good relationship; we talked about everything. I still talk to her when I go home; and we still have a closeness that I appreciate.

Among the same students, 68.7 percent recalled their high school experience as having been very significant, 22 percent somewhat important, and 9 percent unimportant.

FEMALE: I went to a private school in a wealthy neighborhood in Manhattan. Although my family's income was well below that of most of my

In recent samplings, students views on the significance of the school experience rated teacher influence high. (Courtesy of Public Relations Office, State University of New York at Oswego)

friends' families, I never really noticed it. Ninth grade was pretty bad, but the rest of high school was fun. I thought some of the people were phony and superficial, but when I look back, I see that I was like that in some ways, too. I guess it was the age. I hated school itself because I found it boring, so I didn't do as well as I could have done.

Among the same college students, 69.7 percent found the classroom experience very important and 20.3 percent somewhat important.

FEMALE: I have taken classes in the social sciences and have found that I am more open-minded about many social issues because of the broad range of ideas and values of the professors.

Most students (90.7 percent) found their outside-of-class college experience highly significant, and the remainder (9.3 percent) somewhat.

FEMALE: I feel that college experience both inside and outside of classes has influenced me a great deal as a person. Inside class I am gathering unbelievable amounts of knowledge which make me realize things about myself and the whole world that I never knew before. I also take part and witness the professor/student relationship from many viewpoints and learn much from that interaction. The whole atmosphere of the college classroom is so much more distinguished and on an adult level than high school ever was and I like it. Professors are always helpful to me. Outside of class has been one of the greatest influences of all. Living away from home can be traumatic in the beginning and the whole college way of life can turn you off. Learning to cope and get along with others is not easy. You learn a lot about yourself in the process. Responsibilities can be a challenge. It makes the growing up process a quicker one in many instances.

MALE: I've learned a lot about myself, my attitudes, and my ability to cope with others in all sorts of situations. I now know that I can handle my life, but I've decided that I'm a social person. I know I can make it away from home, because I always have, but being at college (away from home) has taught me how very much I love my family. I also realize how much they have helped me.

Causes for Concern

Certain critics today declare the schools to be ineffective. Jonathon Kozol insists that schools have an antihuman bias and teach questionable moral values (Schwartz, 1977). In school, children learn to become passive and mechanically efficient in transacting processes that they do not basically understand. John Holt, in his book *Instead of Education*, perceives the school as dangerously authoritarian and competitive, with its grades, honor rolls, and diplomas.

An important symptom is student dissatisfaction. When students tell what they are getting out of college, classroom activity rates little mention. Here are typical answers to the question, "Do you feel college is offering you anything worthwhile?"

FEMALE: I think college can be worthwhile; but truthfully I'm not getting too much out of this college.

MALE: I'm getting a minimum education; but college offers a good place to meet, to know people, and to experience things like that.

Some of this criticism may be charged to adolescents' tendency to be critical. Moreover, student critics do not always mirror campus sentiment generally.

Critics also cite statistics which suggest that this country's schools are poorer than those in certain others. In a cross-national achievement test which included most countries in Western Europe as well as New Zealand, Australia, Japan, Israel, and the United States, American 14-year-olds were third highest of those in the fifteen nations concerned; however, in reading comprehension they were in the lowest third (Tyler, 1981). Since the early 1960s fewer than half of American 14-year-olds have scored above average on applying computational skills to quantitative problems, such as those involved in making purchases, computing taxes, or making automobile trips. Science scores of American high school seniors were lower than those of the other modern nations, with those from Japan and New Zealand scoring much higher than the others.

In this country scores on the Scholastic Aptitude Test (SAT) for 1979 seniors fell to record lows, continuing a decline that began in 1963. These declines were attributed to everything from "television to Watergate to laxity in the schools" (Woops! SAT scores still falling, 1979, p. 155).

Other research and considerations throw a brighter light on educators' achievement. Contrary to the study cited above, in another cross-national survey the highest percent of American young people achieved the same high scores reached in other industrialized nations where advanced schooling is reserved for elite youth (Tyler, 1981).

Where poorer results are achieved the fault may not lie in the school but in the quality of their student clientele. In Minnesota 300 veteran teachers, averaging 17 years of service, reported significant changes in youth over the past two decades. They reported today's students to be more assertive, outspoken, and concerned with instant gratification and the need to be entertained. They were perceived as being harder to please, having shorter attention spans, greater expectations, less willingness to expend effort to learn, and more motivated by external than internal rewards. Not one of these teachers perceived them as having greater knowledge than in the past (Hedin & Conrad, 1980, p. 702).

Sometimes what may be interpreted as negative effects of schooling may, in the long run, be positive, as in a study which compared 20 male students at State University of New York (SUNY) Buffalo with 20 nonstudent employees of the same age at a large commercial bank in western New York. The results would seem to cast some doubt on the value of college life for late adolescent development (Finkelstein & Gaier, 1983). The nonstudents were more mature emotionally and the college students were more emotionally dependent, perhaps because of their economic dependence on their parents. The students' status also apparently had negative effect on some dimensions of their self-concept, including identity formation. The work culture was a more favorable environment for developing identity formation. Older students, in particular, perceived their bodies as of less worth and they viewed less favorably their physical appearance and their sexuality than did the nonstudents. The students also had feelings of less worth with regard to their social interactions and relationships, and they had feelings of less adequacy. Perhaps, concluded the researchers, this condition derives from the students' relative isolation from, and marginality with regard to, the "social mainstream in which the non-students are already immersed" (p. 126). It may also be due to their greater amount of identity confusion when compared to nonstudents. Their lack of a sense of identity acts as a constraining factor in their interpersonal dealings, and a certain identity confusion prevents them from achieving real intimacy with others.

Further differences were found in the area of vocational maturity. The students seemed to engage in more behaviors than did the nonstudents which characterized the initial phases of crystallizing or actually specifying their vocational ambitions. Overall, the students displayed significantly "less advanced repertoires of vocational developmental behaviors . . ." (p. 126).

The writers question this tendency to assume that all influences impinging on the student are somehow bounded by the campus itself. Rather, students are influenced by "the marginal social role the student plays vis-á-vis the larger society" (p. 127). The results of the study indicated that the student can no more "escape his latent social role as marginal man than the university can escape its latent social function as . . . society's most elaborate device for the artificial postponement of adulthood . . ." (p. 127).

The writers suggest that the impact of the college experience, when seen in broader perspective, may be "considerably less intense and less uniformly positive than believed . . . the university context—in spite of the major upheavals of the past decade—may still be serving as the parental surrogate . . . effectively prolonging adolescence in a double-edged manner; while young adults are reaching puberty earlier, they are retaining their dependent student status for ever-extended periods" (p. 128). The writers also suggest that these data indicate a need to relate the higher education experience to the total life span. It is also seen as giving some ammunition to "proponents of nontraditional study who seek to break up the time-and-place boundedness of higher education and to extend it flexibly over the entire life cycle" (p. 128).

This writer, who has taught college students for many years, questions the conclusions of this study. Obviously, these students may feel a bit emotionally dependent until they finish college; however, they apparently do a quick catch-up afterward. If they appear to possess less self-esteem, perhaps it is because they are a bit more self-critical, which may eventually produce greater achievement and consequently greater improvement in self-concept. If they manifest more identity confusion, perhaps that is desirable too, because those who prematurely foreclose their identities have less room for later growth. This is not the same as saying that such identity diffusion or confusion should continue, but that it may provide the bridge toward greater ultimate growth. With regard to the crystallization of the vocational identities, the bankers may be less satisfied with what they are doing because they are now in a low-paying occupation, whereas the students are not actively involved in their training for some future highly regarded professional specialty. What appears necessary before such conclusions are justified as stated in this article would be a long-term followup. In general, a vast quantity of research shows a clear distinction between college and noncollege adult populations with regard to values and life styles, with the college-trained showing clear advantages in many characteristics ordinarily judged to represent high quality. Also note that the very fact of growing up in the work world tends to establish a certain identity, one which is still tentative for the student. Finally, those individuals who have already settled in the work world might engage in a certain amount of rationalization for not having gone to college and for proving to themselves that they have the best of what the world has to give.

DROPOUTS. Not always have children in America been required by law to attend school. However by 1890 most states and territories had compulsory education laws and by 1918 all of them had. Until 1900 many of these laws were commonly ignored; then the institution of the school census and the employment of truant officers and other measures steadily increased compliance. By the 1920s the mean age of required schooling had been increased to 16 years and 3 months. Many of the poor continued not to comply with attendance requirements and, even in the late 1940s, half of Boston's ninth graders failed to graduate and in New York the figure was over 55 percent (Starr, 1981). Nevertheless, the overall trend of attendance was positive. Just half of those enrolled in the fifth grade in 1942 finished high school in 1950; whereas three-fourths of those enrolled in the fifth grade in 1960 graduated in 1968 (Steinberg, 1982). In the 1980s about three in five youths graduated from high school compared with 30 percent in 1925 and 52 percent in 1950 (Starr, 1981).

In the 1970s, as the country's economic situation worsened, a slight countertrend, toward increase in dropouts, developed. From 1900 to 1978 the percentage of 13- to 17-year-olds enrolled in high school had increased from 11 percent to 94 percent. However, in California dropouts between grades 9 and 12 increased from 12 percent in 1967 to 22 percent in 1976; and the number of male dropouts, ages 16 and 17, increased from 6.2 percent to 9.6 percent between 1970 and 1978. Although greater relative improvements have been made among the minorities in the last decade they are still more inclined to drop out of school than whites. Overall, over the past two decades those dropping out of school before graduation have not fallen below 25 percent a year, despite a great national effort to keep them in school. Nor does their 75 percent graduation record prove that students attend school each day. In some urban schools daily attendance may be as low as 45 percent among those attending, and class cutting and tardiness are common (Starr, 1981). Also, long before they drop out they may cease participation in cocurricular activites. Among a sampling of Georgia high school students (Berryman & Schneider, 1983) the most important finding was that participation in activities declined with age as time devoted to work increased, suggesting that many students begin withdrawing from the educational process before graduation.

Thus, in a sense, the dropping out process often begins long before school leaving actually occurs. One symptom is falling behind in school for reasons of boredom, learning problems, emotional problems, and lack of ability. Those who fall behind are more likely to drop out of school. In 1979 about 6 percent of students were two or more years behind, including 15 percent of Hispanic students and 13 percent of black students, compared with just 5 percent of white students. Within each group more males than females lagged at least two years behind. Students from economic disadvantaged background were almost four times as likely to fall behind and those whose parents did not complete high school twice as likely as those whose parents completed college (Rumberger, 1982).

It should be added that the concept of "dropout" has changed. In former years, when the educational system was fairly rudimentary, a school dropout was anyone who failed to complete elementary school. Now, the dropout is usually perceived as one who fails to earn a high school diploma; increasingly, the term has reference to those who enter but fail to complete college. Here we shall simply define as dropouts those who fail to stay in school as long as their needs and abilities would seem to justify.

Many studies have sought to determine specific characteristics associated with the desire to cease or continue schooling. In a national sampling of youths ages 14 to 21 (Crowley & Shapiro, 1982) to determine educational and fertility expectations, almost all hoped to complete at least high school and almost two thirds wanted to go to college. Factors relating to this desire included parental education attainment, smaller number of siblings, living with both parents, and higher family income. Obviously those with fewer siblings and from intact homes would have more financial resources available for higher education. Those born outside the United States had higher educational expectations than native-born Americans, supporting the view that foreign-born families look on education as a means to upward mobility. Married youth expected less schooling than the unmarried, as did those with children. Women, both married and having a child, expected almost two full years less than single childless women. With regard to religion those of Jewish faith on average expected three-quarters of a year more higher education than did Protestants. Individuals of both sexes who held more traditional attitudes toward women's roles anticipated significantly lower levels of educational attainment. In addition, minorities expected significantly more education than whites, the explanation generally given being that minorities view education as a means, otherwise unattainable, for raising their economic status. This writer might add that their higher expectation of attending college is probably realistic because they may be more likely to be awarded grants for higher education than are whites.

Those individuals who drop out also have their distinctive characteristics. In a study in Melbourne, Australia (Poole & Low, 1982) students who left high school before age 17 were lacking in academic motivation and organization skills, came from poor socioeconomic backgrounds, and had poor verbal ability. Male and female students, whether or not they left school, could be clearly differentiated. The females achieved better grades, were more conforming and more influenced by their teachers. On the other hand, the males were more self-interested, extroverted, and fatalistic. They related their chances of success more highly than the females and were less conforming and conventional in their feelings about school. Boys expected to progress well in life despite low grades; and despite their higher grades, girls saw their chance of success as much lower. Perhaps this difference simply reflects the realistic picture that boys are encouraged by their culture to achieve greater success.

It should be noted that many individuals who drop out later resume schooling. Between 1979 and 1980 about a third of the 14- to 22-year-olds who had dropped out of high school returned, mostly because of their personal characteristics rather than school-related factors (Borus & Carpenter, 1982). Factors that had increased the probability of dropping out of school, such as family background, did not alter the rate of returning, nor did the local unemployment rate or their own personal unemployment status or being from poverty households. Marriage rather than the presence of a child was also a factor in hindering return to school. In general dropouts who had acquired various adult commitments—the married and the older—were less likely to return, and those who desired to attend college were more likely to come back.

Dropping out is only one reaction to dissatisfaction with schooling. Others include frequent absence, running away, suicide, alienation later leading to drug use, physical assaults against teachers, vandalism, and, since the late 1960s, organized protests against school regulations.

Students drop out for various reasons. Girls, especially blacks, most frequently cite pregnancy and marriage as reasons for leaving. Many students, boys especially, leave because they do not like school. About 30 percent of Hispanic boys leave school for economic reasons, including job offers and home responsibilities. Both white and black boys often cite economic reasons. Other reasons for leaving school include poor grades, lack of ability, expulsions, or simply boredom.

An analysis of nonschool factors associated with dropouts of a sampling of 18- to 21-year-olds pointed to several factors. Parental education and the presence of learning materials in the home related to staying in school but parents' earnings did not. Certain variables such as students' ability, education and occupational goals, and the aspirations of their friends were also important.

The fathers' education influenced the dropout rate of their sons but not their daughters; childbirth and early marriage affected the dropout rate of girls more than of boys, and local unemployment rates for minority males but not for others (Rumberger, 1982).

Perhaps some students now drop out who would formerly stay in school because they are more prone to defy compulsory attendance laws. In this modern industrialized technological society youth are more mature and experienced than those in past years—hence, less willing to be dictated to by or dominated by adults (Starr, 1981).

The question arises: Is there any point in trying to keep low achievers in school? Probably college-bound high-achieving students benefit most from attending high school, at least with reference to intellectual development. They have acquired basic skills by the time they reach high school and can benefit from their academic courses. They are more likely than the noncollege bound to take a variety of subjects in high school and, since they have more academic success, they develop a more positive attitude toward learning.

Nevertheless, it may not be wise for low-achieving students to leave school early. Until they have acquired basic skills and arrived at a cognitive level that allows them to behave as responsible adults they will profit little from jobs which do not contribute to these skills. On the other hand, it is hard to justify requiring the least motivated and most educationally handicapped adolescents to attend school when attendance may not significantly improve their basic skills. Moreover, requiring attendance may further impair their attitudes toward education and learning. Perhaps the best solution is compensatory education for such individuals to raise their skills level. Whereas students who have acquired basic skills may benefit from early work experience, those who haven't achieved the degree of intellectual development which would allow them to function responsibly in adulthood, should remain in educational settings which at least have more likelihood of improving their skill levels than the work environment. Programs which combine remedial education and on-the-job training for skills have proved very successful in teaching basic skills. Such programs, in effect, provide a compromise between work and school, especially for low-achieving youth who do not benefit from the regular high school program (Stipek, 1981).

Since many students prefer working to remaining in school, the relative merits of these alternatives should be weighed. In a sampling of Georgia high school youth who held jobs outside the home, almost two thirds (63 percent) received no pay for the work they did at home and just 35 percent received an allowance. They worked for various reasons, mostly for money. Most of them liked their jobs but viewed them as temporary. The students who did not have jobs most often cited as reasons interference with school activities and classwork, or failing to find jobs (Berryman & Schneider, 1983). The latter might have been the lucky ones, for most jobs that youths obtain teach few skills, afford little incentive, and pay low wages (Lewin-Epstein, 1981). In addition, working especially long work hours may negatively impact on youth's work attitudes, social life, and delinquency rates (Johnson, 1980; Greenberger & Steinberg, 1982).

Authorities differ on how long youth should be required to remain in school. The National Commission on the Reform of Secondary Education recommended lowering the school-leaving age to 14; however, a large majority of persons polled support current laws regarding compulsory schooling. In a recent Gallup poll an overwhelming 90 percent approved compulsory school attendance through elementary school and 73 percent through high school. When asked whether students should be allowed to leave school at age 14 if they could pass a test showing that they could "read, write and figure with sufficient skill to get along," just 30 percent agreed and 66 percent disagreed.

Starr (1981) suggests several reasons that the public still favors compulsory schooling. One is that such schooling assures the continued subordination of adolescents to adults. Unions and adults would prefer that adolescents remain out of the regular work force, as distinct from the part-time labor market. Also, many parents rely on schools to take care of their children until they come home from work. Society in general fears the threat to persons and property of unemployed school dropouts. This writer believes that the public supports compulsory schooling mainly because young people cannot become fully effective citizens without it.

DISCIPLINE AND PUNISHMENT   Another problem deserving attention—one with a venerable ancestry—is discipline. During the fourteenth through the seventeenth centuries, the masters whipped students at their own discretion and encouraged them to spy on each other (Ariès, 1962). During the same period, the use of the birch—a practice formerly confined to young children—was gradually extended to all students, sometimes beyond age 20. This extension reflected a corresponding tendency to diminish distinctions between children and adolescents by subjecting them to identical discipline. In the schoolroom, adolescents were placed in the same category as children.

Sixteenth-century English history is full of accounts of young people, ages 16 to 20, being sentenced to whippings. Some English texts of the period referred to the school as "a place of execution" (Watson, 1962). Even at Oxford, tutors could order undergraduates to be whipped like grammar-school boys elsewhere. At Cambridge, corporal punishment was displaced by fines after the age of 18, while at Cardinal College the age limit was 20.

School discipline problems have persisted down the years, though changing in character over time. In eight of the nine annual Gallup Polls of public attitudes toward the schools, from 1969 to 1977, discipline was named as a major problem. This observation, notes Wynne (1978), reflects long-term trends toward increasing desperation, hostility, and disorder among American teenagers. Of course, many youth have little respect for any kind of authority. During recent years, large numbers of teachers have been physically attacked in classrooms, and students often disagree with their teachers (Rosow, 1979).

Kindsvatter (1978) differentiates between discipline problems of normal and disturbed students. When students' misbehaviors are temporary and casual, teachers may, in straightforward fashion, utilize power in whatever degree of intensity is necessary. Typical students will not be unduly affected by such measures. When such behaviors arise from more severe emotional problems, teachers should realize they are pathological and cannot be treated adequately in the classroom. The difficulty is in distinguishing between the normal and the pathological and requires looking into the matter closely. In such a case, a teacher-student conference would seem in order, held after school when the two can be alone.

Psychiatrist William Glasser (1978) believes that the only answer to the discipline problem is to give students a stake in the schools. As it is, many of them come to school only because they have nothing else to do. They are not involved in school acivities and they often make failing grades. Somehow they must be helped to become involved in the school's activities and to make passing grades. They should be helped to learn to read and be given reading matter that makes sense to them. Individuals learn differently and should be encouraged in what they undertake to do. The popular movement of doing away with social promotion will not work with students who have no stake in the schools. For students who break the rules, Glasser recommends loss of privilege and freedom.

DEPENDENCE ON GRADES TO STIMULATE ACHIEVEMENT   Another problem deserving attention is the widespread use of grades as a means of motivating students. The grading practice has its strong points. Much that should be learned is not intrinsically interesting, and in such cases, grades supply the motive. Besides, students must become used to the fact that, throughout life, their performance will be evaluated by others. Students who denounce grading practices will, as adults, choose mechanics and physicians on the basis of performance rather than some pass-or-fail criterion.

On the negative side many teachers rely on competition and awards to induce students to study. Students come to set their sights on winning, not on learning. Their efforts are reduced to a relentless grind for grades. In one sense, observe Light and Laufer (1975), colleges may rob students of their youth because of the constant pressure on them to maintain high grades in order to enter professional schools. Nevertheless, grade pressures have relaxed considerably in recent years. Many studies indicate that *B* grades today are equivalent to the *C* grades of a generation ago. The number of *A*s in selected colleges has doubled since 1974 (Colleges try to halt, 1977).

Despite the pedestal on which grading systems have been placed, there is little consensus about standards to which such systems should relate. If we permit James Joyce to violate conventional writing codes, can a 14-year-old be condemned for doing the same? Or in today's world, can the student who prefers *Death of a Salesman* to *Macbeth* be judged as being less culturally sophisticated than the Shakespeare buff (Long, 1965)?

Goodlad (1979) suggests employing such criteria of evaluation as absence from school for reasons other than illness or insistence on coming to school in spite of illness. School grades simply predict future school grades and little else . . . "neither compassion, good work habits, vocational success, social success, nor happiness" (p. 344).

FACTORS THAT INFLUENCE STUDENTS' LEARNING EXPERIENCE

Teacher-Student Relationships

Efforts to upgrade school programs for adolescents should proceed on a broad front, involving methods, curriculum, guidance, and teacher-student relations. How teachers interact with students, and vice versa, is of utmost significance in learning. In this regard elementary school teachers may do a better

How teachers interact with students, and vice versa, is of utmost significance in learning. (Courtesy of Public Relations Office, State University of New York at Oswego)

job than those in high school. A survey of over 17,000 secondary school students indicated that the general self-concept increases gradually with grade level, but the academic self-concept slightly declines with increasing grade level. Thus, the question: Do lower grade teachers do more than upper grade ones to help children feel positively toward their school work? In the same study, from early elementary grades until senior high school the use of praise, encouragement, correction with guidance, and positive interaction with students decreased by almost half (Benham, Geisen & Oakes, 1980).

THE TEACHERS' ATTITUDE TOWARD STUDENTS COLLECTIVELY Teachers have their own styles of dealing with students. Some teachers "ride herd" on the class but treat their students kindly as individuals. Others manipulate groups with skill but ignore pupils as individuals. A few intrepid souls, with their feet firmly planted in a by-gone era, remain somewhat less benevolent patriarchs in their classroom kingdoms.

Many teachers are more responsive to students in some categories than to those in others. In a certain school setting, the "tribe" boys—not alienated but whose activities were not valued by the cultured—were ignored outside class by all but a few teachers. Only a minority of teachers actively supported them. While the tribe boys were responsive to adults' expressions of concern and straightforwardness, they took advantage of teachers who were tolerant of them but who did not expect much. On the other hand, they rebelled against adults who made arbitrary demands (Todd, 1979).

Apparently, teacher concern for students pays worthwhile dividends. In high schools where students interact with adults across broader settings, students perceive adults as being more concerned about them and embrace their norms more willingly. Paradoxically, there is some pressure against teachers' becoming friendly with students, either inside or outside the classroom. The result is that teachers play a chiefly instructional role and ordinarily have little influence on other aspects of adolescents' socialization (McClintock, 1979).

THE TEACHER'S ATTITUDE TOWARD INDIVIDUALS Where individual students are concerned, teachers may show differential treatment on the basis of intelligence, sex, social class, age, or some other characteristic. Teachers may reject dull students whose lack of capacity threatens their own needs to perceive themselves as successful, especially if their ratings depend on their pupils' performance on standardized tests.

The teacher's capacity to mean something to individual pupils is often greater than he or she thinks. Even, or perhaps especially, in these times, skilled "couriers of culture" win their students' four-star rating. Washington Gladden, a noted minister, said of a teacher,

> He found me a listless and lazy pupil; he left me with a zest for study and a firm purpose of self-improvement. It was a clear case of conversion; and when anyone tells me that character cannot be changed through the operation of spiritual forces, I know better. (Coward, 1959, p. 233)

Calvin Coolidge said of his philosophy professor at Amherst, "To Garman was given a power which took his class up into a high mountain of spiritual life and left them alone with God." On the other hand, Henry Adams' brother, Charles Francis Adams, wrote that Henry's youth and education were a "skillfully arranged series of mistakes."

In a class of 35 upper classmen, the writer found that 11 had at some time in high school or college identified with and received special encouragement from a faculty member, and all 11 reported the experience to have been positive. However, Clark Kerr, chairman of the Carnegie Council on Policy Studies in Higher Education, warns that dropping college enrollments and the consequent decrease in hiring of young professors is raising the average age of faculty members. As a result, the growing age gap between faculty members and students means that students have fewer young adults with whom to identify (Licitra, 1979/1980).

Most teachers relate to students "in a universalistic, not individualistic, fashion, responding less to their emotional needs and more to the necessity for them to become task and achievement oriented" (Gump, 1978, p. 153). While the total number of any particular teacher's students may be so numerous as to preclude spending much time with individuals, there are many things that can be done to keep them from feeling like faceless "blobs" in the classroom. Teachers may greet students by name in the hall or make any sort of personal remark such as "That's a pretty dress" or "I'm glad you raised that question in class." Simply behaving in a warmly concerned fashion conveys an attitude of individual regard.

Although teacher-pupil relations are highly significant, they should not obscure the important effects of pupil-pupil interaction. Peer relations are always important, often in subtle ways. For example, youth may learn from others in effectively led group discussion. While a full-size generation gap may become an unbridgeable chasm, a small one may be the spannable gap that induces progress.

Sex Differences

From earliest years, the differential experiences of the sexes result in distinctively different foundations for future learning. In one study (Harper & Sanders, 1975), when 3- to 5-year-old nursery school children were observed at play, boys used between 1.2 and 1.6 times as much space as girls and entered more play areas. The boys also played more in sand, on a tractor and climbing structures, and around an equipment shed than the girls did. The girls spent more time indoors at craft tables and in the kitchen. Questionnaire data from the children's parents indicated little conscious pressure for sex-differentiated behavior. Nevertheless, they rigged their children's environments in traditionally sex-stereotyped ways.

Causes of boys' problems in school have related mainly to biological factors, lack of male role models, teachers' differential treatment of the sexes, and the feminized school society. In elementary school, boys tend to be more physically active; hence, they have greater problems in the schoolroom. Not all teachers provide adequate role models; nor do all of them tolerate aggressive active behaviors from boys. Women (as well as men) teachers do indeed treat the sexes differently; but in what ways, research is conflicting. Finally, the elementary school is a place where children who are courteous, generous, and obedient are approved and those who are rough, aggressive, and highly active are frowned upon. Boys, more often than girls, are reprimanded for improper behaviors; their academic performance is poorer; and they experience more stress than females do.

Females fare better in grade school than in college. Despite their good grades, they experience various subtle disadvantages. Psychologists Sarah Hall Sternglanz and Shirley Lyberger-Ficek reported, on the basis of observations in 60 college classes, that males dominate action in the classroom, including making comments and asking questions, especially when the teacher is a man. They suggest that girls should be taught to behave more assertively in the presence of male professors and that more women college professors should be hired (Coed competition, 1978).

Colleges provide mostly male-dominated environments, run mainly by male administrators and taught by mostly male professors. Students at women's colleges, reported Westfall (1978/1979), were more aggressive, were more involved, and performed better in their careers, in contrast with the coeducational situation where women were less assertive and outspoken. In men's presence they were more likley to assume a "flirtatious coquettish" role. They could be more themselves when they were educated separately.

Considerable interest has been shown of late in female's inferior mathematics performance and to what degree female academic achievement relates to genetics or experience. Tobias (1982) reports a study by Camilla Benbow and Julian Stanley which compared mathematics scores of seventh and eighth grade males and females who had had similar classroom training and were talented in that subject. They concluded that male superiority was due both to genetic and environmental factors. If such were the case, it would be presumptious to assume that women could ever compete on an even scale with men in technical jobs requiring mathematical skills. However, further analysis of the situation indicates that the differences could have been well accounted for by various extraneous factors. For one thing, the parents had given sons more help than daughters when both were involved in talent searches. They were also more likely to help their sons prepare for the examinations involved in the talent search, which was intended to select highly talented young people for a special program at Johns Hopkins University. In addition, parents of daughters who were accepted into the program had been surprised to learn that their daughters had mathematical talents, although the parents of sons knew it quite well. In consequence, the latter had been more sensitive to developing the son's mathematical skills. Preferential experiences in childhood also make quite a difference such as "fixing mechanical objects, ball play, orienting by compass and rock climbing, a parent who explains math—all can provide important lessons in spatial and mathematical thinking" (p. 16). Sheila Tobias concludes that "until and unless girls are encouraged to experience the world as boys do" it can't simply be assumed that they have had the same exposure to learning mathematics. Note also that the proportion of boys scoring higher than girls has dropped constantly from 1972 until 1979, when the last talent search was reported. Since only 2 or 3 percent of the most talented males now outperform the most talented females the difference can be easily accounted for by environmental factors.

Other research indicated that females' performance in mathematics related to the way they had been socialized into sex roles. In a study of high school girls who enrolled in senior mathematics, the more intellectually ambitious girls were characterized by favorable experiences with mathematics teachers, warm family backgrounds, and sex-role conflict. They valued both future occupational and family roles but felt that the mother's place is in the home. They were ambivalent about being smart and not quite at ease with boys because of their intellectual ability. They had experienced greater conflicts between sex role and achievement in earlier grades, particularly in grade 6 to 9. "Being smart" emerged as a "role," with advantages and disadvantages; and "being smart" depended on the willingness to accept that role (p. 441). Completing a fourth year of theoretical mathematics "automatically marked you as smart," and how that fact impacted on a girl depended on her own personality and the values of her associates. In some same-sex peer groups it was acceptable for girls to be smart; others, mixed or not did not accept her. One straight-A senior girl who planned to be a physician said that the parents of girls she knew encouraged their social activities to a degree that interfered with their study time. These girls saw the chief advantages of being smart as gaining others' respect, finding work easier, and having better vocational opportunities in the future (Sherman, 1982).

Among females academic performance varies greatly according to personality characteristics. A review of the research (Hummel & Roselli, 1983) has consistently shown that high academic achievers have more favorable personality characteristics than do equally bright individuals who achieve below the level that their abilities would allow and that high academic achievers are more often "independent, organized, optimistic, self certain, . . . and have more realistic life goals and values" (p. 18). The same holds for both sexes.

A comparison of female over- and underachievers of the same abilities in a private school for girls in Pittsburgh revealed high academic achievers to be "more purposeful, yet also more flexible and nonarbitrary in their thinking . . . in discussing their own future plans they appeared "more tolerant of uncertainty; being more actively tentative in their beliefs . . ." They were also more likely continually to "examine, clarify and reformulate their own values" (p. 26). In contrast, the underachievers were somewhat vague about their future plans and prospects, and without having thought through them very well, had simply limited themselves to somewhat "narrowly conceived decisions and plans" (Hummel & Roselli, 1983).

Social Class

Another important variable in the educational process is social class. Considerable research has disclosed a positive relationship between social class and vocabulary, achievement test scores, instrumental competencies, and confidence in one's talents. White middle-class students perform better in school and achieve more in adult life than do minority lower-class students who attend equally "good" schools. These findings have been viewed as proof that high schools only moderately influence adult achievement and that such achievement depends chiefly on family background. An alternative explanation is that white middle-class students do better because schools are especially congenial to their values and needs. In contrast, minority students have difficulty internalizing the school's values or utilizing its resources, and thus cannot maximize their own potential (McClintock, 1979).

Apparently whatever academic success these youth may or may not have has little effect on their relationship among their own people. In a study of tenth grade students, ages 15 to 16, in an inner-city high school, with regard to their self-concept relative to family, peers, and academic performance, only academic self-concept related significantly to poor academic performance. In other words, their perception of their relationships with their peers and their families did not significantly relate to their academic performance, contrary to traditional assumptions (Zarb, 1981). This result is hardly surprising when we note that such students, outside school hours, live in the relatively insulated environment of their own neighborhood.

Of recent years increasing numbers of college students in general, including minorities, have received financial aid. In 1979 half received some kind of institutional assistance, including grants, loans, and scholarships. About two thirds received help from friends and relatives. Over a quarter had all living and school expenses paid for them, whereas another quarter had half or more of their expenses given them. Blacks and Hispanics received grants more often than whites; whites more often received assistance from friends and relatives; and women had their expenses paid more often than men (Rumberger, 1982).

The result has been a leveling of educational opportunity. Over the years white males and the well-to-do have gone to college more than others. Recently, at least among high school graduates, the difference in college attendance of various subgroups is slight or small. In 1979 about 40 percent of all high school graduates from ages 14 to 21 attended college. The rate for black graduates was 37 percent and Hispanics and whites 40 percent. White and Hispanic males more often attended; however, among blacks, females attended more often. The rate was higher for children from families below the poverty level than from those above it.

Other factors are also associated with the decision to attend college. These include personal characteristics and family background, especially parental education, income, and family size (Marc, 1980). Additional factors include the nature of the high school curriculum, grades, and characteristics of the college attended, including its location and financial assistance provided (Rumberger, 1982).

Characteristics of the School

Schools vary in their characteristics just as do the students who attend them. They may have important qualities that produce achievement in their students. A school may have a sense of identity, mission, and unity and a generally supportive structure for both teachers and students. For example, during recent years, 5 percent of the all-black schools have produced 21 percent of black PhDs (Goodlad, 1979).

Kelly (1979) reports a study of eighth and eleventh grade boys, all white and middle class, in two schools near Detroit, Michigan. In one of the schools, students shared in decision making; at the other, the parents and school boards had much power and students had but little influence (Rich & Marsh, 1979). At one school, the boys placed great emphasis on sports, while in the other, boys were deeply involved in developing competencies, as in academic work, hobbies, and jobs (Kelly, 1979).

Trickett (1978) calls attention to the significance of social surroundings, or the social ecology of the environmental setting. In a comparison of classroom environments of five types of public schools (urban, rural, suburban, vocational, and alternative) alternative and vocational schools afforded the greatest contrast, where vocational schools emphasized rules and regulations and alternative schools stressed interpersonal classroom experience. The alternative school classroom stressed interpersonal—both student- and teacher-student—relationships; and, though loosely run, they were well organized and task oriented. They were both antiauthority and anticompetitive in quality, consistent with their stress on personal relationships. The vocational schools were competitive, controlled by strict teachers, and the least innovative of all the schools. The rural classrooms seemed moderate in all respects, while the suburban schools stressed supportive teacher relationships, but less than the alternative schools did. They were also far less competitive than the vocational schools. The urban schools did not conform at all to the popular stereotype, being higher than the others in task orientation and highest, except for the alternative schools, in student involvement in class. Such analysis indicates the variation in school environments to which adolescents are exposed; and it may be helpful in designing institutions sensitive to young peoples' developmental needs and aspirations.

Schmiedeck (1979) believes that organizational features of modern high schools have had unfortunate effects on adolescents, at a life stage when they are loosening contacts with adults, and that peer relationships only partly compensate for the safety they have relinquished. Many high schools have grown very large, often encompassing student populations of several thousand. Students selects different subjects each year or semester and find themselves with different peers in almost every course. Also, they do not go through school in small coherent groups where all know each other. Of course, they may belong to cliques of athletes or exceptional students or to special-interest groups. But there is little opportunity for lasting contact with many students, and the cliques are too small and homogeneous to allow varied friendships. As a result, students come to know each other in particular settings, as in science or English but hardly get to know each other as whole persons.

It is commonly believed that students fare better in smaller than in larger schools. In general, classes are smaller, teachers know students more intimately, and students are said to feel a stronger personal identity. However, the larger school has its advocates. Pacheco (1978) believes that the small-town school is often overcrowded and affords a more alienating experience than does the modern large school. Coleman (1978) defends the large school because it is departmentalized, offers specialized advance courses, and allows teachers to focus on their specialty. The school's impersonality might also minimize the practice of teachers' playing up of favorites.

Community Factors

The single most important factor in pupil achievement is the student's background, including family, neighborhood, and social class (Taylor, 1976). These factors far outweigh any variables that the school can manipulate, such as class size, use of technology, or changes in curriculum. Therefore, it seems feasible that the best way to support students' educational needs is to provide support within local neighborhoods and to ensure that families have adequate resources.

Early influences collectively establish the foundation for future school achievement. In the Youth in Transition study (Bachman, et al., 1978), over a 5-year span, students showed a surprising stability from ages 15 to 23. Background variables, such as family, socioeconomic level, intellectual ability, number of siblings, classroom grades, school attitudes, and curriculum (whether college preparatory or not), were strong predictors of school success. Future aspirations, background family variables, and patterns of school success set into motion sequences of life events that followed somewhat naturally and directly from elementary school through high school.

RELATING METHODS AND CURRICULUM TO ADOLESCENTS

Teaching Methods

TRADITIONAL METHODS Creating enthusiasm for learning in students has always constituted a problem. In the early sixteenth-century classroom, the humanist Buchanan observed, "While the master shouts himself hoarse, these lazy children sit dozing and thinking of their pleasures. One boy who is absent has paid one of his companions to answer in his place. Another has lost his breeches while yet another is looking at his foot which is poking through a hole in his shoe" (Ariès, 1962, p. 327).

In the 1960s there was considerable optimism regarding chances of important educational reforms; nevertheless, by the late 1970s there had been few substantial modifications in classroom practice. Teachers have an unusual capacity simply to transform instructional innovations into the more traditional classroom practices (Boocock, 1978). It seems doubtful that new research findings or technological advances will have any truly revolutionary impact on teaching practice, given the climate and situations in which instruction occurs.

Even today, students will sit in the same seat in classrooms for the whole school year (Boocock, 1978). Most of the talking in class is done by the teacher, and almost all the students who talk sit in a small zone in the center part of the room. Seating relates to both social and achievement status of the student. Meantime, the most common method of teaching adolescents continues to be the traditional one of recitation, homework, and term papers, despite a slow trend toward newer modes of instruction. Where term papers are required and topics assigned, the final products are often chunks of material copied and tied together with connective sentences, marvels of "patchwork plagiarism" hardly conducive to feelings of achievement. Another familiar assignment, homework, often involves memorizing what textbooks "say." Some students have very poor home facilities for preparing their assignments. A California boy wrote,

> My problem is studing [sic]. I don't get too good of a grade in school. I trie to study at home but ther is so much noise with the TV and my three little brothers and two sisters. I trie to go in the bedroom. But I have to study on the bed and do more sleeping than studing. I go to this girl's house to study. But we do more talking than studing. (Remmers & Radler, 1957, p. 127)

Traditional education can be quite effective; and it may be superior to more recent methods for some students. Many people maintain that the lecture method is superior to much of the software that has been used in recent years. While instructors should be humanistic and sympathetic, they should uphold academic standards (Colleges try to halt, 1977). Disadvantaged youth, in particular, may profit from a relatively structured classroom and the somewhat firm control of authority. Structured learning often facilitates their scholastic achievement, which is necessary for social mobility.

Teaching strategies become but hollow vehicles if they have little to convey—hence, teachers' knowledge of their fields is essential. Currently, "as life styles become more flexible, the high school remains inflexibly standardized . . . as social problems become more complex the high school curriculum focuses on discrete subject areas and minimal competence" (Tubbs & Beane, 1981, p. 399). However, a large majority (95 percent) of social studies and science specialists agreed that teachers themselves need help in understanding the scope and complexity of major issues as well as strategies for teaching them (Biaga & Cooney, 1981). Moreover, among teacher candidates taking graduate record examinations from 1964 to 1977, 81 percent of those applying to graduate schools of education were below average in the verbal section and 84 percent below average in the quantitative. Fewer than 100 of the 4365 attained grade scores that might be judged distinguished (Frye, 1979).

NEWER APPROACHES Others believe that traditional approaches have failed the test. They claim that the academic disciplines are too narrow in focus for modern society and that traditional methods are impractical because of the knowledge explosion. Some people also assert that the vocational model is better for students who otherwise would not be motivated to learn.

The Coleman II Report (1974) suggests that schools have grown too large and should be broken into smaller, more sensible units. On the other hand, some individuals like the impersonality of the larger institutions. Others favor greater interaction among students of different ages. Coleman notes that the organization of schools by grade creates age-segregated social strata with clear-cut boundaries. The system allows a student little interaction with those of other ages or grades. Moreover, the practice of automatic promotion from grade to grade maintains a very narrow age range.

One once-popular technique, curriculum tracking, or differentiating curricular experiences for students who are or are not going to college, is con-troversial. Those opposed to tracking, as it is currently practiced, argue that students in the noncollege track often suffer from feelings of inferiority and are branded as stupid. They are relegated to curricula which will prevent or impede prospects of ever attending college if they should decide to attend. They also fail to have the kind of education which will truly challenge them or broaden their interests; and they lack the inspiration of being with more able students. Those who support tracking believe that students of less ability can perform more ably in vocational or general tracks and they feel more adequate because they are competing with equals rather than with more able students. Brighter students are more readily challenged by academically-oriented curricula and more nearly achieve their own potential. They can profit from the more advanced material provided and not be held back by slower individuals in the class. They are also motivated through being with more equally matched peers (Alexander, Cook & McDill, 1978).

SOME GENERAL SUGGESTIONS There is no one best pattern of teaching, whether traditional or modern. Each must be adapted to the teacher and situation involved and not just be mechanically employed. Teaching techniques should also be adapted to students' stage of development. Adams and Looft (1977) note that adults and adolescents prefer distinctly different life styles. The adolescent perceives the adult world as instrumental, focusing on competence, achievement, rational thought, and success. Self-regard depends on what one accomplishes and what one becomes. This instrumental culture belongs to the adult and stresses autonomy, confidence, and hard work. In contrast, the adolescent's ideal is the expressive role. Ideals here are self-exploration, sensory experiences, in-timacy, personal meaning, and the here-and-now rather than the future.

Adams and Looft believe that teachers must necessarily realize that life patterns are changing and that for today's youth the product is less significant than the achievement process. Teachers must place more emphasis on social skills and less on academic achievement. They should help youth to attain a sense of identity and feelings of commitment. Teachers must yield some of their authority in exchange for a joint student-teacher meaningful education. They must give up the idea that they, as authority power figures, have all the answers.

Student Reactions

To Poor Instruction   Everhart (1981) comments upon various approaches to describing the lives of adolescents, one being the psychological model which portrays adolescence as a stage when the individual acquires new cognitive competencies, while at the same time experiencing anxieties of self and new relations with people outside the family. There is also the physiological model which emphasizes the rapid changes in physical functioning relating to puberty.

The structural-functional model considers youth in relation to the larger society and the youth subculture. All these approaches, says Everhart, are top-down approaches to studying adolescents. That is, they are based on somewhat broad yet established models; and then researchers categorize adolescents according to that model: "As a psychological being, a neurological entity . . . [or] as a member of a group that fulfills certain functions in relationship to other groups in the larger society" (p. 178). Everhart himself prefers to operate from the bottom up: that is, basing views of adolescent behavior, not on predetermined models, but on what adolescents do and how they perceive their own actions—in short, a phenomelogical approach.

Everhart used this approach to study the goofing off of young adolescents in school—that is, unstructured activities that students use to fill time and to avoid doing what teachers want them to do. He separated students' modes of goofing off into several categories including shooting things (rubber bands, paper clips), throwing things (chalk, erasers, books), bugging the teacher, chewing gum, tapping feet and not doing their work, talking back, wearing hats in class, and so forth, besides miscellaneous ones.

There were three main categories of condition that affected the patterns that students employed in goofing off. One of these was interaction—that is, several friends might be close together and hence engage in such things as throwing chalk or erasers back and forth. And there were the temporal factors, as students appeared to realize that certain times are better for goofing off than others—they would come to realize that teachers might tolerate goofing off up to a point; and spatial factors, depending on matters of location—for example, where one was seated. Students who were seated close together might talk to each other, whereas if they were further apart they might throw things to each other.

Everhart concludes that goofing off is adaptive behavior that students employ. Despite the fact that such behaviors occur in environments that do not ordinarily encourage much initiative, students employ goofoffs in quite remarkable ways. Everhart believes that goofing off is the students' collective response to their role in the hierarchy at school and their response to students' place in the society. That is, adolescents are viewed as "passive, irrational, immature beings; and we arrange their schooling experiences accordingly. Yet adolescents create their own lives within such an environment . . ." (p. 187). To a certain extent "they appropriate some degree of power and control in an organization within which they have been defined formally and symbolically as powerless" (p. 187). Thus, goofing off is a symptom of the "cultural separateness which is accorded them by the society through institutional arrangements at school." The goofing off shows how, through their resistance, students manage to maintain their own collective community within the society. Everhart suggests that if students were included in, and given reasons for, attaining a sense of community within the total enterprise, the need for community which they achieve through goofing off would diminish.

Curriculum

GENERAL PRINCIPLES OF CURRICULUM CONSTRUCTION   There is evidence also that the quality of curriculum declined in the 1960s and 1970s (Ravitch, 1983). A comparison of American high schools in 1974 and 1979 showed that students' involvement in community service and curriculum planning had declined, as well as the teaching of social issues (Tubbs & Bean, 1981). Although a few schools required a foreign language for graduation in 1974, by 1979 that requirement had all but vanished. More science, vocational, career education, and basic skills remedial courses were now provided, but fewer in special subjects, such as art, music, and modern language. In addition, in the era of student freedom of the 1970s, requirements gave way to electives and English "was replaced by courses on the mass media, pop culture and popular fiction. Writing, once a part of every student's daily regime, became a special course. Social studies was often splintered into mini courses in Black history, women's history, or rap sessions about values" (Ravitch, 1983, p. 69). In the mid-70s scores on the SAT fell dramatically as did scores on tests in junior and senior high school. High school students were taking more nonacademic courses and fewer of those required for college. As a result, society began to demand a back-to-basics curriculum, and by 1978 almost 40 states had adopted minimum competency tests for high school graduation. Currently, in the 1980s, society is demanding that American schools stop producing "second-rate brains," else our technologies and innovation will lag in world economic competition.

A strong recent emphasis in curriculum instruction has been on learning skills and on content, such as the classics, that have stood the test of time. Mortimer Adler (1979) recommends preparation for continuing to learn after formal school is complete. Individuals can then, by their own efforts, continuously become better educated throughout adulthood. All individuals should acquire these basics—and that is what quality education is all about. The gifted might learn them through analysis of the great books, while other materials and methods would be appropriate for the less gifted.

Adler advocates a liberalized, unspecialized kind of instruction that introduces youth to the whole cosmos of learning. The curricular content would embrace "basic ideas" that are "pivotal or controlling points" of civilization (p. 6). Even a superficial introduction into this world of learning would afford youth a sense of what they should learn as they pursue their own education after more formal aspects of it are finished.

On the contrary, Goodlad (1979) believes that the current stress on back-to-basics will simply accelerate students' alienation because schools will become even less relevant than they have been. Students need opportunities to derive rich and complex meanings and to devise their own individual creative modes of problem solving. The process becomes more important than the by-product—the means primary and the ends secondary.

In contrast, Anderson (1979) predicts that the only major curriculum changes in the next few years will be greater attention to the so-called basics, especially essay writing, a renewal of core curriculum, the focus on important but more limited goals than in the past, and the usual "curriculum tinkering." This focus on basics, which has gained widespread support of both educators and parents, derives in large part from students' declining performance on certain national standardized examinations.

Many persons are concerned about how schools may cope with the explosion of knowledge, which involves more than simply an increase in quantity. The quality of this explosion must be understood and related to each discipline. The problem will be to organize knowledge into patterns that permit the mind to grasp and retain the most significant concepts and knowledge and to understand their interrelationships.

EXTRA-CURRICULUM   An area in special need of upgrading is the extracurriculum program. Its inadequacies are of such long standing that they are accepted as inevitable. In a study of senior high school students, the amount of their participation in extracurricular activities was not very high (Buser, Long, & Tweedy, 1975). Students already succeeding in academic courses were those most likely to participate in student activities; those with low grades were usually not involved. The students participated for reasons other than those for which the programs had been designed. The educators named as objectives of such programs, "to prepare to become a more effective citizen," "to prepare for a vocation," and "to solve school problems." By contrast, 90 percent of the students said they participated mainly "for fun and personal enjoyment," "for personal achievement," and "for individual needs and special interests" (p. 125). Finally, although many teachers are expected to become involved in such activities, few have had any real training for them.

Interestingly, a reason often cited by schools for maintaining extracurricular activities is to keep certain youths in school. Among students in 22 states, about 70 percent reported participating in cocurricular activities, and interference with such activities was the main reason for giving up a job (Chase, 1982). It appears that extracurricular programs are very attractive to students and often account for their remaining in school. Recently some schools have either trimmed or eliminated such activities, but such procedures may increase the dropout rate. Note, too, that dropping out applies chiefly to those groups for whom schools are the main hope for "upward social and economic mobility" (p. 275). For instance, two-thirds of the black adolescents in this study took part in athletics and almost half of the females, white and black, in clubs. Hence, discontinuing such activities might become a major reason for these individuals to drop out.

According to some persons, the most important curriculum of all is not planned. The essence of the "educational enterprise" is not so much the curriculum of the school as in its "hidden curriculum" (King, 1975). The hidden curriculum involves certain latent assumptions about learning and knowledge. These assumptions are diffuse, representing feelings, beliefs, and images by which "one unconsciously judges events and things without questioning them, or even noticing them" (p. 116).

ADAPTING THE CURRICULUM TO DIFFERENT INTERESTS AND NEEDS   To more adequately meet individual needs high school programs are generally classified into three types: vocational, general, and college preparatory. Students in the college preparatory program have more ability and more advantages, backgrounds, and perform better in school than other students. Vocational students are similar to those in general programs in ability but sometimes perform better in the labor market immediately after leaving school.

In 1979 half of all high school students were in general programs, a third in college preparatory, and about a seventh in vocational. The proportion in each varied little according to sex and race but did by socioeconomic group. Those whose families were below the poverty level were far less likely than others to be in college preparatory programs and those whose parents had not finished high school were twice as likely to follow vocational programs and were less than half as likely to pursue the college preparatory programs as those whose parents had completed college.

The types of courses taken varied more by sex than race. Girls took more courses in foreign languages and boys in mathematics. Girls took most of their vocational courses in home economics and business, boys in business and trades. Overall, differences in the three categories of courses were quite small (Rumberger, 1982).

In college, too, curriculum choices are varied. In 1979 the most popular areas of study were business, physical science, education, and social science. Women more often major in education and health, men in engineering and physical sciences. Blacks more often major in business areas and whites more in the humanities and engineering.

To more adequately meet individual needs high school programs are adapting the curriculum to students' interests and needs. (Courtesy of Public Relations Office, State University of New York at Oswego)

Adapting the curriculum to individuals does not mean that every student should be free to pick and choose from a hodgepodge of subject offerings as casually as he or she selects food in a cafeteria. If students are permitted free choice, they may pick a course because the instructor gives easy grades or avoid a subject they need because the course meets on Saturday. Often students lack the maturity and experience to enable them to plan wisely without adequate guidance.

Tailoring the curriculum to individuals also involves a consideration of their stage of development. Certain modifications are appropriate for adolescents in general although adolescents themselves vary in degree of maturity.

Sizer (1983), former Dean of the Harvard Graduate School of Education, suggests certain measures for improving high school education. First, high schools need a shorter, better defined list of goals, which might involve the demise of some subject areas. For example, the time devoted to driver education might be given to English. Chemistry might not be taught as a subject but integrated with biology and physics. Second, students who enter high school unacquainted with the basics—reading, writing, and mathemtics—would focus exclusively on those subjects since they are the foundations of secondary school work. Third, students would not simply be told how to use higher-order thinking skills such as reasoning and synthesizing—they would become involved in confrontations and dialogue. Fourth, there would be some kind of culminating examination in high school or other proof of mastery before diplomas are granted, in contrast to the present system of dispensing them mainly for "dutiful attendance" (p. 682). Fifth, independent work should be encouraged, including teachers' evaluations of that work. Sixth, more attention should be paid to fundamental skills of thinking and expression which cut across existing academic departments—hence, are often ignored. The "fractionated curriculum that is inherited from the 1890s" would give way to a better coordinated one. Seventh, the chopping of the day into tiny bits of time would become displaced by larger chunks of time which would allow delving more deeply into one's studies. Eighth, age-grading would give way to allowing students to progress at their own rates. Students would not proceed to the next level of difficulty before mastering earlier ones. Ninth, mastery of the basic core of high school work should be for all, and any stereotyping or segregation according to sex, race, or class should cease. That would mean aborting early tracking or decisions on vocational education made by the end of the ninth grade and of magnet programs which actually perpetuate segregation. Tenth, students should learn how to come to connect what they learn in school with the world outside of school. Eleventh, out-of-school experiences should be related somehow to in-school life.

ASPECTS OF STUDENT LIFE TODAY

Violence in the Schools

Of late, society has become increasingly concerned about violence in the schools. In one year over 60,000 incidents of teachers being injured by students were reported (Handleman, 1980). Also common are robberies and acts of vandalism (Ianni & Reussl-Ianni, 1980). The rates of such behaviors as armed robberies, burglaries, aggravated assaults, and rapes in school have leveled off since the 1970s, but vandalism alone still costs education about $600 million a year (McGuire, 1980). In 1974 alone it was estimated that there were about 12,000 armed robberies, 270,000 burglaries, 204,000 aggravated assaults, and 9,000 rapes in public schools.

In a National Education Association teacher opinion poll in 1980 an estimated 5 percent of all public school teachers had been attacked by students in the previous four months; and of those attacked 2500 had been seriously injured. In 90 percent of these cases no charges were filed and in 25 percent no disciplinary action was taken. Also, over half (54 percent) of the nation's teachers say that student behavior interferes with their teaching. Perhaps in consequence, for every year but one between 1969 and 1980, the public ranked lack of discipline as the school's most serious problem, ahead of "lack of proper financial support, problems of integration, teachers' lack of ability, and use of dope or drugs, among other problems" (Starr, 1981, p. 213).

In questionnaires administered to over 300 middle school and high school individuals distinct differences were found between students who did or did not vandalize the schools (Venturini, 1982). It was found that 35 percent admitted vandalizing their schools, the females as often as the males. Most of these adolescents lived with their parents, enjoyed their family life, could communicate with their parents, and said that their parents were interested in their school work. About twice as many of the vandals did not enjoy their family life, and over twice as many felt they did not get enough freedom from home. The writer, however, poses this question: Did they feel they did not have enough freedom, or were they actually accorded little freedom? With regard to their personal lives over twice as many vandals did not feel good about themselves, and 30 percent used drugs compared with 22 percent of the nonvandals. The vandals felt a greater need than nonvandals to get even with someone (80 percent compared with 58 percent), and watched more violent television programs (74 percent compared to 51 percent).

In terms of school-related items, the vandals scored 20 to 32 points lower than nonvandals in terms of liking their teachers and the principal, and liking school and their courses. They also felt they had not been helped by the guidance personnel and that teachers weren't especially interested in them. Almost all the students liked the larger community but twice as many of the vandals disliked it. About half of both groups called the police nice guys. It would appear that those individuals who have family, personal, and school-related problems are more likely to vandalize the schools.

In other research, in an integrated junior high school in Minneapolis, which had a high incidence of antisocial behavior, over half the students (57 percent) reported incidences of fighting, extortion, intimidation, forced selling of regular and marijuana cigarettes; 40 percent complained of problems with the school plant (poor lunches, falling plaster, etc.); and 20 percent named problems with teachers such as poor instruction or being too lenient with those who misbehaved. With regard to personal problems 40 percent had trouble dealing with antisocial behaviors of their peers and 17 percent problems with curriculum (boring courses, and so forth). Most commonly recommended (by 27 percent) was the need for stronger school discipline. Two in five (40 percent), fewer than expected, said that independently working individuals would be interfered with by other students. About one in four (23 percent) indicated that the races did not get along well with each other. Much of the trouble was caused by a relatively small percent of the students, often in cliques of four to seven members. Perhaps these antisocial groups would have been larger had it not been that the students were bussed. Bart (1981) recommended that stricter discipline be coupled with instruction in communication which would teach students from different environmental backgrounds to communicate effectively with each other. Also recommended was human relations training, including open discussion of mixed groups of students which would help them interact positively together, thus reducing the need for behaviors such as intimidation and fighting. In addition, mastery learning projects should be tried to help the more troublesome individuals to achieve academically and thus reduce their need for mastery in less approved ways.

Students' Rights

The concern for student liberties has a long history. The history of student strikes and protests in American high schools stretches back into the 1870s, and in the early 1900s there were frequent strikes supporting student councils (Strauss, 1974). In the 1960s, the matter of student rights became one aspect of the broader civil rights movement. More recently, calm has prevailed; students seem to take for granted certain concessions won by their predecessors.

Issues regarding student rights extend to all aspects of academic and campus life. Educators have made concessions concerning students' extracurricular activities, smoking, and dress. In many schools, hairstyle and dress rules have been abolished, except for safety reasons, and censorship of student publications has been largely abandoned. As a result, student publications may now discuss such topics as sex, drugs, X-rated movies, and birth control devices.

Other issues relate to academic matters. In one case, a San Francisco high school graduate filed a civil suit asking a million dollars from the school district for failing to teach him to read properly (Drive for rights, 1974). Court battles have also been fought over psychological testing programs which involve questions about students' personal lives. As a result, testing programs have either been abandoned or heavily safeguarded to protect student rights.

Students are gradually gaining many of the rights accorded citizens in general. The Supreme Court has ruled that students do not shed their constitutional rights at the schoolhouse gate (Drive for rights, 1974). For example, students have a right to remain silent even if a school authority advises them to talk.

Nevertheless, Starr (1981) believes that most adults seem unconcerned that youths lack the civil liberties that they themselves have. Rather, in the last decade various public opinion polls have shown that most respondents favored stricter discipline of students, more corporal punishment, and parental censorship of textbooks. They suggested that students had too many rights and privileges rather than too few. Adults tended to disapprove allowing married pregnant girls to stay in school, and they opposed lowering the compulsory attendance age for youths not interested in remaining in school.

Starr (1981) concludes that "almost all schools today, despite many progressive innovations over the years, still conform in essential practice to the model of the nineteenth-century asylum." There is an enormous status gap between teachers and students. The latter are matched according to class level, moved around according to a schedule that is set for them, and placed under constant surveillance. All individual movements are monitored and must be approved by an authority. The principal norms of proper student behavior are "to sit quietly, follow directions, and do the assigned work on time." Privacy is nonexistent as "all authorities in the institution share observations of the student's behavior and everything deemed important is entered on a permanent record" (pp. 208–209).

Moreover, students who do not conform, especially those who somehow resist being subordinated, may receive corporal punishment, a practice receiving increasing public support. Within the late 1970s only three states—Massachusetts, New Jersey, and Maryland—expressly forbade such punishment. At the same time, the majority of western European nations, all of Eastern Europe including the Soviet Union, and Japan do not allow such punishment. Although most of such punishment occurs in elementary and junior high school there is some in high school, and it helps account for the growing violence of students toward teachers. Common methods of punishing high school students include keeping them after school, having them perform meaningless tasks until they improve their attitude, and suspending or even permanently expelling them.

School Environments

For children and youth the school environment is of special significance. From kindergarten through the twelfth grade, the average individual spends about 14,000 hours at school; and if preschool and college are added, the total reaches 20,000 (Gump, 1978). This time is not spent exclusively, or even primarily, in dealing with curriculum. Much of it is spent "living" in the school, both inside and outside the classroom.

Every school has its own unique setting, observes Goodlad (1977), and a main goal should be to help schools to develop dynamic environments, the assumption being that they will have a constructive effect on all people relating to them. Students have a right "to be educated in and for a community that goes far beyond what they can see and touch and smell" (p. 103). Hence, schools must become and perceive themselves as part of the ecosystem of all humankind.

Environments embrace "a variety of phenomena . . . physical context, action context, social climate, life space, etc." (Gump, 1978, p. 131). The classroom environment incudes such matters as how much room there is, seating arrangement, feelings of openness, and provision of interesting (or uninteresting) objects; and each individual experiences each aspect of the environment differently. While considerable attention has been paid to environments in elementary school, little has been accorded those in high school or college. College classrooms, especially, are usually drab, uninspiring places.

A school environment is both objective (in terms of both the actual things that exist there and the way they are organized) and subjective (in terms of students' reactions to it—especially to feelings of spaciousness or being hemmed in). All of an individual's former experience, besides intelligence, personality characteristics, and predispositions, modify perceptions of the environment (Wahlberg, 1978).

The growing interest in ecology has created interest in the impact on students of physical and architectural features of campus buildings. Students manifest keen interest in these aspects of their living situations, especially in the dormitories (Moos, 1978). Architectural design variables, such as number of one-person rooms, number of rooms assigned to a single student living group, and the quality of recreational facilities available, do not have immediate impact on behavior. Rather, these factors coupled with others, such as the type of students who live there, determine their particular impact. In a sampling of student living groups drawn from a larger national sampling on 16 college campuses, the architectural characteristics that related most strongly to social climate were the proportion of single rooms in the living group and the centrality of their location on campus. Where the proportion of single rooms was high, there was less emphasis on social interaction, intimate communication, spontaneity, and provision for varied activities. Living groups not centrally located on campus placed greater emphasis on such variables and also more on student control of house rules. Students in the noncentrally located living situations placed less emphasis on dating, partying, academic accomplishments, and formal structure of the living group. These more distant living groups developed a closer, more cohesive situation while neglecting certain aspects of college life that generally contribute to personal growth. In particular, they spent more time with each other, developing close relationships. The larger-sized living groups fared about as well as the small-sized ones, although each had its advantages and disadvantages. While the larger groups were somewhat less cohesive and less friendly, there was greater diversity and heterogeneity so that every student might find at least some compatible friendships.

Dormitory life, including its human and physical features, is an important aspect of youth's experience. Of 165 freshmen and sophomore university students who lived either in their parents' home or in a dormitory, those living at home perceived their parents as viewing them less favorably than did dormitory students (Schwab & Lundgren, 1979). One reason may be that earlier parent-child relationships tend to persist when students live at home, while those between parents and campus residents change. In the latter case, parents accept their almost grown-up children as being more independent and accord them adult status earlier. Students living at home also perceive their friends as evaluating them less favorably. The campus residents apparently develop more satisfying peer relationships and relate more positively to them. On the other hand, parent-peer relationships and self-esteem levels may influence a youth's decision whether to remain at home and go to school or to go away to college.

Munro and Adams (1977) related youth's identity formation to their college experience in its totality. They note that identities within the same person are achieved at different rates. In a comparison of same-aged college and working youth, both categories had achieved similar rates of commitment toward an occupational identity, though in different directions. Over 70 percent of both samplings were in either the identity achievement or moratorium statuses. However, fewer of the college students had achieved political, religious, and ideological commitments. The researchers speculate that the college atmosphere encourages remaining in the diffusion status (no commitments and an absence of crisis); and many of them remain in that status even after four years at a university. Some college students may use college environments and university attendance to avoid commitment. Besides, the college environments are somewhat flexible and open, permitting freedom of expression and thought and providing alternative ideological perspectives which students spend much of their time contemplating. That is, because of the "abstractness" of the college experience, more time is employed to finalize commitment. In contrast, the "concreteness" of the work-a-day world encourages "a right-wrong perspective" which produces earlier commitment.

STUDENT VIEWS OF LIFE ON CAMPUS   In order to determine in some detail how students experience college life, a questionnaire was submitted to students in adolescent psychology classes at the State University College, Oswego, New York (Table 12-1). In this school, as in most other institutions, students have won so much freedom, including emancipation from the old *in loco parentis* role of college administrators, that campus life has changed radically. Women students are no longer required to live on campus; now both sexes may choose where to live. Both sexes generally agree that both dormitory and off-campus life have many advantages, although most of them prefer to live off campus after the first year or two.

> FEMALE: It is a very good experience to live on campus the first year or two of your college years, because you'll meet many new faces there and learn how others live and function. Also, you still need the security of having everything right there for you within easy reach. However, once you've grasped all of this pretty well, you need the challenge and experience of living off campus in an apartment or house to prove to yourself if you're responsible and can handle living and sharing with others. You'll face many more small and large challenges living off campus, and it really is a good test.

> MALE: Most people I know who live off campus complain that they get tired of being with the same 3 or 4 people and do not get the benefit of 50 to 60 different attitudes of people on a floor in the dorm. They also complain of lack of cooperation because you expect so much more from the people than from a roommate or people living on the same floor.

The vast majority of those who live on college campuses prefer living in coed dormitories. Such residency does not produce greater promiscuity; the reverse is true. Almost all student testimony on this point is positive.

> MALE: I really like it. It gives me a chance to meet both males and females. I like seeing and talking with girls. People are more relaxed in a coed dorm than in an all-male or all-female dorm.

> MALE: Living in a coed dorm helps mingling male with female views, and each sex can better understand the other by sharing the same facilities.

Most students find both good and bad features about having roommates, although much depends on the individual student's personal inclinations.

Table 12–1: Extent to Which College Students Find Selected Campus Life Experience Satisfying

TOPIC	FEMALES (N = 60)					MALES (N = 60)					TOTAL (N = 120)				
	V.R.	S.R.	S.U.	D.U.	N.	V.R.	S.R.	S.U.	D.U.	N.	V.R.	S.R.	S.U.	D.U.	N.
	%	%	%	%	%	%	%	%	%	%	%	%	%	%	%
Life on campus, as distinct from life off campus	28	33	11	5	21	33	46	10	0	10	30	40	10	2	15
Life off campus, as distinct from life on campus	33	26	0	1	38	18	41	16	1	21	25	34	8	1	30
Having roommate rather than living alone	43	38	6	3	8	35	45	10	3	6	39	41	8	3	7
Living along rather than having roommate	18	28	8	16	28	8	28	18	11	33	13	28	13	14	30
Having access to good counseling service	38	20	0	1	40	13	50	8	1	26	25	35	4	1	33
Belonging to a sorority or fraternity	10	8	8	10	63	3	6	10	5	73	6	7	9	7	68
Campus peer relationships	70	23	5	0	1	38	55	3	0	3	54	39	4	0	2
Living in a co-ed dorm	45	16	1	0	35	53	33	1	0	11	49	25	1	0	23
Living in a dorm (whether co-ed or not)	26	46	13	5	8	23	53	13	6	3	25	50	13	5	5
College classes	26	56	11	1	3	18	66	11	1	1	22	61	11	1	2
Total college experience	73	23	1	0	1	55	41	1	0	1	64	32	1	0	1
Relationships with adults on campus	25	51	5	1	16	11	61	6	1	18	18	56	5	1	17

V.R.—Very rewarding
S.R.—Somewhat rewarding
S.U.—Somewhat unrewarding
D.U.—Definitely unrewarding
N.—Neutral

MALE: I like having a roommate in the sense of living in the same dwelling. But I also find it advantageous to have my own room. I like having people around, but often enjoy my privacy.

FEMALE: It is good to learn to live with someone else in order to learn about yourself. As you get older, though, your privacy becomes more important to you and having a roommate often causes more problems than it is worth.

Sororities and fraternities are not as important in students' lives today as they were several decades ago. Nevertheless, some students continue to find satisfaction in such experiences.

FEMALE: I never belonged to a sorority and I have a very negative connotation for them. I have a stereotype of them from living in the dorm, one in which they are sexually very loose and look for lushes. Fraternities also turn me off because they spend a large portion of their time talking and being active in sex just for the sake of sex.

FEMALE: Sororities and fraternities are good social groups for those who feel they have difficulties with socializing or wish to have a secure social status. But the majority of college students adapt to the social life around them and do not need a sorority/fraternity to supplement it.

Most students disagree somewhat concerning the value of their academic work. Almost all believe it could be improved; however, the quality of classroom experience varies greatly from one student to another.

MALE: Class is great. I like a relaxed atmosphere in a classroom. I feel more at ease and tend to get more meaning from the lecture.

MALE: I don't enjoy the majority of my classes because most of my teachers are more concerned with themselves than the welfare of the student. Also, many classes are overcrowded.

Students believe that they gain a great deal from campus life and activities outside the classroom.

MALE: I have learned not only from classes but from the many people attending college. College exposes you to a variety of life styles, ideas, and other ways of life.

MALE: I learned more about myself in relation to other people than I ever knew before. It has widened my vision of the whole society.

FUTURE PERSPECTIVES

Schooling has many significant effects upon students' futures. Factors contributing to success later in life include not only family background (especially father's occupation and income and parents' education), but also test scores in school, schooling completed, and such teenage personality characteristics as studiousness (Jencks, 1979). An especially limiting school experience is tracking, which provides different curricula for college-bound and non-college-bound high school students. This practice tends to define students' futures, the jobs they will get, and the social class to which they will belong (Williamson, 1977).

The college experience is often portrayed as having a liberalizing effect (Rich, 1977). While it is true that liberal arts and social science students tend to be more liberal in their views than students majoring in education, physical science, and preprofessional courses, college students in general do not become more liberal than control groups of noncollege graduates. Other long-term benefits of a college education are more clearcut—increased earning power and quality of life style. In general, observes Marvin Wachman, president of Temple University, college educated persons become more active, dedicated citizens and lead fuller lives than nongraduates. They are more likely than others to acquire a life-long interest in the fine arts, great literature, and nature's wonders (The value of college, 1977).

Despite their many accomplishments, schools could do a better job of preparing youth for the future. After surveying a sample of high school students in north and central Georgia, Schab (1979) concluded that much is to be desired in the way that secondary schools prepare youth for the work world. Schools fail to keep pace with the needs of society. Neither in curriculum nor in instructional methodology are students encouraged in the degree of flexibilty, examination of alternatives, or projections about the future required for effective adaptation to a rapidly changing society.

Schools must prepare students to deal with the proliferation of knowledge by teaching them better information retrieval and learning skills, especially in self-directed learning. Those individuals who, as adults, are able to keep up with the times, both on their own or in adult education classes, may well become the elite of the future. Those who emerge into adulthood with little appetite for learning and no real concept of self-as-learner may largely mark time instead of growing during adulthood.

Meantime, education will commonly be viewed as becoming a lifelong enterprise, and the medium for this expansion will be the computer, with stress on individualizing instruction. Teaching in the lower grades will be related, not simply to ability and IQ, but to data showing how a particular brain works best and in what environments. Thus, students who learn best through hearing (through the audio sense) will receive much instruction orally through teacher or computerized recording machine, whereas the more visual learners would devote more time to reading and writing on computer screens. In classrooms students will use desk-top computers to work on individual projects at their own speed. To keep pace with future developments adolescents must come to enjoy learning and perceive themselves as learners so that they will continuously update themselves during all their years ahead.

Finally, more attention should be paid to the influence of the larger school environment. Students perceive that the campus environment, as distinct from classroom experience, is importantly modifying their lives, but there has been little significant research concerning the larger college experience and how it relates to adult life. For example, if more informal discussion groups of social issues were instituted on campuses, might not students, as adults, assume more active roles as citizens?

Looking at the future, the continuing use of polls for determining school policies and issues will, to a certain extent, forestall a revival of faddism, since the public typically espouses more traditional curricular emphases (Ravitch, 1983). In addition, the growing interdependence of all the world makes it hard for schools to ignore the importance of the basics.

Looking ahead, the current preoccupation with excellence will last as long as society believes it is necessary in order to compete effectively in "the international marketplace of goods and ideas" (p. 71). Also, in the future, educators will be concerned, not merely with the traditional basics of reading, writing, and arithmetic, but also with "scientific literacy, cultural and historical literacy" (p. 71). Though fads themselves may "come and go" schools are now concerned with this broader definition of literacy (p. 71).

SUMMARY

Schools have a variety of goals; however, in recent years they have been valued chiefly as vehicles for personal and social development. In fact, despite the recently professed emphasis on academic preparation, schools remain somewhat anti-intellectual and vocationally oriented. However, schools differ among themselves, with some being far more academically oriented than others. Many educators and writers express lofty ideals on the topic, but a considerable gap exists between aim and fulfillment, which is not so much the fault of educators as that of the difficult conditions under which they work.

A second problem is that of dropouts. They may simply be academically retarded and unable to pursue further work, or victims of a personal crisis that forces them to leave school involuntarily; or they may be under-achievers who are capable but perform poorly because of poor motivation or weak early preparation. The effect of dropping out of college depends largely on the circumstances involved. Often it is a positive step, allowing an individual time for a temporary work experience or reassessment of goals. Often college dropouts drop in again later on.

There are at least three main problems. One is discipline, which involves helping the student acquire considerable self-control and maintaining reasonable order within the school. This problem has become especially critical as youth have attained increasing autonomy and responsibility. Its significance differs for normal and disturbed youth. Another problem is motivation. Unfortunately, artificial or extrinsic means of motivating students still prevail that divert them from more solid achievement. A third problem is the kind of guidance that fosters dependency and lack of self-respect in students. This area is one most heavily criticized by adolescents themselves.

Efforts to improve adolescent education involve upgrading methods, curriculum, guidance, and teacher-pupil relationships. Teacher-pupil interaction is especially significant in the learning process, and teachers' attitudes toward their pupils, both collectively and individually, influence how effective these relationships may be. There is probably no one recipe for a good teacher, although certain so-called good teachers apparently possess certain characteristics in common. Typically, they are well rounded individuals with creative, rich personalities. Teachers of lesser stature often have little impact on students.

The influence of most teachers on individual pupils is greater than they realize. Certainly, most of us can think of some teacher who has had a significant effect on our lives. The impact is especially strong and usually quite positive when an instructor becomes a mentor, providing special encouragement and guidance to a student.

The effectiveness of any learning experience relates to students' own personal characteristics, including their sociocultural status and sex. Traditionally, early education has been better adapted to girls and later education has been better suited to boys. It has often been noted that boys are disadvantaged in woman-dominated elementary schools; it has been largely overlooked that most college administrators and instructors, especially the higher status ones, are men. Minority students experience problems on both levels because schools are not especially congenial to their values and needs.

Certain characteristics of schools—for example, whether they are socially or intellectually oriented, large or small, rural or urban—modify their influence on students. Also significant is the demographic composition of schools, which affects the aspirations and activities of the student body. In addition, the adolescent's school experience is limited by factors outside the school, such as the community in which the school exists and the attitudes of parents and peers toward education.

Other factors within the school that affect the educational process are the curricula and teaching techniques employed. The most common methods today continue to be the traditional ones of lecturing, assigning homework and term papers, and giving periodic examinations. Much of the students' energy is dissipated in preparing assignments that have little worth to them. Nevertheless, traditional methods can be quite effective—and superior to less conventional ones with some students.

Traditional schools have their critics who advocate various new approaches for improving the teaching process in terms of both general principles and specific activities. Fortunately, some schools are beginning to experiment with more student-centered approaches. Schools with special programs and philosophies have also been instituted as alternatives to traditional systems. Whatever its philosophical structure or orientation, teaching will be most effective when it is properly articulated with students' stages of development.

The selection of proper curricula for youth is a subject of perennial controversy. In general, it is agreed that young people should learn how to learn and how to locate and deal with all kinds of data. It is also agreed that education should be relevant, although authorities often disagree upon what education is of most worth. In recent years, there has been renewed interest in a return to basics and a rejection of "soft" education. The content and function of extracurricular activities is being reevaluated. Lines are drawn between those who view them as anti-intellectual and those who believe them to be necessary in a well-balanced curriculum.

Lip service is given to the principle that curriculum should be adapted to the individual; however, it is uncertain to what degree students should be granted free choice over the courses they take. In fact, the whole question of how youth may most effectively be educated is under close scrutiny. It is agreed that considerable and continuing revision is necessary, especially regarding student conduct, rights, and responsibilities. Many provocative suggestions deserve a hearing and a trial in schoolrooms.

Students' out-of-class life is receiving increasing attention. Violence in the schools is forcing society to become interested in student activities. Students' insistence on their own rights has also made the broader aspects of school life significant. Students report that out-of-classroom life is more significant for their development than what transpires in the classroom itself. It is not surprising, therefore, that the college environment on campus and in dormitories has significant, though subtle, effects on students. Each college has its own unique complex of influences as reflected in college life on particular campuses.

DISCUSSION QUESTIONS AND ACTIVITIES

1. Topics for panel discussion: (a) What life-adjustment skills should be taught in present-day schools? (b) What are the special strengths and weaknesses of high school and college fraternities and sororities? (c) Would the work-study plan (working part time and attending classes part time) be good for all students? (d) Discuss raising the prestige of academic accomplishment in the schools, including such questions as these: Should school sweaters be given to persons of outstanding scholarly and creative ability as well as to athletes? Should social clubs be deemphasized in favor of discussion groups and scientific, artistic, and other special-interest groups.

2. How would you explain the low rating given by adults and teenagers to the academic function of the school?

3. Should some colleges be created especially for boys and girls of just average performance? How would these colleges differ from others?

4. Should the government pay total expenses of all boys and girls who can profit from college?

5. Would it be ideal if one year of college could be devoted to a world study cruise? How could this idea be made economically possible and educationally successful?

6. Interview dropouts concerning their reasons for not completing high school or college. Report to class.

7. In what respects do effective teachers of adolescents differ from those in lower grades?

8. Is it necessary for teachers to maintain a certain distance if they are to maintain their students' respect?

9. Is it wise for teachers of adolescents to have their students evaluate them anonymously? What are the probable good and bad effects of this procedure?

10. To what extent should a curricular program be elective or prescribed?

11. Write a paragraph assessing your high school counselors' techniques (using no names, of course). A group can collect the paragraphs and report to the class. In general, what do these paragraphs reveal concerning the effectiveness of present-day counselors?

12. List the most common forms of punishment used in the high school you attended. Compiled lists may be discussed in terms of effectiveness.

13. List points in this chapter with which you disagree. Then defend your position.

14. Appraise your own high school and college curricula in terms of students' needs.

15. Debate the issue: It is better not to go directly to graduate school after obtaining a bachelor's degree.

SUGGESTED READINGS

Arnstine, D. (1983). The deterioration of secondary education: Media in ages, administrative nostrums, and college pressures. *Teachers College Record, 85*(5), 9–26. This critique concerns the nature of, and flaws in, current suggestions for improving American education and suggests alternatives.

Borus, M. E., & Carpenter, S. A. (1983). A note on the return of dropouts to high school. *Youth and Society, 14*(4), 501–507. This study of reasons that dropouts do or do not later return to school indicated that, in many respects, the decision is a random event.

Damon, W., & Hart, D. (1982). The development of self-understanding from infancy through adolescence. *Child Development, 53*, 841–864. A review of the literature concerning self-understanding and the cognitive basis for self-conception, yields a description of developmental trends in this characteristic as well as an appreciation of its significance.

Everhart, R. B. (1982). The nature of "goofing off" among junior high school adolescents. *Adolescence, 17*(65), 177–188. This study of goofing off employs the phenomenological approach of examining behaviors from adolescents' perspective instead of imposing theories on them, and suggests that even apparently meaningless behaviors have significance.

Finkelstein, M. J., & Gaier, E. L. (1983). The impact of prolonged student status on late adolescent development. *Adolescence, 18*(69), 115–129. The study reported here indicated that prolonged student status was associated with emotional dependence, negative impact on sense of worth, and slower progress toward adulthood.

Hayes, R. L. (1982). A review of adolescent identity formation: Implications for education. *Adolescence, 17*(65), 153–165. An interactional perspective, based on viewing adolescent thought within the social setting, suggests a revised view of human development and changes in the way people are educated.

Lamke, L. K. (1982). Adjustment and sex-role orientation in adolescence. *Journal of Youth and Adolescence, 11*(3), 247–259. This study of the relationship between sex-role orientation and self-esteem in adolescence raises questions about widely held views of sex-role development.

Murray, H. G. (1983). Low-inference classroom teaching behaviors and student ratings of college teaching effectiveness. *Journal of Educational Psychology, 75*(1), 138–149. Trained observers who visited classes of university lecturers receiving low, medium, or high student ratings found significant differences in manner and method of the three categories.

Nixon, M. (1983). The psychological rights of the child and schooling. *Viewpoints in Teaching and Learning, 58*(1), 99–112. The issue—information about children in school—is discussed to illustrate actions that can be taken to safeguard minors' rights in this area.

Parsons, J. E., Adler, T. F., & Kaczala, C. M. (1982) Socialization of achievement attitudes and beliefs: Parental influences. *Child Development, 53*, 310–321. A questionnaire submitted to students in grades 5 through 11 regarding beliefs and attitudes about mathematics achievement indicated that parents held more positive views regarding this academic area with regard to their sons than their daughters with a correspondingly more positive influence on their sons' self-perceptions.

Piotrkowski, C. S., & Katz, M. H. (1982). Indirect socialization of children: The effects of mothers' jobs on academic behaviors. *Child Development, 53*(6), 1520–1529. A study of 10- to 17-year-olds supported the hypothesis that mothers' skill utilization and job autonomy related significantly to their children's academic behaviors, and somewhat specific relationships were found between parents' employment conditions and certain aspects of their children's school behaviors.

Poole, M. E., & Low, B. C. (1982). Who stays? Who leaves? An examination of sex differences in staying and leaving. *Journal of Youth and Adolescence, 11*(1), 49–63. An analysis of adolescents' statements disclosed factors associated with the predictability of an individual's remaining in or leaving school.

Rumberger, R. W. (1982). Recent high school and college experiences of youth: Variations by race, sex, and social class. *Youth and Society, 13*(4), 449–470. Differences in high school and college participation experiences are analyzed in terms of sex, race, and socioeconomic status.

Scheinfeld, D. R. (1983). Family relationships and school achievement among boys of lower-income urban Black families. *American Journal of Orthopsychiatry, 53*(1), 127–143. A study of 33 poor black urban mothers' views of the ideal relationship between their sons and the world to the sons' academic achievement suggested certain important and related issues in mother-son interaction.

Schneider, F. W., & Coutts, L. M. (1982). The high school environment: A comparison of coeducational and single-sex schools. *Journal of Educational Psychology, 74*(6), 898–906. A study of tenth and twelfth graders from all-male, all-female, and coeducational high schools indicated that students from the coeducational schools had an advantage in terms of social-emotional needs.

Steinbrink, J. E. (1983). Precollege global education: Goals and scenarios. *World Futures 19*, 37–46. A case is made for increasing global-international education, including goals and guidelines for such education.

Travers, E. F. (1983). The role of school in political socialization reconsidered: Evidence from 1970 and 1979. *Youth and Society, 14*(4), 475–500. This study within an academically prestigious and innovative school was designed to determine the effect of schooling and the educational process on adolescents' political attitudes and behaviors.

Yogev, A., & Schrift, R. (1983). Mobility channel preference and educational aspirations in a sponsored mobility system. Adolescence, *18*(69), 71–92. Analysis of personal preferences for alternative mobility channels on educational aspirations of Costa Rican adolescents indicated differences according to sex and social category.

Chapter Thirteen

The Adolescent In The Culture

THE SOCIOCULTURAL
ENVIRONMENT

General Significance

Many researchers have focused on individuals with little regard for their environment. In recent years, however, it has become increasingly recognized that humans continuously interact with and are modified by countless environmental factors. Among these are the economic environment, the moral environment, and the social environment. Collectively, the ecological environment may be portrayed "topologically as a nested arrangement of structures, each contained within the next" (Bronfenbrenner, 1977, p. 14). These structures embrace a microsystem, a mesosystem, and a macrosystem. The **microsystem** refers to relationships between developing persons and their immediate environmental settings, such as home, school, and neighborhood. The **mesosystem** involves interrelationships among major settings of a specific individual at some particular point in life. An adolescent's mesosystem might well include interactions among family, peer groups, school, and perhaps workplace or church. The **exosystem** is an extension of the mesosystem, embracing social structures that do not themselves involve the individual but affect that individual's surroundings. These structures include such social institutions as neighborhood, mass media, social networks, and transportation systems. The **macrosystem** consists of "overarching instructional, legal, and political systems of which the macro, meso and exo systems are the concrete manifestations" (p. 515).

Any particular society has its culture or way of life which stamps all of its members in varying degrees, most of them indelibly. Culture is so pervasive, so much a part of humans themselves that they take it for granted. Just as the oyster builds a shell which becomes part of the organism, so humans construct a culture that in turn molds them. Every individual's basic nature is overlaid by the culture in which he or she grows. Indeed, humans can be molded in so many ways that the temptation arises to view humans as the pawns of innumerable forces. Behavior seems a capricious thing, resistant to intelligent control.

Any intellectually honest sociologists or psychologists who fully accepted this defeatist philosophy would have to abandon their profession. Instead, they perceive humans as selecting from among variables available to them. Thus, individuals are not passively molded, helpless victims of their environment. They choose, consciously or unconsciously, according to past experiences and present needs. What emerges from these interactions is personality. No individual bears the impress of all the minute details of a culture. It is internalized only in certain aspects.

Note, too, that the relationship between youth and their culture is an interactive one. Since adolescents are constantly interacting with their environment, and also impinging upon it, they become "both products and producers of their world" (Lerner, 1981, p. 271).

Often parents are credited with being the main influence on growing children and youth. However, Edwards and Whiting (1980) stress the need to view parental socialization within the context of the broader culture. Parents are able more easily to transmit their values and behaviors to their children because of the broader supportive sociocultural context. Moreover, parents mainly transmit the values of their culture, as filtered through their own experience.

Environment and the Adolescent

Only recently has serious attention been paid to the more subtle ways that youth react to their environments. For one thing, adolescents' territorial space expands, allowing greater distance and autonomy from the family (Germain, 1978). Lower-class youth often have less space in the home and expand their territory to the streets. They are quite sophisticated on matters of gambling, sex, and drinking along their own street, but their domain is limited to the area where their own social class lives.

During adolescence, girls, more often than boys, maintain secret spaces within the mind, that they set down in letters, journals, and diaries. These secret spaces allow greater distance and freedom from the family. Adolescents also maintain secret physical spaces as they seek out places of privacy away from the family, such as in automobiles, on roof tops, in stairwells, or in attics.

The family home signifies one important aspect of space, its walls constituting boundaries between the adolescents' private space and the outer world. An individual feels crowded when the amount of space available is less that he or she requires. Isolation exists when the space is too great so that one is further from others than he or she wishes to be. In overcrowded houses, even bathrooms might not allow retreat. An individual's personal distance or space consists of a zone around the self that constitutes a sort of buffer or protective area and intrusions into that space become threatening.

Also significant is the matter of privacy within the home, especially in a world where populations are mushrooming and in a country where the price of homes makes large ones prohibitive (Parke & Sawin, 1979). The way this factor relates to parent-child interaction is complex. For example, restrictive mothers are also more likely to limit their children's privacy. In homes where parents, not the children, control the closed-or-open status of doors to rooms where their children are, mothers tend to be more coercive. On the other hand, there is a positive relationship between youths' keeping the bathroom door open while they are grooming and the degree of their mothers' affectionate behaviors. In

Individual space and privacy within the home helps the adolescent establish a sense of autonomy and self-identity. (Photo by William J. Butcher)

any case, having their own turf, as it were, and the right to privacy, would seem to help adolescents establish a greater sense of autonomy and self-identity.

THE IMPACT OF
ENVIRONMENTAL SETTINGS

Modern Western Cultures

THE PROTESTANT ETHIC   The formative relationship between personality and culture is complex and subtle. An individual is part of many subcultures, each with its distinctive ways of life. Nevertheless, members of industrialized Western societies long shared certain traditional values, including rationality, individualism, and achievement, a value cluster sometimes called the Protestant ethic. In America, this ethic gave rise to such concepts as "the American dream" and the Horatio Alger myth—that any poor boy can, through his own good character and striving, achieve success. Its ethical orientation may be termed instrumental or task-oriented, coupled with a consuming urge for economic success as the payoff for unrelenting hard work in competing with others.

While most of the older generation still cling to these values, many young people question them. The success of this ethic may have led to its undoing, for the material rewards of such striving resulted in affluence and, with it, the availability of considerable leisure time. The consequent legitimization of a leisure way of life, with stress on recreation and humanism, is in conflict with the relatively joyless Protestant ethic.

ASSESSMENT OF RECENT VALUES   Pervading the subcultures we have already discussed are certain over-all values common to the larger culture of the Western world, some of them positive, some negative, some both. The more positive Western values include altruism, democracy, and concern for the rights of the individual. Margaret Mead cited as advantages its adjustment to a pluralistic society where diversity is respected. In diversity there is strength because in it lie chances for variety and change. She also cited various benefits of modern technology; for example, modern communication has vastly facilitated the acceleration of learning and understanding among peoples of the world (Dangers and hopes for humanity, 1978).

Even divorce, so common in modern Western culture, may have its positive effects. As more family breakups occur and more mothers work outside the home childrearing patterns will change. Neighbors and friends, besides kinspeople and government, will play an active role and more government-financed day care and after school facilities will be provided. As a result children will have "more options, role models and support," predicts Harvard University psychiatrist, Alvin Poussaint; "It can be very positive [for] people must be more communal and cooperative" (p. A4). Furthermore, families will do things more as units—people will not be reared to be so individualistic that they care little for others. "Me-ism will soften and be replaced by we-ism."

Other factors have both positive and negative potential for affecting youth—for example, the fact that life styles are changing so rapidly. Change is one condition necessary for growth. Yet modification that is too swift makes for individual insecurity; inner feelings cannot shift at the pace of current reality. The American culture is also a strange mixture of pressure toward conformity and opportunity for self-expression. Despite its pressures on people to conform, modern culture has its niches for those who are different—surplus commodities in the mass marketplace.

Simpler Cultures

A clearer perspective on modern Western culture as an environment for adolescents may be obtained by comparing it with the culture of certain simpler societies. It has been claimed that modern society inevitably contributes to the difficulties of the adolescent's role. In contrast, Margaret Mead saw the culture in Samoa as a situation favorable to its adolescents.

> Growing up is easier in Samoa than in America because of certain important differences between the cultures. In Samoa all life is casual, unrushed. The world moves at an easy tempo; and close ties, strong personal loyalties, and consuming, driving motives seem absent. This primitive society is quite homogeneous and static; fewer choices are forced upon the child and adult. There is but one religion—not dozens as in America—and but a single moral standard. Sex expression is natural, pleasurable, and largely uninhibited. There are no contradictions between or within the ideologies of different groups. . . . Progression to full adult status comes at a regular time and without interruption. Rites confirming this passage clearly define each person's age stage, both in his or her own eyes and in those of others. Each individual knows what has been accomplished and what remains to be done. Because this new status is officially acknowledged, the adolescent is relieved from guilt about turning away from parental authority. (Mead, 1935, pp. 177–78)

For the children of Western culture, such transitions proceed less smoothly. At adolescence, they lose their status as the kingpins, the biggest children, in a world where play comes first. They must now start over again on the bottom rung of the ladder, and when they reach the top at the close of adolescence, they are thrown down to the bottom again. As fledgling adults they must start struggling up again on this longest of ladders, the ladder of adult achievement or disappointment.

In this society, rituals of marriage and graduation symbolize both for the individual involved and to others that his or her status has changed and that new behaviors, responsibilities, and rewards should be employed. However, the tasks and privileges accruing to such transitions are poorly defined and vary among subcultures—hence, they leave many areas of decision ambiguous for the individuals concerned.

Onyehalu (1981) believes that adolescents in modern complex society, where adults treat them in confusing, often conflicting ways, have a more difficult time achieving an identity than in more traditional simpler societies. In modern societies "prolonged schooling coupled with prolonged disengagement from marriage and from the world of work" presumably provides a moratorium for adolescents to prepare for adulthood. At this time, when they are supposedly sheltered by institutions they are also supposed to attain emotional balance and maturity. In contrast, in simple traditional societies adolescents attain a feeling of real belonging and confidence through initiation rites when they become of age. Then they are encouraged to marry early and thus avoid "the prolonged scourge of sexual pressures." In some less developed societies sexual experimentation by the young may be ignored or even encouraged. Also in such societies, extended family relationships and the comparative ease of entering occupations through a gradual apprenticeship have a relatively easy path to adulthood.

Of course, simple cultures have their disadvantages, too. In them, personality development is retarded in at least two ways. Authoritarianism is often the rule. The pattern of the life curriculum, so to speak, is less flexible. Comfortable niches seldom exist for deviates and there are few alternatives for the realization of individual gifts. Rigid prescription of conduct may lessen anxiety for the individual, but the result is a somewhat static civilization. Such factors are modified, of course, to the extent that foreign influences have penetrated primitive societies.

Even such advantages as may accrue to adolescents in simple cultures could hardly be transferred intact to a modern culture. Therefore, anthropological studies must be considered for what they are—isolated cultural case studies, possibly representing exceptional instances—precarious ground for general theorizing. Nevertheless, providing we preserve some degree of skepticism, such studies do furnish instructive examples of reciprocal interaction between particular child-training practices and adult characteristics. The Eskimos of Alaska, for example, take an interest in others' welfare, which apparently stems from the friendly community atmosphere in which they have been reared.

Cross-cultural Comparisons

Cross-cultural comparisons lend perspective to our own youth's status. In China, hard work is the ideal; the leisure way of life has not arrived. There is also widespread reverence and respect for old age; but in our culture where old age has been devaluated, youth look upon it with fear or dread.

In Germany, Britain, and the United States, Adleson saw in adolescence a steady movement toward realism, and by age 8 they had absorbed the conventional values of their society. The Germans had learned democratic concepts while in school; but they believed that people were "easily confused," and might "get into trouble" without strong leaders and strict laws (Adelson, 1980, p. 64). Of all three categories, the Americans were the most democratic.

A comparison of youth's attitudes in the United States and in Senegal indicated that among the Senegalese positive views toward the elderly on the test given numbered 41.2 percent and negative ones 58.8 percent, and for the Americans positive ones numbered 22.5 percent and negative ones 68.4 percent. The stereotype that emerged for the adolescents in both countries, ages 17 to 20, might be summarized in this manner: being friendly with old people is viewed as good but youth feel inferior to them. Older people are perceived as wanting peace, fearing and expecting death while yearning for paradise. They find work in any form painful because of their physical condition. The young like stories that old people tell of the past but dislike them when they engage in "idle talk."

There are also differences between the two groups. The Senegalese believed the older people had fewer emotional needs and felt less lonely. They held a somewhat subordinate, passive attitude toward their elders, more than did the American youth. More often than the Americans they downgraded their elders' physical appearance, whereas the Americans more often expected older women to feel anxious about their loss of good looks. The Africans were more concerned about older persons' loss of wealth and being willing to work, partly because the life of old people is much harder there (Vandewiele, 1982).

It is important to remember that youth in other countries, as in the United States, vary within subgroups. John Hofman found that Jewish and Arab adolescents living in Israel are both preoccupied with matters of concern to all adolescents—self-esteem, peer relations, and vocational choice. However, the Jewish students scored higher on items measuring need for power (I am glad when I succeed in dominating others) and measures of life satisfaction; and often agreed that "they do as well as most people" and disagreed that they are "a failure" (Guinzburg, 1980, p. 80). The Arab students who are members of the minority in Israel, more often scored themselves higher on items such as, "I would feel better if I had been born elsewhere" and "sometimes I feel I am worthless" (Guinzburg, 1983).

ENVIRONMENTAL SETTINGS IN THE UNITED STATES

The Neighborhood

Of major importance to adolescents is the subculture of their own neighborhood, especially the human beings who compose it. The neighbors may be homogeneous or heterogeneous—persons with similar background, income, and tastes, who belong to the same club, or a varied collection of faces, religions, and national origins, bound to the same locality by such factors as low rents and proximity to jobs.

Sometimes there are special persons or elements within the neighborhood affecting it for better or worse. In one neighborhood, a hard-drinking crowd of young adults seems the ultimate in sophistication to the local youth. The ages of the youth in the neighborhood are important, too. A teenager with few contemporaries at hand associates with those older or younger, or else ranges far afield. One boy who lacked friends his own age tied up with a gang of older boys who spent their time in his neighborhood. Lacking any purposes of his own, he joined them in smoking, annoying passers-by, and playing poker in garages.

Neighborhoods also differ in their effect on self-concept, some producing self-respect, some the opposite. In a certain small southern town, any child from one section is immediately tagged with a lower-class label. The very name by which the neighborhood is called conjures up a picture of run-down homes and backhouses. Here is the reaction of one city child to such a neighborhood.

As I grew up, the neighborhood I lived in seemed to deteriorate. The "El" trains nearby seemed to grow louder, the streets and buildings dirtier. When I became a senior in high school I was often invited to my friends' homes. They all lived in a much more modern neighborhood than I. When it came my turn to entertain I thought I would die from imagining my friends walking up the block—and seeing the "El", the bars, and the thousands of screaming kids.

The structure and location of neighborhoods importantly affects growing youth's development (Berg & Medrich, 1980). In neighborhoods of mostly adults, but few children, friendships are more formal and socialization more private. Recreation areas may, or may not, be suited to particular individuals' needs. Recreation areas may have been created for youth, but the latter often seek out their own undeveloped space. Sometimes areas planned for them are over-supervised, and youth avoid them. As a result streets often become youth's gathering places, despite the dangers involved.

Two special problems are those of mobility and safety. Parents may not grant their adolescent children sufficient autonomy; or ready access to transportation may be lacking. Also, there is the matter of personal safety, especially in certain areas. Some youths come to feel like captives in their own neighborhoods. The truth is, neighborhoods are constructed by adults, for adults, although this society is perceived as youth and child-centered. The result is that individual youths work out their own adaptations as best they can, often against considerable odds.

Of course, all people, including youth, differ with regard to their reactions to particular environmental contexts; however, there is general dissat-

Youths must work out their own adaptations of neighborhoods as best they can, often against considerable odds. (Photo by Michael Sullivan for the OEO)

isfaction with such factors as poor housing facilities, multiple-family dwellings, generally dilapidated appearance, high density, and racial integration. Beyond these generalities what constitutes an ideal configuration of residential factors varies considerably; and yet to be determined is the one optimum for youth, or for the various categories of youth (Galster, 1981). Also uncertain is how much such environments should, or feasibly could, be modified to meet youths' desires and needs, since theirs is a transient life phase.

The neighborhood is of special importance to minority group children. They believe that the neighborhood school belongs to them and is a segment of their territory. In this environment, composed of others like themselves, they feel at home and secure. They are not competing with children who are more favored in terms of parental education and social background.

Neighborhoods differ sharply in rural, urban, and suburban areas. When sixth graders from three contrasting neighborhood schools were asked to name people they knew best outside their immediate families, those from rural schools listed a greater number on the average (16.8) than did urban children (12.2) or suburban children (11.1). Urban children reported less interconnectedness within their networks. The proportion of adults among the top 10 they knew best was 30.9 percent for preadolescents, 19.9 percent for the transitional group between preadolescence and early adolescence, and 11 percent for the early adolescents. It becomes apparent that peers become increasingly important after the transition into adolescence, especially in rural areas (Garbarino et al., 1978).

Neighborhoods also differ in socioeconomic level, suburban neighborhoods being more affluent than the rural ones, and the urban ones least affluent (Garbarino, et al., 1978). Urban children reported fewer people to whom they could go for help with problems (on the average 1.6) than did suburban (2.4) and rural children (2.5). Children on highest socioeconomic levels reported that 3.6 adults took some interest in them, compared with 2 for children in the lowest levels. Many children in suburban neighborhoods named no adults among the 10 people they knew best; and more physically advanced youth reported fewer involvements with adults than did less mature ones (31 percent versus 18 percent). Thus, each child perceives a different "social map" or "network" and these maps vary with age and social class.

The City

Of all types of communities, the city arouses smallest enthusiasm among youth. In a national sampling of college seniors, the majority (54 percent) did not want their children to grow up in a city, and another 16 percent were unsure (Hadden, 1969). Only 25 percent desired that their children live in the central city so that they could go to school with other races. When asked what city, if any, they would prefer to live in, one in four would live in New York, and almost half (48 percent) would pick San Francisco. All in all, concludes Hadden, "it seems fair to infer that the student majority that now joins Pete Seeger in protesting life's 'little boxes' will soon join their parents in suburbia's little boxes" (p. 69).

Even within the same city, the influences that impinge on its inhabitants vary greatly from one section to another. Some sections are affluent, others are poor; some are impersonal, as in much of Manhattan; others are neighborly, as in the Southie community of Boston. The latter is like a village, and its people there are unashamedly provincial.

An important aspect of urban adolescents' experience is the school environment, especially in the inner city. In contrast with suburban schools, inner city ones are large and usually have older facilities, factors which contribute to their anonymity. Often anti-social gangs establish their "turf" in less desirable, "less defensible" school territory such as dim hallways or bathrooms. Such schools tend to produce a certain anomie or normlessness among inner-city students, who often lack supportive environments outside school as well (Wiatrowski, 1983).

The Farm

As an environment for youth, the farm wins no more laurels than the city. Farm communities tend to be very homogeneous in their values and class structures. Farm families have lower incomes than urban families do; their school systems typically lag; and their children are less likely to continue their education beyond high school. When they go to the city, as many must do as opportunities on the farm decrease, they often become shunted into low-prestige occupations. Even those boys who have grown up planning to farm are at a distinct disadvantage in job competition if they must shift to something with which they are unfamiliar. Farm youth, too, are ill-adapted, by reason of their upbringing, to succeed in city jobs. They prefer the freedom of being their own boss. Farm boys prefer to work with things, while boys living in towns prefer working with people. In addition, they experience more feelings of shyness, self-deprecation, and suspicion than do urban youth.

The differential impact of urban and rural environments is considerable, but the relative benefits—or the reverse—of each depend somewhat on the needs of individuals involved (Ulrich, 1981). Youth who are anxious would seem to relax more easily in natural environments when exposed to views of water and vegetation; whereas urban scenes might tend to aggravate their stress. On the other hand, those youths who tend to react more than they act, and suffer from understimulation, might find urban views more helpful. Of course, the optimum might be a combination: rural scenes with a dynamic flavor—tumbling water falls, strong winds, and changes of season or urban areas plentifully dotted with parks and trees.

The Suburbs

Life in the suburbs may have both positive and negative effects. On the negative side, materialism prevails, and a certain rivalry exists among surburban youth over clothing and possessions. They will unite to force their parents to buy the latest model car or television set, or a girl will complain if she feels less stylishly dressed than her friends. The young people of both sexes form exclusive social circles. A favorite pastime is to organize automobile parties to attend various eating or dancing places a dozen or more miles away.

Sociologist Edward Wynne believes that the suburbs may overprotect children, isolating them from reality and diversity, thus producing immaturity and preventing the development of the coping skills needed in adulthood. The school, family, and community all represent homogeneous relationships and values that fail to afford children diversified emotional experiences. While suburbs may indeed be clean, relaxing, and physically safe, they may fail to develop the "negotiating skills" required of adults. Suburban children come from homogeneous backgrounds and have similar attitudes about what is fair. Therefore, they have little opportunity for dealing with people who perceive things from a variety of viewpoints (The sheltered life, 1978).

The idea that they are getting ready for important positions is a major note in suburban adolescents' lives. This concept also implies that they will go to good colleges, will be adept at handling people, and will be resourceful. The last two virtues they exercise by wangling use of the family car and winning parental indulgence for escapades.

Small Towns

Life in small towns, too, has its distinctive features, and it shares certain advantages and drawbacks with both urban and rural life. In small towns, youth get along very well because of kinship networks and certain customs that are integral parts of small-town life. In addition, small-town youth are less restricted than rural boys and girls, and they attend more cosmopolitan schools. However, their power for self-decision may be limited because it is often hard for small-town youth to escape the surveillance of their elders.

A French anthropologist, who studied life in a small midwestern town, suggests some of the implications of small-town U.S.A. life for youth's development (Varenne, 1978). While adolescents in small towns are presumed to experience a somewhat homogeneous environment, such is not the case. There are dominant groups in the community and also fringers who may live on the outskirts and hardly be seen except when producing their food stamps in the supermarket. Young people had their own subgroups in this particular community, from youth of the more affluent to the greasers and the freaks. The members of each of these groups had little to do with the others, although some youth would move from one of these groups to another.

The Fourth Environment

Considerable research testifies to the effect of three environments on growing children and youth—home, playgrounds, and specifically child, or adolescent-oriented institutions (for example, schools and summer camps); however, the role of the "fourth environment has been largely neglected" (Vliet, 1983). This environment consists of shops, trees, buses, restaurants, and other public places which impinge on growing individuals in a variety of ways. These places may provide part-time employment, places of socialization and recreation, identification with role models, and the acquisition of skills that will gradually facilitate induction into the world of adults.

The distance that youth can range from home is in itself of some significance. The further teenagers range from home the more diverse are their activities. Also they possess correspondingly greater knowledge about the resources in their environment. On the other hand, the effect is not straightline—

there is a point beyond which the effect of further ranging may be detrimental. Besides, the quality of the experience may outweigh distance from home in effecting outcomes.

Environmental planners might facilitate growing youth's access to the fourth environment in a variety of ways. For example, they might provide youth with discount fares, or bicycle lanes; or such behavior settings might be integrated into local neighborhoods, providing more differentiated settings.

Subtle Environmental Influences

It is uncertain to what extent young people are affected by subtler environmental forces. For example, to what extent has the growing concern about energy resources and nuclear war contributed to youth's feelings of insecurity? Does population growth tend to reduce youth's search for individual identity or even make such a search useless? To what extent do such factors as climate, geographical features, including elevation or available space, affect youth? Lynch (1977) reports that unprogrammed space—which youth may use as they like— is of special importance. When asked what they would like to do, what places they were interested in, and where they like to spend their time, they did not speak of the school or the playground. Instead they talked about the street, their own room if they had one, and, to a certain extent, sports facilities, open spaces, and the center of the city. Yet students of adolescents rarely study these places, failing to recognize the importance of just hanging around in safe though stimulating environments.

Also important are the resources available to youth in particular environments. Certainly some environments are far more conducive to individual growth and development than others. San Francisco, Paris, and New York have rich and multiple resources for individual development, including cultural opportunities, varied subcultures, and various kinds of therapies; however, their populations must develop a knowledge and appreciation of these opportunities if they are to profit from them.

SEX DIFFERENCES   Because the sexes are not reared alike, environments impact differently on them. Boys have greater access to the world outside the home. Wolf, Schearer, and Laufer (1976) found that boys from age 8 on, more often than girls, described more outdoor places than indoor places other than their own homes. Girls are accorded less opportunity in all communities, but the degree of restriction varies. There is the greatest degree of sex equality in the suburbs, slightly less in the cities, and severe inequality in rural sections (Hart, 1978). The restrictions on rural girls, conjecture Moore and Young (1978) may stem from the parents' wish to protect their daughters or to have them do more chores around the home.

IINDIVIDUAL DIFFERENCES   The foregoing discussion must not be overgeneralized. There are many varieties of cities, villages, and rural areas; and there are wide variations within a region or from one social level to another within the same incorporated area. Furthermore, the impact of any environment depends on what individuals bring to it—that is, their own personalities and their need-fulfilling or need-frustrating habits. In Sweetser's (1941) diagram on the personal acquaintances of residents in a single square block in Bloomington, Indiana, one girl had 3 associates and another had 59. Each girl in effect lived in a different neighborhood. To the first girl, the world outside her door was largely foreign, even hostile; to the other, it was dotted with opportunities for companionship. Both girls lived in the same geographical environment, but their behavioral environments were totally different.

SELECTED SOCIOCULTURAL PROBLEMS

Of the many sociocultural problems with which humanity is confronted today, certain ones stand out as being particularly challenging. The following discussion will treat several that are especially relevant to adolescents.

Cultural Discontinuity

In some societies, especially simpler ones, as well as in certain subcultures within modern society, the tasks of children and adolescents prepare them specifically for their adult roles.

In more complex cultures, sequential age roles in society are discontinuous; that is, expectations for earlier and later roles are contradictory (Mortimer & Simmons, 1978). For example, children, and to a lesser degree adolescents, are "socialized to be submissive, asexual, and nonresponsible while adults are expected to be their opposites. In order to achieve such a sharp transition, considerable socialization of young adults is essential" (p. 421). Or take another example: Despite our urban industrial society's complex network of occupations, the lives of children are relatively holistic. That is, their early training and education concern a broad range of curricula and activities. However, when young people assume jobs, this range narrows quite abruptly and thus requires specific attitudes and behaviors for which youth are psychologically not prepared. Adolescents have grown up as generalists, familiar with symbolic expressions of common life experiences of the members of the society, but now they are confronted with isolated, discrete behaviors associated with a specific job. Finally, after practicing such a specific role for a period of years, young adults lose sight of the diverse life experiences to which they became accustomed as children.

The Pace of Change

Because of rapid change in our society, youth have trouble establishing historical connections with their past and future. They are dislocated in history, unable to identify with the past because it is already out of date. Meanwhile young people must work out a sufficiently flexible identity to relate meaningfully to a shifting environment.

The impact of change will extend to every aspect of daily life style. As youth enter adult society, they adapt their life styles to the necessity of obtaining life's basic essentials, especially food, shelter, and energy. Yet they find that provision of these essentials requires coping with rapid change—"for example, food costs continue to rise. Consumers, facing innumerable supermarket shelves, confront a complicated web of agribusiness, shipping, food preparation and preservation additives, packaging, pricing, shopping, restaurants, etc. New food products are introduced regularly and advertised extensively" (Nourse, 1979, p. 449). Coping with survival needs will require facing rising real estate costs, dealing with pollution wastes, and family mobility. The use of energy resources will require an understanding of conditional and potentially alternative fuels. Without proper knowledge of alternatives, young people will find living very expensive and often overwhelming.

Another problem is adapting one's personal pace to the time system of society. In leisure concerns, people are urged to relax and slow down while being constantly pressured at their vocation to make better time. A continuous stream of inventions, such as jet craft and computers, transform concepts of time. Adolescents must somehow gear their personal time reference system to external timing programs. An individual's internal time concepts have a physiological base, deriving from various internal rhythms, and one must adapt these rhythms to those of the environment (Ashton, 1976).

Mobility of Population

Not all individuals simply fall heir, via birth, to a particular growth setting and remain there. Youth will often find themselves in situations and settings completely different from those in which they have been reared because of currently high rates of geographic mobility. An individual must become familiar with new life styles and viewpoints.

Parents may move not just once but many times; and the over-all effect depends somewhat on their socioeconomic status. Middle-class mobile adolescents—that is, those who move—appear socially poised, mature, and somewhat adult oriented. They spend much leisure time with their families and often select their parents as models, but they are not unusually dependent upon them. Even while severing, or at least loosening, their emotional ties to the family, they are unlikely to use the peer group as a significant medium of transition to independence. Rather, these youth appear to move directly toward independence and, in the process, are constantly encouraged by their parents.

A form of mobility, experienced by increasing numbers of youth—travel in other countries—sometimes produces culture shock when in those countries and re-entry shock when returning home. They often go abroad because they are Peace Corps volunteers, exchange students, or are simply traveling abroad.

Culture shock, experienced through being in an unfamiliar environment, is quite common and can be mitigated through prior knowledge of the cultures to be visited and through recognizing that it is usually transient. An individual may be less vulnerable to culture shock itself by becoming familiar with the language and culture of the region to be visited and also through understanding the phenomenon of culture shock. Anticipating it in advance can help considerably in preparing oneself psychologically.

Re-entry shock may be as stressful as culture shock, and may take the form of antagonism toward the American culture and a "romantic idealization" of the travel abroad. Individuals who experience re-entry shock may be helped by talking with others who have traveled or lived overseas (Locke & Feinsod, 1982).

Cultures Within Cultures

Almost all young people must learn to adapt themselves to at least two kinds of groups, each with its own culture patterns. First, they must adapt to primary groups, those with which they have intimate, face-to-face contacts and fairly permanent relationships, including family, circles of relatives if they are nearby, and even neighborhood associates. Second, they must adapt to secondary groups, those in which predominant relationships are more impersonal—for example, colleagues on the job. In static cultures, children need adjust only to primary groups; they grow to maturity among those they know well. But in modern industrial society, it is nearly everybody's experience to spend much of his or her life among secondary groups.

Usually youth continue to live among primary and secondary groups at the same time. For example, when they take jobs, they may continue to live at home but commute to work. In such cases, the two kinds of environment they face each day may be so contrasting as to be disturbing. At home, the young person may be the center of things, but in the factory he or she is an insignificant cog in just one wheel. In school, one may encounter difficulties, too, for after graduating from a small, homogeneous elementary school, the adolescent may be overwhelmed by a much larger high school population composed of a hodgepodge of races, social classes, and personalities.

One problem is that growing children come to identify with particular national, racial and ethnic groups, and to consider those to which they do not belong as out-groups. Thus they come to establish their identities in terms of contrasts between the groups to which they belong and others. While a study of 6-, 10- and 14-year-olds from ten countries revealed less compartmentalization than expected, parents still emphasize contrasts in bringing up their children (Lambert, 1981).

Logan and O'Hearn (1982) suggest the importance of young people's experiencing both at school and elsewhere a diversity of viewpoints. However, such exposure does not guarantee that one will actively participate in this complex diverse society. Rather, many young people appear bent upon avoiding experiences of complexity and simply going along with currently popular characteristics of youth's life style. As a result, the adolescent life style may be more monolithic than diverse, and consequently not stimulating to reflection upon alternative views.

MEXICAN-AMERICAN YOUTH   The ways of life and the problems of youth from different ethnic backgrounds vary considerably. For example, contrast the status of the Chicano and the Asiatic youth. About 4.5 percent of American youth are of Spanish origin, including Puerto Ricans, Cubans, Mexican-Americans, and Central and South Americans, and all possess a rich cultural heritage. A few of their parents are small businessmen and professionals; however, the children are chiefly from urban working-class homes. A brief portrait of Mexican-American youth will, in effect, constitute a reasonably accurate picture of Spanish-American youth in general (Thornberg & Grinder, 1975).

The family unit of Mexican-Americans is nuclear, and family bonds are of prime importance. The family's power structure is highly traditional: the mother defers to the father; the children, to the father and the mother. The older children boss the younger ones, and the men order the women. Boys are reared in the image of their fathers, and they ordinarily dislike for their mothers to work because it threatens their masculinity. The girl models after the submissive, nurturant role of the mother. At about age 15, a girl ordinarily begins dating at the request of some male, with the consent of her parents. During the courtship period, she is treated as "a queen" by the male; however, after she gets married she dedicates her life to the welfare of her husband and children.

Today's Mexican-American youth are struggling for a sense of identity, and they insist on preserving their individuality, cultural heritage, and language. They are proud of their Mexican heritage and intend to preserve it, but they are affected by the larger Anglo culture as well. They want to prove that they can learn, that they are intelligent, and that they can attain worthwhile future goals.

The schools in the southwest, where 85 percent of Mexican-Americans live, are beginning to recognize their special needs. They are beginning to incorporate into the curriculum units on Mexico and Mexican-American history to foster a better understanding of their customs, to individualize their instruction, and to provide textbooks geared to their interests.

ASIAN-AMERICAN YOUTH Unlike the Mexican-Americans, Asian-American youth, who include Chinese, Japanese, Burmese, Philippinos, and others, constitute an "invisible minority" within the American society. Also unlike

Asian-American youth do well academically and have high achievement aspirations.

Mexican-Americans, blacks, Indians, and Puerto Ricans, who have been awarded all sorts of special opportunities, Asiatic youth have been declared a success, hence, deprived of special consideration. Certainly, compared to other minorities, they have gained higher socioeconomic status. They also do well academically and have high achievement aspirations. On the other hand, since they have close relationships with their families, their cultural orientation is marginal even in the second and third generations. That is, their status is ambivalent; they are astride two cultures, the traditional culture of their parents and the culture of America.

Nevertheless, several factors have tended to create a new generation of Asian-American youth and a sort of third culture, including "the crumbling walls of their ghettos . . . the erosion of traditional authorities, a steadily prosperous economy, a rising middle class, the anachronisms of clan associations, student radicalism . . ." (Liu & Yu, 1975, p. 388). They have grown tired of simply measuring up to their image as a "model minority;" since they are also tired of the "passivity and timidity of their parents, proud of their heritage, and yet reaching into their Asian roots in order to give new meanings to their existence, this sweet-and-sour generation has undoubtedly created new symbols and forged an untrodden path for itself" (p. 388).

Much that is written about Asian-American youth applies only to males; researchers have largely ignored females. Asian women have traditionally been subservient to their men and have remained dependent socially and economically. To what extent the women's liberation movement may influence their motivations and life styles is uncertain.

SPECIAL CONSIDERATIONS   For a better perspective on minority youth, note that they are somewhat less anxious and less fearful than upper middle-class children because they have support from the extended family, the church, and certain cultural and social traditions (Coles & Woodward, 1975). Moreover, childrearing patterns are consistent among these minorities because parents adhere to tradition. As a result, young children in such families find their world relatively calm and steady, even if material resources are scarce. However, as they move into adolescence and find that teachers cater more to children from affluent families, they may get pushed around by authorities. Hence, they may begin to feel powerless and to perceive no real future for themselves.

Because of the increasingly popular concept of cultural pluralism, there is far greater chance now than in the past that such youth will be respected for their own special contributions to society. This concept suggests "that separate groups coexist harmoniously, secure in their distinctive biological, religious, linguistic, or social customs, and equal in their accessibility to natural resources, civil rights, and political power" (Havighurst & Dreyer, 1975, p. 269). This view contrasts with the melting-pot tradition whereby newcomers to the country submerge their identities in the larger American culture.

In order that a pluralistic society be successful, its youth must not only understand and take pride in their own group, but come to understand and accept the existence of other groups. At the same time, they must be made aware of simplistic stereotypes and resist the temptation to regard all other groups as "out-groups" (Havighurst & Dreyer, 1975, p. 275). A delicate balance must be maintained lest they either become encapsulated among their own people, thus depriving themselves of a richer, more varied life, or else reject their own people and their own special contributions in order to identify more completely with the majority group.

SOCIAL CLASS STATUS AND THE ADOLESCENT

Significance of Social Class Status

Subcultural conflicts involving social-status groupings are so complex as to deserve isolation for special analysis. Whether or not they are on the wane, different status levels exist in the United States. Expressions like "the Four Hundred," "the right people," and "the wrong side of the tracks" all bear witness to their existence.

Even in the same school, adolescents of each social class are subject to different motive patterns. Lower-class youth work hard only when immediate gain is in sight; middle-class adolescents strive for a postponed goal and assume that their reward will come later. For lower-class youth, remote rewards appear too uncertain to provide motivation.

Middle-class youth are taught to be pillars of respectability and to do nothing that will hurt the family reputation. They must be clean, respect property, and curb aggression. Lower-class youth express their emotions more freely. Standards of appearance and cleanliness differ, too, by social class. Middle-class adolescents tend to dress conservatively, while the lower classes take pride in flamboyant clothes.

Upper-class Youth

Americans in general are abysmally ignorant about what it's like to grow up in the upper class. The children of the very wealthy, the chairmen of the boards, heads of the old and new upper-class rich dynasties, must incorporate into their life styles riding lessons, ballet lessons, tennis lessons, dancing, parties, socializing, and endless rounds of activities, often meaningless to casual observers. Nevertheless, among the rich, these activities encourage virtues of persistence, self-discipline, and self-possession.

Wealthy parents do not conform to the common stereotype of spoiling or neglecting their children while they pursue their own pleasures. Rather, they instill in their children the responsibilities inherent in privilege and teach them habits of authority and command, beginning with self-control. They instill in them a certain tough-mindedness, including a capacity to cope with obstacles and an acceptance of social-class differences. Parents are not insensitive to class differences or injustices that may exist, but they have no ready answers for how they should be resolved.

Wealthy parents typically have firm ideas about childrearing, in contrast to middle-class parents who are unsure of the values they should transmit to their young. Middle-class parents may be confused about expert advice and even give in to a certain extent, concluding that children must make their own decisions.

Wealthy parents relate to the young the historical legends of their family,

Wealthy parents instill in their children responsibilities inherent in privilege and teach them habits of authority and command. (Courtesy of Public Relations Office, State University of New York at Oswego)

which instill in them a sense of generational continuity lacking in middle-class families. This sense of continuity may decrease as the managerial élite take over from the older propertied upper class. The older bourgeoisie, deriving its position from property instead of salaries, symbolizes the peak of status. While it still owns large real estate holdings and department stores in the West and South, it no longer maintains large corporations or assumes the major role in politics. This class is diminishing and may largely die out.

Nevertheless, even in these times, these families, especially in the West and South, inculcate in their children a strong sense of local pride, to some degree mixed with feelings of concern that outside influences, including government and immigrants to their area, threaten their own power. Ultimately, the children themselves come to identify with the family fortune and the family pride. The children have a feeling of entitlement, derived not solely from wealth but from feelings of historical continuity and place.

Middle-class Youth

Middle-class youth enjoy certain advantages. Certain significant socio-economic developments since 1900 have improved their status, including the growing proportion and the increasing affluence of the middle-class (Wieder & Zimmerman, 1974). Consequently, they not only enjoy the material items that growing individuals value; they can also afford to go to college. In fact, family income determines, in large degree, the kind of institution a youth attends. Those attending prestigious universities and private colleges generally come from well-to-do families and expect to fill managerial, professional, and official positions.

Upper middle-class youth, especially, experience increasingly favorable status and self-enhancement as they move from childhood to adolescence. In early years they are constantly exposed to worried, anxious parents "who frequently have no real faith in much of anything, parents who are bandied about from one child-rearing expert to another . . . from one secular creed to the next" (Coles & Woodward, 1975). Later, after a somewhat difficult childhood, they have a better time. They acquire the stereos, motorcycles, and cars that youth of less affluent families cannot afford, and they take for granted their family's comfortable status in school and community. As a result, they develop increasing effectiveness, authority, and independence.

Of course, in some cases problems do arise. In clinical experiences with over a hundred upper-class families in which the chief wage earner attached primary importance to his corporate role, three major coping patterns emerged among adolescent children (Gulotta & Donahue, 1981). The first pattern was one of compliance; such young people never came to clinics. Instead, they were considered to be perfect children and students, successful academically, athletically, and socially. They were given much attention, many gifts and commendations by their parents. The second pattern was one of quiet resistance, when young individuals simply resisted their parents and experimented on their own in an effort to find out who they were. Often quarrels with their parents were triggered on occasions when the family moved or when their friends moved away. In such transitions they might fail in school, use drugs, or abandon social activities. The third pattern, one of overtly hostile defiance, appeared when their parents' relationship with each other were poor and their own relationship with the parents, especially the father, was strained.

Working-class Youth

With regard to the white working-class, we think of white-collar versus blue-collar, mental work versus manual work, and differences in income, values, and life styles. The lower limit of the white working class is just above the poverty line and the upper limit just below the point where it is automatically assumed that children in the family will complete high school or go on to college. Their family relationships are stable and close, and they grow up mostly in unbroken families.

Boys and girls experience school somewhat differently. After midadolescence, working-class boys begin dropping out of school, although they may return to school for a while. Neither parents nor teachers are surprised if they leave before graduation. The main service of the educational institution is to help them gain some occupational expertise. Girls' situation in school is somewhat different. They remain in the invisible middle of the class and do far better than the boys, academically, more through "good girl" conformity than through any real commitment to learning.

Youth in a Technological Age

All youth, including the disadvantaged, are often portrayed as being trampled under by the onslaught of technology. They are characterized as victims of a machine age, trembling at the confrontation with their own powerlessness, or as the frivolous offspring of the age of psychoanalysis, jazz, and marijuana.

Since young people are especially likely to latch onto new products of technology, they are correspondingly susceptible to whatever dangers may be inherent in their use.

Unfortunately, Americans have felt that science might solve all social problems. The trouble is, concludes Zimmerman, that youth protestors have failed to understand the technology that they distrust. They attacked technology for its waste and pollution; but their attacks were upon technological hardware—and that is not all there is to technology. The core of technology is in treating the universe as "raw material to be exploited by man" (Technology's effect on American society, 1978, p. 442). Nature itself possesses "no intrinsic value" (p. 442). Technology can be employed in either constructive or destructive ways.

From the world view, nature is not to be exploited but is a partner of man. Society must avoid using technological hardware wastefully and ruthlessly or overlooking its hidden social costs. The challenge is to understand and properly control technology so that nature becomes a partner with human beings in their search for fullest self-realization.

To this end, Rosalyn Yalow, Nobel prize winner in physiology and medicine (1982), believes that every high school graduate should be taught enough science to make intelligent political decisions. In this technological age they must, to be good citizens, be well informed about science. Yet, in this country as compared with Japan, "we train 70 times as many lawyers and half as many engineers" (p. 26).

Young people should also understand the special issues relevant to this age. Snyder points out that in earlier times people appeared to worry about such fundamental biological issues as, "will I eat, or be eaten" (Snyder, 1980). However, these days we are confronted with issues of a more "existential nature," one such issue being how to preserve individuality in our increasingly complex, technological, and highly populated society" (p. 90).

Students may gain considerable insight on such issues from the mass media, but only if they have acquired an interest in them and enough knowledge to interpret what they see and read intelligently. Such education is especially important because youth may watch television more on their own, apart from the family. For one thing, as technology improves so will the price of television sets descend. Besides, as broadcasting increasingly decentralizes, and technologies advance, video channels will emerge that are run by and for youth (Larson & Kubey, 1983).

YOUTH'S REACTIONS TO TECHNOLOGICAL CHANGE   The position of youth astride the powder keg of social pressures is uncertain and sometimes ambiguous. Friedenberg (1969) declared that modern youth feel locked in the back seat of a car that has been constructed according to faulty specifications and is being driven at high speed by a middle-aged drunk; youth simply want to get out of the car. On the other hand, certain of the most important characteristics of youth culture—cars, ample spending money, and leisure time—derive from technology. In addition, observes Arthur Clarke, technology provides the potential for becoming more fully human (Technology and the frontiers of knowledge, 1975). Needs of the world's rapidly increasing population cannot be met apart from high technological development; hence, disregard for the possible contributions of technology is irresponsible.

In addition, technology's byproducts have exposed growing numbers of individuals to more intellectual and emotional stimulation than people experienced in any former historical period. On television, they have seen how people around the globe live; they have a ringside seat at events all over the world and even in space. In addition, television has had a large but difficult-to-calculate influence on youth's attitudes and way of life.

Even the assumption of a negative position toward technology is made possible in technological society. Only through the benefits of technology do youth have sufficient leisure time to mull over such things. The demonstration of poverty would lack significance in a society where poverty is routine. Hence, young people exploit technology in their presumed assault upon it. And while they band together to gain a sense of security and a sense of identity, this bonding is made easier by the affluence which permits them to maintain the behaviors and symbols which give them an entity.

THE GENERATION GAP

Much has been written about the so-called generation gap, or differences in values, attitudes, and behaviors of the older and younger generations. **Adultism** refers to older persons' use of power over younger ones because of the special status accorded them by society (Flasher, 1978). Adults have been delegated this extra power because of their greater experience, age, and strength. Adultism suggests that all adults are superior to all children in all skills and character traits. Adults may enjoy their own feeling of extra power, especially men who have little power on the job. In a sense, adults are "parent surrogates" to all children with whom they come in "significant contact" (p. 518). Adultist behavior is encouraged by society's practice of looking on age groups in a hierarchical fashion. It interferes with adults' responsibility to relate more to the maturing aspects of adolescents' personalities than to their status differences.

Some adults, observes Fisher, insist that freedom should always be coupled with responsibility. Nevertheless, this attitude may be a rationalization in order to retain unusual control over the children. Youth can best learn to be responsible through first being given a certain amount of freedom in order to experiment with the rewards, the efforts, and the results of becoming more responsible. Youth do not have a monopoly on making mistakes—trial-and-error learning continues throughout adulthood. Nor do adults have a monopoly on attitudes associated with adultism. Older youth may treat younger ones in a similarly hierarchical manner, taking the same advantage of them.

Differing Views Regarding
the Generation Gap

Authorities differ in their opinions of the reality and extent of the generation gap. Youth and adults, according to the great-gap position, differ in many ways. Not only do youth lead different lives from their parents, but their parents' lives are continuously changing. Thus, both adolescence and adulthood represent processes of continuous change, so youth and adults must continuously readapt to change, both in themselves and in each other.

One subtle factor in creating a gap may be the youth's problem in finding jobs, already filled by adults. Moreover, these older persons, some of whom were activists as youth, will gain greater power, and may win a still greater share from the young in their battle for "the American Pie" (If you live to a hundred, 1983).

The mass media may serve either to widen or narrow the gap. Larson and Kubey (1983) see television as an instrument for "greater social continuity in the transition between generations." However, those youth who are socialized by their own special media, music, may experience a greater generation gap.

Also producing a gap is adults' sense of responsibility for the younger generation, which makes them feel obliged to maintain a measure of authority. Youth often resent having to obey regulations and respect values that, to them, seem outmoded or worthless. Privately, some view their elders as somewhat dull and stodgy, while their elders feel threatened by young people who have more energy and more time in their future than adults have.

Youth see themselves as differing from adults in certain ways. For example, they tend to perceive their parents as having lived somewhat constrained lives from which they "have fortunately escaped" (Yankelovich, 1983, p. 69). They feel, in contrast with their parents, that they have more choices and more freedom to live their lives. Moreover, four in five feel quite confident that they will be able to make these choices and live the kind of lives that they wish. They don't judge their parents as being any worse people than themselves but just view themselves as more fortunate.

A much wider gap separates some adolescents from their parents than others. Wingrove and Slevin (1982) found a larger age gap in attitudes toward the female role in society among adolescents with older mothers than those with younger ones. In addition, and somewhat surprisingly, the daughters of the older mothers had more liberal attitudes than did those of younger ones. In trying to explain this outcome the researchers conjecture that adolescents are more likely to identify with younger mothers and to role model after them, whereas the daughters of older ones might learn from role models outside the home, nearer their age and more contemporary. This writer suggests that daughters of older mothers might be relatively more independent of their mothers' influence, hence more independent in their thinking.

The generation gap may simply reflect growth and change within the society. Successive generations never perceive life quite the same as preceding ones did; and clashes between the generations become, in effect, an important catalyst for social change. Society itself would become static and colorless if new generations did not critically examine and challenge their elders' values. Such conflict also encourages both youth and their elders to clarify and sometimes change their views. Meantime, this examination and subsequent clarification help young people to establish their own separate identity from their parents (Gottlieb & Chafetz, 1977).

Adelson (1979) ascribes presumed generational difference to other factors. Much has been said about the generation gap—the old symbolizing decline; the young, progress; the young were perceived as seeking change, while the old dug in their heels and resisted. But the differences are not generational; they are matters of social class, race, education, and religious background.

A second position stresses continuities between generations and that contemporary concern over generation gap has been overdramatized. This position draws on history to prove the apparently inevitable recurrence of periods of heightened conflict between age groups. Exponents of this position have no difficulty finding research to bolster their point of view. Young people view political matters much the same as do their elders, but on life style issues there are differences (Adelson, 1980). However, by 1981 parents had come, in large measure, to accept behavior patterns that young people were following such as openly living with members of the opposite sex without marriage, joining communal groups, or taking other paths that formerly might have caused parents to feel as failures. That is, as "the new independence and new freedom engendered by all the social change of the past years have taken root," parents are not as anxious as they once were about whether their children would turn out all right (Watts, 1981, p. 41). Thus, it appears that society has adjusted to the new life styles and is less concerned that they will result in unfortunate outcomes. This acceptance may not, in many cases, represent approval so much as resignation to the inevitable. In any case, parents' new attitude does not signify a lack of concern or love for their children, but simply a different relationship between them.

Damon (1983) believes that the parent's role in adolescent development has been underestimated, partly because of earlier studies that popularized the notion that a large gap lies between the adolescent peer culture and the adult world. However, teenagers are oriented to both peers and parents simultaneously—hence, possess a dual orientation (Rutter, 1980). Thus, teenagers respect both parental and peer values and attempt to reconcile them.

Adult Attempts at Rapprochement

Attempts have been made, with varying degrees of success, to bridge the gap that divides generations. The Coleman Panel on Youth of the President's Science Advisory Committee (Coleman, 1974) insisted that the isolation and age segregation that characterize high schools retard youth's acquisition of adult skills and roles. It advised that individuals of all ages be integrated in various enterprises—into the work world, especially. Others call for a more critical approach. Efforts to mix the generations, writes Bernstein (1978), have often been well meaning but inept, even foolish. Adults trying to enter children's games appear childish and silly, and children may be incorporated into adult activities before they are ready for them. It is best to combine the generations in activities befitting both ages. They might well join in leisure activities, such as fishing or camping or in planning youth activities.

Other adults believe that youth need firm guidance and have reasonable confidence in their skill to provide it. Since the roles of guide and guided are essentially hierarchical, these adults defend the generation gap as inevitable and probably desirable. Youth will hardly accept guidance from persons whose status is exactly on a par with their own.

Of late, in a curious reversal of roles, the flow of information and instruction has proceeded from teenagers to adults rather than the reverse. A parallel development has been the erosion of respect for age in American life,

One study has advised that individuals of all ages be integrated in various enterprises, especially the work world. (Courtesy of Public Relations office, State University of New York at Oswego)

along with adults' willingness to learn from youth and to adust to youth's special needs. As a result, some adults abdicate their own authority and allow youth to set the pace, goals, and tastes, while they imitate behaviors of the younger generation. Almost for the first time in history, adults copy teenage music forms and dancing styles and admire teen heroes.

CITIZENSHIP AND POLITICS

In these times especially, when society is facing many crises, the adult's role as citizen is especially important. As life has become increasingly complex and sophisticated, society's requirements for adequate government have become correspondingly more difficult. Hence, the very existence of society depends on the citizen's attitudes and competencies.

Various factors might explain differences in individual adolescents' involvement and interest in politics. About $2\frac{1}{2}$ percent of all adolescents become deeply committed to particular views and dedicate considerable time to it. Other teenagers, with a far lower level of commitment, affiliate with political candidates and parties, locally and nationally, because of the lowering of the voting age to 18. These differences may derive from their differential experiences in the home, in the school, and their own personalities (Damon, 1983). The school, in particular, influences adolescents' general political principles and concepts but not their specific political views. In school students learn about political institutions and processes, and they may be influenced to some extent by attitudes that the teacher consciously or unconsciously reveals in such interpretation.

For whatever reasons, youth's development of political concepts has been inadequate. Psychologist Joseph Adelson (1980) studied adolescents in the United States, Britain, and Germany and found that their ability to handle philosophical and political ideas appears at a later age than does comprehension of earth science and mathematics. Twelve-year-olds might say that the individual who steals should be put to death; but only as they get older—about age 18—do they become capable of open, liberal, humane thinking and of understanding motivations for human action. Nor can 11- and 12-year-olds give abstract definitions of such concepts as law and government although almost 100 percent can do so at around the age of 17 or 18.

In the main American youth have shown little interest in politics, except during the 60s. Until then the middle-class American adolescent was viewed as silly and foolish but contented (Starr, 1981), and colleges and universities still employed an *in loco parentis* concept of administration in which they served as moral guardians of youth. College newspapers were censored, student senates lacked power. Student life, especially for females, was restricted by rules regarding dress, drinking, curfews, and sexuality, and students were constantly watched and given little privacy. Then came the dramatic social movements of the later 1960s which spread to high school and college campuses. As a result "students developed a strong age-group and cohort conscienciousness and embraced new ideological perspectives on society" (Starr, 1981, p. 216).

In the late 1970s it was predicted that youth might effect a political revolution, but they did not do so for several reasons. In the early 1960s adolescents held a highly idealized view of the president, which rapidly declined thereafter. Researchers have concluded that Watergate was responsible for this decline; however, this attitude was already becoming less favorable in the late 1960s, as a result of political events such as Civil Rights protest, and Vietnam, which raised questions about social institutions in general (Carmines, 1981). Also contributing to youth's decreasing interest in politics was that they gained many of the rights they sought to achieve. On other issues they do not differ much in their politics from adults, who are actually farther to the left. Also, they are too immersed in the youth culture to be concerned about the broader scene. Hence, they are much less likely to vote than older people. In 1972 just 53 percent of 18- to 24-year-olds voted, compared with 74 percent of 37- to 69-year-olds.

As the 1980s dawned American youth's relative disinterest in politics persisted. In comparison with youth of other more advanced nations American youth took citizenship more for granted and expressed less concern about it (Tyler, 1981). Nevertheless, there are particular groups and categories of youth who are more politically conscious than others. For example, among undergraduates at a midwestern university in the heart of the Bible belt, of whom 36.2 percent were born-again Christians, 77.2 percent said they would vote in the November election compared with a figure of 54 percent for all eligible voters. A slight majority (52 percent) would join in a street demonstration in order to protest a governmental policy they believed unjust. And 97.7 percent at some time engaged in political discussions with friends and family.

It might appear that college youth are more politically oriented, at least in terms of voting, than the general population. However, one should take into consideration that this college was hardly typical of the country. These youth also had a far higher level of trust in government than the general population or than the youth of the nation, probably because they lived in an environment which was politically conservative and which held strong religious values, associated with high patriotism and support of the political system (Patel & Rose, 1982).

Youth's political interests and concepts also vary from one country to another. In a comparison of American and Irish adolescents' concept of their respective homelands, the Americans showed a pattern of increasing political awareness. The younger ones identified it in terms of its physical features and landmarks and the older ones as "a unique system for the protection of individual liberties" (Egan & Nugent, 1983, p. 197). The Irish discussed it in terms of cultural and psychological values, the Americans in the more specialized sense of political self-awareness and the role of the homeland internationally. Perhaps the Irish had a more difficult time identifying themselves with a country which they had come to realize was somewhat unimportant internationally. Hence, they had come to think of their homeland more in terms of "cultural and moral integrity" (p. 197). In contrast, the Americans perceived their country as politically powerful—hence, identified with it and thus developed a more positive self-image through this identification. The American adolescents also indicated a high degree of commitment to their country's political ideals. Adolescents of both nations demonstrated a transition from concrete to abstract thinking with age. Overall the analysis indicated that quite different sociocultural factors complexly intertwine in the formation of concepts from childhood through adolescence.

In America even the minority of youth who express some desire to become more active admit feelings of futility. What can one individual do, they ask, toward solving the world's energy problems or preventing major wars? One might even question the depth or quality of commitment of some of the politically active youth. Some of them settle for safe, generally popular issues where they can attain excitement and a degree of glory without undue risk. Others selectively choose issues with little concern for the basic philosophies involved. Such individuals lack the curiosity or persistence to unravel the tangled roots of problems with which they are concerned. They prefer to confine their interests to manageable problems while remaining sublimely oblivious to basic issues that defy simple answers.

Young people lack the maturity and experience to temper their political ideals with realism. Not yet are they constrained by adult commitments to work and to family relationships. Hence they can be omnipotent in their desires and imaginations. As a result, they may adopt a highly critical view of the world, which adults may perceive as either "irritatingly naive or refreshingly idealistic" (Baumrind, 1978, p. 259).

Although they professed little interest in politics, 63.2 percent of the author's 98 students felt great pride in being an American; 33.8 percent felt somewhat proud; and only 3.0 percent felt little pride.

MALE: I do not take great pride in being an American because I do not believe that people should identify with their country; rather they should consider themselves a citizen of the world. If a man plans to exist on this earth, then he had better first learn to cooperate with others and with nature.

MALE: I feel it is still true that the United States is the greatest country in the world. We have the good fortune to have the highest standard of living, enjoy more leisure time, and have the best opportunity for advancement in life. If I had to do it all over again, I'd still be an American (especially a New Yorker!!).

Reasons for Youth's Political Disinterest

Other factors also help explain students' political inertia. For one thing, they simply reflect a similar apathy among their elders. Even among adults, only about 5 percent of persons qualified to vote are active politically, reflecting society's failure to arouse any general concern about social problems. In fact, high school students' political responses are about as well integrated as those of adults (Schwartz, 1977). In addition, politicians' appeals to voters, which consist in large measure of sloganizing, backslapping, and other emotional efforts, reflect a political education for citizens involving little more than diffuse descriptions of society's institutions. For another thing, recent history has provided very little to inspire idealistic young people. To the extent that students today have changed, they reflect changes pervading the entire society, as manifested in the new emphasis on social welfare. Also fostering inertia is youth's lack of power. Although even 18-year-olds can vote, youth still lack organized groups to defend their interests.

Youth's Rights

A related question concerns youth's rights as citizens. The concept that knowing the law is important for citizens has been applied mostly to adults, whereas juveniles have been "viewed through the prism of paternalism," because it has been generally believed that the state and its representatives would act in their best interest and protect their rights (Saunders, 1981, p. 714). However, such assumptions are becoming increasingly suspect, and procedural rights for minors have become of growing concern for courts. In consequence, the question arises, how knowledgeable are juveniles regarding their legal rights, a question made more significant because of the ambiguity regarding what is for them legally permissive. Almost everyone knows that the law regards juveniles as adults in some respects and as minors in others.

In a questionnaire study high school students in Oregon indicated less knowledge of major than miscellaneous laws such as those dealing with traffic, possibly because such laws more often touched their lives, although their knowledge differed somewhat according to their sex. The sexes knew the law about equally well, although the males believed they knew it better. Those girls knew it better who were involved in various school and community groups; possibly because of this factor they were likewise involved in a network of communication that aided in disseminating legal information.

The students were also asked which of certain items should not be lawful. Students agreed with the law on almost two-thirds (62.3 percent of the 2531 items); on others they didn't know certain items were already law but thought they should be. With regard to minors' rights in the areas of VD, birth control information, and medical care, almost all believed that they should have legal rights for medical care. Those believing they should have the right of treatment for VD, even without parental consent, numbered 73.4 percent, birth control information 56 percent, and medical care in general 18.8 percent.

In comparing these results with other research both adults and minors favored confidential treatment of minors for VD. The majority of teens as well as adults, favored confidential dissemination of information related to adolescents' sexual activities, but in different numbers. Teenagers overwhelmingly supported such confidential information whereas a considerable minority of adults would deny them such rights. However, more adults than minors would provide juveniles with confidential medical care. Perhaps the minority of teenagers who disfavored juveniles' rights to medical care doubted that they would know how to handle such matters without parental assistance.

The juveniles' greatest ignorance of the law related to procedural rights, nor did they appear to have firm sentiments on this matter. Just 46 percent felt that they should have the right to appeal to a higher court and only 54 percent believed juveniles should have the right to have an attorney to represent them. Perhaps two conditions were involved: first, students were unaware of the significance of procedural safeguards; and second, they may have merely absorbed the "paternalistic premise," that the state will look out for juveniles' welfare. It may be presumed that teenagers' ignorance of such safeguards may lead them simply to succumb, intimidated by authorities—for example, when treatment for VD is involved, fearing that that information will reach their parents. Overall, adolescents who face rapidly fluctuating and complex legal scenes need more information in this area.

Until 1967 there was no clear statement by the Supreme Court that minors are persons with fundamental constitutional rights independent of their parents (Keith-Spiegel & Maas, 1981). Since then the court has zigzagged numerous times in its view of whether minors are complete persons entitled to basic legal rights. This conflicting orientation is based on different assumptions about minors' competence and whether they are capable of sensible, independent, decision-making (Melton, Koocher & Saks, 1983). Lacking evidence to the contrary, many persons argue that adolescents lack the capacity for mature judgment and that their privacy cannot be fully respected.

Hence, it appears desirable that psychologists seek to inform the Supreme Court and other agencies involved as to minors' level of competence in specific contexts. The literature today clearly shows that in most situations adolescents and adults cannot be distinguished from each other on the grounds of competence in decision-making alone (Weithorn, 1982). Nevertheless, seventh and eighth graders are less likely than older adolescents to understand the potential risks and future consequences of their decision (Lewis, 1981).

Considerable literature on adolescents' decision-making in particular contexts is now available. With regard to competence to consent to psychotherapy, adolescents have adult-like concepts of mental health professionals and of mental disorder itself (Koocher, 1983). In a well-designed study Weithorn and Campbell (1982) presented hypothetical situations about psychological and medical treatment decisions to 9-, 14-, 18-, and 21-year-olds, and the replies of the

14-year-olds could not be differentiated from those of adult groups according to any major standard of competency employed. Note, too, that reasons which pregnant minors give for or against abortion were much like those given by pregnant adults (Lewis, 1980). In other words, the Supreme Court's assumptions about adolescent incompetency as decision makers is not supported by current psychological research.

Consider also that there may be some cause to give increased self-determination to minors, even if they are only "marginally competent," if making decisions "per se can be shown to be beneficial" (p. 101). There is evidence to believe that psychological benefits accrue to increased freedom (Melton, 1981). For instance, legal socialization derives largely from actually participating in legal decision-making and experiencing conflicting ideas. Experiencing more freedom may also improve an adolescent's self-confidence.

Respect for adolescents' privacy would also probably have quite positive psychological effects because it would improve their efforts at individuation and provide a sense of control over personal information. Respect for adolescents' privacy may be necessary if adolescents are to voluntarily seek treatment for sensitive problems (Melton, 1981).

Melton (1983) does not argue that adolescents be accorded rights equal to those of adults in all situations. In some cases, as in the use of alcohol, adolescents' liberty may be limited, partly because there is a clear correlation between age and traffic accidents (Wechsler, 1980).

Melton does argue that policy makers should recognize adolescents' personhood. Certainly, the traditional denial of their autonomy has stemmed from assumptions of incompetence that are not supported by research. In contrast, research indicates that adolescents have considerable maturity with regard to liberty and privacy—hence, they should be involved in decision-making about treatment and research. They should participate in decisions regarding matters of "psychotherapy, medical treatment, psychiatric hospitalization, abortion and contraception . . . (p. 102).

True, recognizing adolescent traits in such contexts would require at least a partial reallocation of authority among parents, children, and the state. However, in a study of adolescents and parents in the Los Angeles area both groups supported adolescents' making key decisions at ages often presumed by law to be incompetent. For example, both groups would accept minors' wishes with regard to custody decisions at around age 12, decisions about psychotherapy and medical treatment at about age 14, and decisions about birth control at approximately age 15 (Feshbach & Tremper, 1981).

Youth as World Citizens

The world of childhood is "essentially stable," in that it is "not typically subject to competing world views. . . ." (Baker, 1982, p.168). However, in adolescence an individual is confronted with "previously unknown elements which enter into the social and symbolic world. . . .(p. 168). As a result, "new interpretive modes are called forth; and previously established interpretive modes are likely to give way as new ways of seeing, thinking, acting, and planning are required" (p. 168). That is, adolescents engage in considerable theorizing to adapt to new structures and problems, especially in today's more complex environment and such theorizing is highly consequential for the way that they experience adolescence and anticipate adulthood. In other words, "practical theorizing" involves "negotiating everyday life" and "organizing social interaction—to effect interpretations of the world and the self" (p.177). Adolescents' theorizing is their way of "making sense of the world and the self . . ." (Baker, 1982, p.178). However, Yankelovich (1983) says that Americans are learning that "self-absorption alone is insufficient," but may provide a "transitory feature of a deeper, entirely valid quest, that will allow sufficient flexibility to adapt to the realities of the coming decades" (p. 40).

Even at this time, most of youth's behavioral world is circumscribed, limited to their own community and to a few outside interests—sports, politics, television characters, and the like. Their concern for the larger world is theoretical if it exists at all. What really counts is having some spending money and getting a date for Friday's dance, not the problems of Tibet. Of course, all youth cannot be lumped together, and individuals with broad perspective do exist.

Among college undergraduates, few feel like world citizens in the psychological sense.

> Especially now, with all the troubles we have, I feel more and more close to the United States. I guess I've never really thought about being a citizen of the world. It upsets me to think that we have people here who don't give a damn. I'm not saying that people should go around waving a flag, but as for those who feel that everything about the U.S. and its policies is wrong, as far as I'm concerned they can leave.

> I think very little of my citizenship in the United States and in the world. It has become a dog-eat-dog world. You get everything out of life you can and that's it. No one else really cares what happens to you.

As indicated above it is especially important that students become world-minded or even universe-minded in scope. Increasingly, all countries are becoming interdependent and even reaching beyond into space. If they are to perform effectively in such an interdependent world they should develop an understanding of, and appreciation for, the many cultures of the world (On tap: Faster, easier, more than comfortable travel, 1983).

Another significant factor, rapid change, makes any preparation for adulthood at best conjectural. The emphasis must be on basic learning skills and processes, plus whatever content would seem most essential in the future. Thus, given the growing interdependence of the world's economies, it is necessary for America's youth to become familiar with the metric system.

The generation gap also substantially affects the long-term impact of youth on adulthood. Whenever youth simply soak up their parents' ways, the result is a somewhat static society. Today's youth were granted sufficient autonomy by their parents to gain perspective on their society and to alter it to meet the needs of changing times. A certain gap between youth and their parents acts as a catalyst of change.

In recent years, parents have come to assert their own right to continue developing as persons throughout the life span. Formerly the focus was on their responsibilities to their children. It is to be hoped that the pendulum will not swing so far that adults will go too far in asserting their own rights at the expense of adolescents. For example, will today's youth, as adults endowed with the newly popular idea that they must fulfill themselves, cease to make sacrifices to enable their children to attend college? While such sacrifices can easily go too far, a certain amount is essential if youths are to attain higher education.

Youth commonly move into adulthood with simplistic notions about such topics as technological change, the population problem, ageism, and generation gap. In future years they will have to deal with these problems in complex forms as knowledge continues to proliferate and populations grow. It is common knowledge that most American adults are passive in their citizenship. They may periodically cast a vote, but there is considerable question about how intelligent that vote is. Education for citizenship is critical; American youth's disinterest in citizenship, widely acknowledged by themselves, is a poor omen for their future competency in this area.

Youth's need for a broader world view is becoming increasingly important. The whole world will, in effect, become smaller—for example, the 79-mile trip between Chicago and Milwaukee will require only 32 minutes by a magnetic levitation train (On tap: Faster, easier, more than comfortable travel, 1983). It is also predicted that the United States will become increasingly dependent on the rest of the world in trade, with the most optimistic projections being for East Asia. There will be great expansion of economic opportunities in China and in Australia with its very large mineral reserves. Also capitalizing on their natural resources will be Brazil, Argentina, and Mexico. In contrast, mid-East prosperity may decline as alternative sources of energy are developed. Western Europe will face increasing competition—for example, in world commerce. However, the United States and Canada may continue to thrive in terms of vast resources—Canada, especially in terms of its tremendous potential and huge supply of raw materials (For U.S., an age of reliance on other nations, 1983, p. A28). Obviously, youth's education should involve developing the understanding and attitudes essential for dealing with such a world.

TOWARD HEALTHY CONCEPTS OF WORLD CITIZENSHIP   If schools are to inculcate world-mindedness in youth, the most immediate problem is one of developing awareness, of expanding people's horizons to encompass the entire earth and beyond. A concomitant task is the clarification of the concepts of global security and interrelatedness. Another concept urgently requiring clarification is the problem of nationalism versus internationalism. Youth should learn that our way of life does not automatically commend itself to the people of other lands. Besides, unless we learn to handle our own freedoms intelligently, we will not be able to demonstrate the virtues of citizenship in a free country. Further, unless classroom discussions of controversial issues can be conducted with open-mindedness and impunity, youth cannot acquire habits of free thinking. Examination of significant topics from all angles is requisite to intelligent understanding of the world scene and its problems. Broad-mindedness, in this sense, should not be identified with holding no point of view at all. Nor should youth equate understanding other peoples with approving everything they do.

FUTURE PERSPECTIVES

In particular youth must learn to adapt to an increasingly pluralistic society. Eventually, as technological changes allow people to listen to more and more media channels, and as people can thus limit the news they receive to stories that interest them, there may be a greater "fragmentation of society" (p. A9). Hence it becomes essential that youth be prepared to choose among "cultural options" (The coming revolution in the world of culture, 1983). This same multiplicity of viewing experiences should enrich peoples' lives though a mutual sharing of viewpoints and prevent becoming involved in endless conflicts over differing views (Soon, exciting new ways to stay in touch, 1983).

All life preparation must be from the long-term perspective. The census bureau predicts that, by 2033, life expectancy will increase about 4 years; however, some scientists perceive such estimates as unrealistically conservative. Such prospects suggest that youth should develop habits of anticipatory long-term planning.

Schools should continuously revise their curricula anticipating what effective citizens will need in the future. Shane (1981) emphasizes the importance of becoming committed to something greater than oneself, without which nations do not maintain a high level of moral character. An international panel of distinguished scholars stressed the need for youth to comprehend the "unity or holistic quality of basic laws of nature" (Shane, 1981, p. 353). Youth should come to appreciate that humans are significant environmental change agents and should not exploit the planet. They should comprehend basic scientific principles in this science-dominated world. At the same time principles of equity and justice demand that youth understand concepts of social and economic justice and appreciate that human society is now global in scope. They should absorb concepts of cultural relativism and appreciate the diversity of cultures. It is also important that they know at least one language other than their mother tongue to facilitate cross-cultural communication.

Unfortunately, to date, youth have emerged into adulthood with simplistic ideas about complex topics. They should learn to deal with vast problems, environmental complexity, alternative environments, and how to control them. They should learn to adapt to a complex mesh of culture within cultures and, because of the world trend toward pluralism, to accommodate to various groups and life styles (Rogers, 1982).

In national surveys of high school seniors (Johnston, Bachman & O'-Malley 1980) in both 1975 and 1982 about a third of the seniors agreed with the statement, "When I think about the terible things that have been happening, it is hard for me to hold out much hope for the world." Slightly fewer, at both dates, agreed with the item, "I also wonder if there is any real purpose to my life in light of the world situation." Exactly two thirds agreed with a more optimistic statement, "The human race has come through tough times before and will do so again" (p. 392). Thus, American youth remain optimistic.

In a national survey, when youth were asked if they thought things in the country would be better or worse five years hence, pessimistic responses numbered 55 percent in 1975 and 60 percent in 1982. When asked how they felt their own lives would go in the next five years just 2 percent in 1975 and 4 percent in 1982 felt that it would get worse, while 90 percent said it would get better. Thus, an overwhelming majority of high school seniors have high hopes about their own lives, although they see prospects for the world as "grim and those for their county not very good."

In a national survey of high school seniors the number of those who worried about chances of nuclear war rose from 40 percent in 1975 to 64 percent in 1982 (Smith, 1983). The percent of high school seniors who agreed with the statement "My guess is that this country will be caught up in a major world upheaval in the next ten years" increased from 36 percent in 1975 to 45 percent in 1982; and those believing that "nuclear or biological annihilation would probably be the fate of all mankind within their lifetime" rose from 22 percent to 36 percent (p. 392). Thus, we see that over a third of these high school seniors "expect to join personally in human extinction" (p. 392). A high percent of the nation's high school seniors—47 percent in 1975 and 41 percent in 1982—feel powerless to do anything about the world situation.

Smith (1983) speculates that those who see little hope for the future will turn to the present, with certain inevitable consequences. If they can't do anything about what will transpire, they will simply quit trying to cope. They will resort to present satisfactions, including "careless love" and its "consequences in illegitimacy" (p. 393). They will get their "kicks" where they can, and use chemical assistance.

While growing numbers of researchers are coming to recognize the significance of environmental complexities, little was done until recent years about instructing youth regarding the interrelationships of present and future environments and how best to control them. Adults typically have taken environments too much for granted and either failed to recognize their negative effects or accepted them as inevitable. One technique might be to have students analyze themselves in relation to selected environments and conjecture what are the potential effects of each and also what might be done to alter their relationship to these environments. Societies of the future will need adults with skills for assessing and modifying environments.

Much might also be learned through more adequate cross-cultural research. Unfortunately, most such studies are descriptive and do not deal with how cultural processes work differentially in different environments (Edwards & Whiting, 1980).

Research must also reflect a certain pluralism in "recognizing that generalizations often mask individual and subgroup differences. There are . . . many successful life styles and multiple formulas for appraising progress through life. Both interdisciplinary and multidisciplinary approaches to complex phenomena are necessary if the various facets of adolescence are to be properly sorted out and understood" (Rogers, 1982, p. 422).

Especially in a fast-changing world the study of near and more remote environments—and of adolescents' adaptation to them—is essential. Only through viewing adolescents within the context of a broader life framework can antecedent/consequent relationships be distinguished (Rogers, 1982).

Because of rapid change studies should constantly be replicated and updated, and comparisons should take into account any interim cultural changes. We should also move from descriptive to explanatory research and subject parochial findings to cross-cultural testing (Berardo, 1981).

SUMMARY

Every society has its culture and environment that indelibly mark its members, although in somewhat different ways and in varying degrees. In simpler societies, the relationship between culture and behavior is relatively clear-cut and direct; in modern society it is very complex. Each has its special advantages and disadvantages for youth. Perhaps in neither case is its impact as great as is commonly supposed, for individuals are not mere sponges absorbing any and all influences; they react selectively to the stimuli that impinge upon them. Only recently has any real attention been paid to the way environments impact on adolescents, especially in subtle ways. Cross-cultural comparisons—for example, of youth in China, Israel, and the United States—help to place American youth in clearer perspective.

For better perspective on our own culture, we may compare it with simple societies and with other cultures around the world. By revealing the differences in adolescents from one society or country to another, cross-cultural studies point up the infinite modifiability of human behavior. On the other hand, studies of simple cultures disclose the relationships between particular behaviors and the factors that produce them.

In Western countries, each form of environmental setting tends to exert a characteristic influence. Among these, the neighborhood most intimately affects the adolescent. Its impact varies according to its location, population, and other distinctive features. Youth are also influenced by the wider community, whether it is heterogeneous or homogeneous, large or small. Among the various environments, the city and farm have the least favorable impact, and the suburb the most favorable impact on adolescents. Small towns are especially supportive of their youth; remote communities provide the sanctuary of very close family ties.

Some individuals, both as children and adolescents, move from one community to another. The effects of such mobility relate partly to the individual's social class and to the reasons that the family moves. The influence on adolescents of being in a particular community or succession of communities depends on their own characteristics as well.

The various subcultures of which an individual is a part share certain overall values of the larger culture of the modern Western world. Some of the influences are positive: the existence of niches for different sorts of individuals, the respect for human rights, and the opportunities for self-realization. Other influences are less auspicious, such as the emphasis on competition and the conflict of standards. Many environmental factors, such as threat of nuclear war, shortage of energy resources, climate, and geography, impact on adolescents in complex, subtle, and difficult-to-define ways. Moreover, youth's reactions vary according to their sex, cultural background, and personality.

In the Western world, certain sociocultural problems have emerged as being particularly significant. One such problem is cultural discontinuity. In modern societies, children's experiences are so different from those they will encounter at later stages of life that they are ill prepared for what lies ahead. Youth must also cope with the quickening pace of change and adapt their personal pace.

Another major problem is that of adapting to a complex mesh of cultures-within-cultures, including intimate primary groups (such as family and neighborhood associations) and impersonal secondary groups (such as clubs, labor unions, and colleagues on the job). Minority-group members and children of foreign-born parents experience special difficulties in adapting to secondary groups. However, in some ways their lot is improving, or even superior. Society is coming increasingly to embrace the concept of pluralism by way of accommodating to the varied life styles and needs of such groups. Besides, they often have stronger family and group support than do majority group members. Indeed, some of them take great pride in their group identification, despite its relative low status in the larger society.

Other problems of adjustment relate to social class, even in so-called democratic countries. Adolescents vary in their motive patterns, activities, personal adjustment, and societal status according to their social class. And even within the same social class, various subgroups of adolescents may develop. Contrary to general opinion, lower-class youth possess strong motives to achieve; nevertheless, they encounter formidable obstacles to progress.

Technology, another source of sociocultural problems, is accompanied by automation, constant change, materialism, and exploitation of the individual. The same affluence and leisure that threaten to distort more basic values of society also provide the time and facilities to free humans for higher-level activities. The problem is that youth have not been taught to understand and capitalize upon innovations that they have come to distrust because of their magnitude and complexity. Other matters that youth must understand and adapt to in the future are the miracles of modern medicine, demographic trends, and ageism—discrimination based on their age.

The rapid changes accruing to technology in turn produce a generation gap that makes cross-generational communication difficult. Some authorities perceive this gap as being almost unbridgeable; others believe the gap has been overdramatized; and still others assume an intermediate position. Some adults have come to distrust their own competence to deal with the new generation; others defend adult guidance as necessary and reasonably competent.

Amid such problems, youth's training for citizenship assumes special significance. Yet, despite a politically active minority, most youth apparently remain aloof from personal involvement. Efforts to interest young people in citizenship on local, national, and world levels must take into account their own special needs and competencies, including their idealism, energy, desire for status, and impatience for "results." Adults should set a sound example; youth's apathy toward politics is at least partly a reflection of adults' own disinterest.

DISCUSSION QUESTIONS
AND ACTIVITIES

1. Make a checklist of criteria for evaluating a community in terms of its fitness as an environment for adolescents.
2. Evaluate a community, with which you are familiar, in terms of its potential influence on, and advantages for, youth.
3. Evaluate the over-all American culture as an environment for teenagers and youth.

4. Discuss recent sociocultural developments which are likely to have a large impact on adolescents.

5. Be prepared to join other class members, representing farm, small town, and city backgrounds, in a panel discussion of the relative advantages for youth of these different environments.

6. If you moved more than once during your teens, be prepared to participate in a panel discussion of the relative advantages and disadvantages of changing environments during adolescence.

7. Analyze the college community as a sociocultural milieu for the development of youth.

8. Write on an unsigned slip of paper how you designate the social class to which you think you belong and why, and indicate to which social class you would prefer to belong. Also make up a list of adjectives that come to mind as you think of each social class. These papers may be collected, compiled, and discussed.

9. Write on an unsigned slip of paper your major social prejudices and how you think each was acquired. Papers may be collected and analyzed.

10. Attempt to conjecture how teenagers and youth will be affected (a) if our population quadruples in number; (b) when there is a much higher percentage of the elderly in our population than there is today.

11. In what special ways is technology a boon or a threat to youth?

12. To what degree do college-age youth take an interest in, and prepare intelligently for, voting?

SUGGESTED READINGS

Egan, O., & Nugent, J. K. (1983). Adolescent conceptions of the homeland: A cross-cultural study. *Journal of Youth and Adolescence, 12*(3), 185–201. This study of Irish and United States subjects, ages 8 to 17, disclosed widely different ways of viewing the homeland but a similar trend, with age, in progressing from concrete to abstract levels of thought.

Feurerstein, R., & Hoffman, M. B. (1982). Intergenerational conflict of rights: Cultural imposition and self-realization. *Viewpoints in Teaching and Learning, 58*(1), 1–15. The position, that another individual interprets the world to the young student, is explained, with special attention given influences that impact on an individual's right to be and right to become.

Leahy, R. L. (1983). Development of the conception of economic inequality: II. Explanations, justifications, and concepts of social mobility and change. *Developmental Psychology, 19*(1), 111–125. A study of 6-, 11-, 14-, and 17-year-olds from four social classes, interviewed about concepts of economic inequality, disclosed significant differences according to social class.

Long, S. (1983). Ideology and academic discontent: A study of contemporary university students. *Adolescence, 17*(69), 131–146. A comparison of conservative and liberal students, in terms of their sociopolitical identifications, is discussed within the context of characterizing the university as a quasi-political system.

Melton, G. B. (1983). Toward "personhood" for adolescent autonomy and privacy as values in public policy. *American Psychologist, 38*(1), 99–103. Relevant research concerning rights of adolescents is examined in terms of current concepts, theory, psychological implications, and public policy.

Rosenthal, D. A., Moore, S. M., & Taylor, M. J. (1983) Ethnicity and adjustment: A study of the self-image of Anglo- Greek- and Italian-Austrialian working-class adolescents. *Journal of Youth and Adolescence, 12*(2), 117–135. Differences in adjustment found among Anglo-, Greek-, and Italian-Australian youth are explained in terms of relatively different degrees of culture conflict and assimilation.

Roze, J. A. (1981). The future need for positive and constructive human characteristics. *World Futures, 17,* 251–262. It is suggested that the salvation of the world in the future may well depend upon making better use of human resources as well as developing constructive human qualities and a harmonious human/environment relationship.

Shils, E. (1983/84). Tradition and the generations. *American Scholar,* 27–40. The concept and function of tradition are analyzed as they impact on both older and younger generations and on society.

Teitelbaum, L. E. (1982). The psychological rights of the child and the law. *Viewpoints in Teaching and Learning, 58*(1), 113–127. The controversy over children's rights is considered within the broader context of rights, as well as the relative authority given by the courts to parents, professionals, and minors themselves.

Travers, E. F. (1982). Ideology and political participation among high school students: Changes from 1970 to 1979. *Youth and Society, 13*(3), 327–352. Changes in youth's political participation and ideology from 1970 to 1979 are analyzed in terms of their nature and causation.

Chapter Fourteen

The Future
Wage Earner

THE IMPORTANCE OF VOCATION

Significance for People Generally

Occupation plays an important part in most people's lives. It plays an integral part in personal development generally and not just simply in career choice. It modifies one's whole way of life, even in such details as manner of speaking and style of dress. The banker's wardrobe differs vastly from that of the mechanic. Similarly, a person's job defines one's associates and influences to some extent the kind of thinking one does. The physical education instructor moves among breezy, easygoing extroverts; the longshoreman's workmates are rough and ready.

Jobs also limit an individual's role and status. A lawyer is automatically accorded higher status than a plumber; the schoolteacher is ranked higher than the stenographer; and the surgeon's son who considers teaching in the public schools will move down in the status scale. In addition, work provides a major link to reality, both economic and social. The unemployed person feels outside society. Commitment to work is a characteristic of maturity giving meaning and direction to the search for fulfillment.

Significance for the Adolescent

Adolescents are expected to make considerable progress toward career maturity, a concept which involves knowledge and attitudes about occupations, career decision making, and vocational planning (Krumboltz, Becker-Haven & Burnett, 1979). However, in one sense, a vocational decision is not as critical in adolescence as it was before. At one time, the choice made was considered to be final; now a new pattern is taking shape, as people assume a job, reassess their position, and sometimes change careers (Why millions hate their jobs, 1976). Indeed, youth are counseled not to foreclose or settle on a vocation too early.

The significance of vocation in adolescence can best be appreciated in terms of the total life-span vocational career, a concept illustrated in Levinson's (1978) longitudinal study of a sampling of professional men. At the beginning of the novice phase in the late teens, reports Levinson, a young man's dream is poorly defined and only weakly related to reality. It may embrace concrete goals, such as becoming a great sports star or scientist; it may be dramatic in shape, such as becoming an artist or an executive or great intellect achieving notable honors; or the dream may be to become an ideal husband and father in a particular kind of family, an expert craftsman, or a highly admired citizen in the community. From this stage, an individual's development hinges in considerable measure on whether or not the dream is congruent with his life style. If there is no relation between the two, the dream may simply disappear and, with it, the young man's sense of purpose. Sometimes a conflict develops between life style and dream. At times, an individual's dream is thwarted by his parents, lack of money or educational opportunity, or even aspects of his own personality or the absence of talents required to realize the dream.

In the study, about half of those who were biologists had realized, upon entering their career, that a significant dream had its roots in childhood. They had already decided upon biology as their goal in high school and planned to study it in college. Even when their vocational choice and college studies were congruent with their dream, they often experienced ambivalencies and problems. Sometimes the father wanted them to go into another line of work; at other times, they may have vacillated before firming out the decision to be a biologist.

Certain of the novelists had begun writing even in high school and had looked forward to college training in this field. Already by the end of college, some of them had written books. Others had undertaken writing books later. Some individuals maintained the dream in subdued form, tempting them to combine their dream work (in this case writing) with business or other endeavors.

Certain of the men who became workers were not professionals but had had dreams that they could not achieve. One who wanted to play professional ball had gone into the military instead. For most of the workers, the dream remained unrealized. They continued their fantasy but had no opportunity to explore it and gradually put it aside as they coped with the problems of ordinary living.

Work Versus Leisure

Work relates to activities engaged in primarily for its end product rather than for the satisfactions gained through the processes of effecting such results. Leisure may be defined as "discretionary personal activity in which expressive meanings have primacy over instrumental themes, in the sense that gratification of present needs, wants, desires, or objectives is given precedence over practical preparation for later gratification" (Gordon, et al., 1976, p. 311). Leisure is not equivalent to wasted time or simply idle time. It can be quite meaningful, contributing to continued personal growth and development throughout the life span. Having absorbed this new view, people are becoming avid consumers of leisure (Jones, 1977).

YOUTH AND LEISURE Jones (1977) believes that leisure activities can, if properly employed, help people to live a fuller, more humane life and to free themselves from less rewarding and less pleasant aspects of the human condition. Young people today, liberated from the old notion that leisure is bad, will become social pioneers, affording leadership in the later twentieth and early twenty-first centuries in this area.

Youth itself allows ample peer participation and promotes autonomy from parents, while the mass media permit escape from school work and boredom. Meantime, leisure activities help youth learn to relate to others, to acquire the common language of youth, to learn appropriate sex-role behaviors, and to understand sex better. In the next stage—youth and young adulthood, ages 19 to 29—some individuals experience a prolonged adolescence with a continuation of youth culture activities along with sensory experiences maintained through music, parties, sexual indulgence, drug use, and clothes. Young adults with children have more limited leisure time, and their activities are shaped by their occupational situation, family roles, and money resources (Gordon, et al., 1976). Nevertheless, married couples' leisure activities have become more important than formerly as marital roles have become more equalitarian and as people at all ages have come to place greater value on fun, creativity, and expressiveness (Orthner, 1975).

Leisure acivities help people to live fuller, more humane lives. (Photo by Joseph Franco)

As they look to the future, young people today intend reserving some time for recreation, especially with their colleagues on the jobs, other young adults, and their families. Labor unions have found that many individuals, especially younger ones, prefer more leisure to higher pay and that they would agree to fewer and smaller raises if given more leisure time (Jones, 1977).

Among 98 of the author's students in 1980, an overwhelming majority (73.4 percent) believed they had acquired or were acquiring the sort of leisure skills required for a satisfactory leisure life in the future. The others were doubtful.

MALE: My leisure skills are ones that will remain with me throughout my life. I am a sports nut, you could say. In college I have played tennis, golf, and basketball competitively. Softball, bowling, water skiing, and photography are also some of my interests. Hopefully, my family (future family, that is) will share the same or even more interests than I have.

Among the same students, 73.4 percent expected their leisure pursuits to be as rewarding or more so in the future than their vocation; 8 percent disagreed, while 18.3 percent were uncertain.

FEMALE: I feel it is necessary to have leisure to get a person away from the work syndrome and to be able to have something to look forward to. Everyday work pursuits are important so that the person will feel that he can contribute something that he feels is worth it.

MALE: I want my vocational pursuits to be more enjoyable than leisure. I expect to enjoy my vocation to the point where I can remain motivated about it for sixteen hours a day. I like to work more than play, and I always have. There is something honest and clean about good, hard work, both mentally and physically. I guess I'm a victim of the old Protestant work ethic.

CHANGES IN ATTITUDE TOWARD WORK AND LEISURE   Attitudes toward work and leisure have changed significantly since colonial times. The Puritan tradition endowed successful work and occupational activities with a certain divine grace and religious sanction. This emphasis on work was particularly characteristic of the early rural culture in America and persists now in certain subcultures and families. In contrast many adults today spend as little of themselves as possible, in terms of time and energy, on the job, and deliberately devote the remainder to creating a full life. For many, work has become a less important aspect of life as fun and leisure activity have become increasingly popular. Adults are adopting a more playful way of life, and childrearing is becoming both hobby and profession.

Leisure is coming to play a much greater part in life style than it formerly did, and evidence of this trend abounds. Leisure-related products have proliferated; recreational and public park facilities are rapidly increasing; and colleges are offering courses on the topic. Sports activities, including bowling, tennis, archery, and boating, involve over 700 million people a year. Because of earlier retirement, high unemployment, and shorter work weeks, the constructive employment of leisure time has become an increasingly significant social problem (Recreation for all, 1977).

Nevertheless, most adolescents appear ready to assume adult roles, including work (Steinberg, 1982). Similarities between the values and attitudes of adolescents and adults are far greater than the differences, and this held true even when the generation gap was presumably widest in the 1960s. Furthermore, adolescents' attitudes toward work are as positive as ever and not greatly different from those of adults (Berryman, 1978). Faculties on college campuses are not so much concerned about youth's alienation from the workplace as their preoccupation with preparing for their work roles. Indeed, concludes Steinberg, it is hard "to imagine a cohort of young people who could be more accepting of the values and attitudes of society's mainstream—especially with regard to the workplace" (p. 201).

SIGNIFICANCE OF THE CURRENT WORK ETHIC   In some quarters, the focus on leisure and presumed erosion of the work ethic is regarded with dismay. Erosion of the work ethic may threaten the status of the United States in the world, especially since it has gained in such countries as Russia and China. Historically, countries have declined when they abandoned their commitment to work (*Career Education Resource Guide,* 1972).

Changes in youth's work ethic, while undoubtedly significant, may be less substantial than is often portrayed. A random sampling of 1,992 men, ages 18 to 49, indicated considerable congruence and relatively little difference in their attitudes toward work. In general, the men attached a high value to intrinsic work rewards or those inherent in the work activity itself (Miller & Simon, 1979). They viewed as being very important feelings of challenge, growth, autonomy, and the sense that they were making some meaningful contribution. There was only minimal emphasis on the antiwork ethic which suggests a need to avoid challenge in work and to stress values apart from work. Fewer than a third of the men placed special emphasis on comfortable routines or not having to work too hard; and about half stressed a need to have enough free time to enjoy other things. Despite a slight antiwork ethic among the younger men, there was overall "an impressive continuity of values" between the two age groupings (p. 392). The older men did perceive themselves as having greater access to intrinsic work rewards except for chances for personal growth. More of the younger men reported a gap between their ideal values and the realities of their work experiences. They may be especially impatient to achieve such goals or have an intense need for self-realization. Overall, it seems that youth do want to work and that they value work in much the same way as the older generation does.

The despair experienced by unemployed youth suggests that the work ethic is still strong. In a study of psychological reactions to unemployment (Viney, 1982) in Australia both the adolescent and adult unemployed showed considerable alienation, although some had maintained good morale. Younger ones felt that unemployment had interfered with their efforts to develop a sense of self-reliance or of identity. They also expressed lack of tolerance for others in both indirect and direct expressions of anger.

Asked for specific reactions, one youth said that his father was giving him a hard time about being unemployed; another said he was ashamed for not being able to find a job. He had developed a low opinion of himself, and had quit worrying about his appearance. Some were angered and had become "sick of everything [and] irritated at people in the unemployment office for being so high and mighty." They complained that their elders didn't listen to them anymore and that they were "getting hassled by everybody." Finally, after being unemployed a considerable length of time, they would become somewhat passive, since their "capacities for effective action had been sapped." One said "you just sit around doing nothing. Or you go to an interview; wait, wait . . . no job . . . eventually you need someone to get you out of bed in the morning!" (p. 471). It should be added, in deploring youth's unemployment in the United States, that many youths are simply not willing to do the kinds of work that may be available to them (Kilpatrick, 1981).

VOCATIONAL GUIDANCE

The choice of vocation poses complex problems for youth. Many satisfied workers would have been more effective in some other job. For example, Mr. Thompson is a passibly good chemistry teacher, but with more training he could have been a topnotch laboratory chemist. Matching oneself with a vocation is not easy, partly because of the highly fluid job situation. The demand is for increasingly higher skills, often requiring sophisticated training. Professional opportunities are growing twice as fast as employment generally. The individual must think both in terms of a changing self and a shifting job situation. A young man may decide to be a baseball coach—but will he enjoy such work at age 50? Or he may learn to operate a machine that in time will become obsolete. The young man in the following quotation clearly, though somewhat sadly, recognizes the gap between reality and dreams:

I would live in a red cottage like a peasant with a boat and a net and a bit of land. I would grow purple cabbages with atoes and onions, and garlic and red peppers. I would live with a dark, passionate Dago girl and eat mountains of spaghetti; and I would write a book on the success of failure. . . .

That's just a dream. I'll never do that. I'll be a stodgy professor and prime students with useless knowledge. I'll be a doctor of letters and maybe dean of my college. (Service, 1945, p. 115)

Many youth are not as realistic in terms of career aspirations. Among a youth population, ages 14 to 21, Shapiro and Crowley (1982) reported consistently high educational and employment aspirations. Apparently such aspirations will become revised downward as the youths grow older, because there will not be enough higher-status white-collar jobs available. In particular, female youths' aspirations have dramatically increased their desire for higher status jobs and away from service and clerical occupations. Particular individuals' characteristics and values as well as their family situation, are important determinants of their aspirations. In general, early marriage and parenthood lower educational and occupational aspirations, especially for young women. Blacks and minorities focus on college as a means of reaching educational goals, partly because they feel they have less access to informal networks for advancing their careers (Tinto, 1981).

Unrealistic Vocational Goals

Rubenstein (1978) laments the mismatch between available jobs and youth's skills and calls on educators to help close the gap. In the late 1970s, a survey of major U.S. companies indicated that they planned to hire 3,845 engineering graduates and only 876 liberal arts graduates; yet the colleges gave three times as many degrees to students of the humanities as to those of engineering. Projections also indicate that the number of students receiving bachelors' degrees in psychology will be over ten times the number of openings in that field. There will be three times as many bachelors' degrees in the fine and applied arts as openings in that area, twice as many in the physical sciences, and four times as many in the biological sciences.

Rubenstein offers several suggestions to improve this situation. Colleges should be forced to study the present and probable future job market, to require career-planning courses for students, and to communicate to them projected job opportunities in particular fields four years hence. Business should do its part through working closely with schools and making the most accurate projections possible for the future.

Some youth have special difficulties in attaining vocational goals. Unattractiveness alone may constitute a liability in job seeking or the work world. When photographs of more versus less attractive individuals were appended to standardized job applicant resumés, the more attractive applicants received higher job ratings from both college students and professional interviewers (Dipboye, Fromkin & Wilback, 1975).

MEMBERS OF MINORITY GROUPS Members of sociocultural minority groups, which comprise about a third of the population, also have problems. They identify their self-esteem with work as strongly as do the nonpoor; however, their goals represent extremes, either too low or too high. Such individuals seek present c to compensate for former indignities by aspiring to goals beyond their means. Because of their inadequate career preparation and planning, they experience great gaps between their real and ideal jobs and develop feelings of inadequacy. Often, they settle for occupational foreclosure, taking whatever job they can get. In time, they develop a condition called learned helplessness. They learn to deal with the problems they experience in work by taking refuge in psychosomatic disorders or beliefs that they are ill. Often, individuals with complaints of chronic pains and disability simply have had few rewards in their lives (Skovholt, 1978). A lower-class boy may aim too low because he has never tasted the cultural advantages that make him hunger for more; or he may have attended a segregated school where intellectual standards were low. In general, lower-class youth are perceived as having less potential than they actually do. Such youth also lack detailed knowledge of high-status activities or acquaintance with high-status positions regardless of their own capabilities. Their immediate associates in the home and neighborhood have had little experience with the occupations and opportunities that may be open to them (Super & Hall, 1978).

Since 1960 the United States has developed many programs for disadvantaged youth, perhaps the best known being the Job Corps, the Department of Labor's residential skills-training centers for youth, which offer "meals, counseling, health care, living allowance, clothing and recreation" (Ramsey, 1982, p., 951). A third of these centers are run by the U.S. Department of Agriculture and the U.S. Department of Interior, supported by such "diverse elements as the National Forest Service, the Bureau of Indian Affairs, the National Parks, and the National Fish and Wildlife Service. . . ." (p. 952). About a third are run by industrial corporations with their own training systems including Singer, Teledyne, and RCA. Others are run by nonprofit groups and corporations such as the YWCA, and still others by unions, using their own special systems of apprenticeship and job placement.

Various studies indicate that the Job Corps earns its way. Within 4 to 6 years after graduation students return the cost of their training through taxes paid on the wages they earn; and their entry pay on the labor force is about $1 an hour higher than that of comparable workers. Finally, they are almost one-third less likely than non-job corps graduates "to enter the criminal justice or social services system in later life . . ." (p. 954).

EARLY SCHOOL DROPOUTS   Stevenson (1978) links the problem of school dropouts and youth's unemployment. He takes issue with the common view that periods of unemployment are simply to be expected in youth and that their consequences will be overcome in the long run. A national longitudinal survey that involved cohorts of 5,000 males and 5,000 females for a decade showed that those out of school and out of work as teenagers were far less likely to be employed as young adults. Moreover, their earlier schooling and labor-force status carried over into differential earnings in young adulthood. That is, youth who leave school early and are out of work as teenagers carry disadvantages with them into their adult years. Their earnings are only about half the average for their race and sex. Those individuals having problems as youth also have more difficulty later on. While many unemployed youth do move into good paying permanent jobs, many do not, even by their mid-20s. It appears wise that job creation programs be targeted at youth and that youth employment programs should involve major incentives for completing school. Creation of jobs will have a negative impact if their attractions are so great as to discourage continued schooling.

GIFTED ADOLESCENTS   Gifted adolescents possess definite advantages in vocational adjustment. Secure in the knowledge that they are superior, they can justifiably dream and plan on a more expansive scale. They have a wide range of opportunities from which to choose. Many of them have the confidence that comes from knowing that they possess a trait highly valued by society. The increasing complexity of society's institutions and technology places an ever greater premium on persons with superior qualifications.

However, bright youth are not without vocational problems. They may have so many skills that they have difficulty making a choice. If they prepare for a profession, their training is long and expensive and may delay their attaining the adult role, including marriage. Already in high school preprofessional youth are focusing their attention on goals 4 to 12 years away, getting ready to pursue a useful adulthood (Pachter, 1978). They are simply by-passing youthful rebellion and self-indulgence and living up to the original meaning of the term adolescent—that is, becoming adult. These youth are intent on achieving a good livelihood—they are pragmatists, preferring well-paying and respected careers. At the same time, they have alternative career choices just as they also have colleges to fall back on if denied entrance to the main one they have in mind. They often feel apologetic if they have not decided what they are going to do, although some say that they want to keep their options open.

MALE VOCATIONAL STATUS   Each sex, gifted or otherwise, has its special vocational problems. For the male, such problems loom large because vocation constitutes an important place in his life. From their son's earliest years,

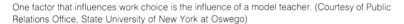

One factor that influences work choice is the influence of a model teacher. (Courtesy of Public Relations Office, State University of New York at Oswego)

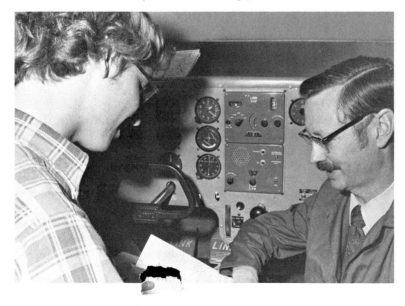

parents emphasize this aspect of his future. They are likely, more in the case of sons than of daughters, to insist that vocation be chosen in terms of status and salary. Their concern may also take the form of pressuring the son into making a premature choice.

In addition, the boy is tempted to subordinate personal satisfaction to economic considerations. He knows that adequate fulfillment of his family's needs will be difficult in a status-oriented, competitive socioeconomic system. Unlike his sister, he accepts primary responsibility for keeping a family and a civilization going. Despite the ever-increasing number of women in the work force, men are still considered the primary providers.

The male's work career ordinarily follows a predictable, regular pattern. It is initiated with choice of career and terminates with retirement. Factors initially influencing work choice are school experience, determination to advance oneself, and the influence of models among teachers, peers, and friends. In the years that follow, men endlessly compete in order to get ahead—and each man's success is another's failure. Especially hurt by this king-of-the-hill game are those individuals who are "at the bottom of the hill looking straight up. Included here are teenage inner-city males and long-term marginal male workers" (Skovholt, 1978, p. 8).

FEMALE VOCATIONAL STATUS   The girl's vocational problems are just as formidable as the boy's, but different. She is concerned with deciding whether or not to have a career (as distinct from a job), what her vocation will be, and whether she should choose something temporary or permanent, part-time or full-time. Several factors complicate the girl's problem of making a choice. Because of traditional beliefs about girl's special abilities and disabilities they have been subtly discouraged from taking advanced courses in science, mathematics, and other presumably masculine areas. Since mathematics, in particular, has traditionally been considered a man's field, girls often develop negative attitudes toward the subject. In a mathematics anxiety clinic at San Diego State University, 80 students sought treatment, two thirds of them women. Such clinics and the gradual dissociation of mathematics from its stereotype as a male-dominated field have expanded women's vocational opportunities. Elyce Rotella of San Diego State found that women in professions requiring mathematics earned 36 percent more than women in professions that did not (Math misery, 1979).

Prior to late adolescence, the girl may have received little orientation to career matters. Her brothers have probably received considerable advice and encouragement concerning their life work, but she is often permitted to drift. In any case, the girl's vocational plans must be tentative and flexible. She does not yet know what kind of a husband she will have, what his own plans for vocation and residence may be, how he will feel about her own career, or whether she will marry soon, late, never, or be divorced. Nevertheless, adolescent girls have come to assume more favorable views toward married women's employment outside the home.

Girls' vocational plans must also take into account possible effects on their future families. Because the factors involved are so complex, girls are able to make fewer long-range vocational plans than boys. Their time perspective in vocation is more limited, and their vocational plans must be more flexible. Hence, they are often willing to work in any of several fields, and they may be less interested in type of work than in other factors, such as flexibility of work schedules.

Government agencies have accorded males greater attention than females regarding career matters. Recent policy directives such as those involved in 1978 CETA reauthorization, have not, in the main, selected young women as a target group for labor market provisions and subsidized jobs. However, their labor market problems are greater than those of young men. Their unemployment rate is higher, and the male-female earnings gap increases from 75 percent at market entry to 61 percent at ages 25 to 26 (Stephenson, 1981).

The sexes are also differentially perceived regarding appropriate work behaviors and suitable types of employment. Although it is generally assumed that women's occupational opportunities have been improving, they are still earning less than men on average, even within the same occupational group (Francesco & Hakel, 1981). Moreover, job interviewers' opinions of how each sex should behave largely determines the criteria by which each sex is judged. However, the sexes do not necessarily act in stereotypic fashion. Among a sampling of college students classified as either cross-sex typed (possessing positive traits considered appropriate for the opposite sex), androgynous (possessing both positive female and male traits), and undifferentiated (possessing few positive male or female traits), the applicant's gender played an important part in determining their ratings as job applicants. The more masculine applicants were preferred for both masculine and feminine jobs, whereas the more feminine applicants were devalued for all kinds of jobs. The androgynous applicants won mediocre ratings for all but the salesperson position. Apparently interviewers prefer, in perspective employees, those characteristics—such as ambition, independence, and self-reliance—commonly identified with the masculine gender. Not merely are masculine traits more highly valued in most occupational situations but society continues to be structured in such a manner that males are more likely to possess these traits. Fewer than half of the college-educated females (45 percent) had a significant number of masculine traits, whereas the majority of males (64 percent) had them.

Career Education

Career development suggests establishing particular goals and deciding what criteria may be desirable. What is adequate development in the work career? "Is it occupational success? Satisfaction? Growth and development of skills? Successful movement through various life stages?" (Super & Hall, 1978, p. 367). Each individual must arrive at a certain personal philosophy about career. Career education, which is charged with youth's career development, as distinct from related courses, embraces aspects of both vocational training and vocational education, although it is closer kin to the latter. Career development involves broad socialization processes that both transform youth into working adults and alter the relationship of the individual as worker to that of other roles as spouse, worker, homemaker, citizen, etc. (Super, 1976). Adults seek self-fulfillment through various combinations of roles, as through homemaking, leisure role, or civic role; and the significance of the work role depends in large measure on the way it becomes integrated in these other roles and into the total life style. In short, occupational career development is one aspect of life career development. In contrast, vocational training relates to the development of skills which may be used in the world of work, ranging from learning the multiplication tables to learning how to use a saw and hammer. However, teaching youth about technology and the world of work is career education.

Career education is reputed to fulfill certain distinct needs, especially these: (1) The student becomes familiar with major categories of occupation. Many occupational roles have poor visibility or may be portrayed inaccurately on television (Mortimer & Simmons, 1978). (2) Theoretically, it helps individuals to become familiar with the values of a work-oriented society and to integrate work values into their personal value structure in order to make work meaningful and satisfying. (3) Career education prepares a young person for a vocation, perhaps more than one, but only after a systematic testing of alternatives. Nevertheless, many young people graduate from school without having any general career goal or marketable skill. (4) Youth come to realize that career choice is an ongoing matter. Technological developments produce a continuous stream of new roles, and many adults find that earlier social and vocational skills are relatively useless (Mortimer & Simmons, 1978). Or they may find that earlier choices are inappropriate later on. (5) Finally, career education may contribute to students' motivation in that those who conceive of their education as relevant to their future work will take it seriously.

Young people, in general, favor some form of career education. Many individuals have some type of occupational training aside from regular school or college—indeed, two-thirds of all respondents did so. Those most likely seeking it are males, minorities, high school dropouts, the unemployed, and those from lower income families. The most frequently mentioned areas included professional, technical, crafts, clerical, and service jobs. Males more often mentioned crafts and females clerical occupations. A majority of those in college said they would like to get further occupational training, as did high school dropouts, especially in the area of skilled trades. Young women have as strong a desire for occupational training as young men, consistent with findings that young women's career aspirations have been rising (Crowley & Shapiro, 1982).

Career education has sustained its share of criticism for several reasons. First, it indoctrinates youth to accept work as it currently exists in society. Career education is also defeatist because we do not know what sort of work world today's youth will face when they grow up. Note, too, that career education has the effect of reducing education to vocational guidance and creating technicians while humanistic goals are overlooked or minimized. In addition, it encourages "a marketplace mentality" in the classroom; and career education programs, as presently designed, help perpetuate traditional capitalistic values. Career educators also convey the impression that education's chief aim should be to provide students with marketable skills, overlooking the enhancement of personality qualities and aesthetic values.

Many authorities advise against too great or too early a focus on the career-oriented mentality. In this rapidly changing world perhaps students should concentrate on establishing a very broad base of understanding their culture and the basic principles of science and mathematics. Otherwise, if they specialize too narrowly they may be unable to adapt to new occupations that will appear in the future (Education? By computer, naturally, 1983).

PART-TIME JOBS   The number of adolescents employed in naturally occurring part-time jobs, as distinct from vocational education programs or government-sponsored employment and training programs, is large and on the rise. The number of 16-year-olds who work increased six-fold among males and sixteen-fold among females between the decades 1940 and 1970. In recent years 43 percent of 16- and 17-year-old males and 37 percent of females were both working and attending school (Steinberg, Greenberger, Vauz & Ruggiero, 1981). Almost all (97 percent) 14- to 16-year-old boys are enrolled in school, and about a fourth of them work, mostly part-time. The major shift to the work force occurs around age 17 and is mostly concluded by age 25, when over 90 percent of youth are working (Gottlieb, 1979). Most of the teenagers are not looking for jobs with career prospects but simply for weekend, summer, or evening work. For both sexes, the trend is away from assuming a full-time job after high school, toward taking part-time jobs, and toward pursuing full-time education through junior college or college.

The advantages to youth of part-time work have been portrayed as learning to budget time well, acquiring useful skills, and developing good work habits, traits which also contribute to the national economy (NAEP, 1981). A study of 100 employed adolescents indicated that part-time work may indeed increase a young person's "sensitivity, social insight and social communication" (p. 154). Some individuals improve more than others, perhaps because of the more advanced cognitive and social skills that they bring with them to the workplace. Besides, certain jobs may be more facilitative of such development than others, because of relatively different demands that various kinds of employment place on workers. To date, however, we have no firm data regarding whether social understandings acquired in the workplace become generalized to nonwork settings (Steinberg, Greenberger, Jacobi & Garduque, 1981).

Steinberg and associates (1981) believe that early work experiences may partially offset adolescent egocentrism and aid in social understanding, besides furthering their cognitive development. In the workplace adolescents must change to quite different roles and must shift from one to another quickly. They might behave authoritatively in relation to customers or workers younger than themselves, perhaps deferentially toward a boss or in an egalitarian manner toward their fellow workers. They must also interact with strangers from highly varied backgrounds. In such situations adolescents' egocentricity and social insensitivity diminish rapidly, if they are rewarded in terms of their willingness to behave in a nonegocentric manner.

Part-time work has other potential benefits as well. The work program helps the youth discover how personal traits bear on success in any vocational role. It is also direct evidence of emancipation, at least in part, from parents, and thus helps cross the threshold into adulthood. In addition, there is benefit in being inducted gradually into the world of work before school and home ties are completely severed. Youth who are bruised by initial skirmishes with the "outer world" find reassurance in the sympathetic shelter of home and school. Continuously braced by the advice and affection they get there, they grow surer of their ability to stand on their own.

Young people also learn to see the world through the eyes of adult associates. As they do so, they acquire numerous skills necessary to adulthood:

the abilities to adapt to many kinds of people, to handle money, to budget time, and to groom themselves properly. Finally, the school-job compromise is one way of having one's cake and eating it too. Schooling provides whatever preparation adolescents still need; part-time jobs curb their impatience to gain a secure footing in the world of adults.

SELECTING A VOCATION

When to Make a Decision

Throughout adolescence, young persons may be subject to pressures from parents, teachers, or guidance counselors to choose a vocation. Once made, a tangible choice does have certain advantages. It relieves a measure of anxiety by dissipating indecision. It affords incentives to learn and creates an atmosphere in which ambition may flourish. An individual need not think of choosing a specific occupation but rather a general field. One may prefer the sciences to the arts, or the reverse, and then gradually narrow the chosen field to a specific choice. In other nations the focus is on early occupational choice; however, in the United States youths are presented a broader range of options—hence are often encouraged to postpone decisions until later in their school careers (Tyler, 1981).

Arguments against early decision are strong. Decisions made when youth have little knowledge of their abilities can put a ceiling on their ambitions and limit their range of interests. In other words, premature commitment unduly foreshortens satisfactory explorations of one's own potential. Nor should it be assumed that, by their early 20s, young people should have made a positive vocational choice, and even to have gained a toehold in the field. This presumption is wrong from two perspectives—first, maturity has not been reached by the end of adolescence (Levinson, 1978); also, vocational decision is not usually a one-time definitive matter. Initial decision does not forever determine sequences within the future vocational career. That is, "the imagery of deciding on an occupation is too narrow and superficial. It is far more useful to speak of forming an occupation, the complex, sociopsychological process that extends over the entire novice phase (the 20s) and often beyond" (p. 101). Most individuals do make their first serious choice between ages 17 and 29; however, it often merely constitutes "a preliminary definition of interest and values" (p. 101). Young adults will need several years, at least, to "sort out [their] multiple interests, discover what occupations, if any, might serve as a vehicle for living out "[their] interests and to commit [themselves] to a particular line of work" (p. 101).

In the process of career selection, youth who change their vocational interests should not be viewed as lacking purpose or proper integration. The decision may indicate a sense of freedom to change or growth toward more responsible or mature job aspirations. Even changes on the job need not indicate personal instability. They may simply derive from changing goals at subsequent stages of personal development.

Factors Affecting Choice
of Vocation

FAMILY FACTORS   Regardless of when one makes a decision, young people should become aware of the factors, conscious or unconscious, which affect their choice. Paramount among these is family influence, although it wanes after early adolescence. By providing certain types of experiences and play materials, parents orient their children's interests from the early years. Family vacations spent in the wild may arouse curiosity about forestry. A large home library may spark a desire to become a librarian. A chemistry set may set a child dreaming of becoming a research scientist.

The parental influence is often direct. Parents may narrow their children's vocational choice by selecting the college they attend. If Joanne is sent to business school, her desire to be an architect may be doomed: Steve is interested in law, but Dad ships him off to his own alma mater, a technical school. By offering or withholding money, parents may control youth's training in some advanced, specialized field.

Many parents are still more concerned about their sons' than their daughters' vocational futures. In a simulation game, which was designed for parents to plan their adolescent children's career goals, 183 families were studied to determine whether traditional sex-role attitudes impacted on their decisions regarding the career goals of teenagers (Peterson, Rollins, Thomas & Heaps, 1982). Eighty percent of the families would give males' career goals priority over the females in a financial crisis situation; and just three of the ninety-six families would not choose one child over another. In the 49 percent of families who would delay the females' career goals, the daughter initiated her own career deferment; and just one of the daughters openly protested the family decision to favor her brother.

A majority of the daughters privately selected a career goal different from their fathers' traditional views; but just one raised objections about the father's views. Although they had beliefs in one direction they decided against making a fuss about such issues. So it appears that they accepted their traditional sex roles and acted accordingly. They might have desired equal priority with their brothers, but accepted their fathers' traditional choices concerning what was appropriate for them.

Without conscious intent, parents may serve as vocational models for children. Many a youth derives positive concepts of vocation from a parent who has achieved a satisfying role in the work world. On the other hand, a son's tie with his father may be so close that, regardless of their differences in ability, the boy tries to follow in his father's footsteps. Close emotional bonds can also create guilt feelings in youth who reject parents' vocational advice.

Identification with the father was apparently an important factor in these cases:

> MALE: I'd like something along the automotive line or testing cars—possibly because my father has a garage and once worked for a fellow who sold Chrysler products. I read about road tests, and compare the

new auto figures with their performance figures, roadability, and handling. I often have ideas on how cars can be improved, even before those improvements appear on the market. I believe I'd be successful in this line because I am intelligent, have good reflexes, and a strong interest in cars.

MALE: I want to go to college and be a forester. My father has a forest, and I have been with him cutting lumber; and I like nature study very much. He hasn't said so directly, but I know he would like me to be a forester.

Identification with the parents may work in reverse fashion. A youth highly suited to his father's occupation may reject it—as well as any vocational advice his father gives him—because he resents his father.

THE SCHOOL EXPERIENCE   Youth choose those colleges that they believe will best help fulfill their personal needs. On the basis of interviews with 384 students from the greater Washington area, who applied for admission to the class of 1982 at Harvard and Radcliffe, the students' chief sources of motivation were status and money. One of the students wanted to be a doctor, partly because it afforded self-esteem. The students were clearly in tune with the times and its focus on materialism and security. They were concerned about their future and often prepared for two lines of work at the same time (Pachter, 1978).

Choice of major and identification with faculty members also relate to career. At the University of Arizona, the same individuals were followed from college entrance until they graduated (Madison, 1971). Among sources of stress were those college experiences that contradicted students' beliefs about themselves. Sidney had made high grades in high school mathematics and science so decided upon a college major in physical science and a future career in medicine.

Students are clearly in tune with the times and are concerned about their future and work choice. (Photo by Carl Purcell, National Education Association)

However, in college, he confronted mathematics theories that he did not understand and found himself enjoying literature and philosophy far more than science and math.

> I took mostly science and math courses ... I found that I was not a scientist and certainly not a mathematician. I was best at the liberal arts. The course I enjoyed most was an introduction to European literature, and my enjoyment was corroborated when I got an A-plus....I found ... that it was the ideas, and not the style which fascinated me. Philosophy, as I suspected in looking over my real interest and abilities, was my subject. (Madison, 1971, pp. 72, 74)

The choice of a college major is simply part of the process of developmental synthesis, the process intervening between the first choice of a college major and the final one. A succession of changes may be necessary to allow for developmental changes in personality that occur in college. Sidney first chose physical science, then philosophy, and finally sociology. His original desire to go into medicine reflected his earlier materialistic outlook. His second choice, philosophy, helped him gain perspective on his situation and to realize that his interest in medicine was largely materialistic. This perspective enabled him to become seriously interested in his third choice, sociology, and a career as a college teacher.

Identification with teachers can also be important in helping students determine and become comfortable with their chosen vocational identities. In Sidney's case, he came to admire certain faculty members and, consequently, was less concerned about earlier preoccupations with material success. As he wrote,

> I saw that these people around me, these intellectuals who were not medical doctors, who were not engaged in materially successful enterprises, were nevertheless happy, healthy, respectable, and highly admirable in the way they were putting their intellects to work. Such a life, then, for the first time, really seemed possible to me. (Madison, 1971, p. 111)

Students who lack such models may, indeed, be at some disadvantage. Making a good vocational choice may be facilitated by having appropriate role models, by receiving occupational information—for example, relating to sex role myths—and by attaining accurate self-knowledge feedback (Krumboltz, et al., 1979).

SOCIOCULTURAL INFLUENCES   Sociocultural factors are just as important as family and school in affecting vocational choice. Cultural settings limit the range of occupations from which one can choose. Besides, each occupation has its own social traditions. Becoming a college teacher may possess a tradition of social value. Being an airplane pilot has about it an aura of glamour; and the electronics technician, as popularly conceived, is a person of mystery. Some occupations may connote the "wrong side of the tracks."

Social class is another factor in vocational choice. Lower-class youth may prefer some form of public assistance to taking jobs that they would not enjoy. Some individuals whose identities are anchored in their work might reject jobs that are not consistent with their identities. Sometimes middle-class individuals are overtrained or can't find jobs in areas for which they were prepared. One strategy would be to promote entry into fields where there are shortages on both high school and undergraduate levels. Scholarships and loans would be available in these areas, while such opportunities would be decreased in areas where jobs are short. Colleges should also provide students with information about where the opportunities are (Boice & Gray, 1978).

On the college level, at least two significant changes have occurred in masculine career orientation. Career, though still significant, plays a lesser role in young men's lives than it formerly did. Young men attach increasing importance to off-the-job aspects of their lives, especially family life and recreation. They have also come to attach correspondingly more importance to work as personal fulfillment and somewhat less to money and status.

Regarding girls' current career orientation, at least three observations are relevant. First, more women are working today and are not as overwhelmingly domestic in their orientation. In addition, the geographic mobility of families has lessened the differentiation of roles within the family. Females tend to be more bicultural than males. Females are also permitted, sometimes encouraged, to relate to the male-dominated achievement system, while males are discouraged from developing expressive skills ordinarily associated with females. Thus, the female has fairly broad options open to her, while the male's alternatives are more limited.

The research reveals a confused, somewhat conflicting picture regarding the realism of adolescent females' vocational outlook. In a study of high school seniors enrolled in a program providing career development assistance to disadvantaged youth, females showed more sex-role flexibility than males, and both sexes more flexibility after program intervention. Their ranking of occupations along a gender-typed continuum corresponded with reality as defined by the census. With regard to vocational aspirations few of either sex would choose female occupations. Unlike former research findings the females did not prefer the traditional female occupations; indeed, over 50 percent of those chosen were traditionally neutral or male (Clemson, 1981). This writer suggests that they now perceive entry into such jobs possible that they did not before.

Oddly enough, girls in ten Milwaukee high schools appeared insensitive to the sex-role implications of aspiring to high occupational status. Nor did girls' own sex role relate to the type of occupations they preferred. They chose occupations on the basis of the jobs' status and their own interests and not sex-role appropriateness (Ridgeway & Jacobson, 1979). Nevertheless, a review of research indicates that those women who select the traditionally male occupations tend to be higher than average on locus of control, self-esteem, mathematical ability, and cognitive complexity, and have less accepting fathers but greater father identification (Krumboltz, et al., 1979).

RACE Another important factor in vocational aspirations is race. A review of research indicates that black females have higher scholastic achievement than black males at the high school level but less than white females. Black female adolescents have higher career and educational aspirations than either black males or white females at the high school level. However, their aspirations decline in college and become lower than those of black males. Moreover, school desegregation affects the black females' aspirations more adversely than it does those of black males. In addition, attending a white college may negatively affect blacks' physical self-concepts and feelings of acceptance. With regard to career, black females, like whites, make career choices in so-called female fields. Black females, ages 16 to 19, have a higher unemployment rate than do either black males or whites of either sex. Finally, black females are more concerned than the white females about employment in contrast to self-fulfillment (Smith, 1982).

PERSONAL CHARACTERISTICS Young people's vocational interests also relate to their fundamental personality characteristics and to their overall concept of themselves. Self-perceptions are selective; those occupations that correspond to felt needs excite interest. The boy who is other-directed may aspire to working in groups; the girl who needs regular pay may choose stenography. An individual who desires personal glamour may choose a job in uniform; the bright social misfit may find sanctuary in a laboratory.

Even characteristics and capabilities demonstrated in earlier years relate to future career. For example, Jencks reported that leadership demonstrated in grades 6 to 10, and general educational attainment in those years, related to achieving prestigious jobs in adulthood (Tyler, 1981).

The realism of youths' choices may be measured by relating their scores on such measures as aptitudes, intelligence, and interests to those of successful people in the occupations concerned (Super & Hall, 1978). However, a majority of occupations involve a variety of tasks which call for people of different personality types and talents (Holland & Holland, 1977). Hence, it is not easy to find the kind of person who might well enter any particular occupation.

The role of personality factors is apparent in these youths' ambitions:

MALE: I plan to be an engineer because I like math and science and the money one makes. It fits my personality because I like things in order.

FEMALE: I'd like to be a school librarian because I like reading and working with other people. There are many job openings, and the pay is good. Besides, for the experienced librarian, there are good jobs overseas.

AVAILABIITY OF VOCATIONAL INFORMATION Another variable affecting vocational choice is availability of occupational information. Adolescents may rate jobs on the basis of limited or distorted information. A girl perceives being an airline hostess as glamourous without realizing the job has a limited future. White-collar illusions obscure the sober advantages of blue-collar jobs. Ignorance of opportunities can as effectively prevent access to them as can obstacles rooted in racial, ethnic, or religious discrimination. Misinformation or illusion explains many a square peg in a round hole.

ROLE MODELS Role models undoubtedly play a significant, though difficult-to-assess, part in career choice. Little is known about the actual impact of role models on adolescents and their occupational decision making. Parents, teachers, and peers are perceived as influencing youth's values through their evaluations of individuals, occupations, and circumstance. These values undoubtedly influence youth's judgments of worthwhileness of occupations. Such individuals may neither know much about these occupations nor exemplify them themselves. However, adolescents can find appropriate role models through part-time jobs, teachers, the media, and contacts with other adults of the community. These contacts will vary in intensity, hence have relatively different impact on youth.

Adequate role models are "a scarce commodity," distributed unevenly among youth according to race, sex, and status. Youth of the lower strata have few role models in their immediate environment who represent the sort of statuses they would like to achieve. In contrast, middle- and upper-status youth have, among their immediate acquaintances, persons in the most desired occupations. Girls' role models are fewer in number and typically lower in status than boys'. Throughout the workplace, few women are found in a great many occupations or in higher statuses in any occupation (Laska & Micklin, 1979).

Television provides career models beyond youth's own personal experiences, perhaps distorted ones. Television's portrayals of the occupational world do not possess much reality. High-prestige occupations are represented three times as often as their actual existence in the job market (Greenberg, 1982).

HELPING YOUTH ADAPT TO THE ADULT OCCUPATIONAL ROLE

Induction Into the Working World

Even in these times of affluence, when work is presumably not so desperate a matter, the transition to worker remains a major task for youth. However, among more advanced nations in Western Europe, as well as Australia, New Zealand, Japan, and Israel, the United States has been least adequate in perfecting a smooth transition from school to work (Tyler, 1981).

The task of entering the work world involves certain conditions that make it difficult for most adolescents. They have undergone a period of prolonged economic dependence resulting from the need for prolonged education required for the type of work they desire. Moreover, they have few visible vocational role models, and they are baffled by the great complexity and impersonality of the work world that confronts them. No matter what occupation they choose, they can anticipate an ever-accelerating pace of occupational innovation and obsolescence (Skovholt, 1978). Meantime, seniority rules often place the inexperienced worker at a disadvantage. In addition, the young worker is vulnerable to current societal conditions. Currently, young people need protection against a capricious labor market; in wartime they are pressured into jobs too soon.

Young adults must be prepared not only to learn the demands of a new job but also to unlearn former expectations. Often they have gained overly idealistic and unrealistic expectations from their schooling and the mass media.

They are unprepared for a certain "hazing phase" which involves being assigned the least desirable tasks during which they are challenged to prove themselves (Mortimer & Simmons, 1978, p. 441). They may also be disillusioned at finding that they are bossed by others when they had expected to be wholly on their own. In general, they can also expect to flounder about somewhat as they move from one job to another in order to find congenial work, a condition especially common at the blue-collar and lower white-collar levels (Gottfredson, 1977). If problems that arise at this stage in the career are effectively handled, there are enduring favorable effects on subsequent vocational adaptation and perform-ance. If they are not, the young adult may display rebellion, withdrawal, or overconformity.

The foregoing discussion has focused on youth who plan to work for someone else; those who want to go into business for themselves also deserve consideration. In an age of big business, the hazards of initiating one's own enterprise are great. Perhaps the government should provide the modern equiv-alent of the free land that enabled former generations of youth to develop a virgin country's resources.

Current obstacles to job entry may conceal a fringe benefit—that of motivating many youth to prolong their education. Because of loans and schol-arships available, today's youth have access to more sophisticated vocational preparation than ever before. Among the disadvantaged, especially, such help means the difference between feeling defeated or challenged.

Preparing for On-the-Job Adjustment

Especially important for all youth, is having realistic information and expectations of the job. Such prior information helps an individual decide on whether a particular job will be appropriate; and it affects initial commitment. Those young people better equipped with prior information feel more respon-sible for their vocational decisions. Realistic information also helps to obtain adequate prior preparation and to avoid attempting a job for which one is unprepared. Individuals who are matched with challenging and appropriate early work assignments both perform better initially and maintain greater com-petence (Super & Hall, 1978).

While youth need help in choosing and adapting to jobs, they must also prepare for the "long haul"—that is, to endure the pressures of working during much of their adult lives. For the first year or so, fledgling workers are often condemned to guerilla action, while their ranks are constantly thinned as their "generals"—or most effective spokesmen—are promoted and defect to the older workers' side. Even later, after the young worker is fully accepted, he or she may work under adverse conditions created by modern technology, including monotony, tension, and frustration. Often, young workers are called on to per-form generally meaningless, highly specific acts, which leave little room for individual creativity and ego involvement. As a result, any tendencies workers may have toward feeling inferior may be increased. Besides, their status is far below that of their bosses. They have little part in decision making and they know they can be replaced. Hence, feelings of resentment erode mental health.

Young workers may develop an unconscious need to get even, especially with the boss-antagonist. Because of such factors, they seek greatest returns with least possible output, an attitude which generalizes to all social institutions.

Youth should also think in terms of integrating their future careers with other life areas. Looking ahead, it seems that there will be pressure for more flexibility in the scheduling of work and nonwork activities through all the years of their lives. Especially in dual-earner families there will be a growing demand for more time off the job, as well as greater discretion to trade extra earnings for more free time. Furthermore, the anticipation of retraining for new vocations in mid-life is, at once, "mixing work experiences into the traditional school years of youth and increasing time given to educational pursuits in later life." In general, there is a growing desire for both shorter work time and more flexible work arrangements. Both sexes would like more free time for vacation; however, women more often than men prefer 50 minutes off one work day a week whereas men are more interested in earlier retirement (Best, 1981). Note, too, that non-traditional family patterns and sex roles are associated with a desire for alter-native work-time arrangements.

The projected changes will importantly impact on women's lives and have almost as much effect on men. Changes in performing the fundamental life chores by either sex will necessitate some adjustment by the other sex and a realignment of sex roles may produce a more flexible and egalitarian assignment of life chores (Best, 1981).

Young women workers must be prepared to cope with discriminations that still exist and motivated to help, in whatever way they can, to erase them. In one study, males devaluated women in some so-called masculine areas such as city planning but not law, which has opened up to women. Also, males de-valuated women who had not achieved status, but did not devaluate them once they had achieved it. It becomes the more difficult for women to prove their abilities since their work will not be judged on an equal basis with that of men. That is, a woman's work is somehow judged inferior until her work achieves special distinction (Isaacs, 1981).

Mortimer and Lorence (1978) review research regarding what youth need for on-the-job adjustment. When young people approach a new job, they must not only learn its specific requirements but also unlearn some of their former, often overidealized, expectations (Van Maanen, 1977). Youth must rec-ognize that the early vocation or career is often characterized by considerable exploration, such as moving from one job to another in hopes of finding more rewarding work (Gottfredson, 1977). They may also expect that their careers will involve many options and transitional points that will permit them consid-erable flexibility. Youth can anticipate that as they proceed through their work life their self-concept and identity will change. That is, work experience produces important personality changes over time regarding matters of internal control, self-esteem, work centrality or its importance in the total life style, and reward values (Mortimer & Lorence, 1978).

A young person also needs to have some idea of career as it relates to the life span. The teens and early 20s are devoted to getting established, trying out jobs, establishing intimacy, and forming commitments. In the 40s the in-dividual cuts ties with mentors and enters into the mid-career, a period of either growth, decline, or plateau. At this time, the individual may become concerned about what he or she is doing that may be of any enduring value for oncoming generations. In the late career, the individual begins to withdraw from work and to plan for retirement (Super & Hall, 1978). Vocational preparation and decisions are often made with limited perspective, without careful consideration of their long-term implications.

FUTURE PERSPECTIVES

Longitudinal studies have shown that adults' vocational pursuits are often rooted in childhood and adolescence. In Levinson's (1978) longitudinal study of young men, ages 35 and 45, four of the novelists had begun writing in high school or earlier and decided in college to choose writing as their vocation. In contrast to the novelists and biologists in the Levinson study, few of the ten executives studied had been motivated by a youthful dream of vocational accomplishment.

Other research pinpoints particular characteristics and adjustments that impact on adult vocational experience. Stevenson (1979) reported that job-holding during school years reduces later unemployment for both black and white youth. Moreover, previous work experience—especially in full-time jobs as a student—relates to increased hourly wage rates on jobs later on.

Holding prestigious jobs in adulthood relates to having done well on academic tests in the sixth grade, having exhibited leadership in grades 6 to 10, and to educational attainment. Relative to other years, the last year of college is especially important; that is, finishing college and getting credentials, rather than what one learns, appears especially important to getting ahead (Jencks, 1979).

There is little in youth that relates more significantly to later life than the acquisition of a proper foundation for the vocational future. A major problem is to identify vocational attitudes and skills that will prove viable in the long run and not rapidly grow obsolete. The attitude that the youth of a country take with them into the adult work world will largely determine that country's ability to retain its standard of living and status in an increasingly competitive work world.

Vocational counsellors and youth themselves must remain sensitive to

The last years of college are especially important to getting ahead. (Courtesy of Public Relations Office, State University of New York at Oswego)

current job markets if they are to be prepared for the years ahead. Often there is an excess of job applicants in one area and a deficit in another. More sophisticated forms of matching youth with jobs must be found, else human resources will be wasted. Youth themselves must develop the flexibility and basic skills required for continuous readaptation on the job.

Few young women prior to adulthood think realistically of problems arising from returning to the work world after taking time out for children. Few of either sex think much about how particular careers will change in appropriateness over the life span. If youth are to function effectively in terms of organizing their life style at successive life stages, they will need to move into adulthood with sophisticated ideas about how to integrate their work and leisure lives and how such activities may be exploited to produce enriched living. As ever-increasing numbers of people are living longer lives, and as years devoted to work become correspondingly reduced, the need for better education for leisure becomes especially critical.

Youth must also habituate throughout their professional career keeping in touch with the ever changing job market. Already the employment picture for the next century is taking shape and by the year 2000 advancing technologies will spell the doom of some jobs but create new employment in such areas as computer maintenance and software design. And as robots eliminate many factory jobs, over 2 million American workers will become employed in monitoring, programming and repairing robots by the year 2000. Many others will be concerned with industry's use of laser equipment. Manufacturing jobs should decline from almost 24 percent in 1980 to 11 percent, and agriculture from 4 percent to 3 percent; whereas service employment will grow from 62 percent to 86 percent. New ways of employing computers will permeate almost every field, from medicine to manufacturing (When job training, 1983, p. A25). Clearly, therefore, adolescents should become comfortable with and knowledgeable about computers. As both wives and husbands work outside home, computers will increasingly become to assume domestic tasks (Education? By computer, naturally, 1983).

In addition, in the next half century robots and computers, which will be able to "think" and analyze tasks, will take over significant roles in government and industry. Super computers will be developed and used by "military planners, code breakers, weather forecasters and space analysts" (p. A21).

Certain types of jobs will be completely new, at least in their environments. By the early 1990s it is anticipated that the first permanent space station will be in orbit, known as Spacehab. The structure will "house as many as 100 scientists, researchers, military analysts and space workers" (p. 18). And space tugs will ferry people and supplies back and forth (A search for life's meaning, 1983).

In the 1970s youth became concerned about the economy and having jobs. However, it may not be inferred that they will, as the economy improves, return to more traditional patterns of behavior—that is, "the search for self fulfillment is not a yo-yo riding up and down on the string of the economy; it is a powerful force working its way into the basic texture of our society" (Yankelovich, 1983, p. 40).

Youths' long-term perspective on career may need to be revised. Since the future elderly will be better educated and healthier physically they will remain more productive, many of them remaining at their jobs until well over age 70. Moreover, says Bernice Neugarten, authority on the elderly, as the era of high technology picks up steam, older people's judgment and experience will be especially needed (If you live to a hundred, 1983).

Overall, youth may find it easier to obtain jobs in the future because of changing views about the ideal number of children and the dramatic rise in employment of women at a period in the life span when they might be otherwise rearing a family (Rice, 1983). In fact there has been a steady decrease in fertility rate from 3.8 children per couple in the late 50s to 1.9 today. If the number of jobs remains the same, the declining number of young entrants into the labor force will create a worker shortage and compel employers to increase wages.

Among occupations predicted for the future, ranked from greatest to least in terms of numbers who will be employed, are telemarketing sales workers, cad'cam workers (computer aided design and manufacturing), software writers, geriatric social workers, housing rehabilitation workers, energy conservation technicians, emergency medical technicians, gerontological aides, hazardous waste technicians, energy auditors, and battery technicians. (When job training, 1983).

Youth must be encouraged to explore various issues of the work place, such as how industry may be organized to promote the personal development of both management and workers. In addition, acquiring an understanding of adult needs should be coupled with feelings of responsibility for what adults should contribute to society. Relatively too great emphasis has been placed on increasing a person's right to work and too little on how best to utilize free time gained through retirement in optimally effective and satisfying ways.

Finally, each generation of young adults must be aware of its own special characteristics as a generation unit. Thus, young people who were born in the baby boom years of the 1950s could not afford the luxury of waiting for the ideal job. Because their numbers vastly exceeded demand in many occupations, large numbers of them settled, at least temporarily, for whatever work they could get.

SUMMARY

An individual's occupation modifies his or her whole way of life. It limits role and status and generally dictates the way one will live and the companions one will keep. Vocation is of special significance for adolescents, who must decide upon and prepare for their commitment to the world of work. Gainful employment has different significance for each of the sexes; it is usually a requirement for manhood, and is rapidly becoming an important part of the woman's role. Just as woman's vocational role is increasing in importance, man's is decreasing somewhat, as compared with their family roles. Indeed, the significance of work has declined somewhat in relation to other interests. The Puritan tradition associated work with such personal characteristics as dependability, integrity, and strong character. Today occupation is still significant, but leisure-time activity has come to rival it in importance. Both leisure and work ethics are changing as youth insist that their future work be meaningful and also leave ample room for varied, personally satisfying leisure activities.

The area of vocation involves special problems for youth. Matching a youth with a vocation is not easy, partly because of the highly fluid job situation. Today's youth also have difficulty establishing a vocational identity because many jobs are highly specialized or largely mechanical in nature. Another problem is young peoples' typically unrealistic vocational aspirations. Often, more youth plan to enter particular professions than openings in those areas permit, and even more aspire to higher jobs than they may feasibly achieve. It is important, however, to distinguish between vocational plans and aspirations. Many times an individual would like to prepare for some job that circumstances do not permit; hence, dreams are one thing, and plans are quite another.

Certain youth, among them the physically handicapped, have special vocational problems. It is important that the physically handicapped be matched properly to jobs to prevent their future discouragement and disillusionment. Racial and sociocultural minorities have their problems as well. Although their problems have received widespread recognition, they are far from solved. In general, minority youth's goals represent the extremes, being either too low or too high. Another youth with vocational problems is the early school dropout, who is at an acute disadvantage in a culture geared to high educational requirements, with routine jobs increasingly consigned to machines. Moreover, as the number of highly trained individuals increases, the school dropout becomes rarer and even more conspicuous than before. At the other extreme, gifted individuals who are also highly educated experience certain disadvantages in vocational adjustment. They may have so many skills that it is hard for them to make a choice of vocation. Also, in certain areas of specialization, the number of highly qualified persons has come to exceed the supply of jobs.

Each sex has its special vocational problems. For the male, vocational choice is difficult because he must prove his success on the job in order to be considered successful as a male. Moreover, his family's welfare and status depend on his vocational success. The female has vocational problems that are just as great but different. She must choose between part-time and full-time vocation and temporary or permanent jobs. She has fewer vocations from which to choose, and she often has less chance for advancement on the job than a male has. She often has had little preparation for making work decisions, incuding how best to integrate future work and family roles. Sexual stereotypes in vocations persist, especially in lower classes. Despite some gains, the work-a-day world is still overwhelmingly a man's world, especially where power and status are concerned. Long-term effects of the women's movement on the relative roles of the sexes in vocation are still uncertain.

The function of the career counselor is to help young people find work congenial to their personal tastes and potential. Counselors must be resource persons, acquainting youth with a broad range of jobs, and also sources of encouragement to youth taking their first stumbling steps toward job choice and preparation. Nevertheless, the counselor must avoid telling the student what to do, for ultimately youth must decide for themselves what their fate will be. The counselor must also avoid prodding the youth to make a premature commitment, for young people need time to become acquainted both with themselves and with various occupations. Counseling is especially effective if coupled with supervised out-of-school work programs. Such programs help youth to develop traits compatible with their future vocational role, and they learn to see the world through the eyes of adult associates. Adolescents generally extol the worth of part-time work and sometimes become business entrepreneurs themselves.

The issue of how long to delay choice of vocation is a difficult one. A relatively early choice tends to produce motivation and commitment, but it also serves to close the door to alternatives. Recently there has been less emphasis on one lifelong choice; rather, the vocational life may involve a succession of choices parallelling changes in development throughout early and middle adulthood.

Many factors affect youth's choice of a vocation, among the most important being parents, college mentors, and other significant persons. The college attended is also a factor, as is choice of a college major. Another factor is the sociocultural setting, which tends to limit the range of occupations from which one can choose. Besides, each occupation has its social traditions that are passed down to youth by their own families. Another factor in vocational choice is sex. In general, girls aim lower than boys, partly because they recognize that their chance to rise is less. Another factor influencing vocational choice is the peer group. Other influences on vocational choice depend on social class and whether the home setting is rural or urban, industrial or agricultural, and so on. A final factor affecting vocational choice is availability of occupational information. Young people cannot select occupations about which they know little.

It is not easy to match youth with jobs; however, certain techniques may be helpful. Among these are various kinds of tests, including intelligence tests, aptitude tests, and vocational interest tests. Often a variety of tests is used, along with personal interviews. These interviews might well involve going over with students various criteria that have been devised for helping to match youth with jobs. In any case, young people are encouraged to understand both themselves and their prospective jobs in order that the two may fit together.

Youth need assistance in entering and successfully adapting to adult occupational roles. Seniority rules often place them at a disadvantage. Youth also need help in adapting to the job once they have chosen and entered upon its duties. To this end, they must be helped to acquire those attitudes and skills which will help them make a satisfactory job adjustment over the years. They must be able continuously to readapt skills to a world of rapidly changing occupations, for only through progressively upgrading skills can a worker be expected to maintain employability. Finally, youth must be helped to attain the sort of personality that facilitates whatever on-the-job adjustments may be required. Regardless of how skilled they may be, if young workers fail in their relations with colleagues, they will hardly find vocational life satisfying or productive. Finally, youth should be encouraged to think of career as it relates to the life span, and vocational choices in terms of their long-term implications.

DISCUSSION QUESTIONS AND ACTIVITIES

1. Share with other members of the class your experiences in attempting to obtain vocational information and advice from guidance counselors or other sources.
2. List the vocations to which you have aspired and why, indicating approximately the age when each ambition was held. Lists may be collected and analyzed, according to changes in ambition by age and reasons for change.
3. Interview someone already engaged in the occupation to which you now aspire. Inquire about satisfactions and drawbacks of the job, as well as qualifications needed for it.

4. Testify concerning types of pressure placed on you directly or indirectly to follow certain occupations.

5. Interview labor union members whom you know, asking about regulations affecting youth entering the working world.

6. How would you advise a youth who cannot seem to make up his or her mind about a vocation?

7. Class members may relate their experiences with part-time work, discussing advantages and disadvantages involved. Develop suggestions for making such work experience more worthwhile.

8. Interview employers who sometimes hire teenage workers. Inquire in what ways these young people have proved their worth or failed to do so. Ask employers what suggestions they would give to parents and school counselors regarding how best to prepare young people for their future work roles.

9. Check help wanted ads in order to determine the relative number and type of jobs that might appeal to, or be available to, youth.

10. Analyze the complex of influences that led to your successive vocational preferences to date.

11. What special opportunities or difficulties existed in your hometown for youth who desired part-time or full-time jobs.?

SUGGESTED READINGS

Baimbridge, W. S., & Hatch, L. R. (1982). Women's access to elite careers: In search of a religion effect. *Journal for the Scientific Study of Religion, 21*(3), 242–255. Census data employed to explore the question whether religion imprisons women in traditional sex roles and denies them high access jobs, gave strong support to this critique in Canada but not the United States.

Blouin, D., Summers, T., Kelley, E., Glee, R., Sweat, S., & Arledge, L. (1982). Recruiter and student evaluation of career appearance. *Adolescence, 17*(68), 821–830. A study in which students and campus recruiters evaluated the importance of physical image for career advancement disclosed certain differences of opinion between these two categories as well as by sex and occupational area concerned.

Ehrenheit, S. M. (1983). No golden age for college graduates. *Challenge*, July–August, 42–50. Although a college degree no longer insures professional employment, it is important for success in a market requiring ever more sophisticated skills and flexibility.

Finkelstein, M. J., & Gaier, E. L. (1983). The impact of prolonged student status on late adolescent development. *Adolescence, 18*(69), 115–129. This study confirmed hypotheses that the prolonged student status encourages emotional independence, has negative affects on feelings of self-worth, and impedes progress toward formation of a vocational identity.

Flick, R. (1983). The new feminism and the world of work. *Public Inquiry*, Spring, *71,* 33–44. Current efforts to narrow the wage gap between the sexes are discussed in terms of their origin, characteristics, and possible effects.

McNair, D., Brown, D. (1983). Predicting the occupational aspirations, occupational expectations, and career maturity of black and white male and female 10th graders. *Vocational Guidance Quarterly, 32*(1), 29–36. This study of tenth graders concerned the relationship of self-concept, perceived parental influence, race, sex, and socioeconomic status to occupational aspirations, expectancies, and career maturity.

Peterson, G. W., Rollins, B. C., Thomas, D. L., & Heaps, L. K. (1982). Social placement of adolescents: Sex-role influences on family decisions regarding the careers of youth. *Journal of Marriage and the Family, 44*(3), 647–658. In a simulation game designed for families to plan adolescents' career goals, family decisions strongly favored male adolescents' career goals over those of females, fathers desired domestic goals for their daughters more often than daughters did for themselves, and daughters were about equally divided among those seeking occupation or homemaking as their primary life goal.

Phillips, S. D. (1982). Career exploration in adulthood. *Journal of Vocational Behavior, 20*(2), 129–140. This study of career development among males, ages 18 to 36 years, indicates earlier career decisions are usually exploratory and later ones of a terminal nature.

Phillips, S. D., & Strohmer, D. C. (1982). Decision-making style and vocational maturity. *Journal of Vocational Behavior, 20*(2), 215–222. This study of college freshmen indicated that, of several variables, only a combination of scholastic achievement and independent decision style related even moderately to vocational maturity.

Ruggiero, M., Greenberger, E., & Steinberg, L. D. (1982). Occupational deviance among adolescent workers. *Youth and Society, 13*(4), 423–448. This study indicated that the workplace provides many opportunities for occupational deviance; nor was there any substantial evidence of benefits to youth of employment.

Steinberg, L. D. (1982). Jumping off the work experience bandwagon. *Journal of Youth and Adolescence, 11*(3), 183–205. A review of the literature on the effect of adolescent work experience suggests that its benefits have been greatly overestimated.

Stewart, A. J., Lykes, M. B., & LaFrance, M. (1982). *Journal of Social Issues, 38*(1), 97–118. Findings from a longitudinal study of educated American women indicate that relationships between work and family variables for women are complex and changing due to the interaction of sweeping social change and processes of individual development.

Subminimum wage for youth. (1983). *New Generation, 81*(2), special issue. This entire issue concerns the advantages and disadvantages of a subminimum wage for youth, in terms of youth themselves, older workers, and society.

Tinsley, H.E.A., Kass, R. A., Moreland, J. R., & Harren, V. A. (1983). A longitudinal study of female college students' occupational decision making. *Vocational Guidance Quarterly, 32*(2), 89–102. A longitudinal study of female college students which involved examining causal relationships among occupational decision-making progress, sex-role attitudes, and cognitive complexity revealed complex relationships among the variables investigated.

Viney, L. L. (1983). Psychological reactions of young people to unemployment. *Youth and Society, 14*(4), 457–474. This interview study of the psychological reactions of unemployed youth disclosed considerable alienation and more differences according to age than sex.

Chapter Fifteen

Induction Into Adulthood

COMING OF AGE

Pubertal Rites

All societies distinguish between the status of child and that of adult. Most simple societies have precise formulas for inducting their youth into adulthood. The youth undergoes certain pubertal rituals, or *rites de passage,* which vary in amount of stress produced, after which the youth is considered an adult. These rites also differ for the sexes in varying manner and degree. Rites may be for one sex only, or they may be more elaborate for one sex than for the other. Societies are more likely to have male puberty rites when the society is more integrated sexually—that is, when the sexes are more jointly involved in various kinds of occupational activities (Kitahara, 1982). Perhaps one reason is that men in such a society desire to maintain a distance between the sexes, even though they are more integrated in the labor force. Thus, male puberty rites keep the sexes from converging even where the labor division is sexually less differentiated.

Such rites may be quite different for both sexes or, in a few cases, much the same. Among the Sepiks in New Guinea, for example, boys can become men only by ritualizing birth and taking over as a collective group the function that women perform naturally (Mead, 1950). More attention is generally given the rites for males, because the man's role in most societies is defined as more important. Besides, the boy undergoes no specific physical event which in itself signals the onset of puberty. His pubertal changes occur slowly, and no developmental events give him an immediate right to say "I am now a man." Therefore, simple societies provide the boy an adult identity by contriving rites of passage which make known his status to his tribe or village. His new social status may be proclaimed by visible signs, including body scars, circumcision, pierced ears, teeth filling, and teeth removal, as well as by special gifts and tattooing. Stressful rites for young males are the rule. For example, the Nandi of East India contrive ingenious tortures during the circumcision of the boy and he is rewarded if he does not show pain. The Apache Indians initiate the boy as though breaking a colt: they compel him to make holes in the ice and bathe, run with water in his mouth, and in general, bully him. Among the Mundugumor of New Guinea, the boy receives blows and curses and is scarred by a crocodile skull.

In contrast, little attention is accorded the girl's puberty. Among the aborigines in Central Australia, elaborate ceremonies are held for the male, but none at all for the female. Since menarche is dramatic and unmistakable, there is no question about the female's new status as a woman. Hence, the girl's rites are usually confined to significant happenings in her development, such as her first menstruation, betrothal, or marriage, and include relatively mundane activities. Only in rare cases—for example, where obesity is considered a sign of feminine beauty—is much attention paid to the girl's growing up. In parts of central Africa, she is separated at puberty from her family and fattened for several years, during which time she performs no physical activities.

Except in rare cases, female rituals are also less stressful, perhaps for similar reasons. During pubertal ceremonies among the Tukuna Indians, a girl's hair is plucked from her head, and the pain may be so great that she faints, but such ordeals for girls are exceptional. In Samoa, which is more typical, there are no taboos surrounding menstruation, and the menstruating girl is even permitted to prepare most foods. Menarche itself is not celebrated at all, although the recognition of defloration, or loss of virginity, is.

Pubertal Rites: Western Style

In modern society, there is no consensus as to what constitutes a rite of passage because growing up by formula is not the rule. Instead of a single ceremony, a sequence of steps leads to adulthood—grade school graduation, high school graduation, and college graduation. Pubertal rites have been displaced by legal definitions of rights and responsibilities. Sometime between the twelfth and the eighteenth birthdays, the protective and restrictive aspects of minor status are progressively removed, and adult privileges and responsibilities are instated. The sacrifice of childhood privileges and the acquisition of mature responsibilities do not always go together. For example, 12-year-olds may pay full fare for airplane tickets; but they may not drive cars.

Perhaps the nearest thing we have to pubertal rites in this culture, writes Joseph Kett in *Rites of Passage*, is leaving home, a ritual that has changed greatly over the past two decades (Goleman, 1980). In the eighteenth and nineteenth centuries youth went through many home leavings before finally setting forth in life. It was a commonplace practice for children, even as young as age 7, to be sent to a neighbor's farm as a boy-of-all-work. Or coast merchants might send their sons to sea as cabin boys even before they were 10 years old. Daughters would go out to work as servant girls. Therefore, the final home leaving was usually preceded by a number of leavings and homecomings. Thus there was a pattern of "semi-dependence," alternating between being subject to the parents' authority at home and much freer on the job.

From about the mid-nineteenth century on, cities grew and employment there increased, which meant that young people who went there to work usually stayed there instead of making regular trips home, because of difficulties and

There is no consensus as to what constitutes a rite of passage because growing up by formula is not the rule. (Courtesy of Public Relations Office, State University of New York at Oswego)

expense of transportation. Then, between 1800 and 1900, certain demographic trends importantly modified the quality and character of American adolescence. Small urban families displaced large families on the farms. People became more affluent, and economic pressures consequently diminished, so that fewer teenagers were compelled to contribute to the family income. In consequence, people began to adopt the "romantic view that the innocent young need protection against the pressures and dangers of modern life," so they were no longer sent away to work but to high school instead (p. 57). The new belief was that parents should carefully look after their teenagers until they were ready for adulthood, which served to prolong adolescence.

These days there are various patterns for children's leaving home. One is to leave home sooner than parents are ready to let their children go. One girl, age 18, did so after she argued with her parents about staying out late. She left and moved into an apartment in Toronto with some friends. She knew that her parents were upset about her leaving but said that she wanted them to see that she was not a child any more. Others leave home in stages, not leaving for good until they have established a secure base away from home. One girl, for example, lived first in her mother's house, then in a small cottage in the backyard, and then in a dormitory on a college campus. By leaving in stages she felt less insecure. Others may feel no pressure to leave at all and may remain at home well into adulthood. For example, in one family five of seven children ages 15, 17, 23, 26, 30 lived at home and the others lived close by. The father said that the family had always been close together and had taken vacations together. Some young people feel ambivalent about leaving home. They may leave but want to be sure there is a home base for them to return to whenever they like.

There is some evidence that leaving home is more difficult for young people these days. Between 1969 and 1979 the proportion of young Americans under age 29 who lived at home grew by 25 percent. One reason may have been economic, another that people are marrying later these days and marriage "has always marked a ceremonial point of no return" in separation from parents.

Psychological counselors in universities indicate that home leaving very often brings students, especially freshmen, to clinics, girls more often than boys. Thus, they may have left home physically but not psychologically. Also only and youngest children have more problems leaving home because parents often hold on to them too long and more tightly.

Another problem is that the home-leaving process is not institutionalized, and there are no firm guidelines. In other words, there is no right time or manner in which to leave. Parents themselves are uncertain about how long to hold their children. It is clear that this matter cannot be understood without studying the family as a whole.

Although mounting evidence indicates that adolescence is not extremely stressful, leaving home presents a problem for most young people, which represents something of a crisis. A major task of the family, especially with parents, is to permit their grownup children to leave home as a natural consequence of their maturity. Successful transactions of this goal usually occur if the parents have strengthened their alliance with each other and with their own siblings. The parents must acknowledge to themselves their adolescent children's maturity and renew their own attachment to each other if they are to avoid feeling depressed.

Wechter (1983), a social worker, told of her own experience in leaving her family in Texas to go to New York. The family perceived her leaving Texas as rejection of her own identity as a southerner, a Texan, and small city girl. She had rejected the family's life style, and her accustomed role as mediator in the family, which tried desperately to get her to stay at home. In her first two years in New York the relationship had swung back and forth between "closeness and distance, enmeshment and alienation, acceptance and rejection" (p. 99). She was torn between her former and present life. The family seemed angry at her seeming rejection and caused her to feel guilty. She was trying to find her own vocational life while, at the same time, trying to retain her parents' encouragement, and she zigzagged between attempting to meet their expectations and developing her own. She gave up the family ideology but, as it dissolved, she was left with conflicting urges to give in to her family's values and to develop her own.

It might be conjectured that youth's permanent departure from home would have varied emotional impact, depending on the individuals involved; however, too little research exists regarding parent-child attachment in adolescence to reach firm conclusions now (Moore & Hotch, 1981).

It should be added that, looking ahead, youth not only perceive the roles of making a living, rearing a family, and maintaining the society but also a life of self-expression, creativity, and adventure. They wish to develop their creative potential for developing "expressive styles of living" (Yankelovich, 1983, p. 39).

Obstacles to Establishing Maturity

One obstacle to maturity is the lack of association between age groups. The adolescent group is often set off by itself to the point of encapsulation, and teenagers spend their time in teen herds. Since they are denied the exercise of genuine responsibility and direct identification with adults, they are correspondingly denied a true apprenticeship for adulthood. Another obstacle to such an apprenticeship is the parent who refuses to acknowledge that his or her child (usually the girl) is growing up. Mothers, especially, may not know how to retire from parenthood, and their children cannot cut parental psychic umbilical cords without guilt feelings.

In addition, much that children learn has little relevance for adulthood. The submissiveness of early years must be changed to independence and even aggressiveness later on. Fun and irresponsibility must give way to serious concerns. Even schools, supposed to train students for the business of life, are highly vicarious in their curricula. That is, they fail adequately to integrate the curriculum with life outside the school. Youth think of graduation as crossing the threshold into real life, as though the years up to that time had been some sort of prolonged prenatal state.

A related problem is difficulty in finding adequate models of adulthood (Porter-Gehrie, 1979). The adults they prefer as models are remote from their experience, such as historical figures or athletic heroes. Hence, their modeling is indirect, as in images of adults presented in films, books, and television.

Another problem of maturing is the lack of any standard for determining when adulthood has been achieved. Standards for achieving maturity vary with social class, sex, culture, and marital status. Children of the lower class are turned loose earlier and become heads of families and wage earners immediately after high school. Despite their later age of puberty, males are accorded recognition as adults earlier than females. College males are often referred to as men, whereas females of the same age are commonly called girls. Marital status also makes a difference. The youth with a wife and family is considered a man, but a single male of the same age is still a boy.

Perhaps youth's slow pace in entering upon adult commitments, such as marriage, parenthood, and final choice of career, also has to do with their culture of the present. That is, they are putting off decisions that would be binding, and focusing on the present which they know. They are delaying making definite choices about matters that formerly were taken for granted, but are perceived today as filled with risky commitments (Smith, 1983).

Contributing further to the confusion are society's capricious standards of responsibility. One teenager is locked up for a crime and held accountable as if he were a man; another of the same age, convicted of an even more serious crime, may be granted reprieve because of his youth. Such ambiguities reinforce young people's uncertainties about themselves. They cannot be sure what privileges they are entitled to or when they will be held accountable.

In the later 1960s and early 1970s young people began to demand their rights and to be treated more maturely, and as a result the voting age was lowered to 18 (Proefrock, 1981). In addition, the jurisdiction of juvenile courts was reduced and there was a trend toward trying adolescents indicted for serious crimes in adult, instead of juvenile, courts. Meantime, technical and trade schools requiring brief periods of training had grown more popular. Thus it appeared that the adolescent period was becoming shorter. Nevertheless, there was no real progress toward giving adolescents a greater share in the benefits they wanted from society. In other words, simply inducting them into adulthood earlier with regard to various privileges did not carry a parallel increase in benefits.

The complex factors involved in establishing recognition as an adult are clearly apparent in students' answers to the question: "At what age do you expect to consider yourself an adult and why?"

> I'll be an adult by age 26, because by then I'll have had experiences as a teacher and as a housewife. I'll have a burden of responsibility and a position of respect.

> I had so many responsibilities during my teens that I was an adult long before I entered college.

> I am young in spirit and will probably not feel like I'm an adult until I am 30.

> I already feel like an adult. I began feeling like one about age 18 and certainly by 21. Why? I first lived away from home and learned what sex was (in theory). Above all, college gave me a personal insight into self.

Factors that Hasten Maturity

Certain factors accelerate youth's progress toward adulthood, one being the constant pressure on high school students to perform well so that they will be admitted to good colleges. For another, many college students feel that they are on their own and cannot depend on their parents for assistance. Also, as early as age 12 or 13, some individuals relate almost exclusively to their peers. Such adolescents simply go underground and develop life styles of their own.

In terms of social role, the transition from adolescence to adulthood is almost always swift for boys, often less so for girls. One day a boy is carefree and protected; the next day, the problems of being an adult are dumped in his lap. Within the span of a few brief months, he may be inducted into the serious adult role of wage earner, husband, provider, and citizen.

Apparently car ownership becomes one route to earlier maturity. In a comparison of male youth, ages 14 to 18, divided into groups of unrestricted drivers, limited drivers, and nondrivers from an urban high school in northeast Kansas, the drivers showed a clear advantage over nondrivers in terms of overall development (Schlecter & Grump, 1983). Driving had helped them become independent of their parents and 45 percent of them said that driving allowed them some financial independence by providing transportation to their place of work. Drivers had access to a larger environment, spent more time with their friends in teenage settings, had more freedom from parental control, and manifested more socially responsible behaviors. Also, the drivers spent more time with their friends, especially with their girl friends. They were less controlled by having to obtain their parents' permission.

Obviously, upon widening their own physical environment they might have a feeling of greater freedom in their own life space, through greater environmental exploration. Also, driving allows development of more and better relationships with peers, partly because they have easier access to their peers, which gives them a certain status. With regard to social responsibility the driving teenagers feel "more mature, less childlike" with relation to their parents and the adult world in general. By obtaining parental permission to drive and leave home they attain a feeling of increased autonomy from their parents. Hence, driving may constitute a significant aspect of shifting from childhood depen-

The transition from adolescence to adulthood is swift for boys and within a few months they may be inducted into serious adult roles. (Courtesy of Public Relations Office, State University of New York at Oswego)

dency to adult autonomy. Of course, it is possible that mature individuals may be allowed the use of the car and that its use is not solely the cause of their greater maturity. On the other hand, we are all well aware of parents who are relatively more or less free with their teenage children, regardless of the latter's manifestations of ability to be responsible.

Of course, the effects of driving a car are not always positive. Young drivers may become involved in accidents, and they spend less time on their school work—and one might assume make lower grades.

ATTITUDES TOWARD GROWING UP

Adults' Attitudes

Among factors serving either to facilitate or obstruct youth's induction into adulthood are adult attitudes. Some parents, unconsciously or otherwise, resist their children's growing up. It is hard to change perceptions which have become habit. Besides, parents' acknowledgment that their children are growing up is to concede that they themselves are aging. Other adults accept their children's changing status because they assume they are expected to or because they look forward to escaping responsibilities incumbent upon the parental role.

Youth's Attitudes

Adolescents hold two distinct concepts of themselves: who I am and who I will be. While the concept of who I am may remain stable through adolescence, concepts of the future self may change during the same period (Coleman, Herzberg & Morris, 1977). Relatively few individuals experience any unusual concern over future identity in early adolescence; however, such concern becomes widespread in later adolescence. The most important developmental change in later adolescence concerns the individual's relationship to the future (Winer, Schwartz & Berger, 1977).

In 1981 younger Americans judged their present lives as lower than the norm. On the other hand, they felt optimistic about their personal lives for the future. Indeed, the present generation is as enthusiastic about its future as were younger generations of former years. This finding appears significant in times judged anxiety-laden, with threat of disasters arising from world-wide economic problems, nuclear attack, and war (Watts, 1981). Youth would feel even more secure about their futures if acquainted with life-span research, despite the common notion that life goes down hill after youth. A national survey indicates that, to some small degree, optimism rises rather than descends with age (Watts, 1981).

Individual reactions vary widely: some adolescents eagerly look ahead; others have mixed feelings; and still others cast a wary eye on approaching adulthood as though flying into the eye of a hurricane. Less than enthusiastic adolescents sympathize with the wit who said, "Adulthood is a time when one stops growing at the ends and starts growing in the middle." Adulthood is the time to settle down; fun seeking as a way of life is over.

Somewhat confused or ambiguous feelings about becoming adult are reflected in these youths' statements:

FEMALE: My perception of the adult world is still ambiguous. Money is very important, too important, as a key to self-actualization. The adult world doesn't place much emphasis on self-actualization. It's too deodorized, too antiseptic. It discriminates against women and frustrates their self-actualization.

MALE: My perception of adult society is complex, and my feelings contradictory. I see a world that says one thing and does another. Adult society says be an individual, make your own choices. It also says don't be a rebel, and follow the rules.

Some individuals have a greater stake in prolonging adolescence than others. The girl may dread choosing between marriage and career. The glamourous female and the male athletic star may lose the worship currently given them. For them, adulthood is anticlimax, not climax. As one 20-year-old youth wrote,

I was a three-letter man in high school and accorded all the honors and privileges that went with my exalted status. I had my pick of dates and invitations to parties. It was wonderful while it lasted, but a football injury put an end to my being a Saturday hero. Now I am a has-been, a used-up athlete, trying to get used to the lack-lustre role that has been forced upon me.

Many adolescents hold a double orientation to adulthood, like young Bazerov in Turgenev's *Fathers and Sons*. Portrayed as the archetype of adolescence, he is described as trembling on the brink of adulthood while also trembling with anger that he was being restrained. In any case, the majority unconsciously accept the fact that they will soon become adults and must prepare themselves accordingly. Whether they perceive adulthood as climax or anticlimax, they accept its inevitability.

Youth's Goals for Adulthood

The life styles most youth would prefer as adults are somewhat traditional, though in some respects they reflect the times. Among 17,000 high school seniors almost three-quarters thought a happy marriage and family life were highly important (Youth on the move, 1981). When college students were asked to anticipate their life styles in 1985, most of them named home ownership, children, marriage, a car or two, and a reasonably well-to-do-life style (Stein, 1976). Young men are coming to attach growing importance to their future role in the family and all but a very few college women still rank motherhood and marriage first among their future priorities, although the majority expect to combine marriage and career (Mash, 1978). Nevertheless, young women no longer look on housewifery, motherhood, and conventional feminine behavior as the be-all and end-all of women's existence. They want flexibility in career plans, with brief interruptions for motherhood or for reducing career commitments when their children are young. On one hand, they intend to maintain intellectual activities and interests outside the home; on the other, they anticipate achieving their most basic satisfactions from home and family.

Indeed, a review of the research (Juhasz, 1980) discloses that adolescents still view legal marriage and nuclear family as the most appropriate setting for childrearing and they see the decision whether or not to have children and how many to have as mainly that of the married couple involved. Slightly over half would prefer two children, the remainder more than two. Most of them believe that their peers are less traditional than they are.

Young women's fertility expectations have fallen more sharply than the fertility ideal. That is, they expect to have fewer children than they ideally would like. Meantime, there has been an increase in women's expectations of working when adult. The decrease in fertility expectation may be linked to a realistic perception of the conflict between having children and holding a job. Decreased fertility expectations are also consistent with their higher educational expectations. Although many young women appear not to regard high level of educational attainment as incompatable with relatively high fertility, expected educational attainment is closely linked to the age when young women begin childbearing. Delay in childbearing is associated with ultimately having fewer children. Moreover, as young women grow older and increase their schooling, they may revise downward their fertility expectations, especially those who obtain attractive positions in the job market. However, this situation may be revised to the extent that child-care programs and flexible policies are provided in the workplace, concepts which are slowly but surely taking hold (Crowley & Shapiro, 1982).

Undergraduates at New York University related the desire to become mothers to three factors: positive aspects of their relationship with their mothers, their degree of femininity, and their feminism through association with the woman's movement. In general, the desire to become mothers related positively to satisfactory experiences with their mothers, perhaps because adult nurturance emerges from the basic trust developed in earlier years between mother and child. Those rating more highly in femininity perceived childrearing as gratifying for both child and parent and as contributing to happiness in family life. On the other hand, association with the woman's liberation movement showed a greater negative correlation with parenthood motivation than any of the several variables studied, possibly because motherhood has been traditionally associated with lower status. The feminists may also be quite cognizant of the problems involved in transacting both career goals and child care responsibilities. It may be added that among all these women a mean of 2.7 and a mode of 3 children were desired, but 9 percent of the subjects wanted no children at all, a slightly smaller percent than reported in other recent studies (Gerson, 1980). Possibly this finding reflects the slight trend, recently, toward greater traditionalism.

In another study, among college students in Jackson, Missisippi (Rao & Rao, 1982) the blacks more often than the whites said that they wanted four children, when given a choice between two or four. Blacks are more likely than whites to associate having children with parental pride and to desire a son. To have children is a sign of maturity and of the man's masculinity (Thompson, 1980). Apparently, sex-role ideology did not affect the white youths' attitude toward childbearing. Students of both races wanted more children than women's birth expectations would suggest, the current lifetime expectation of all women today being 2.1 children, perhaps fewer than required to replace the population.

PREFERRED LIFE STYLES   Undergraduates at the State University College Oswego, New York, indicate the type of the life styles they would prefer as adults.

After college

MALE: I would prefer to wait about 5 to 10 years after school to get married, or possibly just live with someone; and then I would like to have a few children.

FEMALE: My choice would be to get married eventually, but right now I'm not sure that I want to have children. I don't think it is fair to bring a child into a world as problem-oriented as ours. I'd like to adopt a child who needs a home. Society should care for people already living rather than just producing more.

Where to live after college

MALE: Ideally, I would like to live in a small town. I like the easy-going pace, but realize that job opportunities are fewer in small towns. I have to draw a balance between my ideal living conditions and my ideal career aspirations (although I don't even know what they are yet).

FEMALE: I was raised in a rural area and found it very rewarding because I could have pets, as many as I wanted, and always had a place to get away from it all.

Future vocation

FEMALE: I am looking for a job I can be secure in (both financially and job wise) and a place where I can be creative. I am more of a doer than a sitter and both of these two parts have to go together for me to function well.

MALE: After college I plan to become a policeman or federal agent. I would like to get married and have at least three children. However, I want to have good financial status when I get married. I want my children to go to school, and even to college. My sons, I want to be fair, honest, and athletic; my daughters, fair, honest, healthy. I want to live in the country. I want my family to feel like a family, not like a cardboard structure of a family found in suburbs and cities.

CRITERIA FOR MATURITY

Progress toward adulthood is sometimes measured in terms of developmental tasks. That is, an individual must attain particular attitudes, habits, and skills in order to function effectively as an adult. Adulthood often sneaks up on adolescents, catching them unprepared. Various listings of such tasks exist, generally not conflicting but having different emphases. The following points, derived from various lists, have been expressed or implied already but will be summarized here.

1. A basic criterion of maturity is that the normal tasks of adolescence will have been resolved. The young adult must have firm preadult underpinnings; otherwise energies still required for fighting childhood battles and healing old wounds cannot be set free for resolution of adult problems.

2. Youth who are ready for maturity have found healthy channels for expressing emotions and can control them to the extent required. They have learned to inhibit excessive expressions of emotion, as well as to ignore many of the stimuli which, in early years, proved to be stress-producing. This is not to say that they remain emotionally insulated from their environments. On the contrary, they make heavy emotional investments, but are resilient, capable of taking in stride the inevitable frustrations and disappointments of life.

3. Young adults should be able to organize all those factors within their physical and social environments over which they have control in ways that permit maximum self-actualization consistent with long-range social welfare. They relate meaningfully to the world with a sense of commitment and of belonging to the "human enterprise." On the other hand, they manage to maintain personal autonomy or freedom from undue control by others.

4. Mature individuals can maintain their autonomy more easily if they have established a sense of identity and a way of life consistent with their own potential. They are aware of self—not in a self-conscious way, but in a manner that makes for integration of energies and self-respect. Freedom to act is reinforced by the self-understanding, skills, and proclivities needed to act intelligently. Mature individuals make use of their competencies, capitalizing especially on unusual talents, even if the result is an apparently lopsided manner of life.

To maintain autonomy, mature individuals must establish a sense of identity and self. (Photo by William J. Butcher)

5. Another task is to retain the best of the preceding stages, while dispensing with the rest. Adults should preserve the sort of energy, idealism, and *joie de vivre* which is characteristic of youth. However, some aspects of adolescence, if they persist, can become a stumbling block to later adjustment. A case in point is the pressure on American adults to remain pegged at an adolescent stage of sexual development. Marital satisfaction and happiness in American society may decline, partly because adults are expected to perform at 40 or 50 as they did at 20 or 25.

6. Mature individuals have come of age, having established themselves as adults and developed genuine self-determination on their own, outside the childhood home. They have abandoned previous concepts of themselves as sons or daughters, as little or big brothers or sisters, or as students, all of which involve the limitations inherent in immaturity and dependency; or they have integrated their old concepts into fresh versions of self more appropriate to their current situation.

7. They have developed an interest in establishing the next generation, implying a faith in life and in their own place in the total scheme of things. They are prepared to decide when (or whether) to become a parent and what sort of parent to be. "Some people do not apply this gift to offspring but to other forms of altruistic concern and creativity which may absorb their kind of parental responsibility" (Gutmann, 1973, p. 153). This concept subsumes many facets of generation, including all the ways of creating and nurturing new persons, new products, new institutions, and new life styles, through periods of their origin and early existence and early "vulnerability."

8. If not engaged in full-time homemaking, mature individuals have successfully entered a vocation that permits self-actualization, have a reasonably adequate standard of living, and have become good citizens. They have found a place in society and have made satisfactory adjustments to the major social institutions, on both the local and the larger scene.

9. In defining one's relation to the world, the mature individual has developed a rational moral code and a philosophy of life. This philosophy provides the individual with a satisfying concept of the universe and his or her place in it; and the moral code serves as a measuring stick for one's actions. The code must also be flexible, designed to effect its basic purpose—to insure the greatest ultimate good of all concerned.

10. Young adults must also be sufficiently tough, resourceful, and flexible to cope with giant-sized problems. We can prophesy with some degree of certainty that today's young people will ultimately be required to cope with awesome issues, including problems of population, pollution, the bomb, interracial tension, and perhaps interplanetary relationships. Toward such issues young adults should assume a critical though constructive attitude.

11. One fundamental task of young adults is the continuation of exploratory activities already developed—a matter of life styles on trial in a wider arena. They do not find themselves all at once; making final decisions at this age stage is neither immediately necessary nor desirable.

Do Young People Mature "Prematurely"?

Authorities differ on whether youth's admission to maturity is properly timed. Society is assuming healthier attitudes toward youth, observes Robert Coles, and does not prematurely rush them into adult society (For American youth, 1976). Others, including David Elkind (1979), deplore the fact that adults may hurry children into adulthood, believing that the adolescent experience is hollow and without substance. While children may not be growing up faster physically, they are psychologically. Television and peer pressures account in part for this precocity; and many of them must adapt to their parents' divorce and remarriage. Such experiences need not prove unsettling, if too many pressures do not occur at once.

Others believe that youth are held back from maturity too long. They speak of "protracted" or "stretched" adolescence; and they view youth as failures in the developmental task of "abandoning narcissistic fantasies and juvenile dreams of glory" (Keniston, 1975, p. 2). The Coleman Panel (1974) advises that students join the work force earlier than in recent years in order to prepare more effectively for adulthood and to find outlets for their constructive and idealistic impulses.

HELPING YOUTH TO GROW UP

Although most individuals muddle through to maturity reasonably well, some of them, like those quoted here, might be helped to set their compasses more accurately:

> FEMALE: I am only allowed to make unimportant decisions about my life. Most of our decisions are guided by what other people think.
>
> MALE: My perception of the future is mixed. I have trouble striving in college and sometimes I get discouraged. I am afraid of life in a way. I have always concentrated on happiness, but in my childhood I was unhappy and my adolescence is the same. Sometimes I have to stop work and have a good time to sort of regain my childhood. I perceive the college adult world with disdain but when I look at our own generation I am not happy. The world of the businessman I don't like, nor the world of competition.

Assistance for such youth might embrace the following points:

1. Youth should not be forced into maturity too soon. If we indulge in overkill where adolescence is concerned, an individual fails to retain aspects of youth, such as hope and enthusiasm, that should be preserved. The adolescent years may be preserved as a psychosocial moratorium, during which individuals remain relatively free from adult pressures. They need time to engage in identity play and other forms of experimentation to determine who they really are.

2. To be appreciated, adulthood should be earned. Easy induction into adulthood is not identical with optimum adjustment to it. Adults who excessively indulge young people prevent them from understanding that only through becoming competent do they attain true freedom (Baumrind, 1974). That is, they cannot feel that they have a future or that they can make a place in the world without appropriate understandings, skills, and attitudes.

3. Conflicting interests between older and younger generations should be resolved insofar as possible; hence, respective roles of younger and older adults should be clarified. A young Sudanese M.P., on his way to a session of Parliament, expressed this philosophy to the author during a conversation on a Nile steamer:

   The Sudanese parliament is currently divided into the "old guard" and "young bloods." Members of the "old guard" look on us as hotheads. Actually, we will do well to benefit from their greater experience and restraining judgment. But they should acknowledge our greater energy and capacity for fresh ideas.

   Tangential to this discussion is the admonition that neither generation should martyr itself for the other. Parents of young adults should resist the temptation to sacrifice all the fruits of their toil to give their children an effortless start in life. Conversely, young adults must eliminate guilt feelings which tempt them to surrender rights of self-determination to parents who may attempt to run their lives.

4. Training during adolescence should involve a realistic consideration of the period that follows. For example, fledgling adults should be intelligent consumers. Yet a cross-national study of most advanced nations indicated that neither American youth, nor those in other countries, were acquiring the knowledge needed for wise consumption (Tyler, 1981).

5. Youth should be prepared not only to resolve adult problems but to enjoy adulthood actively; yet maturity is rarely pictured as realistic or satisfying. In most television programming, the primary emphasis is on romantic love involving young, good-looking subjects in fictional situations. Hence, youth have fuzzy ideas about adulthood in its most productive and satisfying aspects. Nor are they systematically educated in effective use of leisure time.

6. A more all-embracing goal is that youth should become challenged continuously to develop "new and more inclusive purposes for life" at later ages (p. 438). Nor should they perceive "change" as "threatening, as something that happens to one, but rather something that one's own efforts cause to happen, through explicit purposes, new information and skills" (Menge, pp. 433-439). Their whole emphasis would be "proactive . . . .the future becomes as real as the present . . . the idealistic spirit of youth is maintained . . ." Thus, "life continues to hold out the promise for a better tomorrow and when one feels significantly involved in making that future to happen, the integrity of one's identity and productivity on earth is enhanced" (p. 439).

Menge (1982) points out that current problems are as destructive for the masses and for our institutions as they ever were; and to date humans have proved unable to guide the world "toward a more beautiful, more just, more healthful future" (p. 439). As a result, throughout the years, we have simply rationalized and made excuses for our failures. Such excuses have not helped to solve the problems themselves, partly because the problem-solving approach used to date has not taken into account individual identities and values. Our efforts have been "piecemeal, reactive approaches" to problems (p. 439). This reactive problem-solving approach tends to create a "crisis-oriented mentality" (pp.439-449). To have expected young adults "enthusiastically to embrace the problems created by their elders" is an unrealistic expectation. The past rather than the future has tended to monopolize adult patterns and behaviors.

The alternative is to utilize the future as the starting point, asking "critical questions" to develop goals and direct human efforts, and to ask the sort of questions needed to develop the skills and information required, besides having a "monitoring system" to evaluate attainment of these goals (p. 440). As these processes continue dreams and realities are evaluated against results and then new goals, questions, and information data are produced. In such manner human beings can build a future in the direction of their dreams.

7. A national survey (Watts, 1981) indicated that "parents no longer regard their children as wards, whose future lives they must—or even can—orchestrate and plan" (p. 48). However, adults may earn youth's disrespect by too easily abdicating their own convictions. Some impatient youth champ at the bit; they can already taste the power of running a world; hence, adults should not shirk the responsibility of debating issues with the young. All too many adults have become self-doubting and intimidated by the aggressiveness, impatience, and impulseness of the young and refuse to engage them in vigorous debate on substantive issues.

Perhaps those adults who can best assist youth toward maturity are persons just older than themselves. Under conditions of rapid change, young persons must assume responsibility for the destiny of still younger persons, in ways difficult for older people (and least of all for parents) to perform.

8. Adolescents' efforts to help themselves should be recognized and encouraged. In times of rapid and continuous change, says Spindler (1970), each generation manufactures its own culture. Although each new generation subsides finally to a position roughly resembling that of the preceding generation, the transitional period is marked by a self-invented culture which nudges the whole society in a slightly altered direction. Thus, the generation gap becomes a means to change, if not always to progress.

9. Programs for helping youth grow up should be related to current difficulties in achieving maturity. In these times, youth need a sense of the cosmic and the cataclysmic to avoid fear of being engulfed by forces too big to handle. This aim is utopian and not fully attainable; nevertheless, it can help to establish guidelines for youth's education.

10. It is well, too, for people entering their 20s to look at some of the research being done on people of middle ages and later years. Many middle-aged people look back, wishing that their values had been different in their 20s. Still later, in old age, both physical and mental health status are rooted in habits, skills, and attitudes established in earlier years. Every youth is an old-person-in-the-making and a significant determiner of what that old person will be.

YOUTH AND THE FUTURE

The foregoing recommendations regarding youth's preparation for adulthood have been couched in terms of the world as we know it. The present discussion is more conjectural, in terms of potential and alternative futures.

Youth must be prepared for uncertain futures and events that seem improbable, even impossible, today (Anderson, 1979). They must be prepared for dramatic technical breakthroughs equivalent in significance to the discovery of electricity, the automobile, the airplane, and the computer. It is thought-provoking to examine predictions made by certain highly respected individuals and publications in the past. The *Literary Digest* for October 14, 1899 declared that "the ordinary horseless carriage is at present a luxury for the wealthy; and although its price will probably fall in the future, it will never, of course, come into as common use as the bicycle." *Science Digest* of August 1948 declared that landing on the moon would involve so many serious problems that at least two more centuries would be required to accomplish it (The worst forecasts, 1978).

The following points are intended mainly to establish a habit of thinking that anticipates the future and involves preparation for the most probable scenarios to come. Also essential is the development of abilities needed to cope with new and complex developments and to learn to live with, even be challenged by, ambiguity.

1. Youth should keep abreast of intelligent prediction, as opposed to unscientific "star gazing." Futurist Paul Dickson calls futurism the "fastest growing educational phenomenon in history, the most important new concept of government in a hundred years, invaluable, too, for industry and a major breakthrough in human thinking" (The worst forecasts, 1978, p. 127). Certainly it would seem that perceptions of adolescence would gain greater validity if related to years that follow. As they go through life, individuals must learn to cope with new and growing threats to health that derive from mankind's assault on the environment. The automobile alone accounts for 60 percent of all pollutants in the air of the United States—10,800 metric tons a day in the air surrounding Los Angeles alone (Brower, 1979, p. 20). Roger Revelle points to the threat to human health of new chemicals that never existed before in the natural world (Decades of decision: Alternating currents, 1979, p. 144). There is also the matter of the proper adjustment between society and the individual. As interconnected linkages of computer interactions progress, quantities of data, often very personal, may be made generally

Youths must keep ahead of intelligent prediction in order to deal with future problems. (Courtesy of Public Relations Office. State University of New York at Oswego)

available, thus threatening individual privacy (Decades of decision: Micro/macro, 1979, p. 144).

2. Youth need the emotional health and coping mechanisms essential for dealing with unusual problems and traumas. In the 1960s, there was a 65 percent chance of a major event occurring during any particular year, compared with 90 percent now, and while the probability of a favorable occurrence has declined, the chance for unfavorable ones to occur has almost doubled. Among good events, the chance for foreign travel has shown the greatest increase, and that of becoming a parent, the greatest decrease. Dramatic increases in unfavorable events include becoming a victim of violent crime (up 180 percent) or becoming divorced (up 120 percent). Such figures dramatize the need for adolescents to develop appropriate coping skills and psychological mechanisms for dealing with difficulties (Decades of decision: Quality of life, 1978).

3. Youth need to develop new values if they are to relate properly to a rapidly changing world. Every scientific advance raises new questions of redefining interrelationships in the universe. Sir Eccles, Nobel Laureate in physiology and medicine, speaks of the significance of increased understanding about the origin of the universe and the questions that such discoveries raise about the meaning and purpose of mankind and the place of man in nature (Decades of decision: Micro/macro, 1979). Brower (1979) advises that adults of tomorrow rethink certain values which have been taken for granted—among them, man's right to dominate the environment. Brower suggests that "our attitude toward Earth was healthier when we were pagans who believed that spirits resided in everything, that man and beast were on an equal footing—bears becoming men, occasionally men becoming owls—and that a tree had to be placated before you chopped it down" (p. 20).

4. Because of the growing exploitation of earth's resources, youth need a sense of generativity or concern for future generations, more than ever before. Future generations will hardly forgive us "for the erasure of a large fraction of the species of plants and animals—and unneccesssary wastage of their heritage, which will undoubtedly be ranked as the worst error committed during the twentieth century." Since children and youth have a notoriously limited time sense, they should be helped *imaginatively* to embrace a sufficiently long time span to consider the long-term effects of behaviors (Decades of decision: Alternating currents, 1979.)

5. Adults of the future must have sound interpersonal relationships for their very survival. There is a wide gap between humans' genius in natural discoveries and their inability to resolve conflicts between groupings of humans around the globe (Decades of decision: The human family, 1979).

6. The magnitude of the tasks that lie ahead requires that humans develop their mental potential more fully than they do now. Consider the challenge "to exploit all available energy resources versus the necessity to preserve the fragile balance of nature. The life of the planet is at stake . . ." (Decades of decision: Alternating currents, 1979, p. 96).

7. Schools must continuously update their offerings, attempting to anticipate what their students need for effective living currently and in the future. A panel of youth and adults, commissioned by the National Education Association, defined certain educational goals if youth were to be prepared properly for the future. In addition to more traditional subjects, they should study human relations and communication skills as well as such related skills as computer languages, source, and information processing. Family relationships would be stressed along with group relationships in general. Some of the panel recommended more specific vocational training, while others preferred a more general education as the best preparation for future vocational roles. Specific education was interpreted to embrace comprehension of democratic processes as well as development of world citizenship attitudes. Concepts of work and leisure should be reinterpreted and both become employed as means to greater personal fulfillment. Of special concern to the panel members was the need to develop ethical character, perceived as requiring up-to-date ethical models and redefinition of values of equity and justice (Shane, 1977).

8. Youth must be prepared to think in terms of all the earth and even beyond the earth. Continued developments in transportation and communcation will rapidly increase the tendency, already great, to bring the whole world close together. Author Ray Bradbury concludes that in all the history of the world, nothing is more important than space travel. For him it is "commensurate with the birth of Jesus, Buddha, or Mohammed" (Decades of decision: Micro/macro, 1979, p. 100). Presumably, adults of the late 1900s must deal with the question of how much of the national budget to allocate to searching for life in outer space and what ultimate significance communication with some extraterrestrial intelligence might have for people on earth. Philip Morrison has proposed a

systematic search for radio signals and civilizations that may have far greater expertise than we have (Interview with Philip Morrison, 1979).

9. Tremendous technological advances suggest the potential for greatly enriched lives and vastly increased free time. Merely consider the time saved by the computer. Computers are becoming increasingly simplified and will enable people vastly to simplify coping with problems of managing their daily lives and life styles. To date, society has done too little to help children and youth to develop creative and satisfying ways of spending leisure time for all their years ahead.

    Technological breakthroughs will also necessitate making important personal decisions. For example, through breaking the genetic code, "the master chemical blueprint of life, couples may choose characteristics, including sex, of their children" (Age of miracles, 1983, p. A19). As never before, sophisticated decision-making will be required to maximize benefits and avoid serious errors.

10. Finally, youth should discard the habit of always expecting final, concrete answers. True, psychologists have long associated ambiguity with insecurity and anxiety—people feel more self-assured when their environment is predictable. Nevertheless, it is increasingly clear that the future will require the capacity not only to handle ambiguity but to feel comfortable with uncertainty. Hazel Henderson, economist, points out that new cosmologists are producing "a much more sophisticated in-depth view of reality. We're no longer looking for immutable facts and immutable objects the way we were during the . . . past 300 years. We're learning that uncertainty is the only certainty, and we're learning a happier view of uncertainty. . . . Everything could change in the twinkling of an eye" (Decades of decision: The human family, 1979, p. 102).

Research Needs

No generation in history has been studied more than present-day youth, yet greater knowledge about youth has not been followed by a comparably increased understanding of how to develop worthy young adults. While no answers can be expected to be all-conclusive, the study of adolescence would benefit from a more scientific approach. This field should be combed for questions hitherto investigated inadequately or not at all. One need is to give more attention to subgroupings including upper-class youth, married youth, individualists, and deviates of many kinds. Individuals within the normal range should be differentiated and not simply lumped together and labeled "average." Creating effective adults cannot be an assembly-line job. Youth vary and they resent becoming the creatures of standard equations.

Also deserving special study is the relationship of adolescence to the years that follow. There is plentiful research concerning the fluid character of adolescent personality, but there is little about the final resolution of this diffusion, or how adolescence becomes adulthood. Among pertinent questions are these: How might adolescents' experience best be structured to insure that they will consistently continue to achieve in the future? Most famous people produce little of consequence after the beginning of the middle years, although numerous exceptions prove that productivity can continue to extreme old age. Can the achievement motive become so structured that its impact will continue through-out an individual's life?

No solutions to such questions can ever be accepted as final. Researchers must keep their hands constantly on the pulse of young America. Changing times and conditions inevitably outmode currently sound conclusions. The wisest plan is to appraise data critically and, with an open mind, to use the best of what has been learned to date. Certain persistent principles emerge from the con-sensus of feelings about life and its meaning, giving stability and strength to a scientific approach. For example, it is generally accepted that adults must be concerned about youth, yet they must guard against the overconcern that gen-erates anxiety in those whom they mean to help. Standing by to encourage, they should extend to youth a friendly challenge to "conquer the world" (Halleck, 1948):

> Are the seas then all charted?
> The new trails blazed?
> Are there for the young-hearted
> No pioneer ways?
> Are the stars then all numbered?
> The dragons all slain?
> Lies the earth unencumbered
> With sorrow and pain?
> Up, youth to inherit
> What age has let fall.
> Yours the mantle, now—wear it!
> Godspeed to you all.

SUMMARY

All societies recognize differences between the status of child and that of adult, and all possess ways of inducting youth into adulthood. In modern societies, there is no consensus as to what constitutes an initiation ritual or pubertal rite. Perhaps the requirements of a swiftly changing, complex society have made prescribed formulas for growing up impractical.

There are obstacles to achieving healthy maturity in Western culture, including the discontinuity between training received in childhood and the re-sponsibilities expected of adults. Much that is learned in early years has practically no relevance for adulthood. Adolescents are thereby denied a true apprentice-ship for their responsible role in society. Other obstacles are the lack of asso-ciation between adolescent and adult age groups, the refusal of some parents to acknowledge that their children are growing up, and society's capricious standards for awarding responsibility and for determining when adulthood has been achieved. An individual may be recognized as an adult in terms of military service, while remaining at the subadult level in terms of professional training.

Both adults and youth hold characteristic attitudes about youth's growing up. Adults' attitudes may serve either to facilitate or to obstruct youth's induction into adulthood. Some parents accept their children's changing status because they may desire release from the responsibilities relating to the parental role, or they may resist recognizing their children's increasing maturity because to do so would acknowledge their own aging status. For their part, some youth eagerly anticipate adulthood; others feel anxious about it; still others hold somewhat ambivalent attitudes about it. They may look ahead eagerly, desiring the privileges that customarily accrue to the adult, or they may cling to adolescence because it is more carefree, romantic, and pleasant. Some individuals—among them, college athletes—have a greater stake in prolonging adolescence than others do.

Youth's goals for adulthood are still somewhat traditional, although in certain respects they reflect the times. Almost all expect to marry and have children; a large majority would own their home, living far enough from a city for a measure of privacy and space; and working at a meaningful, reasonably well-paying job. They would like to delay marriage until they are in their late 20s to allow some years for travel and varied experience.

Youth's readiness for maturity may be defined in various ways: for example, in terms of developmental tasks, or the acquisition of those attitudes, habits, and skills required to function effectively as an adult. Youth's progress toward maturity may also be defined in normative terms, or how the individual's progress corresponds with that of others of the same age. For perspective on criteria of maturity, it is well to keep in mind that no one is adequate and that a composite measure might best be used. We must remember, too, that estimates are subjective in nature, depending upon value judgments of the individuals who devise them, as well as the culture or subculture concerned.

There is considerable difference of opinioin concerning how well prepared most youth are for maturity. Some adults have doubts about youth's progress toward maturity; others believe they mature too early and become unduly serious and grim in their attitude toward life. Still others caution that readiness for adulthood is not a once-and-for-all achievement; instead, regressions must be expected from time to time. Individual youth vary greatly in their approaches to and progress toward maturity. Even among the more mature, maturity in all areas is not achieved all at once, and regressions are common.

It is generally conceded that certain measures may help youth in their progress toward maturity. They should not be forced into maturity too soon; they should be permitted a psychosocial moratorium during which to test the ground rules of their society. They also need clear-cut standards of responsibility if their own adult roles are to be adequately defined. Certain customs or rites similar to the aborigines' walkabout, if institutionalized, might facilitate the transition. Certainly, youth must not simply be presented adulthood as a gift; they should earn it if they are to discharge their mature roles adequately. In addition, the adult society should be made more attractive, so that youth are not reluctant to join the ranks of their elders. Adults must present worthy models if youth are to trust their leadership and respect the ranks of those they must ultimately join.

These and other suggestions for helping youth attain a healthy maturity are based on a combination of subjective views and empirical research. Topics heretofore neglected should be investigated, and their scope should be broadened to include youth of all sorts in all countries and subcultures. The research effort should extend backward into the past and forward into the future, anticipating what may lie ahead.

DISCUSSION QUESTIONS
AND ACTIVITIES

1.   Be prepared to participate in a panel discussion of the following: (a) What are the most effective ways of making induction into adulthood more satisfactory? Is the best answer to make adulthood more attractive? If so, how could this recommendation be carried out? (b) Should a single man or woman, age 20 or above, who lives in the same city as his or her parents, continue to live in their home? (c) How do the following experiences affect progress toward maturity: going to college; having a part-time job; getting married while still in college?

2.   Write answers to the following questions on a sheet of paper labeled only with your age and sex: (a) What do you consider the most or least attractive features about growing up? (b) Do you or did you personally mind relinquishing adolescence? Why—or why not? Class groups may collect, compile, and interpret the answers.

3.   Write answers to the following questions on a slip of paper labeled only with your sex: (a) What did you find to be the greatest obstacles to growing up? (b) What types of experiences helped you most to achieve maturity? (c) At what ages did you begin thinking of yourself as fully adult? Why? Class groups may collect, compile, and report on the answers.

4.   Be prepared to participate in a general class discussion of the most important insights gained during this course, including those from class lectures, the textbook, and outside readings.

5.   Just how attractive or unattractive is adulthood in American society?

6.   Rate yourself in relation to the several criteria for maturity as listed in this chapter.

SUGGESTED READINGS

Bloom, M. V. (1980). *Adolescent parental separation.* New York: Gardner Press. The separation process which adolescents and their parents face when young people move into adulthood is discussed and compared with other separation processes.

Cook, A. S., West, J. B., & Hammer, T. J. (1982). Changes in attitudes toward parenting among college women: 1972 and 1979 samples. *Family Relations, 31*(1), Women undergraduates questioned in 1979, in comparison with a 1972 sample, desired fewer children, were more accepting of childless families, and were less concerned about over population.

Crowley, J. E., & Shapiro, D. (1982). Aspirations and expectations of youth in the United States, Part I. Education and fertility. *Youth and Society, 13*(4), 391–422. This report of a National Longitudinal Survey concerns the aspirations and expectations of Americans, ages 14 to 21, for their education and future fertility.

Goleman, D. (1980). Leaving home: Is there a right time to go? *Psychology Today, 14*(3), 52–61. Young persons' leaving home is discussed in terms of its impact on their families, especially the parents and on themselves—with regard to their age at the time, reasons for leaving, and establishing psychological autonomy.

Hendricks, L. E., & Montgomery, T. (1980). A limited population of unmarried adolescent fathers: A preliminary report of their views on fatherhood and their relationship with mothers of their children. *Adolescence, 18*(69), 201–210. Cross-sectional studies are reported of black unmarried adolescent fathers regarding their perceptions of their fatherhood and their relationships with the mothers of their children.

Lee, K. (1982). Age at first marriage in Peninsular Malaysia. *Journal of Marriage and the Family, 44*(3), 785–798. An examination of factors influencing age of first marriage of females in Malaysia, indicated that education, ethnicity, and premarital work duration had the greatest impact on postponing marriage, and, in effect, leaving the family of origin.

Leigh, G. K. (1982). Kinship interaction over the family life span. *Journal of Marriage and the Family, 44*(1), 197–208. If current trends persist young people moving into adulthood can expect to continue having close relationships with parents and siblings, especially if they live nearby, but much less with more distant relatives.

Lewin, B. (1982). Unmarried cohabitation: A marriage form in a changing society. *Journal of Marriage and the Family, 44*(3), 763–773. In view of the now widely accepted practice of unmarried cohabitation among youth in this country, it is interesting to note this practice in Sweden as it persists into adulthood, becomes a form of marriage rather than an alternative to it.

Moore, D., & Hotch, D. F. (1983). The importance of different home-leaving strategies to late adolescents. *Adolescence, 18*(70), 413–416. This brief article describes the results of a study conducted to determine modes of home leaving that adolescents view as most significant indicators of parent-adolescent separation.

National Commission on Youth. (1980). *The transition of youth to adulthood: A bridge too long.* Boulder, Colo.: Westview Press. Recommendations are made for policies that would achieve revitalization of environments for assisting youth in their transition to adulthood and ways are suggested for producing greater cooperation among the agencies involved.

Rubin, Z. (1982). The search for reunion. *Psychology Today, 16*(6), 22–33. As sons grow up and fathers grow older, then relationship becomes one of equals, still complicated to some extent by their respective emotional needs.

Seltzer, V. C. (1982). *Adolescent social development: Dynamic functional interaction.* Lexington, Mass.: D.C. Heath Co. This book concerns the adolescent's search for direction and identity, the peer group as a forum for achieving progress toward adulthood, and implications for parenting and psychotherapy.

Smith, M. B. (1982). Hope and despair: Keep to the socio-psychodynamics of youth. *American Journal of Orthopsychiatry, 53*(3), 388–410. A psychology of hope and despair is related to youth's unrest in the 1960s, their current problem behaviors, and to their feelings about themselves and the future.

Wechter, S. L. (1983). Separation difficulties between parents and young adults. Social casework. *The Journal of Contemporary Social Work, 64*(2), 97–104. The literature is examined regarding separation of young people from their parents and a case illustration is presented.

Wilson, N. H., & Rotter, J. C. (1982). School counseling: A look into the future. *Personnel and Guidance Journal, 60*(6), 353–357. The future school counselors' role is considered in terms of helping young people cope, as adults, with a new civilization, with new ways of thinking and working, family styles, and societal conflicts.

References

Abernathy, T. J. (1981). Adolescent cohabitation: A form of courtship or marriage? *Adolescence, 16*(64), 791–797.

ACE survey (1979). *Phi Delta Kappan, 60*(7), 557.

Achenbach, T. M., & Edelbrock, C. S. (1981). Behavioral problems and competencies reported by parents of normal and disturbed children aged four through sixteen. *Monographs of Social Research and Child Development, 46,* 1082.

Adams, G. R. (1983). Social competence during adolescence: Social sensitivity, locus of control, empathy, and peer popularity. *Journal of Youth and Adolescence, 12*(3), 203–211.

Adams, G. R., & Looft, W. R. (1977). Cultural change: Education and youth. *Adolescence, 12*(46), 137–150.

Adams, V. (1980). Getting at the heart of jealous love. *Psychology Today, 13*(12), 38–47; 102–108.

Adelson, J. (1979). Adolescence and the generation gap. *Psychology Today, 12*(9), 33–37.

Adelson, J. (1980). Children and other political naifs. Interviewed by Elizabeth Hall. *Psychology Today, 14*(6), 56–70.

Adelson, J., & Doehrman, M. J. (1980). The psychodynamic approach to adolescence. In J. Adelson (Ed.) *Handbook of Adolescent Psychology.* New York: John Wiley.

Adler, F. (1975). The rise of the female crook. *Psychology Today, 9*(6), 42–46; 48; 112; 114.

Adler, I., & Kandel, D. B. (1982). A cross-cultural comparison of sociopsychological factors in alcohol use among adolescents in Israel, France, and the United States. *Journal of Youth and Adolescence, 11*(2), 89–113.

Adler, M. J. (1979). Education in a democracy. *American Educator, 3*(1), 6–9.

Age of miracles in science and technology (May 9, 1983). *U.S. News & World Report,* A20–A21.

Agrawal, P. (1978). A cross-cultural study of self-image: Indian, American, Australian, and Irish Adolescents. *Journal of Youth and Adolescence, 7*(1), 107–116.

Akchin, D. (1977/1978). Playing the election game.

Nutshell, the Magazine for the College Community, (1981), 42–44.

Alexander, J., & Cohen, J. (1981). Customs, coupling and the family in a changing culture. *American Journal of Orthopsychiatry, 51*(2), 307–316.

Alexander, K. L., Cook, M., & McDill, E. L. (1978). Curriculum tracking and educational stratification: Some further evidence. *American Sociological Review, 43*(February), 47–66.

Allgeier, A. R., Allgeier, E. R., & Rywick, T. (1981). Orientations toward abortion: Guilt or knowledge? *Adolescence, 16*(62), 273–280.

American Council on Education (1976). *The American freshman: National norms for Fall 1975.* Washington, D.C.: The Council.

American youth: Angry ... bored ... or just confused? (July 18, 1977). *U.S. News & World Report,* 18–20.

A new generation: Where it's heading (September 6, 1976). *U.S. News and World Report,* 45.

Anderson, R., & Nida, S. A. (1978). Effect of physical attractiveness on opposite- and same-sex evaluations. *Journal of Personality, 46*(3), 401–413.

Anderson, S. B. (Summer 1979). Educational measurement in a new decade. *The College Board Review, 112,* 2–23.

Angrist, S. S., & Almquist, E. M. (1975). *Careers and contingencies: How college women juggle with gender.* Port Washington, N.Y.: University Press of Cambridge/Dunellen.

Antin, M. (1912). *The promised land.* Boston: Houghton Mifflin.

Archer, S. L. (1982). The lower age boundaries of identity development. *Child Development, 53,* 1551–1556.

Ariés, P. (1962). *Centuries of childhood.* New York: Vintage Press.

Arlin, P. K. (1975). Cognitive development in adulthood: A fifth stage? *Developmental Psychology, 11*(5), 602–606.

Aronfreed, J. (1976). Moral development from the standpoint of a general psychological theory. In

T. Lickona (Ed.), *Moral development and behavior: Theory, research, and social issues.* New York: Holt, Rinehart & Winston.

A search for life's meaning in a high-tech era. (May 9, 1983). *U.S. News & World Report*, A11.

Ashton, R. (1976). Aspects of timing in child development. *Child Development, 47*(3), 622–626.

Avery, A. W. (1982). Escaping loneliness in adolescence: The case for androgyny. *Journal of Youth and Adolescence, 11*(6), 451–459.

Avery, A. W., Rider, K., & Haynes-Clements, L. A. (1981). Communication skills training for adolescents: A five-month follow-up. *Adolescence, 16*(62), 289–298.

Bachman, J. G., & Johnston, L. D. (September 1979). The freshmen, 1979. *Psychology Today, 13*(4), 26–41.

Bachman, J. G., O'Malley, P. M., & Johnston, J. (1978). *Youth in transition* (Vol. 6). Ann Arbor: Institute for Social Research.

Baizerman, M., Thompson, J., & Stafford-White, K., "An old-young friend" (September-October 1979). Adolescent prostitution. *Children Today, 8*(5), 20–24.

Baker, C. D. (1982). The adolescent as theorist: An interpretive view. *Journal of Youth and Adolescence, 11*(3), 167–181.

Balk, D. (1983). Adolescents' grief reactions and self-concept perceptions following sibling death: A study of 33 teenagers. *Journal of Youth and Adolescence, 12*(2), 137–162.

Balswick, J., & Avertt, C. P. (1977). Differences in expressiveness: Gender, interpersonal orientation, and perceived parental expressiveness as contributing factors. *Journal of Marriage and the Family, 39*(1), 121–127.

Balswick, J. O., & Macrides, C. (1975). Parental stimulus for adolescent rebellion. *Adolescence, 10*(38), 253–266.

Baltes, P. B., Reese, H. W., & Lipsitt, L. P. (1980). Life-span developmental psychology. *Annual Review of Psychology, 21* 65–110.

Baltes, P. B., & Schaie, P. B. (1976). On the plasticity of intelligence in adulthood and old age: Where Horn and Donaldson fail. *American Psychologist, 31*(10), 720–725.

Bamber, J. H. (1973). Adolescent marginality—for further study. *Genetic Psychology Monographs, 88*(first half), 3–21.

Baranowski, M. D. (1978). Adolescents' attempted influence on parental behaviors. *Adolescence, 13*(52), 585–604.

Bardwick, J. M. (1979). *In transition.* New York: Holt, Rinehart & Winston.

Bardwick, J. M. (1971). *Psychology of women: A study of biocultural conflicts.* New York: Harper & Row.

Bart, W. M. (1981). Attention structure, anti-societal behavior, and peer group regulation of behavior among adolescent students. *Adolescence, 16*(62), 433–442.

Barton, J., Chassin, L., Presson, C. C., & Sherman, S. J. (1982). Social image factors as motivators of smoking initiation in early and middle adolescence. *Child Development, 53,* 1499–1511.

Battered families: A growing nightmare (January 15, 1979). *U.S. News & World Report,* 60–61.

Baumrind, D. (1972). From each according to her ability. *School Review, 80*(2), 161–197.

Baumrind, D. (1974). Coleman II: Utopian fantasy and sound social innovation. *School Review, 83*(1), 69–84.

Baumrind, D. (1978). Parental disciplinary patterns and social competence in children. *Youth and Society, 9*(3), 239–276.

Baumrind, D. (1980). New directons in socialization research. *American Psychologist, 35,* 639–652.

Baumrind, D. (1982). Are androgynous individuals more effective persons and parents? *Child Development, 53,* 44–75.

Bayer, A. E., & McDonald, G. W. (1981). Cohabitation among youth: Correlates of support for a new American ethic. *Youth and Society, 12*(4), 387–402.

Bell, R. R. (1966). *Premarital sex in a changing society.* Englewood Cliffs, N. J.: Prentice-Hall.

Bem, S. L. (1975). Androgyny vs. the tight little lives of fluffy women and chesty men. *Psychology Today, 9*(4), 58–59; 61–62.

Benbow, C. P., & Stanley, J. C. (1980). Sex differences in mathematical ability: Fact or artifact? *Science, 210*(12), 1262–1264.

Bengtson, V. L., & Starr, J. M. (1975). Contrast and consensus: A generational analysis of youth in the 1970s. In R. J. Havinghurst & P. H. Dreyer (Eds.), *Youth.* Chicago: University of Chicago Press.

Benham, B. J., Giesen, P., & Oakes, J. (1980). A study of schooling: Students' experiences in schools. *Phi Delta Kappan, 61*(5), 337–340.

Bensman, J., & Lilienfeld, R. (1979). Friendship and alienation. *Psychology Today, 13*(4), 56–66; 114.

Berardo, F. M. (1981). Family research and theory: Emergent topics in the 1970s and the prospects for the 1980s. *Journal of Marriage and the Family, 43*(2), 251–254.

Berg, M., & Medrich, E. A. (1980). Children in four neighborhoods: The physical environment and its effect on play and play patterns. *Environment and Behavior, 12*(5), 320–348.

Berger, B. M., & Hackett, B. M. (1974). On the decline of age grading in rural hippie communes. *Journal of Social Issues, 30*(2), 163–183.

Bergson, H. L. (1946). *The creative mind.* Trans. by M. I. Andison. New York: Philosophical Library.

Bernstein, B. E. (1978). Generational conflict and the family. *Adolescence, 13*(52), 751–754.

Berndt, T. J. (1982). The features and effects of friendship in early adolescence. *Child Development, 53,* 1447–1460.

Berryman, S. (1978). Youth employment and career education: Reasonable expectations. *Public Policy, 26,* 26–69.

Berryman, C., & Schneider, D. O. (1983). Patterns of work experience among high school students: Educational implications. *High School Journal, 66*(4), 267–275.

Berzonsky, M. D. (1978). Formal reasoning in adolescence: An alternative view. *Adolescence, 13*(50), 279–290.

Berzonsky, M. D. (1983). Adolescent research: A life span developmental perspective. *Human Development, 26,* 213–221.

Best, F. (Fall 1981). Changing sex roles and worklife flexibility. *Psychology of Women Quarterly, 6*(1), 55–71.

Big change in adolescent reading (1975). *Intellect, 104*(2367), 8.

Blaga, J. J., & Cooney, T. M. (1981). Teachers need help on science-related social issues. *Phi Delta Kappan, 62*(5), 400.

Blinking at the birds and bees: Moms are still mum about sex (1979). *Human Behavior, 8*(2), 58.

Bloch, D. (1978). Sex education practices of mothers. *Journal of Sex Education Therapy, 4,* 7–12.

Block, J. H., & Block, J. (1983). The role of ego-control and ego-resiliency in the organization of behavior. In W. Damon (Ed.), *Social and personality development: Essays on the growth of the child.* New York: Norton, 282–320.

Block, R., & Langman, L. (1974). Youth and work: The diffusion of "countercultural" values. *Youth and Society, 5*(4), 411–432.

Blume, S. B. (1975). A psychiatrist looks at alcoholism. *Intellect, 104*(2367), 27–30.

Blyth, D. A., Hill, J. P., & Thiel, K. S. (1982). Early adolescents' significant others: Grade and gender differences in perceived relationships with familial and nonfamilial adults and young people. *Journal of Youth and Adolescence, 11*(6), 425–450.

Boice, L. H., & Gray, S. H. (September 1978). Job desirability and the right not to work. *U.S.A. Today, 107*(2400), 44–47.

Boocock, S. S. (1978). The social organization of the classroom. *Annual Review of Sociology, 4,* 1–28.

Bossard, J. H. S. (1954). *The sociology of child development* (2nd ed.) New York: Harper & Row.

Botwinick, J. (1977). Intellectual abilities. In J. E. Birren & K. W. Schaie (Eds.), *Handbook of the psychology of aging.* New York: Van Nostrand Reinhold Co., 580–605.

Bower, D. W., & Christopherson, V. A. (1977). University student cohabitation: A regional comparison of selected attitudes and behavior. *Journal of Marriage and the Family, 39*(3), 447–453.

Bower, T. G. R. (1974). Repetition in human development. *Merrill-Palmer Quarterly, 20*(4), 303–318.

Boyle, H. (June 8, 1951). Associated Press article. Quoted by permission of Wide World Photos, Inc.

Boynton, G. M. (1978). The relation between identity development and attitudes toward motherhood in young married professional women. Unpublished doctoral dissertation. Teachers College, Columbia University.

Braddock, J. H. II. (1981). Race, athletics, and educational attainment: Dispelling the myths. *Youth and Society, 12*(3), 335–350.

Brandt, A. (1982). Avoiding couple karate: Lessons in the marital arts. *Psychology Today, 16*(1), 38–43.

Brandwein, P. F. (1981). *Memorandum: On reviewing schooling and education.* New York: Harcourt Brace Jovanovich.

Brenner, D., & Hinsdale, G. (1978). Body build stereotypes and self-identification in three age groups of females. *Adolescence, 13*(52), 551–561.

Brickman, W. W. (1974). Adolescents and alcoholic abuse. *Intellect, 103*(2361), 165.

Bridgwater, C. A. (1983). Beauties, beasts, and job markets. *Psychology Today, 17*(4), 18.

Brim, O. G. Jr., & Kagan, J. (1980). Constancy and change: A view of the issues. In O. G. Brim J. & J. Kagan (Eds.), *Constancy and change in human development.* Cambridge, Massachusetts: Harvard University Press.

Broad, W. J. (1979). The rebel Einstein. *American Educator, 3*(1), 38–42.

Bronfenbrenner, U. (1977). Toward an experimental ecology of human development. *American Psychologist, 32*(7), 513–531.

Broughton, J. (1977). Beyond formal operations: Theoretical thought in adolescence. *Teachers College Record, 79*(1) 88–97.

Brower, K. (October 1979). In warm blood: Earth. *Omni, 2*(1), 20–22.

Brown, B. B. (1982). The extent and effects of peer pressure among high school students: A retrospective analysis. *Journal of Youth and Adolescence, 11*(2), 121–133.

Brown, S. E., Whitehead, K. R., & Braswell, M. C. (1981). Child maltreatment: An empirical examination of selected conventional hypotheses. *Youth and Society, 13*(1), 77–90.

Bryan, J. W. & Freed, F. W. (1982). Corporal punishment: Normative data and sociological and psychological correlates in a community college population. *Journal of Youth and Adolescence, 11*(2), 77–87.

Buck, L. Z., Walsh, W. F., & Rothman, G. (1981). Relationship between parental moral judgment and socialization. *Youth and Society, 13*(1), 91–116.

Buck, R. W., Savin, V. J., Miller, R. E., & Caul, W. F. (1972). Communication of affect through facial expressions in humans. *Journal of Personal and Social Psychology, 23*, 362–371.

Burleson, B. R. (1982). The development of comforting communication skills in childhood and adolescence. *Child Development, 53*, 1578–1588.

Burquest, B. (1981). The violent girl. *Adolescence, 16*(64), 749–764.

Burstein, B., Bank, L., & Jarvik, L. F. (1980). Sex differences in cognitive functioning: Evidence, determinants, implications. *Human Development, 23*, 289–313.

Burton, R. V. (1975). Honesty and dishonesty. In T. Lickona (Ed.), *Moral development and behavior: Theory, research, and social issues.* New York: Holt, Rinehart & Winston, 173–197.

Buser, R. L., Long, R., & Tweedy, H. (1975). The who, what, why, and why not of student activity participation. *Phi Delta Kappan, 57*(2), 124–125.

Bush, D. E., Simmons, R. G., Hutchinson, B., & Blyth, D. A. (1977–1978). Adolescent perception of sex-roles in 1968 and 1975. *Public Opinion Quarterly, 41*, 459–474.

Bush, S. (1978). Therapy: How not to stop juvenile delinquency. *Psychology Today, 12*(2), 26–27.

Callahan, D., & Callahan, S. (1981). Seven pillars of moral wisdom. *Psychology Today, 15*(8), 84–87.

Candy, S. G., Troll, L. E., & Levy, S. G. (1981). A developmental exploration of friendship functions in women. *Psychology of Women Quarterly, 5*(3), 456–472.

Cannon-Bonventre, K., & Kahn, J. (1979). Interviews with adolescent parents. *Children Today, 8*(5), 17–19; 41.

Caplow, T., & Bahr, H. M. (1979). Half a century of change in adolescent attitudes: Replication of a middle-town survey by the Lynds. *Public Opinion Quarterly, 43*(1), 1–17.

Career education resource guide. (1972). General Learning Corporation.

Carmines, E. G. (1981). Decline in presidential idealization among adolescents: Watergate created? *Adolescence, 16*(62), 487–492.

Carns, D. (1973). Talking about sex: Notes on first coitus and the double sexual standard. *Journal of Marriage and the Family, 35*(4), 677–688.

Carroll, J. B., & Maxwell, S. E. (1979). Individual differences in cognitive abilities. In M. R. Rosenzweig & L. W. Porter (Eds.), *Annual review of psychology, 30*, 603.

Carroll, J. W. (1973). Transcendance and mystery in the youth counterculture. *Journal for the Scientific Study of Religion, 42*, 361–375.

Cernkovich, S. A. (1978). Evaluating two models of delinquency causation: Structural theory and control theory. *Criminology, 16*, 335–352.

Chafetz, J. S. (1981). Family conflict: The application of selected theories of social conflict to an understanding of conflict within families. *Youth and Society, 13*(2), 157–173.

Chapman, R. B. (1978). Academic and behavioral problems of boys in elementary school. *Counseling Psychologist, 7*(4), 37–40.

Chase, C. J. (October/November 1982). Ten thousand students view their high schools. *High School Journal, 66*(1), 36–41.

Chassin, L., & Young, R. D. (1981). Salient self-conceptions in normal and deviant adolescents. *Adolescence, 16*(63), 613–620.

Chico, N. P., & Hartley, S. F. (1981). Widening choices in motherhood of the future. *Psychology of Women Quarterly, 6*(1), 12–25.

Chilman, C. (1979). Adolescent sexuality in a changing society. DHEW publication No. (NIH) 79-1426, National Institute of Child Health and Development, Washington, D.C.

Christensen, H. T., & Gregg, C. F. (1970). Changing sex norms in America and Scandinavia. *Journal of Marriage and the Family, 32*(4), 616–627.

Clarke, A. E., & Ruble, D. N. (1978). Young adolescents' beliefs concerning menstruation. *Child Development, 49*, 231–234.

Cleary, T. A., Humphreys, L. G., Kendrick, S. A., & Wesman, A. (1975). Educational uses of tests with disadvantaged students. *American Psychologist, 30*(1), 15–41.

Clemson, E. (1981). Disadvantaged youth: A study of sex differences in occupational stereotypes and vocational aspirations. *Youth and Society, 13*(1), 39–56.

Climo, L. H. (1975). Acting out of character: Window on the identity crisis. *Journal of Youth and Adolescence, 4*(2), 93–107.

Coed competition: Women miss out on classroom action. (1978). *Human Behavior, 7*(8), 21.

Cogle, F. L., Tasker, G. E., & Morton, D. G. (1982). Adolescent time use in household work. *Adolescence, 17*(66), 451–455.

Cohen, D., & Wilkie, F. (1979). Sex-related differences in cognition among the elderly. In M. A. Wittig & A. C. Petersen (Eds.), *Sex-related differences in cognitive functioning: Developmental issues.* New York: Academic Press.

Colby, A., Gibbs, J., Kohlberg, L., & Lieberman, M. (1983). A longitudinal study of moral development. *Monographs of the Society for Research in Child Development.* Chicago: University of Chicago Press.

Cole, S. (1980). Send our children to work? *Psychology Today, 14*(2), 44–68.

Cole, S. (1983). Red-ucation. *Psychology Today, 17*(2), 76.

Coleman, J., Herzberg, J., & Morris, M. (1977). Identity in adolescence: Present and future self-concepts. *Journal of Youth and Adolescence, 6*(1), 63075.

Coleman, J. C. (1980). Friendship and the peer group in adolescence. In J. Adelson (Ed.) *Handbook of adolescent psychology.* New York: Wiley.

Coleman, J. S. (1961). *The adolescent society.* New York: Free Press.

Coleman, J. S. (1974). Comments on responses to youth: Transition to adulthood. *School Review, 83*(1), 96–97; 139–144.

Coleman, J. S. (1978). Changing the environment for youth. *Phi Delta Kappan, 59*(5), 318–319.

Coleman, J. S. et al. (1974). *Youth: Transition to adulthood.* Chicago: University of Chicago Press.

Coles, R., & Woodward, K. (1975). The cold tough world of the affluent family. *Psychology Today, 9*(6), 67–70; 74–77; 133.

Colleges try to halt meaningless grades (May 3, 1977). *Miami Herald,* 7.

Colletta, N. D. (1979). The impact of divorce: Father absence or poverty. *Journal of Divorce, 3,* 27–36.

Collins, J. K. (1974). Adolescent dating intimacy: Norms and peer expectations. *Journal of Youth and Adolescence, 3*(4), 317–328.

Collins, J. K. (1981). Self-recognition of the body and its parts during late adolescence. *Journal of Youth and Adolescence, 10*(3), 243–254.

Condry, J., & Keith, D. (1983). Educational and recreational uses of computer technology: Computer instruction and video games. *Youth and Society, 15*(1), 87–111.

Conger, R. D. (1980). The child as victim: The emerging issue of child abuse. *Journal of Crime and Justice, 3,* 35–63.

Connolly, L. (1978). Boy fathers. *Human Behavior, 7*(1), 40–43.

Cornish, E. (February 1979). The future of the family: Intimacy in an age of loneliness. *The Futurist, 13*(1), 45–59.

Cornuelle, R. (1975). Society may be kept moving by its misfits. *Psychology Today, 9*(6), 88.

Cory, C. (1981). Power envy. *Psychology Today, 15*(6), 29; 90.

Cosand, B. J., Bourque, L. B., & Kraus, J. F. (1982). Suicide among adolescents in Sacramento County, California 1950–1979. *Adolescence, 17*(68), 917–930.

Coté, J. E., & Levine, C. (1983). Marcia and Erikson: The relationships among ego, identity status, neuroticism, dogmatism, and purpose in life. *Journal of Youth and Adolescence, 12*(1), 43–54.

Cottle, T. J. (1975). Low income youth. In R. J. Havighurst & P. H. Dreyer (Eds.), *Youth.* Chicago: University of Chicago Press.

Coward, R. L. (1959). American autobiographers eye their teachers. *Educational Forum, 23,* 233–238.

Crandall, V. C. (1972). The Fels study: Some contributions to personality development and achievement in childhood and adulthood. *Seminars in Psychiatry, 4*(4), 383–397.

Crites, J. O., & Fitzgerald, L. F. (1978). The competent male. *Counseling Psychologist, 7*(4), 10–14.

Cropley, A. J. (1972). A five-year longitudinal study of the validity of creativity tests. *Developmental Psychology, 6,* 119–124.

Cropper, D. A., Meck, D. S., & Asch, M. J. (1977). The relation between formal operations and a possible fifth stage of cognitive development. *Developmental Psychology, 13*(5), 517–518.

Crosby, J. F. (1980). A critique of divorce statistics and their interpretations. *Family Relations, 29*(1), 51–58.

Crowley, J. E., & Shapiro, D. (1982). Aspirations and expectations of youth in the United States. Part I. Education and fertility. *Youth and Society, 13*(4), 391–422.

Crutchfield, C. F. (1981). Medical treatment for minor children: The roles of parents, the state, the child, and the Supreme Court of the United States. *Family Relations, 30*(2), 165–177.

Csikszentmihalyi, M. & Kubey, R. (1981). Television and the rest of life: A systematic comparison of subjective experience. *Public Opinion Quarterly, 45,* 317–328.

Csikszentmihalyi, M., Larson, R., & Prescott, S. (1977). The ecology of adolescent activity and experience. *Journal of Youth and Adolescence, 6*(3), 281–294.

Curry, J. F., & Hock, R. A. (1981). Sex differences in sex-role ideals in early adolescence. *Adolescence, 16*(64), 779–789.

Curtis, R. (1981). Success and failure, gender differences, and the menstrual cycle. *Psychology of Women Quarterly, 5*(5) Supple., 701–710.

Cutrona, C. E. (1982). Transition to college: Loneliness and the process of social adjustment. In L. A. Peplau & D. Perlman (Eds.), *Loneliness: A sourcebook of current research, theory and therapy.* New York: Wiley-Interscience.

Damon, W. (1983). *Social and personality development.* New York: Norton.

Damon, W., & Hart, D. (1982). The development of self-understanding from infancy through adolescence. *Child Development, 53,* 841–864.

Dangers and hopes for humanity. (October 1978). *USA Today, 107*(2401), 1–2.

Darling, C. A., & Hicks, M. W. (1982). Parental influence on adolescent sexuality: Implications for parents as educators. *Journal of Youth and Adolescence,* *11*(3), 231–245.

Davids, L. (1982). Ethnic identity, religiosity, and youthful deviance: The Toronto computer dating project—1979. *Adolescence, 17*(67), 673–684.

Davidson, S., & Packard, T. (Spring 1981). The therapeutic value of friendship between women. *Psychology of Women Quarterly, 5*(3), 495–510.

Davis, G. A. (1971). Teaching for creativity: Some guiding lights. *Journal of Research and Development in Education, 4*(3), 29–34.

Davis, S. M., & Harris, M. B. Sexual knowledge, sexual interests, and sources of sexual information of rural and urban adolescents from three cultures. *Adolescence, 17*(66), 471–492.

Dean, R. A. (1982). Youth: Moonies, target population. *Adolescence, 17*(67), 567–574.

de Anda, D. (1983). Pregnancy in early and late adolescence. *Journal of Youth and Adolescence, 12*(1), 33–42.

deBeauvoir, S. (1953). *The second sex.* New York: Knopf.

Decades of decision: Alternating currents (October 1979). *Omni, 2*(1), 96; 144.

Decades of decision: The human family (October 1979). *Omni, 2*(1), 102.

Decades of decision: Micro/macro (October 1979). *Omni, 2*(1), 100; 144.

Delong, G. (1975). Inquiry into pre- and early-adolescent interests. *Adolescence, 10*(38), 187–190.

Denno, D. (1982). Sex differences in cognition: A review and critique of the longitudinal evidence. *Adolescence, 17*(68), 779–788.

de Vaux, D. A. (1983). The relative importance of parents and peers for adolescent religious orientation: An Australian study. *Adolescence, 17*(69), 147–158.

De Vogler, K. L., & Ebersole, P. (1983). Young adolescents' meaning in life. *Psychological Reports, 52,* 427–431.

Devos, G., & Romanucci-Ross, L. (Eds.) (1975). *Ethnic identity.* Palo Alto, California: Mayfield, 395.

DeVries, H. A. (1977). Physiology of exercise and aging. In S. H. Zarit (Eds.), *Readings in aging and death: Contemporary perspectives.* New York: Harper & Row, 56–60.

de Wolf, V. A. (Summer 1981). High school mathematics preparation and sex differences in quantitative abilities. *Psychology of Women Quarterly, 5*(4), 555–567.

de Wuffel, F. J. (February 1982). Parent-adolescent interaction and adolescent interpersonal orientation: A research proposal. Unpublished manuscript. Katholieke Universiteit Nijmegen.

Dickinson, G. E. (1978). Adolescent sex information sources: 1964–1974. *Adolescence, 13*(52), 653–658.

Dickinson, G. E. (1982). Changing religious behavior of adolescents 1964–1979. *Youth and Society, 13*(3), 283–288.

Dienstfrey, H. (1982). Clothes power. *Psychology Today, 16*(12), 68–73.

Diets and children's health. (1977). *Children Today, 6*(4), 30.

Dipboye, R. L., Fromkin, H. L., & Wiback, K. (1975). Relative importance of applicant sex, attractiveness, and scholastic standing in evaluation of job applicant resumés. *Journal of Applied Psychology, 60,* 39–43.

Dogmatic teens: Entrenched attitudes at an early age (1978). *Human Behavior, 7*(10), 32.

Donnelly, P. (1981). Athletes and juvenile delinquents: A comparative analysis based on a review of literature. *Adolescence, 16*(62), 415–432.

Donovan, J. M. (1975). Identity status and interpersonal style. *Journal of Youth and Adolescence, 4*(1), 37–55.

Douglas, J. D., & Wong, A. C. (1977). Formal operations: Age and sex differences in Chinese and American children. *Child Development, 48*(2), 689–692.

Douvan, E. (1975). Sex differences in the opportunities, demands, and development of youth. In R. J. Havinghurst, & P. H. Dreyer (Eds.), *Youth.* Chicago: The National Society for the Study of Education.

Douvan, E. (Fall 1976). The role of models in women's professional development. *Psychology of Women Quarterly,* 5–19.

Dozier, J. E., Lewis, S., Kersey, A. G., & Charping, J. W. (1978). Sports groups: An alternative treatment modality for emotionally disturbed adolescents. *Adolescence, 13*(51), 483–493.

Drive for rights of children (1974). *U. S. News, 77*(6), 42–44.

Dudley, E. (February 1979). Rainbows and realities: Current trends in marriage and its alternatives. *The Futurist, 13*(1), 23–32.

Duke, D. L. (1978). Why don't girls misbehave more than boys in schools? *Journal of Youth and Adolescence, 7*(2), 141–157.

Education? By computer, naturally (May 9, 1978). *U. S. News & World Report,* 8.

Edwards, C. P., & Whiting, B. B. (1983). Differential socialization of girls and boys in light of cross-cultural research. In W. Damon (Ed.), *Social and personality development: Essays on the growth of the child.* New York: Norton, 354–363.

Edwards, D. W. (1979). Persons and environments. In J. G. Kelly (Ed.), *Adolescent boys in high school: A psychological study of coping and adaptation.* Hillsdale, New Jersey: Lawrence Erlbaum Associates Publishers, 99–114.

Egan, O., & Nugent, K. (1983). Adolescent conceptions of the homeland: A cross-cultural study. *Journal of Youth and Adolescence, 12*(3), 185–201.

Eisenberg-Berg, N., & Mussen, P. (1978). Empathy and moral development in adolescence. *Developmental Psychology, 14*(2), 185–186.

Eisert, D. C., & Kahle, L. R. (1983). Self-evaluation and social comparison of physical and role change during adolescence: A longitudinal analysis. *Child Development, 53,* 98–104.

Eitzen, D. S. (1975). Athletics in the status system of male adolescents: A replication of Coleman's *The Adolescent Society. Adolescence, 10*(38), 267–276.

Elder, G. H. Jr. (1980). Adolescence in historical perspective. In J. Adelson (Ed.), *Handbook of adolescent psychology.* New York: John Wiley.

Elias, J. E. (1978). Adolescents and sex. *The Humanist, 38*(2), 29–31.

Elkind, D. (1979). Growing up faster. *Psychology Today, 12*(9), 38; 41–42; 45.

Elkind, D. (1983). Strategic interactions in early adolescence. In J. Adelson (Ed.), *Handbook of adolescent psychology.* New York: Wiley.

Elkind, D., & Sameroff, A. (1970). Developmental psychology. In P. H. Mussen, & M. R. Rosenzweig (Eds.), *Review of Child Psychology.* Palo Alto: Annual Review.

Ellis, E. H. (1979). Some problems in the study of adolescent development. *Adolescence, 14*(53), 101–109.

Ellis, D. W., & Davis, L. T. (1982). The development of self-concept boundaries across the adolescent years. *Adolescence, 17*(67), 695–710.

Ellis, G. J., Streeter, S. K., & Englebrecht, J. D. (June 1983). Televison characters as significant others and the process of vicarious role taking. *Journal of Family Issues, 4,* 367–384.

Ellis, W. (1983). Adolescent legend-tripping. *Psychology Today, 17*(1), 68–69.

Eme, R., Maisiak, R., & Goodale, W. (1979). Seriousness of adolescent problems. *Adolescence, 14*(53), 93–99.

Emihovich, C. H., & Gaier, E. L. (1983). Ideology and idealism in early adolescence. *Adolescence, 18*(72), 787–798.

Erikson, E. G. (1950). Growth and crises of the healthy personality. In *Symposium on the Healthy Personality.* Supplement II. New York: Josiah Macy Jr. Foundation, 227–228.

Erikson, E. G. (1959). Growth and crises of the healthy personality. *Psychological Issues, I,* 50–100.

Erikson, E. H. (1968). *Identity: Youth and crisis.* New York: Norton.

Eron, L. D. (1982). Parent-child interaction, television violence, and aggression of children. *American Psychologist, 37*(2), 197–211.

Etaugh, C., & Spandikow, D. B. (Summer 1981). Changing attitudes toward women: A longitudinal study of college students. *Psychology of Women Quarterly, 5*(4), 591–594.

Etzioni, A. (1978). Youth is not a class. *Psychology Today, 11*(9), 20–21.

Eve, R. A., & Bromley, D. G. (1981). Scholastic dishonesty among college undergraduates: Parallel tests of two sociological explanations. *Youth and Society, 13*(1), 3–22.

Everhart, R. B. (1982). The nature of "goofing off" among junior high school adolescents. *Adolescence, 17*(65), 177–188.

Ewing, D. W. (1977). Discovering your problem-solving style. *Psychology Today, 11*(7), 69–73; 138.

Faber, R. J., Brown, J. D., & McLeod, J. M. (1979). Coming of age in the global village: Television and adolescence. In E. Wartella (Ed.), *Children communicating.* Beverly Hills, California: Sage, 215–249.

Falbo, T. (1978). Only children and interpersonal behavior: An experimental and survey study. *Journal of Applied Social Psychology, 8*(3), 244–253.

Falk, R., Gispert, M., & Baucom, D. H. (1981). Personality factors related to black teenage pregnancy and abortion. *Psychology of Women Quarterly, 5*(5) Supple., 737–746.

Fannin, P. N. (1979). The relation between ego-identity status and sex-role attitude, work-role salience, atypicality of major and self-esteem in college women. *Journal of Vocational Behavior, 14,* 12–22.

Farber, B. A., & Morgan, E. (1982). Toward a reformulation of the Eriksonian model of female identity development. *Adolescence, 17*(65), 199–211.

Farrell, W. (1978). The liberated man and woman. *Public Welfare, 36*(1), 22–27.

Farrington, D. P. (1982). Delinquency from 10 to 25. In S. A. Mednick (Ed.), *Antecedents of aggression and antisocial behavior.* Hingham, Mass.: Kluwer Boston.

Fasteau, M. F. (1975). The high price of macho. *Psychology Today, 9*(4), 60.

Feinstein, S. C., & Ardon, M. S. (1973). Trends in dating patterns and adolescent development. *Journal of Youth and Adolescence, 2*(2), 157–166.

Feinstein, S. C., & Giovacchini, P. L. (Eds.) (1978). *Adolescent psychiatry. Developmental and clinical studies* (Vol. VI). Chicago: University of Chicago Press.

Female jocks: Why women are making it in sports. (1978). *Human Behavior, 7*(6), 51.

Fengler, A. P., & Wood, V. (1973). Continuity between the generation: Differential influence of mothers and fathers. *Youth and Society, 4*(3), 359–372.

Ferguson, W. E. (1981). Gifted adolescents, stress, and life changes. *Adolescence, 16*(64), 973–985.

Feshbach, N. D., & Tremper, C. (September 1981).

Attitudes of parents and adolescents toward decision-making by minors. Paper presented at the meeting of the American Psychological Association, Los Angeles.

Fields, A. B. (1981). Perceived parent behavior and the self-evaluations of lower-class black male and female children. *Adolescence, 16*(64), 919–934.

Finkel, M. L., & Finkel, D. J. (1978). Male adolescent contraceptive utilization. *Adolescence, 13*(51), 443–451.

Finkelstein, M. J., & Gaier, E. L. (1983). The impact of prolonged student status on late adolescent development. *Adolescence, 17*(69), 115–129.

Finlay, B. A. (1981). Sex differences in correlates of abortion attitudes among college students. *Journal of Marriage and the Family, 43*(3), 571–582.

Finn, P., & Brown, J. (1981). Risks entailed in teenage intoxication as perceived by junior and senior high school students. *Journal of Youth and Adolescence, 10*(1), 61–76.

Fischer, J. L. (1981). Transitions in relationship style from adolescence to young adulthood. *Journal of Youth and Adolescence, 10*(1), 11–23.

Fischer, J. L., & Narus, L. R. Jr. (Spring 1981). Sex roles and intimacy in same sex and other sex relationships. *Psychology of Women Quarterly, 5*(3), 444–455.

Fisher, W. A. (1983). Why teenagers get pregnant. *Psychology Today, 17*(3), 70–71.

Flasher, J. (1978). Adultism. *Adolescence, 13*(51), 517–523.

Flavell, J. H. (1963). *Developmental psychology of Jean Piaget*. Princeton, New Jersey: Van Nostrand.

Flavell, J. H. (1982). On cognitive development. *Child Development, 53*, 1–10.

Fleischer, B., & Read, M. (1982). Food supplement usage by adolescent males. *Adolescence, 17*(68), 831–845.

Fleming, C. M. (1951). *Adolescence*. New York: International Universities Press.

Folkins, C. H., & Sime, W. E. (April 1981). Physical fitness training and mental health. *American Psychologist, 36*(4), 373–389.

For American youth: Demands no other generation has had to face: Interview with Dr. Robert Coles, (September 6, 1976). *U.S. News & World Report.*

For us, an age of reliance on other nations (May 9, 1983). *U.S. News & World Report, A28.*

Fortes, M. (1974). The first born. *Journal of Child Psychology and Psychiatry, 15*(2), 81–104.

Fox, G. L. (1980). The mother-adolescent daughter relationship as a sexual socialization structure: A research review. *Family Relations, 29*(1), 21–28.

Fox, L. H., Tobin, D., & Brody, L. Sex-role socialization and achievement in mathematics. In M. A. Wittig & A. C. Patterson (Eds.), *Sex related differences in cognitive functioning: Developmental issues.* New York: Academic Press.

Francesco, A. M., & Hakel, M. D. (1981). Gender and sex as determinants of hireability of applicants for gender-typed jobs. *Psychology of Women Quarterly, 5*(5), Supple., 747–757.

Frank, R. E., & Greenberg, M. G. (1979). Zooming in on TV audiences. *Psychology Today, 4*(13), 92–103; 114.

Frank, S., Athey, J., Coulston, S., & Parsons, M. (1982). The relation of ego development to sex-stereotyping in caretakers' expectations for adolescents. *Journal of Youth and Adolescence, 11*(6), 461–477.

Frankel, J., & Dullaert, J. (1977). Is adolescent rebellion universal? *Adolescence, 12*(46), 227–236.

Fraternities bounce back—with big changes. (March 11, 1979). *U.S. News & World Report*, 46.

Freeman, J. (1979). *Their identification and development in a social context.* Lancaster, England: MTP Press.

Friedenberg, E. Z. (1969). Current patterns of a generational conflict. *Journal of Social Issues, 25*(2), 21–38.

Friedrich, W., Reams, R., & Jacobs, J. (1982). Depression and suicidal ideation in early adolescents. *Journal of Youth and Adolescence, 11*(5), 403–407.

Frye, C. M. (September 3, 1979). Who runs the schools? *Newsweek*, 13.

Fulton, J. A. (1979). Parental reports of children's post-divorce adjustment. *Journal of Social Issues, 35*(4), 126–139.

Gadlin, H. (1980). Dialectics and family interaction. *Human Development, 23*, 245–253.

Gagnon, J. H., & Simon, W. (1969). They're going to learn in the street anyway. *Psychology Today, 3*(2), 46–47; 71.

Galanter, M., Rabkin, R., Rabkin, J., & Deutsch, A. (1979). The "moonies": A psychological study of conversion and membership in a contemporary religious sect. *American Journal of Psychiatry, 136*(2), 165–170.

Gallup, G., Jr. (1977). U.S. in early stage of religious revival? *Journal of Current Social Issues, 14*(2), 50–52.

Galster, G. C., & Hesser, G. W. (1981). Residential satisfaction: Compositional and contextual correlates. *Environment and Behavior, 13*(6), 735–758.

Ganong, L., Coleman, M., & Brown, G. (1981). Effect of family structure on marital attitudes of adolescents. *Adolescence, 16*(62), 281–288.

Garbarino, J., Burston, N., Raber, S., Russell, R., & Crouter, A. (1978). The social maps of children approaching adolescence: Studying the ecology of youth development. *Journal of Youth and Adolescence, 7*(4), 417–428.

Gaylin, J. (1978). Learning to suffer—the cultural side of menstruation. *Psychology Today, 11*(12), 36.

Gelman, D. (September 1, 1980). The games teenagers play. *Newsweek*, p. 48.

Genetic differences in intelligence, 1977. *Intellect, 105*(2380), 214–215.

Gerbner, G. L., Gross, L., Morgan, M., & Signorielli, N. (1980). The mainstreaming of America: Violence profile No. 11. *Journal of Communication, 28*, 10–29.

Germain, C. B. (1978). Space: An ecological variable in social work practice. *Social Casework, 59*(9), 515–522.

Gerson, M. J. (1980). The lure of motherhood. *Psychology of Women Quarterly, 5*(2), 207–218.

Glaser, D. (1979). Economic and sociocultural variables affecting rates of youth unemployment, delinquency, and crime. *Youth and Society, 11*(1), 53–82.

Glasgow, E. (1954). *The woman within*. New York: Harcourt, Brace & World.

Glasser, W. (1978). Disorders in our schools: Causes and remedies. *Phi Delta Kappan, 59*(5), 331–333.

Gleser, G., Seligman, R., Winget, C., & Rauh, J. L. (1977). Adolescents view their mental health. *Journal of Youth and Adolescence, 6*(3), 249–263.

Glick, P. C. (1979). Children of divorced parents in demographic perspective. *Journal of Social Issues, 35*(40), 170–182.

Goldberg, S., Blumberg, S. L., & Kriger, A. (1982). Menarche and interest in infants: Biological and social influences. *Child Development, 53*, 1544–1550.

Goldstein, J., Freud, A., & Solnit, A. J. (1979). *Before the best interests of the child*. New York: Free Press.

Goleman, D. (1980). Leaving home: Is there a right time to go? *Psychology Today, 14*(3), 52–61.

Goleman, D. (1980). Leaving later: The invention of adolescence. *Psychology Today, 14*(3), 57.

Goleman, D. (1980a). 1,528 little geniuses and how they grew. *Psychology Today, 13*(9), 28–43.

Goleman, D. (1980b). Still learning from Terman's children. *Psychology Today, 13*(9), 44–53.

Goodlad, J. I. (1979). Can our schools get better? *Phi Delta Kappan, 60*(5), 342–347.

Goodman, H. (1982). Assertiveness breeds attempt. *Psychology Today, 16*(12), 75.

Goodman, N. R., & Barenblatt, L. (1983). Adolescent mobility potential and socio-political attitudes. *Adolescence, 18*(70), 457–472.

Goodstadt, M. S., Lawson, S. L., Langford, E. R. (1982). Role-models regarding smoking and fitness: A survey of youth agencies in Ontario. *Adolescence, 17*(68), 931–938.

Gordon, C., Gaitz, C. M., & Scott, J. (1976). Leisure and lives: Personal expressivity across the life span. In R. H. Binstock & E. Shanas (Eds.), *Handbook of aging and the social sciences*. New York: Van Nostrand Reinhold Co., 310–341.

Gordon, M. (1981). Was Waller ever right? The mating and dating complex reconsidered. *Journal of Marriage and the Family, 43*(1), 67–76.

Gordon, T. H. (1977). Life style of the future: Conspicuous conservatism. *Vital Speeches of the Day, 4*(18), 557–563.

Goswick, R. A., & Jones, W. H. (October 1982). Components of loneliness during adolescence. *Journal of Youth and Adolescence, 11*(5), 355–372.

Gottesman, I. I., & Shields, J. (1972). *Schizophrenia and genetics: A twin study vantage point*. New York: Academic Press.

Gottfredson, G. D. (1977). Career stability and redirection in adulthood. *Journal of Applied Psychology, 62*, 436–446.

Gottlieb, D., & Chafetz, J. S. (1977). Dynamics of familial, generational conflict and reconciliation: A research note. *Youth and Society, 9*(2), 213–224.

Gottlieb, D. (1979). Alienation and adjustment to limited prospects. *Youth and Society, 11*(1), 92–113.

Grady, K. E. (Summer 1981). Sex bias in research design. *Psychology of Women Quarterly, 5*(4), 628–636.

Gray, R. (1979). The changing role of women and adolescent girls in America. *Adolescence, 14*(55), 439–450.

Greenbaum, W. (1974). America in search of a new ideal: An essay on the rise of pluralism. *Harvard Educational Review, 44*(3), 411–440.

Greenberg, B. S. (1982). Television and role socialization. In D. Pearl et al. (Eds.), *Television and behavior: Ten years of scientific progress and implications for the eighties* (Vol. 2). Rockville, Maryland: U.S. Department of Health and Human Services.

Greenberger, E., & Steinberg, L. (1980). Part-time employment of in-school youth: A preliminary assessment of costs and benefits. In *A review of youth employment problems, programs, and policies* (Vol. 1). Washington, D. C.: The Vice President's Task Force on Youth Employment.

Greenberger, E., Steinberg, L., & Vaux, A. (1981). Adolescents who work: Health and behavioral consequences of job stress. *Developmental Psychology, 17*, 691–703.

Greenberger, E., Steinberg, L., Vaux, A., & McAuliffe, S. (1980). Adolescents who work: Effects of part-time employment on family and peer relations. *Journal of Youth and Adolescence, 9*, 189–202.

Greif, E. B., & Ulman, K. J. (1982). The psychological impact of menarche on early adolescent females: A review of the literature. *Child Development, 53*, 1413–1430.

Griffin, N., Chassin, L., & Young, R. D. (1981). Measurement of global self-concept versus multiple role-specific self-concepts in adolescents. *Adolescence, 16*(61), 49–56.

Grinder, R. E. (1975). Epilogue: Two models for the study of youth—1944 versus 1975. In R. J. Havighurst & P. H. Dreyer (Eds.), *Youth*. Chicago: University of Chicago Press.

Grinder, R. E. (1982). Isolationism in adolescent research. *Human Development, 25*, 223–232.

Grob, M. C., Klein, A. A., & Eisen, S. V. (1983). The role of the high school professional in identifying and managing adolescent suicidal behavior. *Journal of Youth and Adolescence, 12*(2), 163–173.

Grotevant, H., Scarr, S., & Weinberg, R. A. (1978). Are career interests inheritable? *Psychology Today, 11*(10), 88; 90.

Group for the Advancement of Psychiatry: Committee on Adolescence (1968). *Normal adolescence in dynamics and impact*. New York: Scribners.

Groves, D. L. (1981). Camping—Its past and future contribution to adolescent development. *Adolescence, 16*(62), 331–344.

Gruber, H. (interviewed by Howard Gardner) (1981). Breakaway minds. *Psychology Today, 15*(7), 64–71.

Gruber, K. J., Jones, R. J., & Freeman, M. H. (1982). Youth reactions to sexual assault. *Adolescence, 17*(67), 541–551.

Guinzburg, S. (1983). Education's earning power. *Psychology Today, 17*(10), 20–21.

Guinzburg, S. (1983). Mideast teens. *Psychology Today, 17*(4), 80.

Gullotta, T. P., Stevens, S. J., Donohue, K. C., & Clark, V. S. (1981). Adolescents in corporate families. *Adolescence, 16*(63), 621–628.

Gullotta, T., & Adams, G. R. (1982). Substance abuse minimization: Conceptualizing prevention in adolescent and youth programs. *Journal of Youth and Adolescence, 11*(5), 409–424.

Gump, P. V. (1978). School environments. In J. Altman & J. F. Wohlwill (Eds.), *Children and the environment*. New York: Plenum Press.

Gunter, B. G., & Moore, H. A. (1975). Youth, leisure, and post-industrial society: Implications for the family. *Family Coordinator, 24*(2), 199–207.

Gutmann, D. L. (1973). The new mythologies and premature aging in the youth culture. *Journal of Youth and Adolescence, 2*(2), 139–155.

Hadden, J. K. (1969). The private generation. *Psychology Today, 3*(5), 32–35.

Hagestad, G. O. (1977). Role change in adulthood: The transition to the empty nest. Unpublished manuscript, Committee on Human Development, University of Chicago.

Hainline, L., & Feig, E. (1978). The correlates of childhood father absence in college-aged women. *Child Development, 49*(1), 37–42.

Hall, G. S. (1905). *Adolescence, II*. New York: Appleton.

Halleck, G. T. (1948). *Take off*. New York: National Tuberculosis Association.

Hallinan, M. T. (1979). Structural effects on chil-

dren's friendships and cliques. *Social Psychology Quarterly, 42*(1), 43–54.

Hamilton, M. L. (1977). Ideal sex roles for children and acceptance of variation from stereotypic sex roles. *Adolescence, 12*(45), 89–96.

Hancock, E. (1980). The dimension of meaning and belonging in the process of divorce. *American Journal of Orthopsychiatry, 50*, 18–27.

Handleman, C. (1980). Teaching and academic standards today. *Adolescence, 15*(59), 723–730.

Hansson, R. O., O'Connor, M. E., Jones, W. H., & Blocker, T. J. (1981). Maternal employment and adolescent sexual behavior. *Journal of Youth and Adolescence, 10*(1), 55–60.

Harper, L. V., & Sanders, K. M. (1975). Preschool children's use of space: Sex differences in outdoor play. *Developmental Psychology, 11*(1), 119.

Harris, M. B. (1970). Reciprocity and generosity: Some determinants of sharing in children. *Child Development, 41*(2), 313–328.

Hart, R. (1978). *Children's sense of place*. New York: Halstead Press.

Haskell, M. (1983). Women in the movies grow up. *Psychology Today, 17*(1), 18–27.

Hauser, J. (1981). Adolescents and religion. *Adolescence, 16*(62), 309–320.

Havighurst, R. J. (1975). Youth in social institutions. In R. J. Havighurst & P. H. Dryer (Eds.), *Youth*. Chicago: University of Chicago Press.

Havighurst, R. J., & Dreyer, P. H. (1975). Youth and cultural pluralism. In R. J. Havighurst & P. H. Dryer (Eds.), *Youth*. Chicago: University of Chicago Press.

Hayes, R. L. (1982). A review of adolescent identity formation: Implications for education. *Adolescence, 17*(65), 153–165.

Hebdige, D. (1979). *Subculture: The meaning of style*. London: Methuen.

Hedin, D., & Conrad, D. (1980). Changes in children and youth over two decades: The perceptions of teachers. *Phi Delta Kappan, 61*(10), 702.

Heilbrun, A. B. Jr., & Landauer, S. P. (1978). Stereotypic and specific attributions of parental characteristics of late adolescent siblings. *Child Development, 48*(4), 1748–1751.

Held, L. (1981). Self-esteem and social network of the young pregnant teenager. *Adolescence, 16*(64), 905–912.

Helson, R., & Mitchell, V. Personality. (1978). In M. R. Rosenzweig & L. P. Porter (Eds.), *Annual review of psychology* (Vol. 20). Palo Alto: Annual Review Inc., 555–585.

Hendin, H. (1975). The new anomie. *Change, 7*(9), 24–29.

Hendricks, L. E., & Montgomery, T. (1983) A limited population of unmarried adolescent fathers: A preliminary report of their views on fatherhood and the relationship with the mothers of their children. *Adolescence, 17*(60), 201–210.

Hendry, L. B., & Gillies, P. (1978). Body type, body esteem, school, and leisure: A study of overweight, average, and underweight adolescents. *Journal of Youth and Adolescence, 7*(2), 181–195.

Hendry, L. B., & Jamie, D. (1978). Pupils' self-esteem and popularity in school. Scottish Educational Review cited in L. B. Hendry & P. Gillies. Body type, body esteem, school and leisure: A study of overweight, average and underweight adolescents. *Journal of Youth and Adolescence, 7*(2), 181–195.

Herman, J. L. (with L. Hirschman) (1981). *Father-daughter incest.* Cambridge, Mass.: Harvard University Press.

Herold, E. S. (1981). Contraceptive embarrassment and contraceptive behavior among young single women. *Journal of Youth and Adolescence, 10*(3), 233–242.

Hetherington, E. M. (1979). Divorce: A child's perspective. *American Psychologist, 34*(10), 851–858.

Hetherington, E. B., Cox, M., & Cox. R. (1979). The development of children in mother-headed families. In D. Reiss & H. A. Hoffman (Eds.), *The American family: Dying or developing?* New York: Plenum Press.

Hettlinger, R. F. (1970). *Sexual maturity.* Belmont, California: Wadsworth.

Higgins, E. T., Ruble, D., & Hartup, W. W. (Eds.) (1980). *Social cognition and cognitive behavior: Developmental perspective.* New York: Cambridge University Press.

Hill, C. T., Peplau, L. A., & Rubin, Z. (1981). Differing perceptions in dating couples: Sex roles vs. alternative explanations. *Psychology of Women Quarterly, 5*(3), 418–434.

Hill, J. P. (1980). The family. In M. Johnson (Ed.), *Toward adolescence: The middle school years.* Chicago: University of Chicago Press.

Hill, J. P. (1982). Guest editorial. *Child Development, 53,* 1409–1412.

Hill, T. B. (1972). Whatever happened to the gifted? *Educational Forum, 36*(3), 323–326.

Hjorth, C. W., & Ostrov, E. (1982). The self-image of physically abused adolescents. *Journal of Youth and Adolescence, 11*(2), 71–76.

Hobbs, N., & Robinson, S. (1982). Adolescent development and public policy. *American Psychologist, 37*(2), 212–223.

Hoffman, L. W. (1974). Effects of maternal employment on the child—a review of the research. *Developmental Psychology, 10*(2), 204–228.

Hoffman, L. W. (1979). Maternal employment: 1979. *American Psychologist, 34*(10), 859–865.

Hoffman, L. W. (1978). Changes in family roles, so-cialization, and sex differences. *Educational Horizons, 57*(1), 10–18.

Hogan, R. (1980). The gifted adolescent. In J. Adelson (Ed.), *Handbook of adolescent psychology.* New York: Wiley.

Hoge, D. R., & Petrillo, G. H. (1978). Determinants of church participation and attitudes among high school youth. *Journal for the Scientific Study of Religion, 17*(4), 359–379.

Hoge, D. R., & Ankney, T. L. (1982). Occupations and attitudes of former student activists 10 years later. *Journal of Youth and Adolescence, 11*(5), 355–372.

Hoge, D. R., Petrillo, G. H., & Smith, E. I. (1982). Transmission of religious and social values from parents to teenage children. *Journal of Marriage and the Family, 44*(3), 569–580.

Holland, J. L., & Holland, J. E. (1977). Distributions of personalities within occupations and fields of study. *Quarterly Vocational Guide, 25,* 226–231.

Holzman, P. S., & Grinker, R. R. Sr. (1974). Schizophrenia in adolescence. *Journal of Youth and Adolescence, 3*(4), 267–279.

Hooper, A. (1980). Egalitarian lip servants. *Psychology Today, 14*(6), 98.

Hoover, E. L. (1979) Far out. *Human Behavior, 8*(1), 16–17.

Hopkins, J. R. (1977). Sexual behavior in adolescence. *Journal of Social Issues, 33*(2), 67–85.

Horn, J. (1975). Reactions to the handicapped—sweaty palms and saccharine words. *Psychology Today, 9*(6), 122–124.

Horowitz, N. H. (1978). Adolescent mourning reactions to infant and fetal loss. *Social Casework, 59*(9), 551–559.

Horowitz, T. (1982). Excitement vs. economy: Fashion and youth culture in Britain. *Adolescence, 17*(67), 627–636.

Horwitt, L. (1979–1980). The boom in student businesses. *Nutshell.* Knoxville, Tennessee: 13–30 Corporation, 49–56.

Houston, L. N. (1981). Romanticism and eroticism among black and white college students. *Adolescence, 16*(62), 263–272.

Hoyenga, K. B., & Hoyenga, K. T. (1979). *The question of sex differences: Psychological, cultural, and biological issues.* Boston: Little Brown.

Hughes, S. P., & Dodder, R. A. (1983). Alcohol-related problems and collegiate drinking patterns. *Journal of Youth and Adolescence, 12*(1), 65–76.

Hummel, R., & Roselli, L. L. (1983). Identity status and academic achievement in female adolescents. *Adolescence, 17*(69), 17–27.

Hunt, J. V., & Eichorn, D. H. (1972). Maternal and child behaviors: A review of data from the Berkeley growth study. *Seminars in Psychiatry, 4*(4), 367–381.

Hunt, M. (1974). *Sexual behavior in the 1970s*. Chicago: Playboy Press.

Hyde, J. S. (1981). How large are cognitive gender differences? A meta analysis using w² and d. *American Psychologist, 36*(8), 892–901.

Ianni, F., & Reuss-Ianni, E. (April–May 1980). What can schools do about violence? *Today's Education.*

If you live to be a hundred—it won't be unusual. (May 9, 1983). *U.S. News & World Report*, A10.

Igra, A., & Moos, R. H. (1979). Alcohol use among college students: Some competing hypotheses. *Journal of Youth and Adolescence, 8*(4), 393–406.

In one ear. . . . (August 1977). *Human Behavior, 6*(8), 46.

Inazu, J. K., & Fox G. L. (March 1980). Maternal influence on the sexual behavior of teen-age daughters direct and indirect sources. *Journal of Family Issues*, 81–102.

Interview: Philip Morrison (October 1979). *Omni, 2*(1), 93–94; 146–147.

Isaacs, M. B. (Winter 1981). Sex-role stereotyping and the evaluation of the performance of women: Changing trends. *Psychology of Women Quarterly, 6*(2), 187–195.

Jacques, J. M., & Chason, K. J. (1979). Cohabitation: Its impact on marital success. *Family Coordinator, 28*(1), 35–39.

Jaffe, J. H. (1975). Drug addiction and drug abuse. In L. S. Goodmand & A. Gilman (Eds.), *The pharmocological basis of therapeutics*, 5th ed. New York: Macmillan.

Jalali, B., Jalali, M., Crocetti, G., & Turner, F. (1981). Adolescents and drug use: Toward a more comprehensive approach. *American Journal of Orthopsychiatry, 51*(1), 120–130.

Janes, C., Hesselbrock, V. M., Myers, D., & Penniman, J. H. (1979). Problem boys in young adulthood: Teachers' ratings and twelve-year follow-up. *Journal of Youth and Adolescence, 8*(4), 453–472.

Janes, C. L., & Hesselbrock, V. M. (1978). Problem children's adult adjustment predicted from teachers' ratings. *American Journal of Orthopsychiatry, 48*(2), 300–309.

Jencks, C. (interviewed by C.T. Cory) (1979). Making it: Can the odds be evened? *Psychology Today, 13*(2), 35–39.

Jensen, R. E., & Moore, S. G. (1977). The effect of attribute statements on cooperativeness and competitiveness in school-age boys. *Child Development, 48*(1), 305–307.

Johnson, C. (1980). Schools and work: Do they ever mix? *Today's Education, 69*, 50–52.

Johnson, M. M. (1981). Heterosexuality, male dominance and the father image. *Sociological Inquiry, 51*(2), 129–139.

Johnson, M. M., Stockard, J., Rothbart, M., & Friedman, L. (1982). Sexual preference, feminism and women's perception of their parents. *Sex Roles, 6*(1), 1–18.

Johnson, R., & Carter, M. M. (1980). Flight of the young: Why children run away from their homes. *Adolescence, 15*(58), 483–489.

Johnston, L., Backman, J., & O'Malley, P. (1980–1983). *Monitoring the future: Questionnaire responses from the nation's high school seniors, 1975–1983* (annual volumes). Ann Arbor, Mich.: Institute for Social Research.

Johnstone, J. W. C. (1978). Juvenile delinquency and the family: A contextual interpretation. *Youth and Society, 9*(3), 299–313.

Jones, M. C. (1957). The later careers of boys who were early- or late-maturing. *Child Development, 28*, 113–128.

Jones, R. S. (1977). Institutional change and socialization research. The school and politicalization. *Youth and Society, 8*(3), 277–298.

Jones, W. H., Freeman, J. E., & Goswick, R. A. (1981). The persistence of loneliness: Self and other determinants. *Journal of Personality, 49*, 27–48.

Juhasz, A. M. (1974). The unmarried adolescent parent. *Adolescence, 9*(34), 263–272.

Kagan, J. (1978). *The growth of the child*. New York: W. W. Norton.

Kagan, J., Kearsley, R. B., & Zelazo, P. R. (1978). *Infancy: Its place in human development*. Cambridge, Massachusetts: Harvard University Press.

Kallen, D. J., & Stephenson, J. J. (July 1980). The purchase of contraceptives by college students. *Family Relations, 29*(3), 358–364.

Kandel, D. B. (1978). On variation in adolescent subcultures. *Youth and Society, 9*(4), 373–384.

Kaplan, A. G., & Sedney, M. A. (1980). *Psychology and sex roles: An androgynous perspective*. Boston: Little Brown.

Kapp, L., Taylor, B. & Edwards, L. (February 1980). Teaching human sexuality in junior high school: An interdisciplinary approach. *Journal of School Health*, 80.

Kargman, M. W. (1979). A court-appointed child advocate (guardian ad litem) reports on her role in contested child custody cases and looks to the future. *Journal of Divorce, 3*, 77–90.

Katchadourian, H. (1977). *The biology of adolescence*. San Francisco: W. H. Freeman and Company.

Katchadourian, H. A., & Lunde, D. T. (1975). *Fundamentals of human sexuality* (2nd ed.). New York: Holt, Rinehart & Winston, 1975.

Keating, D. P. (1980). Thinking processes in adolescence. In J. Adelson (Ed.), *Handbook of adolescent psychology*. New York: Wiley.

Keith-Spiegel, P., & Maas, T. (September 1981). Consent to research: Are there developmental differences? Paper presented at the Meeting of the American Psychological Association, Los Angeles.

Kelly, J. A., O'Brien, G. G., & Hosford, R. (1981). Sex roles and social skills considerations for interpersonal adjustment. *Psychology of Women Quarterly, 5*(5) Supple., 758–766.

Kelly, J. G. (1979). Exploratory behavior, socialization, and the high school environment. In J. G. Kelly (Ed.), *Adolescent boys in high school: A psychological study of coping and adaptation.* Hillsdale, New Jersey: Lawrence Erlbaum Associates Publishers, 245–256.

Keniston, K. (1975). Prologue: Youth as a stage of life. In R. J. Havighurst & P. H. Dreyer (Eds.), *Youth.* Chicago: University of Chicago Press.

Kiesler, S., Sproull, L., & Eccles, J. S. (1983). Second-class citizens? *Psychology Today, 17*(3), 40–48.

Kilpatrick, J. J. (December 3, 1981). The teen-age unemployed. *Atlanta Constitution,* D3.

Kindsvatter, R. (1978). A new view of the dynamics of discipline. *Phi Delta Kappan, 59*(5), 322–325.

King, J. P. (1975). An American perspective on education and change in technological society. *Intellect, 104*(2368), 114–118.

Kitahara, M. (1982). Male puberty rites: A path analytic model. *Adolescence, 17*(66), 293–304.

Klein, M. M., & Shulman, S. (1981). Adolescent masculinity-femininity in relation to parental models of masculinity-femininity and marital adjustment. *Adolescence, 16*(61), 45–48.

Kline, S. A., & Golombek, H. (1974). The incongruous achiever in adolescence. *Journal of Youth and Adolescence, 3*(2), 153–160.

Kloepper, H. W., Leonard, W. M. II, & Huang, L. J. (1981). A comparison of the "only child" and the siblings' perceptions of parental norms and sanctions. *Adolescence, 16*(63), 641–655.

Knox, D., & Wilson, K. (1981). Dating behaviors of university students. *Family Relations, 30*(2), 255–263.

Koff, E., Rierdan, J., & Silverstone, E. (1978). Changes in representation of body image as a function of menarcheal status. *Developmental Psychology, 14*(6), 635–642.

Kohlberg, L. (1975). The cognitive-developmental approach to moral education. *Phi Delta Kappan, 56*(10), 610–677.

Kohlberg, L. (1977). The implications of moral stages for adult education. *Religious Education, 72*(2), 182–201.

Kokenes, B. (1974). Grade level differences in factors of self-esteem. *Developmental Psychology, 10*(6), 954–958.

Konopka, G. (1973). Requirements for healthy development of adolescent youth. *Adolescence, 8*(31), 291–316.

Koocher, G. P. (1983). Competence to consent: Psychotherapy. In G. B. Melton, G. P. Koocher & M. J. Saks (Eds.), *Children's competence to consent.* New York: Plenum.

Kornhaber, A., & Woodward, K. L. (1981). *Grandparents and grandchildren: The vital connection.* Garden City, New York: Anchor Press.

Krech, D., Crutchfield, R. S., & Livson, N. (1974). *Elements of psychology* (3rd ed.). New York: Knopf.

Kretschmer, E. (1951). *Korperbau and character.* Berlin: Springer Verlag.

Krumboltz, J. D., Becker-Haven, J. F., & Burnett, K. F. (1979). Counseling psychology. In M. R. Rosenzweig & L. W. Porter (Eds.), *Annual review of psychology.* Palo Alto: Annual Reviews, Inc., *30,* 555–602.

Kulka, R. A., Kahle, L. R., & Klingel, D. M. (1982). Aggression, deviance, and personality adaptation as antecedents and consequences of alienation and involvement in high school. *Journal of Youth and Adolescence, 11*(3), 261–279.

Kurdek, L. A. (1981). An integrative perspective on children's divorce adjustment. *American Psychologist, 36*(8), 856–866.

Kurdek, L. A., & Krile, D. (1982). A developmental analysis of the relation between peer acceptance and both interpersonal understanding and perceived social self competence. *Child Development, 53,* 1485–1491.

Lambert, T. A. (1972). Generations and change: Toward a theory of generations as a force in historical process. *Youth and Society, 4*(1), 21–45.

Lambert, W. E. (1981). Cross-cultural perspectives on children's development of an identity. *Teachers College Record, 85*(3), 349–364.

Lamke, L. K. (1982). The impact of sex-role orientation on self-esteem in early adolescence. *Child Development, 53,* 1530–1535.

Larson, L. E. (1974). System and subsystem perception of family roles. *Journal of Marriage and the Family, 36*(1), 123–138.

Larson, R., & Kubey, R. (1983). Television and music: Contrasting media in adolescent life. *Youth and Society, 15*(1), 13–32.

Lash, J. (1971). *Eleanor and Franklin: The story of their relationship.* New York: Norton.

Laska, S. B., & Micklin, M. (1979). The knowledge dimension of occupational socialization: Role models and their social influence. *Youth and Society, 10*(4), 360–378.

Laufer, R. S., & Wolfe, M. (1977). Privacy as a concept and a social issue. *Journal of Social Issues, 33,* 22–42.

LaVoie, J. C., & Collins, B. R. (1975). Effect of youth culture music on high school students' academic performance. *Journal of Youth and Adolescence, 4*(1), 57–65.

Lazarus, R. S. (1981). Little hassles can be hazardous to health. *Psychology Today, 15*(7), 58–62.

Lee, P. C., & Gropper, N. B. (1974). Sex-role culture and educational practice. *Harvard Educational Review, 44*(3), 369–410.

Leger, R. G. (1980). Where have all the flowers gone? A sociological analysis of the origins and content of youth values of the seventies. *Adolescence, 15*(58), 283–300.

LeMasters, E. E. (1974). *Parents in modern America* (rev. ed.), Homewood, Illinois: Dorsey Press.

Leona, M. H. (1978). An examination of adolescent clique language in a suburban secondary school. *Adolescence, 13*(51), 495–502.

Lerner, R. M. (1981). Adolescent development: Scientific study in the 1980s. *Youth and Society, 12*(3), 251–275.

Lerner, R. M., Skinner, E. A., & Sorell, G. T. (1980). Methodological implications of contextual/dialectic theories of development. *Human Development, 23*, 225–235.

Lerner, R., Sorell, G., & Brackney, B. (1981). Sex differences in self-concept and self-esteem of late adolescents: A time-lag analysis. *Sex Roles, 7*, 709–722.

Lerner, R. M., & Spanier, G. B. (1980). *Adolescent development: A life-span perspective.* New York: McGraw-Hill.

Lesbian life styles. (1977). *Human Behavior, 6*(11), 51–52.

Leventhal, H., & Cleary, P. (1980). The smoking problem: A review of the research and theory in behavioral risk modification. *Psychological Bulletin, 88*, 370–405.

Levine, H. G., & Stumpf, S. H. (1983). Statements of fear through cultural symbols. *Youth and Society, 14*(4), 417–435.

Levine, J. A. (1978). Real kids vs. "the average" family. *Psychology Today, 12*(1), 14–15.

Levinger, G. (1979). A social psychological perspective on marital dissolution. In G. Levinger & O. Moles (Eds.), *Divorce and separation.* New York: Basic Books.

Levinson, D. J. (1978). Growing up with the dream. *Psychology Today, 11*(8), 20–31; 89.

Levinson, D. J. (1977). The mid-life transition. *Psychiatry, 40*, 96–112.

Lewin-Epstein, N. (1981). *Youth employment during high school.* Washington, D.C.: National Center for Educational Statistics.

Lewis, C. C. (1980). A comparison of minors' and adults' pregnancy decisions. *American Journal of Orthopsychiatry, 50*, 446–453.

Lewis, C. C. (1981). How adolescents approach decisions: Changes over grades seven to twelve and policy implications. *Child Development, 52*, 538–547.

Lewis, R., Casto, R., Aquilino, W., & McGuffin, N. (1978). Developmental transitions in male sexuality. *The Counseling Psychologist, 7*(4), 15–18.

Licitra, A. (1979/1980). Wanted: Students. *Nutshell,* 175–176.

Lickona, T. (1976). Research on Piaget's theory of moral development. In T. Lickona (Ed.), *Moral development and behavior: Theory, research, and social issues.* New York: Holt, Rinehart & Winston, 219–240.

Liebert, R. M., & Poulos, R. W. (1976). Television as a moral teacher. In T. Lickona (Ed.), *Moral development and behavior: Theory, research, and social issues.* New York: Holt, Rinehart & Winston, 284–298.

Light, D., & Laufer, R. S. (1975). College youth: Psychohistory and prospects. In R. J. Havighurst & P. H. Dryer (Eds.), *Youth.* Chicago: University of Chicago Press.

Linn, M. C., de Benedictis, T., & Delucchi, K. (1982). Adolescent reasoning about advertisements: Preliminary investigations. *Child Development, 53*, 1599–1613.

Lipsitz, J. S., (September–October 1979). Adolescent development. *Children Today, 8*(5), 2–7.

Liu, W. T., & Yu, E. S. H. (1975). Asian-American youth. In R. J. Havighurst & P. H. Dreyer (Eds.), *Youth.* Chicago: University of Chicago Press.

Livson, F. B. (1976). Patterns of personality development in middle-aged women: A longitudinal study. *International Journal of Aging and Human Development, 7*(2), 107–115.

Livson, N., & Peskin, H. (1980). Perspectives on adolescence from longitudinal research. In J. Adelson (Ed.), *Handbook of adolescent psychology.* New York: John Wiley.

Locke, S. A., & Feinsod, F. M. (1982). Psychological preparation for young adults traveling abroad. *Adolescence, 17*(68), 815–819.

Loeb, R. (1973). Adolescent groups. *Sociology and Social Research, 58*(1), 13–22.

Loeber, R. (1982). The stability of antisocial and delinquent child behavior: A review. *Child Development, 53*, 1431–1446.

Loftus, E. F. (1980). Alcohol, marijuana, and memory. *Psychology Today, 13*(10), 42–56; 92.

Logan, R. D. (1978). Identity diffusion and psychosocial defense mechanisms. *Adolescence, 13*(51), 503–507.

Logan, R. D. (1980). Identity, purity and ecology. *Adolescence, 15*(58), 409–412.

Logan, R. D., & O'Hearn, G. T. (1982). Thought-style and life-style: Some hypothesized relationships. *Science Education, 66*(4), 515–530.

London, P. (1978). The intimacy gap. *Psychology Today 11*(12), 40–45.

Long, M. J. (1965). Review of David Holbrook's *The secret places*. Alabama: University of Alabama Press, *Teachers College Record, 67*(6), 458.

Lotecka, L., & Lassleben, M. (1981). The high school "smoker": A field study of cigarette-related cognitions and social perceptions. *Adolescence, 16*(63), 513–526.

Loy, P., & Norland, S. (1981). Parent and peer influences on adolescents' gender expectations. *Youth and Society, 13*(2), 175–187.

Lutes, C. J. (1981) Early marriage and identity foreclosure. *Adolescence, 16*(64), 809–815.

Lynch, K. (Ed.) (1977). *Growing up in the cities: Studies of the spatial environment of adolescence in Cracow, Melbourne, Mexico City, Salta, Toluca and Warsaw*. Cambridge, Massachusetts: MIT Press.

McAllister, E. W. C. (1981). Religious attitudes among women college students. *Adolescence, 16*(63), 587–604.

McCall, R. B. (1977). Challenges to a science of developmental psychology. *Child Development, 48*(2), 333–344.

McCall, R. B., Hogarty, P. S., & Hurlbut, N. (1972). Transitions in infant sensorimotor development and the prediction of childhood IQ. *American Psychologist Today, 4*, 40–41; 78–79.

McClelland, D. C., Constantian, C. C., Regalado, D., & Stone, C. (1978). Making it to maturity. *Psychology Today, 12*(1), 42–53; 114.

McClintock, E. (1979). Adolescent socialization and the high school: A selective view of literature. In J. G. Kelly (Ed.) *Adolescent boys in high school: A psychological study of coping and adaptation*. Hillsdale, New Jersey: Lawrence Erlbaum Associates Publishers.

McDonald, G. W. (1982). Parental power perceptions in the family: The influence of adolescent characteristics. *Youth and Society, 14*(1), 3–31.

McGuinness, D., & Pribaum, K. H. (1979). The origins of sensory bias in the development of gender differences in perception and cognition. In M. Bortner (Ed.), *Cognitive growth and development*. New York: Brunner/Mazel.

McGuire, K. D., & Weisz, J. R. (1982). Social cognition and behavior correlates of preadolescent chumship. *Child Development, 53*, 1478–1484.

McIntyre, W. G., Nass, G. D., & Battistone, D. L. (1974). Female misperception of male parenting attitudes and expectancies. *Youth and Society, 6*(1), 104–112.

McMillan, D. W., & Hiltonsmith, R. W. (1982). Adolescents at home: An exploratory study of the relationship between perception of family social climate, general well-being, and actual behavior in the home setting. *Journal of Youth and Adolescence, 11*(4), 301–315.

Maddock, J. W. (1973). Sex in adolescence: Its meaning and its future. *Adolescence, 8*(31), 325–342.

Madison, P. (1971). The campus: Coming of age at college. *Psychology Today, 5*(5), 72–74; 104–111.

Malmquist, C. (1979). Juveniles in adults courts: Unresolved ambivalence. In S. Feinstein, & P. Giovacchini (Eds.), *Adolescent psychiatry* (Vol. VII) Chicago: University of Chicago Press, 444–456.

Manaster, G. J., & Novak, D. (1977). Post high school adolescents: An ecological approach to studying group differences. *Adolescence, 12*(46), 269–275.

Manning, M. L. (1983). Three myths concerning adolescents. *Adolescence, 18*(72), 823–829.

Manning, P. K., & Campbell, B. (1973). Pinball as game, fad and synecdoche. *Youth and Society, 4*(3), 333–358.

Marcia, J. E. (1966). Development and validation of ego identity status. *Journal of Personal and Social Psychology, 3*, 551–566.

Marcia, J. E. (1980). Identity in adolescence. In J. Adelson (Ed.), *Handbook of adolescent psychology*. New York: Wiley.

Mare, R. D. (June 1980). Social background and school continuation decisions. *Journal of American Statistical Association, 75*, 295–305.

Margolis, G. (1981). Moving away: Perspectives on counseling anxious freshman. *Adolescence, 16*(63), 633–640.

Marini, M. M. (1978). The transition to adulthood: Sex differences in educational attainment and age at marriage. *American Sociological Review, 43*, 483–507.

Mark, E. W., & Alper, T. G. (1980). Sex differences in intimacy motivation. *Psychology of Women Quarterly, 5*(2), 164–169.

Marshall, K. P., & Cosby, A. G. (1977). Antecedents of early marital and fertility behavior. *Youth and Society, 9*(2), 191–212.

Marshall, W. A., & Tanner, J. M. (1970). Variations in the pattern of pubertal changes in boys. *Archives of Diseases in Childhood, 45*, 13–23.

Mash, D. J. (Winter 1978). The development of lifestyle preferences of college women. *Journal of National Association of Women Deans and Counselors*, 72–76.

Maslow, A. H. (1954). *Motivation and personality*. New York: Harper.

Massad, C. (1981). Sex role identity and adjustment during adolescence. *Child Development, 52*, 1290–1298.

Math misery: Why can't Jane do calculus? (1979). *Human Behavior, 8*(1), 67.

Matthews, K. L., & Serrano, A. C. (1981). Ecology of adolescence. *Adolescence, 16*(63), 605–612.

Meacham, J. A., & Santilli, N. R. (1982). Interstage relationships in Erikson's theory: Identity and intimacy. *Child Development, 53,* 1461–1467.

Mead, M. (1928). *Coming of age in Samoa.* New York: Morrow.

Mead, M. (1935). *Sex and temperament in three primitive societies.* New York: Morrow. As condensed in R. G. Kuhlen, *The Psychology of adolescence.* New York: Harper, 1952.

Medicine dares to dream of the impossible. (May 9, 1983). *U.S. News & World Report,* A6–A7.

Medora, N., & Woodward, J. C. (1982). Premarital sexual opinions of undergraduate students at a midwestern university. *Adolescence, 17*(65), 213–224.

Medora, N. P., & Burton, M. M. (1981). Extramarital sexual attitudes and norms of an undergraduate student population. *Adolescence, 16*(62), 257–262.

Melton, G. B. (1981). Children's participation in treatment planning: Psychological and legal issues. *Professional Psychology, 12,* 246–252.

Melton, G. B., Koocher, G. P., & Saks, M. J. (Eds.) (1983). *Children's competence to consent.* New York: Plenum.

Menge, C. P. (1982). Dream and reality: Constructive change partners. *Adolescence, 17*(66), 419–442.

Menstrual myths. (1979). *Human Behavior, 8*(4), 60–61.

Metropolitan Life Insurance Company (August 1973). Statistical Bulletin, 9–11.

Meyers, J. H., & Zegans, L. S. (1975). Adolescents perceive their psychotherapy. *Psychiatry, 38*(1), 11–22.

Miller, P. Y., & Simon, W. (1979). Do youth really want to work: A comparison of the work values and job perceptions of younger and older men. *Youth and Society, 10*(4), 379–404.

Miller, P. Y., & Simon, W. (1980). The development of sexuality in adolescence. In J. Adelson (Ed.), *Handbook of adolescent psychology.* New York: Wiley.

Mills, C. J. (1981). Sex roles, personality, and intellectual abilities in adolescents. *Journal of Youth and Adolescence, 10*(2), 85–112.

Misunderstood parents: "Old fogies" fool their own kids (1978). *Human Behavior, 7*(4), 25.

Mitchell, M. E., Schultz, H. G., Eckstein, E. F., Knight, M. A., & Standal, B. R. (1981). Nutritional status and food acceptance of women in the western region: Interrelationships between selected environmental factors and measures of nutritional status and food acceptance. Washington State University College of Agriculture Research Center, Bulletin 0891 (Western Regional Research Project W-116).

Mondale, W. A. (1974). "Family impact statement": A response from the U.S. Senate. *School Review, 83*(1), 11–14.

Money, J. (1977). Destereotyping sex roles. *Society, 14*(5), 25–28.

Money, J., & Ehrhardt, A. A. (1972). *Man and woman, boy and girl.* Baltimore: Johns Hopkins Press.

Monks, F. J., & Ferguson, T. J. (1983). Gifted adolescents: An analysis of their psychosocial development. *Journal of Youth and Adolescence, 12*(1), 1–18.

Montagu, A. (1978). A "Kinsey report" on homosexualities. *Psychology Today, 12*(3), 62–66; 91.

Montemayor, R. (1982). The relationship between parent-adolescent conflict and the amount of time adolescents spend alone and with parents and peers. *Child Development, 53,* 1512–1519.

Montemayor, R., & Eisen, M. (1977). The development of self-conceptions from childhood to adolescence. *Developmental Psychology, 13*(4), 341–319.

Montemayor, R., & Van Komen, R. (1980). Age segregation of adolescents in and out of school. *Journal of Youth and Adolescence, 9,* 371–381.

Moore, D., & Schultz, N. R. Jr. (1983). Loneliness at adolescence: Correlates, attributions, and coping. *Journal of Youth and Adolescence, 12*(2), 95–100.

Moore, R., & Young, D. (1978). Childhood outdoors: Toward a social ecology of the landscape. In A. Irwin & J. F. Wohlwill (Eds.), *Children and the environment.* New York: Plenum Press.

Moos, R. H. (1978). Social environments of university student living groups. Architectural and organized correlates. *Environment and Behavior, 10*(1), 109–137.

Morgan, E., & Farber, B. A. (1982). Toward a reformulation of the Eriksonian model of female identity development. *Adolescence, 17*(65), 199–211.

Mortimer, J. T., & Lorence, J. (1978). Work experience and occupational value socialization: A longitudinal study. Presented at 73rd Annual Meeting of American Sociological Association, San Francisco.

Mortimer, J. T., & Simmons, R. G. (1978). Adult socialization. In R. H. Turner, J. Coleman, & R. C. Fox (Eds.), *Annual review of sociology, 4,* 421–454.

Moustakas, C. E. (1956). *The teacher and the child.* New York: McGraw-Hill.

Munro, G., & Adams, G. R. (1977). Ego-identity formation in college students and working youth. *Developmental Psychology, 13*(5), 523–524.

Murray, J. P. (1980). *Television and youth: 25 years of research and controversy.* Boys Town, Nebraska: Boys Town Center for the Study of Youth Development.

Muson, H. (1978). Teenage violence and the telly. *Psychology Today, 11*(10), 50–51; 53–54.

Muson, H. (1979). Moral thinking: Can it be taught? *Psychology Today, 12*(9), 48–58; 67–68; 92.

Muus, R. E. (1983). Social cognition: Robert Selman's theory of role taking. *Adolescence, 17,* 499–525.

Myers, D. G. (1980). How do I love me? Let me count the ways. *Psychology Today, 13*(12), 16.

Nadler, R. P. (1978). Are we helping? *Adolescence, 13*(51), 453–459.

NAEP (National Assessment of Educational Progress). (1981). *Newsletter, 14*(3), 6.

Nahas, G. G., Paton, W.D.M., & Idanpaan-Heikkila, J. E. (1976). *Marijuana: Chemistry, biochemistry, and cellular effects.* New York: Springer-Verlag.

Nathanson, B. (1979). *Aborting America.* New York: Morrow.

Nation's teenagers becoming conservative. (1977). *Intellect, 106*(2386), 1.

Neapolitan, J. (1981). Parental infuences on aggressive behavior: A social learning approach. *Adolescence, 16*(64), 831–840.

Neugarten, B. L. (1977). Personality and the aging process. In S. H. Garit (Ed.), *Readings in aging and death: Contemporary perspectives.* New York: Harper & Row.

Newcomb, P. R. (August 1979). Cohabitation in America: An assessment of consequences. *Journal of Marriage and the Family,* 597–603.

Newman, B. M. (1979). Coping and adaptation in adolescence. *Human Development, 22,* 255–262.

Newman, B. M., & Newman P. R. (1978). The concept of identity: Research and theory. *Adolescence, 13*(49), 157–166.

Norton, D. L. (1970). The rites of passage from dependency to autonomy. *School Review, 79*(1), 19–41.

Norvell, M., & Guy, R. F. (1977). A comparison of self-concept in adopted and nonadopted adolescents. *Adolescence, 12*(47), 443–448.

Nourse, B. B., Jr. (1979). Students exploring alternative life styles. *Phi Delta Kappan, 60*(6), 448–451.

Nydegger, C. N. (1981). On being caught up in time. *Human Development, 24,* 1–12.

Oberle, W. H., Stowers, K. R., & Falk, W. W. (1978). Place of residence and the role model preferences of black boys and girls. *Adolescence, 13*(49), 13–20.

O'Connell, A. N. (1976). The relationship between life style and identity synthesis and resynthesis in traditional, neotraditional, and nontraditional women. *Journal of Personality, 44,* 675–688.

Offer, D., Ostrov, R., & Howard, K. I. (1977). The self-image of adolescents: A study of four cultures. *Journal of Youth and Adolescence, 6*(3), 265–280.

Offer, D., Ostrov, E., & Howard, K. I. (1981a). *The adolescent: A psychological self-portrait.* New York: Basic Books.

Offer, D., Ostrov, E., & Howard, K. I. (1981b). The mental health professional's concept of the normal adolescent. *Archives of General Psychiatry, 38,* 149–152.

Offer, D., Ostrov, E., & Howard, K. I. (1982). Family perceptions of adolescent self-image. *Journal of Youth and Adolescence, 11*(4), 281–291.

Olday, D. (1977). Some consequences of heterosexual cohabitation for marriage. Unpublished doctoral dissertation, Washington State University.

O'Mara, F. E. (1978). Affiliative processes in military units: Racial and cultural influences. *Youth and Society, 10*(1), 79–96.

One child, two homes. More divorced parents are agreeing to joint custody (January 29, 1979). *Time, 113*(5), 61.

On tap: Faster, easier, more than comfortable travel. (May 9, 1983). *U.S. News & World Report,* A17–18.

Oops! SAT scores still falling: Verbal by two points, math by one in 1978–1979. (1979). *Phi Delta Kappan, 61*(3), 155–156.

Onyehalu, A. S. (1981). Identity crisis in adolescence. *Adolescence, 16*(63), 629–632.

Orthner, D. K. (1975). Leisure activity patterns and marital satisfaction over the marital career. *Journal of Marriage and the Family, 37*(1), 91–104.

Owuamanam, D. O. (1983). Peer and parental influence on sexual activities of school-going adolescents in Nigeria. *Adolescence 17*(69), 169–179.

Pacheco, A. (1978). Alienation: A closer look. *Phi Delta Kappan, 59*(5), 317–318.

Pachter, E. F. (1978). The pre-professionals: A self-portrait by late adolescents. *The Andover Review, 5*(2), 62–75.

Panelas, T. (1983). Adolescents and video games: Consumption of leisure and the social construction of the peer group. *Youth and Society, 15*(1), 51–66.

Parish, T. S. (1981). The impact of divorce on the family. *Adolescence, 16*(63), 577–580.

Parish, T. S., Dostal, J. W., & Parish, J. G. (1981). Evaluations of self and parents as a function of intactness of family and family happiness. *Adolescence, 16*(61), 203–210.

Parke, R. D., & Sawin, D. B. (1979). Children's privacy in the home: Developmental, ecological and child-rearing determinants. *Environment and Behavior, 11*(1), 87–104.

Parsons, J. E., Adler, T. F., & Kaczala, C. M. (1982). Socialization of achievement attitudes and beliefs: Parental infuences. *Child Development, 53,* 310–321.

Parsons, J. E., Kaczala, C. M., & Meece, J. L. (1982). Socialization of achievement attitudes and beliefs: Classroom influences. *Child Development, 53,* 322–339.

Passmore, D. L., & Welch, F. G. (1983). Relationship between preferences for part-time work and characteristics of unemployed youths. *Adolescence, 17*(69), 181–182.

Patel, K., & Rose, G. (1981). Youth, political participation, and alienation: A case study of college students in the Bible belt. *Youth and Society, 13*(1), 57–75.

Patterson, G. R. (1982). *A social learning approach. Coercive family process* (Vol. 3). Eugene, Oregon: Castalia.

Pattison, E. H. (1977). *The experience of dying.* Englewood Cliffs, N.J.: Prentice-Hall, 105–110.

Peabody, E., McKenry, P., & Cordero, L. (1981). Subsequent pregnancy among adolescent mothers. *Adolescence, 16*(63), 563–568.

Pearlin, J. (1980). Life strains and psychological distress among adults. In N. Smelser, & E. Ericksen (Eds.), *Themes of work and love in adulthood.* Cambridge: Harvard University Press.

Peer group replacing family? (1979). *The Futurist, 13*(1), 64.

Permissiveness: A beautiful idea: that didn't work? (September 6, 1976). *U.S. News & World Report, 81*(10), 54–55.

Peskin, H., & Livson, N. (1972). Pre- and postpubertal personality and adult psychological functioning. *Seminars in Psychiatry, 4*(4), 343–353.

Petersen, A. C. (1979). Can puberty come any earlier? *Psychology Today, 12*(9), 45–47.

Petersen, A. C., & Taylor, B. (1980). The biological approach to adolescence. In J. Adelson (Ed.), *Handbook of adolescent psychology.* New York: Wiley.

Peterson, G. W. & Peters, D. F. (1983). Adolescents' construction of social reality: The impact of television and peers. *Youth and Society, 15*(1), 67–86.

Peterson, G. W., Rollins, B. C., Thomas, D. L., & Heaps, L. K. (1982). Social placement of adolescents: Sex-role influences on family decisions regarding the careers of youth. *Journal of Marriage and the Family, 44*(3), 647–658.

Pfeiffer, J. (November 1981). Silliness and survival. *Science 81, 2*(9), 36; 38.

Phelps, L. A. (1978). Turning the gifted on to their talents. *Vocational Education, 53*(7), 26–30.

Philliber, S. G., & Tatum, M. L. (1982). Sex education and the double standard in high school. *Adolescence, 17*(66), 273–283.

Piaget, J. (1948). *The moral judgment of the child.* Glencoe, Ill.: Free Press.

Pines, M. (1979). Superkids. *Psychology Today, 12*(8), 53–61.

Place, D. M. (1975). The dating experience for adolescent girls. *Adolescence, 10*(38), 157–174.

Polansky, L. W., McDonald, G., & Martin, J. (Summer 1978). A comparison of marriage and heterosexual cohabitation on three interpersonal variables: Affective support, mutual knowledge and relationship satisfaction. *Western Sociological Review, 9,* 49–59.

Pomerleau, O. F. (1979). Behavioral factors in the establishment, maintenance, and cessation of smoking. In U.S. Department of Health, Education and Welfare, Public Health Service, *Smoking and health: A report of the Surgeon General.* Washington, D. C.: Government Printing Office, DHEW Publication No. (PHS) 79-50066.

Poole, M. E., & Low, B. C. (1982). Who stays: Who leaves? An examination of sex differences in staying and leaving. *Journal of Youth and Adolescence, 11*(1), 49–63.

Porter, B., & O'Leary, K. D. (1980). Marital discord and childhood behavior. *Journal of Abnormal Child Psychology, 8,* 287–295.

Porter, G. (1979). Models of adulthood: An ethnographic study of an adolescent peer group. *Journal of Youth and Adolescence, 8*(3), 253–269.

Potvin, R. H., & Lee, C. (1982). Adolescent religion: A developmental approach. *Sociological Analysis, 43*(2), 131–144.

Pratt, M. W., Golding, G., & Hunter, W. J. (1983). Aging as ripening: Character and consistency of moral judgment in young, mature and older adults. *Human Development, 26,* 277–288.

Proefrock, D. W. (1981). Adolescence: Social fact and psychological concept. *Adolescence, 16*(64), 851–858.

Ramsey, R. W. (1982). Job corps: Economic renewal through youth development. *Adolescence, 17*(68), 951–954.

Ransford, H. E., & Miller, J. (1983). Race, sex and feminist outlooks. *American Sociological Review, 48,* 46–59.

Ransohoff, R. (1975). Some observations on humor and laughter in young adolescent girls. *Journal of Youth and Adolescence, 4*(2), 155–170.

Rao, V. P., & Rao, V. N. (1981). Family size and sex preference of children: A bi-racial comparison. *Adolescence, 16*(62), 385–401.

Rapin, L. S., & Cooper, M. (1980). Images of men and women: A comparison of feminists and nonfeminists. *Psychology of Women Quarterly, 5*(2), 186–194.

Rating the student diet. (1979/1980). *Nutshell.* Knoxville, Tennessee: 13–30 Corporation, 10.

Ravitch, D. (1983). The educational pendulum. *Psychology Today, 17*(10), 62–71.

Raviv, A., & Bar-Tal, D. (1981). Demographic correlates of adolescents' helping behavior. *Journal of Youth and Adolescence, 10*(1), 45–53.

Recreation for all is latest goal in the cities. (May 25, 1977). *U.S. News & World Report,* 72–73.

Reed, S. K., & Coleman, M. (1981). Female sex-role models in adolescent fiction: Changing over time? *Adolescence, 16*(63), 581–586.

Rees, C. D., & Wilborn, B. L. (1983). Correlates of drug abuse in adolescents: A comparison of families of drug abusers with families of nondrug abusers. *Journal of Youth and Adolescence, 12*(1), 55–64.

Reid, F. (1939). *Peter Waring.* London: Faber.

Reisman, J. M., & Shorr, S. I. (1978). Friendship claims and expectations among children and adults. *Child Development, 49*(3), 913–916.

Remmers, H. H., & Radler, D. H. (1957). *The American teen-ager.* Indianapolis: Bobbs-Merrill.

Renshon, S. A. (1977). "Models of man" and temporal frameworks in political socialization theory. An examination of some assumptions. *Youth and Society, 8*(3), 245–276.

Rest, J. (1983). Morality. In J. H. Flavell & E. Markman (Eds.), *Carmichael's manual of child psychology,* 4th ed. New York: Wiley.

Rest, J. R., Davison, M. L., & Robbins, S. (1978). Age trends in judging moral issues: A review of cross-sectional, longitudinal, and sequential studies of the defining issues test. *Child Development, 49*(2), 263–279.

Rice, B. (1979). Brave new world of intelligence testing. *Psychology Testing, 13*(4), 26–41.

Rice, B. (1983). Good news for future job-hunters. *Psychology Today, 17*(7), 77.

Rice, R. R., & Marsh, M. (1979). The social environments of two high schools: Background data. In J. G. Kelly (Ed.), *Adolescent boys in high school: A psychological study of coping and adaptation.* Hillsdale, New Jersey: Lawrence Erlbaum Associates Publishers.

Rich, H. E. (1977). The liberalizing influence of college: Some new evidence, *Adolescence, 12*(46), 199–211.

Rich, P. (1982). The juvenile justice system and its treatment of the juvenile: An overview. *Adolescence, 17*(65), 141–152.

Ridgeway, C. L. (1978). Predicting college women's aspirations from evaluations of the housewife and work role. *The Sociological Quarterly, 19,* 281–291.

Ridgeway, C. L., & Jacobson, C. K. (1979). The development of female role ideology: Impact of personal confidence and during adolescence. *Youth and Society, 10*(3), 297–315.

Riemer, J. W. (1981). Deviance as fun. *Adolescence, 16*(61), 39–43.

Rienzo, B. A. (1981). The status of sex education: An overview and recommendations. *Phi Delta Kappan, 63*(3), 192–193.

Riesman, D. (1950). *The lonely crowd.* New Haven: Yale University Press.

Roberton, J. (1832). An inquiry into the natural history of the menstrual function. *Edinborough Medical and Surgical Journal, 38,* 227–254.

Roberts, A. R. (1982). Adolescent runaways in suburbia: A new typology. *Adolescence, 17*(66), 387–396.

Robinson, I. E., & Jedlicka, D. (1982). Change in sexual attitudes and behavior of college students from 1965 to 1980: A research note. *Journal of Marriage and the Family, 44*(1), 237–240.

Rodin, J. (1978). The puzzle of obesity. *Human Nature, 1*(2), 38–49.

Rodriguez, J. (January 1980). Youth employment—A needs assessment. In B. Linder, & R. Taggart, (Eds.) *A review of youth employment problems, programs, and policies,* Vol. I: The youth employment problem: Causes and dimensions. Washington, D.C.: Vice-President's Task Force on Youth Employment.

Rogers, D. (1969). *Child psychology.* Belmont, California: Brooks-Cole.

Rogers, D. *Life-span human development.* Monterey, California: Brooks-Cole, 1982.

Roll, S., & Millen, L. (1978). Adolescent males' feeling of being understood by their fathers as revealed through clinical interviews. *Adolescence, 13*(49), 83–94.

Roper, B. S., & Labeff, E. (1977). Sex roles and feminism revisited: An intergenerational attitude comparison. *Journal of Marriage and the Family, 39*(1), 113–119.

Rosenfeld, A. (October 1, 1977). The new SD: Life-span development. *Saturday Review,* 32–33.

Rosow, J. M. (1979). The workplace: A changing scene. *Vocational Education, 54*(2), 22–25.

Ross, S. (1979). *The youth values project.* New York: The Population Institute.

Ross, W. D. (Ed.) (1910). *The works of Aristotle,* Vol. IV. *History of the animals.* Oxford: Clarendon Press.

Rossi, A. (1977). A biosocial perspective on parenting. *Daedalus, 106*(2), 1–32.

Rotter, J. B. (1980). Trust and gullibility. *Psychology Today, 14*(5), 35–42; 102.

Rubenstein, C. (1983). The modern art of courtly love. *Psychology Today, 17*(7), 40–49.

Rubenstein, H. A. (July 1978). Unemployed youth: A ticking bomb. *USA Today, 107*(2398), 42–44.

Rubin, Z. (1979). Seeking a cure for loneliness. *Psychology Today, 13*(4), 82–90.

Rubin, Z. (1982). Friends and lovers. *Psychology Today, 16*(10), 78–79.

Rubinstein, C., Shaver, P., & Peplau, L. A. (1979). Loneliness. *Human Nature, 2*(2), 58–65.

Ruggiero, M., Greenberger, E., & Steinberg, L. D. (1982). Occupational deviance among adolescent workers. *Youth and Society, 13*(4), 423–448.

Rumberger, R. W. (1981). Experiences in high school and college. In M. E. Borus (Ed.), *Pathways to the future.* Columbus: The Ohio State University Center for Human Resource Research.

Rushton, J. P. (1982). Television and prosocial behavior. In D. Pearl, et al (Eds.) *Television and behavior: Ten years of scientific progress and implications for the eighties* (Vol. 2). Rockville, Maryland: U S. Department of Health and Human Services.

Russ-eft, D., Sprenger, M., & Beever, A. (1979). Antecedents of adolescent parenthood and consequences at age 30. *Family Coordinator, 28*(2), 173–179.

Russell, D., Peplau, L. A., & Cutrona, C. E. (1980). The reviewed UCLA loneliness scale: Concurrent and discriminant validity evidence. *Journal of Personality and Social Psychology, 39,* 472–480.

Rust, J. O., & Lloyd, M. W. (1982). Sex-role attitudes and preferences of junior high school age adolescents. *Adolescence, 17*(65), 37–43.

Rutter, M. (1980). Attachment and the development of social relationships. In M. Rutter (Ed.), *Scientific foundations of developmental psychiatry.* London: William Heinemann.

Sabatino, D. A., Heald, J. E., Rothman, S. G., & Miller, T. L. (1978). Destructive norm-violating school behavior among adolescents: A review of protective and preventive efforts. *Adolescence, 13*(52), 675–686.

Santrock, J. W., & Warshak, R. A. (1979). Father custody and social development in boys and girls. *Journal of Social Issues, 35*(4), 112–125.

Saucier, J., & Ambert, A. (1982). Parent-marital status and adolescents' optimism about their future. *Journal of Youth and Adolescence, 11*(5), 345–354.

Saunders, L. E. (1981). Ignorance of the law among teenagers: Is it a barrier to the exertion of their rights as citizens? *Adolescence, 16*(63), 711–726.

Savage, B. M., & Wells, F. L. (1948). A note on singularity in given names. *Journal of Social Psychology, 27,* 271–272.

Scanlon, J. (1979). *Young adulthood.* New York: Academy for Educational Development.

Scanzoni, J. (1979). A historical perspective on husband-wife bargaining power and marital dissolution. In Levinger, G., & Moles, O. (Eds.), *Divorce and separation.* New York: Basic Books.

Scanzoni, J., & Fox, G. L. (1980). Sex roles, family, and society: The seventies and beyond. *Journal of Marriage and the Family, 42,* 743–756.

Scarr, S., & Weinberg, R. A. (1978). The influence of "family background" on intellectual attainment. *American Sociological Review, 43,* 674–692.

Schab, F. (1979). Adolescence in the South: A comparison of blacks and whites not prepared for the world of work. *Adolescence, 14*(55), 599–606.

Schab, F. (1982). Early adolescence in the South: Attitudes regarding the home and religion. *Adolescence, 17*(67), 605–612.

Schaffer, H. R., & Hargreaves, D. (1978). Young people in society: A research initiative by the SSRC. *Bulletin of British Psychology and Sociology, 31,* 91–94.

Schaffer, K. F. (1980). *Sex role issues in mental health.* Reading, Massachusetts: Addison-Wesley.

Schippers, L. (1978). The permanence of change and the adolescent experience. *Adolescence, 13*(49), 143–148.

Schmiedeck, R. A. (1979). Adolescent identity formation and the organizational structure of high schools. *Adolescence, 14*(53), 191–196.

Schneller, R. (1982). The science-religion problem: Attitudes of religious Israeli youth. *Youth and Society, 13*(3), 251–282.

Schooler, C. (1972). Birth order effects: Not here, not now! *Psychological Bulletin, 78,* 161–175.

Schwab, M. R., & Lundgren, D. C. (1979). The impact of college on students: Residential context, relations with parents and peers, and self-esteem. *Youth and Society, 10*(3), 227–235.

Schwartz, S. K. (1977). The validity of adolescents' political reponses. *Youth and Society, 8*(3), 212–243.

Sebald, H. (Spring 1981). Adolescents' concept of popularity and unpopularity. *Adolescence, 16*(61), 187–193.

Segrave, J. O., & Hastad, D. N. (1983). Evaluating structural and control models of delinquency causation. *Youth and Society, 14*(4), 437–456.

Selman, R. L. (1980). *The growth of interpersonal understanding: Developmental and clinical analysis.* New York: Academic Press.

Seltzer, V. C. (1982). *Adolescent social development: Dynamic functional interaction.* Lexington, Mass., Heath.

Service, R. (1945). *Ploughman of the moon.* New York: Dodd, Mead.

Sewell, T., Farley, F. H., Manni, J., & Hunt, P. (1982). Motivation, social reinforcement, and intelligence as predictors of academic achievement in black adolescents. *Adolescence, 17*(67), 647–656.

Sex and the homosexual. (April 30, 1979). *Newsweek,* 81–82.

Sexton, P. C. (1969). *The feminized male: Classrooms, white collars, and the decline of manliness.* New York: Random House.

Shane, H. G. (1981). Significant writings that have influenced the curriculum: 1906–1981. *Phi Delta Kappan, 62*(5), 311–314.

Shapero, A. (f1975). The displaced, uncomfortable entrepreneur. *Psychology Today, 9*(6), 83–86; 88; 133.

Shapiro, D., & Crowley, J. E. (1982). Aspirations and expectations of youth in the United States. Part 2. Employment activity. *Youth and Society, 14*(1), 33–58.

Shapiro, H. (1974). Kids take on "William's Doll." *Ms. Magazine, 2,* 42–44.

Sharabany, R., Gershoni, R., & Hofman, J. E. (1981). Girlfriend, boyfriend: Age and sex differences in intimate friendship. *Developmental Psychology, 17,* 800–808.

Sheldon, W. H., Stevens, S. S., & Tucker, W. B. (1940). *The varieties of human physique.* New York: Harper.

Shenker, I. R., & Schildkrout, M. (1975). Physical and emotional health of youth. In R. J. Havighurst & P. H. Dreyer (Eds.), *Youth.* Chicago: The National Society for the Study of Education.

Sherman, J. A. (Summer 1982). Mathematics the critical filter: A look at some residues. *Psychology of Women Quarterly, 6*(4), 428–444.

Shields, J. J. Jr. (1979). The return to gray flannel thinking. *USA Today, 107*(2404), 49–52.

Shlechter, T. M., & Gump, P. A. (1983). Car availability and the daily life of the teenage male. *Adolescence, 17*(69), 101–113.

Shore, M. F. (1981). Non-traditional mental health services for youth in six European countries: Some general observations. *Adolescence, 16*(61), 195–201.

Silber, T. J. (1981). Ethical consideration in the medical care of adolescents who consult for treatment of gonorrhea. *Adolescence, 17*(66), 267–271.

Silbert, M. H., & Pines, A. M. (1982). Entrance into prostitution. *Youth and Society, 13*(4), 471–500.

Silverman, R. E. (1974). *Psychology.* Englewood Cliffs, New Jersey: Prentice-Hall.

Simmons, C. H., & Parsons, R. J. (1983). Empowerment for role alternatives in adolescence. *Adolescence, 17*(69), 193–200.

Sizer, T. R. (1983). High school reform: The need for engineering. *Phi Delta Kappan, 64*(10), 679–683.

Skolnick, A. (1978). The myth of the vulnerable child. *Psychology Today, 11*(9), 56–65.

Skovholt, T. M. (1978). Feminism and men's lives. *The Counseling Psychologist, 7*(4), 3–10.

Slavson, S. R. (1947). *The practice of group therapy.* New York: International Universities Press.

Smith, C., & Lloyd, B. (1978). Maternal behavior and perceived sex of infant: Revisited. *Child Development, 49*(4), 1263–1265.

Smith, C. P., Berkman, D. J., & Fraser, W. M. (1980). *Reports of the National Juvenile Justice Assessment Centers.* Washington, D.C.: American Justice Institute.

Smith, E. J. (1981). The career development of young black females. *Youth and Society, 12*(3), 277–312.

Smith, E. J. (1982). The Black female adolescent: A review of the educational, career and psychological literature. *Psychology of Women Quarterly, 6*(3), 261–288.

Smith, M. B. (1983). Hope and despair: Keys to the social psychodynamics of youth. *American Journal of Orthopsychiatry, 53*(3), 388–399.

Smith, M. J. (1980). The social consequences of single parenthood. A longitudinal perspective. *Family Relations, 29*, 75–81.

Smith, P. B., Nenney, S. W., Weinman, M. L., & Mumford, D. M. (1982). Factors affecting perception of pregnancy risk in the adolescent. *Journal of Youth and Adolescence, 11*(3), 207–215.

Snyder, C. R. (1980). The uniqueness mystique. *Psychology Today, 13*(10), 86–90.

Snyder, M. (1980). The many me's of the self-monitor. *Psychology Today, 13*(10), 33–40; 92.

Solway, K. S., & Hays, J. R. (1978). An intellectual and personality study of juveniles who are petitioned for waiver of juvenile jurisdiction. *Journal of Youth and Adolescence, 7*(3), 319–325.

Soon, exciting new ways to stay in touch. (May 9, 1983). *U.S. News & World Report,* A19.

Spanier, G. B. (1975). Sexualization and premarital sexual behavior. *Family Coordinator, 24*(1), 33–41.

Spence, J. T. & Helmreich, R. L. (1980). Masculine instrumentality and feminine expressiveness: Their relationships with sex-role attitudes and behaviors. *Psychology of Women Quarterly, 5*(2), 147–163.

Spender, S. (1951). *World within world.* London: Hamish Hamilton.

Spindler, G. D. (1970). The education of adolescents: An anthropological perspective. In E. D. Evans, (Ed.), *Adolescence: Readings in behavior and development.* Hinsdale, Illinois: Dryden Press.

Starr, J. M. (1981). Adolescents and resistance to schooling: A dialectic. *Youth and Society, 13*(2), 189–227.

Stein, S. L., & Weston, L. C. (1982). College women's attitudes toward women and identity achievement. *Adolescence, 17*(68), 895–899.

Steinberg, L. D. (1982). Jumping off the work experience bandwagon. *Journal of Youth and Adolescence, 11*(3), 183–205.

Steinberg, L. D. (1981). Transformations in family relations of puberty. *Developmental Psychology, 17,* 833–840.

Steinberg, L. D., Greenberger, E., Jacobi, M., & Garduque, L. (1981). Early work experience: A partial antidote for adolescent egocentrism. *Journal of Youth and Adolescence, 10*(2), 141–157.

Steinberg, L. D., Greenberger, E., Vaux, A., & Ruggiero, M. (1981). Early work experience: Effects on adolescent occupational socialization. *Youth and Society, 12*(4), 403–422.

Stekel, W. (1926). *Frigidity in woman* (Vol. 1). Trans. by J. S. Van Teslaar. New York: Liveright.

Stempfel, R. S. (1967). The question of sex hormone therapy in cases of delayed puberty. *Journal of Pediatrics, 70*(6), 1023–1024.

Stephenson, S. P. (1979). From school to work: A transition with job search information. *Youth and Society, 11*(1), 114–132.

Stephenson, S. P. Jr. (1981). Young women and labor: In-school labor force status and early postschool labor market outcomes. *Youth and Society, 13*(2), 123–155.

Stevenson, W. (1978). Causes and consequences of youth unemployment. *USA Today, 107*(2398), 46.

Stipek, D. J. (1981). Adolescents—Too young to earn, too old to learn? Compulsory school attendance and intellectual development. *Journal of Youth and Adolescence, 10*(2), 113–139.

Stone, L. J.., & Church, J. (1973). *Childhood and adolescence* (3rd ed.) New York: Random House.

Story, M. D. (1982). A comparison of university student experience with various sexual outlets in 1974 and 1980. *Adolescence, 17*(68), 737–747.

Storz, N. S. (1982). Body image of obese adolescent girls in a high school and clinical setting. *Adolescence, 17*(67), 667–672.

Strauss, G. H. (1974). Two perspectives on high school student politics: Political objects versus political actors. *Youth and Society, 5*(3), 360–376.

Strauss, J. S. (1979). Social and cultural influences on psychopathology. In M. R. Rosenzweig & L. W. Porter (Eds.), *Annual review of psychology*. Palo Alto: Annual Reviews, Inc., 30; 396–416.

Strong, L. D. (1978). Alternative marital and family forms: Their relative attractiveness to college students and correlates of willingness to participate in nontraditional forms. *Journal of Marriage and the Family, 40*(3), 493–503.

Stubbs, M. L. (1982). Period piece. *Adolescence, 17*(65), 45–55.

Student apathy and cynicism. (1974). *Intellect, 102*(2358), 483.

Student spirits: A new look at drinking on campus. (1979). *Human Behavior, 8*(1), 67.

Students returning to Western form of worship. (1978). *Intellect, 106*(2396), 439.

Super, D. E. (1976). *Career education and the meaning of work*. Washington, D.C.: U.S. Office of Education.

Super, D. E., & Hall, D. T. (1978). Career development: Exploration and planning. In M. R. Rosenzweig & L. R. Porter (Eds.), *Annual review of psychology*. Vol. 29. Palo Alto: Annual Reviews, Inc., 333–372.

Sussman, M. (1978). The family today: Is it an endangered species? *Children Today, March-April*, 33; 37; 45.

Svobodny, L. A. (1982). Biographical self-concept and educational factors among chemically dependent adolescents. *Adolescence, 17*(68), 847–853.

Swanson, R. B., Massey, R. H., & Payne, I. R. (1972). Ordinal position, family size, and personal adjustment. *Journal of Psychology, 81*, 53–58.

Sweat, S., Kelley, E., Blouin, D., & Glee, R. (1981). Career appearance perceptions of selected university students. *Adolescence, 16*(62), 359–370.

Sweetser, F. L. (1941). Neighborhood acquaintanceship and association. Published by the author.

Tanner, J. M. (1968). Earlier maturation in man. *Scientific American, 218*, 21–27.

Tanner, J. (1978a). New directions for subcultural theory: An analysis of British working-class youth culture. *Youth and Society, 9*(4), 343–372.

Tanner, J. M. (1978b). *Education and physical growth* (2nd ed.) London: University of London Press.

Tanner, J. M., & Taylor, G. R., and the editors of Time-Life Books. (1969). *Growth*. New York: Time-Life Books.

Taylor, R. L. (1976). Psychosocial development among black children and youth: A reexamination. *American Journal of Orthopsychiatry, 46*(1), 4–19.

Technology and the frontiers of knowledge. (1975). The Franklin Doubleday lectures. First series. New York: Doubleday.

Technology's effect on American society. (1978). *USA Today, 106*(2396), 441–442.

Teenagers in the 60s. (1974). *Children Today, 3*(1), 31.

The coming revolution in the world of culture. (May 9, 1983). *U.S. News & World Report*, A8–A9.

The sheltered life: Adulthood sometimes comes hard. (1978). *Human Behavior, 7*(10), 61.

The significance of shyness. (1975). *Intellect, 104*(2368), 81.

The "unsilent generation" breaks silence. (February 17, 1958). *Life*, 112–126. From *The Unsilent Generation* compiled and edited by O. Butz. Copyright 1958 by Otto Butz. Reprinted by permission of Holt, Rinehart & Winston, Publishers.

The worst forecasts. (April 1978). *The Futurist*, 127–128.

Thomas, A., & Chess, S. (1977). *Temperament and development*. New York: Brunner/Mazel.

Thompson, K. S. (1980). A comparison of black and white adolescents' beliefs about having children. *Journal of Marriage and the Family, 42*(1), 133–140.

Thompson, V. D. (1974). Family size: Implicit policies and assumed psychological outcomes. *Journal of Social Issues, 30*(4), 93–124.

Thomson, E. (1982). Socialization for sexual and contraceptive behavior: Moral absolutes versus relative consequences. *Youth and Society, 14*(1), 103–128.

Thorbecke, W., & Grotevant, H. D. (1982). Gender differences in adolescent interpersonal identity formation. *Journal of Youth and Adolescence, 11*(6), 479–492.

Thornburg, H. D., & Grinder, R. E. (1975). Children of Aztitlan: The Mexican-American experience. In R. J. Havighurst & P. H. Dreyer (Eds.), *Youth*. Chicago: University of Chicago Press.

Thornton, A., & Freedman, D. (1980). Changes in the sex-role attitudes of women, 1962–1977: Evidence from a panel study. *American Sociological Review, 29*, 831–842.

Thornton, W. E. (1981). Marijuana use and delinquency: A reexamination. *Youth and Society, 13*(1), 23–37.

Thornton, W. E. (1982). Gender traits and delinquency involvement of boys and girls. *Adolescence, 17*(68), 749–768.

"Three R's" in schools now: Retrenchment, results, realism. (September 6, 1976). *U.S. News & World Report, 81*(10, 50–51.

Thurnher, M. (1983). Turning points and developmental change: Subjective and "objective" assessments. *American Journal of Orthopsychiatry, 53*(1), 52–59.

Tiger, L. (1978). Omnigamy: The new kinship system. *Psychology Today, 12*(2), 14; 17.

Tinto, V. (1981). High education and occupational attainment in segmented labor markets: Recent evidence from the United States. *Higher Education, 10,* 499–516.

Tischler, C. L., McHenry, P. C., & Morgan, K. C. (1981). Adolescent suicide attempts: Some significant factors. *Suicide and Life-threatening Behavior, 11*(2), 86–92.

Tobias, J., & Lablanc, T. (1977). Malicious destruction of property in the suburbs—1975. *Adolescence, 12*(45), 111–114.

Tobias, S. (1982). Sexist equations. *Psychology Today, 16*(1), 14–17.

Todd, D. M. (1979). Contrasting adaptations to the social environment of a high school: Implications of a case study of helping behavior in two adolescent subcultures. In J. G. Kelly (Ed.), *Adolescent boys in high school: A psychological study of coping and adaptation.* Hillsdale, New Jersey: Lawrence Erlbaum Associates Publishers.

Toffler, A. (1980). *The third wave.* New York: Morrow.

Tognolli, J. (1980). Male friendship and intimacy across the life span. *Family Relations, 29*(3), 273–279.

Tolor, A. (1983). Perceptions of quality of life of college students and their faculty. *Adolescence, 18*(71), 585–594.

Tooley, K. M. (1977). Johnny, I hardly knew ye: Toward revision of the theory of male psychosexual development. *American Journal of Orthopsychiatry, 47,* 184–195.

Torgerson, E. (1977). What teen-agers watch . . . and why. *TV Guide, 25*(7), 4–7.

Trachtman, L. E. (1975). Creative people, creative times. *Journal of Creative Behavior, 9*(1), 35–50.

Trickett, E. J. (1978). Toward a social-ecological conception of adolescent socialization: Normative data on contrasting types of public school classrooms. *Child Development, 49*(2), 408–414.

Troll, L. E., & Turner, B. (1978). Impact of changing sex-roles upon the family of later life. In C. Safilios-Rothschild (Ed.), *Impact of changing sex roles upon the family.*

Tubbs,, M. P., & Beane, J. A. (1981). A second look at the U.S. high school. *Phi Delta Kappan, 62*(5) 399–400.

Tyack, D. (1978). Socialization to what? *Phi Delta Kappan, 59*(5), 316–317.

Tyler, R. W. (1981). The U.S. versus the world: A comparison of educational performance. *Phi Delta Kappan, 62*(5), 307–210.

Ullian, D. (1984). Why girls are good: A constructionist view. *American Journal of Orthopsychiatry, 54*(1), 71–82.

Ulrich, R. S. (1981). Natural versus urban scenes. *Environment And Behavior, 13*(5), 523–556.

U.S. Department of Health and Human Services. (1982). Socialization and conceptions of social reality. In D. Pearl et al. (Eds.), *Television and behavior: Ten years of scientific progress and implications for the eighties.* Rockville, Md: published by the author.

U.S. National Center for Health Statistics (1975). *Self-reported health behavior and attitudes of youths, 12–17 years, United States.* Washington, D.C.: Vital Health Statistics, Series 11, No. 147.

Unger, R. K. (1981). Sex as a social reality: Field and laboratory research. *Psychology of Women Quarterly, 5*(4), 645–653.

Vaillant, G. E. (1977a). The climb to maturity: How the best and the brightest came of age. *Psychology Today, 11*(4), 34–41; 107–108; 110.

Vaillant, G. E. (1977b). *Adaptation to life.* Boston: Little, Brown, & Co.

Vaillant, G. E., & McArthur, C. C. (1972). Natural history of male psychological health. The adult life cycle from 18–50. *Seminars in Psychiatry, 4*(4), 415–427.

Value of college education to jobless graduates. (January 1977). *Intellect, 105*(2380), 210–211.

Vander Mey, B. J., & Neff, R. L. (1982). Adult-child incest: A review of research and treatment. *Adolescence, 17*(68), 717–735.

Vandewiele, M. (1982). Wolof adolescents' attitudes toward old people. *Adolescence, 17*(68), 863–869.

VanDusen, R. A., & Sheldon, E. B. (1976). The changing status of American women. A life cycle perspective. *American Psychologist, 31*(2), 106–116.

VanMaanen, J. (Ed.) (1977). *Organizational careers: Some new perspectives.* New York: Wiley.

Van Ornum, W., Foley, J. M., Burns, P. R., DeWolfe, A. S., & Kennedy, E. C. (1981). Empathy, altruism, and self-interest in college students. *Adolescence, 16*(64), 799–808.

Varenne, H. (1978). La Vie en Appleton. *Psychology Today, 11*(9), 66–74.

Venturini, J. L. (1982). A survey on causes of school vandalism. *High School Journal, 66*(1), 7–9.

Veysey, L. (May 1, 1976). Rejoice! Some of what ails us may not be so. *The National Observer,* 31–32.

Viernstein, M. C., McGinn, P. V., & Hogan, R. (1977). The personality correlates of differential verbal and mathematical ability in talented adolescents. *Journal of Youth and Adolescence, 6*(2), 169–178.

Vincent, C. E. (1972). An open letter to the caught generation. *Family Coordinator, 21*(2), 143–150.

Viney, L. L. (1983). Psychological reactions of young people to employment. *Youth and Society, 14*(4), 457–474.

Vinter, R. (1979). Trends in state correction: Juveniles and the violent young offender. *Crime and Delinquency, 25*(2), 145–161.

Virginia Slims American women's opinion polls. (1970–1980).

Vliet, W. V. (1983). Exploring the fourth environment. An examination of the home range of city and suburban teenagers. *Environment and Behavior, 15*(5), 567–588.

Wagner, C. A. (1980). Sexuality of American adolescents. *Adolescence, 15*(59), 567–580.

Wahlberg, H. J. (1978). Psychology of learning environments: Behavioral, structural, or perceptual? In L. S. Shulman (Ed.), *Review of research in education,* (Vol. 4). Itasca, Illinois: F. E. Peacock.

Walker, L. (1983). Sex differences in the development of moral reasoning. *Child Development, 54,* 1103–1141.

Wallerstein, J. S., & Kelly, J. B. (1980). *Surviving the breakup: How children and parents cope with divorce.* New York: Basic Books.

Ward, W. C., Kogan, N., & Pankove, E. (1972). Incentive effects in children's creativity. *Child Development, 43,* 669–676.

Waterman, A. S. (1982). Identity development from adolescence to adulthood: An extension of theory and a review of research. *Developmental Psychology, 18,* 341–358.

Waterman, A. S. (1981). Individualism and independence. *American Psychologist, 36*(7), 762–773.

Watrous, P. (1983). Me generation II. *Psychology Today, 17*(4), 75.

Watson, F. (1962). The English grammar schools in 1660. Cited in P. Ariès, *Centuries of childhood.* New York: Vintage.

Watts, W. (1981). The future can fend for itself. *Psychology Today, 15*(9), 36–48.

Wechsler, H. (Ed.) (1980). *Minimum drinking-age laws: An evaluation.* Lexington, Massachusetts: Lexington Books.

Wechter, S. L. (February 1983). Separation difficulties between parents and young adults. *Social Casework, 64*(2), 97–104.

Weintraub, P. (April 1981). The brain: His and hers. *Discover,* 15–20.

Weiss, R. S. (1979). *Going in alone.* New York: Basic Books.

Weithorn, L. A., & Campbell, S. B. (1982). The competency of children and adolescents to make informed treatment decisions. *Child Development, 53*(6), 1589–1598.

Welch, E. (1980). In breast size, small is smart. *Psychology Today, 14*(7), 27–28.

Western world's "silent revolution." (1978). *Intellect, 106*(2396), 436–437.

Westfall, P. (1978/1979). What does college do to your head? *Nutshell,* 21; 23–24.

What the next 50 years will bring. (May 9, 1983). *U.S. News and World Report,* A1–A42.

When "family" will have a new definition. (May 9, 1983). *U.S. News & World Report,* A1–A4.

When job training will be a lifelong process. (May 9, 1983). *U.S. News & World Report,* A25–A26.

White, L. K., & Brinkerhoff, D. B. (1981). Children's work in the family: Its significance and meaning. *Journal of Marriage and the Family, 43*(4), 789–798.

Why millions hate their jobs—and what's afoot to help. (September 27, 1976). *U.S. News & World Report,* 87–90.

Wiatrowski, M. D., & Gottfredson, G. (1983). Understanding school behavior disruption: Classifying school environments. *Environment and Behavior, 15*(1), 53–76.

Wieder, D. L., & Zimmerman, D. A. (1974). Generational experience and the development of freak culture. *Journal of Social Issues, 30*(2), 137–161.

Williamson, R. C. (1977). Variables in adjustment and life goals among high school students. *Adolescence, 12*(46), 213–225.

Willis, M. R. (1981). The maligning of adolescence: Why? *Adolescence, 16*(64), 953–958.

Wilson, G., & Nias, D. (1976). Beauty can't be beat. *Psychology Today, 10*(4), 96–98; 103.

Wilson, G. T., & Davison, G. C. (1975). A road to self-control. *Psychology Today, 9*(5), 54; 58–60.

Wilson, H. (1980). Parental supervision: A neglected aspect of delinquency. *British Journal of Criminology, 20,* 203–235.

Winer, J. A., Schwartz, L. H., & Berger, A. S. (1977). Sexual problems found in users of a student mental health clinic. *Journal of Youth and Adolescence, 6*(2), 117–126.

Wingrove, C. R., & Slevin, K. F. (1982). Age differences and generational gaps: College women and their mothers' attitudes toward female roles in society. *Youth and Society, 13*(3), 289–301.

Wilkerson, J., Protinsky, H. O. Jr., Maxwell, J. W., & Lentner, M. (1982). Alienation and ego identity in adolescents. *Adolescence, 17*(65), 133–139.

Wilson, G., & Nias, D. (1976). Beauty can't be beat. *Psychology Today, 10*(4), 96–98; 103.

Wogan, M., & Elliott, J. P. (1972). Drug use and level of anxiety among college students. *Journal of Youth and Adolescence, 1*(4), 325–331.

Wolf, F. M., & Larson, G. L. (1981). On why adolescent formal operators may not be creative thinkers. *Adolescence, 16*(62), 345–348.

Wolfe, M. (1978). Childhood and privacy. In I. Altman & J. F. Wohlwill (Eds.), *Children and the environment* (Vol. 3). New York: Plenum Press, 175–222.

Wolfe, M., Schearer, M., & Laufer, R. S. (May 1976). Private places: The concept of privacy in childhood and adolescence. Paper presented at the meeting of the Environmental Design Research Association, Vancouver, British Columbia; City University of New York Graduate School: Center for Human Environments, No. 76–178.

Wolfgang, M. E. (1973). Because they're young. *Mental Hygiene, 57*(2), 4–9.

Wolfstetter-Kausch, H., & Gaier, E. L. (1981). Alienation among black adolescents. *Adolescence, 16*(62), 471–485.

Wright, J. D. (1975). The socio-political attitudes of white, college-educated youth. *Youth and Society, 6*(3), 251–296.

Wright, L. S. (1982). Parental permission to date and its relationship to drug use and suicidal thoughts among adolescents. *Adolescence, 17*(66), 409–418.

Wright, P. H., & Keple, T. W. (1981). Friends and parents of a sample of high school juniors: An exploratory study of relationship intensity and interpersonal rewards. *Journal of Marriage and the Family, 43*(3), 559–570.

Wynne, E. A. (1978). Behind the discipline problem: Youth suicide as a measure of alienation. *Phi Delta Kappan, 59*(5), 307–315.

Wynne, L., & Frader, L. (1979). Female adolescence and the family: A historical view. In M. Sugar (Ed.) *Female adolescent development.* New York: Bruner/Mazel.

Yalow, R. S. (1982). Physiology/medicine, 1977. *Psychology Today, 16*(12), 26.

Yankelovich, D. (1981). New rules in American life: Searching for fulfillment in a world turned upside down. *Psychology Today, 15*(4), 35–91.

Yarrow, M. R., Scott, P. M., & Waxler, C. Z. (1973). Learning concern for others. *Developmental Psychology, 8,* 240–260.

Yoon, G. (1978). The natural history of friendships: Sex differences in best-friendship patterns. Unpublished doctoral dissertation, St. Louis University.

Youniss, J. (1980). *Parents and peers in social development.* Chicago: University of Chicago Press.

Youth on the move. (1980). *U.S. News & World Report, 89*(26), 72–73.

Zarb, J. M. (1981). Non-academic predictors of successful academic achievement in a normal adolescent sample. *Adolescence, 16*(64), 891–904.

Zeldin, R. S., Small, S. A., & Savin-Williams, R. C. (1982). Prosocial interactions in two mixed-sex adolescent groups. *Child Development, 53,* 1492–1498.

Ziomkowski, L., Mulder, R., & Williams, D. (1975). Drug use variations between delinquent and nondelinquent youth. *Intellect, 104*(2367), 36–38.

Glossary

ability   comprises intelligence plus attitude, persistence, accumulated learning experience, and coping skills.

achievement status   the situation of having arrived at vocational decisions after having examined awaitable alternatives in terms of one's own special talents and needs.

acculturation   the process by which an individual learns the attitudes, modes of thinking, and behaviors characteristic of the larger social group or culture.

acute gastritis   inflammation of the stomach, with a relatively short but severe course.

adolescence   the period of life from the beginning of puberty until maturity.

adrenals   glands located above the kidneys, consisting of an outer layer (the cortex) and an inner portion (the medulla) which secretes adrenalin thereby affecting body responses in emotion.

adult   an individual who has achieved maximum physical growth and who has legally come of age.

adultism   the assumption by adults of undue authority over, and arrogance toward, children and youth.

affiliative   characterized by a close relationship to others.

ageism   the process of systematically stereotyping and discriminating against people on the basis of age.

agrarian   relating to land or landed property.

alienated youth   young people characterized by feelings of distinctiveness and isolation from the dominant social group.

alienation   the condition of feeling distinct from, isolated from, and to some degree opposed to the dominant social group.

alternative family   any of the family living styles other than the traditional two-parent nuclear family.

altruism   unselfish concern for the welfare of others.

amphetamines   synthetic drugs customarily used as inhalants, as sprays for head colds, hay fever, etc., and as diet pills. Amphetamine sulfate is a white, odorless powder that acts as a stimulant to the nervous system.

analgesic   a remedy that relieves or reduces pain.

andante   moderately slow and even.

androgen   a hormone secreted in both sexes, though far more abundantly in males, that influences maleness of structure, function, and, to an unknown extent, behavior.

androgynous   possessing both male and female characteristics.

anthropological method   the research approach which involves studying the physical and cultural aspects of humans.

anthropology   the comparative study of the chief characteristics of humans, including somatic characteristics, social habits, customs, and language.

antiestablishment   against the existing power structure.

anxiety   generalized feelings of worry and apprehension, present in many conflict situations.

apathy   extreme lack of interest, concern, or involvement.

aptitude   a natural ability in some particular skills or area of learning.

archetype   the pattern or model from which other things of the same kind are made.

asynchrony   a lack of concurrence in timing.

atheist   one who disbelieves in the existence of God.

attitude   a consistent tendency to react in a particular way—either positively or negatively—to an object or event. Attitude possesses both cognitive and emotional components.

autonomic   pertaining to that division of the nervous system concerned with the largely automatic regulation of smooth muscles and glands.

autonomic balance   a status of harmony between the sympathetic and parasympathetic divisions of the nervous system, suggesting stabilized emotion.

axillary   underarm.

barbiturate   a crystalline acid or salt used as a hypnotic or sedative.

behavior modification   the process of altering or managing behavior which involves the rewarding of desired responses and ignoring or punishing disapproved ones.

behaviorism   an approach, or school, of psychology that treats objective, observable manifestations as critical for understanding human behavior. Subjective consciousness and feeling are dismissed as unessential or considered mediating processes between stimulus and response.

biosphere the portion of the earth's crust, waters, and atmosphere where living organisms can subsist.

body image the mental picture an individual has of his or her own body, derived from internal sensation, others' reactions, and one's personal goals.

bohemian unconventional; arty.

bureaucrat an official of a government who functions through bureaus and petty officials.

butch a lesbian who behaves in a somewhat masculine manner.

cadence rhythmic flow of a sequence of sounds or words.

cardiovascular pertaining to the heart and blood vessels.

case-study method a technique that involves obtaining all significant past and present evidence relating to a subject.

catamenia menses.

central traits see traits, central or core.

cirrhosis a disease of the liver.

clique a close-knit, unisexual social group, most characteristic of early adolescents, especially girls, but occurring sometimes among children as young as 8 or 9 years.

cognitive pertaining to the process of knowing and thinking.

cognitive style the characteristic way individuals organize their approaches to mental tasks, including specific ways of relating to the problem at hand.

cohort category of persons who share some characteristic, such as age or period in history.

commitment the act of pledging oneself in dedicated fashion to some set of values or course of action.

commune a close-knit community of people who share common interests and activities, as in the area of child rearing.

concrete operations period (Piaget) the period (between ages 7 and 11) when reasoning processes have begun to appear logical. By this stage the child can perceive structural similarities and categorize items on the basis of perceptual cues.

consortium any association, partnership, or union.

constancy of IQ the degree to which a specific individual's intelligence remains approximately the same relative to that of others of his own age status across the years.

conventional stage (Kohlberg) the second stage of moral development, occurring during later childhood, when good and evil are first identified with the concepts of "good girl" and "good boy," and the concepts themselves are allied with social standards of law and order.

convergent (thinking) process involves surveying available data and narrowing the alternatives in order to find a predetermined "correct" solution.

cosmologist a philosopher who is concerned with the origin and general structure of the universe.

counterculture a culture, or way of life, which develops within a larger culture and has no real substance of its own. Its only function is to criticize the major culture, and its activities reflect reactions to that culture.

creativity the ability to devise new solutions or novel syntheses of familiar ideas.

critical-period hypothesis the proposal that if certain experiences occur during specified periods they will have unusual and lasting effects.

cross-cultural research the study of the dynamics of particular behaviors within the context of different cultures.

cross-sectional studies research involving a number of persons in terms of one or more variables at a given time.

crowd a large, loose-knit group, sometimes containing several cliques.

cult devoted attachment to a person, principle, or whatever, particularly when perceived as a fad.

cultural discontinuity a characteristic of a culture in which childhood roles are unrelated to those of adulthood.

cultural pluralism diversity of ways of life within a particular society.

culture-fair test an instrument of evaluation specifically designed to minimize differences in ability attributable to membership in particular subgroups or classes of society.

culture lag the delay between some social change and the society's adaptation to it.

demography the study of human populations, with reference to population trends, distribution, and differential birth rates in subcultural groupings.

depolarization the reversal of the tendency to assume opposing positions.

depression an emotional condition characterized by gloomy thoughts, lowered initiative, and relative inaccessibility to stimulation.

deprogram to utilize psychological techniques that reverse or undo the affects of brainwashing.

deterministic perceiving events as the inevitable or logical results of natural causes.

development a process involving all the many changes, both qualitative and quantitative, that occur during progress toward maturity. It embraces both changes inherent in the maturing process and those resulting from interaction between individuals and their environment.

developmental psychology the branch of psychology concerned with characteristic behaviors at successive stages of development and the processes involved in moving from one state to another.

developmental task a skill or accomplishment that

should be satisfactorily mastered at a particular age stage if an individual is to be ready for the next stage.

dichotomy   division into two discrete parts.

disadvantaged   persons who because of some characteristic of the group to which they belong—for example, its social class, race, or creed—are denied the advantages normally enjoyed by members of the society.

discontinuity   a characteristic of a culture which suggests that childhood roles are unrelated to those of adulthood.

displacement   transfer of emotions from objects or ideas to which they were originally attached to others.

dissociation   a splitting of the mind or consciousness so that the remainder of the mind has no control over the split-off portion.

divergent   contrasting; varying from the norm.

double sex standard   in the psychosexual sense, distinctly different moral codes for the sexes.

ecological   pertaining to that branch of biology that concerns the relationship between living organisms and their environment.

ecology, social   the study of the environmental impact of social factors.

ectomorph   an individual with a body build characterized by linearity, fragility, and thin muscles.

EEG (electroencephalogram)   a graphic record of wavelike changes in electric potential, made by attaching electrodes to either the skull or the exposed brain.

ego   self, as distinguished from other; the aspect of the psyche (general psychological function) that is conscious and most in touch with reality.

ego-ideal   aspect of an individual's moral code that serves as a guide to his or her behavior.

ego identity   the perception of self as a distinctive individual.

egocentrism   self-centeredness.

egoistic   self-centered and concerned with one's own gratification.

electra complex   the repressed desire of a daughter for sex relations with her father.

emasculated   deprived of virility or manhood.

emotion   a complex feeling state with characteristic glandular and motor accompaniments.

emotional maturity   achievement of emotional patterns characteristic of well-adjusted adults.

empathy   the comprehension of another's feelings without possessing those feelings oneself.

empirical   based on experience, careful experiment and/or observation.

encounter group   a group characterized by frank, intimate, often emotional interaction.

endemic   characteristic of a particular locality or group.

endocrine gland   a ductless gland which discharges a secretion directly into the blood stream or lymph glands.

endocrines   internal secretion, applied to glands or organs whose function is to secrete substances into the lymph or blood.

endocrinologist   a specialist in the study of the endocrine glands and their secretions.

endomorph   an individual with a body build characterized by large accumulations of fat, large trunk and thighs, tapering extremities, and relatively weak bones and muscles.

entrepreneurial   showing initiative and risk in the management of some enterprise.

Erikson, Erik   a psychoanalyst who is well known for his theories and writings relating to human development.

esoteric   understood by only a select few who possess special knowledge and interest in a subject.

estrogen   any of several estrus-producing compounds, estrus being the sexual excitement, or heat, of female mammals.

ethic   moral code.

ethical   conforming to standards of conduct.

existential   of, or based on, existence.

exosystem   social structures that do not in themselves involve the individual but impact on an individual's immediate surroundings and somehow influence or even determine what goes on there.

expressive subculture   a grouping within a society concerned with emotions, feelings, and freely expressed behaviors.

fad   a passing fashion or interest.

fantasy   a daydream or wishful imagining.

fem   the individual who assumes a feminine role in lesbian pair relationships.

feminist   one who is especially interested in women's rights.

field dependent   incapable of isolating an object from compelling background forces.

field independent   capable of isolating an object from compelling background forces.

foreclosure status   a state of having formed conclusions without prior examination of alternatives.

formal operations stage (Piaget)   the period, between ages 11 and 15, when truly logical thinking begins and the final step is taken toward abstract thinking and conceptualization.

Freud, Sigmund (1856–1939)   The Austrian neurologist and psychiatrist who devised the technique that became the standard procedure for psychoanalysis. His theories stressed the critical significance of childhood experiences.

friendship   a relationship between two persons, characterized by mutual attraction and intimacy, usually without erotic overtones.

fundamentalist (religion)   one who adheres strictly to the tenets of religious doctrine.

gang   a formalized social group, more typical of boys than girls, characterized by organization, secrecy, high activity, and adventure.

gay   homosexual.

generation effect   the differential impact on successive age cohorts, not merely because of age difference, but because they have experienced different historical events.

generation unit   a grouping within the same generation that organizes its common experience in distinctive ways.

geriatric   relating to the disorders of old age.

genius   an individual of exceptionally high mental ability or one who possesses exceptional ability in some special skill, as music or art.

gerontocracy   a governing group composed of old men.

gonad   the primary sex gland—the ovary in the female and the testis in the male.

group marriage   a marital arrangement in which two or three couples live together and share sex partners.

Hall, G. Stanley (1846–1924)   American educator and psychologist, especially important in the history of adolescent psychology.

hallucinogen   chemical substance capable of producing hallucinations.

hedonism   the doctrine that pleasure is the chief goal in life.

heterogeneous   composed of dissimilar ingredients or elements.

heterosexuality   sexual attraction toward members of the opposite sex.

hippie   a 1960s version of the Bohemian, who believes in liberty, living for the moment, and completely free self-expression.

homophobia   a fear of one's own kind, as of persons of one's own sex.

homosexuality   sexual attraction toward members of the same sex.

hot line   an arrangement whereby persons with particular problems may find assistance by telephoning a person, persons, or organization designated to provide support.

humanist   one who is philosophically concerned with the ideas and ideals of human beings.

hypochondriac   a person unusually preoccupied with his or her own health.

hypothesis   an admittedly tentative explanation of a body of data.

hypothetical   based on supposition.

IQ (see intelligent quotient)

id   in psychoanalytic terminology, the deepest, most primitive stratum of the mind.

ideals   those aspects of an individual's moral code that serve as guideposts for behavior.

identical twins   monozygotic twins; developed from a single fertilized ovum.

identification   the merging of one's own purposes and goals with those of another, or modeling one's goals after those of another.

identity   a sense of uniqueness as a person and distinctiveness from others, equivalent to answering the question "Who am I?"

identity crisis   a major turning point, or situation, relating to the determination of what and who one is.

identity diffusion (Erikson)   instability; lack of framework for resolving inner and outer demands.

ideology   the doctrines, opinions, or philosophy of an individual or group.

in loco parentis   in the place of a parent; said of a person acting temporarily with parental authority.

instrumental   characterized by goal-directed activity.

instrumentalism   active employment of means to reach goals.

intelligence   the ability to learn and to apply what one learns, especially in new situations.

intelligence quotient (IQ)   a value assigned to an individual's mental ability which represents one's capacity as compared to that of others of the same age or stage of development.

intrinsic   deriving from the nature of the thing concerned.

Jung, C. J. (1875–1961)   a Swiss psychologist who made significant contributions to personality theory.

juvenile delinquents   individuals, not yet legally mature, who violate the law.

ketosteroid   male and female hormones.

kibbutz (plural, kibbutzim)   collective farm settlement(s) in Israel.

kosher   fit or allowed to be eaten according to particular dietary or ceremonial laws.

larynx   the structure in which the vocal cords are located.

leisure   time spent doing what one desires to do at one's own pace.

life cycle   the complete set of phenomena and events that comprise the total life span.

life style   the overall pattern of motives, coping techniques, and behaviors that generally characterize an individual's activity.

longitudinal studies   research relating to the same persons, objects, or situations over a period of time.

LSD (lysergic acid diethylamide)   a powerful hallucinogen used illegally by people and also on a very limited basis in some types of psychotherapy.

machismo   delusion of power and strength, often associated with excessive pride in one's own masculinity or a false sense of superiority.

macro   prefix meaning large-scale, enlarged, or elongated (Opposite: micro).

macrosystem   an overall prototype, within the culture or subculture that sets the pattern for activities and structures occurring at the concrete level, thus indirectly impacting on the individual.

marginal personality   caught between two cultures, not feeling at home in, or fully accepted by, either. Examples would be the newly arrived immigrant, the black child in an integrated school, and the poor child in a wealthy school.

marijuana　the dried leaves of hemp which have a narcotic effect when smoked in cigarettes called "joints."

masochistic　gaining gratification from being cruelly treated.

matristic　oriented toward, or dominated by, women.

maturity (physical)　the stage of development when maximum development has been reached and growth has ceased.

megadorm　a very large or high-rise dormitory.

menarche　the establishment or beginning of the menstrual function.

menses　flow of blood, normally every month; from the female uterus.

mentor　a wise, trusted, and helpful counselor.

mesomorph　an individual having a muscular, athletic build.

mesosystem　as used in the text, relationships between persons and intermediate-range environmental settings.

metabolic　characterized by, or resulting from, metabolism, the physical and chemical processes that proceed continuously in living organisms and cells, by which assimilated food is built into protoplasm (anabolism) and broken down into waste and simpler substances (catabolism), as energy is released for vital processes.

metamorphosis　a complete change in form or structure.

metaphor　the application of a word or phrase to a concept or an object which it does not literally denote, in order to suggest comparisons.

microsystem　as used in the text, relationships between persons and their immediate environmental settings.

mid-life (middle age) crisis　a critical period, during middle age, when an individual is induced by the culmination of personal, physical, and social factors to examine his or her life, which may result in important modifications of life style and philosophy.

momism　concept of the maternal relationship as characterized by an unhealthy overly emotional influence on the offspring.

moratorium　delay, usually for a specified period of time.

narcissistic　self-loving.

negative identity　an identity composed of feared yet fascinating qualities.

neoatavistic　relating to the characteristics of some near or immediate ancestor.

neofreudian　follower of Freud, who has nevertheless substantially modified the orthodox Freudian doctrine.

network　a loosely connected system of interrelated groups.

neurologist　one who specializes in the study of the nervous system and treatment of related diseases.

neurosis　see psychoneurosis.

neurotic (also psychoneurotic)　Tending to behave in predominantly emotional rather than rational ways.

nihilistic　with intent to destroy, as in terroristic movements.

normality　in the statistical sense, the condition of being average or typical; in the psychological sense, the status of acceptable adjustment, free of unhealthy deviations.

nostalgic　having, or causing, nostalgia (longing for home, homeland, or something of long ago).

nuclear family　the family composed only of the father, mother, and children, as opposed to the extended family which also includes all the descendants of a common grandparent and all their relatives.

nurturance　an attitude of warmth and assistance on the part of a parent, usually the mother, toward a child.

nurturant　characterized by warmth and involvement (personal love and compassion).

obesity　condition of extreme overweight.

obsession　persistent idea.

obsolescence　the process or state of becoming out of date or going out of use.

occultism　belief in secret, esoteric powers.

Oedipus complex (Freud)　the repressed desire of an individual for sex relations with the parent of the opposite sex. Specifically, the term relates to the boy's incestuous desire for his mother, but it often subsumes an analogous desire of the girl for her father (more properly, the Electra complex).

oligarchy　a form of government in which power is invested in a few persons or a dominant class or clique.

omnigamy　the kinship system produced by divorce and remarriage.

open-class society　sociocultural grouping in which channels exist for changing one's social class status.

ovulation　the physiological process by which a mature ovum (female germ cell) escapes from a ruptured follicle (sac or cavity).

pancreatitis　inflammation of the pancreas, a gland located near the stomach which secretes a digestive fluid into the intestines.

paranoia　a functional psychosis characterized by delusions of persecution or grandeur.

parasympathetic dominance　a condition of emotional "balance" suggesting that the portion of the nervous system which is more active in everyday functions of the organism and which tends to preserve an individual's emotional equilibrium is prevalent over the sympathetic nervous system, which is concerned with reactions to stress.

parent surrogates　anyone other than the natural parent who fulfills that role.

pathological　pertaining to a diseased or abnormal condition of the organism or its parts.

patriarchy　a sociocultural grouping, such as a family or tribe, in which the father or oldest male is recognized as head, and descent is traced through the male line.

patristic　oriented toward, or dominated by, men.

peer   a person of one's own age or status.

peer culture   technically, the way of life of a group of equals; the term is applied especially to adolescent groups.

personality   the total pattern of an individual's characteristic traits, constituting his or her distinctive ways of adapting to the environment.

personality inventory   an instrument for measuring an individual's personal characteristics, arranged for self-rating or rating by other persons.

phallus   representation of the penis or testes especially as a symbol in decoration or cult worship.

pharmacological   pertaining to the science of dealing with the preparation, use, and effects of drugs.

phenomenological   pertaining to an individual's own perceptions of an object or experience.

phobia   irrational fear; the individual may realize its irrationality but nevertheless be unable to dispel it.

Piaget, Jean (1896–1980)   a Swiss psychologist who was perhaps this century's most significant writer and theorist on child development and developmental processes.

pimp   an individual who solicits customers for a prostitute.

pineal gland   a small body in the brain having no known function, but believed to retard sexual development during childhood.

pituitary   an important endocrine gland, about the size of a pea, located at the base of the brain; sometimes called the master gland because of its important effects on the other endocrines.

pluralistic society   a society characterized by more than one relatively distinctive subculture.

polarization   the tendency to assume diametrically opposing positions.

positive reinforcement   the strengthening of a response through associating it with reward.

postconventional stage (Kohlberg)   the highest stage of moral development, during which the individual adheres to personal principles, transcending not only conventional morality but even a social contract.

preadolescence   a stage in development spanning approximately two years before puberty; also called pubescence.

precocity   unusually early or rapid development.

preconventional stage (Kohlberg)   the lowest stage of moral development, which involves relatively egocentric or self-centered concepts of right and wrong concerning what one can do without getting caught or what leads to greatest personal gratification.

preoperational thought stage (Piaget)   a period (ages 2 to 7) divided into the preconceptual stage (ages 2 to 3) when the child is eccentric and uses himself as the standard of judgment, and the intutive stage (ages 4 to 7) when the child conceptualizes more, and groups objects into classes.

prepotent   pre-eminent in power, authority, or influence.

primary sex organs   those parts of the body directly concerned with reproduction.

proclivities   natural or habitual inclinations or tendencies.

projection   attribution of one's own ideas or impulses to another.

projective technique   a procedure for discovering an individual's characteristic modes of behavior by analyzing his or her responses to relatively ambiguous, unstructured stimuli or situations.

proselytizing   seeking converts.

prosocial   approved by, or favorable to, society in general.

Protestant ethic   a set of ideas about man's spiritual relationships that emphasizes hard work, personal stewardship, pleasurelessness, and individual enterprise.

prototype   model; pattern; archetype.

psychasthenia   an inability to resist abnormal fears, obsessions, or compulsions that one knows are irrational.

psychedelic drugs   chemicals or narcotics which produce extreme reactions including visual stimulation, flights of rapid thought, and hallucinations.

psychiatrist   a physician who specializes in the diagnosis and treatment of mental disease.

psychic   beyond natural or known physical processes; pertaining to the psyche, or mind.

psychoanalytic   relating to a body of doctrine associated with Freud and modified by his followers: a special technique for disovering hidden motivation.

psychometric test   an instrument designed to measure one or more psychological characteristics.

psychoneurosis   a somewhat poorly defined mental disorder, less serious than psychosis, and leaving the personality relatively intact.

psychopath   an individual with a pattern of immature and pathological behaviors.

psychopathology   the science that deals with mental disease or disorders.

psychosis   the scientific name for severe mental disturbance, commonly called insanity.

psychosomatic   pertaining to the mind-body relationship; having bodily symptoms of mental or emotional origin.

psychotherapy   the use of any psychological technique in treating maladjustment or mental disorders.

pubertal rites   a program of precepts and rituals by which an individual, on reaching sexual maturity, is initiated into the adult life of the community.

puberty   the period during which the individual's reproductive organs approach readiness to function and secondary sex characteristics develop.

pubes   (1) lower part of the abdomen; (2) the hair appearing in this region at puberty.

pubescence   the period of about two years preceding puberty, or the time span of physiological development during which the reproductive system matures.

quasi as if or in the manner of.

rapprochement restoration of harmony.

recidivism habitual or chronic relapse, as in committing crime.

Reformation theologian a religious movement of the sixteenth century which had for its objective the reform of the Roman Catholic Church.

Renaissance a movement of the fourteenth through the seventeenth centuries characterized by an impressive revival of art, literature, and learning.

rites de passage rituals associated with induction into the adult society.

role model an individual whose portrayal of some pattern of behavior is so exemplary as to make him or her worthy of emulation.

roles socially accepted patterns of behavior associated with functions in various groups. Among the most important for children are age, sex, pupil, and family roles.

Rorschach test a psychological test consisting of inkblots of various designs and colors, shown to subjects for their interpretations from which inferences about personality characteristics and mental function are drawn.

saliency the quality of being prominent or conspicuous.

schizophrenia a group of psychotic reactions characterized by distortions of reality and by extreme intellectual, emotional, and behavioral disturbances.

secondary-group relationships associations with people who are less closely attached, as on the job or in the broader community.

secondary sex characteristics those physical traits that emerge in each sex at the time of puberty and symbolize sexual maturity but not essential for reproduction.

secular pertaining to worldly or nonreligious matters.

self-actualization the process of moving through sequentially higher stages of motivation and organization to adequate achievement of one's potential.

self concept an individual's view of the self, reflecting the subjective experience of uniqueness.

self-deprecation representation of oneself in disparaging terms ("throwing off" on oneself).

sensitive period hypothesis the tentative suggestion that there is a particular time during which particular experiences may have especially profound and enduring effects.

sensorimotor activity behavior that depends upon the integrated functioning of sense organs and motor mechanisms.

set certain crowd, or combination of crowds, that distinguishes a particular status within the youth hierarchy in a high school.

sex drive a genetically determined psychic factor which, when operative, causes one to seek release of tension through sexual behaviors.

sex role the pattern of behaviors characteristic of male or female in a particular society.

shamanistic pertaining to certain people's religions and cultures of southeastern Asia.

sibling brother or sister.

social adolescence conception of this stage of development as the time when an individual becomes ready to assume the privileges and obligations of that society.

social distance the variable gap that exists between one or more individuals and others in interpersonal relationships.

social sex role the stereotyped composite portrait of male or female, defining the behavior patterns deemed proper for each sex.

socialization the process by which an individual learns to behave like, and to get along with, others in one's society and culture.

sociometric test a quantitative study of group relationships, often involving determination of how group members perceive and feel about each other.

spermatozoa mature male reproductive cells.

stage theory the conceptualization of human development as involving several relatively discrete stages which can be identified physiologically, psychologically, and sociologically.

Stanford Binet one of the best known intelligence test scales, designed for oral administration to individuals.

status the position accorded an individual, formally or informally, within a group, carrying with it privileges, duties, and responsibilities and reflecting the way others view him or her.

status offender a minor whose offense is illegal, though it would not be so deemed if he or she had already attained legal adulthood.

stereotype a preconceived, prejudiced picture of the members of some particular group.

storm-and-stress theory the view, first popularized by G. Stanley Hall, that adolescence is a period of unusual emotional turbulence.

straight individuals who follow the conventional pattern.

streaking a brief fad of the late 1960s, characterized by dashing, completely nude, through some public place.

sublimation the substitution of behaviors approved by society for disapproved ones, that serve the same, or similar, underlying need.

superego conscience; the aspect of the psyche that holds the id (primitive impulses) in check.

suppression conscious exclusion of disapproved thoughts, as opposed to repression which is an unconscious process of barring such thoughts.

sympathetic dominance the condition within the nervous system of being primarily oriented, in the neurological sense, toward stress, suggesting that the portion of the nervous system which mobilizes body resources to deal with emergencies and emotional states is prevalent over the parasympathetic division, which is chiefly concerned with ongoing, everyday functions of the body.

Taoistic pertaining to a certain Chinese philosophical system that advocated simplicity, naturalness, and noninterference with the course of natural events.

territorial space the area in which a particular person or group normally operates.

Thematic Apperception Test (TAT) a projective test in which the subject is asked to make up stories about each of 19 somewhat vague unstructured pictures.

therapeutic healing; curative.

Third World the aggregate of all smaller unaligned nations as distinct from the more powerful communist and democratic blocs.

throwaway kids children or adolescents who have been encouraged or driven by their parents to leave home.

thymus a gland, located in the throat, which presumably inhibits precocious sexual development and which gradually disappears in late childhood.

thyroid an endocrine gland located on either side of the upper windpipe, of special importance in growth and in controlling the metabolic rate.

topological relating to the mapping or charting of features of a relatively small geographic area.

trachea the principle passage (from the larynx to the bronchi) conveying air to and from the lungs.

tracking the practice of organizing students into ability groups for purposes of instruction.

tracking, curriculum the division of studies pursued through high school into two programs for those who do, or do not, intend to go to college.

traits, central or core characteristics most typical of an individual, most difficult to change, and most closely related to achievement of one's fundamental goals.

traits, peripheral or secondary characteristics less typical of an individual, more modifiable, and presumably less likely to be based on heredity than central or core traits.

transactional analysis a process of cross communication of each member of a relationship or group with the other member or members; or the dynamic two-way interaction between a therapist and patient.

transcendence quality or state of going beyond ordinary limits.

transescence the stage of development initiated with puberty and extending through early adolescence.

values clarification an approach to moral education which involves eliciting children's own judgment of issues in which values conflict instead of imposing values on them. It is assumed that simply becoming more self-aware of values is a highly desirable goal in itself.

vandalism the deliberate and malicious damage or destruction of property.

vicarious characterized by imagined instead of actual participation in an experience.

walkabout the custom, employed by Australian aborigines, of requiring youth to prove their ability to survive for a period of time, alone, in isolated areas before being accorded adult status.

youth ordinarily, an individual in the late teens or early twenties who has not yet assumed the responsibilities of adulthood.

youth culture the way of life characteristic of adolescents.

Index